Notable Books Council Award
from the American Library Association
for one of the top twelve Best Nonfiction Books of 2008

Washington Post Best Book of 2008

Honorable Mention, Gustavus Myers
Center for Human Rights Book Award

More praise for DEFYING DIXIE

"A sweeping, fresh consideration of pre-movement civil rights activism . . . full of informative gems." —*Publishers Weekly*

"Strikingly fresh. . . . Instead of taking the traditional path and examining the South in isolation, Gilmore situates the region in a national and international framework. She is adept at drawing character studies and uses this talent to follow the lives of several Southerners, white and black, who were forced to flee their native region. [These] individual vignettes are compelling." —Kevin M. Kruse, *The Nation*

"A complex narrative of people and movements whose common purpose was defying the Dixie of [the author's] childhood." —*Boston Globe*

"In her well-researched history, Yale professor Gilmore shines a light on some lesser-known chapters of the Civil Rights Movement." —*New York Post*

"The fascinating story of how communists, socialists, liberals, legal and labor activists helped lay the groundwork for the mainstream civil-rights breakthroughs." —*Kirkus Reviews*

"*Defying Dixie* tells of the most marginal of Southerners: fierce radicals who at the height of Jim Crow dared to demand a world free of racial oppression and economic exploitation. Scorned and scarred for their beliefs, these courageous men and women risked everything to build a civil rights movement that shook the South to its core—and transformed the nation. Glenda Gilmore's evocative, sensitive account endows their extraordinary story with the majesty it deserves."

—Kevin Boyle, Ohio State University

"Gilmore weaves her many participants nimbly into and out of a forward-flowing narrative told in the most personable voice."   —*Gay City News*

"A valuable, engaging, and important study from one of the most talented and accomplished historians of the American South."

—Walter Russell Mead, *Foreign Affairs*

"A fine example of history writing, deserving a large readership."

—Don Flynn, *Chartist*

"*Defying Dixie* offers a valuable lesson to Americans with short memories: The civil rights movement did not start with Rosa Parks in 1955."

—*Journal of Blacks in Higher Education*

"In re-creating the lives and dreams of courageous Southerners, black and white, who posed an alternative vision for their tortured region based on social justice and racial equality, Glenda Gilmore has forever changed the way historians will write and teach about the roots of the modern civil rights movement. Elegantly written, chock full of historical nuggets, *Defying Dixie* is a work of stunning originality."

—David Oshinsky, University of Texas

"*Defying Dixie* is a singular triumph. Glenda Gilmore has stretched our notion of the civil rights movement, moving its start point back to the 1920s, broadening the cast of characters to include labor leaders and 'Red' preachers, and seeing the Southland from the milltowns of North Carolina to the inter-chambers of the Kremlin. All of this, by itself, makes the book a major contribution to Southern, American, and even global history. But even more, Gilmore has written an achingly beautiful account. This is history at its finest, full of pain and pathos."

—Bryant Simon, Temple University

"The map of the history of the Civil Rights movement will never look the same. Professor Gilmore has given us a new highway. Bypassed are all the biblically named exits; gone too are all those black men guarding the ramps. The terrain is now radical country. Communists, once trolls under the bridge, are now sentinels of the new route. And Pauli Murray leads the way. A wonderful book." —William S. McFeely,
Pulitzer Prize–winning author of
Grant: A Biography

"*Defying Dixie* unearths the radical roots of the freedom movement and thereby recasts American history, drawing the American South onto the world stage where drama, irony, achievement and tragedy all take their place. This is an electrifying work of history, all the better for its fully human cast of characters." —Timothy Tyson, Duke University

"Glenda Gilmore's fascinating account gives us the civil rights struggle from the Left—its more vigorous side before the 1950s—with the individuals and all their quirks left in. Lovett Fort-Whiteman and Pauli Murray head the cast of intriguing activists, whose personal character *and* their historic achievements Gilmore presents in her signature lively prose."
—Nell Irvin Painter, Princeton University

"Glenda Gilmore's *Defying Dixie* is a triumph of narrative synthesis, a powerful meld of storytelling and interpretation that puts the radical and too often marginalized forerunners of the post-WWII civil rights generation front and center where they belong."
—David Levering Lewis, New York University

"Masterful. . . . This gracefully written, thoroughly researched book will be indispensable reading for students of civil rights and US history."
—*Choice*

DEFYING DIXIE

Glenda Elizabeth Gilmore

DEFYING DIXIE

THE RADICAL ROOTS OF CIVIL RIGHTS, 1919–1950

W. W. NORTON & COMPANY

NEW YORK   LONDON

Since this page cannot legibly accommodate all the copright notices,
page 621 constitutes an extension of the copyright page.

For information about permission to reproduce selections from this book, write to
Permissions, W. W. Norton & Company Inc., 500 Fifth Avenue, New York, NY 10110

For information about special discounts for bulk purchases, please contact
W. W. Norton Special Sales at specialsales@wwnorton.com or 800-233-4830

Manufacturing by RR Donnelley, Bloomsburg
Book design by Dana Sloan
Production manager: Julia Druskin

Library of Congress Cataloging-in-Publication Data

Gilmore, Glenda Elizabeth.
Defying Dixie : the radical roots of civil rights, 1919–1950 / by
Glenda Elizabeth Gilmore. — 1st ed.
p. cm.
Includes bibliographical references and index.
ISBN 978-0-393-06244-1 (hardcover)
1. Social justice—Southern States—History—20th century. 2. Social movements—
Southern States—History—20th century. 3. Radicalism—Southern States—
History—20th century. 4. Civil rights movements—Southern
States—History—20th century. 5. African Americans—Civil rights—Southern
States—History—20th century. 6. Political activists—Southern States—History—
20th century. 7. Social reformers—Southern States—History—20th century.
8. Southern States—Politics and government—1865–1950. 9. Southern States—
Race relations—History—20th century. 10. Southern States—Social conditions—
20th century. I. Title.
HN79.A13G54 2008
303.48'409750904—dc22 2007010237

ISBN 978-0-393-33532-3 pbk.

W. W. Norton & Company Inc., 500 Fifth Avenue, New York, NY 10110
www.wwnorton.com

W. W. Norton & Company Ltd., Castle House, 75/76 Wells Street, London W1T 3QT

1 2 3 4 5 6 7 8 9 0

To Ben, who hung the moon over Magpieland,

and to Miles, Derry, and Mia-lia,

who dance with us by its light

CONTENTS

"The South" under Siege • What *Does* the Negro
Want? • The Agony of White Southern Liberals •
Pauli Murray's Sit-Ins • "I Am an American, Too"

LIST OF ILLUSTRATIONS

DEFYING DIXIE

Introduction

SUNSET IN DIXIE

The Sun
Is gonna go down
In Dixie
Some of these days
With such a splash
That everybody who ever knew
What yesterday was
Is gonna forget—
When that sun goes down in Dixie.

—LANGSTON HUGHES, "SUNSET IN DIXIE,"
SEPTEMBER 1941[1]

When African Americans used the word "Dixie" in the first half of the twentieth century, they pronounced the South another country, with its own political and social institutions, upheld by a white supremacist regime. The sun went down in Dixie in the great splash of the civil rights movement of the 1950s and 1960s, and for a while "everybody who ever knew/What yesterday was" forgot. In the simplified story broadcast across the nation on black-and-white televisions, the heroes of the movement arose directly from the ashes of slavery as the first African Americans ever to challenge the South's archaic and long-undisturbed system of racial management. With the exception of Rosa Parks, the first woman who ever refused to give up her seat on a bus, the heroes were men, and those men came from black churches, where they had kept the light of freedom burning for a very long time. These nonviolent heroes wanted to vote, send their little children to school, sit down after a weary day, and order a grilled cheese sandwich at Woolworth's. According to this view, the civil rights movement started when it burst into white people's living rooms, brought to them by white media.[2]

African Americans knew better. Asked by an interviewer in the 1990s when he joined the civil rights movement, an elderly black man in Louisiana responded, "Been involved in the movement all my life."[3] In the three decades that followed World War I, black Southerners and their allies relentlessly battled Jim Crow, the South's system of racial hierarchy. Challenges to segregation happened daily on buses across the South, and people went to jail and sometimes died over seating arrangements. There was never a time when black Southerners gave up their political aspirations, and increasing numbers voted in urban areas throughout the 1930s and 1940s. The legal campaign to desegregate education began in 1933.[4] These issues, however, never stood as separate goals. They were part of a much larger push for economic justice and a broad vision of human rights that made up what historian Jacquelyn Dowd Hall has called "the long Civil Rights Movement."[5]

When I was growing up in the dimming rays of Dixie's sunset in the 1950s in Greensboro, North Carolina, I came across clues that a battle had been fought on my home ground. Our long, baking hot drives to Myrtle Beach were punctuated by three strange roadside billboards: THIS IS KLAN KOUNTRY, IMPEACH EARL WARREN, and U.S. OUT OF THE U.N. As a white child I understood the first two as foregone conclusions. THIS IS KLAN KOUNTRY declared the proximate boundaries of southern localism. IMPEACH EARL WARREN warned that the judicial power of the national state stopped here, short of fulfilling its mandate in *Brown v. Board of Education*. But the third—U.S. OUT OF THE U.N.—gave me pause. I learned all about the United Nations at Sternberger Elementary School, where we made cardboard models of its shiny new headquarters. My teachers told me that it was a beacon beaming U.S. democracy into the dark corners of the world. It might even prevent another war like the one my daddy had fought in. But what did the UN have to do with the South?

Although I could not understand the connections at the time, all three billboards drew the boundaries of the mythical country in which I lived. The nation we knew as Dixie survived into the 1950s because it zealously policed its borders. Within those borders, racial oppression reigned supreme, controlling not only public space but public conversation and private conscience and narrowing the political imagination of even its most defiant subjects. Those who openly protested white domination had to leave, one way or another. Once they left, they could no longer be Southerners. Those who did not grow up within the South would always be outsiders, for they could never be Southerners either. I rose and stood for "Dixie" until I was twenty years old, when I finally made the connection between my mythical country and racial oppression.

Grown-up white Southerners had always known that Dixie depended on localism, on their right to be left alone to manage their unique "Negro Problem." On the eve of the 1950s civil rights movement, the South's rulers continued successfully to broker deals with both political parties, Congress, and the executive branch to reinforce local power. But for the first time since the Reconstruction amendments the federal judiciary began to recognize black civil rights by extending constitutional guarantees throughout the nation. The remedy? Impeach Earl Warren.

As the third billboard proclaimed, white supremacists took the threat issuing from the court of world opinion just as seriously. After the UN Charter incorporated provisions for human rights, and almost a century after the first secessionist movement, white southern conservatives proposed to secede again: to get the United States out of the United Nations. Since World War I African Americans and their white allies had increasingly brought global politics to bear on domestic racial oppression. In the late 1930s and 1940s a domestic ideal of racial tolerance, necessitated by the demands of fighting Fascism, became the American way, at least rhetorically. If advocating political isolationism in the "American century" ultimately proved a futile exercise, it was not because southern segregationists did not vigorously pursue it.

When I was about eight, I visited an abandoned mansion in our neighborhood. Here, everyone whispered, was where the Communist had lived. No one really understood what a Communist was; rather, the lesson lay in what became of them. They left their homes, they lost their families, and they went to prison. That's what had happened to Junius Scales, the rich golden-haired boy who had grown up in that house. That's what would happen to white Southerners who betrayed their own people and way of life. In the 1920s and early 1930s the Communists alone argued for complete equality between the races. Their racial ideal eventually became America's ideal. Years later I came to know Junius Scales. A sweet, gentle man, he joined the Communist Party in 1939 because it was only among Communists that he found nonracist people who cared about the poor.[6] I never told him how his house, silent, empty, and dark, behind boxwoods grown massive and wisteria run amok, haunted my memory.

Defying Dixie begins at the radical edges of a human rights movement after World War I, with Communists who promoted and practiced racial equality and considered the South crucial to their success in elevating labor and overthrowing the capitalist system. They were joined in the late 1930s by a radical Left to form a southern Popular Front that sought to overturn Jim Crow, elevate the working class, and promote civil rights and civil liberties. During and after World War II a growing number of grassroots activists protested directly against white supremacy and imagined it poised to fall of its own weight. They gave it a shove.

Many of those Southerners who attacked Jim Crow lived outside the South. Some, like Junius Scales, defied Dixie and found themselves banished, but others chose to leave. Whenever I pressed the preeminent southern historian C. Vann Woodward to tell about the South—why he left it and how he felt about it—he would draw himself up and declare forcefully, with just a tinge of hurt pride, "I am an expatriate." Although he appreciated the collard greens, the fried chicken, and the banana pudding I served him, they never once extracted from him an ounce of nostalgia. He saw the South clearly, and he loved it, but he preferred to love it from afar.

During the first half of the twentieth century Dixie regularly purged itself of dissenters and counted them out of the polity. Many protesters remained, but to acknowledge only those Southerners who stayed behind produces a distorted view of the place. The South could remain the South only by chasing out some of its brightest minds and most bountiful spirits, generation after generation. Many of those who left did so, directly or indirectly, because they opposed white supremacy. Counting them back into southern history reveals an insurgent South and shows some Southerners to be a revolutionary lot that fought longer and harder than anyone else to defeat Dixie.[7] The outside agitators upon whom this book focuses all are native Southerners who returned, either physically or through their intellectual reach to redeem the place they loved but where they could not stand. *Defying Dixie* presents region as a state of mind as well as an actual place.

Writing a history of the South that includes its expatriates leads one to reconsider places, ideas, and organizations generally thought of as distinctly *un*southern. I came to think of Washington, D.C., as a border post from which black Southerners kept one eye on their country. Chicago became a cache pool up the Mississippi River that harbored refugees fleeing the Deep South. So many black North Carolinians settled within a few blocks of one another in New York that the Harlem Renaissance might have been the Raleigh Renaissance, North.

Ideologies looked different when I considered their southern sources. For example, six years after twenty-two-year-old A. Philip Randolph arrived in New York from Crescent City, Florida, he joined another freshly expatriated black Southerner, Chandler Owen from Warrenton, North Carolina, to found the "radical," "northern," Socialist newspaper the *Messenger*.[8] Or consider Ben Davis, Communist and councilman from Harlem—well, actually, Atlanta. Black Northerner W. E. B. Du Bois edited *Crisis* during the adolescence of the National Association for the Advancement of Colored People (NAACP), but two black Southerners, James Weldon Johnson of Jacksonville and Walter White of Atlanta, ran the association. When I dwelt on these characters' southern roots, I realized how growing up under Jim Crow had shaped their politics. They were similar to governments in exile. Jim Crow's black daughters and sons established beachheads in the North and around the world to gain safe ground from which to fire back at those occupying their country. They regularly, if sometimes covertly, joined the friends and family they left behind in the South who fought daily battles. In this book southern history becomes a national, even international story.

The mythical, isolated nation that I thought I grew up in existed *only* as an imagined community. The image of the benighted, static South with its peculiar ways, the place that opened just a crack after World War II mobilizations, Cold War politics, and air conditioning wafted into its humid miasmas, was the creation of the white supremacists themselves. From one world war through another, Southerners always interacted with the nation and the world, and Jim Crow's resisters took every opportunity to bring down the weight of world opinion on white supremacy. Jim Crow's supporters exported their system politically, economically, and culturally. Just as their grandfathers and great-grandfathers before them had bargained to extend slavery, so white supremacists in the 1910s and 1920s hoped to extend segregation and black disfranchisement to the nation and the world. When the Great Migration, the Great Depression, the New Deal, and Fascism put an end to those hopes, they circled their wagons to defend Jim Crow. This difficult task required them to emphasize the South's difference, its separateness from the rest of the world. The more the outside world impinged, the more separate and "southern" Jim Crow's defenders had to become.

What is at stake if we chart the movement against Jim Crow beginning in World War I, if we take into account exiled white and black Southerners, and if we see both resistance to and support for Jim Crow as international? First, it becomes clear that the presence of a radical Left, in this case a Communist Left, redefined the debate over white supremacy and hastened its end. By brooking no compromise with full social equality for a decade after they entered the South in 1929, the Communists gave Southerners a vision and a threat. Their small numbers mattered less than their very existence. It was Communists who stood up to say that black and white people should organize together, eat together, go to school together, and marry each other if they chose.

It has been a scholarly challenge to identify the people who stood up as Communists, but with the opening of the Comintern archive in Moscow and the Communist Party USA papers in the United States in the late 1990s, it became possible to identify Communists and understand their work in the South. Whether or not a Southerner joined the Party mattered because it meant that he or she sought the most radical solution available to change the South and one that called for complete racial equality. Tying together the history of southern Communism with the Kremlin's actual involvement dispels the myth of robotic spies roaming the region, funded and controlled by Moscow gold. Black and white Southerners helped forge Soviet policy on race and revolution before Stalin consolidated his power, and they returned impoverished from Moscow to implement those policies in the South.

Moreover, once we acknowledge the Communist Left in the South, we can assess its significance as a catalyst for change and as a force that moved Socialists and liberals to action through the southern Popular Front.[9] If the Communists are omitted from this story, the National Association for the Advancement of Colored People looks radical and the Commission on Interracial Cooperation (CIC) appears to be the only home for white Southerners uneasy with Jim Crow's excesses. If the Communists are included, we can see the conservative aspects of the NAACP's litigation strategy and the bankruptcy of moderate organizations such as the CIC in the face of European Fascism. A more insurgent South emerges.

Another advantage in expanding the temporal and geographical boundaries of the war against Jim Crow is that this clarifies the connections between foreign affairs and domestic racial struggles. African Americans always used geopolitics to fight domestic racism. They exposed U.S. imperialism and Jim Crow as two sides of the same coin in their protests over the American occupation of Haiti. They debated and followed Gandhi's methods of passive resistance from the 1920s onward. They critiqued European colonialism and theorized black Southerners as a captive colonial people. Their most forceful arguments compared the Nazis and Dixie. African Americans realized as early as 1933 that Hitler posed an unparalleled evil and made his persecution of the Jews front-page news throughout the decade. Moreover, they frankly and repeatedly compared Jim Crow with Fascism, thereby helping forge an ideal of tolerance that would carry the United States into the fight against the Führer. Their critique left white Southerners defending the sort of racial order they were enlisting to fight against, and the contradictions undercut Jim Crow's apologists during World War II. For the first time since Reconstruction, the federal government intervened in the southern system of segregation by ordering the desegregation of war work.

The internationalist civil rights struggle also allows us to reassess recent works on the Cold War's role in the civil rights struggle of the 1950s that argue that the Cold War facilitated the civil rights movement. Since the United States could ill afford the publicity that exposed Jim Crow at a time when it hoped to win the world for democracy, the federal government slowly moved to support for civil rights.[10] But this argument inflates the Cold War's contributions and discounts its costs. The State

Department's concern for civil rights counted for little on the ground since with the exception of sending troops to Little Rock in 1957, the federal government failed to intervene in civil rights struggles during the height of McCarthyism.

Seen through the lens of African American history, the influence of the Cold War weakens further. African Americans had long exposed the abuses of the antidemocratic South. Global demonstrations protested the prison sentences of the Scottsboro "Boys," newspapers from Melbourne to Moscow customarily ran stories and photographs of lynchings in the 1920s and 1930s, and freedom fighters everywhere condemned Jim Crow.[11] On the other hand, those who sought to persecute ethnic groups outside the United States—for instance, in Nazi Germany and South Africa—held up Dixie as a good example of pragmatic racial politics in a democratic setting. Thus the publicity that Jim Crow drew during the Cold War era was nothing new. What was new was the State Department's determination to do something about the most overt forms of black oppression. Even then that response was measured, distant, and largely rhetorical until the end of John F. Kennedy's presidency.

Against this federal response the Cold War unleashed a virulent southern anti-Communism that eviscerated postwar social justice movements and truncated the civil rights movement that emerged in the 1950s. White southerners who opposed integration linked Communism and civil rights, almost destroyed white southern liberalism, and narrowed the civil rights movement's agenda. Anti-Communism swept economic and public policy issues off the table and forced limited change only within the system. Those who had defied Dixie before the Cold War had vowed to change the system, but anti-Communism meant that the possibilities of the 1930s were labeled "Red" after 1950.[12]

Setting the 1950s civil rights movement in the context of the fights against southern injustice that preceded it reveals new insights into the sources of social change. If one believes that the civil rights movement arose in the 1950s, when the majority of white people noticed it for the first time, then those catalysts for social change that managed to survive anti-Communism take on exaggerated importance. Seeing the 1950s vestige of the movement as the actual movement itself makes it appear that middle-class black men in ties radicalized the nation. Thus many historians have found the roots of the civil rights movement in the black church since it was the strongest visible black institution in the mid-1950s. Cold War anti-Communism had destroyed some of the other broad catalysts for civil rights—for example, southern Communism and labor radicalism. Moreover, liberal organizations, such as the NAACP and Tennessee's Highlander Folk School, found themselves persecuted by anti-Communist scrutiny. White liberals who had been active before World War II became "fellow travelers" to be hounded out of their jobs and homes, not to mention out of public life. By giving the movement a 1950s start, we discount the forces that generated and sustained human rights during the 1930s and 1940s and privilege its religious, middle-class, and male roots.

A focus on the mid-century civil rights movement suggests that African Americans simply wanted desegregation and highlights NAACP school litigation and the Montgomery bus boycott. On the contrary, African Americans had worked for decades to secure social justice in broader terms. The NAACP's litigation campaign that resulted in *Brown v. Board of Education* in 1954 was only part of a much larger campaign, even within the NAACP, for economic opportunity and a thoroughgoing reordering of society to recognize universal human rights. In the simplified stories that the media told of the movement, civil rights came to mean school integration, access to public accommodations, and voting rights. This view erased the complexity of a drive to eliminate the economic injustices wrought by slavery, debt peonage, and a wage labor system based on degraded black labor. It took residential desegregation off the agenda, apparently once and for all. It swept away connections among civil liberties, labor rights, and civil rights that liberals and radicals had carefully forged from the mid-1930s onward. Taking this narrow view, Black Power betrayed the movement of which it had always been part, and the cries from Watts for equal economic opportunity were anti-American.

Perhaps most sadly, the erasure of the first civil rights movement left an enormous burden on *Brown v. Board of Education*. I believe that *Brown* was the single most important moment in the civil rights movement, its most enforceable intervention, and its most powerful statement. But *Brown* was not all that we could have had or all that was due the South. Before *Brown*, activists dreamed a viable dream of true equality among the

races, an equality that encompassed politics, education, economics, housing, personal interactions, and legal access. *Brown* squeaked through in
the anti-Communist period, but without a southern Left to shelter it, it
stood alone, under attack, for almost a decade until the Civil Rights Act of
1964. Full implementation of *Brown* did not occur until after 1970, but by
then the South's integrated public schools had been supplanted by segregated private ones.

Through *Brown*, the weight of Jim Crow's destruction fell on the
backs of schoolchildren. If the first civil rights movement had had its way,
there would have been a *Brown* for every aspect of its agenda, backed up by
powerful liberal forces on the ground in the heart of Dixie. It was not
within *Brown*'s power to right all the racial inequalities of the preceding
fifty years, a fact that has prompted criticisms that it was somehow
"wrong." It wasn't wrong; it was simply limited. Like the black children
who marched into Little Rock High, *Brown* marched into a Cold War
America that eventually overturned earlier visions of a more just society.
Brown went out alone on that beautiful Black Monday, and it met a mob.[13]

Defying Dixie is divided into three sections—"Incursions," "Resistance,"
and "Rebellion"—and each section encompasses three chapters. "Incursions" evokes the border crossings that took place from 1919 to 1930.
White Southerners sought to export Jim Crow to the nation and the
world, and expatriate Southerners, including Communists, led patrols
into the heart of Dixie to overcome racial oppression. Part 2, "Resistance,"
demonstrates that the Great Depression, anti-Fascism, and the Popular
Front created a new Left in the South that brought together liberals and
Communists. Part 3, "Rebellion," documents a time when Southerners
mounted a full-fledged, yet largely forgotten civil rights movement
against Jim Crow just before and during World War II. It follows the
undoing of civil rights leaders as the Cold War equated racial justice with
Soviet Communism.

The book's structure demonstrates the internationalism of the interwar social justice movements, as chapters cross borders to weave together
international and domestic racial politics. The world changed the South
as Southerners traveled to meet it. *Defying Dixie*'s itinerary is an extensive one. It starts in the South, moves to Haiti, takes an international tour

with the Ku Klux Klan, and returns to Broadway. It moves back south to Tuskegee, then west and north to St. Louis and Chicago, and sojourns in Moscow, before returning to Gastonia, North Carolina. It visits Chattanooga, Birmingham, and Charlotte, while it scatters the seeds of Scottsboro around the world. Then its protagonists travel to the USSR, stopping off in Moscow, Odessa, and Central Asia, before the journey ends for one black Southerner in Kolyma, Siberia. When civil liberties come under siege in Atlanta, black Southerners visit the Third Reich and bring home its example. As a southern Popular Front grows, moderate interracial cooperation as a political strategy crumbles in Chapel Hill and Cape Town. World War II plunges the nation into a global conflict, and black Southerners in New York and Washington declare war on racial inequality. Southern African Americans join them in countless confrontations with Jim Crow.

Defying Dixie is a history in which ideas are embodied in a collective biography of activist black and white Southerners. The central core of protagonists includes well-known figures, such as NAACP Secretary James Weldon Johnson, and those more obscure, such as civil rights activist Pauli Murray and the first American-born black Communist, Lovett Fort-Whiteman. In life, as in the book, characters forged ties with one another, and the interconnectedness of their stories ensures that they surface again and again in these pages. Many who defied Dixie are missing altogether, however, and important events that changed the course of white supremacy are not included. To illustrate my points, I have chosen characters and events to provide deep local context for broad historical changes. In attempting to connect the international and the local, I have included only a fraction of the stories that could have been told. Except where key to understanding the meaning, I have avoided inserting *sic* in quotations.

The book's organization also slights the local people who lived in the South and who started the civil rights movement in the 1950s. Those who do emerge in these pages may not have been able to take credit for that civil rights movement, but they knew in their hearts that they had helped pave the way for it, even if it left behind some of their goals. Some of them lived to watch the movement turn back in the late 1960s and early 1970s toward many of the goals for which they had fought in the 1930s and 1940s. As Pauli Murray described her early activism, "Each new attempt was linked with a previous effort. . . . Once begun, this debate would not be silenced. . . ."[14]

Two characters in this book, Lovett Fort-Whiteman and Pauli Murray, never allowed themselves to be silenced. From their examples and those of other characters, I have learned something of the dialectics of patience and impatience, of anger and fear, of working hard and daring much. In July 1867 Murray's grandfather Robert Fitzgerald wrote in his diary: "The past is the key of the present and the mirror of the future."[15] If we look into the mirror of the future and see people there like the ones in *Defying Dixie*, then everything will be all right.

PART ONE

INCURSIONS

1

JIM CROW MEETS KARL MARX

In the first three decades of the twentieth century most white Southerners believed that taken at the flood, the racial caste system they had recently institutionalized would spread across the nation and around the world. As black Southerners moved north, and European nations experimented with ways to manage their colonized subjects, white Southerners imagined they heard a long-awaited distress signal that summoned them to rescue a white race drowning in a rising tide of color. Southern experience counted for something: In the most democratic country in the world white Southerners had counted a minority group out of a constitutionally guaranteed political process by legal and extralegal measures.

By World War I white Southerners had created an intricate racial system of breathtaking complexity that left no action to chance. In the first place, it disfranchised African Americans and legislated them into segregation. Then it moved from the political to the personal to guarantee white supremacy. The system, which most people simply called Jim Crow, offered a color-coded solution for every human deed and thought, from where one might urinate to how far one's ambition might soar. Because it was so all-encompassing, it required constant policing and terrible, swift punishment of violations, willful or not. Taken piecemeal, Jim Crow might have seemed arbitrary. Why was it wrong for a white man to sit down and eat supper with the black woman who had nursed him as a baby? If a black man must step off a sidewalk to make way for important white men, should he not also pull his car off the road to make way for white drivers who overtook him on the highway? And why did a little white boy grow up to be mister and a little black boy grow up to be, simply, boy? These weren't the kinds of things a white man could learn overnight if suddenly confronted with black people on the streets of New York, London, or Cape Town. Maintaining this sort of reality required instruction and practice.

Southern white people would have gone mad if they had thought that they were spending a considerable portion of their daily lives imposing a cruel, artificial system on their fellow human beings, but few saw it that way. Jim Crow's success depended on its capacity for self-justification. Everywhere white Southerners looked, they saw black Southerners behaving according to white supremacy's dictates, and they took that behavior as an indication of black people's inferiority. Whites failed to fathom the antidemocratic nature of their regime or to acknowledge that it required both arbitrary violence and institutionalized police power to enforce it. They told themselves that African Americans—except for a few crazy ones—welcomed their leadership. And Jim Crow dealt ruthlessly with the crazy ones to avoid jeopardizing the imagined happiness of all.

Many white Southerners believed that they possessed the intimate knowledge, practical skills, and moral compass to minimize friction between the races everywhere. They could tell white New Yorkers what "Negroes" were really like, how they should treat them, and why they should feel good about treating them that way. They could clean up the mess in Haiti, the only black republic in the Western Hemisphere, by grafting on white dominion. They could remind Europeans that if they did not police their domestic racial hierarchies, they could kiss their colonies good-bye.

Jim Crow's success offered a persuasive final solution to what whites commonly called the race problem. In the South whites did not have to resort to genocide or ethnic cleansing to keep African Americans in their place. If managed properly, the system would produce more tractable black subjects in each succeeding generation. Indeed, those who instituted Jim Crow expected it to last for a thousand years, allowing black Southerners ample time to move up the evolutionary ladder. It seemed a modern, well-organized, and efficient way to line up the races in the worldwide contest for advancement.[1]

In the 1910s and 1920s the comprehensive system of segregation and disfranchisement that white Southerners had perfected in the 1890s and 1900s surged over the borders of the region, spilled into the nation, and lapped at the edges of the outside world. From New York to New Zealand, those whites who found themselves challenged by race relations looked to the American South for advice. A whirlwind tour of Jim Crow's flight—from North Carolina to Haiti to Mexico to Europe and back to Broadway—illustrates that white supremacy was not a vestigial, dying system; instead it was a vigorous, growing one.

The Southern Solution

The South was never another country, even though for much of its history it may have felt and acted like one. African Americans could cross the South's border without passports to escape its repression. Indeed, the movement of over one million southern blacks to the North in the 1910s and 1920s, known as the Great Migration, constituted one of the largest movements of a civilian population ever in a time of peace and prosperity.[2] At first migration simply secured African Americans northern asylum. Later it produced enemy agents who infiltrated Dixie's borders, helping undermine oppression's defenses. Because the South was not sovereign, Jim Crow's health depended on the federal government's support of its administration and on positive public opinion or at least public indifference outside the South. The first task came relatively easily after the Supreme Court ruled for segregation in *Plessy v. Ferguson* in 1896, after legal challenges to disfranchising laws failed at the turn of the century, and after the Congress failed to approve federal antilynching legislation in the 1920s.

A modern and efficient model of Jim Crow nested into Washington when native Southerner Woodrow Wilson moved into the White House in 1913. One hundred people were lynched in 1915, most of them in the South. Wilson did nothing. In the Wilson administration's first congressional session "there were no less than twenty bills advocating 'Jim Crow' cars in the District of Columbia, race segregation of Federal employees, excluding Negroes from commissions in the army and navy, forbidding the intermarriage of Negroes and whites, and excluding all immigrants of

Negro descent." When that legislation failed, Wilson issued an executive order to segregate the federal government's operations in the city.[3] He appointed to high offices white Southerners, many of whom owed their prominence to their role in disfranchising black voters back home. At the end of Wilson's second term one worried African American veteran exclaimed, "Confederate-Americanism has gained such headway that it now threatens to become the dominant Americanism."[4]

Once the United States entered World War I, in April 1917, southern states attempted to fill their quotas by drafting African Americans in disproportionate numbers, even though some warned about the prospect of black men in the armed services. Moreover, black recruits from the North quickly found themselves in poorly provisioned military camps in the South. The ensuing tension between black northern troops and local whites resulted in violence across the South, most notably in a race riot in Houston and a near riot in Spartanburg, South Carolina.[5] When black soldiers went to France, army officials tried to force the French to establish segregation, despite the fact that it "seem[ed] questionable to the French mind." There should be no eating together, no shaking hands, no "sign of intimacy in public between white women and black men," the army ordered.[6]

For African Americans, World War I was a turning point. After "fighting the savage Hun," they returned to fight the "treacherous Cracker." W. E. B. Du Bois, editor of *Crisis*, the magazine of the National Association for the Advancement of Colored People (NAACP), put it this way: "We Return. We return from fighting. We return fighting. Make Way for Democracy!"[7]

Democracy aside, white men singled out and attacked uniformed black veterans across the nation, and twenty-six full-fledged race riots occurred in the summer of 1919.[8] A racial massacre in Chicago raged for days. Whites attacked African Americans, who fought back with guns. White Southerners mocked northern riots as "the chickens coming home to roost"—the result of too much permissiveness toward black southern migrants—but violence broke out in the South as well. White planters tortured and massacred scores of black sharecroppers who had joined together in a union in Elaine, Arkansas.[9] Obsessed with the idea that black troops had consorted with Frenchwomen, the white South was gripped by a widespread sexual panic. Jim Crow, it seemed, needed constant refinement, and white Southerners were up to the task. Now they would have to purge the South of what one white southern U.S. senator called "French-women-ruined niggers."[10]

Amid the bloody chaos that followed World War I a group of white Southerners founded the Commission on Interracial Cooperation (CIC) in 1919. Building on contact between black and white Southerners in the recent war effort, Young Men's Christian Association (YMCA) workers, ministers, and community leaders joined together to alleviate "friction and strife." As racial clashes became "daily occurrences," the CIC inspired more than one-half of the South's 1,293 counties to organize interracial committees under a state and regional hierarchy. The commission sought "legal and economic justice" and "better educational and living conditions" for black Southerners, but it never meant to overturn Jim Crow, nor did it support African American political participation for the next decade. Instead it meant to make Jim Crow work more smoothly. Its black and white members devoted themselves to understanding each other, improving African American living conditions, and forming community structures that would deter racial violence.[11]

The Commission on Interracial Cooperation represented an indigenous solution designed to prove that Southerners themselves could steer a middle course between racial violence and interracial democracy. It attracted the talents of middle-class, educated black and white people, who pursued various strategies to "uplift" African Americans. As time went on, many of its white members and most of its black members personally supported African American suffrage in limited degrees, but the commission did not endorse voting rights as a goal. Moreover, the coalition coalesced because of its members' refusal to declare, even to one another, where they stood on segregation. They simply worked around it.[12] If integration became an issue, one segregationist among them could put a stop to their initiatives. For example, when the commission's director, Will Alexander, condemned Jim Crow railroad cars as "an injustice" in a 1926 speech in Birmingham, he "was ordered out of town."[13] Alexander avoided such forthright proclamations for the next decade. He "knew he could get them [white people] to cooperate with him in programs if he didn't raise this spectre. Because if he raised it, they'd have to discuss it," one observer remembered.[14]

It was important to moderate Jim Crow because most southern whites expected it to last a very long time. That's certainly what the foremost authority on the "Negro Problem" in the South, sociologist Howard Odum at the University of North Carolina, believed. According to Odum, change came only over generations since people behaved according to folkways forged in a regional context. Born in 1884 on a small farm in Georgia, Odum grew to intellectual maturity during the Progressive Era. While earning an MA in classics at the University of Mississippi in 1906, he began to collect black folk songs and record observations on black life. He left Mississippi in 1908 for Clark University in Massachusetts, where he studied under psychologist G. Stanley Hall and attended a seminar on psychoanalysis taught by Sigmund Freud himself that seems not to have made even the slightest impression on him. He earned a PhD at Clark in twelve months and another at Columbia University with sociologist Franklin H. Giddings. Both his dissertations were impressionistic accounts of black life laced with unfounded generalizations.[15]

In 1920 Odum founded the School of Public Welfare (later Social Work) and the Sociology Department at the University of North Carolina. He was still chair of the Sociology Department when the Supreme Court handed down its *Brown v. Board of Education* decision thirty-four years later. He had enormous influence on the study of social problems in the South and successfully brokered most of the research money that flowed south from philanthropies and the federal government. He saw himself as a liberal, joined the Commission on Interracial Cooperation, headed its North Carolina branch, and ultimately became president of the regional commission.[16]

Odum's intellectual journey paralleled that of many educated white Southerners. He migrated from a belief in inherent racial differences in the 1910s to a celebration of black folklore in the 1920s and on to an unshakable faith in culture as a frozen formation in the 1930s.[17] Odum's 1910 *Social and Mental Traits of the Negro* reflected his early belief in the permanence of black inferiority. He wrote of the African American: "He has little conception of the meaning of virtue, truth, honor, manhood integrity. He is shiftless, untidy, and indolent." While there might be individual exceptions, "Negroes . . . are nevertheless of a race that cannot share the communal life of whites."[18] Odum concluded: "As a rule after Negro children become older than ten or twelve years, their development is physical rather than mental."[19]

Odum's identification with the "common folk in the South," by which he meant white people, made him the strongest proponent among U.S. sociologists of the German psychologist Wilhelm Wundt's *Volkerpsychologie*.[20] Transferring Wundt's beliefs to the South, Odum believed that white Southerners and African Americans lived according to traditional mores that changed slowly, over decades or centuries. African Americans' folkways lagged behind whites' in all measures. Slaves had occupied a childlike rung on the ladder of evolution, Odum argued; thus "the short span of his adult status" simply had not given the black Southerner much time to progress. Educated, middle–class white Southerners must oversee black Southerners' projected social evolution and, in the meantime, keep common white Southerners from engaging in violence against them.[21] Odum's theory, which he named regional sociology, meshed with the actions of the CIC to offer a moderate, incremental Southern Solution to the Negro Problem. As the 1920s went on, many whites around the world looked upon the Southern Solution as reasonable, permanent, and intellectually sound.

Snapshots from Jim Crow's World Tour

The Southern Solution stood in contrast with eugenicists' dire predictions of a worldwide white demographic disaster.[22] In 1921 President Warren G. Harding told whites in Birmingham, Alabama, that "the time has passed when you are entitled to assume that this problem of the races is peculiarly . . . your problem." The southern "problem" "is becoming a problem of the north . . . the problem of Africa, of South America, of the Pacific, of the South seas." With the fate of the white world hanging in the balance, the Southern Solution, which rejected "every suggestion of social equality," offered the best hope for white people around the world.[23] The North increasingly adopted segregation, and it came as no surprise when in 1928 the Republican Party excluded black delegates from official national convention hotels, an innovation that would have been scandalous twenty years earlier.[24] Segregation began to appear in venues that had been previously integrated. At the same time, national anxiety over race escalated with international events.

When Woodrow Wilson advocated self-determination in World War I, he conveniently ignored the empire that had resulted from the 1898

Spanish-Cuban-American War. Nor did he mention his recent escapade in Haiti in his Fourteen Points. The federal government had been managing people of color in places such as Cuba and the Philippines for almost two decades when Wilson sent U.S. troops to quell unrest in Haiti in 1915, an occupation that continued until 1934. As a black republic near the United States Haiti had long evoked hope and fear among Americans.[25] As a symbol of black power Haiti itself testified to the capability of ex-slaves. As an example of armed manhood, self-determination, and classical education for black citizens it posed a challenge to the Southern Solution. To whites who believed in Negro inferiority, Haiti was the world turned upside down. Wilson's future secretary of state, William Jennings Bryan, was said to have put it this way in 1912: "Dear me! Think of it! Niggers speaking French!"[26] To African Americans, Haiti represented the city on a hill.

Jim Crow took flight with the U.S. occupation of Haiti, and white Southerners rushed in to extend all aspects of the system. Secretary of the Navy Josephus Daniels functioned as the occupation's chief executive officer, and he installed a group of white Southerners to govern the country. An ambitious newspaper editor and Democratic Party climber, Daniels had masterminded North Carolina's bloody white supremacy campaign in 1898. Within four years black North Carolinians had lost the right to vote and found themselves under Jim Crow's talon. One black Southerner called Daniels "this unspeakable Southern bureaucrat of North Carolina" with an "anti-Negro virus." W. E. B. Du Bois laid the blame for the Haitian occupation at Daniels's feet: "Josephus Daniels has illegally and unjustly occupied a free foreign land and murdered its inhabitants by the thousands. . . . He is carrying on a reign of terror, browbeating, and cruelty at the hands of southern white naval officers and marines."[27] Teetotaler Daniels even considered ordering the military governor to impose Prohibition, since the "natives drink rum," but decided that might be going too far.[28]

Because of Daniels's involvement, the presence of a large number of white southern administrators, and a Marine Corps occupying force made up of largely white Southerners, African Americans regarded the Haitian occupation as an extension of Jim Crow. Within months Americans had segregated facilities in urban areas, provoking one correspondent to report, "Jim Crow had arrived in Haiti!"[29] Atrocities abounded in the occupation's initial stages. Visiting African Americans remarked on the marines' "cracker" accents and on the fact that the marines called the Haitians Gooks.[30] John McIlhenny of New Orleans became the occupation's leading civilian official on the ground and controlled the flow of money in and out of Haiti. Upon meeting the Haitian minister of agriculture, McIlhenny thought "that that man would have brought $1,500 at auction in New Orleans in 1860 for stud purposes."[31]

The marines impressed Haitians into forced labor on the island's infrastructure, justifying the practice by "the obsolete Haitian *corvée*," a vestige of French colonialism that required citizens to work a number of days each year on the roads. Similar to the southern convict labor system, groups of Haitians worked under guard for months at a time. If they tried to escape, they could be shot. The marines enforced the corvée "with all the vindictiveness that a Southern American Negro Hater could put into it."[32]

The most hated white Southerner in Haiti was the Alabamian George Freeman, who had come to the island to impose the southern model of black vocational education. The classical curriculum survived in the Haitian public school system for the first seven years of the occupation, but in 1922 the U.S. Senate forced the substitution of "agricultural instruction." Vocational education, identified with Booker T. Washington's Tuskegee Institute, undergirded Jim Crow. Freeman, who had been working as head of the Texas Agricultural Experiment Station, eagerly exported the Tuskegee model to Haiti. He formed the Service Technique de l'Agriculture et de l'Enseignement Professionnel, a teacher-training school for vocational education. He closed forty classical schools and substituted twelve industrial schools. There was just one problem: Freeman never learned to speak French or Creole. As Freeman ordered his Haitian students to dumb down and set to plowing, bilingual Haitians stood beside him and translated his lectures.[33] Freeman mused: "I believe I am the most disliked man in Haiti. . . . Why am I hated? Because I don't teach what they want me to teach—the classics." He hoped to reap "a fine class of young men to take charge of rural farm teaching," but he sowed a fine field of black revolutionaries instead.[34]

Haiti's young men saw the Tuskegee model as a step backward toward slavery. In his nationalist newspaper *Le Petit Impartial*, young, European-

educated Jacques Roumain argued that George Freeman was determined
to transform Port-au-Prince's lycée "into a vulgar workshop . . . dominated by a regressive and pernicious utilitarianism." Roumain founded the
League of Young Haitian Patriots and took every opportunity to be a
thorn in the side of the Americans. He soon found himself tried for *délit de
presse* (misdeeds in the press) for advocating the return of the rule of law to
Haiti. He served six months.[35] By 1929 his protests had inspired a strike
against Freeman's regime that soon exploded into a nationwide protest
against American rule. The Americans had "deprived them of legal schol-
arships [and] forced them into manual labor," and Haitians "resented
being taught by teachers who could not speak their language." Roumain
became the head of the Comité de Grève, which coordinated the strike and
explicitly protested occupation abuses. When the U.S. forces crushed the
strike, the League of Young Haitian Patriots made contact with African
American Communists, and the Comintern sent a "comrade to Haiti" to
spur the "nascent revolutionary movement." Roumain visited African
American Communists in 1932 and, upon his return to Haiti, founded the
Parti Communiste Haïtien in 1932.[36]

Outraged African Americans called Haiti America's Ireland and
America's India and pronounced the occupation "more shameless and
inexcusable than the German rape of Belgium."[37] As the federal government talked of "great advances" under white troops, African Americans
turned to the black press and the NAACP to learn the truth. NAACP Secretary and ex-Floridian James Weldon Johnson, who spoke fluent
French, set up a black foreign policy that shadowed the occupation's
administration and brought him into close contact with Haitians. He
became "*l'homme plus populaire en Haïti*" and kept the issue in front of the
American public for over a decade.[38] Johnson was a force behind the
Women's International League for Peace and Freedom's fact-finding
mission to the island in 1927. The mission concluded that "the Occupation should be ended for the sake of Haiti, for the sake of the United
States, and especially for the sake of good relations among all American
republics, and finally because it is in itself an unjustified use of power."[39]
Instead it continued for another seven years.

Domestically the U.S. occupation of Haiti served as a warning to
African Americans and a reassurance to white Southerners of national

commitment to white supremacy over democracy. It lent federal imprimatur to the racial regime that white southern disfranchisers, Josephus Daniels chief among them, had created at the turn of the century. The occupation incorporated violence as a vital part of white supremacy, and it portrayed the gap between white civilization and black degeneration as unbridgeable. Through the occupation of Haiti, the Southern Solution became U.S. foreign policy, much as it had become domestic policy in the early days of the Wilson administration.

While the federal government extended Jim Crow by military occupation, the Ku Klux Klan extended white supremacy by ideological conversion. As white people worried about the rising tide of color throughout the 1920s, international attention focused on the recently revived KKK. The Atlanta-based reincarnation of the nineteenth-century Klan swept the nation and went out into the world, adding anti-Catholicism and anti-Semitism to its program of racial hatred. One black Southerner, returning to New York in 1922 after an eight-thousand-mile cross-country journey, reported, "The South has triumphed! The spirit of Dixie holds the nation in its grip." Everywhere he went he had observed KKK advertisements in local newspapers and segregation spreading.[40]

Americans watched as rogues and politicians around the world turned to the Klan to stir up religious and racial prejudice. To the north, western Canadians employed the KKK against Catholics and to discourage African American immigration.[41] To the south, where Cubans had long accused Americans of trying to foment racial discord, a would-be coup leader imported the Klan to organize resistance to the incumbent government. Even farther south, when a Mexico City newspaper editor published an anti-Klan piece, the KKK kidnapped him and released him only when he published a retraction. Across the Pacific, a thousand hooded New Zealanders formed a Klan chapter to control the native Maoris.[42] Secrecy, race-baiting, kidnapping: These methods worked as well in Auckland as in Atlanta. Around the world people looked on southern white supremacy as a desirable import, the most protean of products, adaptable to their own pesky racial situations.

The Klan's exportation provoked international scrutiny of southern white supremacy. A Japanese newspaper declared that "lynching is possible in the United States because the spirit of America is in favor of it. If this were not true, this foul crime would never have grown to its present proportions."[43] A Hindu newspaper in Madras pointed out that a racial massacre in Florida was not an isolated "street brawl"; rather, it resulted from the "racial animosity [that] is artificially kept up by Jim Crow institutions."[44] When U.S. Klansmen founded *Der deutsche Orden des feurigen Kreuzes* (The German Order of the Fiery Cross) in Berlin in 1925, the Germans scoffed at those who joined as "ill-balanced and romantic youths" and quickly extinguished the organization.[45]

Certainly racial and ethnic prejudice existed around the world, but outside the South no one had perfected such a thoroughgoing system of white supremacy.[46] Colonial nations did not always draw the color line in the metropole. One amazed African American observed, "In South Africa or in India, the Negro or the Hindu who must get off the sidewalk at the approach of a white person, can go anywhere his money will take him when in England."[47] Sporadic English attempts at segregation in public places made the news, and authorities frequently investigated the incidents.[48] For example, actor Paul Robeson found himself "barred from a grill room," and *Chicago Defender* owner Robert S. Abbott was refused by twenty hotels before he found a place to stay. "There is apparently something new here," one observer reported as he warned that these practices would harm Britain's relations with its colonial subjects, "turbaned men of dark complexion."[49] African Americans considered segregation abroad a southern import. In fact segregation owed more to colonial experience than African Americans acknowledged.[50]

While the Haitian occupation and the international KKK are the most obvious examples of Jim Crow's flight, the white South's most thoroughgoing success lay in its cultural imperialism. During the 1920s white Southerners' depictions of black life contested those of black writers in the Harlem Renaissance in a battle between Harlem's New Negro and white Southerners' fictive Old Negro. The Great Migration created an audience for southern white cultural production of black life as northern whites came into daily contact with southern-born blacks. By the 1920s minstrelsy, based on highly stylized images and played by white actors in blackface, was offering northern whites few clues about their new black neighbors. As minstrel shows faded (and it was a slow fade) light musicals, such as *Harlem at the*

Apollo, starring actual black people, flourished. Both forms continued alongside the dramas and musicals that white Southerners staged.[51]

White Southerners' work packed Broadway theaters in the 1920s and swept up five Pulitzers. For example, Charlestonian DuBose Heyward wrote the novel *Porgy* in 1925. Two years later, in collaboration with his wife, Dorothy, he rewrote it as a play.[52] North Carolina playwright Paul Green won the Pulitzer in 1927 for *In Abraham's Bosom,* a play of black life based on Green's attempt to "interpret the Negro." The passionate young Green portrayed the black sharecropper Abraham as Christ-like. He believed that Jesus would never tolerate white supremacy or "go slow, be careful, soft pedal" the way the best white Southerners around him did when faced with the "Negro Problem." James Weldon Johnson found Green's play, which depicted the plight of a sharecropper driven to murder his landlord, to be "closer and truer to actual Negro life . . . than any drama of the kind."[53]

Other white southern writers produced tamer work. South Carolinian Julia Peterkin took the Pulitzer in literature in 1929 for her portrayal of black life in the South Carolina low country. When her *Scarlet Sister Mary* became a play, it included whites in blackface and only a "few Negroes in that 'Negro' drama."[54] By contrast, when *Porgy* opened on Broadway in October 1927, its cast was all black. The play toured the world and enjoyed an extended run in London.[55]

White Southerners who depicted African Americans competed with white Northerners, most notably Eugene O'Neill, whose successful *The Emperor Jones* depicted a black man's regression to primitivism on an island nation much like Haiti. But O'Neill went too far for most white Southerners in *All God's Chillun Got Wings* when he included a marriage between a black man and a white woman.[56]

In 1930 the "best loved play of the century," *The Green Pastures,* offered up the least threatening type of Negroes possible, dead ones in a black heaven. Instead of white people with black faces, most of its actors were black people with white wings, governed by a righteous black "Lawd." *The Green Pastures* was a southern white stepchild of Mississippian Roark Bradford's folkloric dialect sketches adapted by New Yorker Marc Connelly.[57] There has rarely been such an unequivocal success among both white and black, northern and southern, critical and popular audiences as *The Green Pastures* first as a play, then as a 1936 film. Heywood Broun said,

"Mind you, I am not saying that this is more than 'Hamlet,' though in all candor I've seen no Hamlet who could hold me if I had tickets for [The Green Pastures]." Robert Benchley raved about it in the New Yorker. African Americans tempered their criticism because of the dignified and lovable Richard Harrison, who played De Lawd, and because entire families toiled in the play, working, they joked, for "Massa Connelly."[58] Nonetheless, a few black viewers criticized it as "the height of absurdity." These white southern plays portrayed "the Negro not as he sees himself, but as he is seen through the condescending eyes of the detached observer," black viewers complained.[59] One black critic observed, "[White] Authors are too anxious to have it said, 'Here is the Negro,' rather than here are a few Negroes whom I have seen."[60]

On the contrary, white Southerners bragged that the plays gave black Southerners the chance to be themselves onstage.[61] White Southerner Eleanor Mercein dubbed The Green Pastures "the first result of the recent Negroid invasion of our allied arts which can give no possible offence to the inborn tastes and tabus of Southern-bred people." She thought Connelly had portrayed the "black psychology, . . . Negro soul-stuff," realistically, but she knew he could never have done that without using a white Southerner's book. "Such insight does not and cannot come out of New York, even out of Harlem. It is a product of the South alone, the deep South, where civilization has not yet obliterated the . . . the race-marks, the race memories." When Mercein referred to the South, she did not mean the black South: "Only a white man of that South could come so closely and so tenderly into the truth of a race . . . [to the truth of] 'our people,'" conveying the ownership of African Americans that she felt.[62]

Black Southerners fled white southern ownership in the Great Migration, taking a chance that they could become their own people in the North. Radical white Texan Robert Minor drew a beautiful cartoon, captioned "Exodus from Dixie," that showed black men and women climbing out of a dry Red Sea. They shook their fists as they turned to look at the lynched bodies and KKK slogans back in Egypt.[63] Yet as African American migrants watched Jim Crow spread its wings across the nation and fly over Haiti, some began to wonder if they had fled far enough. A few decided to look farther.

The Communist Solution

In the 1910s and 1920s the Bolsheviks believed that taken at the flood, the system of Communism they had recently institutionalized would spread across their new nation and around the world. As Russians, Georgians, and Uzbeks threw off feudal regimes and seized their own countries, Communists thought that they heard the long-awaited distress signal that would validate Karl Marx's predictions and destroy capitalism. In this system, racism would be outlawed as "social poison," workers would own the means of production, and town meetings, called soviets, would ensure that everyone's voice was heard. Ethnic differences and historic hatreds would be banished through the multicultural practice of nurturing each group's language and culture. No one would have too much, and no one would have too little. Like Jim Crow, this system also had wings. It promised to liberate colonized peoples and demonstrate to poor white Southerners their class solidarity with poor black Southerners. The Bolsheviks believed that their experience counted for something; in what had been the most autocratic country in the world, Bolsheviks had put workers in control of their own destinies.

A decade after the Bolshevik Revolution, Communists in the USSR and the USA created a Negro Policy that left no action to chance. In the first place, there must be absolute equality between individuals in all social relations. Then it moved from the personal to the political to guarantee equality to all ethnic groups. The system, which most people called social equality, offered a simple mandate for all human activity, from whom one should ask to dance to where workers should sit at union meetings. Because it was so all-encompassing, it required constant, vigorous policing and swift punishment of violations, willful or not. In theory, equality extended to every phase of public and private life. Why shouldn't a black person be able to love and marry a white person? Why shouldn't poor white cotton millworkers be able to unite with poor black workers to stand up to the bosses who exploited them? And why shouldn't a little white boy and a little black boy grow up to be comrades? These weren't the kinds of things one could learn overnight if suddenly confronted with black and white Communists on the streets of Moscow, Charlotte, or Atlanta. Living this new reality required practice.

Black and white Communists in the U.S. South would have gone mad if they had thought that they were spending a considerable portion of their daily lives at an impossible task, but few saw it that way. Communism's success depended on its capacity for self-justification. Everywhere Communists looked, they saw the economy behaving according to the dictates of Marx, and they took that behavior as an indication of Communism's manifest destiny. They watched unemployed black and white Southerners march in the streets together to demand relief in the Great Depression. In the mid-1930s they rejoiced that liberals, Socialists, and Communists united against Fascism and against Jim Crow. In the late 1930s southern Communists failed to fathom the increasingly dictatorial nature of the Soviet regime or to acknowledge that Joseph Stalin applied arbitrary and institutionalized police power to enforce it. They told themselves that the workers welcomed their leadership. There were a few crazy ones who refused to take up the line, but after Stalin had consolidated his power, it was fitting that he dealt ruthlessly with the crazy ones to avoid jeopardizing the happiness of all.

The Bolshevik Revolution's success offered a persuasive final solution to the labor problem. Communists did not have to resort to ethnic cleansing to bring minorities into their nation, and social equality could elevate racially diverse workers to their rightful place. If managed properly, the system would produce ever more committed Communists in each succeeding generation. Indeed, those who instituted Communism expected it to last forever. It was a modern, well-organized, and efficient way to remove the stumbling blocks of race and class in the worldwide contest for advancement.

Because the South represented the least industrialized and least unionized part of the United States, the region weighed heavily on Communist minds. In 1920, 9 million African Americans lived within the confines of the Old Confederacy, the border states of Kentucky and Oklahoma, and the mid-Atlantic states of Maryland and Delaware. Only 1.5 million African Americans lived outside those bounds.[64] If southern African Americans became Communists, they could lead the revolution in their region. If they did not, they could provide a reserve labor force to be used by reactionary planters and industrialists, North and South. Moreover, if the Communists did not conquer racism, they could not organize the poorest, yet fastest industrializing, region of the United States. That is why the South loomed large in Communist imaginations, sometimes as a threat, sometimes as an insurmountable impediment, but most often as a possibility. Black Southerners might open the door to that possibility.

From Tuskegee to Moscow

If Lovett Fort-Whiteman had let himself think too hard about it, the trek from Tuskegee to Moscow might have seemed insurmountable. At the beginning, when he took pleasure in going barefoot, red dust sifted up between his toes. At the end the icy cold from frozen cobblestones penetrated his soles, arching up through his legs despite his knee-high felt boots. Back at Tuskegee Normal and Industrial Institute in 1906, he sometimes had gone for days without seeing a white person, but at the University of the Toilers of the East, he rarely spotted a black person.[65] In Alabama, when he traveled forty miles to bustling Montgomery, Fort-Whiteman stepped aside carefully for white women and children, knowing that trouble might follow if he caught a white person's eye. But as he walked through the streets of Moscow in 1924, curious Russian eyes searched his face, and friendly women and children reached out to touch him.[66] He shed the narrow neckties and white shirts of Tuskegee for a *robochka*, a long shirt sashed with a fancy belt. Now he tucked his trousers into his high boots and adopted a fur hat that sat like a 'possum on his freshly shaved head.[67]

From tomatoes and butter beans to cabbage and beets, from breakfasts of hot buttered grits to *zavtraki* of cold hard-boiled eggs, from four-story brick buildings on campus to two-room log cabins in the heart of Moscow, from the back seat on the streetcar to the one up front, from listening to spiteful white men whistle "Dixie" to watching grown men cry as they sang "Mother Russia," his head spun from the changes.

His greatest adjustment came from escaping to a place where racism, or "social poison," as the Russians called it, was illegal. The Russian Revolution shortened the distance between the South and the Soviets and built a bridge that beckoned those who deplored Jim Crow. The receding southern shore legislated racial discrimination. The looming Soviet horizon legislated the social equality of the races. In the 1920s and early 1930s the Communists encouraged friendship, love, and marriage between blacks and whites.[68] The thoroughgoing ideal of racial and ethnic equality that existed in the USSR sprang both from an ideological impetus to cast off czarist prejudices and from a practical desire to unite people as Communists, not as Jewish or Uzbek.[69] Many black Southerners imagined the USSR as the one place in the world free of racial prejudice.

To Communists in the 1920s, race trouble, such as that in the United States, simply camouflaged class disparity; racism was a byproduct of economic competition between groups.[70] The international Soviet governing body, the Comintern, welcomed the "rising tide of color" that it could turn against imperialist nations. Those whom the eugenicists feared the Soviets welcomed as comrades. To the Soviets, racism wafted off the capitalist enterprise like noxious smoke, an indication of something rotten and smoldering at the core. Where there was smoke, the Comintern thought, fire would soon follow, a revolution kindled by class solidarity that would incinerate discrimination worldwide.[71]

Southern-born people, those who spoke "Russian with a Mississippi accent," helped make the South and African Americans central to Soviet policy.[72] In speaking for the southern masses, African American Communists had an influence on domestic and international Communist policy disproportionate to their meager numbers.[73] As delegates to the international congresses, as students in Moscow, and as radical editors, the fifty or so Communist African Americans and their occasional white southern ally found highly placed Communists in New York and Moscow eager to listen to their advice. After 1928 well-positioned African Americans in the Negro Commission of the Comintern's Executive Committee (ECCI) helped set policy for Communist organizing around the world.

Lovett Fort-Whiteman, a black man from Dallas, Texas, became the first American-born black Communist. Earning the title of the "reddest of the blacks," Fort-Whiteman came to Communism through Socialism, radical labor activism, and race consciousness.[74] As a man Fort-Whiteman embodied the excesses of radicalism; white Southerners would have called him one of the crazy ones. He took enormous risks that promised little in return. He maintained an abiding faith that total victory lay just around the corner. He exhibited a stubborn resistance to alter his course once he headed off toward a goal. Sometimes he was foolish, sometimes he was overbearing, and sometimes he seemed to go around in circles. His comrades often found themselves out of patience with him. Skeptics wondered how he could believe so fervently in something so unlikely. Vexing, curious, and theatrical, he was never commonplace.

Born in December 1889 in Dallas, Lovett Fort-Whiteman grew up in a "radical family." His father, Moses, born in slavery in South Carolina, arrived in the promised land of Texas sometime before 1887. He settled in Dallas, where he worked as a stockman and janitor and owned a house and some cattle. At thirty-five he married Elizabeth Fort, a Texas girl of fifteen, and they prospered. Children came quickly: first Lovett Huey Whiteman and then his sister, Hazel.[75] In time Lovett would seek his own promised land, just as Moses had.

Lovett was a "medium brown color" and grew to be a tall man with "very square shoulders" who "spoke with a Texas accent." He was "shrewd and well educated," having benefited from living in Dallas, where school lasted nine months, instead of the usual three or four, and where African Americans could attend one of the few black high schools in the South.[76] Lovett entered Tuskegee Institute around 1906 and graduated as a machinist. His science background served him well enough to allow him to enter Meharry Medical School in Nashville, Tennessee, but he did not graduate. Instead by 1910 he was in the heart of Harlem, living on West 135th Street, with his widowed mother and sister, Hazel. They lived a little over a block away from the corner of 135th Street and Lenox, called the crossroads of the black world, where radical black speakers such as A. Philip Randolph lectured in the open air. Lovett became, if he did say so himself, a "very successful . . . amateur actor." He was not successful enough, however, to quit his day job as a hotel bellman.[77]

Sometime after the Mexican Revolution began in 1910, Lovett abandoned his acting career and his country to go to Mexico. Perhaps he was on the run from something or perhaps he simply sought adventure. Perhaps he joined the "relatives" whom he mentioned as living there. Perhaps he feared being drafted if the United States entered the Great War.[78] Whatever the explanation, he jumped Jim Crow. He spent the next two or three years in one of the nearest faraway places in the Western Hemisphere, the Yucatán. He worked as an accounting clerk in the hemp industry, spoke fluent Spanish, and learned to read French "fairly well."[79]

In March 1915 the Mexican Revolution arrived in the Yucatán, spurring a coalition of middle-class landowners, workers, and merchants to experiment with homegrown Socialism. Lovett watched as its leaders reformed prostitution, established schools, fought the Catholic Church, and regularly jailed elite landowners for such infractions as "public displays of arrogance" toward their former Indian workers. Fort-Whiteman became a self-described syndicalist and Socialist in the anarcho-syndicalist Casa del Obrero Mundial (House of the World Worker). When the COM called for a strike against the revolutionary government, the government destroyed it.[80]

In 1917, Fort-Whiteman beat a fast retreat and signed on as a sailor on the *Bonita Pintada*, bound for Havana. From there he sailed to Halifax, Nova Scotia, a popular port for West Indian and African American sailors; he next went to Montreal, using the name Harry W. Fort.[81] Then he had to sneak back across the U.S. border since he had entered Mexico without a passport. Black porters, chefs, and waiters on the Boston & Maine railroad line dressed him up as a dining car waiter, and he smiled and mumbled "yassa" as the diners swayed from Montreal to New York. Henry W. Fort rolled into New York City without a nickel in his pocket but full of renewed ambition to become a Shakespearean actor. In the meantime he took a job as a salesclerk. On June 6, 1917, twenty-seven-year-old Lovett Huey Whiteman registered for the draft, as the law required of every man between twenty-one and thirty.[82] Catching a break, he joined the Shakespeare Negro Players and performed the title role in *Othello* in cities up and down the northeastern seaboard.[83] He did so under a new name, Lovett Fort-Whiteman, that combined his mother's and father's surnames. This one stuck.

As he revivified his stage career, he launched his political career when he joined the Socialist Party of New York in the fall of 1917. He quickly made friends with black expatriate Southerners A. Philip Randolph and Chandler Owen of the Socialist magazine the *Messenger*, a radical alternative to the National Association for the Advancement of Colored People's *Crisis*. They belonged to the Socialist Party's interracial Harlem branch, which Fort-Whiteman eagerly joined.[84] Randolph and Owen lectured at the Socialist Rand School of Social Science, and Fort-Whiteman enrolled to hear his professors laugh at Woodrow Wilson's New Freedom, taunting it as the "New DeMOCKracy," and jeer at the "Southern Bourbon ignoramus."[85]

At the Rand School, Fort-Whiteman took the six-month training class for "effective service in the Socialist and radical labor movement" and was graduated "specially equipped to . . . overturn . . . the capitalist system of exploitation." At Rand he met such leading radicals as Sen Katayama, a Japanese Socialist, and Otto Huiswoud, a black man from British Guiana.[86] He spent time with radical Socialist Rose Pastor Stokes, carried around revolutionist Emma Goldman's home address, and preened when future Communist Elizabeth Gurley Flynn judged him capable of "splendid work."[87]

In addition to passions for politics and acting, Fort-Whiteman felt "ambitious to write" and in 1917 became "Dramatic Editor" at the *Messenger*. In its pages, he represented the leading edge of the Harlem Renaissance. "Let the stage for Negroes be dominated by Negroes," he argued, as he demanded that it be black playwrights who wrote the plays in which those actors would work. Eight years before the term *New Negro* became popular currency, Fort-Whiteman wrote, "We, of the New Negro, demand that if the white man comes into our communities to make a living, he must not altogether be on the taking side."[88] When the war ended in November 1918, Fort-Whiteman was twenty-eight and the consummate New Negro: passionate, political, impatient, and searching for racial equality.

Fort-Whiteman tried his hand at fiction that incorporated racial themes. The two short stories he published in the *Messenger* would have almost certainly gotten him lynched back home in Dallas. In "The Nemesis," a Haitian woman first seduces the white southern marine who killed her lover and then takes her revenge on him. In "Wild Flowers," a wealthy northern white woman falls for a poor southern black man working at a Massachusetts seaside resort. He returns to college; she bears his child. To hide their affair, she accuses her New Orleans–born white husband of having black blood, a proposition he readily accepts. When the black lover becomes a college professor, he returns to Massachusetts, but he spurns the white woman and his child, declaring that "my way is to the South."[89]

By 1919 Fort-Whiteman's way back to the South would be radicalism, but it was uncertain what sort of radicalism it would be. In January the Bolsheviks proclaimed the Third Communist International and invited U. S. Socialists to Moscow to attend its First Congress. The next month the Left Wing of the Socialist Party in New York declared its support of the Bolsheviks and claimed seventy thousand "members or sympathizers."[90] One of them was Lovett Fort-Whiteman. He became acquainted with Ludwig C. A. K. Martens, the Bolsheviks' representative in New York. Martens tried to strengthen direct Soviet influence over the Left Wing Socialists and had a particular interest in "propaganda among the negroes." He promised to send Fort-Whiteman to the Soviet Union for a year "in preparation for his work in America."[91]

The "Reddest of the Blacks"

Before Fort-Whiteman could travel to the USSR, however, the Red Scare taught him a lesson in the cost of radicalism. He was still in New York for the National Conference of the Left Wing Socialists in June 1919 but had left by late summer, when the Socialist Party expelled the Left Wingers. Those expelled promptly formed not one but two Communist parties. The Communist Labor Party of America (CLP) worked through the Industrial Workers of the World (IWW) and even the American Federation of Labor (AFL), but the Communist Party of America (CPA) argued that Communists should found their own unions.[92] The CPA included Fort-Whiteman's acquaintances Otto Huiswoud and Cyril Briggs, both black Americans born in the Caribbean.[93] Fort-Whiteman later claimed that he became a Communist in the fall of 1919, but he may not have actually been present at either party's formation since he was traveling south. He joined the IWW after a few weeks on the road, suggesting that when he did officially sign up as a Communist, he probably joined the Communist Labor Party. Organizing black labor was Fort-Whiteman's foremost concern, and he dreamed of founding a black labor magazine.[94]

The 1919 Red Scare and the upsurge of racial violence against African Americans might have daunted a lesser man than Lovett Fort-Whiteman. J. Edgar Hoover, of the Bureau of Investigation, had been closely watching African American radicals. Now all his fears merged into the figure of Fort-Whiteman: black, Socialist, IWW, and probably Communist.[95] After a prolonged and bloody racial battle in Chicago, the bureau sprang into action to search not for the whites who had perpetrated the violence but for the Communistic African Americans who they thought had fomented it. Across the country people asked, "Have the Blacks Turned Red?" and throughout that "Red Summer" white Southerners anxiously awaited racial violence. From Houston, Nashville, Mobile, and Wilmington, North Carolina, reports came in of armed, radical African Americans ready to run amok.[96] Southern congressmen called for an investigation, fully expecting to find that the Socialists, the Bolsheviks, or even the suddenly scary National Association for the Advancement of Colored People (NAACP) were behind this newfound Negro militancy. South Carolina Congressman James Byrnes wanted to suppress three "radical" black periodicals, the NAACP magazine, *Crisis*, Owen and Randolph's Socialist publication, the *Messenger*, and Cyril Briggs's newspaper, the *Crusader*.[97]

If they had read it, the *Crusader* would have frightened southern white readers the most. It was the newspaper of the African Blood Brotherhood. An armed self-defense association shrouded in secrecy, the ABB was a small, New York–based group of radicals founded by Cyril Briggs as a "peace-loving, but red-blooded organization created to afford immediate protection and for Immediate Ultimate Liberation to Negroes Everywhere."[98] When white Southerners asked for federal help to ferret out black radicals, Briggs mocked their hypocrisy. *Now* they demanded a congressional investigation on the "Negro question," he noted wryly. For decades white Southerners had been saying, "We want no interference in our affairs. We can settle this nigger problem ourselves," as they lynched black men. But when they thought that armed black men were headed their way, white Southerners hotfooted it straight to Congress, screaming, "Hey! Help! This nigger problem has changed."[99]

Dixie's dilemma was Fort-Whiteman's delight, and he plunged into this tense moment of opportunity determined to organize black and white southern workers. He planned to make Dallas his base, but first he had to earn his way home by speaking to radical organizations. Armed with a pitifully short list of mostly Socialist "comrades" in the South, he left New York in late August 1919, first for Pennsylvania and then for Ohio, where he watched leaders of the CLA and CPA debate.[100] Youngstown police seized him at an IWW meeting where he was trying unsuccessfully to help future Communist William Z. Foster recruit African Americans to join striking steelworkers.[101]

In late September Fort-Whiteman arrived in St. Louis with Robert Minor, a New York friend and a transgressive Texan like Fort-Whiteman, albeit a white one. Minor's mother was descended directly from Sam Houston, and his father was a frontier lawyer in San Antonio. Poverty and artistic ability had driven him from school and into sign painting at fourteen. Cartooning and journalism had led him to a St. Louis newspaper, where he became friendly with a Russian Jew who converted him to Socialism. In 1918 he went to Moscow, where he witnessed the Russian Revolution, interviewed Lenin, and questioned the centralized state that the Bolsheviks were building. Minor's skepticism gave way to discipleship only slowly, but ultimately he renounced the "Socialist party with its childish drivel about getting a majority vote," something he knew would never happen. In September 1919 he was months away from joining the Communist Party. Minor and Fort-Whiteman had become friends in New York. The bond between the white man from San Antonio and the black man from Dallas was so strong that Otto Huiswoud derisively called Fort-Whiteman "Minor's man Friday."[102]

Minor told twelve hundred white people in St. Louis about his bird's-eye view of the Russian Revolution, while Fort-Whiteman met with white members of the St. Louis Communist Labor Party and talked about Communism to any African Americans who would listen.[103] After two weeks of groundwork, Fort-Whiteman hoped for a packed house at his first public speech, "The Negro and the Social Revolution," but he drew only CLP regulars and an undercover military intelligence officer. He launched into a speech on "the revolution," "Soviets," and "the dictatorship of the proletariat" and pushed copies of the IWW's "Justice for the Negro: How We Can Get It" and an outdated Left-Wing Socialist pamphlet.[104] Suddenly, on a signal from the informer, detectives swarmed into the room, arrested the assembled dozen, and confiscated Fort-Whiteman's stacks of literature.[105]

The St. Louis police crowed that they had captured the "St. Louis Soviet" of the Communist Labor Party. Everyone except Fort-Whiteman was white, four were IWW members, three belonged to the Society for Technical Aid to Soviet Russia, three swore that they had simply wandered in out of curiosity, and one was the government informer.[106] The "foreign influence" abounded. Five Romanians, four Russians, and an Austrian sat in jail. The only American-born attendees were Fort-Whiteman and the military intelligence officer who had infiltrated the group.[107] Government agents declared Fort-Whiteman "a dangerous agitator," and J. Edgar Hoover personally detailed a special agent to handle the case. The local chief of detectives scolded Whiteman: "It has been only since you came here that there has been talk of an uprising against the whites." Fort-Whiteman protested: "It's all wrong, chief, my work is to harmonize the two races." A local black police detective warned that "there is no trouble here and the races have no complaints to make of each other. . . . We don't want you here."[108]

The prosecution cobbled together accounts of Fort-Whiteman's speech and charged him with violating the federal Espionage Act by advocating "resistance to the United States." Fort-Whiteman swore he had never spoken those words.[109] The government also hoped to charge him with failing to register for the draft, a federal crime punishable by a prison sentence. When the agent asked if he had registered for the draft, Fort-Whiteman fictively extended his stay in Mexico by two years and told them he had sat out World War I there. On that sleepy peninsula, he remembered "very little press service, and . . . not much said about the war." Under interrogation he admitted to being a Socialist, an IWW member, and a syndicalist, but he denied being a member of the Communist Labor Party, perhaps technically true at that point.[110]

Meanwhile Justice Department officials widened their net and dispatched agents to Fort-Whiteman's sister's house in Dallas. Married to a wealthy, illiterate man twenty-five years her senior, Hazel Whiteman Harris disarmed the agents. The white Dallas agent described her as "an educated and stylish negress, the mistress of a rich and elegantly furnished home . . . [who] mingles only with the aristocracy in darktown." Furthermore, the agent reported confidently, Harris obeyed her husband when he forbade "any mixing of his wife with these 'niggers what wants to be on equal footing with the white folks.'" The agent admired Harris's Tuskegee degree and reported that she "realized as an educated woman of the colored that her position was not among the whites and that the whites were her and her husband's best friends." The sister was completely in the clear, the Dallas agent assured the bureau, since Hazel had heard from her brother only twice in the past few years, and she swore he could not be involved in politics. Instead he was on his way home to become her handyman to maintain her "fine home and other property," the agent reported.[111]

In fact Hazel Whiteman Harris had been secretly taking money from her husband and sending it to her brother to finance his radical activities. Fort-Whiteman sent her radical publications in return, and A. Philip Randolph depended on her to distribute the *Messenger*. In the summer of 1919, when she sent Fort-Whiteman the money to come to Dallas, she felt that the city was holding its breath, expecting a riot at any moment. She urged her brother to be careful since she knew that he "would not mind dying for his race, nevertheless his death would not better conditions, the masses of Negroes would have . . . to fight for justice." She was doing her part in that fight by distributing the "news and papers" he was sending to her. Hazel Whiteman Harris had completely bamboozled the white agent and apparently her husband as well.[112]

Fort-Whiteman had been in the St. Louis jail for two weeks when federal authorities raided Communist offices and meetings across the country. Both the Communist Party of America and the Communist Labor Party went underground for the next two years. Lovett Fort-Whiteman stayed in jail for months.[113] Finally, in December 1921, the two factions came together to found the Workers Party of America to serve as the "legal," or public, face of the Communist movement.[114] A little over a year later, in February 1923, Fort-Whiteman's name reappeared on the masthead of the *Messenger*, but A. Philip Randolph and Chandler Owen probably did not know yet that Fort-Whiteman was a Communist.[115] Their early admiration for the "Bolsheviki and Lenine," as "extreme radicals," had rapidly turned into disdain.[116] By the time that Fort-Whiteman reappeared, Randolph and Owen saw the Communists as union "wreckers," politically suicidal, and oblivious of the Negro, judgments that aptly described the Communists during their two years underground.[117]

Agitating the Uplifters

Fort-Whiteman came out as a Communist in January 1924, when he published an article in the *Daily Worker* and the Workers Party elected him a delegate to a national "All-Race Assembly" coming up in Chicago the next month.[118] Billed as the "Negro Sanhedrin," after the biblical Hebrew supreme council, the assembly was to give a voice to a broad variety of black organizations and to promote unity among those organizations. It marked the first black event in which Communists openly participated.[119] Cyril Briggs of the African Blood Brotherhood (ABB) had joined with the Boston-based National Equal Rights League to propose the idea to other black organizations. To his dismay, the conservative Howard University professor Kelly Miller was elected chairman. Miller, who believed in Booker T. Washington's uplift strategies, had opposed the founding of the NAACP as too radical. Needless to say, he condemned Bolshevism, Socialism, and the IWW.[120]

Kelly Miller struggled to control the radicals among the planners, specifically ABB leaders and Communists Briggs and Huiswoud.[121] After 1921 the ABB had served as a recruiting arm for the Workers Party and reached out to about four thousand through its newspaper, the *Crusader*, although its active membership fell far short of that figure. The African Blood Brotherhood brought together West Indian émigrés and native-born African Americans. Known as "the angry blond Negro," Briggs was "not distinguishable from a white man." Eloquent on the page, Briggs stuttered so badly in conversation that his speech was incomprehensible, but he wrote at a high pitch of anger. He tied domestic racism to imperialism and saw Communism as the antidote for both.[122] Most of his metaphors were military ones; for example, he wanted the ABB to build a "vanguard and general staff of the negro race" and smuggle "modern arms" into Africa. Briggs was an unabashed radical who advised, "Don't mind being called 'Bolsheviki' by the same people who call you 'nigger.' "[123] As secretary of the Sanhedrin planning committee he sat side by side with mainstream leaders such as James Weldon Johnson, secretary of the NAACP.[124] Fort-Whiteman and Robert Minor beat the Sanhedrin delegates to Chicago by a few days to celebrate the Workers Party's "Negro Week."[125]

In February 1924, 250 people, representing more than sixty-one black organizations, assembled in Chicago. Five black Communists and a handful of ABB members attended the Sanhedrin, and Fort-Whiteman led them all.[126] The *Daily Worker* heralded "the zeal for unity" at the meeting, but if there was any zeal for unity, it vanished when Fort-Whiteman put forward the Workers Party resolutions.[127] He called for U.S. recognition of the Soviet Union, recognition of "The International" [*sic*] as the "anthem of Negro freedom," an end to segregated housing and to colonialism in Africa, freedom of speech in America, legal contracts for tenant farmers, an end to miscegenation laws, and more. The resolutions attacked the American Federation of Labor for its exclusion of African Americans and called on the Sanhedrin delegates to join the Farmer-Labor Party.[128] When Kelly Miller appointed an official of the Chicago Chamber of Commerce to head the Labor Committee, Fort-Whiteman "protested with eloquent vehemence."[129] When the ABB and the Workers Party representatives could not get their resolutions heard, Fort-Whiteman demanded that their issues be put before the conference. Huiswoud jumped to his defense, screaming that "labor is as outcast here as it is outside," while Miller "tried vainly to shut him up."[130] The Communists concluded that "Miller never had any intention to give labor any consideration at the Sanhedrin." They were right. Labor's only success was a resolution condemning segregated AFL locals.[131] Minor castigated the Sanhedrin for ignoring the South, and Miller fielded questions from angry black Southerners about his failure to include African American farmers and workers.[132] The Sanhedrin accomplished little, save to expose class differences among African Americans.

Fort-Whiteman remained in Chicago to become a full-time Communist organizer, focusing on local issues close to working people. In March he led the Chicago Negro Tenants Protective League as it fought against the black and white "rent hogs" who profited from the city's acute housing shortage and growing segregation. By June twenty "little Negro Boy Scouts" had set aside their merit badges and become "twenty little Negro Communists" in a Young Workers League.[133]

As reports floated south about Fort-Whiteman's Communist organizing in Chicago, the largest white newspaper in South Carolina scoffed: "Rouge et noir! Fe Fi Fo Fum!" There might be "in the festering masses of Chicago's Black Hole, or in the rabbit-hutch tenements of darker Harlem," perhaps a "negro . . . of the black-and-tan intelligentsia, who has ingested more propaganda than he can digest," but the "Negro masses, like the race leaders who hold their trust, are far removed from the Communists."[134] South Carolina whites did not know that Fort-Whiteman had launched an all-out campaign in that "Black Hole" for better housing.[135] For a little while longer smug white Southerners might amuse themselves with their coded jokes about the "festering masses," the sexual promiscuity of "rabbit-hutch" tenements, and the sons and daughters of white planters and raped black slave women who had become the "black-and-tan intelligentsia."

Race as Class in the USSR

In mid-June 1924 Fort-Whiteman traveled from Chicago to Moscow as one of roughly five hundred delegates to the Fifth World Congress of the Third International. In Red Square the delegates viewed Lenin's body. Down the hill from the Kremlin, men rowed small skiffs up and down the river, and people on the streets had a more prosperous air about them than any time since the revolution. Some conceded that "events have not developed with quite the speed we expected."[136] The session at which Fort-Whiteman spoke was devoted to "discussion on national and colonial question[s]." Since colonies had not yet industrialized, Fifth Congress delegates debated under what conditions Communists should organize rural peasants like those in Vietnam, Africa, or the American South. Simultaneously, they thrashed out an anti-imperial policy.[137]

On July 1, a long, warm summer day, Fort-Whiteman rose to educate listeners, including Joseph Stalin and Ho Chi Minh, on the Negro question. He outlined the Great Migration of black Southerners to the North and pointed out that these new black industrial workers were difficult to organize. He advised the Party to move into the South and "exploit" rising dissatisfaction among sharecroppers, a strategy that would pay off, since the "negroes are destined to be the most revolutionary class in America." Yet he tried to explain that "even the wealthy bourgeoisie among the negroes suffer from persecution"; thus African Americans "are not discriminated against as a class, but as a race." This was not exactly the right thing to say to a Marxist gathering. Such talk made some warn Fort-Whiteman that he must be careful not to emphasize race over class. Class came first; indeed, it created race.[138] For now Fort-Whiteman began his education by listening to Fifth Congress delegates call "national and race prejudices . . . [the] product of slavery." The Fifth Congress institutionalized a permanent Negro Commission in the Comintern, chaired by an American Communist.[139]

Fort-Whiteman did not return immediately to the United States but enrolled in the school for colonized peoples, the Kommunisticheskii Universitet Trudiashchiknsia Vostoka (Communist University of Toilers of the East), known by the acronym KUTV.[140] He focused on the treatment of minorities within the USSR, which he found extraordinarily encouraging.

For example, he marveled that until the Bolshevik Revolution "the Jew was the Negro of Russia subjected to periodic wholesale lynchings, termed in Russia 'pogroms.' " Now the Jew, Fort-Whiteman concluded, "has become a complete integer of national life. . . . He lives where he chooses." He overlooked the fact that the Bolsheviks suppressed Jewish religious practice.[141]

Fort-Whiteman admired the separate administrative homelands where a particular ethnic group was in the majority and where, theoretically, the group could retain and develop its culture. He saw the homelands as necessary breathing spaces. With territorial "realignment," he reported, Soviets had created "republics in which each of these races may enjoy group autonomy. . . . [Thus] every trace of racial friction is obliterated." Previously it had been "Tatar against Turk; . . . Georgian against Armenian," with "strict segregation." In Tashkent, for example, wooden partitions had "separated natives from Europeans" on streetcars. Fort-Whiteman argued that the Soviets had "approached these racial problems with a directness and a scientific understanding" unsurpassed in the world. The Muslims gained access to schools in Turkestan, and the Uzbeks, crushed under the czar, were, according to Fort-Whiteman, "quite free and independent and a politically important people." This ethnic freedom did not include retaining religious customs; for example, Fort-Whiteman supported the campaign to convince Uzbek women to lift their veils.[142]

Naturally, he filtered his perceptions of racism in the USSR through his memories of racism in the United States. In the Soviet Union he saw nothing of lynching, Jim Crow accommodations, racial slurs in public spaces, or ethnic disfranchisement. The openness of the Soviet people astonished him. In the Ukraine the Third Cossack Division made him an honorary member. In Turkestan residents of Kaufmansky voted to rename their city Whitemansky in his honor. Audiences everywhere listened raptly as Fort-Whiteman told them of the racial hierarchy in the U.S. South; audiences everywhere disavowed racism in the new Soviet society. Fort-Whiteman became convinced that the USSR had become the "first state in the history of the world which ha[d] actually solved the problem of racial discrimination."[143] Under his Party name, James Jackson, he wrote to W. E. B. Du Bois "from a village deep in the heart of Russia." He marveled that in the Soviet Union women and men from all over the world "live as one large family, look upon one another simply as human beings. . . . Here life is poetry itself!" Fort-Whiteman exclaimed.[144]

His studies at KUTV and experience on the ground slowly convinced Fort-Whiteman that he had been wrong to say that African Americans were discriminated against as a race, not as a class. It helped to realize that racism was a man-made rather than a natural phenomenon. Racial oppression sprang from slavery and shored up the postbellum southern economic structure. Freedpeople provided a vital cheap labor force, and whites honed new measures to keep them there. "Race prejudice is not an inherent thing in the mental makeup of the individual," Fort-Whiteman discovered; it was not "transmitted thru the blood." Instead "race prejudice . . . springs from the capitalist order of the society," he declared. White capitalists knew all too well how to "divide and rule" poor whites and blacks. Moreover, a few black people were successful capitalists themselves.[145] It was the "Negro proletariat," rather than the black middle class, that held "the key of salvation of the race."[146]

A senior official in the Comintern provided the intellectual compass for journeys such as Fort-Whiteman's. Sen Katayama, whom Fort-Whiteman had met in New York, was a Japanese revolutionary, an honorary Southerner, and an honorary African American. In the early 1890s Katayama had attended Presbyterian Maryville College in Maryville, Tennessee. Set atop a mountain near Knoxville, Maryville was one of the very few predominantly white southern schools that admitted African American students. Some held it up as a success story, but Katayama had found the racial situation in Maryville abysmal. While Japanese students found acceptance on campus—a countryman captained the football team—only a few African Americans attended the school. Katayama thought that the administration treated those black students as tokens.[147] Himself a "small, dark-brown" man, Katayama was appalled by southern white supremacy when he ventured into town. He did not specifically record what the white men sitting by the cracker barrel said to the "small, dark-brown man" when he went into the store. Did they call him boy? Outside, did they demand that he step off the sidewalk when a white woman passed? Whatever they did, Katayama hated them for a lifetime. After three semesters at Maryville, he could stand it no more and transferred to Grinnell College in Iowa.[148] Converted to Social Gospel activism at Grinnell, Katayama then graduated from Yale Divinity School in 1895 and returned to Japan, where he became a labor activist and eventually a Socialist.[149]

Katayama moved to New York in 1914 and put himself in the heart of radical politics. He encountered Fort-Whiteman and Huiswoud at New York's Rand School during World War I and met with Nikolai Bukharin and Leon Trotsky in Brooklyn. Closely watched by military intelligence during World War I, Katayama leaped the Socialist Party fissures, joined the Communist Party of America, and ran a popcorn stand on Coney Island.[150] The Bolsheviks in 1920 called him to Moscow, where they revered him as a father of Communism and ensconced him in the halls of power.[151] Throughout this dazzling life Katayama never forgot his bitter experience at Maryville. As one African American Communist recalled, " 'Old Man' Katayama knew all about white folks."[152]

In 1921 Katayama had "placed the American Negro problem first upon his full agenda." He spoke in a "squeaky grandmotherly voice about Negro problems and kept the African American cause before the Soviet councils."[153] He held three positions that helped him promote that cause: He was chief of the "American Bureau" of the Comintern, was a member of its powerful Executive Committee (ECCI), and served alongside Ho Chi Minh on the executive committee of the Krestintern, the commission that dealt with peasant issues. The latter position lent him a bully pulpit to point out the potential for revolution among black sharecroppers and tenant farmers.[154]

Moreover, Katayama hoped to link black farmers' struggles with international agrarian travails. He sponsored a successful Resolution on the Negro Question and won approval for a World Negro Congress from the Fourth Congress in 1922. The Comintern's focus on African Americans complemented its "turn to the East," which argued for liberating the oppressed colonial subjects of European imperialism, rather than focus exclusively on European proletarians.[155]

According to Katayama, African Americans would be in the vanguard of the American struggle. He believed that urban, ethnic white Communists gravely failed their party and obstructed revolution when they "neglect[ed]" and "postpone[d] Negro problems again and again." They had not protested the "wholesale massacre of the Negro population of the city of Talsus [Tulsa], Oklahoma by the armed whites of that city" in 1921. Nor had they lobbied for an antilynching bill before the U.S. Congress.[156] "The American Negroes are proletarian," Katayama pointed out, "and they are engaged in heavy works like dockers, railway porters and now many Negroes are in factories of the North." The Comintern could no longer give in to the "petty objections put up by the American Comrades who are too sensitive and irritable about the prejudice of the Southern people and . . . Communists who are yet unable to get rid of racial antagonism." The Party would be doomed in the United States, Katayama warned, unless it solved its own "Negro problem."[157]

Learning to Be Black Bolsheviks

One spring day in 1925 Oliver Golden, of Yazoo City, Mississippi, Tuskegee, Alabama, and, most recently, Chicago, Illinois, spotted his old friend Fort-Whiteman walking down the street. Golden could not believe his eyes. Fort-Whiteman's shaved head reflected the cold spring sun. He sported a *robochka*, knee-high felt boots, and a small mustache. Golden laughed. "What the hell are you wearing?" he asked. "Have you just come off the stage?" Fort-Whiteman told him that he had just returned from the USSR. Golden shared the news that he had just married and was working as a chef on the railroad. But, he complained, the railway companies demanded long routes of black workers, withheld amenities, and failed to pay them for all the hours they worked. Fort-Whiteman shot back: "Then why don't you go to school in Moscow next year?" Golden reported, "At first I thought he was kidding, man, but I would have done anything to get off those dining cars." When Fort-Whiteman said that Golden's wife, Bessie, could go too, the deal was sealed for the Goldens to join eight other new black recruits to KUTV.[158] After eight months in the Soviet Union, Fort-Whiteman had returned to the United States to recruit other African Americans—some already Communists; others, like Golden, merely aggrieved—to study and work in Moscow. Members of the Comintern believed that this core of black students would return to the United States to recruit new black Communists.

In reality, Golden was more traveled and more political than his account of the meeting suggests. Two years older than Fort-Whiteman, Golden had served in France during World War I with the Ninety-second Division of African American soldiers. His best friend had been signal corpsman James Ford, born in 1893 in Pratt City, Alabama. After the war Ford had joined Golden in Chicago, worked in the post office, and tried to organize through the Chicago Federation of Labor for black postal workers' rights.[159]

Both the Golden and the Ford families had been driven from the South. Oliver Golden's grandfather owned a large farm in the Delta, but whites twice burned down his house, once in the 1890s and again in 1909. The last fire proved a blow from which the family never recovered. James Ford had an even more tragic family story: A white mob in Georgia had lynched his grandfather. Golden graduated from Tuskegee, and Ford from Fisk, where his running skills on the football field earned him the nickname Rabbit. Both men had followed the Great Migration stream to Chicago, where they joined the army during World War I. In France, Ford and Golden had protested against discrimination. After they mustered out, they arrived back home just in time to witness the 1919 Chicago race riot. Finding themselves shut out of the jobs for which the army had trained them, the two ex-soldiers worked on the rails and in the post office, where they came into contact with other educated black workers in jobs incommensurate with their educations.[160] Fort-Whiteman's experience in the USSR provided a bridge for Golden to cross in 1925; subsequently Ford would follow.

Fort-Whiteman succeeded in recruiting three black women and seven black men to KUTV. They included the Goldens and Otto Hall, a former African Blood Brotherhood member, whose younger brother, Haywood, joined him in a few months, changing his name to Harry Haywood. Soon Oliver Golden was learning Russian, and Bessie took a new name, Jane.[161] Black Americans joined white Americans who traveled to Moscow after World War I to escape the labor, racial, and class repression of the Red Scare. U.S. citizens poured into the USSR in the late 1920s and 1930s at a rate of five thousand each year. Many were simply tourists. Others were dissidents who sought a place where labor had dignity, where the people ruled over the bosses, where races coexisted peacefully, and where fulfilling basic human needs took precedence over capitalist accumulation. They thought they might find such a place in the USSR.[162]

African Americans, especially, wanted to see the Soviet experiment in racial equality. NAACP founder W. E. B. Du Bois wrote from Moscow in the summer of 1926, "I stand in astonishment and wonder at the revelation of Russia that has come to me." After "less than two months . . . and two thousand miles" in the country, he allowed that he might "be partially deceived and half-informed. . . . But if what I have seen with my eyes and heard with my ears in Russia is Bolshevism, I am a Bolshevik."[163] George Tynes came from Roanoke, Virginia, by way of Wilberforce University, with an agricultural degree. He stayed the rest of his life and became the Soviet authority on the breeding of Peking ducks.[164]

The "racial equality" that African Americans found there turned out to be "so abundant that it proved . . . to amount to almost . . . racial inequality." One black émigré recalled: "If a Negro was standing in line at a shop, some Russian was sure to tug him by the arm and lead him to the front of the line. If it was a matter of a dance with a Russian girl, a Russian man would always give way. . . . In a barber shop or restaurant, although a Russian might long have been waiting his turn, he would always be willing to relinquish it to a Negro."[165] Another black visitor, William Pickens of the NAACP, described such treatment as "almost embarrassing courtesy."[166]

Part of this extraordinary reaction came from the rarity of black faces on the streets, but plenty had appeared on the stage. Before and after the revolution, minstrel and vaudeville shows toured St. Petersburg and Moscow regularly. In the 1920s black jazz bands proved a regular attraction; in fact one could pick and choose from two or three gigs with black performers in a single week.[167] When a group of children followed black students down a street in 1926 shouting, *"Jass Band . . . Jass Band,"* the students suddenly realized that the children thought that *"Jass Band"* meant black people.[168] In addition to the handful of African American and African delegates to the Comintern, there were usually between five and ten African American students in residence in Moscow in the 1920s. By the early 1930s those numbers had swelled with skilled black workers recruited for new Soviet factories.[169]

At KUTV, African Americans joined Indians, Indonesians, Koreans, Filipinos, Persians, Egyptians, Middle Easterners, Africans, Chinese, and Japanese in Marxist theory classes taught in English, French, and Chinese.[170] KUTV actually functioned as a segregated university for "colonized" peoples, usually of color; white Americans attended other schools, such as the Lenin School.[171] In fourteen months African Americans could become "theoretically trained workers," who might be "summon[ed] to Moscow for a prolonged period" to influence Soviet policy on oppressed peoples, but most of their time would be spent organizing in their home countries.[172] Conditions at KUTV shocked African American students. They reported that the dorms were freezing and declared the "sanitary conditions . . . INTOLERABLE." They lacked lighting to study, and despite the fact that they slept on boards, they suffered from bedbugs. They finally asked the Comintern for "separate rooms in the dormitory, the habits and conditions of living of the Eastern students being totally different from what the Americans are accustomed to."[173] In other words, they asked for segregation within the segregated university. William Patterson, a black lawyer from California by way of Harlem, argued that white, not black, U.S. Communists should study at KUTV so that they could learn about people of color and imperialism.[174] The student protest was not the only protest in paradise. Lovett Fort-Whiteman had deplored the fact that "[t]hroughout Russia, it is common to notice prints of caricatured faces of Negroes advertising cigarettes, films, pictures, etc." He knew that there were "no anti-Negro feelings behind it" and that most of the promotions originated abroad, but, he concluded, "the results are the same.[175]

Fort-Whiteman told the press that he had been recruiting African Americans for three years' training for the Russian "diplomatic service."[176] From Moscow, the *Herald Tribune* reported: "Soviet Trains Negroes Here for Uprising." The story quoted Fort-Whiteman as he assured recruits that he would provide them with forged passports and announced his plans to open a KUTV branch in Harlem. The idea was "fantastic," "grotesque," and designed to teach African Americans to "do some real upheaving when they come home."[177] A liberal magazine for white Americans, the *Independent*, concluded that the point of such an education must be to "spread Communism among the colored people of the entire world." The editor of the *Independent* reflexively held up the image of Tuskegee as a totem to ward off such radical Negroes. After all, it was at Tuskegee that African Americans took their first slice of the great capitalist pie. With African American capital in the United States now amounting to over two billion dollars, "it would be hard for a Communistic agitator to fool" such sober, not to mention wealthy, Negroes, the *Independent* said. The editor imagined the KUTV recruiters as "white [and] mysterious," with purses full of Moscow gold. The truth—that by now Tuskegee itself had produced several of those *black* and "mysterious" Communist agitators—would have made Booker T. Washington spin in his grave. [178] If Jim Crow produced black Bolsheviks, then southern white supremacy threatened the entire nation.

Building a Black Communist Base

After he had returned to Chicago to recruit KUTV students, Fort-Whiteman founded the American Negro Labor Congress (ANLC). [179] The Party ordered the African Blood Brotherhood disbanded and made the ANLC the official black Communist organization, a move that made Fort-Whiteman forever the enemy of ABB founder Cyril Briggs. [180] Fort-Whiteman hit the Chicago streets, a leader without any followers. He announced that the ANLC would fight lynching and discrimination in housing and employment and end disfranchisement and sharecropping, which he described as a "peonage system." Enmeshing his early sentiments with Communist policy, Fort-Whiteman called for the lifting of the "steel heel of American imperialism in Haiti." He would force the American Federation of Labor to "abolish the colour line," organize black and white farm workers together, and "institute a vigorous campaign" to defeat the Ku Klux Klan, which he described as an "American fascist organization." [181] In the early spring of 1925 Fort-Whiteman launched a tour to promote the American Negro Labor Congress in the Northeast and the South, seeking to organize "Negro LABOR connections." [182] Fort-Whiteman stayed so far underground on the southern leg of his tour that it is unclear if he went at all.

Instead of organizing the South, Fort-Whiteman returned to Chicago to set up a national ANLC conference. [183] The Comintern expected him to "rally the proletarian elements as the vanguard of the Negro Movement and to bring about their rapprochement with the revolutionary section of the American proletariat." [184] As he sat in his South Side Chicago office with a photograph of Lenin staring down at him, Fort-Whiteman must have found these great expectations—nothing less than a charge to solve the U.S. race problem through a working-class revolution led by African

Americans—a tall order for an organization that existed mainly in his head. The conference was to be held in Chicago in the fall of 1925.[185]

As Fort-Whiteman publicized the ANLC, A. Philip Randolph organized the Brotherhood of Sleeping Car Porters (BSCP), which became the most effective trade union among African American workers.[186] A sympathetic W. E. B. Du Bois argued that both the BSCP and the ANLC "found opposition . . . from the same source."[187] If Du Bois saw similarities between the Brotherhood of Sleeping Car Porters and the American Negro Labor Congress, Randolph put distance between them. He knew that the Communists looked for the opportunity to join the BSCP and push it to the left.[188] He warned the brotherhood, "We cannot temporize with the Communist menace. It's a sinister and destructive crowd. . . . We shall kill this reptile at the very outset."[189]

Randolph hoped for BSCP inclusion in the American Federation of Labor, but only 45 of the organization's 111 affiliated unions admitted African Americans, and most of those forced their black members into Jim Crow locals.[190] The antipathy reflected the pervasive national racism through which white workers protected their jobs. While the AFL recognized BSCP chapters individually, it delayed granting it an international charter and voting rights for seven more years. Some AFL leaders began to reach out to black workers, sponsoring conferences on African American labor, but black AFL membership stayed low because of white workers' resistance on the ground.[191]

While it might not accept African Americans on equal terms or even at all, the AFL nevertheless wanted to control all laborers. Its president, William Green, warned his segregated black locals that if they attended the ANLC, they would be expelled from the AFL. The ANLC would simply distract African Americans and make them think "all their grievances will be remedied by overturning the government of the United States and establishing a Soviet Republic."[192] The *Messenger* purged Fort-Whiteman and opened its pages to Green, who told African Americans not to be "lured" away by the Communist distraction.[193] Communist Robert Minor pronounced Green's order to boycott the ANLC a throwback to "open-shop, union-hating labor-grinding bosses" and predicted that black workers would rally against it. The mainstream *Afro-American* did: "If the American Federation of Labor has something better to offer the American

Negro than the Communists of Moscow, then they need not fear any widespread development of this radicalism."[194]

Nonetheless, the AFL's ban on participation by its black unionists stunted the ANLC conference's outreach. Nor did it seem likely that many black Southerners would attend. Many of the ANLC's planning committee members were southern-born, but only two of the seventeen still lived in the South: a longshoreman from New Orleans and the head of the "Neighborhood Protective Association, Toomsuba, Mississippi."[195]

Fort-Whiteman might have taken the conference's opening night in late October 1925 as a hint of even more trouble to come. His love for Moscow and his flair for the dramatic prompted him to plan an opening night extravaganza of Russian ballet and theater. Five hundred African Americans packed a hall on the South Side of Chicago, and as an expectant hush fell on the crowd, an all-white female ballet troupe entered. Shocked to see a mostly black audience, one of the ballerinas exclaimed in a loud southern accent, "Ah'm not goin' ta dance for these niggahs!" To which someone in the audience shouted, "Throw the cracker bitches out," and the "Russian" ballet corps scooted out of the hall. Then came the pièce de résistance, a Pushkin play, performed by real Russian actors. Pushkin, who was part African, was revered as Russia's greatest poet. To Fort-Whiteman's dismay, disaster struck again when the actors began to speak . . . in Russian.[196]

When Fort-Whiteman finally rose to welcome the delegates, standing under a banner that read ORGANIZATION IS THE FIRST STEP TO FREEDOM, he faced a confused and agitated audience. But he saved the night with a fiery speech, telling them, "The aim of the American Negro Labor Congress is to gather, to mobilize, and to co-ordinate into a fighting machine the most enlightened and militant and class conscious workers of the race."[197] Ten white men lurking on the fringes of the hall, "Mr. Coolidge's federal dicks," took down his every word.[198]

The opening night crowd of five hundred vanished the next morning, turning out to have been mostly local people seeking entertainment. When the credentials committee met, they seated about "forty Black and white delegates, mainly Communists and close sympathizers," most of them from Chicago.[199] The absence of black southern farmers and sharecroppers left an embarrassing void at the conference since the Cominern had ordered the council to report on southern farmers for Sen Katayama's peasant council, the Krestintern.[200] In fact no "Negro peasants" showed up in Chicago. Only three black Southerners attended at all: a dockworker from Galveston, Texas, a freight handler from Lake Charles, Louisiana, and a woman who led the 250-member chapter of the African Blood Brotherhood in Montgomery, Alabama.[201] Robert Minor tried to put the best face on things by arguing that repression had depressed attendance, but he had to admit a "very serious weakness lay in the complete absence of representation of Negro farmers."[202]

The delegates met in a hall decorated to evoke a radical past and to cement a radical present. Portraits of imagined likenesses of slave rebels Nat Turner and Denmark Vesey hung near another of Toussaint L'Ouverture of Haiti. Close by, representations of Abd el-Krim, the Moroccan revolutionary, and Sun Yat-sen, the Chinese revolutionary, stood as "resisters of white imperialism." A Ukrainian chorus sang, a Mexican immigrant coal miner spoke, and a Chinese student spoke of the "British and Japanese imperialism" under which his country suffered. Over the podium hung a six-foot banner illustrating a black man and a white man shaking hands. That handshake could become reality only if the AFL ended segregation.[203] Until then the ANLC would forge "inter-racial committees" between black and white unionists.[204]

The ANLC pointed out that Jim Crow had taken flight and drew analogies between the Ku Klux Klan and the U.S. Congress. For example, the U.S. Congress opposed immigration and the labor movement; so did the KKK. And the KKK kept Congress on its side by enforcing disfranchising laws and instigating terror at the polls, so that politicians had nothing to gain by courting black Southerners. "The Klan is not dying. The Klan is going ahead by leaps and bounds," one speaker told the delegates.[205]

On its last day the conference endorsed "full social equality," a taboo phrase even among the most liberal black leaders. The delegates demanded repeal of interracial marriage prohibitions since they were "schemes to preserve the property of the whites at the expense of Negro womanhood" because they made children illegitimate and ineligible to inherit from their white fathers. The delegates also called for desegregation of public places, residential housing, and the army and the navy, along with the right of free speech and jury service for African Americans.[206] They linked domestic struggles over race to struggles against imperialism and hailed the USSR as a model of equality.[207] The delegates finished off their celebration with a "Grand International Halloween Ball," a perfect ending for Fort-Whiteman, who loved to dress in costume.[208]

When all was said and done, Robert Minor declared the convention a "splendid foundation." Heretofore, Minor argued, black conventions had been hopelessly petty bourgeois. Church conventions simply promoted "the blight of organized superstition." Negro businessmen met regularly "to pose in the attitude of 'optimism' of the white Babbitt-bourgeoisie." Teachers assembled "suffering under the sorest grievances but fearfully avoiding all suggestions of the only remedies which exist." The NAACP held its convention in border states to pander to white philanthropists' interests and to further the Republican Party at election time. Now, Minor concluded, the ANLC had broken the cycle of "prominent persons"—Head Negroes—speaking for "Negro workers." Here the workers spoke for themselves.[209] While Minor mischaracterized the black middle class, at least one non-Communist who covered the conference was impressed. "They really believe that society is upon the threshold of the millennium," he reported. "I rushed into the street expecting to behold a great proletarian uprising."[210]

Although Fort-Whiteman told the Comintern that the conference signaled the start of "real revolutionary work among Negroes," it actually exposed the Communists' weaknesses.[211] Geographically limited to a few large northern cities, small in numbers, unaffiliated with the masses of black workers, and unable to penetrate the South, the ANLC faced insurmountable obstacles. As of January 1926, only one branch existed: in Chicago, with a membership of fifty.[212] One recruiting success stood out: James Ford began his long Communist career at the conference. Fort-Whiteman headed out to recruit comrades to join him.[213] After Fort-Whiteman spoke in Baltimore, the *Afro-American* concluded, "If this is red propaganda, then for God's sake let all our leaders supply themselves with a pot and brush and give 12,000,000 colored people in this country a generous coating."[214] Other African Americans who heard Fort-Whiteman on tour disagreed. According to one, he suffered from an "astral enthusiasm" that would "die aborning."[215]

The white press reacted as if Lovett Fort-Whiteman were Nat Turner and Vladimir Lenin rolled into one. "The Reddest of the Blacks," *Time* magazine called him. Communists were "Bolshevizing the American Negro" and "Boring into Negro Labor." The boring "appears to be directed by the Cvommunist Internationale in Moscow as part of its world-wide propaganda among backward and 'oppressed' colored races."[216] Fort-Whiteman's own motivation, education, and ideology counted for nothing in the white press, where he appeared as a member of a "backward and 'oppressed' colored race," a dog that barked when it heard its Comintern master's voice. The *Literary Digest* could not resist laughing at black workers even as it shuddered to think they might turn Communist. A cartoon in the *Digest*'s pages showed a white man offering a spick-and-span Sambo figure "Bolshevik Pills" and a bucket of red paint. The Samboesque workman rejected the offer, saying, "Excuse me, Mister Bolshiviki, but ah reckon ah's goin' to keep the color the good Lord give me."[217] For his part, Fort-Whiteman complained that not a single black journal had supported the ANLC, but he exaggerated.[218] In *Crisis*, Du Bois upheld the "right . . . to investigate and sympathize with any industrial reform, whether it springs from Russia, China or the South Seas."[219]

The ANLC launched the *Negro Champion*, which took as its motto "The New Negro Acknowledges No 'Superior' Race."[220] Editor Cyril Briggs and contributing editor Lovett Fort-Whiteman reported on the black side of labor stories—for example, the key role that black workers played in the mostly white textile strike in Passaic, New Jersey, in 1926.[221] The *Negro Champion*'s news seemed to jump off the page; it excited, it exhorted, it encouraged. No wonder "one of the younger fellows on the farm" wrote from Alabama, "I understand that all of the city young people are in unions and are getting higher wages and are perfectly satisfied with life. . . . How should we go about organizing?"[222]

Ironically, if "one of the younger fellows on the farm" got a glimpse of the world through the *Negro Champion*, Katayama and the other peasant council Krestintern members decried the fact that they couldn't get a glimpse of the younger fellows on the farm in its pages. Even Fort-Whiteman saw the rural South only in his memories. His lectures remained limited to a few border states, even though he was aware of Katayama and the Krestintern's displeasure with his failure to bring in black southern farmers. He wrote to Robert Minor in the USSR, "I shall insist upon you always being my champion in Moscow. You tell me of some criticisms that are being stated against me."[223] Those criticisms multiplied in the late 1920s.

The Conundrum of Race, Class, and Nation

Three ideological issues divided Communists when they thought about organizing African Americans: the direction of the economy, whether black peasants or proletarians should be organized first, and how much black Southerners' condition resembled that of minorities in the Soviet republics. If one believed that U.S. capitalism was flourishing and the revolution remained far off in the future, it might be prudent to wait for the Great Migration to bring African Americans to the North and organize them there as proletarians. Indeed, they already made up 20 percent of the nation's industrial workforce. But if the economy was collapsing, it made more sense to go at once to the South and organize black sharecroppers even though that would be the tougher task in the short run. The third question involved an analogy to the Soviet Union: Did southern black people represent an oppressed group similar to the USSR's ethnic minorities? If one believed that African Americans constituted a nation within a nation, then the question became how to give them a democratic voice and cultural autonomy. It might be necessary to plot a second southern secession. Fort-Whiteman's difficulties at the grass roots reflected and fueled a debate in the halls of the Kremlin.[224]

In 1927 the Executive Committee of the Comintern (ECCI) expressed its displeasure that Fort-Whiteman "sadly neglected" southern work among farmers. That year he claimed forty-five ANLC chapters, but none in the South. The two strongest were in Chicago and Harlem, where the ANLC had recently recruited a law student named Malcolm Meredith Nurse. Under the name George Padmore, Nurse became first a famous Communist and then a famous ex-Communist.[225] But such victories were small. Critics said that the ANLC was not a "real fighting organization"; it was "merely a propaganda club." There was no "practical plan of building up local councils in the South," either for "unorganized Negro workers in the new southern industries" or for the "Negro tenant and 'share' farmer."[226] The ECCI fired the organizer Fort-

Whiteman had appointed and named West Indian Richard B. Moore, a former leader of the African Blood Brotherhood, general secretary and national organizer of the ANLC.[227]

People had long whispered about Fort-Whiteman. Moore characterized him as a "Bohemian . . . appearing far removed from the workers whom he was expected to organize."[228] Otto Huiswoud thought that he was making "grave blunders."[229] James Ford, whom Fort-Whiteman had brought into the Party, remembered the period of Fort-Whiteman's leadership as one in which "sincere Negroes were driven away from the organization by bad methods of work." Harry Haywood had mixed feelings: "I was both repelled and fascinated by the excessive flamboyance of the man."[230] As the ANLC floundered, black Communists burned with "smoldering dissatisfaction" and found themselves divided into "cliques."[231] In this confusing period some tried to stick "the Trotsky label" on Fort-Whiteman.[232]

It might seem that a black man from Dallas, especially a Tuskegee graduate, would have excelled at southern organizing. But when Fort-Whiteman left the South as a teenager, he had become a true *ex*patriate. His imagination had long ago outgrown the region's boundaries. In the South, Lovett Fort-Whiteman was unthinkable. In the South, black people did not write short stories portraying interracial sex or pen manifestos advocating social equality. Black southern men did not presume to play Othello or walk down the street dressed like Cossacks. Dixie could neither fathom Lovett Fort-Whiteman, the man, nor abide his ideas. Perhaps he failed precisely because he *was* a black Communist from Dallas by way of Tuskegee, a man who knew the limits of the possible in his homeland and found them intolerable. Perhaps he saw too clearly the danger of moving in and out of sharecroppers' shacks, running from a lynch mob, languishing in jail, or, more likely, dying there.

Suddenly emancipated from Party duties and confused about his failures, Fort-Whiteman sought solace in the summer of 1927 by enrolling in Robert Harry Lowie's anthropology class at Columbia University. Lowie, a former student of acclaimed sociologist Franz Boas, taught that race was a variable, unstable concept that obscured individual characteristics rather than illuminate them.[233] Moreover, cultural diffusion, the spread of ideas and practices from one group to another, meant that minority groups did not have distinct, fixed cultures, an argument that countered the Soviet idea of ethnic nationhood. As Boas put it, "a close connection between race and personality has never been established."[234] As a marker of a distinct people race simply did not exist.

Fort-Whiteman now reversed his thinking on the best way to produce black Communists. From now on Communists should not establish separate organizations, such as the ANLC, nor should they try to organize southern rural African Americans. Action should proceed on class lines, not racial lines. But as usual, he went overboard. The "Negro," he argued, "has no peculiar role to play as a race in the American proletarian revolution. He holds no strategic place in our industrial system, nor will he attain to such a position on the eve of the revolution." That did not mean that black people should not be organized, but that it occur only alongside white people, according to their class interests. It did mean that Soviets should temper their expectations of southern African Americans as a revolutionary group-in-waiting.

As he prepared for the upcoming Sixth Congress in Moscow in the early summer of 1928, Fort-Whiteman coauthored a paper entitled "Thesis for a New Negro Policy." Taking on Katayama and most of the Comintern, he argued that it was counterrevolutionary to organize black southern farmers; since white southern farmers would never join them, class solidarity among poor rural Southerners was impossible. Fort-Whiteman's "Thesis" also bore the signatures of William L. Patterson and Jay Lovestone, the white general secretary of the Workers Party.[235]

The preceding year Lovestone had written a controversial article on the Great Negro Migration, in which he argued that only continued black migration to the North would bring African Americans into the Communist Party because only then would they share the class perspective of white workers. Then, as the standard of living for African Americans improved in the North, lynchings would decrease, and the South, facing an agricultural labor shortage, would industrialize. Those African Americans who remained in the South would grow more militant since their labor would be in shorter supply, and they would become proletarians in the new factories. It would therefore be premature to enter the South now. Soon, as blacks filled northern factories, and later, when they filled southern ones, white workers everywhere would jettison racial prejudice and recognize their shared class interests with African Americans.[236]

For the time being, Communists did not need to go to the South since the South, or at least its African Americans, would come to them. The South did not stand as a powder keg awaiting a Red match; rather, the southern problem would wither away.[237] The explanation comforted Fort-Whiteman. He had wasted his time organizing black workers separately; he should have been organizing black and white workers together.

The Lovestone–Fort-Whiteman position antagonized three powerful ideological groups at home and abroad. First, there were those who supported Lovestone's competitor and rising party star William Z. Foster. Then there were black Communists, such as Briggs and Huiswoud, who had come into the party through the African Blood Brotherhood. That group, which embraced a form of black nationalism that the Party tolerated in the 1920s, also believed in the immediacy of the revolution, making them allies of Foster.[238] Third, the Lovestone-Foster breach in the U.S. party mirrored a breach among the Soviets that was partly personal, partly ideological. Having just dispatched Leon Trotsky to internal exile, Joseph Stalin now turned to eliminating Nikolai Bukharin from the chairmanship of the Executive Committee of the Comintern. Bukharin argued that capitalism had gained, not lost, ground in the United States, and Lovestone agreed with him. In the spring of 1928 Stalin disputed them and decided that the revolution was at hand. Foster supported Stalin.[239]

All this esoteric thinking carried heavy practical implications. If the revolution remained, say, a decade away, it made sense for Communists to join non-Communist organizations and unions and gradually to try to persuade other people to join the Party by boring from within. On the other hand, if the economy was going to collapse forthwith, now was the time to establish separate Communist unions and organizations so that revolutionary cadres would be ready and willing to step in when the time came.[240] Fort-Whiteman knew Bukharin well and, as a Lovestone supporter, settled into his deferred revolution camp at the Sixth Congress in the summer of 1928.[241] The meeting marked "the culmination of the struggle for power and policy which had racked the Soviet Party since Lenin's death."[242]

Foster planned a showdown with Lovestone at the congress, and he needed friendly African American Communists on the spot to defend him.

Lovestone originally chose Fort-Whiteman and a black Chicago organizer loyal to him as the only black delegates. Outraged, Foster supporter and ANLC national organizer Richard Moore telegrammed the Executive Committee of the Comintern demanding that Moscow require Lovestone to appoint him and three other black Fosterites. The ECCI secretary noted that the congress planned to give "full discussion to the Negro question" and appointed Foster supporter James Ford to join the U.S. delegation. African American students already in Moscow participated in the congress as well. These included Harry [Hall] Haywood and his brother, Otto Hall, along with William L. Patterson.[243]

The intricate relationships among those who would organize African Americans alongside whites or in a separate group, who would stay in the urban North or venture into the rural South, who believed in the health of capitalism or its sickness, who followed Lovestone or Foster, who bet on Bukharin's strategies or Stalin's ruthlessness all nestled within one another like Russian matrioshka dolls. Fort-Whiteman's future lay hidden in the innermost void. His position on a seemingly small issue of grassroots politics—the way the Party should go about organizing southern black people—thus had resounding implications for individuals, U.S. party factions, and even Soviet history. At the same time, Stalin's attempt to undercut Bukharin, Foster's attempt to oust Lovestone, and Moore's replacement of Fort-Whiteman at the ANLC had resounding implications for the South.[244]

Self-Determination for the Black Belt

With characteristic valor and habitual indiscretion, Fort-Whiteman walked straight into the tempest of the Sixth Congress, his "Thesis for a New Negro Policy" in hand. He attacked William Z. Foster unfairly for maintaining the old Socialist Party prejudice against recruiting African Americans and blamed him for "the Party's half-hearted work among Negroes."[245] Harry Haywood wrote a diverging thesis that supported Foster, one that Stalin would be much more likely to support. He argued that the revolution was imminent and that a swath of black majority areas of the South, the Black Belt, constituted a nation unto itself.[246]

Haywood, the son of slaves from Kentucky and Tennessee, had grown up in Omaha and Minneapolis, just about as far away as one could get from the Black Belt. But he had raised hell through Dixie while traveling with his regiment during World War I, as the black soldiers looted segregated restaurants and punished white insults. If a white Southerner drawled, "Where you boys going?" the soldiers answered, "Goin' to see your momma, you cracker-son-of-a-bitch."[247] Coming from Nebraska, Haywood passed through Dixie as if it were another country. He got away with a lot because he kept moving, but he learned little about southern reality on his way.

Sen Katayama had long supported the idea of African Americans as a separate nation, which meant that they should have geographical, cultural, and some political integrity, but Haywood had resisted the theory when he was a KUTV student.[248] Stalin himself had tried to convince Haywood's brother, Otto Hall, of the same thing.[249] After graduating from KUTV, Haywood had advanced to the Lenin School, where his Marxist theory teacher was Nikolai "Charlie" Nasanov. Just back from two years in the United States, Nasanov argued that black Southerners were an oppressed nation, Haywood began to listen to him.[250] According to Nasanov, the North had won the Civil War, but the South had won the peace, short-circuited Reconstruction, and incorporated the freed slaves as a separate entity that functioned as a captive source of cheap labor. Southern African Americans constituted a nation within the United States; as such they had "the right of self-determination even to separation."[251]

Nasanov followed Lenin, who had written of "the right of nations to self-determination," and included black Southerners as "an oppressed nation . . . (e.g., in Ireland, among the American Negroes etc.)."[252] Stalin had written on the national problem within the USSR, defining a nation as "an historically evolved stable community of language, territory, economic life, and psychological make-up manifested in a community of culture."[253] Across the United States, African Americans should have political rights, but since they met Stalin's definition of a nation in the Black Belt, they could secede from the United States if it did not accord them their rights.[254]

Haywood's thesis, which became known as self-determination for the Black Belt, capitalized on the Soviet "turn to the East" that emphasized organizing colonized peasants.[255] Into this Marxist discussion, Haywood blended strains of American composition. He recognized that the idea of self-determination resonated with Woodrow Wilson's Fourteen Points and that African Americans had deplored Wilson's failure to apply his international philosophy to his native region, the South. Moreover, he knew of the long history of southern black nationalism that grew from slave cultivation of the land, black Southerners' disappointment at Reconstruction's failure to redistribute it, and Pan-African longings. There were newer riffs to play as well. The separatist teachings of Marcus Garvey had attracted many black Americans, to the dismay of the Communists. The idea of black folk culture as a separate genius of the African American people appealed to the white Southerners who misappropriated it and inspired many African Americans in the Harlem Renaissance.[256]

If Fort-Whiteman's new thesis wrote off the South, Haywood's theory of black nationhood made the region a cornerstone of American Communist policy. It would be "the beginning of systematic work in the South."[257] The slogan "Self-determination" would encourage black Southerners to confiscate white planters' land and institute "democratic land redivision." The argument over race and nation divided brothers Otto Hall and Harry Haywood. Hall called his brother Haywood's thesis "criminally stupid" and argued that it "would only serve to drive the Negro masses away." African Americans, he warned, would see it as self-imposed segregation, sort of "revolutionary Jim Crowism," or, as one historian later put it, "a red-winged Jim Crow."[258]

Fort-Whiteman's and Haywood's theses went to the new thirty-two-member Negro Commission, chaired by Stalin faithful Otto Kuusinen. The debate lasted for three days in early August 1928.[259] Haywood and his brother, Otto Hall, joined James Ford, William Patterson, Sen Katayama, Jay Lovestone, and William Foster.[260] Fort-Whiteman appeared before the general session, but his voice is conspicuously absent from the minutes of the self-determination debate, perhaps demonstrating Foster's power to exclude him.[261] Haywood argued that rural black Southerners were "the natural allies of the revolutionary proletariat" and that going South constituted "one of . . . [the Comintern's] principal tasks." The first thing to do would be to "establish a new district in Birmingham, Alabama . . . and gradually . . . spread to the rural districts."[262]

The Negro Commission quickly rejected Fort-Whiteman's argument to wait out the Great Migration, but some were shocked by Haywood's thesis as well. As they parsed Haywood's phrase *oppressed nation*, everyone acknowledged the oppression; it was the nation part that confounded them. Otto Hall was far from alone when he argued, "The Negroes in America are not a national minority; our slogan should be full social and political equality." Many believed "the whole theoretical basis of the thesis wrong."[263] James Ford, from Pratt City, Alabama, wondered out loud if the South could be penetrated. "We have practically no Negro party members," Ford said, mentioning some fifty black Communists out of twelve million African Americans. Someone else pointed out that "the Party has no organizer in the South."[264]

The policy ultimately incorporated four imperatives. First, the Party would emphasize "Negro work." Second, this work would have to be done in the South since most of the black population remained there and industry was moving there. Third, the problem of the black southern population was part of a "general international Negro problem." Fourth, the delegates approved wording that argued that black Southerners "may" seek self-determination, a controversial idea that some argued would fail to win black Southerners while antagonizing poor white Southerners who might have become Party members.[265]

Much drafting and redrafting were to follow, but it was at this moment that the Communist line of self-determination for African Americans in the South emerged. Self-determination did not *mandate* secession; rather, it argued that the black majority in the Black Belt could determine for themselves its political future. The Negro Commission seized the moment to adopt the same theoretical imperative for "an independent native South African republic." A white South African who sat on the Negro Commission warned that white South African trade unionists would "howl them down" and "bricks would fly" when they advocated such a slogan.[266]

A few days later Otto Hall delivered his own dissenting opinion before the Sixth Congress. "If we consider the American Negro a national minority ... we should advocate immediately for an independent Negro republic in the United States," Hall acknowledged, but that would be the wrong move for a number of reasons. First, he argued, African Americans were not a nation culturally, and he portrayed the current celebration of folk songs, traditions of slavery, literature, and "so forth, an idealization of all things black," as "the fabrication of Negro history." Second, the Negro "does not want separate autonomy"; rather, "He wants social and political equality and this is what we have to fight for." Third, the self-determination idea would backfire. It wasn't the black sharecropper but the "southern white worker . . . [who] would welcome this slogan," the idea of "which he would interpret as a means of segregation."[267] One might dream of a "Negro Soviet Republic," but now the Negro question was "not what will be done with them after the revolution," but what it will take to make them revolt in the first place. Social equality, not self-determination, should be the "central slogan around which we can rally the Negro masses."[268]

But it was too late to abandon self-determination. Hall's demurral resulted in an amendment that " 'social equality' remain the central slogan of our party for work among the masses," but a countermotion proposed that "to the point of separation and organization of a separate state" be added to the Haywood self-determination policy.[269] What the commission had avoided when drafting the line, the possibility that black self-determination might mean secession from the South, now put teeth in its resolution. Both amending motions passed by one vote each, whereupon "Old Man" Katayama closed the proceedings by warning dissidents, such as Hall, that "it is your duty to carry out the instructions of the Comintern."[270]

Despite, or perhaps because of, his forthright opposition to self-determination, African American Otto Hall became one of the Communist shock troops in a southern invasion.[271] The Communists' first chance to implement the new Negro policy came a few months later, in Gastonia, North Carolina, when Communist-organized textile workers, 95 percent of them white, struck. In Gastonia the Communists would touch a southern powder keg with a Red match. It proved a trial by fire for the new self-determination policy.

Lovett Fort-Whiteman did not go to Gastonia. Nor did he go back to America, despite the presence of his name on the Workers Party ticket for comptroller of New York State. Without saying good-bye to the 12,370 who voted for him, he took a two-year fellowship to study ethnology at Moscow University, where he hoped to combine his interests in Marxism and anthropology.[272] He could walk the streets of Moscow dressed like a character in the story he was writing in his head, dreaming of a world that would have room enough to hold him. Turning the title of Claude McKay's *Home to Harlem* upside down, Fort-Whiteman grew fond of saying that he went "home to Moscow."[273] He felt free there, whole there. As he had so often in the past, again he judged the risky path safe enough.

2

RAISING THE RED FLAG
IN THE SOUTH

When a black man joined the Communist Party in the 1920s, he often brought the spirit of his grandfather along. The grandfather might have been killed long ago during a terror-filled night on a remote southern farm, but his ghost sang the story of that night in his grandson's ear. James Ford's grandfather hung at the end of a rope in Georgia, Oliver Golden's grandfather twice watched his Mississippi homestead burn down, and Otto Hall's grandfather blew a Tennessee Klansman's head off as the Klansman barged through the family's cabin door. Grandfather Hall was "much of a man," but even he could never remain in the South after proving it.[1]

As the Halls fled their home, they carried home in their hearts all the way from Tennessee to Nebraska, where they traded ribs for runzas in South Omaha. The Hall brothers, Otto and Haywood, grew up in a white world, living and learning beside hardworking Czech and Irish families. Otto was an excellent student, but he dropped out of high school during his senior year in 1908, just before he was to become the only black graduate of South Omaha High. He dropped into black life in North Omaha, where he matriculated on the streets.[2]

For young black men like Otto Hall, World War I shone a light on racial inequality in the United States. He got his first glimpse of his grandfather's South when he served as a stevedore under abusive southern white noncommissioned officers in Newport News, Virginia. In the coldest winter for years he lived in a tent without floors or heat, unable to change clothes or bathe for four months. Ultimately the black soldiers protested until they won barracks and mess halls. Then Hall shipped out to France to help supply the troops abroad. When the war ended, his white officers refused to let him see Paris, so he went AWOL to do it. Ultimately, black men like Hall returned from the war nursing angry hangovers from the injustice they faced while making the world safe for democracy. In 1919 the Hall brothers arrived in Chicago just in time to witness what whites labeled the Chicago race riot, but what Haywood more accurately termed the Chicago rebellion, an event that he recalled as "a pivotal experience in my life."[3]

Otto Hall combed Chicago looking for a radical organization that welcomed blacks. First, he joined Cyril Briggs's African Blood Brotherhood (ABB); then he moved into the Communist Workers Party. Working with Lovett Fort-Whiteman throughout the 1920s, Otto brought into the Party his little brother, Haywood, who took the name Harry Haywood. By the time Otto Hall stood up to Harry Haywood in 1928 over the self-determination policy at the Kremlin, both were seasoned Communists. Hall left Moscow upset about the adoption of self-determination as the new Communist line but buoyed by the Comintern's turn to the South. His grandfather's ghost warned him of the dangers of southern organizing, yet he took the risk. When the Communist National Textile Workers Union (NTWU) entered the South in 1929 by organizing textile mills in Gastonia and Bessemer City, North Carolina, Otto Hall went with them.

The southern textile industry employed an overwhelmingly white workforce. If one takes at face value that textile mills were "white" space, then one might assume that what happened there had nothing to do with race, yet the fact that a certain southern space was designated as white offers a telling clue that race lies at the center of the story. Cotton mills claimed to offer protection for white working people, especially women and children, from the competition of cheap black labor. In this paternal fairy tale, textile millowners also safeguarded white women's virtue by giving them incomes, sheltered them within the mill's walls from the black men who lurked outside, and even chaperoned them inside the factory by keeping them in low-paying women's work away from white men. If this fictive white paternalism was not enough to test the Communists' new Negro Policy, there were four hundred living, breathing black textile workers in Gaston County.+ One organizer recalled that "we could easily have made the decision . . . to hell with the Negroes temporarily . . . but we didn't . . . we made the decision that one of the key things of our policy must be equal wages for equal work—white or black or anything like that."[5]

Reconsidering the 1929 Gastonia strike in light of the Sixth World Congress's commitment to organizing southern African Americans infuses race in a story that has been told as one of unions versus capital, mill hands versus preachers, and patriotic insiders versus subversive outsiders. The Gastonia strike meant all those things, but it meant much more to the history of southern radicalism. The new Communist line on absolute social equality meant that African Americans had a symbolic as well as real role to play in the Party's first foray south. National and international developments in the history of the Party impinged on the way organizers conducted the strike, and many of those developments centered on the worldwide Communist debate about how to recruit people of color. But most important, trying to organize black and white workers together made Gastonia the first southern skirmish in what became a long Communist battle for black equality. Communists came away from the experience espousing a doctrine of black civil rights and social equality because they believed in it, because the Party backed it, and because they believed that only people who embraced that policy could be good Communists.

From Comintern to Cotton Mill

For Communists, the road to Gastonia, North Carolina, began at the Kremlin. In the aftermath of the 1928 Sixth World Congress, the U.S. Workers Party was in an uproar. Stalin had lost patience with Jay Lovestone, and black Party members had lost patience with Lovett Fort-Whiteman. Moreover, delegates had dispersed without a clear idea of what self-determination for the Black Belt actually meant. Stalin had forced Nikolai Bukharin, Lovestone's most important ally in Moscow, to resign the chairmanship of the Executive Committee of the Comintern and had accused him and his followers of representing a Right-Wing antirevolutionary danger. Stalin began to tighten his grip on U.S. Communists and pressured Lovestone and the U.S. Communists to renounce Bukharin by March 1929. Back in Moscow, black Communists like William Patterson and Harry Haywood tried to gain Stalin's favor, and they began to avoid Fort-Whiteman, whom they saw as loyal to Bukharin.[6]

African American Communists returned home from Moscow in the fall of 1928 with new power, and at the next Party convention, Cyril Briggs, Otto Hall, and Otto Huiswoud all won election to the Party's Central Committee. Hall also served in the newly formed Negro Department, headed by Huiswoud and now in charge of the American Negro Labor Congress (ANLC). In the hands of Fort-Whiteman's rivals, the ANLC provided a perfect platform from which his detractors could vilify him. Huiswoud reported that the ANLC was in "bankruptcy," with fully functioning branches in only five cities, none of them in the South.[7] The South had proved to be Fort-Whiteman's Waterloo, even though he had refused to travel there to meet it. It was time to rectify that failure.

In January 1929 the leaders of the Negro Department took up the Sixth Congress's mandate to enter "the South—the hotbed of reaction and race prejudice" and the land of opportunity for Communism. If they established even "one or two units . . . with white and Negro members in the same unit . . . [that would be] in itself an achievement," they reckoned. But how? Otto Hall found eager ANLC recruits in the urban North and Midwest, but his occasional forays into the border states found him facing audiences filled with "pessimism and defeatism."[8] Although they understood the imperative to go south, black Communists were divided on which direction to take. Hall wanted to go where the Communists would most likely find support—for example, among longshoremen in such port cities as Galveston and New Orleans or among black steelworkers in Birmingham, Alabama. Cyril Briggs, remembering the Tulsa racial massacre, wanted to set up an "illegal Party apparatus . . . and [make] plans for an interracial defense corps." Otto Huiswoud argued for the importance of organizing sharecroppers in rural areas.[9]

The Negro Department turned for help to the Red International of Labor Unions (RILU), created as part of what Communists called the Third Period. Embodying the Sixth Congress's belief that capitalism was in crisis and the revolution was at hand, the Third Period signified a more militant, separatist Communism and a push to the left.[10] Stalin deplored the U.S. labor policy of "boring from within the established unions" as futile and antirevolutionary; thus during 1928 the RILU forced U.S. Communists to abandon their efforts to push the American Federation of Labor (AFL) to the left. Instead they would form new Communist unions, called dual unions, to compete with the AFL, an enormous departure from the past.[11] This was good news for African Americans since the AFL largely excluded black workers anyway. Moreover, the new dual unionism policy provided an opportunity to organize the black reserve labor force on southern farms. The RILU addressed the exploitation of workers of color around the world. In March 1929 the RILU Committee of Negro Workers demanded that the U.S. Workers Party focus on the "Negro peasantry of the Southern States of U.S.A.," where black convicts were leased to mine and plantation owners. Convict leasing represented "camouflaged slavery," just like that of blacks under the "Mosanbique [sic] Treaty," and resembled the "corvee labour" that the U.S. Marines imposed on Haitians.[12]

The RILU program for the international liberation of black labor called for the eight-hour day, equal pay for equal work, an end to lynching, abolition of the poll tax, universal education, and special labor consideration for women and children. Then it layered Communist objectives onto those liberal goals—for example, the support of the right of self-determination of Negroes in South Africa, the West Indies, and the U.S. South and a fight against the influence of the church "befogging the minds of the Negro workers and peasants." The RILU's Communist objectives would have been anathema to white Southerners; however, much of its program read like a combination of the 1880s Knights of Labor Constitution and a 1920s southern woman's club agenda. A progressive white North Carolinian would have been able to embrace many of the remedies.[13]

A progressive white North Carolinian had in fact helped craft the manifesto. Paul Crouch had attended the 1928 RILU meeting in Moscow to advise General Secretary Solomon Lozovsky on how Communist unionists might enter the South. Lozovsky was ready to turn south. He believed that the U.S. Workers Party had mishandled black workers and that the Party had thrown away the victory that it had won organizing white textile workers in Passaic, New Jersey, when it handed those workers off to an AFL union. He imagined a Communist union's rushing in where AFL unions had feared to tread to convert newly proletarianized Southerners.[14]

Crouch's personal journey to Communism testifies to its appeal to indigenous southern radicals. His family had lived in rugged Wilkes County in western North Carolina since the eighteenth century, farming on Brushy Mountain and sometimes living in the tiny villages of Moravian Falls and Boomer below. These were places where people had opposed secession and voted Republican after the Civil War. Shortly before Crouch's birth in 1903, North Carolina Republicans had tried unsuccessfully to fight off the disfranchisement of their black allies in the eastern part of the state. The last child of an old farmer and his young second wife, Crouch was surrounded by scores of relatives. Oddly, given their remote location, his relatives ran two nationally circulated newspapers. A male cousin sent two hundred thousand subscribers the *Yellow Jacket*, a Republican paper filled with anti-Catholic diatribes, pro–Ku Klux Klan editorials, and sneers at "nigger equality."[15]

Incredulous at the size of the *Yellow Jacket*'s subscription base and dismayed by its narrow-mindedness, Crouch's neighbor and distant relative James Larkin Pearson decided to put out the *Fool-Killer*, which reached forty thousand readers by the early 1920s. It was an irreverent Socialist paper, filled with "Idiotorials," sympathy for the theory of evolutionism, scorn for religious hypocrisy, and hard-hitting jabs at capitalism. While the *Yellow Jacket* jeered at "nigger equality," the *Fool-Killer* put together a critique of race and class structures: "A nigger is a colored person who has no money."[16] If the *Yellow Jacket* printed "A Klansman's Creed," the *Fool-Killer* castigated "The Ku Klux Klucks." Pearson asked in reference to the Klan: "But say! haven't the pluto papers been telling us that the—the—eh—Bolsheviks have been conducting a secret movement to obtain control of our beloved country . . . ? Now," he reasoned, "if a secret movement is so dangerous to America, it seems a little funny that the '100 per cent Americans' would grasp the same red-hot iron that they fear so much." Pearson saw himself as a Socialist, even if he formed a party of one. He revered Eugene V. Debs and kept up a hot correspondence with Upton Sinclair.[17]

In May 1923 Crouch became the associate editor of the *Fool-Killer*, then operating for a short time under the title *Pearson's Paper*. In twenty-year-old Crouch's first editorial, he embraced vegetarianism, positive thinking, hard work in the open air, and Esperanto. Up on Brushy Mountain, young Paul Crouch had come to believe he could change the world through Socialism. "Let us not be chained to religious or other beliefs because of prejudice or the fact that our parents believed in them," he exhorted. After all, "They might be wrong."[18] Crouch believed that a great crisis was at hand. "Capitalism," he argued, was "the great power as well as the curse of our modern civilization. . . . Only the working class" could bring about change. Capitalism contained "evils" that would gnaw at it from within. After "a total collapse of the governments of the world," there would be "an earthly paradise," where "the UNIVERSAL BROTHERHOOD OF MAN will become a reality and not a dream." When he wrote those words, Crouch probably had never seen a city or a bustling factory. The next year he saw both when he headed to New York to work for the Socialist paper the *Call*. Within months he joined the army and shipped out to Honolulu.[19]

Private Crouch quickly found out that exercising his right to free speech in the army was an altogether different matter from exercising his right to free speech back home in North Carolina. Soon after he arrived, he wrote a letter to the *Honolulu Star-Bulletin* defending the Bolshevik Revolution and Communist ideals. He had learned more about Communism when he organized an Esperanto study group that used *International Language Magazine* as a textbook. The magazine included "stories from Russia that excited comment among the men," and they discussed the revolution. At that point Crouch had never met an actual Communist. He was stunned when the military police arrested him for "conduct prejudicial to good order and military discipline." He sent a desperate appeal to the Comintern, which military authorities promptly confiscated. The court sentenced him to forty years at hard labor at the military disciplinary barracks on Alcatraz, but his commandant recommended cutting the sentence to one year.[20] Brushy Mountain people might have thought of Paul Crouch as a lovable, if misguided, character. Waikiki people thought of Paul Crouch as a dangerous radical. So he became one.

On Alcatraz Crouch finally met a bona fide Communist and joined the Party. Once released, he headed straight to Moscow. He arrived in December 1927, and he rocketed from private to honorary commander of the Red Army. The only southern white delegate to the 1928 RILU conference, he found himself in a strategic position to advise on organizing the South. Later he counseled the Party on applying the policies of self-determination and dual unionism in Dixie.[21]

Once he returned to the United States in the fall of 1928, the Party sent Crouch on a scouting trip to find the best spot from which to organize the South. He chose Charlotte, North Carolina, a place with a relatively diversified economy in the center of a textile region. Charlotte, about ninety miles southeast of his home in Wilkes County, must have seemed full of possibility to Crouch, while it reassured him by offering a modicum of security. It was large enough for organizers to blend in with workers. It had tall buildings. Unlike some southern cities—Birmingham or Gastonia, for example—Charlotte's diversification and size prevented one company or a handful of elites from using city government and the police force as personal fiefdoms. A boosterish air hung over the city, and banking, service, and distribution industries burnished a gloss on its base as a cotton mill town. Charlotte had a thriving and educated black middle class, a black and white proletarian workforce, and it sat smack-dab in the middle of the Piedmont industrial crescent that stretched north to Danville, Virginia, and south to Atlanta, Georgia.

Crouch decided that the best tool to pry open the South would be the National Textile Workers Union of America. The NTWU was one of the first unions created by the RILU shift to separate openly Communist unions, and union leaders Crouch, Albert Weisbord, and Amy Schechter had recently been arrested during a major organizing effort in New Bedford, Massachusetts. Now they were itching to advance into a region that was stealing jobs from northern textile factories. "Most of the cotton workers, 243,000 out of the 445,000, are in the south," the NTWU told the Comintern, "and the south is especially difficult and dangerous to organize."[22] Few in the South, white or black, would have considered it even a remote possibility that white mill hands would ever join a union that espoused racial equality, nor did the Communists give much thought to how they would execute their new Negro Policy on the ground. For his part Paul Crouch did not linger over the contradictions.

In December 1928 the NTWU sent Fred Beal, a heavyset, motorcycle-riding white man, to Charlotte. A self-described Yankee, he had entered the mills as a child in Lawrence, Massachusetts. At the IWW-led strike there in 1912, he heard the legendary labor radical Big Bill Haywood speak. Beal lingered to touch Haywood's coat as he descended the stage, and Big Bill reached down and ruffled the towheaded fifteen-year-old's hair to ignite Beal's career as a labor organizer. His work as a Communist began in 1927, when he traveled to Boston to protest the executions of Sacco and Vanzetti. He then took part in the New Bedford strike the next year.[23] Now he was to lead the NTWU's strike in a most unlikely place, Gastonia, North Carolina, twenty-three miles to the west of Charlotte.[24]

If capitalism wore seersucker suits, white bucks, and panama hats in Charlotte, in Gastonia it didn't bother to dress up. Charlotte's urban sparkle passed quickly from sight as Beal guided his motorcycle toward Gastonia across the bridge that spanned the wide and muddy Catawba River. The river separated more than Mecklenburg and Gaston counties; it separated two New Souths. Had the Communists searched the South over for a tougher place to start, they could not have found one. Beal was quick to realize the differences between the two cities, and he refused to spend the night in Gastonia, retreating at the end of each day to Charlotte.

Gaston County's 112 mills may have reminded Beal of the factories in his native New England. The Loray Mill, the largest mill complex in the South, sat behind an iron fence and resembled a "fortress." But if the factories looked familiar, the housing for millworkers reminded Beal that he was not in Massachusetts anymore. Workers lived in company-owned mill villages, from which they could be evicted in an instant, giving mill-owners "almost feudal power."[25] "Poor, shabby, squalid, a typical mill village," was the description one organizer gave of the Loray village, where seven thousand people lived.[26] In the daytime "hardly a sound" could be heard, since mill mothers worked at night and shushed their children so that they could sleep in the day. Unlike New England mill towns, Gastonia added race segregation to class segregation. In the company-owned "Negro section," black people lived in shotgun shacks, so named because you could stand on the front porch and fire a shot through three rooms in a row and out the back door. White millworkers, by contrast, lived in double-wide shotgun shacks, where you could stand on the front porch and fire a shot out the back door but miss the two bedrooms on the side. Four-room mill houses rented for eight dollars a month. A bathtub in the house bumped up the rent by fifty cents a week. Eight dollars and fifty cents was a sizable chunk out of a woman's twelve-dollar weekly paycheck. Mosquitoes and flies multiplied in the standing water under the houses and swarmed through the screenless windows to cover helpless babies. Those who worked the night shift said the buzzing was so loud in the daytime, they couldn't sleep.[27] Close to downtown, the white middle and upper classes lived on tree-lined paved streets in brick Georgian houses that would have been at home in any upper-class residential area from Philadelphia to Portland.

If anyone ever joined the middle class by working their way up through the Loray Mill, the historical record does not reveal it. Owned by the Rhode Island–based Manville-Jenckes Company, the mill had a reputation for handing down the harshest of "hard rules." There young women tended mill machinery for twelve hours each night, with no supper break. The workweek lasted sixty hours. All of Gastonia's people, black and white, rich and poor, depended directly or indirectly on the mills for their living. The millowners owned more than the factories; they owned the town's commerce, its preachers, and its police force too.[28]

Despite, and perhaps also because of, the ironfisted management, Beal quickly recruited forty-seven white NTWU members in February 1929. His task had been made easier by the former Loray manager, Gordon Johnstone, who deserved his reputation as one of the hardest-driving managers in the South. Johnstone thought that his efficiency drives could not succeed without total control of the workers. He employed labor spies in mill jobs to report on their "coworkers."[29] After Johnstone himself, Loray hands hated the hank clock most. According to one organizer, a millworker described the hank clock as "an invention of the devil. It measures the yarn you're spinnin'. They tells you how much you got to spin, but you cain't make it." The mill linked wages to the impossible production standards as measured by the hank clock, but the workers had no method of verifying its measurements and did not trust it.[30] They responded at first with street protests, not strikes. For example, they paraded down Gastonia's main street with a coffin carried by eight pallbearers. Inside lay a mill operative dressed as Johnstone. Every few feet the "dead" Johnstone would sit up and shout, "How many men are carrying this thing?" The pallbearers would answer, "Eight." The "dead" Johnstone would order: "Lay off two, six can do the work."[31] Yielding to worker complaints, Manville-Jenckes fired Johnstone a few months before Beal's arrival, but Loray retained the spies, the hank clock, and the high production goals. Further trouble seemed almost inevitable.

The Communist Party officially entered the South when Fred Beal called a strike at the Loray Mill on April Fool's Day 1929. The strike came prematurely. Unbeknownst to Beal, one of his early recruits was a company spy who caused five of the forty-seven union members to be fired. On Saturday, March 30, Beal opened an NTWU headquarters and issued a public call for a union meeting. Members voted to strike, and workers at the Loray Mill walked out the following Monday. Fully half of Loray's workforce, eleven hundred people, struck.[32] The strike evenly divided the Loray workforce, even as it divided families. When an "aged striker," Anna Funderburk, tried to stop her daughter from going back into the mill, her son-in-law knocked her to the floor. Beal had been busy in other Piedmont cities as well. In Pineville, Charlotte, and Lexington, millworkers joined the Loray strikers and walked off their jobs.[33]

Beale looked to the Party in New York for more organizers. Crouch was sidelined with pneumonia and missed most of the action. Among those sent south was George Pershing, whom Paul Crouch had recruited into the Party in Alcatraz, now dispatched by the Young Communist League.[34] Pershing had been an idealistic young soldier who joined his mates to burn down the biggest brothel in Honolulu. According to Crouch, Pershing had acted to save the community's morality and to liberate the prostitutes. Beal, who did not like Pershing, told a different story. According to Beal, as a frisky young soldier Pershing had joined some other soldiers to enjoy a night on the town and accidentally ended up burning down the brothel. In any case, the army sent Pershing to Alcatraz. Amy Schechter, who would be in charge of strike relief, was a British-born woman who had been a teacher in a commune in the Soviet Union.[35]

The National Textile Workers Union secretary Albert Weisbord buzzed in and out of Gastonia, but his lover, Vera Buch, stayed in the thick of things. They had met in the 1925 Passaic strike, when Weisbord coolly informed twenty-eight-year-old Buch that he wanted to live with her, never mentioning the word *love*. Buch was madly in love with Weisbord and also in awe of him. When he "proposed" to her, he told her, "You have the courage, intelligence, and the desire to be a Bolshevik." Now she threw herself into organizing the Gastonia workers to prove herself worthy of his prediction.[36]

Black Equality, Red Scare

About four hundred African Americans worked in the textile industry in Gaston County, some in unskilled jobs, such as preparing the cotton for production and sweeping the mill floors. The successful operation of the mill depended on these jobs, menial as they were. If the cotton was not cleaned before it entered the mill, it could not be spun. Likewise, in the dusty mills the crucial, constant job of sweeping and lint control was done by black scrubbers. Loray employed perhaps ten African Americans inside the mill, but a good many more worked in the preparation department "outside" the mill. In Bessemer City, sixteen miles away, the racial dynamics were quite different. Roughly a hundred African Americans worked in American Mill No. 1, which also employed as many white workers but segregated the workforce within job classifications. American Mill No. 2 used a totally black workforce of about one hundred to recover the post-production cotton remnants. The remaining black Gaston County textile workers were scattered at other mills in preparation or sweeping jobs.[37] More African Americans worked in textiles in Gaston County than in some other places in the South, and their presence would test the Communist commitment to interracial organizing.

Two African Americans who worked inside Loray walked out with the white strikers, but the Gastonia police came to their homes and forced them back to work. Those blacks "outside" in preparation tasks stayed on the job, as did a few more inside the mill. But a few days later in Bessemer City, black and white employees at American Mill No. 1 walked off their jobs. Everyone expected American Mill No. 2, which relied exclusively on black labor, to be next. If there were black textile workers, the Communists would have to organize them alongside whites in the same unions. The policies adopted at the Sixth Congress made that clear.[38]

Moreover, U.S. Communists rushed to tell Moscow that they would organize blacks and whites together. NTWU Secretary Weisbord and Robert Minor excitedly cabled RILU General Secretary Lozovsky in

Moscow: "Native American Southern workers awakening everywhere greatest potentialities . . . workers absolutely destitute fighting starvation full weight state machinery treachery AFL and liberals." They planned a "rolling strike wave" in the Carolinas that would require "maximum forces party attention." They assured Lozovsky, "Negro question raised policy no retreat. . . . Main question funds."[39] Thus, when the Communists first ventured into the South, they brought along the Sixth Congress's commitment to black organizing.

In New York the Negro Department met with Weisbord, and together they issued orders to make African American John Owens a full member of the strike committee. Weisbord directed the union to publicize "the fact that the NTWU has sent a Negro organizer into the Southern strike zone . . . to organize the Negro on a basis of full equality." Lest everyone get too carried away, Cyril Briggs suggested that the Party furnish Owens train fare home in case he had to beat a hasty retreat.[40] On Weisbord's first visit to Gastonia on April 7, he publicly advised white strikers to "go say, 'come on brother white and black.' Our union knows no political or religious distinction. We have no color line, although the bosses wish you did."[41] Now Owens was to personify that equality.

When Owens arrived in Gastonia around April 10, Beal invited him to address the white strikers at once. Owens told them, "Negroes are just as good material for struggle in the working class battles as workers of other races." Capitalists used race prejudice to keep workers apart, he argued. He claimed to have impressed the white strikers, but the main result of the speech was to mark him as the most recognizable man in Gastonia within two hours of his arrival. Owens did not know what to do next and decried a lack of direction from New York. Was he representing the ANLC, the Workers Party, or the NTWU? He begged party leaders for "a line to follow out."[42]

Ultimately, Owens, accompanied by a white striker, hit the streets. The mill's private detectives watched their every move. At the end of the day Owens had earned a hole in his shoe—"since 'niggertown' doesn't boast any street cars," he said—and little else. Thoroughly shaken by the surveillance, the white striker told Owens that he was on his own from there on out and that Owens was "due for a bullet at any time and no investigation would be made." Owens headed for the black Ministers Alliance to try to form "some sort of interracial committee to investigate the conditions at the mill, and help Negro workers formulate demands." The ministers wanted nothing to do with the idea or with Owens. Finally, when he gathered a number of black workers together, they "express[ed] a keen interest in some form of organization." It wasn't a union they wanted, however, but an armed "defense organization."[43]

Owens fled after only a few days. He surprised Cyril Briggs and Otto Hall by showing up in New York, telling them that they had no idea what he had faced down there. Henceforth, he suggested, the Negro organizers sent to the South be "given a degree of latitude consistent with the conditions in the penetrated regions" to modify "proper Communist discipline." Briggs reprimanded Owens: "There is only one sort of Communist discipline": to stay at one's post. As a labor journalist put it, "Owen[s] went after one smell of the place."[44]

The Communists' interracial message, as evidenced by Owens's address to white workers and Weisbord's calls for racial equality, sent some white strikers back into the mill within the first two weeks of the strike. Itinerant preacher and striker B. A. Mull announced on April 12 that he was returning to work because union membership conflicted with "my obligation, which is to put the Anglo Saxon race first and to have no mixing of colors." Mull reported that "a number" of Ku Klux Klansmen living in the mill village felt the same way.[45]

The local heat melted the white Communists' resolve. Fred Beal began to vacillate and even reprimanded a fellow organizer when he championed racial equality in an address to the strikers. Worse, Beal broke with the Communist line and proposed that separate black locals be formed in a concession to white workers. New York and Moscow quickly condemned his idea. Another organizer saw cowardice: "Comrades in the field had retreated completely before the prejudices of the white workers." The critical moment came when George Pershing met with the striking white and black workers in Bessemer City and the whites ran a wire across the hall to separate the races. Pershing did not stop them.[46]

When news of the wired segregation got out, NTWU Secretary Weisbord called up Beal and "bawled ... [him] out" for implementing segregation and failing to demand interracial locals. Beal could only reply: "Workers don't like Negroes here. . . . They don't understand much about white chauvinism down here."[47] Another organizer complained that they did not understand how "to apply correctly the new line for the U.S.A." in such a racially charged situation. But for officers of the Negro Department, such as Briggs and Hall, there was no wavering; the policy of complete equality must be followed. The Central Committee recalled Pershing because of the incident, and Otto Hall set out for Gastonia.[48]

If Gastonia workers did not "understand much" about white chauvinism, the Party did not understand the extent of the hostility that Communists would meet in Gastonia. On April 2, the second day of the strike, North Carolina Governor O. Max Gardner, himself a millowner from nearby Shelby, had sent in the National Guard. The *Gastonia Gazette* reported that the troops had arrived to "quell" the strike, but Weisbord welcomed their arrival as a way to keep the peace.[49] As long as the National Guard was there, observers from around the state commented on the "good order" in town. From Brushy Mountain, Crouch's erstwhile mentor James Larkin Pearson pointed out: "The strikers and their leaders [have] so conducted themselves as to win the respect and sympathy of the public, and even, to a large extent, of the newspapers." He also couldn't resist kicking the Gastonia millowners who had "moved [the millworkers] . . . with the toe of a capitalist boot." They got what they deserved: "This time it wasn't the old conservative labor union that came, but a reeking Red union of the sort that gets its color from Moscow."[50]

But the governor withdrew most of the National Guard troops after a week, leaving the strikers in the hands of hastily deputized local World War I veterans by April 10. When a mob of masked men attacked union headquarters and tore it down, board by board, police arrested the strikers who had run out of the building and left the mob alone.[51] Then, as Paul Crouch addressed the strikers on the ruins of the union headquarters, Gastonia officials deputized an additional fifty local men and armed them with bayonets and blackjacks. The first thing that the new deputies did was beat up and stab a reporter from a Charlotte newspaper. Major Alfred Lee Bulwinkle, a former congressman, World War I veteran, and the Loray Mill's lawyer, presided over the temporary deputies, who called themselves the Committee of One Hundred.[52]

The local newspaper, the *Gastonia Gazette*, spouted hysterical anti-Communist propaganda and incited violence. It harped on four themes:

The Communists were "foreigners" who did not truly care about the strikers, they advocated violence, they opposed religion, and, worst of all, they supported racial equality. The organizers, according to the *Gazette*, were "Russianized, Red[s]," and "long-haired fanatics of Petrograd. Shall men and women of the type of Beal . . . with their Bolshevik ideas, with their calls for violence and bloodshed, be permitted to remain in Gaston county? . . . The so-called union that Beal has organized is nothing more or less than a cloak to disguise the Bolshevik principles which he advertises," the *Gazette* reasoned.[53] It published a drawing by a "young man employed in the Loray Mill" of a snake throttling the American flag, with the words "Communism in the South, Kill it."[54]

Gastonia's white elite was proud to equate white supremacy with Americanism and racial equality with Communism. Indeed, the *Gazette* printed the platform of the ANLC as proof that Communists believed in "racial equality, intermarriage of whites and blacks, abolition of all laws discriminating between whites and blacks, etc., etc."[55] Spies reported that a white woman with Workers International Relief "introduced a Negro as her brother," at a union meeting.[56] In a full-page ad entitled "Red Russianism Lifts Its Gory Hands Right Here in Gastonia," the *Gazette* reprinted the announcement of a New York fundraiser for the ANLC's new newspaper, the *Negro Champion*, edited by Cyril Briggs. "Another opportunity for white and black workers to get together socially will be given Friday evening," Briggs's invitation began cheerfully. "Workers of all races . . . [come] together at the dance and help break down capitalist-instilled prejudices and race hatreds."[57] Such an affair, the *Gazette* argued, proved once and for all that Communists "condemn[ed] all religion and loyalty and believe[d] in free love and social equality."[58] The newspaper mused: "How our good mill people can be led by these people who are not our kind, who defy God, flout religion, denounce our government, and who are working for social equality among white and black, is a mystery." The press counted on millworkers' racism to end their labor activism. "These people who are on a strike would be among the first to resent undue familiarity from a Negro," newspaper columnist "Aunt Becky," allegedly a former millworker, reported. "About the first time a Negro presumed to claim equality as a 'member of the union and of the communist party,' blood will be shed," she happily predicted.[59]

For its part, the rival American Federation of Labor decried the strike's racial politics as dangerous for the strikers, even though the AFL had never helped Loray workers. It argued that the NTWU had never meant to start a union in Gastonia; it had meant to start a revolution. "They brought in with them numbers of negroes and they put them on the platforms and patted them on the back," an AFL representative observed. Adhering to racial equality destroyed white Loray workers' chances for a successful strike, alleged the AFL, and had "created a state of mind . . . which was hostile to the workers." Some argued that instead of improving life for those who placed their faith in them, the Communists made matters worse. But the atmosphere in Gastonia had always been "hostile to the workers," black and white, and it was only the Communists who stood up for them.[60]

When the Communist Party dispatched Otto Hall to Gastonia around the end of April, he found tensions at the breaking point and the strikes in disarray. He discovered that the Loray day shift had returned to normal operations fifteen days earlier.[61] After a week on the ground, Hall realized that about 75 percent of the strikers were back at work, with three hundred still outside. In Pineville strikers had given up ten days after they went out, muttering that Beal had promised to feed them but that "he hasn't turned up with a cent . . . my kids are getting hungry." Strikers in Lexington, where one mill remained closed, took heart when they listened to Crouch speak.[62] Crouch took heart from his encounter with Sylvia McMahon, a young striker, with whom he fell in love.

The three hundred Gastonia and Bessemer City strikers continued to picket and to hold open-air meetings. Picketing had been difficult because Gastonia required a permit to "parade," and the deputies enforced the law with bayonets and fists, routinely beating up women. The Communists would not let the male strikers picket armed, and the male millworkers did not like to give up their guns to picket. Therefore a disproportionate number of mill women walked the picket lines and went to jail with female Communist strike leaders.[63] In the women's cellblock, verses of "The Red Flag" lapped and twined with those of mountain ballads like "Barbara Allen," tightening the knot between workers and organizers.[64] Despite the abandonment of the strike by many workers, the strikers were now building a real union, one with dedicated members whose numbers would grow.[65]

Once in Gastonia, Hall received a chilly reception from some of his fellow Communists. Despite his public support of racial equality in the strike, NTWU leader Weisbord was suspicious of Hall. Weisbord was a Lovestonite, Hall was not, and Weisbord was afraid of him. Weisbord refused to release NTWU organizing funds to him since Hall technically represented the Negro Committee and the ANLC, not the textile union.[66] Beal became defensive immediately and continually asked Hall what *he* "would have done about the 'Jim-Crow' wire," if he had been there. Everyone was distracted by the ongoing confrontation between Workers Party head Lovestone and Stalin, and they were suspicious of one another. The Central Committee replaced George Pershing, who condoned the wire, with nineteen-year-old Sophie Melvin, a veteran of the Passaic strike.[67]

Jockeying for position at the top of the Party caused suffering on the ground in Gastonia. The organizers did not have enough money to feed and house the strikers, in part because of the Lovestone controversy. To win the strike, the NTWU would have had to put its money where the workers' mouths were and care immediately for the thousand people who surged out of Loray's gates on April Fool's Day, feeding and housing them when the mill began evictions. When the workers held their first mass meeting, one young woman carried a sign proclaiming, THE INTERNATIONAL WILL FEED US.[68] "Workers flocked out of the mills, already hungry and without a cent of money, expecting and demanding that the Union feed them from the first day and every day," Gastonia organizers reported to RILU Secretary Lozovsky in Moscow. But the Workers International Relief sent Amy Schechter, its representative in Gastonia, only two hundred dollars per day, "a drop in the bucket." Even then organizers had to wait every day for the CP in New York to wire money before they bought food for supper that night. The tents that Beal had promised in April did not arrive until May.[69]

When they did arrive, dispossessed strikers such as Daisy Mae McDonald moved into the tent city. McDonald had left her home in the Smoky Mountains as a teenager to work in South Carolina mills and ended up in Gastonia. By the time she was a thirty-seven-year-old striker, she had given birth to eight children; two had died, and three were old enough to work in the mill. Striking must have been an incredible hardship since she and her six children were penniless. When the strike committee suggested sending one of those children, James Elmer, to the Soviet Union on a tour with the Young Pioneers, McDonald did not even hesitate. She thought it was the "opportunity of a lifetime."[70]

To support families like the McDonalds, organizers begged Lovestone for money, but he was loath to send any. When Beal described his own worn-out clothes in an attempt to get cash from New York, Lovestone sent him an old suit. Beal sent it back to him.[71] When black organizer John Owens complained to the Negro Department that he had not been paid for his work in Gastonia, Briggs responded that the Party was in a "financial crisis." Too bad, Owens decided, "I have been handed a dirty deal. . . . The Party is bunk."[72] Beal was convinced that something was wrong: "Money literally poured into the New York Headquarters of the Workers International Relief and there were sufficient funds to carry on the strike indefinitely." The money never reached the strikers; instead, he alleged, it went to pay back salaries for Party functionaries.[73]

Despite its spotty resources, the NTWU made demands that would assure a long strike. For example, the Communists argued for a forty-hour week, which represented a cut of twenty to thirty-two hours from the current workweek. The NTWU called for a minimum wage of twenty dollars per week when workers were lucky to take home thirteen. In an industry based on the exploitation of women and children, the NTWU demanded that women and children be paid as much as the men in the same jobs. The union should have known that it would never win such an agenda, yet it had no fallback plan. Earl Browder, a rising young Communist who supported William Z. Foster over Lovestone, complained about Weisbord's management: There was no "practical program whatever of ending such strikes, except to see the workers driven back, demoralized and beaten, under the worst possible conditions for building a permanent trade union."[74] The union did demand a few realistic improvements in the mill village: the installation of bathtubs, reduction of charges for lights and water in mill housing, and window screens. In addition, it requested that the toilets in the mill be fixed and that the hank clocks be abolished.[75]

As the embattled Gastonia strikers entered their sixth week outside the mill in mid-May, Lovestone returned to Moscow one more time to jump into the ring with Stalin. He brought along what he thought would be a knockout punch, a vote indicating the support of 90 percent of the

Workers Party, now renamed the Communist Party USA (CPUSA). Lovestone noticed that Moscow had become a much grimmer place in the ten months since the Sixth World Congress. Now people stood in long lines for food and supplies. At the Hotel Lux bar, comrades no longer greeted one another with hearty shouts but spoke in worried whispers.[76] Lovestone lost every round he fought with Stalin, and in committees the Soviets criticized the Americans for their failure to recruit large numbers of African Americans to the party. In the Kremlin, Stalin raged from the podium against Lovestone, capping his outburst with a chilling portent of the future. "Who do you think you are?" Stalin asked Lovestone. "Trotsky defied me. Where is he? Zinoviev defied me. Where is he? Bukharin defied me. Where is he? And you? Who are you?" Then Stalin turned and stormed out of the packed hall, past the American delegation. When he came to Edward Welsh, a black American, Stalin stopped and reached out for Welsh's hand. Confounded, Welsh drew it back and turned to Lovestone, asking, "What the hell does this guy want?"[77]

Before he left for Moscow, Lovestone had anticipated his ouster as head of the CPUSA and had counted on acting Party secretary Robert Minor to change the locks at Party headquarters and freeze the bank accounts. But when the Comintern directed Minor to hand everything over to William Z. Foster, he did so, double-crossing Lovestone, whom the party ultimately expelled.[78] Since many of those involved in Gastonia—Albert Weisbord and Vera Buch, for example—were Lovestonites, the strike leadership was split. Lovestone protested vociferously and accused his enemies of undermining the Gastonia strikers.[79] Amid the controversy everyone in Moscow talked about Gastonia.

Lovett Fort-Whiteman and his colleagues in the Negro Department of the Comintern celebrated reports of Otto Hall's progress in Gastonia, but Hall himself despaired. The diminished numbers of Loray strikers held firm at three hundred, and Bessemer City looked promising, but Hall was appalled at the task before him.[80] He called Weisbord's reports to New York and Moscow about the racial equality of the Gastonia strike "bunk." Hall observed that "the attitude of these cracker strikers toward the Negro has not been changed a bit."[81] He had to convince the remaining strikers that organizing black workers would be in their interest. Sensibly, Hall began organizing any African Americans he found, inside or outside the mills. For those who worked in the service economy, he founded a chapter of the ANLC. Moreover, he worked among those in cotton preparation and began to convince the white strikers that this job was critical to the mill's operation since it controlled the mill's supply of raw materials. [82]

Hall tried to keep a low profile, but he stepped into the limelight during the Communist National Negro Week, May 10–20, when the white press learned that "several Northern Negroes said to have been brought here by the union might address the strikers' mass meeting this evening." Hall talked to the mostly white crowd about those African Americans who prepared the cotton: "If these Negroes quit, the mill can not run."[83] Weisbord arrived to reinforce Hall's efforts and to uphold racial equality: "Every man and woman, white or black, tan, yellow or red, that comes into this organization comes in on an equal footing."[84]

Otto Hall joined forces with Ella May Wiggins, a white striker who lived among African American workers in a shack in Stumptown, a Bessemer City neighborhood. Black and white workers in American Mill No. 1 had walked out on April 15. About the time that Hall arrived at the end of April there was a strike at American No. 2, the all-black cotton waste mill. Subsequently, the overwhelmingly white Osage Mill closed its doors. Two days later part of the white workforce at the remaining unorganized Bessemer City mill, Gambrill and Melville Mills, walked out.[85] The action had shifted from Gastonia to Bessemer City, with its black textile workers.

After watching the repression of the Loray strike, Bessemer City workers understood exactly what they were in for. A non-Communist visitor from the North walked up to a crowd of striking Bessemer City workers and asked a "middle-aged [white] woman" "if she was a Communist." "Sure I am," she answered. "I joined the minute I heard of it in my section and came right on strike with the others." Then the visitor quoted the Gastonia newspaper's characterization of the union—" 'Negro lovers, against America, free love[rs], northern agitators, Russian reds' "—and asked, "Do you mean to say you are lined up with a bunch like that?" The woman responded, "Say you! Listen to me. These people are helping us. They are feeding us. That paper is a liar, and so are you, if you say things like that." While the interlocutor took this to mean that she did not have "enough time or energy to analyze complicated problems of political economy," it also meant that she understood Bessemer City's political economy, and her place in it, all too well.[86] Or as another worker put it, "workers don't give a damn what the union organizers believes in as long as they sticks by the workers."[87]

For example, Ella May Wiggins earned nine dollars a week, four of her nine children had died, she was pregnant, and she had not yet seen her thirtieth birthday. Poverty had been her teacher; now she used it to teach black workers about the union. "I know the colored don't like us," Wiggins told Communist organizer Vera Buch. "But if they see you're poor and humble like themselves, they'll listen to you." As Buch later recalled of Wiggins, "She understood immediately without argument the value of our union principle of racial equality."[88]

For these desperate people, the Communist policy of interracial organizing meant that race wouldn't always separate workers, robbing mill managers of one of their most potent tools. Moreover, the policy had begun to work by the end of May, and Otto Hall and Ella May Wiggins were building an interracial base in Bessemer City. To accept interracial unionism, white workers had to reject everything they had ever been taught and face condemnation and terror. Nevertheless, white millwork-ers such as Red Hendricks, Daisy Mae McDonald, Sylvia McMahon, and Ella May Wiggins came to believe that bringing workers together across racial lines was one way to win their fight. Some of the most ardent strik-ers became Communists after the strike ended. Hendricks joined the CP and became a lifelong organizer. Loray striker Dewey Martin became a district organizer in Charlotte. Daisy Mae McDonald's son Elmer returned from the USSR to find his mother in the CPUSA. After Paul Crouch and Sylvia McMahon married, Sylvia devoted most of her life to working in factory jobs to support Paul while he served as an underpaid organizer in the Communist cause.[89]

The NTWU sent Ella May Wiggins, Kelly Yale "Red" Hendricks, and ten other strikers to Washington to lobby Congress. Hendricks was a charismatic figure whose striking pompadour of bright red hair had earned him his nickname long before his politics did. When North Car-olina Senator Lee Overman told thirteen-year-old, sixty-nine-pound Bin-nie Green, "You ought to be in school," it was Ella May Wiggins who turned on him. She wheeled around, put one hand on her hip, and demanded to know, "How can I send my children to school when I can't make enough to clothe them decently? When I go to the mill at night I have to lock them up at night all by their lone selves." Bertha Crawford burst into tears and asked Overman why she could not earn enough to keep her children in school. He sputtered and became "incoherent." Newspapers across the nation painted a sympathetic picture of Ella May's little ones locked up all by their lone selves.[90]

Saved by the "Crackers"

On June 7, as Otto Hall worked among black Bessemer City workers, Loray Mill strikers gathered to plan their first evening picket line. Vera Buch and Fred Beal were outlining the plans for the march at a union meeting when they were showered by eggs thrown by a heckler. It was the first sign of tension that day. Strikers mobbed the heckler, and a shot rang out, but the heckler escaped, and order returned. As dusk descended, about two hundred strikers marched toward the mill. Three women, Vera Buch, Sophie Melvin, and Edith Miller, led the group. Police beat up several women, and the picket line scattered. From there the police and their deputies, led by Chief of Police Orville Aderholt, turned toward union headquarters at the tent city. Striker Red Hendricks spotted them, jumped up on a tree stump, and crowed like a rooster in warning. The police brushed off the armed sentries' demand for a warrant and threw open the front door of the shack that was the union office. They found themselves facing four shotguns, one held by Fred Beal. Chief Aderholt stepped back off the stoop and began walking away, and shooting broke out. After a few chaotic minutes a striker and Aderholt lay dead.[91]

Some said that the chief's own deputies shot him in the back by mistake; indeed, at his funeral one deputy accidentally shot another deputy as both fired at the strikers in attendance. From Brushy Mountain, James Pearson called it a "deep blood-red catastrophe" and found "the moral" in ending brute force on both sides. "I guess the mills are wishing some they'd let the pale pink unions come," Pearson said, "thus heading off the rabid Reds that come hell-bent and cracking heads." He must have known that Paul Crouch, his protégé, was among the rabid Reds. In H. L. Mencken's *American Mercury*, a little-known reporter from Charlotte, Wilbur J. Cash, reflected on the Gastonia strike as "The War in the South."

Gastonia would be, Cash predicted, "the Lexington from which historians of the future will reckon the industrial struggle, the war of a thousand battles, which, I so believe, will convulse the South during the next decade."[92]

Otto Hall had been unaware of the shooting as he headed back toward Gastonia from Bessemer City until a group of white strikers flagged him down. They warned that if he returned to town, he would surely be lynched since deputies were on a rampage, rounding up strike leaders. Fred Beal could not be found, so Hall would qualify as a perfect scapegoat for Chief Aderholt's death. The white millworkers helped Hall into the trunk of their car and drove him over to the train station in Charlotte.[93]

As he waited in the station's "colored" waiting room, Hall knew that he owed his life to those he had formerly known only as those "cracker strikers." The full-equality policy had cost the union white members, but it had worked. Blacks and whites had joined the union in Bessemer City. Moreover, the white Gastonia workers who had stayed in the union were the sort who could put a black man in the trunk of their car and drive like bats out of hell toward safety, expecting to be stopped and searched any moment. Had they been stopped by a mob, all, white and black alike, would have died. The day after the shootings the *Gazette* actually called for blood: "The blood of these men cries out to the high heaven for vengeance. This community has been too lenient with these despicable curs and snakes from the dives of Passaic, Hoboken, and New York. . . . We dare Beal to show his face again."[94]

The story of white workers saving a black worker's life became a parable of Communist possibility. A few months later, when Harlem residents gathered in a memorial tribute to Nat Turner, they heard "the thrilling story of Gastonia . . . fighting race hostility and hatred in the South and in organizing white and Negro workers side by side in the same unions." A black organizer in Baltimore was arrested when he told a crowd that the Gastonia experience "brought home to the white workers the necessity of open cooperation with colored workers to secure protection from exploitation."[95] Boston's ANLC newsletter proclaimed, "White Workers Help Negro to Escape Bosses' Thugs" and "Solidarity of White and Colored Workers against Southern Mill Owners."[96]

At the end of the day interracial solidarity triumphed in memory over the incredible difficulty of organizing blacks and whites together. In the

Communist press, Myra Page, a white southern woman, retold the story of Gastonia so that its theme was the triumph of class solidarity over traditional racial divisions. She noted that the first question white workers asked when they heard about the Communist program of racial equality was "Would you want to marry a nigger?" or "Would you want your sister [or daughter] to marry a nigger?" Page observed sternly, "This is clearly a bourgeois prejudice, yet we have to deal with it among southern workers." The Communist answer, she said, should be the true one: There had always been a great deal of "intermixture" in the South, "due primarily to the aggressiveness of white males toward Negro women.... The establishment of personal relations, like those of sex, should be left to the choice of the individuals concerned."[97] Such prim jargon most likely would have left Page's hypothetical hecklers dumbfounded, but other Communists formulated the answer in slightly more proletarian terms. The white CP organizer William F. Dunne heard the question once too often and was said to have replied, "Listen, mister, my daughter will marry any man she likes whether white, Negro or Chinese. That will be her affair, not mine. But one thing you can rest assured of: I would rather that she jump into a lake than to marry such a yellow-bellied Negro-hater like you."[98]

To many Communists, the Gastonia strike "demonstrated the correctness of our party line and the readiness of Southern workers to follow it." Once southern white workers realized that "race prejudice is one of the curses which systems of exploitation have visited on the toilers," their conversion to racial equality would make them better Communists.[99] Thus the story began to flow in heroic channels of courage and retribution to end up like this: White CP organizers originally capitulated to southern racism, but Otto Hall's practical approach and hard work won over the white strikers, who ultimately recognized their class interests and saved his life.[100]

If the story of Gastonia became redemption from race prejudice within the Party through the grace of class struggle, there had to be guilt to be cleansed. The organizer who had put down the segregating wire, George Pershing, presented an easy target, and the Negro Department voted to censure him on Hall's advice.[101] But the buck stopped with Lovestonite Weisbord, who found himself accused of "running away from the South" because he had not remained full-time in Gastonia to lead the strike. From Moscow, RILU officials sneered at him: "Now they are only segregating by ropes the Negroes from the Whites at union meetings," an improvement over wires, no doubt. Moreover, Secretary Lozovsky told an RILU assembly, "Weisbord, arguing at a meeting in favour of the Negroes being in one union with the Whites, has told his White listeners that to be in one union with Negroes does not yet mean to feed at one and the same restaurant, to live with them in one hotel, and to travel in one street car with them. Such 'communists' should be chased out of our ranks." Weisbord, whom Passiac strikers had called Little Jesus three years earlier, now found himself transubstantiated, in Lozovsky's words, into "a rag, an alien element to be banished from our ranks." With that, the Communists used the Negro Policy to oust their Lovestonite enemy, even though Weisbord had called for equality in his Gastonia speeches. The price that he paid would serve as a warning to others in the South. Communist organizing demanded complete racial equality. If they should forget, Lozovsky would remind them that "white chauvinism is a serious disease in America . . . it is no joke."[102]

"We Will Never . . . Let Our Leaders Die"

The Communist International Labor Defense (ILD) meanwhile rushed to hire lawyers to defend the strikers jailed after the shootout. Police had quickly apprehended Fred Beal in Spartanburg, South Carolina, and a total of seventy-one people had been arrested.[103] Twelve men, including Beal and Red Hendricks, were charged with murder, punishable by the death penalty. Three northern Communist women, Vera Buch, Sophie Melvin, and Amy Schechter, were also charged with murder. Eight more local strikers charged with assault with a deadly weapon charge made bond.[104] While in jail awaiting trial, Red Hendricks read Marx and named his newborn son Lenin Hendricks. Striker Will McGinnis read nothing in jail; he could not read. By trial time another striker, Clarence Miller, had been charged with murder as well. At a July hearing on change of venue, the judge agreed to move the trial to Charlotte and set it to begin in late August. Moreover, the prosecution reduced the charges against the women to second-degree murder and allowed them to post bail. The women promptly left the state.[105]

After their experience in Gastonia those organizers who were not in jail argued that the ILD must become the "mass organization" leading the Communists in the South. Sending organizers to the South was not enough; the Party must also send lawyers, guns, and money. Only in this way could they expose the "system of police persecution as part of the machinery of class and racial oppression in the south." Organizers related that in Gaston County, some people thought that it was normal for 50 percent of the white workers to "pass through the hands of the police, the courts, the jails and the chain gang" in any given year. For black workers, it was "much worse . . . class oppression of the most vicious kind." The capitalists used "state power" to "cow the workers and keep them in constant subjection by the daily threats of conviction and imprisonment for alleged offenses." The rule of thumb among the police was "When in doubt, arrest a Negro."[106] The South could be organized only with a huge monetary contribution from the Comintern to hire "young, energetic and ambitious lawyers," who would work "for a moderate weekly salary on the immense amount of legal work that will soon pile up."[107] A brave Charlotte lawyer associated with the ILD and took the strikers' cases, but the Comintern did not send money for a southern legal defense network.

The ILD used the weak cases against the strikers to showcase southern injustice at home and around the world. They sponsored rallies across the country for the Gastonia defendants. Reporters from around the world covered the trial. Workers in Mexico, London, Copenhagen, Canada, and South America protested. From France, a Communist editor compared the Gastonia police and North Carolina with the new Fascist threat that French workers felt emanating from Germany.[108]

Ella May Wiggins carried on without Otto Hall in Bessemer City. At an ILD picnic on the eve of the trial, three thousand millworkers from all over the Piedmont heard May sing her own composition, "Mill Mother's Lament," "in her throaty voice" as if lining out a hymn, "with the sudden upward jerk at the end of each line in mountain style." Her new "song ballet," as Wiggins called her ballads, was an even bigger hit that day:

> Come all of you good people, and list to what I tell;
> The story of Chief Adderholt, the man you all knew well.

It was on one Friday evening, the Seventh Day of June,
He went down to the union ground, he met his fatal doom.

They locked up all our leaders, and they put them all in jail,
They shoved them into prison, and refused to give them bail.
The workers join together, and this was their reply;
"We will never, no, we will never, let our leaders die." [109]

The strikers' murder trial resumed August 26, with thirteen men charged with capital murder and three women charged with second-degree murder. But fifteen days later the judge declared a mistrial because a juror went insane. Angry Gastonia rowdies and company thugs began roving the streets of Charlotte and Gastonia.[110] If Otto Hall's blackness had made him a marked man, Wiggins's whiteness had made her a marked woman. A white woman who organized blacks into unions would not have been tolerated even if she had been a Methodist preacher's wife, much less a single mother, pregnant for the tenth time, who cast her lot with Communists.

A week after the mistrial, a band of armed men in cars chased a pickup truck in which Wiggins and other unarmed strikers rode, standing in the open bed. Careening down the road at high speed, Wiggins's group had almost made it home when there was a huge crash. Armed men poured from their cars as strikers jumped out and ran across the fields. A "volley of shots" rained down. One man aimed his pistol straight at Ella May and shot her through the heart at close range. "Oh Lord, he's shot me," she cried out, and died. Even in death Gastonia mobs tormented her, following her coffin home from the funeral parlor. Authorities scattered her little children to several orphanages, to be left forever by "their lone selves."[111]

White supremacy could be vicious to the whites who challenged it as well as to the blacks whom it suppressed. Organizer Vera Buch lamented: "Even more than Communism, it was the appeal to the black people, and especially her [Wiggins's] role in their organization, that incensed mill owners and like-minded people in the South. I am certain it was as an organizer of the Negroes that [she] ... was killed."[112] There were eyewitnesses to Ella May Wiggins's murder, and every one of them recognized her attackers. Several people knew who had pulled the trigger. From New York to San

Francisco, Communists organized protests to "smash the fascist rule of the South," yet a Gaston County grand jury refused to indict anyone.[113]

At that point Governor Gardner intervened and moved the case to Charlotte. Gardner had the courage to argue that "in North Carolina a man may join whatever he wants to join, even the Communist party, and not forfeit his right to the protection of his property and his person." Another hearing in Charlotte resulted in indictments of fourteen men. Yet when five of Ella May Wiggins's murderers came to trial months later, their Loray-paid defense attorneys, led by Major Alfred Lee Bulwinkle, made a simple argument: "Their clients ought not to be found guilty because the slain woman believed in communism." Out for only thirty minutes, the jury set them free.[114]

Meanwhile, on September 30, the Aderholt slaying case went to trial for a second time before Judge Maurice Victor Barnhill. This time around, prosecutors nol-prossed nine of the defendants' cases and tried seven other men for second-degree murder. Beal, Hendricks, Miller, and McGinnis were among the seven charged. The Communists sent a "labor jury" that included two black members and some Gastonia strikers, who sat down together in the courtroom, but the bailiffs quickly strong-armed the whole group up to the Jim Crow balcony. The two black "jury" members had just arrived from New York and tested the limits of segregation by "insist[ing] on staying" in the white district organizer's house. The organizer expected immediate eviction. In New York, Robert Minor worried that they might be lynched.[115]

At one point in the trial the prosecution asked white striker Dewey Martin whether he had ever addressed a union meeting along with a "Negro, Otto Hall." When the defense objected, the prosecution argued that it was an "impeaching question." Martin's testimony could be disregarded if he was foolish enough to believe in "the social equality of whites and Negroes." Judge Barnhill overruled that line of questioning, refusing to allow a defendant's racial ideology to stand as a test of veracity. But after witness Edith Miller kissed the Bible with a resounding "smack," the judge allowed the prosecutor to ask, "Do you believe in the Bible?"[116] The prosecutor wound up his closing argument by asking the jury, "Do you believe in the flag of your country floating in the breeze, kissing the sunlight singing the song of freedom? Do you believe in North Carolina?"

Into this paradise, he told them, "union organizers came, fiends incarnate, stripped of their hoofs and horns, bearing guns instead of pitchforks . . . sweeping like a cyclone and tornado to sink damnable fangs into the heart and lifeblood of my community."[117]

The jury, all white, of course, was out for fifty-seven minutes before it found the defendants "guilty of murder in the first degree." Judge Barnhill looked dumbfounded. "They are not charged with murder in the first degree!" he blurted out. Ultimately, Barnhill sentenced the northern Communist defendants, including Fred Beal, to seventeen to twenty years in prison. Red Hendricks got five to seven years. The ACLU provided bond for Beal and Hendricks, and the ILD appealed the cases to the North Carolina Supreme Court. The two planned to leave Charlotte on speaking tours to raise money for their appeal.[118]

First, however, Hendricks went straight back to Gastonia. "Sorta thought it would do me more good than anything else," he said. In front of Johnson's drugstore, at Greasy Corner, half a block from the mill, Hendricks bragged, "I talked as much union as I could" to two hundred workers who gathered.[119] From Greasy Corner, Hendricks went to Madison Square Garden, where he addressed ten thousand people on the anniversary of the Russian Revolution. Observers reported that he made "a picturesque appearance" with his "abundance of flaming red hair." He told the assembled ten thousand: "I've come back to give you the plea for bail of my six comrades. . . . You'll have to hurry up or they will be taken out and lynched," he cautioned. "They want our lives just as much as they did Ella May Wiggins's," Hendricks warned.[120]

Setting Down Communist Roots

After the Gastonia strike and trials, the Communist Party sustained a permanent presence in the South and committed itself to racial equality in the service of class struggle. On January 1, 1930, the Party officially set up two southern districts, District 17, which included Alabama, Tennessee, Georgia, Mississippi, and Florida, with headquarters in Birmingham, and District 16, which included Virginia, North Carolina, and South Carolina and was usually headquartered in Charlotte, sometimes in Greensboro or Winston-Salem.[121]

Southern Communists continued to declare themselves openly despite the violence they had met in Gastonia. Dispatched to organize millworkers in Greenville, South Carolina, Sophie Melvin drummed up a large crowd for her first Communist NTWU meeting by putting an ad in the paper.[122] The Communists also publicized the ILD's First Southern Conference in Charlotte in December 1929. Sixty-two delegates attended, but there was only one African American, B.W. Miller, from Atlanta. Daisy Mae McDonald, former Gastonia striker, served as secretary of the conference. Red Hendricks, out on bail, was there. The *Labor Defender* published a photograph of the delegates. The people in the crowd wear clothes so big that they hang off their emaciated bodies. The timber storefront behind them is typical of the textile neighborhood of North Charlotte, with porches upstairs and down, hugging the corner of Belmont and Caldwell streets and "edging on the Negro neighborhood." The loopy smiles and self-conscious poses recall a Sunday school picnic. But the signs that the delegates hold arrest the viewer who thought she knew the South. DOWN WITH FASCIST TERRORISM AND ANTI LABOR LEGISLATION; ABOLISH LYNCHING/END DISCRIMINATION AGAINST NEGRO WORKERS; FREE ALL CLASS-WAR PRISONERS; and the calmer, but no less astonishing, WE GREET THE WORKERS OF THE USSR.[123]

Under ideal conditions, each southern district had a district organizer and three other staffers, but vacancies were the norm. The Communists who were on the ground spread themselves thin to cover several states.[124] By December 1929 District 16's first "Negro organizer," Solomon Harper, arrived in Charlotte from Harlem. He had been south twice before, once as a member of the labor jury at the strikers' trial and then at the rather extravagantly named General Southern Textile Conference, held by the NTWU in Charlotte the past October. Harper had been an organizer of the Harlem Tenants League; now he was to organize black labor. He went at once to Bessemer City to deliver NTWU cards to black textile workers there, and he contacted the Negro Workers Relief to send help to black strikers in Leaksville. Harper organized a mass meeting to show support for the end of the U.S. occupation of Haiti, but he despaired of its success because "only a very few of the Negro workers in the South ever heard that Haiti is a Negro land . . . (Southern papers do not publish that fact)." To boost local interest, he combined the Haitian protest with one against a recent Charlotte lynching.[125]

The Communists tried hard to link white working-class rights and black civil rights. When a black tenant farmer was lynched in the small town of Tarboro in 1930, Charlotte Communists put out a flyer alleging that "a mob of landlords and storekeepers" had committed the crime. The lynchers' "excuse" was that "a Negro worker was supposed to have 'attacked' a white woman." Then the broadside argued, "The lynchings and terrorism that is now taking place throughout the South against Negro and white workers is incited by the mill owners Landlords and capitalist." This was a "bosses lynching" and black and white workers must organize themselves into "defense organizations to fight the big bosses lynching mobs."[126] Moreover, the Communists compared these lynchings with "terror" against strikers and the murder of Ella May Wiggins. "It is clear now that terrorism and lynching is being organized by mill owners and their agents," a pamphlet pointed out. A strong "defense organization" of blacks and whites would be the only way to stop lawlessness against the poor in the South.[127] The American Negro Labor Congress urged: "Negro and white workers—organize to fight: The Bosses, The Landlord, The Police, The Lynch Gang"—to them, all birds of a feather.[128]

For its part, the Comintern proposed: "One of the First Communist Party demands is: death penalty for Negro lynching."[129] Twenty-five whites and fifteen African Americans held a Conference against Lynching in Charlotte and asserted the "solidarity of all workers and . . . the full social, economic and political equality and the right of self-determination for the Negro nation." Throughout 1930 Communist antilynching meetings drew growing audiences. In Winston-Salem three hundred black and white workers showed up in front of the Reynolds Tobacco Factory No. 9 to protest lynching.[130]

At first blush, it is astonishing to think of "mobs of landlords" running through the streets lynching black men. The popular wisdom claimed that poor white farmers and millworkers, not their landlords and bosses, led lynch mobs, and then only to punish black criminals, usually rapists. But even those who were most carried away with the myth of black men's perpetual lust for white women knew that often the first step in a lynching was an African American's argument with a landlord or boss over earnings. They knew too that black women were lynched, along with established members of the black community who had run afoul of white elites over some commercial transaction.[131] Moreover, poor black transients looking for work often found themselves accused of crimes by people they had never met in places they had only visited. The Communists realized that white Southerners used the criminal justice system to enforce their political economy. Lynching a black man taught other black men to stay in their places at the bottom of the economic ladder.

Organizing around issues such as lynching helped bring southern African Americans into the Party. After Otto Hall left Gastonia, he traveled to Baltimore, Atlanta, Richmond, Birmingham, and throughout North Carolina. He hoped to turn radical preexisting black organizations into American Negro Labor Congress chapters.[132] At the close of 1929 the ANLC had forty-six locals, including twelve in the South, an amazing increase over the five northern locals it had had when the Gastonia strike began. The next year, "for the first time in the five years' history of the A.N.L.C. since its founding in Chicago in 1925, a delegation came from the South." Hall had succeeded where Lovett Fort-Whiteman had failed.[133]

New ANLC branches should have furnished black CP members to integrated Party units, but getting the local white Party members to accept black people proved a difficult task. For example, in Norfolk, Virginia, Party members were Jewish small businessmen who conducted meetings in Yiddish. A young white Communist organizer built a union among black women who worked in a bedspring factory there, only to be charged with a violation of Virginia's law against "conspiracy to incite the colored population to insurrection against the white population."[134] Moreover, he reported, the local Jewish Communists adopted an "open antagonistic attitude towards Negro Comrades." The practice of interracial Communism proved too much for the Jewish members, who feared their own arrests would come next. They voted to "disband the branch in the face of all the terror." The Party called them "petty-bourgeois elements" and expelled them.[135] The Party had to impress the Negro Policy's importance on their white members.

The interracial League of Struggle for Negro Rights (LSNR) was a step in that direction. It replaced the all-black American Negro Labor Congress with an organization that would be "more broad and all-inclusive" and include "white workers standing on the program of Negro Liberation."[136] By the end of 1931 ferreting out racism in the Party had become a constant preoccupation of those at the top. For example, Otto Hall made a formal complaint about the white women comrades who refused to dance with "Negro workers" at a Christmas Day dance in New York. Four months later Earl Browder declared "War against White Chauvinism."[137] Do not, the Central Committee warned organizers, "look upon the LSNR as a substitute for the Party . . . and relegate all work among Negroes to Negro comrades and to the LSNR." At the same time, assigning Negro organizers only to Negro work was an "opportunist tendenc[y]." Since integrated groups increased the personal danger in which southern organizers found themselves, it took courage to stay on the path of integration and equality. The Central Committee reinforced that courage with a firm hand: "The opportunist deviations in practice from that line must now be decisively corrected in every district."[138]

Although the Party committed itself to racial integration and "the beginning of systematic work in the south as one of its main tasks," some remained openly skeptical that integrated organizations would work in Dixie.[139] Some Soviets encouraged establishing showy national integrated organizations instead and argued that aiming for integrated branches in the South would prohibit work among whites. But Earl Browder explained to those Soviet doubters that the race question was not peripheral but central: "Nobody is indifferent to this issue in America. . . . There are no indifferent people. . . . Precisely *because* we are raising this issue in the sharpest form, our party is growing stronger, not only among the Negroes but among the whites generally."[140] In a letter to the Politburo, Birmingham organizer Tom Johnson seconded him: "I do not agree" with "the formation of separate organizations of Negroes and whites. . . . In this organization . . . we have to raise the slogan of social equality and full equality for Negroes, and how [if we have separate organizations] do we reconcile the slogan with our practice?" As hard as it was to organize blacks and whites together in the South, many of those who worked there believed in it so strongly that they pushed for integrated organizing as hard as, and sometimes harder than, Moscow did.[141]

Meanwhile until 1931 southern organizers let the self-determination line languish. As Cyril Briggs paused to evaluate southern work, he saw obstacles. He deplored the lack of a "self-defense corps" that could go underground and proposed the establishment of something called the

Ethiopian Mutual Aid League to do the job. Moreover, Briggs could not figure out how the organizing of white millworkers would bring southern African Americans into the Communist Party. Moreover, the ILD was a fine organization, but Briggs feared that legal defense rearguard actions would take the place of organizing workers. Finally, he demanded, what had happened to the policy of self-determination?[142]

What indeed? For two years following the Sixth World Congress, the effort to explain self-determination took many twists and turns. The idea of a minority as a nation became entwined internationally with anticolonialist efforts and complicated by an argument against black "nationalism" of the Garvey variety.[143] Although the line was not working out in the South, it was the argument over self-determination at the Sixth World Congress that had first made the "Negro Question" important to the CPUSA. It had brought the Party into the South standing firm on racial equality and propelled African Americans to national and international party offices. For example, the Red International of Labor Unions World Conference in the summer of 1930 required that one-third of the American delegates be "black proletarians."[144]

In August 1930 the Comintern's Negro Commission reaffirmed self-determination, including the right to secede, as the line to be used in the U.S. South.[145] Harry Haywood criticized those southern organizers who neglected the line and accused them of a "deep lack of faith in the Negro masses."[146] In February 1931 the Comintern ordered all U.S. Communists to get behind the idea whether they liked it or not.[147] To Comintern leaders, the "struggle for the right of self-determination" was now an article of faith. They believed that a zeal for self-determination must be inherent in southern Negro toilers. Self-determination was a bonfire that the masses had built, and it simply awaited an organizer's match. If it wasn't catching fire, it was because the organizers had failed to strike that match. Self-determination went from being an idea to being a line to being an immutable truth ignored at one's peril.

For the most part, those trying to organize grassroots party members didn't like the self-determination line. It was ambiguous at best and segregationist at worst. Field organizers explained self-determination most easily as majority rule, which it was in part, and they rarely ventured into long discussions upholding the right of secession. That was grist for the mills of their enemies, who probably brought up self-determination more often than did the southern Communist organizers. One prominent white Southerner, who had read up on the issue, thought self-determination proved that the Communists could not be serious about organizing poor whites at all; they simply wanted to organize "the negroes under European direction."[148] An African American organizer in District 16 warned that "if we raise the slogan of self-determination we will be driven under ground."[149] Otto Hall put it more gently: "We have neglected to put this slogan forward and really clarify this slogan." Although he had opposed it in Moscow, after Gastonia he argued, as he had to, that it would be a good tool to "utilize this national spirit that exists among Negro peasantry."[150]

The Comintern ignored the facts of southern landownership after adopting self-determination. They imagined Dixie as a land in which white large landowners held African Americans as serfs, even though they collected troves of census and economic data about the South. The messy reality of southern farming negated their fantasy. Among the rural poor, many white farmers rented some of their land to black and/or white tenant farmers or had on the place black and/or white sharecroppers who owned no land; some blacks owned some land, but it might not be enough to support their families, so they were tenants on a little more; some poor white farmers owned no land and sharecropped or rented land themselves; some poor white farmers tended their land without any help from black sharecroppers or tenants. Although he professed to support the line, Birmingham organizer Tom Johnson urged the Politburo "to decide whose land is to be confiscated, and to whom does it go. . . . If you come in [here] . . . with a demand for confiscation of land, these fellows who are starving on their 40 acres, and renting the other half to their brother, will lynch you." He tactfully suggested sparing these southern kulaks and asked the Politburo to "frame our demand as the confiscation of the land of the big landowners." Southern small farming, tenancy, and sharecropping proved too complicated for self-determination, and many organizers ignored it, even as they stood up against racism and for social equality.[151]

On the heels of the Gastonia strike trials, James Ford headed down south. The black Communist had served with Otto Hall in France and joined the Party through Lovett Fort-Whiteman's efforts at the first ANLC conference. Now he was appalled by the condition of the workers he addressed in Birmingham. Red Hendricks, awaiting his appeal, joined Ford on the platform in Chattanooga, where the crowd looked better, "more of a healthy aggressive proletarian type." In Atlanta, Ford's uncle Ben was among a crowd of whites and blacks who turned out to hear his speech. Ben Ford had been a steelworker in Birmingham and was "eager for organization, reliable, religious but militant."[152] The tour, with its integrated audiences, encouraged Communists in the South and in Moscow.

From Cotton Mill to Comintern

As the Gastonia defendants waited for the North Carolina Supreme Court to hear their appeals in the late spring of 1930, seven of the defendants met in New York with the CPUSA Central Committee. Fred Beal hoped to persuade the committee to send them on vacations in the Soviet Union while they awaited the outcome of their appeals. Clarence Miller hoped to skip bail and move there permanently. The committee refused to pay for a trip and adamantly opposed any of the defendants' skipping bail. Subsequently, five met secretly and decided to leave the country in defiance of the Central Committee. With the help of an ally, they secured false passports and money and disobeyed the Party.[153] Fred Beal, Clarence Miller, Red Hendricks, William McGinnis, and Joe Harrison planned to go to Berlin, where they would throw themselves on the mercy of the German Communist Party and beg it to arrange their entry into the USSR.[154]

On the voyage across the Atlantic, Beal tortured himself with self-doubt. When the news broke that he had left the country, he speculated, "[h]ow pleased the forces of reaction in the South would be!" He thought he heard the ship's engine humming, "Go . . . back. Don't run. Go . . . back. Don't . . . run." But he kept on running. Beal and Hendricks felt a thrill when they finally glimpsed the "Red Flag flying over factories—big, huge, giant factories owned by *workers*." Beal thought: "How silly of America not to have a revolution and put the Red Flag on the White House!" To Hendricks, it was "all the more reason why we should return to America. We must return and fight for a Soviet America." A crowd of ragged beggars at Leningrad gave them pause; so did the enormous numbers of jostling filthy orphans.[155]

In Moscow, Beal and Hendricks realized, too late, that the Comintern considered them residents, not visitors, and they began to petition to go back to the South, to keep their promise to southern workers. The Finn Otto Kuusinen, who had served as secretary for the meeting that drafted the Negro resolution, decided their fate. Beal recalled, "How futile I felt there before Kuusinen. State of North Carolina vs. Fred Beal. Comintern vs. Fred Beal. . . . How was Judge Kuusinen to understand my feelings any more than Judge Barnhill?"[156] In August 1930 the North Carolina Supreme Court confirmed their sentences and ordered Beal and Hendricks to appear in court and begin serving their terms. The ACLU, which had provided their bail, made the same demand, but Beal and Hendricks would be staying in the Soviet Union.[157]

From Moscow, Lovett Fort-Whiteman had watched carefully as the Communist Party finally brought a radical alternative to the South. Perhaps he had been wrong to oppose self-determination since it had, after all, brought the Party into the South. Yet the problems the Party encountered there certainly underscored the fact that it would have been easier to organize whites separately. He probably breathed a sigh of relief that he had not been in Otto Hall's shoes, and he decided to stay in Moscow on a permanent basis. He asked for a transfer of his membership from the Workers Party to the Communist Party of the Soviet Union, a move many expatriates took to gain voting rights and power in their new home. He used his fellowship to First Moscow State University to study ethnology; then he capitalized on courses he had taken at Chicago's Armour Institute of Technology to get a job in research on fish breeding at the University of Moscow. He married a twenty-nine-year-old Jewish Russian woman who also worked as a scientific researcher, and they moved into a dark one-room apartment. He struggled, unsuccessfully, to improve his very bad Russian. His wife spoke very bad English. He even managed to swallow the self-determination line, which, as a Lovestonite, he had originally opposed.[158]

His most highly visible job was as a science teacher at the American School in Moscow, teaching the white children of foreign workers. The poet Yevgeny Dolmatovsky visited one of his classes and commemorated its spirit in verse:

> . . . Change rumbles up the staircase
> The bell reestablishes order

Children of English and American workers
Sit side by side.
The lesson—electrical current.
Let's start studying.
The classroom is quiet. The black teacher Whiteman
Leads the lesson.
From in my heart I draw my words
From the deepest reaches within
I see again, and again, and again
You, my black Comrade![159]

Going "home to Moscow" had brought Fort-Whiteman happiness, success, and even veneration. As pleased as he was to hear of the Communist progress in the South, he was delighted to be otherwise occupied in the revolution.

If Fred Beal, Red Hendricks, and Fort-Whiteman needed any reassurance about the wisdom of their decisions, they could find it in a comparison of the Loray Mill in Gastonia with the new cotton mill in Ashkhabad, Turkmenistan. In Gastonia the workweek lasted sixty hours, but in Ashkhabad seven-hour shifts and five-day workweeks left everyone time and energy to go to the new adult literacy center in the evening. Gastonia workers like Daisy Mae McDonald had left behind sweet mountain air for stagnant water, flies, and knee-deep mud. Ashkhabad workers had left behind sandy tents for a workers' village with landscaped grounds and a lovely park. If a bathtub cost an extra fifty cents each week in Gastonia, electric lights in Ashkhabad illuminated brand-new cottages. In Gastonia the only vacation that workers earned was when they quit. In Ashkhabad everyone had a month each year off with pay.[160] It must have seemed obvious to Beal, Hendricks, and Fort-Whiteman which system would prevail.

3

FROM THE GREAT DEPRESSION TO THE GREAT TERROR

In the hot Georgia summer of 1930 an Atlanta men's clothing store advertised a remarkable piece of attire: "Black Shirts. American Fascisti: We have just what you want! Why not wear one at the meeting Monday night at Lakewood Heights?" Several prior Black Shirt rallies had already whetted consumer demand.[1] The ad invited "every 'HE' white man in Atlanta" to "have all the fun we please . . . and carry forward the sublime principles of the Blackshirts."[2] While the Fascisti left the definition of "HE men" and "fun" to the imagination, their "sublime principle" was to "inculcate and foster in the minds of its members and the public generally, white supremacy." The group quickly spread to four other Georgia cities, where corner newsboys shouted: "Another *Black Shirt* sold, who'll be the next to pay a nickel for a white man's paper?"[3]

The *Black Shirt* attacked "the doctrines of race equality being sponsored by Communists among the Negroes of the South."[4] The Communists had predicted this union seven years earlier: "The Fascisti, with their black shirts, and the Ku Klux, with their night shirts, are still battling heroically for the right to save the white man's civilization. . . . The result may be a combination between the two brokerage firms in bigotry, intolerance and race hate."[5] For their part, the Black Shirts worried about the "chastity of American Women," which the Communists' version of social equality threatened.[6] The shaky racial solidarity of the Gastonia strike reinforced the Black Shirts' fear that the Communists posed "the greatest menace to this country that we have ever known."[7] In addition to chastity, the Black Shirts worried that black and white cooperation in unionization would result in integrated workforces and cost some whites their jobs. They discounted the Communist argument that working-class solidarity over racial lines would strengthen workers' bargaining power.[8]

Fascism festered in the second Ku Klux Klan's hometown of Atlanta as the Black Shirts linked race, economics, and politics in ways that would have made Mussolini proud. Within weeks the Black Shirts claimed twenty-seven thousand members in Georgia and served notice on African Americans: "Before Christmas there isn't going to be a black bell boy or black truck driver in Atlanta." The problem, according to the Black Shirts, was that blacks lived and worked in American cities at all. They belonged on farms. The group saw their proposed apartheid as a simple solution to the Great Depression. "If white men would assert their rights there would be no unemployment in Atlanta and other cities of the South," they predicted confidently.[9]

As the Depression deepened in 1930, urban migrants watched opportunities transform into dangers. The prospects that once lay before them so glittering, so new, now beckoned like the gates of hell. In one decade 1,750,000 country people, many of them African Americans, had come to towns across the South. If once they had thought they might die of hard work on the farm, now they thought they might die of no work in the city. If they delighted in trading sharecroppers' shacks for drafty shotgun houses, now the rent came due not at harvesttime but every week. If they had slipped the itchy ropes of rural communities to frolic on city streets with anonymity, now they found themselves unknown, hungry, and dependent on the kindness of strangers while the dribble of relief from Community Chests and municipal governments sputtered, creaked, and ran as dry as the old hand pump back home.[10]

In 1930 the emptiness of the New South promise—that cheap labor and a laissez-faire state would ultimately bring prosperity—became clear to millions of farmers and wage laborers caught in the tightening grip of what became a Great Depression. The southern economy rested on a pedestal of debased black labor and cheap white labor, throwing Jim Crow capitalism into sharp relief as the gloom gathered. The low wages that employers paid to African Americans undervalued vital work, segregated black workers in the most menial jobs, and compressed the wage scale for whites as well. "As long as we have a great reservoir of unused black labor in the South, there will always be low wages and low economic conditions for the poor white man in the South," the president of all-black Howard University told the students at the all-white University of North Carolina in 1931.[11]

In good times white workers could feel superior to African Americans who dug ditches, stripped tobacco leaves in factories, or swept up cotton lint; all that was "nigger work." In bad times whites wanted those jobs. "White men in the South today are driving trucks and express wagons once driven by Negroes, repairing streets, delivering ice on their own backs," one observer reported. Whites were "doing other tasks once regarded fit only for Negroes." Moreover, there had always been a paucity of state and municipal services in the South, in part to keep white taxpayers' money out of black hands. An entire biracial working class now faced unemployment and eviction.[12]

What the Communists called the black reserve proletariat, the southern-bred Fascists now called "niggers taking our jobs." Needless to say, their solutions diverged. While the Fascists advocated expelling African Americans from industry and cities, the Communists advocated the unity of black and white workers.[13] Just as some white workers joined the Black Shirts, others crossed racial lines to join the Communist-sponsored organizations called Unemployed Councils, which fought for municipal relief. The Communists had learned the lesson of Gastonia and during the 1930s never again compromised on the principle of organizing black and white workers together.

Challenges from the Left and the Right threatened the racialized economic structure, and whites in power struck back by criminalizing behaviors on both sides. Dismayed by the Black Shirt challenge, the Communist-led Unemployed Councils, and the severity of the economic downturn, elite whites struggled to shore up the rickety racist hierarchy that guaranteed them cheap labor. In 1930 the American Civil Liberties

Union found itself in Atlanta, fighting for both the Black Shirts' and the Communists' rights to march, distribute literature, and hold public meetings. Powerful white Southerners dispatched the Black Shirts quickly, but the Communists proved more tenacious. From 1930 to 1932 the white power structure launched a southern Red Scare.

As the Great Depression deepened, the Communists' ever-rising profile had impact beyond the Party's small, ever-shifting membership base. The Communist legal defense of nine African Americans charged with rape in 1931, the Scottsboro "Boys," provoked a crisis in southern justice. The CP's political campaign to free them, deeply resented by most of the white South, caused a few white Southerners and many white Northerners to question the southern legal system. It also focused world opinion on antidemocratic practices in the South. In addition to its far-reaching ripples, the publicity surrounding the Scottsboro cases, coupled with the economic emergency, brought African Americans into the Party in substantial numbers for the first time.

The Scottsboro defense heralded the Communist Party's commitment to racial justice and prompted some black and white Southerners to visit the Soviet Union. They wanted to see firsthand its famed social equality, study its vaunted workers' paradise, and bring back lessons to teach the bosses and racists back home. As the USSR attempted to gain U.S. recognition and Stalin tightened his grip on the Comintern in the early 1930s, Southerners bustled about Red Square. In 1932 twenty-two young African Americans journeyed to Moscow to make a film to drive home the lessons of Scottsboro. A few went to stay. They immediately confronted Stalin's growing paranoia and ambition. Lovett Fort-Whiteman, Old Bolshevik and true believer, realized too late that Stalin's "revolution from above" spelled doom for popular African American input into Communist policy.

The Politics of Hunger on the Right

The Black Shirts offered starving white workers an easy solution to unemployment: the extension of segregation. Taking white supremacy to its next logical step, it advocated the relocation of African Americans to rural areas, thus reserving urban wage labor for whites. Scarce jobs and miserly municipal relief would be reserved for whites, while agriculture would flourish with an ample supply of cheap black labor. The white working-class men who joined the Black Shirts abhorred the paternalistic relationship between comfortable white men and their black servants, and they resented the monopoly that black men had on certain service jobs. "You men who freely tip your caddies, your bootblack, your waiter, and anyone else who happens to serve you," the *Black Shirt* asked, "do you realize the fact that there are several thousand unemployed white men in Atlanta?"[14] In a quandary on how to replace your black servants? *"The Black Shirt* can furnish you any kind of white help," the organization boasted.[15]

Across the South white men attacked black men at work. In Texas an unemployed white man, "incensed because a Negro was working and he was not, shot and killed the Negro." In Florida white men kidnapped and flogged five black bellhops until they promised not to return to work. In Arkansas gangs of white men attacked groups of African Americans doing road construction. The Black Shirts threatened Rich's Department Store and the Coca-Cola Company with violence and a boycott if they did not fire their black employees. White Atlantan and Commission on Interracial Cooperation (CIC) employee Clark Foreman summed it up this way: "When you have unemployment in the South, you have race trouble." [16]

It did not take long for the Black Shirts to feel the wrath of Atlanta's affluent white people, led by the women. Alerted by their "greatly disturbed . . . cooks, nurses, and other domestic help, . . . alarmed housewives" complained to police about the Black Shirts. White businessmen and housewives panicked at the thought of their black domestic workers, janitors, and chauffeurs being shipped off to some remote tenant farm.[17] Who would drive Miss Daisy? A leading white man mused that firing a thousand experienced African Americans and replacing them with a thousand inexperienced whites would be downright ridiculous. To their credit, some cared about fairness as much as about their own convenience. One white minister on Atlanta's outskirts, shaken by a Black Shirt demonstration five hundred strong, spoke out for black labor: "Any man, white or black, is entitled to hold a job that he is qualified for and earn an honest living for his family."[18]

Eager to avoid violence, the decade-old Atlanta-based Commission on Interracial Cooperation (CIC), led by Will Alexander, urged the press to cover Black Shirt rallies firsthand. What they saw alarmed them.

"Negroes were referred to in the speeches as 'burr heads' and 'nuts.' " One man spoke of "Buck niggers bellyin' down the streets pushing white women off the side-walks." The CIC knew that this sort of talk often orchestrated the prelude to a racial massacre; a 1906 mass slaughter cast a long shadow over Atlanta. "Trouble would mean but one thing, rioting and bloodshed," a CIC observer reported. The CIC sent undercover agents into neighborhoods sympathetic to the Black Shirts and rallied the city's ministers against the organization. The mayor ultimately told "all citizens of Atlanta, white or black, to set their faces against every person and faction seeking to embroil the races in trouble."[19]

The Black Shirts met such criticism by impugning the critics' honor. When the mayor of Athens confiscated copies of the *Black Shirt* from a "helpless, hungry and half-clothed news boy and made a bon-fire of them," the Fascists ridiculed him as a "real He-Man." They implied that he was less than robustly masculine, threatening him with "a few facts about him that wouldn't be exactly to his advantage . . . we can only hold contempt for you and your ilk." In Atlanta they threatened to expose graft in city government and generally ridiculed the business classes: THE MASSES ORGANIZE AND THE CHAMBER OF COMMERCE IS HORRIFIED, one *Black Shirt* headline read.[20]

The horrified Chamber of Commerce and the Commission on Interracial Cooperation closed ranks against the Fascists. The white Fulton County grand jury urged the city to deny them a parade permit and the state to withhold their charter.[21] The grand jury scolded the Black Shirts: "We insist that this particular kind of haberdashery be worn in the home land of fascism and not in America, as our people could be at better business than aping the reactionary institutions of Europe." In most white Atlantans' eyes, white supremacy was the modern solution, and Fascism a feudal one led by "misguided men who endeavor to organize prejudice, hatred and intimidation."[22] To put a finer point on it, the *Atlanta Constitution* reminded its readers that "white supremacy means the legitimate rule by lawful methods of the greatly major race," not "sinister and dangerous propaganda."[23]

Elsewhere less patrician capitalists welcomed the Black Shirts. In contrast with Atlanta's business leadership, millowners in Charlotte, North Carolina, a city reeling from the Depression and the Gastonia strike and trials, eagerly opened their gates to the Black Shirts in hopes of stemming Communist activity. In the fall of 1930 an Atlanta attorney lectured fifty Charlotte workers "on the horrors of the Russian Bolsheviki, and the terrible crime of social equality for Negroes" and "praised Mussolini for his 'good' government in Italy."[24] At the Louise Mill, where the National Textile Workers Union tried to organize, an attorney recruited Black Shirts and denounced the "Reds who 'incite our good Negroes and make them discontented with the station in life in which it has pleased God to call them."[25]

The Black Shirts' doctrine of saving jobs for working-class white men offered one great white hope during the worst economic crisis in memory. One millworker recruited by the Communists in Greenville, South Carolina, told them that one of his "old schoolmate[s]" had proclaimed, 'This country needs a Mosselini.' " The millworker and proto-Communist went on to say, "I don't know if I spelled his name right but you know who I mean the Big Dago." He predicted a coming revolution as laborers "pressed" capitalists because "they can get no jobs."[26] A "Mosselini" seemed the answer to many people's prayers in the summer of 1930.

The Communists watched in horror as the Black Shirts recruited a few National Textile Workers Union members to a meeting in Charlotte.[27] When Major Alfred Lee Bulwinkle, the Loray Mill lawyer who had successfully defended Ella May Wiggins's murderers, ran for Congress in 1930, an odd amalgamation of anti-Communist bedfellows—the Black Shirts, the Charlotte Central Labor Union, and the state AFL—endorsed him against a former Gastonia striker running a vigorous campaign on the Communist ticket.[28] Some millowners threatened to fire workers if they didn't vote for Bulwinkle; others simply put an extra two dollars in the pay envelopes of those who did. Bulwinkle went to Washington, where he became a conservative ally of the New Deal. To Communists, his election signified "the further fascisation of the state."[29]

The Politics of Hunger on the Left

The Black Shirts' rearguard action responded in part to the Communists' success in the spring and summer of 1930. As the Depression became acute, starvation brought black and white workers to the Communist table. CP leaders organized Unemployed Councils, theoretically modeled on revolutionary groups that had sprung up in St. Petersburg under the czar in 1906 but practically possible because of the acute economic crisis.[30] The councils demanded that municipal authorities create a safety net for the unemployed, some of which later became vital parts of the New Deal: relief, free rent, free electricity and water, free milk and hot lunches for their children, free medical attention, and, most important, unemployment and social insurance. While those issues made sense to an unemployed painter in Atlanta, the Party added some that probably didn't: recognition of the Soviet Union, driving "out social fascists, AFL and SP [Socialist Party] agents of the bosses," and fighting "against imperialist war."[31] The Party declared March 6, 1930, International Unemployment Day, and hunger marches took place from San Francisco to Baltimore. More than thirty-five thousand paraded in New York.[32]

The CP, well informed on the Depression in the South, made Unemployed Councils there a priority. Despite "police threats," in Charlotte, 3,000 marched to harassers' jeers.[33] In Winston-Salem, 140 belonged to the council; many of them were black women who worked in the tobacco factories organized by Gastonia striker Red Hendricks before he escaped to the USSR. On the day of their planned march, almost 2,000 walked, amid rumors that white bystanders would beat up black marchers.[34] For many, the councils were their first contact with Communists, "transmission belts" that propelled people deeper into the Party. "United We Eat," the Communists declared. By April 3, 1930, Otto Hall reported, "nearly a thousand Negroes" had joined the party.[35] Many came in through Unemployed Councils in the South.

Birmingham-based district organizer Tom Johnson set up Unemployed Councils in Birmingham, Chattanooga, and Atlanta, but he dared not stage a march on International Unemployment Day in his home city; the "terror [was] too real."[36] In September 1930 one hundred rifle-toting police surrounded an unemployment demonstration, and Johnson found himself "carried 50 miles out in the country, before they let me go." He reported: "We had to devise new methods," as the party abandoned open recruiting.[37] Despite tales, then and now, of Soviet gold pouring into the United States, the Party practically starved southern organizers. "It makes it a lot harder not to have a dollar in your pocket in a spot like this,"

Johnson told the Central Committee after an arrest. Moreover, the police chief had just told Johnson that he would routinely arrest him for vagrancy every ten days. If he didn't have bail money in his pocket, he would go to jail, from which the warden released Communists into the hands of a waiting KKK posse. [38]

In contrast with Birmingham, Atlanta looked like a more promising Communist seedbed in the spring of 1930. Joseph Carr and M. H. Powers, white Communists, recruited two hundred Atlantans into an Unemployed Council. At first they avoided talk of Communism and spoke only of hunger. They stayed in the background since they wanted the police to "think to the last minute that it is a spontaneous revolt of the workers themselves." Carr and Powers predicted that ten thousand people would take to Atlanta's streets on International Unemployment Day, March 6, but the police refused to issue them a parade permit and threatened to arrest anyone who participated.[39] That morning the police raided the council's headquarters twice and stood by to arrest demonstrators. As a heavy rain fell, the organizers were horrified, then mortified when no one showed up to march.[40]

An interracial meeting three days later brought out one hundred people, people of a sort ill advised to mingle, as the *Atlanta Constitution* pointed out: "whites and blacks, men and women."[41] The police threw a tear gas bomb into the room, arrested Carr and Powers, and charged them under an 1866 Reconstruction law with "inciting insurrection." Only one person had been charged under the law since 1866, when the legislature updated an 1833 antebellum law designed to quell slave rebellions.[42] The statute forbade "any attempt, by persuasion or otherwise, to induce others to join in any combined resistance to the lawful authority of the State."[43] The cost of violating the vague law included the death penalty.

Atlanta's white newspapers applauded the arrests of Carr and Powers, but the Atlanta-mocking *Macon Telegraph* warned that "such treatment of Communists is the only way to insure the growth of Communism in the United States."[44] Indeed, the Communists quickly made connections among a recent lynching in Sherman, Texas, in which the victim was burned alive, the murder of Ella May Wiggins in Gastonia the year before, and "the capitalists and their court in Georgia [who were] . . . trying to lynch 'legally' " Powers and Carr, who posted bond and disappeared.[45]

Delegates to the American Negro Labor Congress *(*Workers Monthly, *December 1925)*

Lovett Fort-Whiteman addressing the American Negro Labor Congress *(Workers Monthly, December 1925)*

Sen Katayama *(Rose Pastor Stokes Papers, Manuscripts and Archives Department, Sterling Memorial Library, Yale University)*

Fred Beal *(Labor Defender, August 1929)*

Kelly Yale "Red" Hendricks *(Labor Defender, August 1929)*

Ella May Wiggins's children after her death *(Labor Defender, October 1929)*

Delegates to the General Southern Textile Conference, Charlotte, NC
(Labor Defender, *November 1929*).

Application form, American Fascisti, Order of the Black Shirts, 1930
(Labor Defender, *April 1931*)

Black and White cast members in the USSR *(Langston Hughes Collection, Yale Collection of American Literature, Beinecke Rare Book and Manuscript Library, Yale University)*

John Hope *(Robert W. Woodruff Library, Atlanta University Center, Archives and Special Collections)*

Demonstration on behalf of the Scottsboro "Boys" (Labor Defender, *June 1932*)

Lovett Fort-Whiteman in a meeting in the USSR, possibly regarding the *Black and White* script *(Langston Hughes Papers, Yale Collection of American Literature, Beinecke Rare Book and Manuscript Library, Yale University)*

Langston Hughes with a Russian copy of *Not Without Laughter*, entitled *Laughter through Tears (Langston Hughes Papers, Yale Collection of American Literature, Beinecke Rare Book and Manuscript Library, Yale University)*

Louise Thompson, circa 1932, "To Lang, My best pal. Lou" *(Langston Hughes Papers, Yale Collection of American Literature, Beinecke Rare Book and Manuscript Library, Yale University)*

The Scottsboro "Boys" in jail in Birmingham *(Langston Hughes Papers, Yale Collection of American Literature, Beinecke Rare Book and Manuscript Library, Yale University)*

"The nine Negro Scottsboro 'Boys' and a mass demonstration on their behalf" (Labor Defender, *May 1932*)

Although the Communist Central Committee mounted an international publicity campaign focused on Powers' and Carr's arrest, it spent little time or money in Atlanta. The International Labor Defense (ILD), a defense league with heavy Communist participation, hired an Atlanta lawyer for the two, but despite Tom Johnson's pleas, it failed to send funds to start a defense committee. Johnson bravely announced a May Day parade in support of Powers and Carr. [46] ATLANTA REDS DEFY MAYOR, headlines screamed. The city warned that they would parade "at their own peril," an ominous phrase that meant that police might arrest them or, worse, refuse to protect them from the Black Shirts or the KKK. [47] The *Atlanta Journal* alleged that Tom Johnson warned, "We'll be awfully sore if we don't parade," to which Chief of Police James Beavers purportedly replied, "You'll be awfully sore if you do, and I am not referring to your pride or disposition." [48] It seemed like a recurring nightmare when a mere twenty-two people showed up for the highly publicized May Day demonstration, only to be outnumbered by policemen. [49] Yet the ILD national secretary told the *Atlanta Constitution* that "hundreds of thousands" had demonstrated across the nation in support of Powers and Carr and compared the upcoming trial with "the Gastonia case in North Carolina and the Sacco-Vanzetti case in Massachusetts." [50]

Tom Johnson sent more organizers to rebuild the party in Atlanta. Two northern white women, Anne Burlak and Mary Dalton, came from Chattanooga, Tennessee, and Greenville, South Carolina, to organize National Textile Workers Union locals at the Atlanta Woolen Mill and the Fulton Bag and Cotton Mill, two of the city's harshest employers. Burlak, only nineteen and known as the Red flame for her long red hair, fiery spirit, and Marxist politics, had organized in the Passaic strike and spent time in the USSR. Twenty-year-old Dalton first drew police attention when she repeatedly disrupted a local speech by the AFL president William Green by yelling that he was "selling out to the bosses." [51] Then she pushed the police over the brink at a subsequent interracial "free rent while idle" meeting of forty-five people. When police demanded that the meeting break up, Dalton demanded that they show her a warrant. They arrested six: Burlak, Dalton, a white Atlanta couple, and two African American men, one a local printer and the other an organizer for the League of Struggle for Negro Rights. [52]

The incarcerated white couple turned out to be live-in housekeepers for the president of the Atlanta Women's Civic Council, who sprang them at once, arguing that they were "courteous, industrious, and active in charitable work." Moreover, she predicted an impending Christian conversion for the Jewish pair, since "despite their lack of beliefs in divine guidance, she . . . noted a consecration to the spirit of service." The desire to help others that the clubwoman saw in her handyman as a "gradual unfolding of the knowledge of God through the spirit of Christ" actually sprang from his secret Party membership. The police denied bail to the "girl 'Reds,' " Dalton and Burlak, and to the two African Americans and sent them to jail. Now the four, along with Powers and Carr, faced insurrection charges that could send them all to an "electric chair lynching."[53] A police spokesman reminded the Atlanta Six, "This is not Boston," as if they did not know.[54]

By the end of May Tom Johnson still had no money to pay their local counsel and asked Party leadership to "get Roger Baldwin or some other big shot of the Civil Liberties down here for a protest meeting under our leadership." He scrawled on the bottom of a letter to the Central Committee: "It is now six p.m.—no money yet. It seems useless to spend more money on wires—I cannot live here or get out." Johnson had to create his own allies, even as he begged for gas money to travel from Birmingham to Atlanta.[55] The last straw came when the *Daily Worker* failed to print a story that Johnson sent in on the Atlanta Six, and he bemoaned the paper's "miserable handling all material from South."[56] Someone listened, and the next month the Central Committee decided to found a southern Communist newspaper, the *Southern Worker*. The remedy arrived too late to rescue Johnson. He suffered a nervous collapse and left the South.[57]

The ACLU, not the International Labor Defense, ultimately rescued the Six. Roger Baldwin sent a field agent to Atlanta to organize local liberal whites and retain counsel for the defendants.[58] They won bond for the Six, who left the state at once. Thereafter their attorneys won postponements and filed demurrers, and the state seemed reluctant to pursue the cases of Powers and Carr and of the other four defendants.[59] The ACLU fought for the Black Shirts' right to protest Communist activity even as it supported the Atlanta Six.[60]

While the state hesitated, the ACLU mobilized support among

middle-class white Atlantans against the insurrection law. Citing the principles of Jeffersonian democracy, sixty-one local white opinion leaders remonstrated in the *Atlanta Journal* that "a policy of repression will exaggerate the importance of false ideas, and it is likely to open the flood gates for future repression of progressive social movements."[61] Fifteen women signed, including Mary Raoul Millis, Atlanta's own socialite Socialist and sister of the local president of the League of Women Voters. Future historian Comer Vann Woodward, then a twenty-one-year-old English instructor at Georgia Tech, signed. So did his uncle, an Emory University dean. Even Will Alexander, secretary of the Commission on Interracial Cooperation, signed, although he groused that "the Communists really deserved no help because they were foolish enough to talk Negro social equality in the South."[62]

As defenders of free speech mobilized, liberal African American leaders sought to distance themselves from the Communists. Congressional hearings on the Communist menace in 1930 had delved extensively into black Reds, and now the NAACP, which had branches in fourteen southern cities, sought to position itself as an anti-Communist moderate organization.[63] The nation's only black congressman, Oscar DePriest, told an Atlanta audience in the spring of 1931, "Negro, lend no ear to Communism; it is not good for you because the Negro depends upon the white man for a job." Ironically, he should have been making that speech back home in Chicago since his district contained the largest number of black Communists in the nation. Communist and white Southerner Robert Minor responded that DePriest was an "instrument . . . for the anti-Negro and imperialist Republican Party." To Communists, DePriest's advice to African Americans boiled down to the same "old crap about their existence depending on the boss; he is trying to drag them back to slavery."[64]

The tension in Atlanta that spring dissipated as local authorities backed away from prosecuting the Communists whom they had charged. It might be better for the city, and certainly for business, if the whole thing went away, especially since so many of the city's leading white people opposed the insurrection law. June came and went without any more Communist rallies. Besides, in the past two months the Atlanta prosecutors had seen a Communist trial in Scottsboro, Alabama, generate worldwide headlines. It seemed prudent to let the Atlanta cases languish.

Derailing the Rape Myth in Scottsboro

The trial of the Scottsboro "Boys," which began in late March 1931, has become a historical icon, "one of the great defining moments of the twentieth century," and "a central episode in the global racial politics of the 1930s." The term *Scottsboro* has also become shorthand for Communist involvement in the South, eclipsing Gastonia, the Atlanta Six, and Tom Johnson's battles with the Birmingham police. Scottsboro is a kaleidoscope through which the images of the southern "race problem" reshuffled themselves as they passed from hand to hand. The NAACP, the Communist Party, white liberals, and dedicated white supremacists all read different narratives in its shards. Scottsboro did, however, project a few panoramic shots of the southern racial landscape that bedazzled everyone. From those projections came new ways to frame the future of the South. [65]

We might never have heard of the Scottsboro case if Sol Auerbach, using his Party name, James S. Allen, had not arrived in Chattanooga, Tennessee, in mid-July 1930. A fervent supporter of self-determination for the Black Belt who had spent time in the USSR, he planned to start the new Communist paper for which Tom Johnson had begged funds, the *Southern Worker*. Red Hendricks, out on bond after the Gastonia trial, had arrived the preceding February with Gastonia millworker Fred Totherow and Party organizer Amy Schechter. They rented an office on South Broad and "started signing up white and negro laborers" through interracial meetings that included both sexes. They made no attempt to avoid publicity, and Hendricks and Totherow posed, smiling, in front of their headquarters for the local newspaper.[66] The Central Committee had sent two hundred dollars along with Allen, who had edited the ILD's *Labor Defender*.[67]

On Allen's first trip south, his optimism overflowed. "It will not be so difficult" to persuade one of Chattanooga's thirty printers to produce the paper, he thought. But when he finally located a printer across the state line in Georgia, Allen worried that the firm would "not be reliable once in a tight situation" since one of the owners was the "local kleagle of the Ku Klux Klan." The *Southern Worker* used a fictitious Birmingham address to defy that city's "police and terror" campaign and to throw the authorities off the track of its true location, which was actually Allen's Chattanooga apartment.[68]

Beginning in August 1930, Allen printed twenty-five hundred copies a week, with the slogans "White and Colored Workers, Unite!" and "Issued Weekly by Communist Party of U.S.A." on the masthead. Two months later he had garnered only forty subscriptions, and organizers handed out the rest for free. [69] Or they didn't. Southerners were too scared to subscribe to the *Southern Worker*, and organizers were too scared to distribute it. Allen's successor found "hundreds and even thousands of old copies laying in rubbish piles." Moreover, most weeks the Central Committee delayed or failed to send the money to print it. [70] Before six months was up, Allen's new realism became abject despondency, and he begged to be relieved of his "extremely monotonous" and "depressing" job. [71]

As he pined away in Chattanooga in March 1931, Allen heard on the radio that the Paint Rock, Alabama, police had pulled nine black men from a freight train and charged them with rape. When a grand jury convened in Scottsboro, Alabama, to charge the African Americans, Isabelle, Jim Allen's wife, and Lowell Wakefield, the southern ILD representative, sat in the courtroom. [72] Allen's early and relentless coverage of the Scottsboro "Boys" made his reputation. It probably saved them from execution. Without the spotlight that Jim Allen quickly focused on the trials it is most likely that the "Boys" would have been dead by fall, lost among the thousands of unknown southern black men executed legally and illegally. [73]

Allen's base in Chattanooga was the hometown of four of the "Boys," which allowed the Communists to be in close touch with their families, who developed trust in Allen and the ILD. The timing was fortunate for the CPUSA as well since Scottsboro exploded only days after the Party expelled New York CP member August Yokinen for "white chauvinism," because he had excluded black Communists from a dance at the Finnish Workers Club. African Americans demonstrated their power within the Party by protesting and recalled the Comintern's commitment to destroy racism "branch and root." [74] Earl Browder stated flatly at the time that "without the prelude of the Yokinen case, the Scottsboro case would never have been heard of." [75] If white Alabamians had meant to stage the Scottsboro prosecution as a show trial to prove the beastiality of African Americans, the Communists used it as a show trial to prove their commitment to racial equality.

The nine black men were *really* boys—the oldest twenty, the youngest thirteen—who had hopped a freight train traveling through Tennessee to look for work. They were not traveling as a group; some did not know the others until they met in jail. It was late March, early spring in the mountains, and they were bundled up against the cold. Desperate people packed the train, hoboing around to find work, and fights broke out between black and white riders. The bloodied whites got off at Stevens, Alabama, and the stationmaster wired ahead to the next stop to "capture every negro on the train." As the train approached Paint Rock, a few of the black riders saw an angry crowd waiting and jumped off before the train pulled into the station. A mob of over two hundred whites met the train, searched it, and discovered the remaining nine black teenagers, who had been scattered in different cars.[76]

They also discovered two white women, Ruby Bates and Victoria Price. The women, sometime millworkers, found themselves in a pickle. Riding the rails, dressed in men's overalls, consorting with rowdy white men, they could have been charged with vagrancy or worse. Bates and Price, sitting calmly under a shade tree, chatting with Paint Rock women, slowly realized the seriousness of their situation. Price had once been jailed for adultery, and both had been picked up previously for vagrancy. If they were arrested now as prostitutes, Price could be tried in federal court under the Mann Act, since Bates was under eighteen, and Price had "transported" her across state lines. To make matters worse, Bates was drunk. One can only imagine their responses to the questioning of the good Paint Rock white women. Bates and Price must have quickly recognized their stark choices. They could either go to jail or claim to be victims. They cried rape.[77]

With that choice, Bates and Price had a lot of explaining to do. First, they had been riding with several white men in an open gondola half filled with gravel when several black men hopped in. It was one thing for southern white women to ride in a car with white men; it was another to ride in the same conveyance with black men, even though the gondola had no roof. A white woman's reputation might stand up to hoboing, cross-dressing, and one or two wild times with white men. It could never survive traveling in the same railroad car with black men. Second, in the hours that followed their allegations, a doctor examined Bates and Price and determined that they had had sex, but not recently. Medical exams were a new twist on the old rape story. In the past a white woman of good reputation could simply swear that she had been raped by a black man, and no one would have questioned it, much less hinted at a medical examination. However, Paint Rock authorities would not take the women's word that rape had occurred since they doubted that two women could have been raped by nine men in a moving gondola half filled with gravel and emerged without a blemish. When the exam showed that Bates and Price had had sex, they had to stick with the rape story or run afoul of the Mann Act and prostitution charges. Bates and Price found themselves on a runaway train.[78]

Quickly the entire South hopped on board. The Communist *Southern Worker* identified the women as "notorious prostitutes," while the *Chattanooga News* sounded the familiar call to white men's anxieties. "How far has our vaunted Southern chivalry sunk? How far has humanity sunk when we must contemplate the frightful things that occurred in that gravel car? How is it possible that in the venture of man can exist souls like these nine?" implored the *News*.[79] Alerted by Jim Allen, the International Labor Defense sent a telegram to the presiding judge demanding a change of venue and threatening to hold him "personally responsible," for what might happen if the trials weren't moved. The ILD sent an investigator and a black organizer for the League of Struggle for Negro Rights to witness the proceedings.[80]

The prosecution separated the defendants into four trials that lasted a total of four days. Within two weeks of their arrests, eight of the Scottsboro Nine had received the death penalty, and the judge had declared a mistrial in the case of thirteen-year-old Roy Wright because the jury was determined to execute him when the state had asked only for life imprisonment. Dismayed, unprepared, and worried that the "Boys" might actually be guilty, the NAACP flailed about. By the time that the NAACP secretary Walter White met with the defendants, three weeks after their convictions, five hundred mostly white Communists had marched in Harlem to support the "Boys," while five thousand mostly African American spectators looked on. The ILD hired a Chattanooga attorney to appeal the cases.[81]

By February 1932 Ruby Bates had recanted her testimony in a letter to her boyfriend that found its way into the hands of authorities. She admitted she had feared a jail term: "Those policeman made me tell a lie. . . . You will be sorry some day if you had too stay in jail with 8 Negroes you would tell a lie too. . . . Those Negroes did not touch me or those white boys. I hope you will belive me the law don't," Bates implored. "I was drunk at the time and did not know what I was doing. . . . I wish those Negroes are not Burnt on account of me it is these white boys fault," she confessed. The white man who had been on the train with Bates subsequently testified that the fight had not been in their car but in an adjacent one. Bates repeated the recantation at subsequent trials and joined ILD publicity campaigns to free the Scottsboro "Boys."[82] But most white Southerners no longer believed Ruby Bates and thought that the Communists had corrupted her. When she was a white sexually active hobo draped in the gauze of white southern womanhood, she could not tell a lie. When she was a white sexually active hobo involved with the Communist Party, they thought the truth was not in her.[83]

During 1932 two juveniles had been severed from the rest, the U.S. Supreme Court reversed the remaining seven convictions, and retrials and convictions separated the "Boys." One, Haywood Patterson, was ultimately sentenced to death in three separate trials, and the Supreme Court reversed the death penalty twice. In his fourth trial he got seventy-five years. In 1937 a deal between the defense and the prosecution dropped the charges against one defendant, set four free after six years in jail with a nol-pros, and kept four in jail, three with long sentences, one facing execution. The next year the Alabama governor commuted that sentence. Several of the defendants served time until the end of World War II, and one until 1950.[84] They all were totally innocent.

The worldwide publicity surrounding the Scottsboro appeals and retrials served the purposes of both the Communists and the NAACP. The association repeatedly tried to convince the Scottsboro Nine to hire attorneys other than those from the ILD. The battle over representation also brought out Will Alexander of the Commission on Interracial Cooperation, who thought it would be best if a local white lawyer or the NAACP took over the defense from the ILD.[85] When the Communists argued that the cases were emblematic of the class struggle and labor oppression, Alexander derided them. Ignoring the brutal economic crisis that compelled the defendants and alleged victims to ride the rails in the first place, as well as the political uses of racially inflected rape scares to control the white working class, Alexander argued that the case had absolutely nothing to do with the political economy. "It originally grew out of contacts between low-class whites and low-class Negroes, who happened to be bumming their way on a freight train," Alexander wrote. Even though his one-sentence description fairly screams "class struggle," he declared, "The Scottsboro case has nothing of class struggle in it."[86]

The NAACP, which was initially hesitant even to get involved, accused the ILD of caring only for publicity and not at all for the Nine's fate. The association tried to convince the defendants to let it engage Clarence Darrow to represent them, but they refused, whereupon Darrow issued the verdict: "You can't mix politics with a law case."[87] Still, the NAACP realized that the trials' politicalization could work in its own interest. Early in 1932 Walter White informed James Weldon Johnson that the Nine had refused NAACP help. "For your private ear," White whispered, "this is the last thing the Communists wanted, and if they win, they lose." In other words, if the southern court system set the Scottsboro Nine free, the Communists had lost the cases' propaganda value. If the courts continued to find them guilty and punish them harshly, people would always believe that the NAACP and Darrow could have done better. "Privately, I am much relieved" to be out of the case, White said, especially since he believed "the thing is going to turn out all right eventually."[88]

The NAACP seized upon the Communists' zealous representation of the Scottsboro Nine to position its organization as a most reasonable alternative to Communism. Although White had been friendly with Communists in the 1920s, the CP and the NAACP had become bitter enemies by late 1931, when he first began to brandish the Communist threat as a fundraising tool. The Communists, White argued, "seek to capitalize [on] unrest among Negroes, which is born of lynching, unemployment, and other things from which the Negro especially suffers."[89] W. E. B. Du Bois, editor of the NAACP magazine *Crisis*, acknowledged that the Scottsboro cases "have brought squarely before the American Negro the question of his attitude toward Communism." Although he admired the Soviet Union as "increasingly successful," Du Bois condemned American Communists as "young jackasses" who doomed the Scottsboro Nine by "threatening judges and yelling for mass action on the part of white southern workers."[90]

The dislike was mutual, since the Communists saw the NAACP as the worst example of the "Negro reformism [that] has become an active agent of the ruling imperialist bourgeoisie in helping to prepare the way for fascism."[91] They denounced the NAACP leaders as "tools of the capitalists" and "Negro misleaders," whose representation of the "Boys" would lead them to the electric chair. The Communists believed that black workers "evidenced" a "leftward trend" and that the "Negro Reformists" tried to "stem and head off their rising struggles."[92]

The Communists used the Scottsboro cause to build contacts with northern white liberals and a few white Southerners. Writer Theodore Dreiser began a fundraising effort that attracted black and white writers on the Left from across the country. Although Paul Green later joined the National Committee for the Defense of Political Prisoners, which grew out of this effort, at the time he thought that the Communists were simply making a horrible situation worse. He begged Dreiser to "throw away your politics and your theories this once . . . for it would be an everlasting sin for you to use the bones of seven Negro boys to hammer the drums of a social revolution."[93]

Scottsboro became central to the CP's recruiting strategy among African Americans as well. Hosea Hudson, a black man working in the steel mills in Birmingham, explained how the ILD defense moved him: "Whenever Negroes was frame-up, I always would look for somebody else to say something about it." Sometimes the white interracialists would protest, "but it wouldn't amount to nothing" until the Scottsboro case; "then," Hudson remembered, "I could see some hope."[94] In 1932 the ILD appointed William Patterson, the black lawyer now back from Moscow, national secretary. Communist lore had it that the Scottsboro "Boys" sang in their cells:

> *I looked over yonder and what did I see*
> *Comin' for to carry me home?*
> *Mr. William Patterson and the I.L.D.*
> *Comin' for to carry me home.*[95]

Looking past Scottsboro's immediate fractiousness, we can now see the tectonic shifts that it produced on the southern landscape. First, the cases disrupted the long-standing political usefulness of southern white women's purported purity. Through a coolly concocted and heatedly publicized rape scare in the 1890s, upper-class white men had destroyed the populist coalitions between white and black working-class men by arguing that such interracial alliances put white women at the mercy of black men's lust. The bargain theoretically extended chivalry and protection to all white women; in effect it paid working-class white women, in the mills and on the farms, a whiteness bonus through which they purchased the assumption of lily-white innocence formerly reserved for upper-class white women. Even at that, the pedestal was only for public consumption during political moments, and poor white women lived a different reality, one that included all the possibilities and pitfalls that beset Price and Bates. Despite their daily dangers, poor white women still risked a lot when they failed to behave in respectable ways. Victoria Price and Ruby Bates put up their whiteness cards as a ticket to ride the rails, to drink and have sex with men while sleeping rough and wearing overalls.[96]

When the white woman's character was questioned, occasionally black men were acquitted in rape cases. In this case, however, the allegation was so outrageous (rape by nine men) that it quickly became a political issue. Prosecutors and their supporters could not afford to admit doubt, even as they stared at a mountain of contradictory evidence. Price and Bates's ordeal—and it must have been an ordeal for them, if a self-inflicted one—marked the moment from which a hite woman's cry of black rape would no longer reflexively be taken up as a political club without someone's questioning just what sort of white woman was crying rape. The Scottsboro Nine were so pitiful and so clearly innocent, Bates was so heroic for her recantation, and the litigation lasted so long that stories of southern injustice slowly began to replace the overheated rape myths in the political arena of the 1930s.

Before Scottsboro, white Southerners used deliberately vague and suggestive language to discuss the crime of black on white rape in the South. Terms like *outrage, brute, unspeakable horrors, ravished,* and *violating white womanhood* blurred the facts of the case and licensed white imaginations to run wild.[97] Historian Jacquelyn Dowd Hall has called it "folk pornography." In the Scottsboro cases the Communists used frank language, including the words *rape* and *prostitute,* to dispel the discursive fog that surrounded the purported victims and condemned the alleged perpetrators.

Moreover, the Scottsboro cases taught many southern whites something that African Americans and members of the Commission on Interracial Cooperation already knew: A trial might be a lynching in disguise. The transparent unfairness of the original Scottsboro trials, followed by the fact that Bates's recantation had little influence on subsequent litigation, shook some whites' trust in the southern judicial system. White moderates like those on the Commission on Interracial Cooperation worked to prevent lynching by getting accused blacks in jail and in court. Just prior to the Scottsboro affair, the CIC had sponsored the formation of the Association of Southern Women for the Prevention of Lynching (ASWPL).[98] The women of the ASWPL headed off lynchings and worked to get trials for alleged perpetrators. Yet the CIC's white leaders consistently failed to endorse publicly the two positions that their black interracialist counterparts urged upon them—black suffrage and black representation on juries—which might have assured fairer trials.

The Scottsboro verdicts suggested that it was not simply lawlessness that jeopardized black safety but lawfulness as well. The CP referred to the prosecution as the "persecution," and to the Scottsboro trials as lynchings. The Scottsboro cases shook the ASWPL's founder, Jessie Daniel Ames, and she began to confront what she called "the Prostitution of the Courts" in these instances.[99] The world's scrutiny of the Scottsboro cases focused attention on the flaws in the southern judicial system rather than on the mythical flaws in southern black men.

Of course the Communist party exploited the Scottsboro case, and the Anglo-American section of the Comintern pushed the publicity campaign. They did so skillfully and toward two ends: winning the Nine's freedom and pressing Communist gains. Scottsboro demonstrations brought people into the world's streets in front of American consulates in Europe, South Africa, and Latin America. In the United States, Scottsboro sympathizers marched on Washington and in Harlem.[100] From Haiti, Jacques Roumain, who had led the student strike against vocational education, raised money for their appeals. For this and other radical action, the Haitian government charged him with treason and imprisoned him.[101] The ILD publicity strategy helped save the lives of the Nine and held up southern "justice" to mockery. Around the world the publicity drew attention to the South in much the same way that Theophilus Eugene "Bull" Connor's fire hoses did three decades later.

With ample evidence gathered from their own experiences in Gastonia and in the jails and courts of Atlanta and Birmingham, the Communists understood that appeals must be made in two venues, before the law and before the people. They put their faith in the masses and believed their own headlines, such as MASS PROTESTS AGAIN SNATCH SCOTTSBORO BOY FROM DEATH CHAIR. Earl Browder called the Scottsboro case "a great political success for our Party."[102] Haywood Patterson, one of the Nine understood that the publicity surrounding his case was part of something bigger: "I guess my people gained more off the Scottsboro case than any of us boys did. . . . Our case opened up a lot of politics in the country."[103] Scottsboro helped elevate black Communist James Ford to the vice presidential slot on William Foster's presidential ticket in May 1932.[104] It even seemed to have opened, ever so slightly, the politics of white millworkers. From Concord, Gastonia, Burlington, and Danville came telegrams of protest to the Supreme Court and the governor of Alabama, who received two thousand missives within three months of the Nine's convictions. A Communist argued that the greatest value of Scottsboro could be found in this connection of race and class: "We have had hundreds of such cases [rape charges] . . . but they were not considered problems of the labour movements. . . . [With Scottsboro we] demonstrated in practice what was before theory . . . that the struggle of the Negro masses was part and parcel of the struggle of the American working class."[105]

As part of this mass action Communist writers joined non-Communist black writers of the Harlem Renaissance to land the deathblow against Dixie's monopoly on cultural representation of "*the* Negro." White playwright John Wexley wrote *They Shall Not Die*, a play based on the Scottsboro case, which opened in New York in February 1934. If the wildly popular "Negro dialect" play *The Green Pastures* depicted God as a "white plantation owner" happily presiding over his black angels' fish fry in heaven, *They Shall Not Die* mocked southern white dialect in similarly offensive ways. Tom Ewell as Red, a down-on-his-luck white worker in jail, uttered such lines as "Same way them trash gals carry on with them niggers." Ruth Gordon played Ruby Bates as a pathetic, slow-witted,

semiprostitute with a halting, gooey caramel way of speaking: "Yeah, maw
... I'm a-feelin' might low. . . ." Claude Rains appeared as the eloquent Jewish northern lawyer who had no accent at all: "We're only beginning. I
don't care how many times you try to kill this Negro boy. . . . I'll make the
fair name of this state stink to high heaven with its lynch justice. . . . These
boys, *they shall not die!*"[106] Carl Van Vechten, white patron of the Harlem
Renaissance, reported that radical Emma Goldman pronounced it "very
bad propaganda."[107]

By the spring of 1932 the Scottsboro case had traveled around the
world and back again. Schoolchildren from Moscow to Milwaukee began
to think of Dixie as an antidemocratic place, a place where a black man
could not get a witness and where justice was a stranger. Black poet
Langston Hughes, deeply influenced by the Scottsboro trials and retrials
in 1932, spoke for many when he wrote:

> *That Justice is a blind goddess*
> *Is a thing to which we poor are wise:*
> *Her bandage hides two festering sores*
> *That once perhaps were eyes.*[108]

Sons and Daughters of Scottsboro

From the Scottsboro cases, the Communists developed a model that operated at two levels. An intensely local effort pitted the ILD against southern judges and lawyers at the same time that a publicity campaign reached
internationally to attract other Communists. They put it to good use in
Camp Hill, Alabama, where sharecroppers in the Communist-organized
Share Croppers' Union were massacred and the survivors criminally prosecuted.[109] The lessons of Scottsboro and Camp Hill, where the ILD fought
for black people whom everyone else had abandoned, proved to starving
black Southerners that the CP had something to offer them. In July 1931,
for example, five hundred people turned up at an outdoor meeting in
Charlotte, North Carolina, to "demand the release of the Scottsboro
Nine."[110] According to the one set of southern membership records, it
appears that Scottsboro drew African Americans to the Party in District
16 in the fall of 1931. The Party Registration and Control Forms verify

membership in Virginia, North Carolina, and South Carolina at one moment in time and are unique among southern CPUSA records. Other membership estimates come from organizers, who counted in inconsistent and incomplete ways.[111] Likewise, the Party forms may not include all members in District 16, but the data tell us a great deal about members in particular places at a particular time. For example, sixty-two of the district's ninety-five members belonged to an Unemployed Council.[112]

Thirty-two women and sixty-three men joined for a total of ninety-five Party members in District 16, but nine did not disclose their location. Three women did not provide their race on the form, but sixty of the ninety-five members were certainly African Americans, thirty-seven men and twenty-three women.[113] Only four of the female members identified themselves as white. U.S. Communists had informed the Comintern of the importance of organizing black women, on the basis of the high percentage of married black women who worked. Moreover, they had noted that black women could be counted on during strikes because they "show[ed] a fighting spirit with which the bosses must reckon."[114]

District 16 membership reveals that the local demography reflected local concerns. Party star Amy Schechter, a veteran of the USSR and Gastonia, organized a group of all-white members in Danville, Virginia, through an AFL United Textile Workers strike. She criticized the AFL's failure to provide adequate strike relief and its compromising settlement, claiming, by contrast, that the Communist National Textile Workers Union was "a fighting union." In Danville eight Party members worked in textiles, two women appear to be married to textile worker members, and a plumber joined.[115]

While Danville was white, in Greenville, South Carolina, veteran organizer Clara Holden recruited an integrated membership of employed and unemployed. In February 1931 she organized a march of two thousand workers, including two hundred African Americans, protested against discrimination in relief by the American Red Cross, and packed city council meetings with black and white workers who "sat side by side. . . . Like rats," frightened city councilmen "sneaked out the back door."[116] Holden put black and white workers on the same committees and organized interracial action groups to prevent evictions. Still, at unit meetings, Holden noted, the "Negro workers do not sit with the white workers.

They come in and sit apart." Nevertheless, she thought things were going well. "I think we will have social equality to a limited extent in dances, affairs, etc., in a few months," she predicted to the Anglo-American Section of the Comintern. "We must send more forces to the South," she wrote to her comrades in the Soviet Union on April 7.[117]

Holden was optimistic in the face of terrors. A few days before she cheerily reported to Moscow, Unemployed Council members protested at a city council meeting in West Greenville. The mayor briefly left the room and returned with members of the Ku Klux Klan in "full regalia." As the unemployed attempted to speak, the local newspaper reported that the Klansmen "took charge" and warned the workers to "leave the Unemployed Council if they hoped to get aid or jobs." Two days later the KKK showed up at an interracial Unemployed Council meeting at Workers' Hall and began to beat up the African Americans there. When white Communist workers jumped in to defend them, a free-for-all ensued, while three police officers watched.[118] In September, Klansmen broke up an Unemployed Council meeting, and "mill thugs" kidnapped Clara Holden and beat her up.[119] By then Holden reported a diminished five hundred members in the Unemployed Council. The forty-six party members whom Holden counted in April had dropped to eighteen; ten were white, eight black. Only five members, including an African American, worked in textile plants. In October 1931 Holden left Greenville for Straight Creek, Harlan County, Kentucky.[120] The white terror had succeeded.

In Charlotte, African Americans, drawn by Communist support of the Scottsboro "Boys" and by local protests on behalf of the unemployed, predominated in party membership. Of fifty-seven members, only eight were white. Of the eight white members, three were Russian-born; they included the blind Jewish junk dealer who had welcomed Fred Beal two years earlier. Of the remaining five white members, one was a printer at a newspaper, one ran a lunch stand, and one worked in a textile mill. The remaining two white members were Dewey Martin and W. G. Binkley, both Gastonia strikers who became CP organizers. The other forty-nine African American members joined because of neighborhood or "street" organizing through Unemployed Councils.[121] A year earlier the Charlotte Unemployed Council had brought out three thousand protesters demanding jobs and welfare. Charlotte's mayor played right into their hands when he appointed the owner of one of the largest mills to the unemployment relief commission; that millowner had just given his workers a 10 percent wage cut.[122] A few days later an integrated mass of a thousand people demanding relief marched to city hall to see the mayor, whereupon the police beat them up with baseball bats. An organizer complained, "If the chamber of commerce or a group of bankers or the A. F. of L. fakers wanted to see the mayor they would be greeted by a special reception committee, but when we workers come here to demand relief we are greeted with police billies." The workers came back for more: "DEMONSTRATE FEB. 28 For Lower Rent, For Unemployed Relief and Unemployed Insurance From the Government! Against Evictions of Unemloyed [sic]!"[123]

Twenty-one black women belonged to the Party in Charlotte, but not a single white woman did.[124] The Young Communist League of the First Ward unit, operating in one of the most crowded black neighborhoods abutting the white mill villages in North Charlotte, held an interracial dance in the summer of 1931. Although it reported that the dance was "successfully held and well attended," it seems unlikely that any local white women were there.[125] The Communists were probably the only people who celebrated International Woman's Day in Charlotte that year, and they called for "equal pay for equal work for more pay." A poster broadcast: "We are forced to do mens jobs at less pay. In Charlotte we slave in the mills, laundrys and do all the house work for the rich. Working Women don't stand for it. Join together with the men workers." Since black women most often did not work in mills and white women most often did not work in laundries or the homes of the rich, the poster spoke to both groups, even if white women were not listening.[126]

Unlike black women, white women had little chance to hear the CP message in their neighborhoods. Since the Party insisted on interracial meetings, it was an enormous risk for white women to attend, and their presence would call unwelcome attention to the Party as well. African Americans rarely entered white neighborhoods after dark, but white men more often entered black ones, so unit meetings were held in black homes. If a white woman was spotted in a black neighborhood, everyone would be exposed. Robert Minor, who had emerged as the CPUSA's top officer in charge of the South after the Lovestone purge, deplored the "extremely bad prejudice" that had to be "broken down among white men" and pointed out that "[white] women in the South, when they do get going, often . . . become the very best leaders."[127]

These poisonous gender dynamics did not silence the CP in the South. The Communists' vocal protests against Jim Crow never wavered as they held integrated antilynching conferences and marches. They made connections among "lynch law, mob violence, and bosses' terrorism" that pointed up the lack of protection for anyone, white or black, who lived in a society that condoned lawlessness and failed to protect the powerless.[128] No doubt the courage of the white organizer and the black worker who stood for Charlotte City Council elections on the Communist ticket in April 1931 also helped draw African Americans to the Party. The Communist platform demanded $10 per week relief for the unemployed and free transportation to school, along with free lunches and textbooks for their children. They appealed to municipal workers with an eight-hour day and a $20 weekly minimum wage and to everyone else by advocating that the city manager's salary be reduced from $12,500 to $2,500 annually.[129] The black Communist who dared stand for the council was the first African American to run on any ticket in Charlotte since disfranchisement at the turn of the century.

By the spring of 1932 the question of what the Communists offered them interested African Americans across the country, and the NAACP's magazine, *Crisis*, devoted a symposium to it. The editor of the *Afro-American* argued that the CP was "as radical as the N.A.A.C.P. were twenty years ago. . . . The Communists are going our way, for which Allah be praised." Frank M. Davis, editor of the *Atlanta Daily World*, dramatized the powerful appeal that the CP held for southern African Americans caught in the two-fisted grip of white supremacy and the Great Depression. "If, when the United States awoke some morning, it were suddenly discovered that everybody claimed as a Negro had gone Red, it would cause an immediate change in race relations," Davis observed. "There might be trouble for a day or so, but it would not long last. Whites, thoroughly aroused and afraid, would attempt to remove those injustices heaped upon Afro-America that cradled black Communists," because "12,000,000 souls, backed by the U.S.S.R. and possibly other jealous nations . . . , would be too big a group [for the whites] to deal with by force." In the next line Davis called this scenario "remote and improbable."[130]

Yet the Communists were in the South, and many people wanted to know more about them. The Communists ran for office, helped hungry people, and weren't afraid to take on a rape trial to save the lives of nine black men. The publicity surrounding the Scottsboro case meant that every Southerner, black or white, heard about Communism, and it inspired some to head to the USSR to see for themselves how it worked. Conversely, the publicity surrounding the Scottsboro case meant that every Muscovite had heard of southern white supremacy, and some of them were eager to learn more about how that worked.

Seeking Solutions in the USSR

If a Communist takeover seemed "remote and improbable" in Atlanta, in the summer of 1932 Atlantans took over Red Square. Atlantan Clark Foreman, who had worked at the Commission for Interracial Cooperation and recently completed a PhD at Columbia University, spent seven months in the Soviet Union, carefully observing its racial practices. John Hope, the black president of Atlanta University, and Ira De A. Reid, a young black sociologist there, went as well.[131] Embittered by the fight for the Atlanta Six's right to free speech and disgusted with the Scottsboro trial, C. Vann Woodward itched to see for himself the Socialist experiment. At twenty-three, the tall, handsome native Arkansan resembled the archetypical white Southerner on the outside, but on the inside he was already an outsider.

Once in Moscow, Woodward found himself inundated with criticism of the South's persecution of African Americans, but the Soviets liked him well enough to offer him a teaching job. He had thought he might be "ready to embrace some such philosophy" as Communism, but thanks to his traveling companion, a woman fluent in Russian, two incidents deterred him. In a factory a worker broke from the ranks and ran over to tell the tour group that he was a slave. Then, during a trip by rail, a peasant jumped up, denounced the Soviet system, and jumped off the car. Immediately upon leaving the USSR, however, Woodward wrote to a friend back home, "If I had not acquired some very capitalistic debts . . . I would have remained in Russia. . . . Might go back next year. No place in the world could be so interesting." He warned his correspondent to "use your discretion about ... communicating my Soviet enthusiasm."[132] When he returned home, he was determined to "get in on" the next opportunity to defend civil rights. Only much later did Woodward forget his enthusiasm and recall that the trip "was important in sobering me up."[133]

As Woodward left the South to look at the Soviets, the Soviets made plans to look more closely at the South. Scottsboro had become a cause célèbre in Moscow, and Russians were eager to know more about black Southerners. In the spring of 1932 James Ford, the African American running for vice president of the United States on the Communist ticket, learned that the Soviets were eager to make a movie depicting working conditions in Birmingham, Alabama. Titled *Black and White*, it would be made by the German film company Meschrabpom with the cooperation of the Comintern. The Soviets charged Ford with recruiting African American cast members who could come to Moscow, paying their own ways and bringing their own props, in the summer of 1932.[134]

It must have been a dream come true for Lovett Fort-Whiteman when he got a chance to work on the script with Russian screenwriter Georgi Grebner and German director Carl Junghans. After all, hadn't he played Othello with the Negro Shakespeare Company? And he had written those awkwardly realized short stories depicting interracial love in New England and interracial lust in Haiti. Most important, Fort-Whiteman was a true Southerner—not a Nebraskan like Harry Haywood or a West Indian like Otto Huiswoud, two other African Americans then living in Moscow. Although Fort-Whiteman may never have actually dared organize in Birmingham, he had grown up in Dallas and spent time in jail in St. Louis. The Comintern would have to depend on him for deep southern background and local color.[135] His collaborators, Grebner and Junghans, had the Comintern's confidence, but the three spoke different languages. With the help of a translator, Fort-Whiteman helped Grebner write the Russian script, which was translated into English. Then Fort-Whiteman was supposed to make the dialogue believable.[136]

Communist Party vice-presidential candidate Ford deputized New Yorker Louise Alone Thompson to recruit the cast. Born in Chicago in 1901, Thompson had graduated from the University of California at Berkeley and gone to teach in the South in 1923. She ended up at Hampton, Virginia, during a student strike against the racism of the school's white principal. This demoralizing period filled her with a radical desire to over-throw southern white supremacy from without, since her experience had convinced her that the time was not ripe to do it from within.[137] There had been one bright spot at Hampton: Thompson met visiting speaker William Patterson and expressed an interest in going to study at the KUTV in Moscow. When Patterson forwarded her a KUTV application, she realized that she was not yet ready to commit to being a "revolutionist."[138]

Instead of moving from Hampton to Moscow, Thompson decamped to Harlem, where she quickly joined the circle of writers, artists, and performers who were making the Harlem Renaissance. She married Wallace Thurman, a talented writer, but the couple lived together a bare six months before, convinced that he was gay, she left him. "Wally and I didn't have any very satisfactory sexual contact," Thompson recalled. "Why did you marry me, Wally? Why?" she would ask, and he would say, "'I love you.'" "That's all I could ever get out of that man. 'I love you.' He would never admit he was a homosexual."[139] Thompson had been crushed by the ordeal of her improbable marriage. After that, she put her trust in groups and institutions, not in individuals. To stay afloat, she worked as a secretary for Langston Hughes and Zora Neale Hurston while they collaborated on the play *Mule Bone*. Hurston resented Thompson, whom she saw as a cheeky clerical worker who attracted too much of Hughes's attention.[140] Indeed, Hughes quickly became the most important person in Thompson's life.[141]

Fed up with the "little or no action" of seminars on interracial cooperation, the ILD's Scottsboro defense prompted Thompson to search "for an alternative."[142] She found it in the National Committee for the Defense of Political Prisoners, where she could support the Scottsboro Nine. Subsequently she formed a Harlem chapter of the Friends of the Soviet Union, an organization that then worked for U.S. recognition of the USSR.[143]

Thompson knew scores of other young African Americans who had been activated by the Scottsboro trials, but only a few who would be able to pay their passage to Moscow, even though the film company, Meschrabpom, would pay them a salary once they were there and provide their return fare. For example, Pauli Murray, a young woman from Durham, North Carolina, found the trip too pricey. "It was my last year in college, and because getting through had been such a struggle, I decided not to go. . . ." It was one of the few adventures Murray ever declined, and she marked missing the Moscow trip as one of two lifetime opportunities that "I wonder if I will regret."[144] Thompson recruited college students, raised money for their passages, and made it clear that one did not have to be a Communist to go.[145] In her fundraising material, she characterized *Black and White* as the "first authentic picture of Negro life in America," one that would show black life "devoid of sentimentality as well as of buffoonery."[146]

Finally twenty-two people signed on. Only one was a member of the CPUSA; some had worked in leftist causes alongside Communists; a few had never met a Communist before.[147] The Scottsboro case had radicalized Homer Smith, who was working his way through journalism school in the Minneapolis post office, and he had read everything he could about the USSR. He hoped to secure permanent work there. No one could guarantee that, but James Ford told him that Lovett Fort-Whiteman could probably help him. Lloyd Patterson, a house painter expelled from Hampton for participating in the student strike, and Wayland Rudd, an actor who had appeared in DuBose Heyward's *Porgy*, Eugene O'Neill's *The Emperor Jones*, and Paul Green's *In Abraham's Bosom*, wanted to remain in the USSR as well.[148]

Several other cast members had appeared as bit players in the southern white depictions of Negro life as well, and now they itched to depict their own lives more realistically. Twenty-two-year-old Dorothy West, a promising writer, had toured in a bit part in *Porgy*.[149] Sylvia Garner, a singer, had appeared in *Scarlet Sister Mary*, another woman had sung spirituals with the Hall Johnson Choir, and one of the men had been in *Ham's Daughters*. Alan MacKenzie, a salesman, was the only CP member in the group.[150] Others were college kids, for example, Mildred Jones and Mollie Lewis. Loren Miller, Ted Poston, and Henry Lee Moon were journalists.[151] The previous summer Moon had written an article on Scottsboro that took the NAACP to task: "Is the Negro race in America to continue to accept the reformist philosophy of the association as its most advanced and militant expression?"[152]

Langston Hughes represented the Harlem literati. Like Thompson, Hughes had connections to the CP—he had endorsed the Foster/Ford ticket—but he was not a Party member. His pamphlet *Scottsboro Limited*, which included a one-act play that depicted "Reds" rushing to the aid of the Scottsboro Nine, was just out, and his volume of poetry *Good Morning, Revolution* would appear in the United States while he was in the USSR.[153] Though Thompson and Hughes didn't carry Party cards in their pockets, they draped themselves in Communist accessories, calling each other comrade and teasing a mutual friend about being a "damn bourgeois," even as Louise admitted a case of the jitters before her "debut as a revolutionary speaker."[154] Hughes drove like a madman from California to New York and cabled Thompson from that crossroads in the desert Yuma, Arizona: "You hold that boat cause its an ark to me."[155]

By coincidence, that boat also carried Howard University professors Alain Locke and Ralph Bunche up in first class, and the young radicals in third class took special pleasure enjoying themselves under their disapproving gazes. Locke sniffed at the "wild crowd of young Negroes," while the young Harlem literati mocked him unmercifully. Louise Thompson's husband, Wallace Thurman, had once called him "a perfect symbol of the Aframerican rococo in his personality as much as in his prose style."[156] Zora Neale Hurston complained that Locke, who had published an anthology of New Negro literature, tried to run "a mental pawnshop." She observed: "He lends out his patronage and takes in ideas which he soon passes off as his own." The "wild crowd of young Negroes" might have agreed with Hurston that Locke was "a malicious, spiteful little snot."[157]

Perhaps Alain Locke protested too much about the "wild crowd" to hide from himself and others his attraction to his former protégé and traveling companion Langston Hughes. It took all his willpower to avoid losing himself in the glare of Hughes's sunny spirit. Locke called these moments when he lost his head "Langston eclipses."[158] Hughes, as always, played the life of the party and the center of attention. A black man who met him in Moscow commented on "his zest for life and love of people. He was as easygoing and charming, perceptive and intelligent in person as was the best of his poetry." He "enjoyed a good time, and if he could not find one, he would make one on the spot, with his hearty infectious laughter."[159]

In early summer 1932 Fort-Whiteman welcomed the group when they embarked on Soviet soil. He had brought along a brass band to play "The Internationale," and some cast members promptly kissed the ground.[160] When Hughes met Fort-Whiteman, who had now lived in

Moscow four years, he held him up as an example of Soviet robustness: "Certainly Comrade Whiteman didn't look anything like *A motherless chile, A long ways from home.'* And he has lived in Moscow for years."[161] After a grand feast, the cast rode by train from Leningrad to Moscow, where they were greeted by four African Americans, including Emma Harris, the "Mammy of Moscow," who had been born in Reconstruction Georgia and stranded in Moscow in 1901 by a vaudeville troupe known as the Louisiana Amazons. Misled by a Russian "charlatan" who wooed her but then exhibited her as a slave whom he had captured in Africa, Harris had found the American consul unhelpful when she tried to leave. She decided to stay in Russia, sang as the Black Nightingale, and married a Russian. She supported the revolution and eventually learned to speak fluent Russian. If white Southerners in Moscow called her Mammy, Soviets called her Tovaritsch Emma.[162] Upon seeing the cast, Emma "crowed, 'Lord a'mighty, my people don' arrived.' "[163]

After they had settled into Moscow's Grand Hotel, the cast went to the Park of Culture and Rest to take part in a Scottsboro demonstration.[164] Emma Harris, introduced as "our own beloved Negro comrade, Emma, who before she came to the Soviet motherland, knew the stinging lash of race hatred in her native America," starred at these occasions. She would "denounce race prejudice . . . in fluent Russian" and "hail the workers of the world, the Soviet Union, and Stalin, in traditional form." Then she would march off the stage and murmur to Hughes and company, "They ought to turn them colored boys loose," adding, "I wish I was back home."[165]

Langston Hughes was annoyed to discover that Fort-Whiteman had failed to complete the translation of the Russian movie script. "Russian time is worse than CPT," Louise Thompson said.[166] It took another two weeks to produce an English version. In the meantime the cast members explored Moscow and enjoyed their status as honored guests. They went to the head of the queue, shopped at special stores reserved for foreigners, and, instead of sitting at the back of the bus, moved to the front as friendly Russian riders sprang up to accommodate them.[167]

From afar their friends and family envied their freedom from the color line and their relative luxury as the Depression deepened in America. From New York, black writer Countee Cullen wrote a despairing letter to Dorothy West, chronicling his most recent day from hell, one that culminated with his discovery that his bank had failed with his money in it. He "rejoiced" for West, "so far removed from bad gin, the color question, number playing, even spirituals." He suggested that she write an article on "How It Feels to Be in an Unprejudiced Country." [168] West's father told her "to stay there as long as you can where you will be treated like a human." Her mother added, "You could never live in this country after Russia." Her cousin Helene asked, "How does it feel to be a woman and not a curiosity?" She couldn't resist adding, "How charming is Langston?" [169] Langston was inordinately charming, and he found the Soviets charming as well: "I find myself forgetting that the Russians are white folks. They're too damn decent and polite." On one of her letters home, Louise Thompson drew a smiley face and captioned it "me in the USSR." [170]

When he finally got to read Fort-Whiteman's English script, Hughes pronounced it "improbable to the point of ludicrousness." He must have known it was Fort-Whiteman's translation, since Grebner refers to "Comrade Whiteman" in script notes, but Hughes later referred to it as written by a "Russian writer who had never been in America." [171] One of the ludicrous parts involved a "beautiful colored girl," a servant in the home of a white steel magnate in Birmingham. The magnate's son goes up to the girl at a party and says, "Honey, put down your tray; come, let's dance." The scene bears a resemblance to Fort-Whiteman's short story on interracial love in New England, and the sexual exploitation recalls his story on interracial lust in Haiti. Other problematic scenarios suggest Fort-Whiteman's judgment and hand. When white workers begin to massacre African Americans, wealthy blacks go to their radio station (!) and broadcast a cry for help to the North. Unionized white workers "jump into their cars and buses and head straight for Alabama to save their Negro brothers." [172] Parts of the script rang true, however. It included many references to Scottsboro and centered on the arrest and lynching of a young black boy for rape. [173]

Stranger than fiction, but then, so had been Fort-Whiteman's 1925 ANLC meeting in Chicago, with its "Russian" ballerinas and its incomprehensible play—in Russian. Foolishly optimistic, but then, so had been the banner over the ANLC stage of white and black hands clasped. Larger than life, but then, so had been Fort-Whiteman strolling down the streets of Chicago dressed in a *robochka*, with his head shaved in the Soviet futurist style. In his writing and in his performance of daily life, Fort-Whiteman composed scripts of racial fiction. Harry Haywood characterized him as "a showman; he always seemed to be acting out a part he had chosen for himself."[174] Those scripts enabled him to escape the pain of white oppression by moving to an imagined world in his mind, long before he ever moved to the real and imagined world of Moscow. Homer Smith, cast member and would-be journalist, later excused Fort-Whiteman's failure by arguing that "he was a Negro intellectual and so steeped in party dogma that he had completely lost touch with America."[175]

Fort-Whiteman's countervision allowed him to expand the limits of the possible, but this time his job had been to see the world the way it was. The Comintern had counted on him to guide Georgi Grebner to write "the first authentic picture of Negro life in America."[176] Fort-Whiteman had not counted on Langston Hughes, a professional writer whose supreme self-confidence enabled him to tell the Russians what they didn't want to hear: The script was worthless.

The second draft, written by German director Carl Junghans in consultation with Hughes, represented relatively accurately the South's economic desperation and Communist hopes for the region in 1931 and 1932.[177] On his own, Junghans could never have written this saga of AFL "social fascism," racial oppression, and true-to-life working conditions in southern industry, all capped by a realistic interracial march of the unemployed through the streets of a southern city. The script depicts the Dixie that Communist organizers defied every day, from a false rape charge and lynching by burning of an innocent black man to a noble white worker who crosses the color line to march with the black workers. The marchers shout, "Black and White Unite to Fight," and carry signs reading DOWN WITH LEGAL LYNCHING OF NEGROES AND RACE DISCRIMINATION and TO HELL WITH CHARITY, WE WANT UNEMPLOYMENT INSURANCE.[178] It's doubtful that Lovett Fort-Whiteman collaborated on this version. The scenes are up-to-the-minute and read as if they were written by an eyewitness to the Atlanta Six's efforts or at least a reader of the *Southern Worker*, and Fort-Whiteman had not been in the United States since 1928.

Even though the script aptly depicted a southern Communist's point of view, it was turgid and too short, even if it was now free of the howlers that had unhinged Hughes. Hughes often later denied writing the second script, but one time he conceded he had written the sparse dialogue. Ultimately, though, Hughes didn't *write* it; no one really wrote it. When it was "finished," the Comintern and Meschrabpom held it back for weeks, refusing to allow the cast to see it.

Meanwhile Meschrabpom expected Lovett Fort-Whiteman to act as the group's host. The cast was, in Thompson's words, "living like royalty used to be entertained in Tsarist Russia," even though they heard rumors of a terrible famine in the surrounding countryside. Idle, they toured Moscow, took Russian lessons, and divided up into cliques. One group— Louise Thompson, Loren Miller, Langston Hughes, and Matt Crawford —became more impressed with the Soviet society each day and socialized with Harry Haywood and Otto Huiswoud.[179] Thompson became so enthralled with the Communist system that other cast members nicknamed her Madam Moscow.[180]

Aspiring writer Dorothy West and South Carolinian Mildred Jones stayed together at the Grand Hotel, which West termed "truly magnificent," in a room overlooking Red Square. Emma Harris did their laundry and occasionally cooked supper for them.[181] Dorothy awaited Countee Cullen's periodic love letters, even as she fell under Langston Hughes's spell when he called her "darlink." There were rumors that she proposed to Langston, but one reason that people loved Hughes was that he rarely talked about his affairs of the heart, and when he did, he did so at a very safe distance. For example, Hughes wrote to Carl Van Vechten from Moscow that his "girl friend at the moment" was Sylvia Chen, the West Indian–Chinese daughter of a Chinese radical, but he avoided mention of romantic attachments to Chen, West, or Thompson in his published memoir of the trip.[182] "Chic, bob-haired, peach colored" Mildred Jones dallied with Constantine Oumansky, who headed the Soviet Press Office. He fell madly in love with her.[183] Teacher Mollie Lewis had an affair with a German diplomat.[184] Spiritual singer and preacher's daughter Sylvia Garner entered her first lesbian relationship with another cast member, who broke her heart by taking up with a Russian female translator.[185] The cast saw other African Americans who came to town, including Ira De A. Reid and John Hope.[186]

For their part, Meschrabpom representatives deplored the fact that only two cast members could sing and that when they did sing, they sang

spirituals that included references to God. Perhaps worse, the troupe simply did not look like "Negroes" because of their light complexions. "Russians," Thompson reported, "think Negro means literally black, and our
group has been the subject of much discussion on this point." Homer
Smith heard a Russian murmur, "We needed genuine Negroes and they
sent us a bunch of *metisi.*" As Hughes put it, the cast was "not *quite* what
they had expected."[187]

Sylvia Garner, one of the two professional singers, resolved the religious clash by inserting the word *dog* for *God*, so that the Russians would
not recognize the lyrics: "Rise and shine, And Give Dog the glory!
Glory!"[188] The color issue was clearly more difficult to address. Thompson
had asked applicants, "Kindly telegraph description yourself size complexion," and "Kindly telegraph description yourself particularly color."
Had she hoped to screen out darker voyagers or to recruit more?[189] She
had ended up with twenty-two people with a "wide range of skin colors,"
from "peach-colored" to "dark brown" with "hands, so soft, they don't feel
like workers hands."[190] If the African Americans weren't playing to the
Soviet idea of type, the white man whom the Russians cast as the burly
labor leader, Californian John Bovington, a vegan nudist dancer in the
style of Isadora Duncan, didn't fit the African Americans' stereotype of a
white steelworker.[191]

Fort-Whiteman resented Langston Hughes's scathing condemnation
of the script on which he collaborated, and perhaps he said so. For some
reason, Louise Thompson loathed Fort-Whiteman, even as she found
Hughes irresistible. "Whiteman turns out to be an awful person and such
a person that one can only have contempt for," Thompson wrote home,
without saying why, exactly. She considered him a "real opportunist." She
deplored the fact that he sat on park benches with white prostitutes. After
reporters Henry Lee Moon and Ted Poston, along with actor Thurston
Lewis, fell in with Lovett Fort-Whiteman, they spent too much time proving "all the things white Americans say about Negro men and white
women," Thompson wrote.[192]

The cast's newfound sexual freedom—across the color line and across
the heterosexual line—might have suited the Soviets in the 1920s, but by
the early 1930s the Bolsheviks had tightened their control of private life.
They began analyzing social and sexual practices, called *byt*, a word that

translates roughly to "lifestyles," to see which ones represented the Communist way of life. Others would be labeled monstrous maladaptations from their czarist past. The U.S. Red Scare of the 1920s had promulgated the idea that the Soviets had "nationalized" women, making them "common property . . . as they had of land, railroads, and public utilities," a myth that carried over into the Cold War as the doctrine that the Communists had outlawed marriage and the family. On the contrary, it was women's "self-reliance and economic independence," not their subjugation, that struck cast members most forcefully.[193] Still, in 1932 and 1933 the Soviets sorted out sex as Stalin's authoritarianism reordered *byt*. Prostitution remained legal but heartily discouraged; "hardened female prostitutes were routinely sent to labor colonies." Their behavior was "socially anomalous," not to mention capitalist. The next year Moscow and Leningrad police cracked down on gay men who met in public places and, in 1934, criminalized homosexuality among men, condemning it as "antisocial."[194] But fear of gay life was rising even before the prohibition. For example, when Sylvia Garner's female lover threw her over for the Russian woman who served as their translator, the secret police (NKVD) confiscated their love letters and quickly exiled the translator and her family to Siberia.[195]

Still legally married to a man she regarded as a homosexual, Thompson was no prude, nor was she naive. She didn't object when cast members bathed naked "among the nude Russians" in the Moscow River, but she fretted when some ran naked down a nonnude beach in Odessa. As a group the cast was young, beautiful, high-spirited, and deliciously avant-garde when it stepped up to life's experiences. Sophisticate Thompson did not comment negatively on the interracial liaisons that other cast members embraced. She did, however, warn them "to uphold the honor of our race." She may have known about the *byt* wars when she condemned Fort-Whiteman as a sexual libertine, but she uncritically embraced Hughes, rumored to have had affairs with many, male and female.[196] There seems to have been something about Fort-Whiteman that Thompson wasn't telling her momma in her letters home, something that was odious to her.

Whether he walked the streets of Chicago or the streets of Moscow, Lovett Fort-Whiteman drew disapproval as readily as Langston Hughes drew adoration. People just did not like Fort-Whiteman's dress, his "flamboyance," his actions. In 1928 U.S. Communists had criticized his ANLC organizing in particularly vituperative language. While he proved to be an abysmal manager of the ANLC, it existed only because of his vision. One thing about him stands out: He lived a radical life, without a drop of caution, lacking any measure of judiciousness, never able to marshal much self-restraint. He dressed in Cossack costume in the middle of a Red Scare in Chicago. He arrived in Leningrad with a brass band. He bragged about his contacts, notably Jay Lovestone and Nikolai Bukharin, even as they stood to be purged.[197] He said and did exactly what he wanted to say and do with no thought to the consequences. He dared people to dislike him, and many took him up on it. Fort-Whiteman was a one-man brass band playing discordant notes in an increasingly stifling Soviet state. Perhaps he thought he could get away with it because he was the United States' very own Old Bolshevik, one who had been true since shortly after the revolution.[198] But under Stalin it was precisely Old Bolsheviks who were in real trouble now.

In mid-August, as most of the cast vacationed in Odessa, Henry Lee Moon arrived bearing the *New York Herald Tribune* and bad news. "Comrades, we've been screwed!" he declared as he read the headline: NEGROES ADRIFT IN 'UNCLE TOM'S' RUSSIAN CABIN, SOVIET ABANDONS SLAVERY FILM PREACHMENT TO WOO U.S. FAVOR IN THE FAR EAST.[199] The Meschrabpom representative in Odessa assured them that it was simply a postponement. The company would pay for a tour of the USSR and for their trips home, or they could stay and become Soviet citizens. He cited "scenario difficulties" and the approaching winter, but the cast wasn't buying those excuses, because nothing had been done for weeks.[200]

They sped back to Moscow on August 20, falling into factions. Henry Lee Moon, Ted Poston, and Thurston Lewis, "encourage[d]" by Lovett Fort-Whiteman, cried racism and insisted that the Comintern had "sold us out. . . . because the Soviet Union wants American recognition and does not want to offend American opinion."[201] In a fraught meeting with Meschrabpom officials, Fort-Whiteman, Poston, and Moon read an indictment in which they attributed the cancellation to "political reasons"; worse yet, they labeled those political reasons "Right Opportunism."[202] Finally, they charged the "Meschrabpom Film Corporation and any other organization which may support it in this stand, with sabotage against the Revolution." The cast fought it out in hours-long "son of a bitch" meetings.[203] Thompson called the Fort-Whiteman faction "ridiculous" and condemned it for showing "colossal ignorance." She wrote to her mother that "a few of the group . . . have sworn that we have been betrayed and that all the Negro people in the world have been betrayed. . . . It will be, and has already been, used in the bourgeois press to further counter revolution propaganda."[204]

Finally two cast members confessed that "weeks ago, over drinks in the Metropol Bar," Colonel Raymond Robins, a white American then in Moscow to negotiate U.S. recognition of the USSR, had told them that the film "would be a black mark" and that they should withdraw from the cast.[205] Others told the U.S. press that the American Colonel Hugh Cooper, who was then in the USSR building the Dnieperstroy Dam, had gone to V. M. Molotov in protest when he learned of the nature of the script. According to this scenario, Molotov had had the film called off within twenty-four hours.[206] The United Press reported that "several Americans interested in obtaining a speedy rapprochement between their country and the Soviet Union" had convinced the Comintern to kill the film.[207] Certainly the Lovett Fort-Whiteman faction thought something of that sort was afoot, and its manifesto put it bluntly: "We believe that this cancellation is a compromise with the racial prejudice of American Capitalism and World Imperialism, sacrificing the furtherance of the permanent revolution among the 12,000,000 Negroes of America and all of the darker exploited colonial people of the world."[208]

The Comintern called both factions before it. Langston Hughes and Loren Miller spoke for the majority: "We greatly deplore and emphatically deny all slanderous charges and rumors concerning the postponement of the film 'Black and White' and the subsequent welfare of our group." They continued: "The statement that the picture has been cancelled for political reasons . . . is without foundation." What a terrible charge to level in the "Soviet Union . . . where exploitation and oppression of racial minorities have been eliminated." Moon and Poston followed them and repeated their charges of Soviet betrayal in front of the Comintern, whose members could not have been pleased.[209] Louise Thompson settled on a commonplace explanation. "The scenario proved unacceptable," she told her mother, and assured her that the film would surely be made next year.[210] "We know that the workers in the Soviet Union are helping the fight of the Negro masses in America for social, political and economic equality," Thompson asserted. "Their persistent struggle for the defense of the Scottsboro boys is only one proof."[211]

The warm welcome that the cast had received in the USSR discouraged them from questioning their hosts' motives for abandoning the film. For the first time in their lives, they walked down the street, danced, talked, thought, lived, and loved as equals to those around them. If there was a color line in the USSR in 1932, following it led to the head of the queue rather than outside the circle. Many cast members fell in love with the Soviet Union, remained blind to its faults, and plighted their troths to its racial politics. "This is the equality we will fight for when we return to America," Thompson told the press.[212] If Stalin had sold out black Americans to curry the favor of white Americans who oppressed them, it meant that their love affair had been a lie. Worse, it meant that there was nowhere on earth where they could be really free.

The cast went to their deaths never knowing that Fort-Whiteman was right about the cancellation. Correspondence made public decades later from the American consul general in Berlin and Stalin's private papers reveals that Colonel Cooper did indeed meet with Molotov, who in turn cabled Stalin on July 31. Cooper, who later built the TVA dam at Muscle Shoals, Alabama, was arranging a "visit of 10 famous American businessmen to the Soviet Union," and he "spent one hour arguing persistently that the anti-American propaganda film would be a serious barrier to U.S.-Soviet relations." Cooper told Molotov that if the film went ahead, he would personally "refuse to help the USSR" get U.S. recognition.[213]

Then, on August 3, as the unsuspecting cast vacationed in Odessa, the Politburo met to discuss the "Negro Question." A telegram to Stalin reported its verdict: "We think that maybe it is possible to do without this film. Mezchrabpom did this without the permission of the Central Committee." By the time that cast members appeared before the Comintern, Stalin had arranged for Hugh Cooper to be awarded the Order of Labor Red Banner and a Certificate of Honor. FDR announced recognition of the USSR on November 16, 1933, and Cooper served as toastmaster at a gala celebration at the Waldorf-Astoria for the visiting delegation from the USSR.[214]

Louise Thompson, however, thought that Fort-Whiteman and his allies within the cast members had besmirched the USSR's reputation by accusing it of racism. She laid much of the blame on Fort-Whiteman's shoulders: "Instead of helping us, he encouraged Ted [Poston] and Thurston [Lewis] in their escapades." Fort-Whiteman was insufficiently mindful of his advantages, Thompson thought. "Here we come from a country where everything is denied us—work, protection of life and property, freedom to go where we will and to live where we will—where we are despised and humiliated at every turn. And here we are [in the USSR], accorded every courtesy—free to go where we will and eagerly welcomed—given every opportunity to enjoy ourselves and to travel—free to pursue any work that we choose." Then she employed the language of racialized manhood to her own end: "And these *boys* play right into the hands of American newspaper *men* who of course do everything they can to turn Negroes against the only land that gives them perfect equality."[215] Poston, Lewis, and Moon headed back to the United States, where they sold their version of the story to the white and black press.[216] Thompson countered with outraged letters that defended the USSR and promised that the film would be made.[217]

The cast dispersed. Sylvia Garner and Mollie Lewis headed for Berlin. Dorothy West and Mildred Jones stayed put in Moscow for another year. West worked under contract for Meschrabpom as a writer, and Jones worked for the *Moscow News*.[218] Wayland Rudd, Lloyd Patterson, and Homer Smith joined Fort-Whiteman as Muscovites. Langston Hughes took a tour of Central Asia, which he immortalized in *I Wonder as I Wander*. Eleven others, including Thompson, accompanied him through Kazakhstan and Turkestan.[219]

Hughes drew a parallel between "Going South in Russia" and going south in the United States. He wanted to see how "the yellow and brown peoples live and work" in the USSR. "There is no Jim Crow on the trains of the Soviet Union," he reported triumphantly.[220] He spent Christmas on an Uzbek cotton plantation. There, with the help of George Washington Carver, black Communist Oliver Golden had recruited nine African Americans from Tuskegee and elsewhere to provide expert assistance to the USSR. A homesick Hughes remembered: "Three or four jovial colored wives, who had come from Dixie to this" made pumpkin pies for Christmas dinner.[221]

Thompson sailed for home in early November and quickly assured *Crisis* readers that the film was on Meschrabpom's calendar for the summer of 1933. W. A. Domingo, a seasoned Communist, pointed out to her the possibility that "postponement . . . is, in Russia, tantamount to abandonment." He told her, "Whatever happens now THE PICTURE MUST BE MADE," to save faith in the USSR among African Americans.[222] Of course, it never was, and the cast recast the trip in their memories as the years went by. Pauli Murray recalled that "the glamour which surrounded the group . . . lingered for a number of years." Langston Hughes issued the venture's valedictory: "As for me, I've had a swell time."[223]

Finding the Great Terror

The cast's swell time coincided with the onset of the Great Soviet Famine of 1932–1934, but the rumors that reached them of a great starvation simply did not register as true. Emma Harris, in between dishing up "corn bread and greens," told them there was "a famine in the Ukraine." She exclaimed: "Why, down around Kharkov, people's so hungry they are slicing hams off each other's butts and eating them. That's no lie!"[224] Despite the cast's rejection of her news, it wasn't a lie. Scores of cases of cannibalism occurred, and the famine constituted one of the worst human disasters in history.[225] Harris must have heard those stories in the spring and early summer of 1932, before the cast arrived, since the situation had eased somewhat during that summer.

Atlanta University president John Hope visited a collective farm that summer and reported that peasants were happy to be free of the kulaks, who had been "terrible exploiters of the farmers." But C. Vann Woodward, with the help of his traveling companion who was fluent in Russian, realized what was going on: "There was a famine and there was violence and there was oppression of kulaks."[226] The famine became a crisis only after Hope, Woodward, and most of the cast members had left in the winter of 1932–1933. Clark Foreman, who had spent his time in Moscow studying Russian, saw "near starvation" while he was traveling through the Ukraine in the spring of 1933 and became convinced that the USSR would fail.[227] But Stalin tried to hide it, and Communist Sam Adams Darcy characterized it years later as "a certain amount of deprivation and maybe even hunger."[228] Despite the Soviet-imposed reporting ban in the Ukraine, two foreign reporters broke the story.[229]

Fred Beal, the organizer of the Loray Mill strike in Gastonia, was working at the Kharkov Tractor Works during the famine. Since June 1930, when he and Red Hendricks arrived in the Soviet Union, he had found himself under control of Soviet bureaucrats. The Party prepared documents on U.S. politics and forced him to sign them. In one such exchange, Comrade Otto Kuusinen, secretary of the Comintern, called him on the carpet when he refused to sign a statement that Roger Baldwin and the American Civil Liberties Union had "come out for unrestricted activity of the KKK." Kuusinen actually referred to the ACLU's intervention on behalf of the Black Shirts' right to parade in Atlanta. Kuusinen browbeat Beal, but Beal argued back pugnaciously: "I cannot see why, when the [A]CLU was aiding the KKK all the[se] years, all of a sudden now the Party discovers it and breaks with them." Kuusinen never revealed to Beal that the ACLU had championed the Atlanta Six as well.[230]

Then Kuusinen dropped another bomb on Beal. Roger Baldwin, head of the ACLU, had been quoted in the *Washington Post* as saying, "I have been in correspondence with Beal, and he is unhappy in Russia." Baldwin told the press that Beal thought that "an American jail is to be preferred to Soviet freedom."[231] Beal denied complaining to Baldwin, but he was in deep trouble. Because of the publicity, Kuusinen in January 1931 allowed Beal to return to the United States. Once he was there, the CPUSA sent Beal to hide out in Connecticut and cut off his communication with Hendricks back in Moscow. Beal then decided to return to the USSR rather than go to jail in the United States and forgo ever again seeing Red Hendricks, the man he most loved.

By 1932 Beal's work at the Kharkov Tractor Works had demonstrated to him the failures of Stalin's 1929 Five-Year Plan. It was worse than the Loray Mill. He watched a supervisor turn away a peasant, taunting, "Go away, old man . . . go to the field and die."[232] The peasants who used the tractors didn't know how to repair them, and the Ukrainian soil sifted into every gear. Collectivization and the kulak purge had taken their tolls. Rapid industrialization took untrained farmers and put them in Beal's factory, where they proved to be poor workers. The six hundred foreigners with whom Beal worked proved little better, and the Americans in the plant dared protest openly and criticize Stalin. To camouflage the famine, Stalin kept exporting grain and importing little, while barring visitors from the Ukraine.[233] Beal's nightmarish life grew darker on a walking tour in the area around Kharkov in the fall of 1932. As he stepped off the beaten path, he saw a corpse lying by a creek and was accosted by starving peasants. In the spring of 1933 he found a "dead horse and a dead man upon the side of the road. . . . The man was holding the reins." In some villages he could see dead people seated at their windows, where they had died, gazing out on nothing.[234] The journey that had begun in 1929, when Beal rode his motorcycle across the Catawba River in North Carolina, ended as he walked through this devastated Ukrainian land. Now, more than ever, he desperately wanted to return to the United States.

As for Lovett Fort-Whiteman, his extraordinary life took a turn toward the ordinary, ordinary for a Soviet citizen in the 1930s. Like Beal, Fort-Whiteman decided that he wanted to go home, and on October 27, 1933, he wrote directly to the CPUSA to tell it so. Addressing the Party secretary in New York, Fort-Whiteman said, "I wish to return to America and desire a place as instructor in the Party School." He felt qualified to teach "General Scientific Method and Fundamentals of Modern Biology and Social Problems." Authorities must have been screening his mail since his letter never left the USSR and someone sent copies to the "Cadre Department" and the "Party Membership" committee in Moscow. A typed copy of his handwritten letter went into his file within three days, and "Brigadier" wrote instructions in English on the bottom of the letter: "Com. Sherer, Write a note to Whiteman, requesting him to call and see me."[235] After all, when Fort-Whiteman transferred his membership to the CPSU in 1928, he had come under its discipline.[236]

Always outspoken, Fort-Whiteman continued to be so, even after the *Black and White* debacle. He had asked officials, "Where is the money to bring American Negroes to school in Moscow that the Far Eastern section appropriated?" There is no record of a response.[237] He "considered himself the mentor" of a "small group of American Negroes living in Russia" and took them regularly to lunch, where he "did his best to proselytize and indoctrinate them." He lectured his guests on the Negro as a reserve proletariat and on "the inevitability of the coming proletarian revolution" in the United States.[238] He boasted of his close connections with Nikolai

Bukharin. The Bukharin reference only served to remind his listeners that Fort-Whiteman had come to Moscow in 1928 as a member of the now-purged CPUSA Lovestone delegation.[239]

Then, in June 1934, the year after Fort-Whiteman had tried to leave the USSR, Communists became immersed in an argument about privileging race over class. George Padmore, editor of the *Negro Worker* in Hamburg, used the *Black and White* incident to support his "charge that the Communist International had deserted the African liberation struggle." Harry Haywood immediately characterized the charge as "flimsy."[240] The party expelled Padmore for "stressing race rather than class in his interpretations on current issues."[241] Lovett Fort-Whiteman had made similar charges when he argued that the cancellation of *Black and White* represented a "compromise with the racial prejudice of American Capitalism and World Imperialism." Moreover, now, it was the Trotskyites, the "left opposition," who were arguing in 1933 and 1934 that African Americans were an oppressed race, not an oppressed nation.[242] At the same time, Fort-Whiteman began to tell African Americans in Moscow that "the group should maintain a high degree of consciousness of their color and always remember that they were Negroes." Most African American Muscovites, breathing in the heady air of equality for the first time, thought it ridiculous that he kept harping on race. Variously, they called him a "Red racist" and a "Communist Uncle Tom" and asked "why he didn't go to Mississippi if he was 'going around with a black chip on his shoulder.'"[243]

Why *didn't* Fort-Whiteman go back to Mississippi? He *had* tried to go back to the United States, if not to Mississippi. Why did he go around with a black chip on his shoulder? Fort-Whiteman came to believe that the Comintern was wavering on its commitment to African Americans. Five years earlier, when he moved to the USSR, Fort-Whiteman trusted the Soviets enough to argue that U.S. organizing should proceed on a class basis and separate organizations such as the American Negro Labor Congress should be abolished. But as his trust ebbed, he began to believe that the Comintern, and especially Stalin, would jettison African American interests on a whim, as they had jettisoned *Black and White*. Fort-Whiteman wanted to win equality for African Americans in Montgomery, not Moscow. It was up to Communist African Americans to keep the race issue in the United States from fading from Soviet view.

In early August 1935, as black and white delegates gathered for the Seventh Comintern Congress and hung out at the Foreign Workers Club, Lovett Fort-Whiteman complained loudly in the bar about Langston Hughes. Fort-Whiteman deplored Hughes's recently published *The Ways of White Folks*, which Hughes had begun in Moscow and completed four months after his return to the United States.[244] It is easy to see what Fort-Whiteman disliked about this collection of short stories. For starters, the *New Masses* Communist critic found them bereft of any "anti-bourgeois or revolutionary" themes.[245] Several of them, most notably "Rejuvenation through Joy," riff on white people's craze for discovering a primitive essentialism in black people and appropriating it as a path to self-actualization. Other stories play on white people's smugness in assuming knowledge of the ways of black folks, casting the white characters as hapless anthropologists who stumble, hopelessly lost, through Darkest America.[246] Certainly Fort-Whiteman missed the irony, just as Hughes missed a class critique. Carl Van Vechten, one of Hughes's white friends in Harlem, loved the collection explicitly for this reason. He wrote to Hughes's publisher: "All of it is good and some of it, I should think is great.... I am glad to feel this way after my reaction to that Communist book of poetry."[247] Surely Fort-Whiteman disagreed. He preferred Hughes's *Good Morning, Revolution* to the cultural relativity that permeates *The Ways of White Folks*.

William Patterson, who overheard Fort-Whiteman's tirade at the Foreign Workers Club, immediately pronounced it "counter-revolutionary," an ominous turn of phrase in 1935 Moscow.[248] Moreover, Patterson pointed out that the Foreign Workers Club was a "hot-bed" of spying by the American Embassy.[249] Next, Earl Browder met with several others who were in town for the Seventh Congress to discuss the "disposition of Negro comrades" at a subcommittee meeting of the CPUSA on August 25, 1935.[250]

The timing is significant since in the preceding few weeks the Seventh Comintern Congress had pulled an "about-face" and announced an extraordinary change in policy: cooperation in a worldwide Popular Front to fight Fascism. For the CPUSA, this meant that reformists like FDR were no longer "social fascists"; rather, "it was FDR's right-wing critics who represented the fascist danger."[251] Fort-Whiteman stepped up his criticism of the Communist stand on the race question in response to the Popular Front, since he believed that cooperation with Democrats and liberals, white or black, would inevitably sell out the black working class. He told Homer Smith privately that he "felt the present Stalinist rule was becoming more and more deviationist—that is, was leading the revolution away from, and betraying the basic ideals and aims of, Marxism and Leninism." Lovett Fort-Whiteman had not yet learned that a private conversation could not remain private in Stalin's Moscow.[252]

Browder's subcommittee on the "disposition of the Negro comrades" complained of "reported efforts of Lovett Whiteman to mislead some" of them. They ordered William Patterson and James Ford to hold a "meeting with all the Negro comrades to discuss the question before they leave." The meeting likely included new black Bolsheviks dispatched as delegates to the Congress, as well as the old-timers Patterson and Ford.[253]

For Lovett Fort-Whiteman, the meeting's solution to his "disposition" was disastrous news. The NKVD, the Soviet secret police, informed him sometime late in 1935 that his "counterrevolutionary" talk meant that he was banished from Moscow. "He was ordered to be in a certain town on a specific date, and immediately upon arrival to report to the local police," an African American friend who lived in Moscow later learned.[254] By early 1936 Fort-Whiteman was living in exile in Alma-Ata, a beautiful small town in southeast Kazakhstan in mountainous Central Asia. Tashkent, three hundred miles away, was the largest nearby city.[255] While it may have been difficult for Fort-Whiteman to be out of the Moscow limelight, he taught school and boxing and possibly returned to Moscow for visits.[256]

Eight months after Fort-Whiteman went to Alma-Ata, in August 1936, his close contacts Nikolai Bukharin and Karl Radek, now an editor at *Izvestia*, were named as a " 'reserve group' for terrorist activity." Thus began a series of show trials and the Great Purge. By January 23, 1937, Radek, of whom Fort-Whiteman had often spoken fondly, faced false charges as a Trotskyite and confessed to continuing contact with Trotsky as late as 1935.[257] Fort-Whiteman had boasted as well of close ties with Bukharin, who was expelled from the party at the 1937 February–March Plenum.[258]

By summer the purges had spread to regional levels, as "Stalin and Molotov took a personal hand in whipping up the hysteria" over "wreckers" and spies within the party. In July, Moscow put seventy-two thousand names on execution lists and sent them to regional authorities. In addition, Stalin left it up to local officials to root out those with "anti-Soviet" attitudes and established quotas of exiles for each region.[259] The police arrested Lovett Fort-Whiteman. The authorities sentenced him to hard labor.[260]

Fort-Whiteman's new address was Sevvostlag Prison Labor Camp, Magadan, Kolyma, Siberia. The camp system reached a new low in 1937–1938, and Kolyma was the worst of the worst. Sevvostlag wasn't actually a place; it was a traveling hell, where prisoners dug *lagpunkts*, or holes, in the frozen tundra in which to sleep, as their work shifted up and down the Kolyma Highway. The temperature dipped to sixty degrees below zero; it could get as cold as the South Pole there. Often one-half of those sentenced to Kolyma died before they arrived. Then the mortality rate increased.[261]

On January 13, 1939, Lovett Fort-Whiteman of Dallas, Texas, died in the gulag. It was an ordinary death for the place. Fort-Whiteman had not been able to meet the work quota; for this, he "was severely beaten many times."[262] When a prisoner could not make the quota, his food rations were decreased, in a blatant attempt to mark the weaker prisoners for death.[263] A man who had witnessed his death said that "he died of starvation . . . a broken man."[264] They said his heart stopped, but that didn't explain why they had knocked out all his teeth first, perhaps to shut him up once and for all.[265]

Deep disappointments, crushing blows, starvation: It took them all to break Lovett Fort-Whiteman. Did he dream, there in a frozen hole in the tundra, of hot nights on Sweet Ellum Street back home in Dallas? Of midday classes at Tuskegee, where sweating students performed the heavy work of uplift? Of humid mornings in the Yucatán spent imbibing Socialism? Of escaping J. Edgar Hoover's men in St. Louis? Or did he dream his own "dream deferred," of bringing the revolution to Chicago streets, equality to the South, and black liberation to the Kremlin? There in Kolyma no one mourned him, no one knew that he was the first African American Communist. No one knew of his eagerness, his recklessness, his abiding faith in poor working people. In the final, perfect equality of the gulag, it mattered not a whit that he was a black man, only that he was a broken man.

PART TWO

RESISTANCE

4

THE NAZIS AND DIXIE

As the would-be cast of *Black and White* straggled out of the USSR in the fall of 1932, Mollie Lewis turned up in Berlin. A lifetime ago, back in New York, Lewis had been a student at Columbia University's Teachers College. In Moscow a German diplomat had fallen hard for her, and the lighthearted Lewis had simply ignored most of the political controversy that swirled around the cast.[1] After the film's "postponement," she headed off for her lover's fatherland, where she landed a job in a Berlin cabaret. Decked out as "Mona the Indian girl," she wore a feathery headdress and worked as a barmaid for 10 percent commission on the drinks she sold.[2] She set about to meet men, preferably one who could be her "sugar daddy," she wrote to a friend. To her shock, she found she had landed in the wrong place: "Unfortunately, the place where I work is mostly for the Lesbians." She met beaus elsewhere who saw her as "a black Marlene Dietrich." Lewis reported that her dates showered her with "candy flowers, etc.—but money is very scarce." Ultimately, she observed, "Berlin has cured me of the habit of being surprised and shocked."[3]

"Life is divine," she mused in June 1933, four months after the Reichstag blaze, three months after the March Enabling Act had given Adolf Hitler dictatorial power, and two months after Hitler had purged the civil service of all Jews except war veterans. Dachau already held political prisoners in the summer of 1933, when Lewis wrote to Dorothy West in

Moscow, urging her to come to Berlin: "Things are not as bad in Germany as you read about."[4] In the summer of 1933 blithe Mollie Lewis did not yet know that she lived in the belly of a newborn beast.

More discerning black visitors, however, began to send home troubling reports. The same year, the black American sociologist Horace Cayton stood aghast on the streets of Cologne, watching "at least a dozen arms snap into the air with the cry, 'Heil Hitler!' " in a single city block. When he sat down on a bench in a city park in Hamburg, a police officer accosted him with questions he did not understand. He finally realized that the officer was asking if he was a Jew. "No," Cayton replied, "I am an American." The officer responded, "If you are not a Jew, you don't have to sit on this bench. It is for Jews only." When Cayton replied, "I like it here," and remained seated, the officer became bewildered. Cayton continued to sit for half an hour. He recalled, "I had, of course, heard of the persecution of Jews, but this seemed to me even sillier than Mississippi, where discrimination was at least based on color differences. Here they couldn't even be sure what a Jew looked like." Cayton looked back on his protest as a "broad gesture . . . against prejudice in any form."[5] The moment was a formative one for him, since he had never really thought of Jews as anything but white people, some of whom he knew to be prejudiced against African Americans. But on the park bench that day he recognized the horror of systemic discrimination as an evil power, one that might target any group.

Habituated to hatred and accustomed to state structures of oppression, many African Americans recognized at once the catastrophic danger that the Nazis posed for German Jews. The prevailing argument—that Americans remained relatively unaware of Hitler's persecution of the Jews—does not hold up when one reads the black press, even as early as 1933. The persecution of the Jews was never "beyond belief" for African Americans; rather, it was the big story in the black press throughout the remainder of the 1930s.[6]

African Americans watched in horror as Nazi oppression grew, and they worked with U.S. Jews to fashion an anti-Fascist rhetoric to alert other Americans to the dangers.[7] Although Fascism was more than anti-Semitism, African Americans took Fascism's anti-Semitism to be the driving force of Nazi power. Moreover, they saw it as only one form of minority hatred that might appear in a Fascist state; abomination of blacks and others with "differences" would surely accompany it.[8]

Although African Americans opposed Fascism out of humanitarian concerns and an aversion to ethnic hatred in general, they also capitalized on the opportunity that Fascism presented to discredit southern white supremacy. Both Communist and non-Communist African Americans used white Americans' recognition of the threat of a racist totalitarian system in Germany to redefine Jim Crow as a systemic, antidemocratic malignancy that could destroy the nation. In 1933 a white Southerner could glibly refer to the "Negro Problem" and blame the South's troubles on black deficiency. As events in Germany proved that racial hatred was a dangerous force that degraded its perpetrator, many Americans began to reverse the agency in that southern conundrum. The "Southern Problem" became white racial discrimination, not black deficiency.[9]

Moreover, as the white southern industrialists and planters resisted New Deal legislation and fought to keep their hold on southern labor, especially white millworkers and black sharecroppers, the coercive nature of their politics became more apparent. The virulence of anti-Communism among southern authorities after the Scottsboro cases stunned and frightened some liberal white Southerners as well. White supremacy depended upon pervasive control of public and private life, upon racial subordination of blacks, and upon economic subordination of the poor. Southern white liberals thought they saw the possibility of domestic Fascism rising around them in the Great Depression's deepening chaos. By 1938 many had become convinced that unless the South extended basic civil rights to all, Dixie could provide a beachhead for the growing Fascist threat.

Black Americans and white liberals shuffled evidentiary cards from Germany's and Dixie's decks to try to tell democracy's fortune. Did the failure to pass a federal antilynching bill trump the enactment of the Nuremberg Laws? African Americans and their allies divined in Fascism portents of southern politics.[10] Communists made the leap between Nazi persecution and Jim Crow oppression early.[11] But other, non-Communist African American leaders drew nuanced comparisons between anti-Semitism and white supremacy and used those comparisons to the best advantage with the greatest numbers of Americans. While the Communists critiqued Fascism more generally, non-Communist African Americans most often focused on the treatment of the Jews. Watching Hitler closely, black leaders such as W. E. B. Du Bois, James Weldon Johnson, and Kelly Miller applied the lessons of Jewish persecution that unfolded in Germany to the practice of white supremacy in Dixie.

This is not to say that the southern system of white supremacy was a Fascist system or that German Fascism can be reduced to racism. In the South, Jim Crow lost out to the civil rights movement. In Germany, Fascism caused the Holocaust. Prior to the Nazi takeover, Jews enjoyed full civil rights. By contrast, southern African Americans had lived under a legal system of racial segregation and persecution for at least three decades before Hitler came to power. A Jewish man strolling past the Glockenspiel in Munich in 1930 could assume that he would arrive safely at his lunch. In Atlanta a black man walking down Decatur Street might be lynched for accidentally brushing against a white woman. Before the Great Depression, abundant economic opportunities existed for Jews in Germany, while southern blacks found themselves relegated to sharecropping, domestic work, and the basest industrial jobs. Yet as Atlanta's Black Shirts discovered in 1930, the white South depended on black labor, in part because it was so debased. White middle-class and upper-class Southerners had no intention of expelling their large black labor force and dramatically altering their daily lives. Those same southern whites who would keep blacks close at hand sanctioned, often by sins of silence, pervasive terror to keep them in line. In Germany, Jewish capital could simply be seized.

The Jews' relation to the Nazis was, in many ways, a reversal of the southern case. African Americans, at least theoretically, could be recognized by their color; the Jew, as Horace Cayton observed, might not be recognized at all. Southern African Americans occupied a place of permanent inferiority made conspicuous by color, but the Nazi image of the Jew was one of hidden conspiracy, manipulation, and abuse of power. The Nazis thought subordination might not be possible; elimination offered a more permanent solution.

African Americans compared Jim Crow with Nazi oppression to unsettle white supremacy's place in a democratic system. They wanted their fellow Americans to stop thinking of Jim Crow as a vestige of the past and to start thinking that it had the potential to become the vanguard of the future.

In 1930 white supremacy's face remained partially masked by the nostalgic glow that white Southerners had painted over it when they disfranchised and segregated African Americans at the turn of the century. Then white Southerners portrayed Jim Crow as the best answer to the legacy of slavery, which had produced a "Negro Problem" that threatened democracy. But by 1938 African American anti-Fascism had stripped off the South's veil to reveal a modern monster, a region of the United States that seemed to have more in common with the Führer than with the Founders. African Americans sought to destroy the notion that southern white supremacy offered the best solution to a difficult question and to recharacterize it as an up-to-date threat to U. S. democracy at home and abroad.

The Trials of Angelo Herndon

The case of Angelo Herndon, a black Communist, opened as another episode in southern anti-Communism and racial oppression but ended as a touchstone for anti-Fascism. Herndon was arrested in Atlanta in 1932 while picking up his mail and found himself charged with the capital crime of "attempting to incite insurrection."[12] There wasn't much argument over what he had done: He had organized the unemployed through speeches, literature, and protests; he received Communist publications in the mail; and he boasted of his membership in the Communist Party. The argument was over his civil rights: Could a black Communist exercise constitutionally protected free speech in Atlanta? The Herndon case took the measure of southern—and national—democracy.

Coming a little over a year after the original Scottsboro trial, the Herndon case seems to take place in an entirely different era. Scottsboro evoked turn-of-the-century rhetoric of southern pure white womanhood. The Herndon case pointed out the dangers of white women workers joining the Communist Party. The Scottsboro Nine personified provincialism. Angelo Herndon exuded urbanity. The Scottsboro Nine wrote awkwardly and often found themselves tongue-tied; others spoke for them. Angelo Herndon wrote eloquently and made his own brilliant speeches. If the Scottsboro cases recalled the South's past, the Herndon case foretold its future.[13]

During the disfranchisement campaign at the turn of the century, white supremacists had deployed two stereotypes of dangerous African

Americans: the black incubus who raped white women and the Town Negro who got above his raising by wearing glasses. The first would mongrelize the white race; the second would outsmart it. While fighting the incubus of the Scottsboro "Boys," white Southerners also turned to prosecuting the second stereotype, Angelo Herndon, Communist and Town Negro. Along with his tweed sport coats, crisp white shirts, and flashy red tie, Herndon wore snappy little owlish glasses.[14]

When he was little more than sixteen, Herndon and his brother jumped a freight to travel around the South to find work. Starting in their hometown of Wyoming, Ohio, they ended up in their father's hometown of Birmingham, Alabama, just at the height of Communist Party district organizer Tom Johnson's mass demonstrations in the summer of 1930. Herndon found a job at Birmingham's Tennessee Coal, Iron, and Railroad Company.[15] Communist leaflets circulated, and Herndon pored over a pamphlet on interracial organizing in Gastonia. To his great surprise, for the first time in his life, he felt sympathy for white workers: "I could see that the methods of exploiters and sweaters of labor were the same everywhere and that our problems were their problems." He joined the Party, and District 17 organizers quickly sent him to Atlanta in September 1931, six months after the first Scottsboro trials. "Gene's address is—Angelo Herndon (name he is using) box 339 Atlanta. I think he is pretty reliable to carry out instructions," wrote a Birmingham CP organizer.[16] Gene, Gelo (his nickname), or ultimately Angelo had just turned eighteen. The name he was using, the post office box, and Herndon's ability to carry out instructions became an international legend soon enough.

Atlanta held promise for Communists. An organizer who arrived to work with Herndon exclaimed, "Gee, you have a hell of a sight better place to work here. In fact it is a paradise in comparison with Birmingham." Within two years, that same man was dead, gunned down in a Kentucky coal strike.[17] A paradise Atlanta was not, but in contrast with many parts of the South Atlantans maintained a long tradition of strong trade unions, particularly in the crafts, a labor newspaper, and thriving labor politics. The Atlanta Six cases had mobilized moderate Atlantans to protect free speech and the right to assembly, and many of them had publicly denounced the state's anti-insurrection law, particularly in light of the fact that it carried the death penalty. Even as Herndon appreciated the city's opportunities—for example, the trade unionists let him use a room on the second floor of their Labor Temple—he kept in mind the recent arrest of the Atlanta Six for insurrection. They had been out of the state on bail for several months before Herndon arrived.[18]

In that time the Depression had deepened, and many hungry Atlantans cared not whether help arrived from the left or the right. One white woman recalled: "The soup line stretched down Edgewood Avenue almost to Five Points. . . . You could see black and white folks in that line . . . just to get something to eat." Herndon responded with a barrage of broadsides, "To All Workers of the Atlanta Woolen Mill: Organize and Demand a Living Wage-Better Conditions," and a petition to the city "For Immediate Relief for the Unemployed." These attest to Angelo Herndon's passion and organizational skills and also suggest Otto Hall's experienced hand. After Gastonia, Hall had traveled around the South for the League of Struggle for Negro Rights before he joined Herndon in Atlanta late in 1931 or early in 1932.[19] One particularly pointed leaflet defending the Atlanta Six suggested that "the money spent in sending these comrades to the electric chair be spent in providing unemployment relief."[20] Despite the harsh treatment middle-class white Atlantans had meted out to them in 1930, the Black Shirts still found considerable support among the white working class. "As an organizer for the Unemployment Council," Herndon recalled, "I had to fight mighty hard against this poison."[21]

In late June the city and county relief pump ran dry, ending its dribs and drabs of relief to 21,730 people. Herndon retold it like this: "The city and county authorities decided to drop twenty-three thousand families from the relief rolls. In consequence, those who had been driven by starvation from the farms were to be rounded up and shipped back again." Herndon exaggerated. When faced with a delegation of black and white unemployed, a county commissioner agreed to meet only with the white group. He urged them to go back to the country to live with relatives and suggested that the city might pay their transportation.[22] By the time federal relief reached Atlanta in July 1933, only 11,000 families qualified and at least another 10,000 went hungry. On July 10 Herndon led 1,000 people to the courthouse in the largest integrated march Atlanta had ever seen.[23]

Police arrested him the next evening when he went to get his mail at P.O. Box 339. Then they searched his room without a warrant. At first booked simply "on suspicion" and signed into custody as a "Communist," after two weeks Herndon was charged by the assistant solicitor general under the insurrection statute. The charge cited his interracial meetings and his distribution of Communist literature as revolutionary goads. To support the last charge, the authorities proffered Herndon's mail and reading material, including George Padmore's *The Life and Struggles of Negro Toilers* and copies of the *Southern Worker*.[24] On the other hand, Otto Hall escaped arrest, just as he had in Gastonia. Soon, however, Hall would not be so lucky. Three months later the KKK kidnapped and savagely beat him in Birmingham.[25]

The southern Red Scare that netted Herndon had begun in Gastonia in 1929 and spread across the South as the economy worsened. One white southern liberal put it hyperbolically: "It is not the economics of Communism that frightens the white Southerner; it is the racialism of Communism that frightens him."[26] In fact it was probably both and more. After Herndon's arrest, prosecutor John Hudson announced that he would seek the death penalty for "every Communist who comes to the State and publicly preaches the doctrine of violent opposition to the State." To prove it, he brought the languishing two-year-old Atlanta Six cases up for trial.[27] A Fulton County superior court judge found the indictments against the Six too vague and threw out the charges, but the grand jury responded with new, more specific indictments. Hudson defended the anti-insurrection act: "If we wait until they seize the Capitol and the courts before we consider it an overt act, there will be no government left to punish insurrection."[28]

In the Herndon case, the International Labor Defense at first fell back on its Scottsboro strategy. It proposed to hire its own outside lawyers, publicize the case internationally, and use it as an organizing tool in Atlanta. Distraught at the prospect of Atlanta's becoming another Scottsboro, Will Alexander of the Commission on Interracial Cooperation (CIC) tried to enlist Walter White of the NAACP and Roger Baldwin of the ACLU to manage the case and to find a local white moderate to represent Herndon. Alexander made little headway. Baldwin responded: "We have ceased writing bail in all Communist cases since our experience in Gastonia." Herndon languished in jail.[29]

William Patterson, fresh from Moscow and three months into his tenure as national secretary of the ILD, hurried to Atlanta to arrange

Herndon's defense on the free speech issue. Sidestepping Alexander's choices, but conceding to hiring local counsel, Patterson engaged two young black Atlanta lawyers, Ben Davis, Jr., and John Geer, to represent Herndon.[30] Ben Davis's father, whom W. E. B. Du Bois called a "fearless and forceful man," had been a Republican national committeeman and fiery Atlanta newspaper editor. Ben Davis, Jr., had grown up in comfort and entered Morehouse's preparatory school when he was eleven; later he attended Amherst College and Harvard Law School. When the Herndon case came his way, Davis had been practicing law for just a year.[31]

Ben Davis, Morehouse man, Amherst alumnus, and Harvard Law(yer), walked into the packed courtroom a nominal Republican. He strode out a card-carrying Communist. Prosecutor Hudson demanded not only that the jurors find Herndon guilty but that they sentence him to death.[32] Although joining the Communist Party was legal in Georgia, "The theory of Communism is on trial as well as Herndon," Hudson argued. "This is not a trial of Herndon, but of Lenin, Stalin, Trotsky, and Kerensky."[33] Then Hudson argued that Herndon's literature "appealed to southern Negroes to 'smash the National guard,' take over the state government, withdraw from the Union and set up a nation of their own." For his part, Davis opened by challenging the jury selection system as unconstitutional since only two blacks had ever been called to serve, and those only fourteen days earlier.[34]

The next morning a cross smoldered on Ben Davis's front yard. In court that day he fought like a tiger to prevent state witnesses from calling Herndon a "darkey"—"the darkey with glasses on"—and a "nigger." The prosecutor issued an apocalyptic charge to fight this "red army of infidels." Two Emory University professors testified that Herndon's reading material could hardly be evidence of insurrection; the public library circulated similar books. The CIC's Will Alexander characterized the trial as "an argument between Herndon and his lawyers and an ignorant, fanatical prosecutor as to the merits and demerits of communism."[35]

The defense gave as good as it got. Davis argued that Padmore's *Negro Toilers* "should have been written in the blood of Negroes who were burned at the stake by mobs. I say lynching is insurrection." More mildly, Davis said: "You can't kill a man because of the books he reads." He argued: "The only offense Herndon committed was that he asked for bread for children. His only crime is his color."[36] At the end of a dramatic day Herndon himself took the stand to say: "You may do what you will with Angelo Herndon. You may indict him. You may put him in jail. But there will come other thousands of Angelo Herndons."[37]

That night Ben Davis joined the Party. "Credit for recruiting me into the Communist Party goes to Judge Lee B. Wyatt, who had been summoned from the backwoods hinterland of the state to hear the case," Davis recalled. "So crude and viciously unconstitutional and anti-Negro were his rulings," Davis said, "that my instant joining of the Communist Party was the only effective reply I could give." Davis admired the CP for "its practice of the equality it preaches, with its policy of unity between Negro and white on the lowest economic level." He did not announce his membership.[38]

The next day, in his closing argument before Judge Wyatt, Davis told the jury that Prosecutor Hudson knew "as much about communism as a pig knows about a full-dress suit." Then he called for a verdict of not guilty, stating that "any other verdict will be catering to the basest passion of race prejudice . . . making a scrap of paper out of the Bill of Rights, the Constitution of the United States and the State of Georgia."[39] A man's life depended on Davis's words; indeed, he would not have been vain to entertain the thought that many people's lives depended on his words. Davis spoke like a man, like an equal, because he was demanding that his client be treated as one. Three jurors turned their backs on him as he spoke; Ben Davis kept talking to those jurors' backs.[40]

The jurors faced front when they pronounced Angelo Herndon guilty and sentenced him to eighteen to twenty years. This was the mercy verdict, something of a slap in the face to the prosecutor, who had tied the case to the death penalty, which only two jurors had favored. In January nineteen-year-old Herndon went to Fulton Tower, the county jail, to await the outcome of his appeal. For over two years the state refused to set bond.[41] Meanwhile the Atlanta Six's challenges to the insurrection statute wound through the courts. The Georgia Supreme Court upheld one of those indictments under the same statute, concluding that "a state may penalize utterances which openly advocate the overthrow of the government."[42] Both cases alarmed southern liberals, black and white, who began to speak out for broader civil rights and civil liberties in the South as a means of fighting Fascism.

Fighting Fire with Fire, ADOLPH HITLER, K. K. K.

Adolf Hitler took power two months after Angelo Herndon had gone to jail. Herndon's appeals soon tapped into the budding anti-Fascist sensibility. Reaction to the guilty verdict came from all sides. The Ku Klux Klan announced that it was reviving itself in order to "wage war on Communism in the south," using its "own system of espionage, which keeps radical agitators under surveillance."[43] The governor worried about "threatening" letters "from a good many sections" in support of Herndon. Ben Davis became an instant celebrity and spoke around the nation.[44]

In the midst of the Herndon publicity, the NAACP positioned itself as a moderate alternative to revolution. When the Communists denounced the NAACP, the editors of the black *Atlanta World* argued in 1934 that "Communism Kills Itself" by "taking Potshots at the N.A.A.C.P."[45] James Weldon Johnson, the former NAACP secretary, handled the issue carefully in his 1934 book *Negro Americans, What Now?* "Communism is coming to be regarded as the infallible solution by an increasing number of us," he wrote. Some, Johnson said, embraced Communism because they saw the "Soviet Union as a land in which there is absolutely no prejudice against Negroes. This is an unquestioned fact, but I can see no grounds on which to attribute it to Communism." He warned "against childlike trust in the miraculous efficacy on our racial situation of any economic or social theory of government—Communism or Socialism or Fascism or Nazism or New Deals. . . . It would be positively foolhardy for us, as a group, to take up the cause of Communistic revolution."[46]

The NAACP dreaded the publicity that the Herndon appeal would afford the Communists. Walter White, the current NAACP secretary, wanted the association to take over the Herndon appeal to avoid "having it distorted by injection of the Communist angle."[47] After its embarrassing fight with the ILD over whether a Communist defense would taint the Scottsboro "Boys," this overture reveals the NAACP's anti-Communism even as it points toward a drive on the part of the organization's leaders to dictate all challenges to Jim Crow. White knew that this time the defendant embodied the "Communist angle" but supposed that Herndon would remain silent with proper NAACP direction. Nothing came of White's request at the time.[48]

As the NAACP stood against Communism, international Fascism handed the association a mirror to hold up to Jim Crow's visage. While James Weldon Johnson sought to distance African Americans from Communism, he brought Fascism closer to home. He saw "no apparent probability that the United States will go over to Communism; . . . the same cannot be said about Fascism." He reminded his fellow African Americans that "most of us, it is true, have for long years lived in the Fascist South." If full-blown Fascism arrived on U.S. shores, Johnson mused, "it is hardly possible that we could fare worse" under a national Fascist government, but things would get worse for "other minorities." Therefore African Americans had "both a practical and a moral obligation" to everyone "to defend the rights of other minorities, as well as our own," by opposing Fascism "with our utmost strength."[49]

Until Hitler's takeover, African American intellectuals had respected Germany for its intellectual and artistic life. In 1893 W. E. B. Du Bois had studied at the University of Berlin, where he felt free of the color line for the only time in his life. In Germany he could meet people "not [as] white folks, but [as] folks." He described his return home this way: "I dropped suddenly back into 'nigger'-hating America." In 1930 singer and actor Paul Robeson, fresh from playing Othello in London, announced, "Germany is now the gateway of all Europe." In Germany and Eastern Europe, Robeson's mix of high art and folk culture garnered great acclaim, and he enthralled packed concert halls with his Negro spirituals. Robeson announced his plans to "live a long time in Germany," but Hitler's ascent dashed his plans.[50]

African Americans who believed that black uplift strategies would ameliorate white supremacy were astonished that Germans could turn against such a successful minority. In May 1933 Du Bois wondered how "in the middle of the twentieth century a country like Germany could turn to race hate as a political expedient." He reminded Americans of what "the Jew has done for German civilization."[51] In Germany, Jewish success brought on persecution. The Communist *Negro Worker*, published in Germany, warned in the spring of 1933, "Today Negroes like Jews are the daily victims of fascist terrorism." It implored its readers to "Smash U.S. Fascist Terror." and free Angelo Herndon. The African American *Philadelphia Tribune* made the suggestion when it ran a cartoon of Hitler shadowed by a Klansman and pronounced him "Another Klansman."[52]

At first some argued that the South was worse than Germany. In September 1933 the *Chicago Tribune*'s Paris edition ran a vigorous debate on whether Jews or African Americans were more oppressed, with opinions falling on both sides. The litmus test was the use of violence. A white American expatriate argued, "No Jews have been chased through the streets by mobs and when caught lynched or riddled with bullets as in the Southern States of the U.S.A." In those early days of the Reich, some debated if the American South's violence would *spread* to Germany. One black man spoke in terms of cultural traits and national character: "Hitler, at his worst, is but a poor imitator of the cracker methods. Your average southerner . . . is a half-baked savage while the Germans . . . are a very kind and cultural people."[53] The next month the *Philadelphia Tribune* argued, "To be a Jew in Germany is hell. . . . To be a Negro in America is twice as bad."[54] That calculus changed as German anti-Semitism became more virulent.

The International League against Anti-Semitism alerted African Americans to "Negro victims of Hitlerism" in December 1934. A little over a year after Mollie Lewis urged Dorothy West to come to Berlin because "life is divine," the Nazis "deprived [blacks] of all forms of employment. . . . Those who are married to German women are forced to break up their homes," and "Negroes" had to abide by curfews. Many of the black victims were African soldiers who had fought for the French in World War I, settled on the Rhine, and then found themselves under Nazi control.[55]

African Americans responded in their own self-interest as they became anti-Fascist, even as they acted out of concern for Jews. From their own particular experience with discrimination, African Americans forged a universal condemnation of it. The *Afro-American*'s editor summed up the way in which altruism and self-interest went hand in hand: "We think Hitler is a tyrant and a brute, a ruffian and a cur. We detest him for the way in which he is crushing the Jew. . . . But we can't forget there is a man right here at home who has his heel on our neck."[56] The Ku Klux Klan kept its heel on black necks, and African Americans realized that the shoe fit Hitler as well. As soon as Hitler assumed power in 1933, the *Afro-American* ran the headline ADOLPH HITLER, K.K.K. "Germany is doing to its Jewish people what the South does to the Negro in spite of the law," the editor declared.[57]

Even relatively conservative African Americans such as Kelly Miller, the black sociologist who organized the Sanhedrin, argued that "the racial policy of the Hitler movement is strikingly similar to that of the neo–Ku Klux Klanism of America."[58] He pointed out that residential segregation was spreading across the United States. While it was illegal to segregate living space by ordinance, it was acceptable by deed covenant. "Germany has not yet decreed residential segregation for its Jewish population," Miller noted. But he knew what must come: "The other restrictions, based on race prejudice, must inevitably lead to the reestablishment of the Ghetto known by Germany in a former day." Miller used Dixie's pervasive violence to argue that black Southerners suffered worse than German Jews. African Americans were "often lynched and burned at [the] stake ... [but] the German people have not yet reached such depths of depravity." He hoped that "the ruthless and inhuman regime of Hitler may be spared this stigma of infamy which has stained the fair name of America in the eyes of the world."[59]

Black columnists set out to make it difficult for white Americans to condemn Germany without condemning Dixie's despotism. Soon "America [must] awake to the fact that when they maintain color discrimination here they are aiding the very ones they are supposed to be fighting," one black journalist warned.[60] When, in 1934, the Senate debated a resolution disapproving of discrimination against German Jews, the *Afro-American* observed that maybe the Germans would heed such a resolution when the Senate approved an antilynching bill. A black columnist commented, "We have our Hitlers here," just as Germany had its "mutton-headed heinies."[61]

As African Americans compared Germany with the South, so too did Hitler. Dining with colleagues in the summer of 1933, according to an apostate Nazi's later account, Hitler praised U.S. white supremacy and lynching: "The wholesome aversion for the Negroes and the colored races in general, including the Jews, the existence of popular justice [lynching] ... are an assurance that the sound elements of the United States will one day awaken as they have awakened in Germany." Paul Joseph Goebbels is reported to have excitedly agreed: "Nothing will be easier than to produce a bloody revolution in North America. ... No other country has so many social and racial tensions," he continued. "We shall be able to play on many strings there."[62]

Moreover, the Nazis invoked the Jim Crow system as a defense. Until late 1936 they argued that Germany was not as bad as the American South. Julius Streicher, publisher of the stridently anti-Semitic magazine *Der Stürmer*, proclaimed to an audience of twenty-five thousands Nazis in 1935: "We do not kill Jews in Germany. Perhaps they would like for us to do so, that is the Jews, but we have other and more civilized methods of punishing them. In America," Streicher pointed out, "Negroes are killed by mobs without fear of punishment and for the most trivial reason." He declared, "The treatment of Negroes in America [is] far worse than that accorded Jews by the Nazis and America's criticism should be turned in that direction rather than toward Germany. Here in Germany we say that when a Negro is lynched for assaulting a white woman he gets what is coming to him," Streicher gloated. "As we do not bother about executions of Negroes, you [Americans] should not bother when we lead a race desecrator through the streets."[63]

In addition to their growing horror at German events, many shared James Weldon Johnson's worry that the combustible mix of southern white supremacy and domestic Fascism might ignite in America. Before the 1934 Nuremberg Laws, a white writer argued in the NAACP magazine, *Crisis*, that if Fascism came to America, "Fascist leaders will order the wholesale discharge of Negro workers. . . . Negro professional and business men will find themselves boycotted. . . . Negroes who lift up their voices in protest will be herded off to filthy prisons and concentration camps, there to be killed outright or slowly tortured to death."[64] When domestic Fascist groups actually appeared in the United States, African Americans marveled at the ways they coupled Jews and blacks. For example, this fantastic amalgam took root in the minds of the Fascist Connecticut-based James True Associates: "You take the hiring of 'big buck niggers' by Jews to attack white women in the South. That's right in the *Talmud*. . . . Only recently a police chief had to shoot one of these 'niggers' and he found out that he was hired by a Jew to rape a white woman."[65]

Congress pursued more than 100 possible domestic Fascist organizations through the McCormack-Dickstein Committee. Samuel Dickstein, a New York congressman and a Lithuanian-born Jew, succeeded in making the committee a permanent feature of Congress by 1936, when it became the House Un-American Activities Committee (HUAC). But when con-

servative Texas Democrat Martin Dies became chairman, he denied the
liberal Dickstein a seat and turned HUAC to the pursuit of Communists
and radicals [66].

That same year investigation of a grisly Detroit murder brought to
light a secret group known as the Black Legion. For more than two years
its members had secretly been killing "anarchist[s], Communist[s], the
Roman hierarchy," and unionists.[67] The black press termed it a "new Ku
Klux Klan."[68] Even the KKK disavowed it, but the Black Legion, which
claimed a membership of sixty to one hundred thousand, had indeed originated in an outcast Ohio Klan chapter. The chapter's founder, an Ohio
physician and former Klansman, vowed, "I tried to run it right on the principles of the Old South. I believed we ought to maintain southern chivalry
and the ideas of the South before the Civil War."[69] No southern chapters of
the Black Legion existed, yet when Michigan authorities interviewed several hundred members, their composite Black Legionnaire "came from a
small farm in the South" to work in the industrial Midwest.[70] It went without saying that he was white. Explicitly violent, it advocated in the voice of
its "general" as early as 1935 "the mass extermination of American Jewry"
through poison gas canisters touched off in synagogues on Yom Kippur.[71]

By 1937 Germans imagined the Klan as the perfect Fascist launching
pad in the United States. That year Baron Manfred von Killinger, the Nazi
consul general in San Francisco, directed a woman using the alias Mrs.
Leslie Fry to buy the Ku Klux Klan outright. At least part of her seventy-
five thousand dollars in purchase money came from the German Ministry
for Propaganda and Public Enlightenment. She planned to unify domestic
Fascist groups under the KKK cross and recruited a member of the Silver
Shirts, an organization that attracted many former Klansmen, to approach
the KKK's Imperial Wizard. The FBI chased her out of the country before
she could succeed.[72]

Some whites "scoffed at the idea that there would ever rise to power in
this democracy anything even remotely resembling the Fascist dictatorships of Europe." When whites did debate the danger of Fascism's taking
hold in the United States, they generally based their arguments on the
robustness of America's liberty. For example, Sinclair Lewis's famous *It
Can't Happen Here* underscored the duty of Americans to be vigilant. Some
pointed to the Depression as a Fascist seedbed or argued that FDR's

attempts to concentrate power paved the way for Fascism. Amid all these concerns, most white people managed to ignore the millions of black Americans to whom liberty was a stranger.[73]

Meanwhile, as non-Communist African Americans marshaled to fight Fascism, Communists drove home its similarities to the Scottsboro injustice and the Herndon case's totalitarian issues. In June 1934 the *Labor Defender* reported that Ada Wright, one of the Scottsboro mothers, could not get served by a "pro-Nazi" restaurant manager in Cleveland. When challenged by the Communists, the manager shrieked, "We need a Hitler here!"[74] Angelo Herndon made the connection explicit in a letter he wrote: "The Fascist dogs are trying to kill me even before I get out." As if to prove him right, authorities arrested Ben Davis for "trying to smuggle insurrectionary material" when he took the letter out of Fulton Tower to mail it.[75] Herndon came to be characterized as "America's young Dimitroff." Georgi Dimitrov was the Bulgarian Communist whom Hermann Göring accused of burning the Reichstag. At his trial the proud Dimitrov "stood before the court as an accuser." Ultimately acquitted, Dimitrov became a symbol of Communist courage in the face of Fascism.[76] Herndon and Dimitrov both proudly proclaimed their faith in Communism and spoke past the courts and to the people.

Homegrown Radicals

Against this backdrop of Fascism abroad and fear of Fascism at home, many Southerners began more robustly to protect free speech, even Communist free speech. Prosecutor Hudson's use of the insurrection statute in the Herndon case caused great concern, as did the fact that Angelo Herndon faced many years in prison. The most public manifestation of this concern occurred when a group of white and black Atlantans formed the Provisional Committee for the Defense of Angelo Herndon, drawing members from those who had previously defended the Atlanta Six's right to free speech. Ben Davis characterized the committee in late 1933 as "united on the one issue of freeing Angelo Herndon . . . there being no requirements whatever that the members be either Republicans, Democrats, Socialists, or Communists."[77] If the American Civil Liberties Committee had come to town to organize a defense committee for free speech, Hudson and his cronies could have complained about Yankee interference, but the homegrown Provisional Committee attracted all sorts of prestigious Atlantans and prefigured the cooperation between groups on the left in the Popular Front.

This was C. Vann Woodward's big chance to honor the pledge he had made in the USSR and "get in on" the next opportunity to defend civil rights. In the spring of 1933 Woodward worked closely with Ben Davis to organize the Provisional Committee. Socialist socialite Mary Raoul Millis chaired it. At an early meeting, when the Communist ILD representative called her a social Fascist, she retorted that she was "not going to put up with any kind of that nonsense." When he did it a second time, she walked out of the meeting and quit the committee. On the spot, Woodward found himself presiding and "holding the bag." The committee coalition proved unstable, and several prominent African Americans resigned.[78]

Ben Davis assured Will Alexander of the CIC that there were no Communists on the committee, but Alexander still refused to join. When Woodward wrote to Ben Davis that Alexander "is so conservative that he's hopeless in this case," Davis quoted Woodward's confidential missive. The powerful Alexander was a Woodward family friend, and the humiliated Woodward decided that he "couldn't trust" Communists.[79] At the end of the school term Georgia Tech refused to renew his contract, and he left for graduate school at Columbia University.[80]

As Herndon languished in Fulton Tower, prosecutor Hudson expanded Atlanta's Red Scare, turning his attention to Don West, a white Georgia native who had replaced Herndon as the CP organizer.[81] West had grown up in a one-room cabin in Devil's Hollow in the North Georgia mountains. At six feet two inches and 180 pounds, with slightly wavy blond hair, he was handsome and smart as a whip. A friend described him as a "north Georgia movie idol sort of fellow."[82] West's great-grandmother was a Cherokee, and various family members made moonshine: "pure corn. None of this diluted stuff." West's family "went down out of the mountains" in a serial exodus, lured by the promise of work in the cotton mills. But his mother refused to put the children to work in the mills, and West's father became a sharecropper. Like so many other mountain people, West's father never became reconciled to life away from the Blue Ridge. "He always wanted to go back. All my life as a kid . . . that was dad's hope," West recalled. The only way that most migratory mountaineers went back was in a coffin, and then only if they got their last wish.[83]

At fifteen, with only five years of schooling, West followed other impoverished, smart, and lucky mountain children to the Martha Berry Schools in Rome, Georgia. The Boys Industrial School was a Tuskegee for whites, where students traded labor for learning and where, with the school's blessing, Henry Ford recruited students to work in his Detroit auto plants. Eventually West came to see the Berry Schools as a capitalist plot to keep "the mountain people separated from any kind of ideas of organization, union." The administration instilled racism as well; the film *Birth of a Nation* served as a history text. West protested when the administration fired his favorite teacher and got expelled for his trouble.[84] In 1929 West entered Vanderbilt Divinity School, a place awash in Christian Social Gospel teachings. Finally he flourished. He wrote poetry, worked in a rural settlement school, and won ordination as a Congregational minister. Then he spent two years in Europe, where he studied the Danish folk school movement, which used native arts and crafts skills and cultural expressions to empower communities.[85]

West met his middle-class counterpart in Tennessee-born Myles Horton. A young Union Theological Seminary graduate, Horton was a follower of Reinhold Niebuhr and a member of the Socialist Party. In 1932 he came back South with the vague idea of organizing a "southern folk school," and Will Alexander introduced him to Don West.[86] Recently returned from Denmark as well, Horton planned to weld a "successful adaptation of the high school idea to the needs of a labor school." This would be no vocational training site like the Berry School; instead, it would embrace a "curriculum for stimulating and awakening people rather than imparting practical information."[87] As southern industrialization matured, Horton's trained labor organizers would unionize the workers. He jotted down his strategy: "Cap. [italism] flows—therefore, it will flow to the lowest of the lowest area. . . . 1. Mountaineers 2. Negroes. These are the groups to work with."[88] To eliminate class prejudice, the school would be a commune, where everyone acted out "an idea of the kind of world we would like to have."[89]

Together West and Horton founded Tennessee's Highlander Folk School in the fall of 1932. Highlander, one Tennessee woman recalled, embodied "clean living and high thinking if I ever saw it."[90] Horton pledged to live life "abundantly and daringly" since life was "too spiritual to be dragged down by the material." He "insist[ed] on the right of others to live that kind of life, too." For his part, twenty-four-year-old West became the state organizer of the Socialist Party for Tennessee.[91]

A snowy winter on Highlander's isolated mountain plateau with the unceasingly reflective Horton made West long for action. "I guess Horton and I just had a different way of looking at things," West recalled. When West brought "poor, raggedy people," up to Highlander, Horton would say, "Oh, that's one of Don's friends."[92] Soon West met Communists in Chattanooga, and by April 1933 he was hitchhiking to Atlanta, arriving a few weeks after the Angelo Herndon trial. Once there, West founded the Southern Folk School and Library to "conduct study classes in socialism." He met with mountain people like himself, whom he found "hungry for what we . . . [had] to offer."[93]

At some point after meeting Chattanooga's Communists and before establishing himself in Atlanta, West had joined the Communist Party and taken the position of state organizer for Georgia. Some Atlantans realized that he was radical—"I was labeled right off as a red," he recalled—but he did not publicly announce his Party membership.[94] Because West came into the party as a state organizer, not as a regular Party member, and retained strong local ties, he never quite conformed to Party discipline. He remained a Christian, built affiliations with liberals before the Popular Front, and seemed to see himself as a Party of One. As 1933 waned, West wrote to Myles Horton, asking, "Have the Reds got any hold around your place?" West did not tell Horton that he had become a Communist, only that he had "drawn . . . many local people. Part of them are Negroes also. I don't go in for the Jim Crow idea any."[95] As "Jim Gray," he visited New York and the Communist National Training School, where he played volleyball, studied Marxism, and taught Hosea Hudson, a black Communist from Birmingham, how to read.[96] West reconciled his abiding faith in Jesus with his faith in Marx and invented his own brand of Christian Communism. He used the Communist Party without being consumed by it.

It was his old nemesis the Martha Berry Schools that brought West to John Hudson's attention. West's cousin attended Berry and organized some students to announce to neighboring "farmers and workers" that the school was "free from all taxes," paid the students little, and made "it hard for you farmers to get anything for what you raise." The students especially resented Berry's money-grubbing magazine, sent to wealthy Northeasterners and full of " 'sob tales' about 'poor little country boys and girls.' " School officials did not allow the students to read it since "they don't want us . . . to know about the crooked tales they tell about us."[97] West turned to the National Student League (NSL) to help organize a strike at the school. The police promptly arrested West's cousin, and Berry officials warned West that "if you ever come on the campus again we are going to string you up to the first limb we can get you to." After that, West recalled that the police tailed him, "and it got so that I could hardly move around."[98] When prosecutor Hudson finally issued a warrant for West's arrest under the insurrection statute, West escaped Atlanta in the back seat of Ben Davis's car.[99] A couple of months after his escape, West published this poem in the *Daily Worker*:

> *Dream on, Angelo Herndon,*
> *Dream and rot*
> *Behind steel bars*
> *In Fulton Tower. . . .*
> *Dream of black kids and white*
> *Singing songs together. . . !*
>
> *Kids will have a story book,*
> *Angelo Herndon.*
> *To read tales of the revolution . . .*
> *Tales of a black boy*
> *Rotting*
> *In Fulton Tower. . . .*[100]

West left Vann Woodward behind in Atlanta to work for Herndon's appeal; however, it was tough going. The Provisional Committee for the Defense of Angelo Herndon raised only one hundred dollars, but the ACLU finally decided to pay Herndon's lawyers, and money to guarantee his bond fell as manna in the form of small individual contributions from around the world, totaling eighteen thousand dollars. ACLU president Roger Baldwin admired Herndon, saying of him that "he had a winsome sweetness which concealed real guts." As Herndon sat in jail in the summer of 1934, a real insurrection, led by white millworkers, broke out across the South.[101]

GEORGIA OFFICIALS APE HITLER TERROR

In September 1934 two-thirds of the South's textile workers, some 170,000 people, most of them white, joined in the general textile strike. Organized by the AFL's United Textile Workers of America, it stretched from Maine to Alabama. In North Carolina 64,000 struck; in South Carolina strikers numbered 40,000. Across the South governors called out the National Guard, whom the mostly female strikers taunted as "Boy Scouts" and "Tin Soldiers."[102] Flying squads, automobile convoys, of workers drove from one mill to the next, calling out operatives. One millworker described the scene this way: "There were a power of men and women in the streets. The flying squad from the union had come. They went over the mill fences like rabbits. . . . We stopped the looms and shut off the power, and came out into the streets."[103] On Labor Day 1934 an estimated 5,000 people paraded down Gastonia's main street. One observer called it "the closest thing to a revolution I've seen in this country." Most called it an "uprising." No one could fail to realize that it was a massive political demonstration.[104] For its part, the AFL disavowed any Communist involvement and proclaimed the strikers "100 per cent Americans."[105]

Communist organizers tried to join in, but on the eve of the strike in District 16, only five CPUSA members were textile workers. Nonetheless, Communist officials bragged hyperbolically that it was they who had activated the flying squads, and a few Communists managed to join AFL unions surreptitiously.[106] When District 16 organizer Paul Crouch called a rally on the courthouse steps in Charlotte to show Communist solidarity with the strikers, an angry crowd of three hundred white workers showed up, shouting, "Let us have him; we'll take care of him!" As a North Carolina mountain boy Crouch was no outside agitator, but the Charlotte police took him into "precautionary custody" anyway.[107] In Atlanta native white Georgians and sisters Nannie Leah Young and Annie Mae Young

Leathers handed out the *Daily Worker* on the picket line at Exposition Mill. They were "grabbed by the law [and] carried to the police station as two red agents," Young recalled. The women sang "The Internationale" all the way to jail, where they were charged under the insurrection statute. Angelo Herndon had recruited Young to the CP two years earlier. The white women shocked all Atlanta by choosing a black man, Ben Davis's co-counsel, John Geer, to represent them.[108]

Whatever the Communists might sing or say, the general textile strike of 1934 was not a Communist uprising. Buoyed by FDR's National Industrial Recovery Act, which established the National Recovery Administration (NRA), the American Federation of Labor moved to organize southern textile workers eager to share in the fair wages and reasonable working hours that the New Deal promised. Although textile executives had forced the NRA chief to declare that "it is not the duty of the administration to act as an agent to unionize labor in any industry," the AFL quickly announced, "The President wants you to join a union!"[109] Just two months after the NIRA became law in June 1933, the AFL reported a 25 percent increase in membership in the South. The southern AFL representative vowed to "forestall the possibility of organization of the workers into Communist and other radical groups."[110]

Some 7,562 Georgia employers adopted NRA guidelines for a minimum wage and caused a one-day increase in state payrolls of "approximately [a] half million dollars a year." Despite the spike, most southern mills quickly brought their payrolls back down by implementing the stretch-out, increasing piecework, and laying off workers. They adamantly opposed collective bargaining.[111]

While some textile workers saw the NRA as "a mouthful of promises," others saw it as a great opportunity, and labor unrest became ubiquitous in the fall of 1933. Emboldened by the NRA codes, millworkers saw unionism as Americanism. "The Laboring People here are trying to uphold our President and also the code," a Charlotte, North Carolina, woman wrote to Franklin Roosevelt.[112] African Americans remained generally skeptical of the NRA since it did not apply to many of the jobs that they held. Moreover, as wages rose, employers fired black workers first and hired whites. African Americans began to call it the "Negro Removal Act." The Communists dubbed it the "Negro Repressive Act" and the

"Negro Run Around." The NRA compliance logo, the blue eagle, became known to African Americans as that "Jim Crow bird."[113]

The general textile strike quickly generated violent repression. In Honea Path, South Carolina, authorities shot and killed seven unarmed strikers. Ten thousand attended their funeral.[114] In Georgia, Governor Eugene Talmadge called out the National Guard, declared martial law, and set up an "internment camp" for strikers at Fort McPherson. He announced that "where rebellion or violence or insurrection is going on," strikers could be arrested by the National Guard and tried in military courts. The Guard intercepted flying squadrons and transported workers to Fort McPherson.[115] There 140 strikers were incarcerated without charges—"the men behind barbed wire and the women in a barn—until the strike emergency" ended.[116]

WOMEN HELD IN CONCENTRATION CAMP, the front page of the *New York Times* reported as it showed four stylishly dressed women standing in front of an armed soldier. The same photograph ran in the *Atlanta Journal* with the caption "Atlanta's Own Detention Camp for Pugnacious Strikers Is Seen Here in Smooth Operation Tuesday." Then the *Atlanta Journal* bested its hypocrisy of the previous day with "Pickets Having Good Time in Internment Camp Here," even as it added, "Eight machine gun pits command all entrances to the camp" and "heavy patrols guard all borders."[117] The ACLU petitioned the federal court for a writ of habeas corpus for the internees. The *New Republic* commented, "The suppression of all liberties in Georgia and the killing of sixteen workers . . . suggest that in certain areas of our fair land even the Nazis might learn a trick or two."[118]

In fact the Nazis had a field day with the Georgia news. "Page-wide banner headlines" in Berlin newspapers announced that "concentration camps are being established in America for strikers and 'insurrectionists,' and that men and women, whites and 'negroes' are being confined in the same camps near Atlanta." The German press used Talmadge's impromptu concentration camps as evidence that "Germany is decades ahead of the rest of the world," and it predicted U.S. authorities would move "more and more into fascist direction," to quell the growing social unrest.[119]

Atlanta prosecutor John Hudson capitalized on the upheaval to step up his anti-Communist activities. He raided the ILD's Atlanta office, where he met an angry Ben Davis, who demanded a warrant. Then the Fulton and DeKalb County police forces raided the interracial Urban League office, the black YMCA, and even meetings in private homes. One gathering at the home of a white female public school teacher netted copies of the *New Republic, Redbook* magazine, and her teenage daughter's copy of "Are Petting Parties Dangerous?" The southern field secretary of the Urban League issued a tongue-in-cheek statement instructing Atlantans that "the Urban League is regarded by many as ultra-conservative and by the Communists as reactionary. Our stock now should go up considerably in the community when we are suspected of being 'Reds.'"[120] A Fulton County grand jury began an investigation into the Red menace, but the neighboring DeKalb County grand jury dismissed the charges against those rounded up there. An Emory University student who had been ensnared commented, "I used to think this was a free country, but I know better now."[121]

The authorities' draconian measures against the 1934 strikers, coupled with the travesty of the Angelo Herndon case and the new wave of Red-baiting, exacerbated moderates' and liberals' fears of domestic Fascism and connected labor and race struggles in new ways. The editor of Atlanta's venerable *Journal of Labor* and the Atlanta Federation of Trades argued that the Herndon case "opens the way to impose slavery not only on the black, but on the white."[122] The Scottsboro and Herndon cases came to be seen in the context of the growing Fascist threat. A columnist in the *Nation* argued that if Herndon's conviction "sticks and if the Atlanta Six are sent to prison, the forces of reaction and fascism in Georgia will have temporarily triumphed. The entire labor movement, communist and otherwise, . . . will be driven underground just as surely as in Nazi Germany."[123]

Southern excesses provided a powerful tool for Communists to turn a spotlight on the South and recruit support outside the Party. For example, novelist Theodore Dreiser served as secretary of a national committee to support the Scottsboro "Boys" and became interested in the Herndon case as well.[124] When a white prisoner warned Herndon that he would be kidnapped on the courthouse steps and lynched if he accepted bail, Dreiser telephoned Governor Eugene Talmadge to demand Herndon's protection. Talmadge assured him, "People down here don't get excited about things like that. We never molest a nigger unless he rapes a white woman." Talmadge volunteered to put his "nigger servants" on the phone to verify that statement, but Dreiser said, "Thank you very much. I just wanted to be sure."[125]

Langston Hughes, now president of the League of Struggle for Negro Rights, organized a campaign for the Scottsboro and Herndon defenses through the National Committee for the Defense of Political Prisoners. White southern playwrights DuBose Heyward of Charleston and Paul Green of Chapel Hill responded to the appeal with donations.[126] White southerners like Heyward, Green, and Woodward were willing to risk their reputations for the release of a black Communist because they thought that their region risked substitution of totalitarianism for liberty. Hughes also found time to organize a successful campaign to "Free Jacques Roumain," the nationalist turned Communist who languished in a Haitian prison for fighting the U.S. occupation.[127]

The campaign ultimately bore fruit when Herndon finally left Fulton Tower on bond in August 1934. He was twenty-one. He headed at once for New York, where seven thousand received him with wild enthusiasm. Later, at a meeting of three thousand in Rockland Palace in Harlem, "a group of friends, Negro and white, bore Herndon into the hall, and up the central aisle to the stage." He told the crowd that "the Southern ruling class thought they had just another 'nigger' case . . . but they discovered they had to take notice of millions of protests that came in from the masses all over the world." Then he "pointed out the close connection between his own case and the case of the nine innocent Scottsboro boys."[128]

Herndon connected the Nazis and Dixie: "They say Angelo shall go to the sure death of the chain gang. They say that the Scottsboro boys shall die. Their brother Fascists say that Ernest Thaelmann, courageous leader of the German working class, shall die." Blending call and response with the Communist line, Herndon continued: "But we the workers, reply . . ." The audience responded, "They shall not die."[129] The Nazis had arrested, tortured, and imprisoned Ernst Thälmann, the head of the German Communist Party (KPD), in March 1933. Don West had compared Thälmann with Herndon the month before in an article in the *Labor Defender* bearing the powerful headline GEORGIA OFFICIALS APE HITLER TERROR.[130]

African Americans Confront Fascism

As African Americans observed from afar Hitler's repression of the Jews and compared Germany with Dixie, Mussolini's aggression toward Ethiopia in 1935 proved their fears that Fascist racism would spread. Many American blacks held Ethiopia in the highest esteem, regarding it as "the spiritual fatherland of Negroes throughout the world." *Crisis* declared: "From Bahia to Birmingham, and from New York to Nigeria, peoples of African descent . . . [were] stirred to unparalleled unity of thought" as Mussolini threatened Ethiopia.[131] An Ethiopian told African Americans, "You are not NEGROES, but sons and daughters of Africa."[132]

In the summer of 1935 fights erupted between African Americans and Italian Americans in Jersey City, New Jersey, after the "Brown Bomber," Joe Louis, knocked out Italian great white hope Primo Carnera, known as the Ambling Alp, before sixty thousand fans in New York's Yankee Stadium. By fight time Italy had been rattling its sabers at Ethiopia for seven months. The next month, for good measure, Louis knocked out the great U.S. white hope, Max Baer, in four. Richard Wright, a young black writer from Mississippi who had joined the Communist Party, watched his neighbors pour into the streets of Chicago's South Side, screaming, "LOUIS! LOUIS! LOUIS!" Their exuberance moved him to write, "Say, Comrade, here's the wild river that's got to be harnessed and directed. . . . Here's the fluid something that's like iron." That "wild river" took a political turn on October 4, 1935, the day after Italian troops invaded Ethiopia, and riots between Italian Americans and African Americans in New York brought out more than a thousand policemen. When the conflict began, Italian Americans owned most of the bars in Harlem, and "Mussolini's picture hung over almost every Italian cash register." African Americans boycotted the bars until one by one, they closed.[133]

Black Americans also squared off against Italian Fascists in more academic settings and jabbed at them in the popular press. Two weeks after the New York riot, NAACP secretary Walter White debated an Italian Fascist before a college audience.[134] In the pages of *Foreign Affairs*, W. E. B. Du Bois marveled that Italy could so "brazenly" declare "that she needs the land of the Ethiopians for her own peasants."[135] African Americans, from the Fraternal Council of Negro Churches to the remnants of Marcus

Garvey's United Negro Improvement Association, mounted organized protests that clearly identified racism as a key explanation behind the invasion. Moreover, they argued, it was racism, not diplomacy, that restrained the white world from coming to Ethiopia's aid.[136] In New York, black and white marchers carried signs reading: FREE ANGELO HERNDON, DEFEND ETHIOPIA, and DOWN WITH THE ITALIAN IMPERIALISM.[137]

The Ethiopian invasion and the passive response of white Americans and Europeans alerted African Americans to a gathering international crisis that would connect Fascism, colonialism, and the German persecution of the Jews. The invasion of Ethiopia rang for African Americans as a fire bell in the night, and it destroyed their faith in the League of Nations, where as Paul Robeson put it, countries' delegates remained "deaf to Haile Selassie's desperate plea for sanctions."[138] No one took action; even the USSR continued to ship wheat and oil to Italy. League of Nations members remained mired in self-interest, foreclosing an effective response while Mussolini grabbed Ethiopia. It was an ominous lesson for African Americans. Du Bois asked: "[I]f Italy takes her pound of flesh by force, does anyone suppose that Germany will not make a similar attempt?"[139]

African Americans boiled down the complicated geopolitical rationales of the League members to two factors, racism and imperialism. Du Bois closed the circle: "Economic exploitation based on the excuse of race prejudice is the program of the white world. Italy states it openly and plainly. . . . Negroes in the United States . . . have lost faith in an appeal for justice."[140] James Weldon Johnson argued that imperialism must console itself with the belief that colonized people were inferior, a rationale that led to "Germany's treatment of the Jewish people, and . . . Italy's affronts to the Ethiopian state."[141] Walter White uttered a dark prophecy: "Italy, brazenly, has set fire under the powder keg of white arrogance and greed which seems destined to become an act of suicide for the so-called white world."[142] African Americans in the streets of New York shouted a rallying cry that brought it all home: "Stop Mussolini's lynchings."[143]

The Negro Commission of the Comintern connected the dots between worldwide injustices, linking Italian invaders to southern white supremacists: "The war makers are those who raped Africa . . . they are the lynchers of black men and the despoilers of black women . . . they have jailed Thaelmann and . . . Herndon. They are torturing the best sons and daughters of the people everywhere." The *Southern Worker* made the Ethiopian crisis front-page news. The Communist International Negro Liberation Committee urged "all categories of the Negro peoples" around the world, including sharecroppers and tenant farmers, to throw themselves into "action against the menace of war in Abyssinia." And the Comintern's Negro Commission used Scottsboro as a way of "linking up the struggle of the Negro toilers in the USA with that of the colonial toilers on the terror regime of the European imperialist powers."[144]

A Southern Popular Front

By the time that Angelo Herndon's appeal reached the U.S. Supreme Court for the first time in the spring of 1935, many liberals had begun to downplay anti-Communism to embrace anti-Fascism. Reconciled in this instance with the ILD, the NAACP's Charles Hamilton Houston argued before the justices for Herndon's release. In May the Court refused to uphold Herndon's challenge to irregularities in his trial, but he remained free throughout the summer, as from New York he petitioned the Supreme Court for a rehearing.[145]

By August 1935, when the Seventh Comintern Congress announced the Popular Front to unite liberals, Socialists, and Communists to fight Fascism, black and white southern Communists and non-Communists had been cooperating for months on free speech issues. The Seventh Congress had decided to affiliate with a wide variety of leftists. Georgi Dimitrov, the Bulgarian Herndon, dominated the Seventh Congress. His imprisonment and trial for burning the Reichstag had convinced the delegates and, more important, Stalin that it would take a coalition to stop Fascism.[146] That coalition moved people into the Communist Party. After the Popular Front, CPUSA membership grew from twenty-six thousand in 1934 to eighty-five thousand in 1939.[147]

The southern Popular Front drew together black organizations, the Socialist Party, free speech advocates, and the new labor organization, the Congress of Industrial Organizations (CIO), a competitor of the AFL's then turning toward Dixie. The CP's new policy proclaimed "sustained and fraternal cooperation . . . with the NAACP, the Urban League, and the Black church."[148] In 1932 roughly 20,000 Southerners had voted for

Socialist Norman Thomas for president. If one includes Kentucky and West Virginia, the total swells by 9,000 votes. According to CP organizers, the Socialist Party's dismal performance resulted from "the unwillingness of its heads to 'go after the Negroes.' " Now the Communists could show them how, even though the Communist Party ticket of William Z. Foster and James Ford had received only 2,117 votes compared with the Socialists' 29,000.[149] The existing Socialist Party units in the South—most mid-size to large towns had small ones—provided a starting point for CP outreach in the Popular Front.[150]

There were few southern ACLU members, but on a national level the organization had maintained a long, usually fraught association with the Communist ILD. The ACLU had provided bail for the Gastonia defendants and lost its money, it had consulted with the ILD on the Scottsboro cases, and it had raised funds for the Herndon defense from the beginning. ACLU director Roger Baldwin described the connection this way: "We must necessarily work in very close cooperation with this defense organization [the ILD], although we do so from the point-of-view of civil liberties,—that is, of civil rights regardless of whom they affect."[151] With the coming of the Popular Front, southern CP organizers made contacts with the few ACLU members across the South. They also offered to lend their experience to the CIO: "The Communists must help the C.I.O. leaders nationally and locally, and impress upon them the need for extra vigilance in combating racial prejudice."[152]

After the announcement of the Popular Front, Herndon's defenders celebrated with a New York rally, including many whom the CP might have denounced as "social fascists" a scant three months earlier. Reinhold Niebuhr "took Herndon's hand, saying, 'You are a victim of oppression and we sympathize with you. But you are a challenge , and so for that we envy you. . . . You are the omen of a United Labor Party in America.' " By now the NAACP, the ACLU, and the Justice Commission of the Central Conference of American Rabbis had filed friends of the court briefs in Herndon's appeal.[153]

When the Court refused him a rehearing in October 1935, Herndon left New York by train for Atlanta and a jail cell in Fulton Tower. A crowd of two thousand sent him off from Union Square. Herndon could have stayed in New York, but he would have forfeited eighteen thousand dollars in bail money, along with his working-class heroism. Asked why he had decided to return to Atlanta, Herndon replied, "[B]rother, there is no running away for me. If I run away and you run and everybody else who loves freedom and truth runs away, who will be left to fight the good battle?"[154] Rather than book a sleeper car, from which he would have been evicted at the Virginia border, Herndon chose to sit up for the roughly thousand-mile trip. His ride inspired a Communist journalist to write a play in which Herndon hears workers' spirituals drifting through the train window: "Yes, Angelo, it's–us a-cryin', it's-a us a-cryin . . . 'cause you're our soul."[155] When the nonfictional Herndon entered the Tower, his attorneys filed a challenge to the constitutionality of the insurrection law in Fulton County Superior Court, on the ground that its standard of guilt was so vague that it infringed on the right of free speech.[156]

As Herndon awaited his second appeal, a journalist interviewed Governor Talmadge, whom Herndon called "the South's leading contender for the Hitler role." The journalist's Fascist hunt succeeded beyond his wildest expectations: "He [Talmadge] did think a heap of Hitler and Mussolini for they are strong men, and they must be 'he'pin'' their people or their people wouldn't have them." Asked what he thought about the Nazi persecution of the Jews, Talmadge replied, "Shucks, Hitler ain't so small as to do a thing like that." Talmadge kept talking, as if determined to hoist himself on his own petard. "How small a crime is wife-beating?" the journalist asked. Talmadge responded, "Depends on how hard you hit her." The journalist said, "That reminds me of Hitler who says woman's place is in the kitchen." Talmadge replied: "I don't know for sure, since I haven't ever been in Germany, but folks I know been there and they think a good deal of Hitler." Talmadge's interviewer concluded, "If Herndon goes to the chain gang you have one step further toward outright Fascism or military dictatorship."[157]

Talmadge's demagoguery set off alarm bells among liberals. The journalist interviewed "a number of Georgia liberals, Negro and white." One "upper middle-class [white] man said, "We have, in effect, what can be called Fascism." He figured that by trying to usurp black civil rights, the state had finally threatened "the rights of even middle-class whites."[158] African American Kelly Miller compared southern demagogues like Talmadge with Hitler and predicted that "the normal German mind, freed

from revolutionary frenzy . . . will doubtless repudiate Hitler and his dia-
bolical persecution of the Jew." He had less faith in the normal white
Southerner's mind but argued that southern demagogues' rise to national
power would be impossible because more sensible Northerners and West-
erners would not succumb to such an appeal. [159]

Setting a benchmark in the annals of irony in southern history, it was
Hugh M. Dorsey who was to hear Herndon's new appeal in Fulton
County Superior Court. As a young prosecutor Dorsey had vigorously
prosecuted Jewish businessman Leo Frank for a murder he had not committed. Now Dorsey ruled the insurrection law unconstitutional and freed
Herndon on eight thousand dollars' bond. The defense tried to keep the
focus on the constitutionality of the insurrection law; the prosecution
tried Communism. Communism's worst offense, it argued, was that "Russia ordered the American Communists to confiscate property from the
white people to establish a state in the black belt," where the "white minority in the state would have been made to submit to the will of the
Negroes." Dorsey chose to rule on the case, not the cause. The law, according to him, was "too vague and too indefinite" and violated the Fourteenth
Amendment. [160] The Georgia Supreme Court quickly ruled that Dorsey
had erred, and once again Herndon appealed to the U.S. Supreme Court.

The "pig" in a "full dress suit" now donned a Brown Shirt as Herndon's
prosecutor, John Hudson, and American Legion members followed the
state court ruling with a huge book burning of "Red literature." Purging
books occupied many Georgia citizens during the 1930s. Governor Talmadge had appointed a textbook committee to root out "subversive doctrines or philosophies which were not in harmony with the South." The
committee "voted to expurgate" from the schools Frederick Allen's *Only
Yesterday*, Howard Odum's *Southern Regions of the United States,* and Albert
Bushnell Hart's *American History Told by Contemporaries.* [161]

Free on bail as his case for a second time wound up to the U.S. Supreme
Court, Angelo Herndon became the representative victim of domestic
Fascism. When he returned to Manhattan in the winter of 1935, Rabbi
Stephen S. Wise, Roger Baldwin of the ACLU, and Walter White, executive secretary of the NAACP, welcomed him at a huge rally. [162] Herndon
spoke in 1936 to the American Youth Congress (AYC), which represented
the Young Communist League, the Young People's Socialist League, the

YMCA, the YWCA, and the Methodist youth federation.[163] The fear of domestic Fascism occupied the delegates that year as the AYC president warned that "we may see our youth listening to the first skillful demagogue to appeal to them and swept into a Fascist youth movement dedicated to violence."[164] American Communists reported to Moscow that they had "penetrated" the American Youth Congress "with the understanding of . . . the basic features of our Negro program." Their success "crystallized particularly around the personality of Comrade Herndon."[165] The next year the AYC sent seven delegates to visit Franklin Delano Roosevelt. When the president asked them what they thought about his Supreme Court packing scheme, one delegate responded, "Well, Mr. President, that all depends on how the Supreme Court decides my case." Then Angelo Herndon introduced himself to FDR.[166]

Herndon's lawyers based his new appeal on the same grounds that had led Judge Dorsey to overturn his conviction. Their brief argued that the insurrection statute "unreasonably restricts appellant's freedom of speech and assembly" and that it "prescribes a standard of guilt which is so vague and indefinite that it is not susceptible of reasonable ascertainment."[167] As if to underscore the importance of Herndon's appeal, Atlanta police arrested eighteen blacks and whites on charges of inciting insurrection at a private meeting in May 1936. At this point the AFL, at its national convention, endorsed the efforts of its Georgia chapter to lobby for repeal of the statute.[168]

Fair Play and the Fascists

Since Hitler was hosting the 1936 Olympics in Berlin, sports provided a logical ground to measure the respective treatments of German Jews and African Americans. In the South, teams at all levels were completely segregated and never competed across the color line; in the North, integrated teams often benched black athletes if whites on the opposing team objected to playing against them. In 1924 Ben Davis, a tackle on the Amherst football team, encountered such a game against Princeton, but the Amherst team captain refused Princeton's demand that Amherst's four black players be benched.[169] African Americans used the 1936 Olympics to set new standards for fair play and Americanism in the face of

Nazi oppression. If the United States was to hold itself up as an alternative to Fascism, African Americans were determined to hold the United States to its rhetorical ideal.

At first African Americans discussed boycotting the "Nazi Olympics." One proboycott black editor argued that black athletes should stay away because "Germany today stands for everything that is repugnant . . . racial hate and intolerance . . . oppression, intimidation and persecution of a minority group." Then he connected Hitler's persecution of the Jews and African Americans: "No American Negro can support or sanction the monstrous theory of Aryanism . . . [for] on this theory the Nazi government justifies its shameless treatment of its Jewish citizens and by the same token condemns the Negro to perpetual oppression and subjugation throughout the world."[170]

Others, however, thought that participation by African Americans would send a pointed message back home. Ben Johnson, a black Columbia University track star, argued, "The Negro in the South is discriminated against as much as the Jews in Germany," and for that reason he supported the exposure that competing in Berlin would bring.[171] If black Americans could not compete with white Americans in the South, they would have to travel to Nazi Germany to find an even playing field.

Avery Brundage, president of the American Olympic Committee, fought the boycott movement by connecting it to Communism and portraying it as "un-American," because "those alien agitators and their American stooges . . . would deny our athletes their birthright as American citizens." Brundage collaborated in decisions to strike Jews from Olympic teams; he was virulently anti-Semitic and probably racist as well. But it suited his larger purpose—to press on to Berlin—to include African Americans and prevent a boycott. He inadvertently played right into the hands of African Americans who wanted to publicize simultaneously the injustices of discrimination and the capabilities of African Americans. They would *exercise* "their birthright as American citizens," while the spotlight fell equally on them and on the Jim Crow South. On July 4, 1936, the day that Angelo Herndon warned delegates to the American Youth Congress of the Fascist danger, black athletes performed spectacularly at the Olympic trials.[172]

In the past African Americans had used the rhetoric of national unity that accompanied war to claim the full citizenship; now they used the Olympics in a similar way. Talk of boycotting faded, as racial harmony came into focus. *Time* magazine praised "Ohio State's dusky Jesse Owens." The tryouts bespoke religious, ethnic, regional, and racial diversity: "They came from the deep South . . . [and] from the eastern seaboard. . . . They were Jew and Gentile—black and white."[173] In the end, fourteen African Americans suited up for Hitler's Olympics. "All America wants to see these young Negroes victorious," the black press proclaimed. Led by "the amazing Owens," the twelve black men and two women would "be the living refutation of the sinister doctrine of racial superiority by which the dark people of earth would be thrust beyond the outer pale of civilization and progress."[174]

If the part of America occupied by Atlanta wanted "to see these young Negroes victorious," you couldn't tell it by reading the hometown newspapers. As the *Atlanta Journal* covered the Olympic trials, its editors skipped over Owens to choose their own light horse, Forrest "Spec" Towns, a white University of Georgia student. When forced to use an Associated Press (AP) story with the lead "Jesse Owens, Ohio State's triple Olympic threat, led America's athletic march toward Berlin," the *Journal* put the piece under its own headline: TOWNS WINS HEAT IN 14.3; WALKER LOSES IN 100 METERS. When the big news in another AP wire announced that Owens was the "only man to gain three places," the *Journal* headlined the story TOWNS AND PACKARD GO TO OLYMPICS. And when ten "Negro athletes" made the male track and field team of sixty-six, the paper's focus was nonetheless on white Southerners. SOUTH DOUBLES ITS ENTRIES IN OLYMPICS IN FOUR YEARS, the *Journal* boasted, as it counted the whites and left out Alabama-born Jesse Owens and all other black Southerners.[175]

In Germany discrimination took the field, even though Hitler had removed all overt signs of anti-Jewish propaganda in Berlin during the games. The black athletes stood as gladiators in the as yet undeclared race war. German world heavyweight champion Max Schmeling sought out American black track star Jesse Owens in the Olympic Village, if only to rub in his month-old victory against Joe Louis. Owens remembered, "Inwardly many of us were trying to atone for Joe's loss."[176] Although Hitler had ordered everyone else to soft-pedal anti-Semitism and racism, he could not stomach remaining in the stands and inviting black American high jump victor Cornelius Johnson to his box, as he had the previous three white gold medalists. "Americans ought to be ashamed of themselves for letting their medals be won by Negroes," the Führer reportedly said. "I myself would never even shake hands with one of them."[177] Hitler's actions confirmed that Jews and African Americans shared a global enemy.

By the time Jesse Owens captured a gold medal the following day, the Olympic Committee had warned Hitler to shake black hands or shake no hands at all. From then on Hitler chose to forgo issuing personal congratulations. One white writer captured the scene: "We like to think of that moment: Hitler, his racial dogma made ridiculous by the performances on the track before him, scurrying under the stands to get away from the truth, while Jesse Owens, great Negro, walked in the sun before a cheering German crowd."[178] Before the games ended, Owens won four gold medals and tied two world records. For his part, Owens played straight to the stands back home in his victory message: "Maybe more people will now realize that the Negro is trying to do his full part as an American citizen. Please send word back that I am grateful for the opportunity America gave me."[179]

Perhaps the black press was too exuberant when it implied that African American Olympic performance softened even Nazi racism. But Owens may have become the second most popular man in Germany. Under the caption "Color Line Fades" German bronze medallist Lutz Long and Jesse Owens lay side by side on the ground, heads up, watching the broad jump. A German cigarette manufacturer distributed the photo of Owens and Long as a collectible card, and Owens dominated Leni Riefenstahl's film *Olympia*.[180]

The marathon to equate diversity with democracy took a great leap forward on the Berlin track. The contrast of the United States' integrated Olympic team competing against Hitler's Aryan athletes gave Americans a model they had not had in the past. This time the "us" in "us against them" included both black and white Americans. Many white Americans found it easy to hate Hitler; meanwhile most black Americans worked to keep Hitler's racism front and center. They could only hope that their white fellow Americans would connect the two and hate the sin as much as they hated the sinner. If Hitler, even Hitler, had been shamed into briefly taking down anti-Semitic graffiti and posters, what of those "colored" and "white" signs on Atlanta's water fountains?

Only when Owens had won his first gold medal did the *Atlanta Journal* mention him in a headline. It never ran his photograph. *Journal* editors bragged that they "cover[ed] Dixie like the Dew," routinely referred to African Americans as "darkies," and, to judge from their Olympic calculus, considered all Southerners white.[181] It is certain that they themselves would never have shaken hands with a black man in 1936; one wonders if they agreed with Hitler that "Americans ought to be ashamed of themselves for letting their medals be won by Negroes," rather than by white Southerners like Spec Towns, who won a gold medal for the 110-meter hurdles.[182]

African Americans writing about the Olympics used an old tactic: They overstated America's racial opportunity to encourage whites to hearken to their better angels, to maximize the American model of tolerance. "It was modern America the Germans . . . were looking at when Uncle Sam's representatives took possession of the field. . . . Nazi flag-toters couldn't understand how black boys could ride over the ocean in a boat, eating and drinking at the same table with white people," one black columnist reported, painting a transitory moment as the rule. Du Bois wrote of Owens and Cornelius Johnson, "They typified a new conception of the American Negro for Europe, and also a new idea of race relations in the United States."[183] White Americans who had cheered when black athletes defied Hitler's racism would now have to put up or shut up. At a 1936 Republican rally in Philadelphia, Jesse Owens asked: "Roosevelt didn't think enough of me to even send congratulations, what do you think he will do for you?" At least Hitler had "warmly showered" the German medalists with personal affection, Owens pointed out.[184]

"What Else Are Jim-Crow Laws but Fascist Laws?"

After the Olympics, as the Nazis stepped up and legalized their repression of the Jews, the Scottsboro and Herndon cases loomed even more important in the fight against Fascism. Jim Crow laws and southern injustice in the courts inspired comparisons with Nazi legislation. Black columnist J. A. Rogers mused, "Recently I heard a very prominent white speaker say

that Fascism would not win in America as the American people were tem-
peramentally opposed to it." Yet the best argument that Fascism could succeed here was the fact that it was *already* here: "Not only is there Fascism in
America now but Mussolini and Hitler copied it from us. What else are jim-
crow laws but Fascist laws? . . . It is difficult to believe that Hitler to save
time did not copy them directly from the Southern statues and from the
unwritten laws of America against Negroes." A 1936 review of Hitler's legal
restrictions of the Jews ran under the heading "The Nazis and Dixie."[185]

Although Hitler did not actually use southern laws as an explicit
model for Jewish persecution, he was reported to admire Dixie's dictates
for enforcing day-to-day white supremacy. Hitler believed that the Bill of
Rights was irrelevant to American life and that the United States owed its
secret strength to state laws that legally institutionalized segregation and
oppression. In 1940 he studied the Nazi Heinz Kloss's survey of racial
laws in the United States, *Das Volksgruppenrecht in den Vereinigten Staaten
von Amerika.* According to Kloss, "a unified national America was an illusion"; state legislation had worked to keep races separate and minority
groups pure.[186] Others quoted Hitler as believing that America's national
promise had died when the Confederacy lost the Civil War. According to
an ex-Nazi's memoir, Hiter thought that "historical logic and sound
sense" dictated that the Confederacy emerge victorious. The Union victory was a perversion of history that left the United States structurally
damaged.[187] With *Das Volksgruppenrecht*, Jewish and African American
comparisons came full circle: Nazi Germany held up the U.S. South as a
model for its racial persecution. The comparison that many U.S. whites
were unwilling to draw, the Nazis drew for them.

After the 1936 Olympics, as the Nazis moved more boldly against the
Jews, they argued that they were merely following the example of the
American South. In 1939, *Das Schwarze Korps*, the newspaper of the German secret police, argued that Jews should be forced to ride on separate
train cars, Jim Crow cars. After all, to do so would "follow a democratic
example" good enough "for the world's freest country, where even presidents denounce the devilish invention of race consciousness." In America
it did not matter if the black person was "a world boxing champion or
other national hero," like Joe Louis. Louis, the Germans gloated, could not
sit, much less sleep, beside any white man, even a lowly "sewage worker."

If Negroes tried that in America, *Das Schwarze Korps* noted triumphantly, "The colored people [would] be relentlessly driven by an equally colored conductor into their own rolling kraal."[188]

Finally, on April 26, 1937, in a five to four vote, the United States Supreme Court declared Georgia's insurrection statute unconstitutional, voiding once and for all Angelo Herndon's conviction. Justice Owen Roberts read every piece of literature that the police had confiscated from Herndon six years earlier and carefully parsed the differences between insurrection, revolution, and organizing. Herndon's membership in the CP and "his solicitation of a few members," according to Roberts, "wholly fails to establish an attempt to incite others to insurrection." Moreover, he found that the statute "does not furnish a sufficiently ascertainable standard of guilt." Writing for the majority, he compared the statute with a "dragnet which might enmesh any one who agitates for a change of government if a jury can be persuaded that he ought to have foreseen his words would have some effect in the future conduct of others."[189] Herndon called the verdict "a decisive victory for all the progressive forces in the country" and argued that it "strikes another heavy blow at the Jim Crow oppression of the Negro people." [190]

The Herndon verdict reflects the influence of domestic and international politics on the courts. FDR announced his plan to add justices to the Court in February 1937. The Court ruled on Herndon's appeal that April, the month in which it changed direction and began to uphold key New Deal measures. Thus the *Herndon* decision was part of the "switch in time that saved nine."[191] Moreover, Herndon's case also traveled through the courts as Hitler stripped Jews of civil rights and Stalin stripped the USSR of dissent, real and imagined, through the purge trials. Herndon's arrest had occurred before Hitler came to power. By the time he went free, African Americans had fought in Spain against Fascism.[192]

Two months after Herndon's acquittal, the popular legal front convened at the annual meeting of the International Labor Defense organization. Leon Ransom, a Howard law professor and NAACP lawyer, spoke on antilynching legislation and civil rights along with Angelo Herndon and Ben Davis. Thirteen organizations supported the conference that year; they included the NAACP and the ACLU.[193] In the spring of 1937 Ben Davis basked in the successes of the Popular Front and the uncompromising Communist position on black equality. With Herndon, Otto Hall, Harry Haywood, and James Ford at his side, he summed up their experiences of the past five years: "Certainly if Communism is 20th Century Americanism, it also is 20th Century Abolitionism"[194]

Intimations of the Holocaust

After 1936 those who read the black press, along with increasing numbers of white Americans, began to realize that German Jews were doomed if Hitler could not be stopped. When African Americans began to predict the worst for Jews in Germany, they could not imagine exactly what the worst might be. *Crisis* pointed out that African Americans had "the right to protest and work to improve their lot. In Germany the Jew has no such privilege." Few, if any, predicted mass genocide, but there were intimations. If Jews could not protest, *Crisis* predicted, for them "there is no hope."[195]

Du Bois had lived in Germany for nearly six months in 1936, but Gestapo tactics muted his usual eloquent outrage. His beloved Germany had become monstrous, but he hoped that his experience with prejudice in America might fortify him there. Daily life for a black man in Nazi Germany seemed calm enough on the surface, but Du Bois realized that the Nazis watched his every move, and they opened his mail. At first he self-censored the weekly columns that he sent to the *Pittsburgh Courier*, and he let loose only after he knew he would be safely out of the country when his words were printed. Although he had encountered not a single instance of prejudice directed against him, he was overwhelmed by Nazi racism in general: "There is a campaign of race prejudice carried on, openly, continuously and determinedly against all non-Nordic races, but specifically against the Jews, which surpasses in vindictive cruelty and public insult anything I have ever seen; and I have seen much."[196]

For Du Bois, there was no contest in the villainous competition between German anti-Semitism and white southern racism. On his return to the United States, he told an interviewer, "The treatment of the Negro here cannot be compared to the German situation."[197] The pause in anti-Semitism during the Olympics, he argued, was a false spring, for Hitler's ultimate aim was to launch "world war on Jews." Du Bois recognized the power of Nazi propaganda. "Adolph Hitler hardly ever makes a speech today . . . without belittling, blaming or cursing Jews," he wrote. And the German magazine *Der Stürmer* was "the most shameless, lying advocate of race hate in the world, not excluding Florida." Du Bois spoke pointedly when he mentioned Florida; German newspapers had run photographs of Claude Neal's lynched black body in Greenwood, Florida, in 1934. The "lynching party" had been planned and publicized, and thousands had attended. The mob tortured Neal all day, cut off his penis and testicles, and made him eat them. He did not die until evening.[198]

Despite Jim Crow's attendant horrors, Du Bois argued in December 1936, "There has been no tragedy in modern times equal in its awful effects to the fight on the Jew in Germany." Only two other "attack[s] on civilization" in all history compared with it: the Spanish Inquisition and the African slave trade.[199] By making this linkage, Du Bois demonstrated his identification of the common destiny of Jews and blacks.

Throughout the 1930s U.S. Jews and African Americans built on an old and special relationship. The spread of segregation in the 1890s inspired Jewish philanthropists such as Julius Rosenwald, whose contributions helped build schoolhouses for African American children when southern states drastically cut funds for black education. From its inception in 1909 the NAACP counted on Jews to serve as board members, committee members, and benefactors. Historian David Levering Lewis argues that the relationship strengthened after Leo Frank's conviction and lynching in Atlanta in 1915, when Jews began to realize that the southern white supremacist system threatened every minority. The Anti-Defamation League was founded in response to the Frank lynching, and Jewish support for black civil rights leaders switched from black accommodationist leaders to those who more directly challenged the racial status quo.[200] Still, it was not a close relationship during the 1920s and early 1930s. But after Hitler's rise to power, Jews made the link between Nazism and southern white supremacy, just as African Americans did. Rabbi Stephen S. Wise, a NAACP founder who moved left during the interwar years, told 1934 NAACP annual meeting delegates: "I do not know whether Aryanism is going to survive. We have tried it in America. When are we going to learn that members of every race have exactly the same right to be themselves that the members of any other race do?"[201]

A few months later, as James Weldon Johnson agreed to speak at a seminar sponsored by the National Conference of Jews and Christians in 1935, he found himself assigned a new topic, "The Totalitarian Idea." He complained that such a subject did not have much "appeal" for him. But the NCJC director explained: "It was I who suggested that title ... [because] the old order has imbued ... a vestige of tribal thought ... exhibited in the ideology of Nazism in Germany today." In other words, an exclusionary, nationalistic race pride lived in Fascism and in southern white supremacy. "In the United States one sees lynching as an evidence of the totalitarian idea abiding in this land," the NCJC director pointed out. "If ever there was a nation in which cultural pluralism must be taught and maintained, it is ours."[202] Johnson rethought his decision and quickly realized the value of such an approach for both groups.

Discussions of how to improve the African American–Jewish relationship frequently found their way into print, and some historians have taken this public discourse to mean that African Americans were anti-Semitic before and during World War II.[203] However, years earlier than most non-Jewish white Americans, many African American leaders recognized and vigorously denounced Nazi persecution of Jews. When a handful of anti-Semitic black Fascists surfaced in the United States, the vast majority of African Americans promptly condemned them. In black leaders' comparisons of Germany and the American South, they took care not to denigrate the Jewish case.[204]

Certainly, African Americans were not immune to anti-Semitism, but they understood their common political interest and the similarities of their situation as minority groups. Black journals ran articles that promoted tolerance between the two groups, for example, "Jew Hatred among Negroes," written by Rabbi Edward L. Israel in 1936.[205] Israel relayed anti-Semitic stereotypes that average African Americans held in daily life. His purpose was not to condemn African Americans as anti-Semitic; rather, he hoped to sensitize African Americans to anti-Semitism in daily life. In the context of race relations—when "Jew" and "nigger" jokes regularly passed Gentile whites' lips—these columns represented an extraordinary attempt to set a higher standard for relations between Jews and blacks. *Crisis* added this encouragement: "At least two of the minority groups in this country ought to understand each other better and unite against the common enemies of both."[206]

By 1938 the links between Fascists and southern white supremacists and Jews and African Americans had been firmly forged. The American Anthropological Association unanimously passed a resolution condemning racism.[207] That year James Weldon Johnson was asked to write an article on "Fascist Trends in the United States," in "reference to the Negro." He responded that Fascism was not a *trend* but a fact for African Americans. Black Southerners had "lived under a certain and very definite form of Fascism for the past sixty years.[208] Despite this analogy, Johnson and most African Americans now thought Nazi persecution of the Jews a greater evil than Jim Crow. As a black writer pointed out, "Doctor Du Bois lives in Atlanta and he can say and do things in Georgia which Freud cannot say and do in Germany."[209]

At the same time, many Jews aggressively articulated their commitment to African American advancement, even as their own persecution grew in Germany. "The Jewish stake in removing the blot of white racialism from American life is clear," an editor at the Reconstructionist Society for the Advancement of Judaism argued. He reasoned: "Both self-interest and our holiest traditions demand our making common cause with the Negro in his fight for equality of status with the white."[210] The *Jewish Frontier* proclaimed: "We Must Stand Together." Reviewing the black presses' condemnation of Fascism, it said, "Negroes can understand the plight of the Jewry more keenly than many others and their sympathy has the sincerity of people who share a similar fate." By 1939 "many a Jew in Germany might be inclined to look with envy upon the status of the Negro in the U.S. today," but considering the desperation of the German Jews, now there was "no time to compare grievances." The *Frontier* saw dark days ahead and predicted that European Nazis would "no doubt seek to organize forces of racial intolerance in this country." Only by standing together could blacks and Jews ever hope to succeed in "eradicating the cancer of racial intolerance."[211]

By the end of the decade African Americans and Jews had planted the seeds of a new public discourse of tolerance. In 1939 the *Atlanta Journal*, which had customarily used the word *darkie* and slighted Jesse Owens four years earlier, argued, astonishingly: "There is no greater threat to real democracy than the cancer of racial discrimination. . . . We condemn properly, the persecution of minorities in the dictator-ruled countries of

Europe. Yet there are those among us, not a few who would deny equal justice in the courts, equal educational opportunities, equal chances for making a living, to racial minorities in this country." Then the editor, sounding downright Du Boisian, declared "Such beliefs and attitudes constitute a cancer on the heart of democracy that will, unless cured, bring death."[212] In less than a decade the national discourse had transformed southern white supremacy from race pride to intolerance and from intolerance into a cancer.

Writing in 1939, before segregation and oppression turned to extermination, one American Jew reflected: "If the injustices inflicted upon Jews in Germany will arouse the conscience of America to do justice to the Negro racial minority, it will be some consolation to us Jews. We shall at least have the satisfaction of feeling that we are, to some extent, performing the traditional role of the 'servant of the Lord,' that our suffering is, in some measure an expiation for the sins of the world, that 'by *our* stripes' others are healed."[213] If black Southerners were not healed, then at least they were inspired on their own journey to be made whole.

5

MOVING LEFT FROM CHAPEL HILL TO CAPE TOWN

Looking out from Chapel Hill in 1935, Communist organizer Don West could see in every direction. To the south, toward rural Chatham County, green farms, speckled with cattle, fanned out. To the east was Raleigh, where state legislators made law in the daytime and raised hell at the Sir Walter Raleigh Hotel at night. To the northwest, all of Burlington's mostly white cotton millworkers had filed back through the gates after the 1934 general textile strike—all, that is, except the six men who faced charges of dynamiting the mill.[1] If West drove north twelve miles, he whiffed the sweet, sharp smell of Durham's tobacco factories, where thousands of African Americans worked. "The Durham streets at dusk,/Are swarmed with color," a black poet wrote. The "tobacco scented" bodies owed their livelihood to the industry that drove their town and pervaded their lives.[2]

When you looked out from Chapel Hill, you could see all sides of things, and that, some people said, was precisely the problem with the place. More than one white North Carolina boy, yearning to get off the farm and into the classroom, heard his father say, "You'll go to Red Hill over my dead body!" During the Popular Front varying shades of liberals, Socialists, anti-Fascists, and new Communists came together to create a hotbed of agitation among students and professors at the University of North Carolina. Some of it even spilled over among the Methodists at

Duke University in Durham, which, with its large black working class and black middle class, fomented its own radicalism. African American editor Louis Austin published Don West's columns in his newspaper, the *Carolina Times*, and white UNC and Duke students began reading a "black" newspaper.[3] Inside The Intimate Bookshop on Franklin Street in Chapel Hill, C. Vann Woodward, self-exiled from Atlanta and late of New York City, often sat reading. Skeptical townspeople and some wary professors took The Intimate to be the source of all sedition in the little town, but they got the story only partly right.

When sociologist Howard Odum walked to work at UNC's Institute for Research in Social Science (IRSS), he could tell himself that nothing could be finer than to be in North Carolina, especially in Chapel Hill, where black and white people were friendly and worked hard for each other's good. Now and in the foreseeable future, as Odum saw it, that good included segregation. Odum was a man who believed in being realistic. Change came achingly slowly since people behaved according to regional customs. These behaviors, which he called folkways, would change only over generations, not overnight. He had boosted the Sociology and Social Work departments at Chapel Hill to national prominence. His IRSS served as Chapel Hill's very own think tank. There, largely in the absence of workers or African Americans, scholars from across the South produced studies of labor and race problems.[4]

After Woodward found himself unimpressed with political science at Columbia University, Odum secured a fellowship for him to pursue the PhD in history. Woodward entered UNC in the fall of 1934, but after a few months Odum heard gossip about Woodward's hanging out at The Intimate Bookshop. He telephoned Woodward and told him that he had fallen in "with the wrong crowd." If Woodward valued his fellowship, he should fall out of it, Odum warned. Nothing could have made Woodward more determined to spend time in the bookstore, which he dubbed "more or less leftist."[5]

The Popular Front prompted those "more or less leftist" Southerners to abandon the best existing model of race relations, the Commission on Interracial Cooperation (CICs). In the 1920s and 1930s white and black leaders worked to ameliorate Jim Crow's worst features through state organizations and a regional CIC based in Atlanta. For some white Southerners, the CIC provided a forum for interracial understanding that served as an incubator for a broader vision of civil rights. Others stayed within the model's confines, tacitly supporting segregation, while they advocated generosity and good manners toward those less fortunate than they. What had been an extremely useful way of managing racial oppression gave way to a Popular Front that directly challenged the racial caste system.[6]

With the emergence of a southern Left and the threat of Fascism in Europe, the CIC's refusal to push for black voting rights and its failure to condemn segregation began to appear obstructionist. As Nazi persecution of the Jews made racism seem un-American, CIC members found themselves in the awkward position of making segregation and disfranchisement more palatable even as they condemned Fascism. The apolitical stance that had enabled their work seemed outmoded in a world careening toward a racially driven cataclysm.[7]

By the late 1930s some moderate and liberal white Southerners had begun to consider more radical measures than the model that the CIC offered. Some moved leftward because of the interracial understanding that they gained in CIC work. A growing body of anthropological and sociological theory on race influenced others. The Communist alternative attracted some and opened up space on the left. Some came to support black civil rights through labor organizing. Moreover, the New Deal influenced many Southerners who went to Washington. It was a symbiotic relationship: Sometimes the New Deal moved Southerners to the left, and sometimes Southerners moved the New Deal to the left by keeping it focused on southern poverty and political repression.

Many of the same forces that moved Southerners to the left were at work internationally, and the crisis of confidence in the interracial cooperation model occurred in the Union of South Africa as well as in the U.S. South. In the 1920s and 1930s white Southerners exported the interracial cooperation model as the best possible system of race relations, but the colonized quickly realized its limits. Max Yergan, a black man from Raleigh, North Carolina, spent fifteen years with the international Young Men's Christian Association in an increasingly repressive South African environment. By 1936 a radicalized Yergan had returned to the United States. Following Yergan to South Africa and back again—from exuberant YMCA worker to disillusioned expatriate, from Christian social worker to budding

Communist—illustrates the politicization of those who moved from seeking interracial understanding to demanding human rights.[8]

By 1937 one could see a new spectrum of opinion on race relations in the American South. At one end the Communist Party advocated immediate social, economic, and political equality. Closest to it was a group of activist black and white progressive Southerners, Vann Woodward among them, who foresaw full labor and civil rights and thought that mass action might be necessary to change the system. Standing next to them, but apart, was the NAACP, which garnered both criticism and support from progressive activists as it sought change primarily through the courts. Commission on Interracial Cooperation members began to split. Some supported black voting rights and limited integration; some migrated even further to the left. Others, like Howard Odum, who became CIC president in 1937, found themselves in the fraught position of fostering gradualism while they argued, convincingly enough, that white Southerners were not ready for integration. To these groups' right stood Odum's *folk*, a majority of white Southerners, who vowed to fight to the death for Jim Crow. The significance of this spectrum lies not in the size of its bands but in its very existence. The South was anything but solid.

Liberals Meet the Left

That spectrum hung like a rainbow over Chapel Hill, where the local newspaper boasted: "We can use comfortably a few more radicals whose roots are set deeply into native soil." By 1935 the college town was hosting several groups of "native radicals," an active Communist Party, collaborating Socialists, lots of liberals, and a phalanx of moderates.[9] University of North Carolina Professor Frank Porter Graham danced nimbly across the kaleidoscopic rainbow, and he made sure that others noted its display across Carolina's blue sky. A strikingly handsome young man, Frank was five feet six inches and 125 pounds. All his life he wore boys' shoes. Graham had finished his BA at UNC, where his Bs and Cs did not stop him from becoming president of both the senior class and the YMCA. Graham's sweetness and empathy made him a charismatic leader. His fellow students called him "everyman's friend, confidant, and playfellow." One professor recalled that "he was just too darn good. . . . He loved people so."[10] In 1917 he enlisted in the Marine Corps as a private and departed a first lieutenant in 1919. Graham returned to UNC that year, first as dean of students, then as a history professor. He realized that he could not continue with just a BA and left to complete course work for his doctorate at the University of Chicago in southern history. But he became more interested in the southern economy than in the southern past and studied at the Brookings Institute during a fellowship year, ending up at the London School of Economics. There he took seminars with the Socialist political scientist Harold Laski, who "taught tolerance, the willingness to listen although one disagreed, the value of ideas being confronted." His favorite professor was R. H. Tawney, a Fabian Socialist. After four years outside the South, Graham returned in 1925 to teach history at UNC once again.[11]

In 1929 Graham avidly followed the Gastonia strike, and Ella May Wiggins's death crushed him. "I have never felt more depressed and bewildered in my life than I did reading the Sunday's paper with the story of Mrs. Wiggins' death," he declared. "The sheer power of the figure of this woman shining out from the facts is simple, beautiful, terrible! . . . Her death is upon the heads of us all . . . what I see in her is not Communism but Americanism." Ella May's embrace of "alien doctrines," Graham reasoned, was a search for "answers to her aspirations for her children. . . . It is we who are responsible for the void of leadership into which" the Communists came.[12] "We" meant the good, progressive, white people of North Carolina, and to them Graham turned three months later to ask for their signatures on an Industrial Bill of Rights that affirmed the right of free speech and proposed labor reforms to guide North Carolina. More than three hundred of the state's most prominent white liberals signed Graham's petition in 1930.[13]

Graham's characterization of Ella May Wiggins and his petition brought down a firestorm of criticism on the university. President Harry W. Chase deflected calls to fire Graham from the History Department. The Gastonia prosecutor upbraided Graham for coming to the defense of those who associated with Communists.[14] The editor of the *Southern Textile Bulletin* complained that within the faculty at UNC, "'Tis a small group of radicals who are, in an insidious manner, eternally fighting that which they fanatically call 'capitalism.' "[15]

Despite the furor, the university tapped Frank Porter Graham to be its president in 1930, and every day thereafter he tapped the courage of his convictions to blur the class and race-based divisions in southern society. His political ideology followed the Golden Rule. To Graham, every person, without exception, deserved equal opportunity and respect. His kindness lent dignity to others. Vann Woodward recalled of Graham that "he was all but irresistible."[16] If Graham was Peter Pan, UNC was a southern academic Neverland. Under the shield that Graham projected over the campus, differences of opinion flourished.

Woodward's newfound friends, or Odum's "wrong crowd," took it upon themselves to turn up the volume of free speech and burnish the local liberal glow. The Intimate Bookshop was North Carolina's Algonquin, its Greenwich Village, its Bloomsbury, its City Lights, all contained within four walls on the town's main street. Entering for the first time, a small-town Southerner might stop and gasp. In the former grocery store, as far as the eye could see, were books. These were not books like those back home in the Carnegie Library, all bound and sitting well behaved in their places, but books unaligned in towering stacks and riotous colors.[17] These books called to you and told you things your momma didn't want you to know. One woman remembered The Intimate as "the guts of the town's intellectual life," and its owner, Milton Abernethy, known as Ab, as Chapel Hill's "gatekeeper to imagination." Equally important, she recalled, the store was "a concordance to sex. People looked up 'orgasm' and were amazed."[18] One graduate student characterized Ab as a "congenial, fat, little bastard, hardly a Communist," accompanied always by "his lazy old dog with hair over his eyes."[19]

"Ab's existence gave us a sense of our own importance, justifying our subversion," one of the store's young devotees recollected. The Intimate was an oasis in the Sahara of the Bozart. Ab had started the store in his dorm room, and in 1931 playwright and UNC professor Paul Green gave him and his business partner, Anthony Buttitta, some books and probably a loan. Ab and Buttitta happily announced their new public location on Franklin Street, "where any cautious co-ed may now join the booklovers on their daily pilgrimage." By 1935 patrons might find fifteen-year-old high school student Junius Scales amid "piles of textbooks . . . curled up" reading. Scales, the son of a distinguished North Carolina family, breathed in the radical politics that mingled with the bookstore's dust. In 1939 he joined the Communist Party.[20]

Ab and Buttitta began publishing a "little magazine," *Contempo*, backed by Paul Green. With dazzling chutzpah, since they had no money to pay authors, they recruited scores of famous writers as diverse as James Joyce and William Faulkner. The result was plainspoken criticism of the South and Jim Crow, published from within the South, rather than from a border post such as H. L. Mencken's Baltimore.[21]

Thanks in part to Ab and Buttitta, Chapel Hill had its own "Langston Eclipse" in 1931. As he planned a southern lecture tour, Hughes saw Paul Green's *The House of Connelly* on the New York stage. He characterized it (at least to its author) as "the most interesting dramatization of Southern life that the theater has given us." *Vanity Fair* called Green "next to O'Neill . . . America's most significant playwright" and an "ardent gentleman farmer." Green's national reputation, coupled with his deep North Carolina roots, protected him when he flouted southern white convention. Hughes asked Green, "Have any of the Negro poets read their poems at Chapel Hill?" Enthusiastic about Hughes's inquiry, Green prevailed upon Guy Johnson, a sociologist who worked closely with Howard Odum, to raise an honorarium for Hughes among the faculty.[22] Things were calm when UNC's student newspaper announced the reading: "J. Langston Hughes Has Won Many Prizes and Is Listed in 'Who's Who.' "[23]

It was, however, the calm before the storm. Just before Hughes's November 19 visit, *Contempo* published his new poem on Scottsboro, "Christ in Alabama." Ab and Buttitta were capitalists enough to print an extra five thousand copies.

Christ is a Nigger,
Beaten and black—
O, bare your back.

Mary is His Mother—
Mammy of the South,
Silence your Mouth.

God's His Father—
White Master above
Grant us your love.

Most holy bastard of the bleeding mouth:
Nigger Christ
On the cross of the South.[24]

Hughes's poem inverts the story of the Virgin Birth to replace Mary
with a silenced black woman, raped by her white master, who bears a different kind of Christ child, one who will be crucified by lynching. An outrage of epic proportions ensued. "It's bad enough to call Christ a bastard,
but to call Him a Nigger—that's too much," one reader protested. [25] As if
the poem were not enough, alongside it was printed Langston Hughes's
take on Scottsboro, published as the provocative "Southern Gentlemen,
White Prostitutes, Mill-Owners, and Negroes." Millowners, Hughes
argued, should "pay their women decent wages so they won't need to be
prostitutes. . . . The sensible citizens of Alabama" should fund schools for
"the black populace of their state," and while they were at it, they should
include "the mulatto children of gentlemen."[26] Paul Green observed, "My
boys—as I presume to call them—the *Contempo* two seem bent on stirring
up a little fun. I try to guard them as much as possible, but expect a showdown before long."[27]

On the day of his visit Hughes read poetry and gave an autobiographical lecture, serenaded by the local black singers, the Silver Tongue Quartet.
Predictably, more students showed up for the football team's pep rally than
for Hughes's reading. It did not matter much since Hughes had his usual
marvelous time and wowed everyone. The *Daily Tar Heel* described him as
"that refined, and culture [*sic*] young Negro poet" and, daringly, called him
Mr. Hughes.[28] Green reported that he "had Hughes out to my house for the
evening, reading, and talking," but he thought Ab and Buttitta went too far
when they took Hughes to the segregated fancy cafeteria in town. "They
are a tactless two," Green lamented.[29] Yet eating at the cafeteria was a mas-
terstroke against segregation. In a cafeteria they did not have to wait to be
served, it was packed with gawking white students, and the "Negro waiters
and waitresses" who brought the sweet iced tea over "were particularly
pleased." For his part, Hughes commented, "If they were willing to go
through with dinner in a public restaurant in the tense atmosphere of that
small town, I was willing, too." Buttitta recalled: "Much was made of this,"

even as he revealed that one of the town's leading matrons "thought Hughes was darling, cute, and wanted to have him out to dinner."[30]

But most white North Carolinians, including "a small circle of Negro haters on the [UNC] Board of Trustees," did not find the affair "cute." Hughes recalled he never got paid the "fee agreed on." The editor of the *Southern Textile Bulletin*, who hated Frank Porter Graham, reprinted "Christ in Alabama" and "Southern Gentlemen, White Prostitutes, Mill-Owners, and Negroes," as "examples of student journalism" and misled readers into thinking that *Contempo* was a university-sponsored "Communist Paper."[31] Scores of North Carolinians, sniping from high and low places, clamored for the dismissal of the "man who had brought" Hughes. Frank Graham refused to identify Hughes's sponsor and declared, "I am responsible for what happens on this campus. You fire me."[32] Following the many Americans who wanted to see firsthand the Soviet Union's unprecedented experiment in action, Ab headed to Moscow for a visit early in 1932. When he returned, he and Buttitta dissolved their partnership, possibly over political issues, possibly over the determination of Ab's new bride, Minna, to clean up the cluttered bookstore.[33]

By the time that Don West and Vann Woodward arrived on the scene in 1934, The Intimate was beating as North Carolina's radical heart. West proved as irresistible as Ab was. Vann Woodward had not been in graduate school a week before he fell in with West, whom he had known in Atlanta, where they worked together on the Angelo Herndon defense committee. The first three weeks of Woodward's Chapel Hill sojourn coincided with the general textile strike of September 1934. Instead of hitting the books, Woodward traveled around with West, who used the Party name Jim Weaver. Woodward knew that West/Weaver was a Communist using an alias and boasted that there were "warrants for his arrest in three Southern states." He and West set out to "organize some protest of terrorism" in the general textile strike. Owners had employed "every method of Fascism" against the strikers, Woodward observed, and "Communism was pretty much eclipsed in the strike; much weaker than in '29. . . . Still," he added, "it is stronger than you might suspect."[34] During the strike, in fact, there had been one Communist in the Loray Mill and twelve in the mills in Concord. Several workers in Burlington, including those charged with hurling the "dynamite bomb" from a car, joined the Party after West came to their defense.[35]

West worked under North Carolinian Paul Crouch, who had returned to the state in 1934 as the District 16 organizer. Crouch's wife, Sylvia, a former Gastonia striker, served as organizer of the Young Communist League. West complained about them to the Central Committee: Paul was "a sick man," and Sylvia was "very nervous and high tempered."[36] In turn, the Central Committee complained to Crouch about West's poor administrative abilities. West resented writing "regular reports smearing on the bull about wonderful work with the rank and file worker." He did not make a good Party bureaucrat: "God damn it, I'm sore enough already over this unceasing work and labor . . . by golly my nerves are just about shot or something. I'm doing about everything I can to stick by the strict party line and carry out every detail." Flat broke like all CP organizers, West drove around in "an old wreck of a jalopy," of which Woodward said that "the only trouble is it leaks; the roof leaks, the tires leak, the radiator leaks, the gas line leaks, the car leaks."[37]

During the general textile strike in Burlington, dynamite exploded outside one of the mill buildings and caused minor damage. Six union activists were arrested, tried, and sentenced to long prison terms. The defense of the Burlington strikers became the point of convergence—a southern Popular Front—between the Communist Party, Socialists, and local free-range radicals in early 1935. The Burlington sheriff claimed that Communists had masterminded the explosions; that seemed unlikely since the defendants were members of an American Federation of Labor union. A cross section of liberals and radicals formed the Burlington Defense Committee to protest the overly long sentences. Although one Communist complained that the Defense Committee was "dominated by Socialists," Don West served as "assistant chairman."[38] Vann Woodward joined, and Paul Green got involved because, he said, "ninety-odd years" was excessive punishment for breaking "out twelve dollars worth of window panes." The committee hired lawyers and raised money for an appeal to the Supreme Court. West pleaded for justice for the defendants at Methodist, Baptist, and Presbyterian churches across the North Carolina Piedmont.[39]

The official Popular Front, announced in Moscow in August 1935, ratified what was already happening among the anti-Fascist Left on the ground in the South. It liberated the Communists to work with others and marked the high tide of recruiting white southerners to the Party. Perhaps most important to the South, where actual numbers of Communists were few, the Popular Front created a national culture attentive to labor rights, international anti-Fascism, and the global problems of people of color upon which non-Communist Southerners could draw.[40] In the South the Popular Front gave people courage, comparative perspective, and a new way to talk about local issues. While the Burlington strike had been spectacularly unsuccessful, the Burlington Defense Committee succeeded in bringing together those in the Left around issues of free speech and criminal rights. West did not come out as a Communist to them.[41] Paul Green didn't know and recalled that West "seemed more interested in justice for the mill defendants than in pushing any political point of view." Green observed, perhaps disingenuously, that "there might have been Communist influence in these meetings, but if it was apparent, I was too blind to see it. . . . Our interest was not Communism, but justice."[42]

In fact, when West organized the Burlington Defense Committee, he also organized a unit of the Communist Party, which Green did not join. "Boy, but have we done things with this S.P. [Socialist Party] here!" West wrote in 1935. "Did we organize a real unit Sunday in Chapel Hill!" he exclaimed. "If we had picked the whole place over we could not possibly have chosen 5 fellows who are better material. And they know how to carry on too. Of course, they are intellectuals, but nevertheless very important."[43]

If Green did not know that West was a Communist, he did know that the Party aided the Burlington Defense Committee. In March 1935 Green went to New York with attorney Major John Henderson and UNC English professor Eston Everett Ericson to meet with Earl Browder and coordinate representation of the strikers by the International Labor Defense. Taking a lesson from Scottsboro, Green protested that the ILD should not send lawyers into North Carolina and warned that a local defense attorney would be more likely to prevail.[44] Ericson had been a Socialist. Using the code name Spartacus, he became an underground member of the CP in the fall of 1934 but maintained publicly that he was a Socialist. For his part, Green knew that "everybody said" Ericson was a Communist, "and we sort of tried to tame him down a little bit."[45]

By February 1935 West had organized the Chapel Hill CP unit, an ILD branch, and a Young Communist League in Burlington, helped by "the faint driblet of liberalism coming from Chapel Hill and other universities around here." Elsewhere in District 16, under Crouch's leadership, units existed in Danville, Virginia, Concord, Charlotte, and Gastonia, North Carolina, and Columbia, South Carolina. Despite these inroads, party members in the district totaled fewer than 100.[46]

Communists joined eagerly with the small numbers of southern Socialists who had been around since the collapse of the Populist Party at the turn of the century. In North Carolina in 1935 there were six SP locals with a total membership of about seventy-five. Several urban areas had small Socialist parties, and every four years disgruntled farmers and agrarian intellectuals joined them to vote for the SP candidate for president, Norman Thomas.[47] By the early 1930s a new strain of Christian Socialism had begun emerging in the Appalachians and western Tennessee as well. Many of its advocates, including Howard Kester of the Southern Tenant Farmers' Union, Myles Horton, founder of Tennessee's Highlander Folk School, and James Dombrowski, a Columbia PhD who joined Highlander in 1933 after Don West left, were ministers who had been influenced by the Socialist Reinhold Niebuhr of Union Theological Seminary.[48] Although West became a Communist, Kester, Horton, and Dombrowski remained Socialists and came together through a loosely structured organization called the Conference of Younger Churchmen of the South. In 1934 the Younger Churchmen condemned "the manifest injustices to the Negro," including discrimination in employment, unions, the courts, and education. It stopped short of calling for integration.[49] Many Younger Churchmen joined interested laypeople in the Fellowship of Reconciliation, Kester reported, and he claimed that it had "built a strong Socialist movement which cuts across all racial and religious lines."[50]

In the spring of 1935 southern Socialists and Communists cooperated to organize the All Southern Conference for Civil and Trade Union Rights.[51] Not all Socialists and liberals were willing to make alliances with Communists in the face of the Fascist threat. Warned by a liberal that the Communists were "not to be trusted," Jim Dombrowski responded that he had once felt the same way. Now, however, he considered "a United Front . . . of vast importance. . . . Huey [Long] may cause people to laugh now, but I was in Germany in 1932 . . . and you know that people even then were laughing off Hitler."[52] Communists stayed in the background at the All Southern Conference, while Dombrowski and Kester's Conference of Younger Churchmen of the South and Highlander Folk School came to the fore. Conference organizers called for "immediate repeal and defeat of all existing and proposed sedition and anti-labor laws," the right to unionize and strike, "the right of all citizens, white and Negro, to vote without payment of the poll tax," drastic penalties for lynching, "disbanding all armed fascist bands (K.K.K., etc.)," and "freedom of the Burlington textile workers, the Arkansas sharecroppers, the Scottsboro boys, Angelo Herndon, Tom Mooney, and all other victims of capitalist persecution."[53] The excited group that converged on Chattanooga in May 1935 included Don West, who brought along several Burlington millworkers and an unidentified UNC student.[54]

If Southerners on the left were ready for a united front, the Chattanooga American Legion was already united against them. The Legion called the conference "red," forced it out of the Odd Fellows Hall, and prevented organizers from renting the "Negro Pythian Hall." When the beleaguered delegates finally convened in another space, Legionnaires surrounded them there. The justifiably frightened landlord ordered the delegates to leave, and they split up and tried to reach the Highlander Folk School. The intimidation and violence justified the conference to its participants. "It was in such incidents as this . . . that the Fascist dictatorships of Germany and Italy began," Dombrowski pointed out.[55]

In North Carolina the new Popular Front coalition included African Americans. When West began writing for Louis Austin's *Carolina Times* in March 1935, Austin knew that Jim Weaver, the Communist, was actually Don West, and he thanked him for "your great work toward liberating the fettered masses of the south." For his part, West was delighted at the opportunity to reach African American workers in print.[56] By the early summer of 1935 Communist Party membership in North Carolina had reached 155, with units in Greensboro, Charlotte, Burlington, and Durham. Like all good academics, the Chapel Hill members did not meet in the summer.[57]

The Intimate provided a safe haven to print Communist publications. West and Ericson convinced Ab and a group of his friends to buy a press that would be housed in the back of the bookstore, ostensibly to publish liberal tracts. There the CP revived the *Southern Worker*, printing it secretly at night. "The paper has already been driven out of Alabama, Georgia and Tennessee," one Communist observed.[58] "At last," he trumpeted, "the Party has a complete print-shop in the South. . . . The liberals who signed our note at the Morris Plan Bank here don't know, of course, who controls the press."[59] Paul Green was one of those liberal benefactors. The *Southern Worker* resumed publication in late 1935 or early 1936 under the slogan "The Paper of the Southern Toilers," a phrase quickly supplanted by "The Magazine of the Common People of the South."[60]

Of course, Milton and Minna Abernethy knew that the *Southern Worker* and Party pamphlets came off the press in their back room, but theirs was also a money-making venture that also produced liberal publications. Nor did housing the press prove that the Abernethys were Communists; the CP had always published its newspaper using non-Communist printers. Later Paul Crouch claimed that Ab and Minna were "Communists who accepted party decisions without having membership books at that time." In other words, they did not actually join the Communist Party. If they had wished to, they could have joined as underground members and paid their dues directly to Crouch, just as Ericson did.[61] The "Communist press" at The Intimate quickly became North Carolina folklore. "The rumor was he [Ab] let people use that mimeograph machine behind the curtained partition to print up leftish flyers," one student remembered. Another remembered the equipment as "a joke," since it constantly broke down and was Ab's way of making a "buck."[62]

The roots of the southern Popular Front, represented by The Intimate, the Burlington Defense Committee, the All Southern Conference for Civil and Trade Union Rights, newly energized Socialists, and Don West himself, went deep into southern soil. Some of its Communist members embraced Christian venues and Christians themselves. It flourished in a time when the local newspaper could agitate for a few more home-grown radicals. It was a moment in which one didn't call in the FBI when one's colleague was rumored to be a Communist; instead one tried to "tame him down a little bit." The South's new Left nourished old believers, unsettled the complacency of their liberal allies, and produced a fresh crop of indigenous radicals.

Outside Agitation and Southern Conversions

Native white Southerners who had attended northern universities and traveled abroad swelled the ranks of the southern Popular Front. For example, Olive "Polly" Stone was a former Young Women's Christian Association worker among southern working-class white women. Her search for answers to the plight of those women began at University of Chicago summer school in 1924. At registration she saw a sign that read " 'social service administration.' I wondered what that was?" She told the lady registrar, who "looked like a little old grandmother, quite innocent," that she had worked with the YWCA. "Well now," the lady replied, "I think it would be very nice if you came down to school. You can have a little course with Miss Abbott." Only later did Stone realize that her registrar had been Sophonisba Preston Breckinridge, JD, PhD, and a founder of the discipline of social work. Stone's "little course" with Edith Abbott led Stone to an MA in social work at the University of Chicago. She had stumbled upon the gods of women's activism in the Progressive Era. What seemed to be their twilight was simply the passing of the torch to a new generation of women. For her part, Stone studied and worked with black families that were recent migrants to Chicago from the rural South, and in the summer she worked on a Children's Bureau project in Kentucky. She returned to Alabama in 1927 to train child welfare workers, and in 1929 she became a professor of social work at Woman's College of Alabama in Montgomery.[63]

Ensconced in her dream job, Stone began to question things "beyond just the Y.W.C.A.-type of human interest in other races, other religions, and other nationalities." She wondered if "maybe we should do something about the government and the discriminations and so on." Her curiosity took her to the Soviet Union in the summer of 1931. Upon sailing, she discovered that her fellow travelers defied political labels: a preacher and his wife, a midwestern farmer eager to see collectivized farms, a Wall Street heiress who wrote for *Fortune*. "The Russians," Stone recalled, "never claimed in those days that the country was Communist; they were 'on the road to communism.' " Stone watched people on the streets suddenly jump up, click their heels, and sing out, "It's my country now."[64]

When she returned to Montgomery, Stone founded what she described as a "study group" or a "hospitality group for a lot of people" that some began to call a Marxist cell.[65] With an Episcopal bishop's widow, Mary Martin "Dolly" Craik Speed, her Viennese-educated daughter Jane, the local rabbi, and about eight other "professional people," Stone read Marxist literature. Dolly and the rest were "liberals," Stone explained, but Jane, at least, joined the CP. The group hosted Communist organizers who came through Montgomery on their way from Chattanooga to Birmingham and found themselves moved by the plight of the Communist-organized Share Croppers' Union in nearby Tallapoosa County.[66] Stone secretly passed money-filled envelopes to a black CP organizer in the post office, and a CP organizer took Stone's social work students to meet the striking sharecroppers.[67] Stone also dabbled in Socialism and arranged interracial speaking tours for black and white members of the predominantly Socialist Fellowship of Reconciliation (FOR). She went on a FOR tour to India to study "the nonviolent Gandhian approach," since "India's barriers were not unlike those we had in the USA."[68]

In 1933 book club member Jane Speed tried to get a permit for an integrated May Day meeting in Birmingham. The city commissioner refused, saying that, "we are sitting on a barrel of dynamite, and this is no time to have the whites and the Negroes mixing and mingling together." Nonetheless, Speed called a meeting in the park across from 16th Street Baptist Church, but a young policeman named Theophilus Eugene "Bull" Connor forcibly broke up the meeting.[69] Speed, who called herself "a truly Southern girl," jumped on a car and began to yell "in a shrill voice" to the three thousand assembled. "Fellow workers, this is the way they do us," she cried as the police tried to drag her away, calling her a "nigger lover." Black women in the crowd began yelling, "Let her speak," and a black man attacked the police. When they grabbed him, the black women screamed, "Turn him aloose," and hit the police with their parasols. Police finally took Speed to jail. Her mother, Mary Martin Craik Speed, the bishop's widow, came to court to see her convicted of disorderly conduct, speaking without a permit, and "speaking to a public assembly of mixed races without physical barriers of separation." Defiant, Jane Speed decided to serve time rather than pay the fine.[70]

CIC director Will Alexander was astonished to learn that Speed was "indeed of the best that Montgomery has"; in fact her aunt was the town's "social dictator." The consensus in Speed's hometown was that she had "succumbed to radicalism in Vienna," brought home an Austrian husband, and "was a woman emotionally deranged" who might have "turned to religion, if she had not taken communism as a hobby." If locals thought Jane "emotionally deranged," they could not explain her mother's conduct. After Jane's arrest, Mary Craik Speed appeared at a mass rally in Harlem with black Alabamian and Communist James Ford. "Down home," she told the crowd, "we never have any meetings like this. Why, I guess a gathering this large would just about frighten Montgomery to death."[71] The bishop's widow joined Harry Haywood, Cyril Briggs, Louise Thompson, and Langston Hughes on the national council of the League of Struggle for Negro Rights.[72]

Stone hoped that her associations with radicals, some of whom she knew to be Communists, would not endanger her new position as dean of women at Alabama's Methodist woman's college, but that hope proved naive. Mary Craik reported that "we are watched. Our every move is followed. . . . [O]ur smallest action may endanger the lives of our comrades." Yet Olive Stone took chances. For example, she gave copies of her Tennessee Valley Authority–funded research to Jim Allen, editor of the *Southern Worker*, even though it "might create difficulties for her at the college" if anyone found out.[73] Stone walked a tightrope and began to believe that Woman's College, perhaps even Alabama itself, was too "parochial."[74] In 1934 she decided to pursue a PhD in Howard Odum's sociology program at UNC.

In the summer before she enrolled in UNC, Stone attended two historic integrated conferences. The first, the Swarthmore Institute of Race Relations, sponsored by the Pennsylvania Society of Friends, lasted twenty-nine days and featured twenty-nine African American speakers. The institute originated as a reaction against a suggestion by CIC director Will Alexander that the Friends start an Interracial Committee of the North. They rejected Alexander's colonization attempt and sought their own, more thoroughgoing solution to race relations.[75]

Alexander must have been surprised that the Pennsylvanians declined his overture, since he had exported the Commission on Interracial Cooperation to Africa. Alexander believed that if "America is to render a service to a world vexed by race problems, we of the South must assume responsibility." He became a "warm friend" of Anson Phelps Stokes, head of the Phelps

Stokes Fund, which devoted its efforts to education and interracial cooperation in Africa.[76] The southern CIC branches inspired interracial joint
councils in thirty South African cities. One white member characterized
the councils as places where "Native extremists are brought to a reasonable
frame of mind by having their wild views firmly but sympathetically criticized by thoughtful Europeans . . . [who] afford the Native members their
superior knowledge and show them the inevitable outcome of unsound
views." The Phelps Stokes Fund also exported Howard Odum's Institute
of Human Relations lecture series to the all-white University of Cape
Town as the Lectureship on Interracial Problems.[77]

In 1930 Will Alexander met with the South African general and
politician Jan Christiaan Smuts to recommend that the South Africans
establish Commissions on Interracial Cooperation. Smuts told Alexander
that "instead of mixing up white and black in the old haphazard way . . . we
are trying to keep them apart."[78] Smuts saw the commissions as a way to
"work out" segregation, and he warned: "You in America must not make
any mistakes in dealing with these matters, because the rest of the world
will follow you." Alexander agreed: "This is our great opportunity."[79]

The organizers of the Swarthmore Institute rejected Alexander's
overture and the Society of Friends formed its own Committee on Race
Relations, headed by Helen R. Bryan, a white Quaker, and Crystal Bird
Fauset, a black YWCA organizer. Throughout the spring of 1933 the two
women worked closely with Franz Boas, the renowned white anthropolo-
gist, and Charles S. Johnson, the black sociologist from Fisk.[80] The first
Swarthmore Institute that summer included Will Alexander and Howard
Odum, along with South Africa's black YMCA director, Max Yergan.[81]

Yergan embodied Will Alexander's "great opportunity" on the ground
at Fort Hare College, Alice, Cape Province, South Africa.[82] He had been
born in 1892 in Raleigh, North Carolina. His mother was a dressmaker,
and his grandfather a successful carpenter who had been born a slave.[83]
They could read and write and owned their home. Max could barely
remember black political participation in North Carolina before the white
supremacy campaigns of 1898 and disfranchisement in 1900. In his adolescence and college years, it seemed as if the only way that North Carolina's African Americans could move forward was through education and
interracial cooperation.[84] A committed Christian, Yergan attended St.

Ambrose Academy, operated by white Episcopalians, and then Baptist-affiliated Shaw University. Meanwhile his mother had to abandon dressmaking and become a domestic worker.[85] At Shaw, from which he graduated in 1914, Max Yergan starred on the football field and became a student YMCA leader.[86]

When World War I broke out in Europe, Yergan answered the YMCA call for paid volunteers to work among soldiers in India. He made friends among his white shipmates during the crossing, and one remarked: "Truly Jesus Christ does transcend all racial and color lines." After a few months in Bangalore, India, Yergan leaped at the opportunity to work among African troops in Dar es Salaam, Tanganyika (now Tanzania), British East Africa.[87] In this beautiful city Yergan learned some Swahili, organized religious services for the troops, set up night schools for literacy education and clerical skills, and roused Africans to foot races and a "cocoanut-tree climbing contest."[88] The troops flocked nightly to his movies from the United States, which often portrayed African American progress. One night an African soldier asked him, "You say you have this thing called ambition, hope, and you . . . are our brothers and sisters? . . . Then why . . . are there so few of you here?" Yergan returned to the United States in 1918, became an army chaplain, and later served with the YMCA in France.[89]

He yearned to return to Africa, where he believed that he could best combine his Christian principles and YMCA methods. In 1919 the YMCA offered him the national secretaryship for British East Africa, based in Kenya. But Kenya had "set an embargo against any Negro of greater education or higher sophistication than Kenyan Africans."[90] That left South Africa, where Yergan headed the Young Men's Christian Association among African students from 1922 to 1936. By the time he arrived at the Swarthmore Institute, he had already led South Africa's most historic conference on interracial cooperation, the 1930 Bantu-European Student Conference.[91]

Helen Bryan had visited Yergan in South Africa in the year preceding the first Swarthmore Institute. She recalled the Bantu-European Student Conference as "the greatest step forward in understanding among South African youth in the history of that country." It had, she waxed hyperbolically, "acted as a bomb shell in the accepted mores of South African life."[92]

Bryan hoped that the Swarthmore conference would do the same for the United States, and she hoped to bring to it "students from Gandhi's Ashram . . . and Max Yergan's Student Center."[93]

Under the direction of Bryan and Fauset, the Swarthmore Institute drew on Quaker tradition and differed in three ways from southern interracial conferences: It was truly integrated, it questioned the category of race, and it emphasized the international oppression of people of color. First, the institute served as a "demonstration center . . . of both races living and working and thinking together," which "might ultimately act as an integrating force."[94] Away from Jim Crow's sharp eye, black and white participants lived, swam, and talked together for an entire month. Second, black sociologist Charles Johnson argued that race was not a meaningful category, other teachers debunked biological differences, and everyone took on "fact and fancy in race classification."[95] Third, participants framed questions internationally, rather than within the U.S. South's narrow possibilities. "The problems of race contact in our American life are but fragments of a world problem," the organizers argued. Participants learned about "race prejudice as an historic and current phenomenon" in Japan, China, India, Africa, and the United States.[96] These controversial stands drove away the philanthropies usually interested in funding interracial work. Will Alexander and Howard Odum quickly distanced themselves from the institute after its first year.[97]

Participant Olive Stone marveled over the differences between the Swarthmore Institute and southern interracial conferences. Swarthmore's activities lacked the "patronizing approach on the part of the whites and the ingratiating appeal from the Negroes." Absent as well was the emotional fervor of the southern meetings that sprang from the "confessional value . . . [of the] Negroes . . . bursting with a smoldering sense of injustice and the ease of conscience . . . which the whites get from their benevolent gestures." Instead of individual catharsis, Swarthmore participants focused on "scholarly, scientific analysis," Stone reported, and students never stooped to "an emotional or agitational level." Instead of patron/client relationships, they formed "permanent friendships."[98]

Moreover, they deliberately steered past becalmed civility and into troubled waters. Sociologist Robert Park welcomed contestation, since "racial animosities" sprang from African Americans' discontent with their "subordinate position." Where Odum saw danger in upsetting white folk-ways, Park argued that tension preceded change. Of Park, Stone recalled, "we all sat at his feet, more or less."[99] After that summer's success, Helen Bryan and Crystal Fauset sponsored a seminar on segregation that Yer-gan attended. A small group took up the question "If to date the results of segregation do not warrant its continuance, what steps should be taken to eradicate it?"[100]

Yergan and Stone followed up the institute by taking a version of it to Yergan's alma mater, Shaw University in Raleigh. The Negro-White Conference was the first southern interracial conference that dared endorse integration. Organized in the fall of 1934 under the auspices of the International Student Service, a Socialist organization, the Shaw con-ference sought to convince existing interracial organizations like the CIC "to work for complete social, political, and economic equality of the races," to organize the "masses," and to "change their character and structure" to meet those goals. James Dombrowski of the Highlander Folk School recounted to Reinhold Niebuhr that the Shaw conference tried to "pro-mote a revolutionary viewpoint particularly among Negroes, . . . and bring some pressure from the left upon the existing organizations in the field, e.g. NAACP, and others." Loren Miller and Henry Lee Moon, *Black and White* cast members back from Moscow, attended. The scattering of southern whites included Dombrowski and Howard Kester.[101] The Shaw participants debated "the inadequacy of present organizations" in inter-racial work and questioned their methods.[102] It was a radical intervention in race relations.

Building a New Left in the New South

After the Shaw conference, Stone entered Odum's Sociology Department as a part-time PhD student, and she worked for the Southern Committee for People's Rights. The committee provided a homegrown alternative to the northern ACLU and had been organized in Atlanta during the Hern-don prosecution. Don West, who had known Stone in Atlanta, was thrilled to hear of her impending arrival in Chapel Hill. "She should be able to swing a lot of interest our way," he predicted.[103] She recruited members from the Burlington Defense Committee and the university to join the

Southern Committee for People's Rights "to protect civil and human rights for all people in the South."[104] The committee used a sophisticated anti-Fascist, pro–free speech critique of "the right of minority groups, whether religious, political, or racial, to voice their convictions" and espoused a reformist agenda of labor legislation.[105]

Members of the Southern Committee for People's Rights illustrated the vibrancy of the southern Popular Front. Vann Woodward had dropped in on the committee in Atlanta and then joined it in Chapel Hill. So did Paul Green, the Abernethys, Raleigh *News and Observer* editor Jonathan Daniels, several English professors, and numerous graduate students.[106] Jonathan Daniels was the son of Josephus Daniels, a heavy mantle that he wore well. Josephus had made the *News and Observer* the leading purveyor of white supremacy in the 1890s; then, as secretary of the navy, he had exported Jim Crow to Haiti. Jonathan spent his first decade in Raleigh, living in an integrated neighborhood across the street from Shaw University and playing with its grammar school students. Ten-year-old Daniels perhaps watched Max Yergan practicing on the football field or running his early-morning mile. Daniels used the *News and Observer* throughout the 1930s to condemn police brutality against African Americans and to argue for fairer trials.[107] Thirty-two years old when he joined the committee, Daniels represented a new generation of white southern liberals.

The committee published an alternative newspaper, widely available on campus and mailed to a thousand more subscribers. It tracked Herndon's appeals, the Atlanta Red Scare, the Burlington dynamiters' case, and civil rights for labor and African Americans.[108] The committee kept liberals and radicals on the alert to protect free speech. They found an excellent opportunity to do so after an interracial student-labor conference held in Durham, where the keynote speaker was African American James Ford, the Communist candidate for vice president. Professor Eston Ericson, aka Spartacus, gave young Junius Scales a ride to the meeting. Scales, who had grown up in The Intimate, followed the path of least resistance and enrolled in the university. When he realized the banality of his new classmates during freshman orientation, he tried to kill himself. Radical politics held out a lifeline to Scales. The student-labor conference astonished him, and he ate his first integrated meal in the cafeteria of the

Durham Y.[109] Ford appreciated the interracial nature of the meeting, but he also hoped to recruit a "good leading type of comrade in Durham" who was African American. In this he failed.[110]

As black and white students ate together in the integrated cafeteria, Ericson dined with James Ford in his hotel suite. Fred Smethurst, the managing editor of Jonathan Daniels's *News and Observer*, exploded when he heard of Ericson's dinner, even though it did not take place in public. To listen to Ford might be "distinctly creditable," but to eat with him was beyond the pale. As a faculty member at UNC Ericson had "no right to engage in even purely personal practices which offend the spirit of our laws and the conventions of our people," Smethurst argued. Daniels agreed.[111] Ericson countered that he had the right to dine with whom he pleased and that he had acted as an individual, not as a representative of the university. He admitted to being a "Socialist" and told the press that politics never entered his classroom. Alumni called for this "liberal exhibitionist" to be fired since "such an act violated the sensibilities and social traditions of thousands of university alumni and taxpayers." The university, they advised, should conduct a "general house cleaning."[112]

To save Ericson, the Southern Committee for People's Rights blanketed the campus with leaflets repudiating "utterly the doctrine that no white person may eat with a Negro without lowering himself in some way."[113] This simple statement shook the cornerstone of Jim Crow. To Southerners, eating was a familial act, not a public one. Because it embodied both intimacy and equality, those who ate together were practicing social equality. In the minds of some Southerners, that was just one step away from interracial sex. Rupert Vance, a researcher in Odum's IRSS, recalled his mother's pronouncement when she learned that he had dined with black sociologist Charles Johnson: "Well, I've always heard that those that'll eat with them will sleep with them."[114]

The Southern Committee for People's Rights regarded the Ericson case as an issue of "academic freedom" and a chance to "reiterate our fundamental disapproval of racial discrimination." Frank Porter Graham kept mum on the dining incident, but the committee reported that he "continues to uphold the right of a man to govern his own private actions in accordance with his own convictions."[115] Howard K. Beale, Woodward's favorite history professor and one of only two northern-born men teach-

ing history at the college level in the entire South, spoke on academic freedom at a committee event.[116] The committee condemned the *News and
Observer*'s coverage of the Ericson affair but included Jonathan Daniels's
name in the condemnation leaflet as a committee "sponsor." A little irri-
tated, but mostly bemused, by this apparent contradiction, Daniels published an editorial in which he characterized himself as "one apparently
both shot at and shooting from the same gun." However, he insisted "on
the absolute quality of the right of these Chapel Hill peoples to shoot at
him on sight, at will or through the mails." As for Ericson, Daniels
thought that the university should "put no chains on any man's mind. But
neither is the University a sanctuary for folly."[117] Daniels saw two
admirable elements at odds: free speech and civility. To Daniels, Ericson
had foolishly ignored the latter at his own peril.

Unlike the Commission on Interracial Cooperation, which used civility to avoid disruption among its members on the issue of integration, the
Southern Committee for People's Rights saw civility as the grease that
clogged the workings of free speech, hence, of change. The incident
proved to be a turning point for Daniels. Confronted with the novel argument that his commitment to civility stood in the way of free speech and
the committee's uncivil practice of calling the question of his racism, he
began, ever so slowly, to support desegregation.[118]

But the committee did more than simply protect professors. The
Shropshire and Barnes incident illustrates the way in which it tied
together civil liberties violations and African American rights. The grue-
some case bristles with contradictions between New South problems and
Old South remedies. Paul Green called the committee together and told
its members the sordid story so eloquently that Olive Stone remembered
his words for the rest of her life. In 1935, Woodrow Wilson Shropshire
and Robert Barnes had been arrested in Charlotte for drunken driving
and sentenced to four months at the Mecklenburg County prison camp.
Things went from bad to worse for the two black twenty-year-olds. They
were banished from the prison farm to a punishment camp, one for "shov-
eling too slowly," the other for "warming his feet." Chained "spread-eagle
against the bars from sun-up to five-thirty in the afternoon" in a cold
room, their feet swelled. Shropshire's "shoe laces snapped, and 'he came
out of them brogans.' " When they returned from the punishment camp

after twelve days, the prison farm doctor treated them for athlete's foot. After their feet had rotted for another eighteen days, the warden finally sent them to Charlotte's black hospital, where doctors amputated their feet. Five prison officials were indicted. Two of the indictments were dropped, and the remaining three officials were tried and found innocent. All this had taken place in one of North Carolina's most progressive counties. Then the state failed to deliver on its promises of artificial limbs and jobs for Shropshire and Barnes. The Southern Committee for People's Rights refused to let the case die, demanding compensation for the victims and lobbying against the southern chain gang system, which operated out of county prison farms.[119]

While the case represents a continuation of liberal agitation against southern punishment systems—convict leasing or the chain gang—it also marks a subtle new departure in lobbying for the rights of individual prisoners, guilty or not. Paul Green pioneered this approach in the South, and his membership on the National Committee for the Defense of Political Prisoners (NCDPP) signifies that he considered people like Shropshire and Barnes victims of brutally unjust court and incarceration systems.[120] Earlier Green had worked to spare Emmanuel "Spice" Bittings from the electric chair, to which he had been sentenced for the murder of his landlord, an incident that followed the plot of Green's Pulitzer Prize–winning play, *In Abraham's Bosom*.[121] In the Bittings case, life had followed art. Now, with the Shropshire and Barnes cases, art followed life when Green wrote a one-act play, *Hymn to the Rising Sun*, about the horror of the North Carolina chain gang. It became Green's "most frequently performed" play, and he sent the script to legislators, judges, and editors across the region.[122] Four years later Carson McCullers wrote about "Willie and other footless victims of the chain gang" in *The Heart Is a Lonely Hunter*. McCullers argued that her novel was "an ironic parable of Fascism," but critics then and now disputed her claim that it was about Fascism and argued it was about the South instead. No one appears to have considered that McCullers meant to connect the two.[123]

Against a background of anti-Fascism, the Southern Committee for People's Rights connected constitutionally guaranteed civil liberties for all Americans and African American civil rights. The inclusive name People's Rights and the committee's occasional use of the term *human rights* demonstrate its determination to use a new rhetoric in its colorblind defense of liberty. In contrast with CIC members, who sought to work more smoothly within the limits of white supremacy, the Southern Committee for People's Rights sought to overturn white supremacy. "How could you have true race relations," Stone asked, "when one group is not given the ballot, or is in other ways a second-class citizen?"[124] Christian goodwill was not enough. The white paternalism, the interracial conferences, the uplift strategy all represented inadequate attempts to compensate for the simple fact that African Americans lacked equality under the law.

The committee published Stone's survey of "civil rights [violations] in the South" during the years 1934 and 1935. Strikingly, the survey conflated the position of white people and black people as victims of those who abused the Constitution. For example, Part One, "Legal Invasions of Civil Rights," brought together such problems as the requirement of loyalty oaths for public school teachers, prosecution for distributing literature, and the exclusion of African Americans from juries and from party primaries. Political parties, the Supreme Court had recently ruled, were "private or voluntary associations" and could exclude whomever they wished from primaries. Part Two, "Extra-Legal Terrorism and Intimidation," grouped together police brutality, abuses on the chain gang, lynchings, and super-patriot" organizations such as the Black Shirts. Stone's final category, "Legal and Extra-Legal Encroachments upon Right to Organize and to Bargain Collectively," provided an analytical structure through which one could recognize the commonality of the murders during the general textile strike, violence against the black and Communist-led Share Croppers' Union, and the detention of "political prisoners," from Kelly Yale "Red" Hendricks of the Gastonia strike to Angelo Herndon to the Burlington dynamite case defendants.[125] In Stone's analysis, race relations conferences didn't guarantee human rights or protect the innocent. Even the guilty deserved equality before the law and their rights upheld, even in confinement.

The Bankruptcy of the Interracial Cooperation Model

Although Olive Stone understood that it was the southern system that needed fixing, she pursued her PhD in Odum's Sociology Department, where she was taught that it was the southern people who needed fixing; moreover, among them, the black people should get fixed first. "The Odum point of view, I had heard," Stone recalled, "was to discuss more than to act."[126] Odum and Guy Johnson taught courses on "Folk Sociology" and "The Negro," but by then Odum had disavowed the sweeping claims of black inferiority that he had espoused in his 1910 book *Social and Mental Traits of the Negro*. UNC sociologist Rupert Vance recalled that "the further he got, the further he saw that that race psychology business was just foolish determinism."[127] He replaced genetic infallibility with geographically determined cultural authority. By the mid-1930s Odum believed in "group . . . differentials," and "the cumulative power of regional and cultural conditioning." He headed the North Carolina Commission on Interracial Cooperation during the tumultuous period 1933–1937 and became CIC regional president in 1937.[128]

Woodward pronounced Odum's ventures at UNC "the most thriving academic empire in the South," and in 1935 UNC's Sociology Department ranked among the top five in the country. Odum's close links with private foundations and his cautious diplomacy tided his enterprise over the shoals of the Depression. Odum understood himself to be saving the South through liberalism, and he competed with Frank Porter Graham to see, as Vance put it, "who could best establish themselves as leader of the children of light."[129] Odum supervised students and researchers who were more liberal than he on race and labor issues, even as he drew fire from many white Southerners more conservative than he. Yet he cared the most for those conservative white Southerners. As a common farmer from Georgia he understood "why certain people joined the Ku Klux Klan, lynched Negroes, and did other unjust things. . . . But for the Grace of God you or I might be doing these same things. Let us condemn their evil deeds, but still love the people," he told his colleagues.[130]

Because Odum believed that the vast cultural differences between blacks and whites would take decades to change, by the mid-1930s white southern liberals had begun moving too fast for him. He urged caution. "The insistence of many irresponsible ideologists and front-page seekers to force on the South stereotyped reconstruction is bad," he wrote in 1938. "It is because I know and love these millions of common [white] folk in the South that I must stand with them. . . . The Negro question means to them 'For God, for home, and country.' . . . We can do a great deal of harm here."[131]

Odum disdained legal and political challenges to Jim Crow that would force white Southerners to change since he believed that folkways trumped "formally organized society," including government and the law. Without the support of the folk, law could not force social change. Odum tried repeatedly to demonstrate to outsiders the power of white southern folkways. For example, in an article entitled "Lynchings, Fears, and Folkways," he took the viewpoint of a lyncher. After musing that "we" worried that "the Negro" was rising, he wrote: "We struggle with fear and misgivings and rage that we should get into such a fix. And the Negro must pay. And then we are afraid of what we have done. Our conscience is the conscience of a religious people. . . . We have done right and will stand by it and . . . the sacred whiteness of our race." "The Negro must pay," "what we have done," and "it" all are euphemisms for lynching.[132] When Odum explained lynching, he made it seem normal, and his critique remained muted or missing.

As for how those nearly immutable folkways came about in the first place, Odum created a tautological explanation that he called regionalism. He defined regional influence as "both natural and human." Once accreted in a region, folkways calcified into an almost immovable stubbornness, Odum believed.[133] By 1930 Odum said "race prejudice [was] an acquired social attitude," but the fact that racism was learned did not matter much to his politics because it would be generations before white and black Southerners unlearned it. Stone was right when she recalled, "Odum wanted to go slow."[134] Hence regionalism helped Odum explain why the South did *not* change. He used these explanations to attract funding for progressive projects within the South, but one couldn't expect much to change as a result of them. Regionalism would not explain much if the South actually began to change. Odum looked at the present, mistook it for the past, and predicted it to be the future. For his sociology to be of any value, Odum would have to stop history in its tracks.[135] Instead history roared past him in the 1930s.

Fascism alarmed Odum, and he worried that the South was ripe for a dictator. Despite the fact that regionalism was a theory of stasis, Odum declared himself ready to consult with political leaders on a "transitional society between epochs or between crises or between changing cultures." His cautious solution involved bringing such societies back into equilibrium, forcing them to slouch slowly forward.[136] On the Nazis, Odum was as decisive as he ever was: "The folk doesn't necessarily have to win or deserve to win in this contest."[137] It was simply not in Odum to write that the folk must not win, nor deserve to win, this contest, even when the folk were Nazis.

When Odum became the first southern president of the American Sociological Society (ASS, therefore referred to by members as SS) in 1930, his regionalism and gradualism in race relations did not represent all, or even most, sociologists' and anthropologists' views. As early as the 1920s some sociologists had condemned the "racial basis of civilization" as fallacious and identified it as support for the "Nordic doctrine" and the root of Fascism. Franz Boas destabilized the idea that there was a biological basis for race separation and deplored Odum's *Social and Mental Traits of the Negro*. Boas's concept of culture was far more malleable, materially based, and historically contingent than was Odum's.[138]

No incident better illustrates Odum's awkward straddle across the racial breach than one that occurred when James Weldon Johnson, then executive secretary of the NAACP, addressed the UNC Institute of Human Relations in 1927. Jointly planned by students and faculty, the biennial meetings addressed social "problems," such as African Americans and labor rights. Will Alexander had taken it to be a good sign that "college men are thinking and speaking for the new South" and considered Johnson's appearance at the first session "epoch-making."[139] The trouble came when Odum introduced the NAACP secretary to the audience at Memorial Hall as *Mr.* Johnson. To Odum's horror, the chairman of the History Department, J. G. de Roulhac Hamilton, jumped to his feet and stalked out.[140] Jim Crow custom decreed that a white man never "mister" a black man. In history classes, Hamilton spent "much time talking about the inferiority of the Negro," arguing, according to his colleague Guion Johnson, that the Negro's "mind freezes at the age of twelve. And he never develops beyond the age of twelve."[141]

Mr. Johnson ignored the rude clamor and met with small groups of "southern white young men" after his address. He recalled that he "felt a greater desire to win them over than I had felt with any other group I ever talked to," and ultimately, he decided, "I did." As a finale, Johnson addressed an open meeting of students and Chapel Hill residents and read his poem "Go Down, Death." Will Alexander approved of the performance; "art is ultimately more powerful than argument and propaganda." Johnson recalled it as "one of the most interesting episodes in my whole career" and called UNC "the focus of the greatest liberal forces of the state."[142] If James Weldon Johnson appreciated this sort of interracial experience in the early 1930s, as the decade went on, black sociologist Charles Johnson took his place in working with white interracialists "who counsel[ed] time and patience."[143] But Charles Johnson also worked in the New Deal, from which Southerners began to draw new lessons in urgency and activism.

Southern New Dealers Imagine a New South

The New Deal opened up new intellectual and political space for a broad range of Southerners. For example, Will Alexander began to abandon the interracial cooperation model when he went to Washington to serve in the Roosevelt administration. As northern New Dealers began to search for solutions to the Depression, they turned to regional representatives like Alexander and Howard Odum. Many liberal Democrats believed that if the nation was sick, the South was the site of infection. Federal money poured into Odum's Institute for Research in Social Science, beginning with funds for a study on the effects of the Depression in North Carolina and then for fourteen more studies on the South's economic problems.[144] FDR recommended that Frank Porter Graham serve as chairman of the federal Advisory Council on Economic Security, which became the National Conference on Economic Security and influenced the passage of the Social Security Act. Commission on Interracial Cooperation representatives, including Alexander, rushed to Washington to plan "the work of re-habilitation in the South." There they insisted that every New Deal agency "embody in its policies a racial nondiscrimination clause."[145] Clark Howell Foreman of Atlanta went first in 1933. Foreman, who had worked for Will Alexander at the CIC, became special adviser on the economic status of negroes in the U.S. Interior Department. He considered the effects of New Deal programs on black Southerners with an eye to improving the southern economy from the bottom up.[146]

Through a variety of New Deal agencies and philanthropies, money flowed south to fund studies that directly or indirectly blamed segregation for economic problems. So many studies focused on black southern life that one white newspaperman dubbed the process "Porkbarrelensis Africanus." Reports criticized the region's two-tiered, segregated wage system and the rural tenancy and sharecropping that linked Jim Crow and poverty. When the Rockefeller Foundation created the Committee on Negroes in the Economic Reconstruction in 1934, it tapped Charles Johnson and Will Alexander to lead it.[147] They in turn, called on black Chicago sociologist Horace Cayton, back from his tour of Nazi Germany the previous year, to study the National Recovery Act's effect on black industrial workers. They also commissioned Howard Odum's IRSS researchers to conduct a survey of agriculture and tenancy under the Agricultural Adjustment Act. Rural sociologist Arthur Raper summarized their findings this way: "We were saying: Now look here, you're sending down AAA money and . . . these sharecroppers aren't getting it." Repeatedly, white and black Southerners exposed the shortcomings of early New Deal approaches to the region.[148] In 1935 Will Alexander became deputy administrator of the federal Resettlement Administration, which sought to redirect sharecroppers and tenants who had been displaced by the Agricultural Adjustment Act's policy of curbing cotton production.[149] It was one of the most farsighted and radical agencies in the New Deal.

Away from the South and the CIC, Alexander began to blame segregation for the South's economic problems and openly to promote black voting rights. When the Resettlement Administration became the Farm Security Administration, he took heat from both sides of the ideological spectrum. Georgia's Eugene Talmadge called Alexander a Socialist and a Communist interchangeably, at the same time that the Communists called him "fat, aging, soft-looking, stupid, but powerful." They said: "There is nothing to Will Alexander except a soft voice and an oily manner."[150] But this was a misplaced critique that failed to fathom the dynamic changes at work within the old CIC warhorse. The distance between Washington and Atlanta and the challenge of the New Deal liberated Alexander. He no longer had to tiptoe through the minefields of southern race relations. From Washington he began to work against the poll tax and put together an interracial coalition to discuss the "disadvantage to democracy . . . whenever any large number of citizens are excluded from participation."[151]

The flurry of activity was not simply academic or advisory; Southerners wrote New Deal legislation and implemented policy. After IRSS researcher Guy Johnson worked closely with black sociologists Charles Johnson of Fisk and Ira De A. Reid of Atlanta University on the Commission on the Study of the Participation of Negroes in Southern Life, he met with Will Alexander to plan the sale of farms to tenants through federal loans.[152] In 1936, when Will Alexander escorted Secretary of Agriculture Henry Wallace on a southern tour to see firsthand the region's poverty, Wallace was "visibly shocked."[153]

In 1938 Clark Foreman and his southern New Deal allies wrote a report on economic problems in the South that they issued under the signatures of a group of twenty-two southern liberals who were not in government. Frank Porter Graham headed the nongovernmental Advisory Committee on Economic Conditions in the South, whose members ultimately signed the *Report on Economic Conditions of the South*. Franklin Roosevelt was deeply involved in the advisory committee's work and wrote to it: "The South presents right now the Nation's No. 1 economic problem—the Nation's problem, not merely the South's."[154] In a striking departure from southern tradition, the report did not separate economic data by race. The South had to take responsibility for its own problems; it could no longer hide behind its usual excuse, the "Negro Problem."

Moreover, the committee had strong labor representation through Lucy Randolph Mason, the southern organizer for the Committee for Industrial Organization (CIO). "Miss Lucy," of Richmond, Virginia, descended from two signers of the Constitution. "Her name has magic below the Mason and Dixon Line," one supporter announced.[155] A former member of the Richmond Commission on Interracial Cooperation and the National Consumers' League general secretary, Mason accepted a position in 1937 as a southern organizer for the CIO the year after it had been formed by breakaway AFL unions. The CIO planned to organize southern miners, Atlanta automobile workers, tobacco workers, and textile workers. Mason wrote to tell Frank Graham about her new job and asked his thoughts on it. He confided that he believed that industrial democracy represented the next stage of societal evolution and that "collective agreements" between managers and workers were inevitable. Highly regarded by the most liberal forces in the South, Mason had Eleanor's ear and a fast track to Franklin.[156]

The Roosevelts understood the importance of keeping the South in the Democratic Party, and they relied on people like Miss Lucy and Will Alexander to help them do it.[157] Armed with the *Report on Economic Conditions of the South*, Roosevelt marched through Georgia in the summer of 1938. The president deplored the South's "feudal economic system" and boldly attacked the myth of white southern economic paternalism. "When you come down to it, there is little difference between the feudal system and the Fascist system," he declared. "If you believe in the one, you lean to the other."[158] In the heart of Dixie, Roosevelt declared the South "the nation's number one economic problem."[159]

Franklin Delano Roosevelt believed that the Democratic Party's success and the nation's economic health depended on extending more democracy to the South and restructuring its economy. After his reelection in 1936, he tried to pry Democratic political power out of the hands of southern industrialists who thrived on cheap labor, exploited poor whites and African Americans, and held enormous political power. Southern Democratic politicians turned on FDR, arguing that he had allowed "Communists and Socialists and reactionary Republicans to seize control of our party."[160] But poor white people, especially those in rural areas, often supported him. When the American Manufacturers' Association hired a Vanderbilt University professor to brand Roosevelt a Socialist scourge, a farmer rose from the audience and proclaimed: "We're not going to listen to any more of that. We have the only President of the United States that's ever paid a damn bit of attention to what happens to the farmer in all these swings of the cycle, and you're trying to tell us that this is nothing but a dirty Communist trick. We don't believe it."[161]

Howard Odum, who enjoyed New Deal funding and a secure professorship was much more timid than the forceful farmer. His researchers had contributed to the *Report on Economic Conditions of the South*, but Odum himself remained in the background. Careful not to expose himself to criticism, he did not leave his fingerprints on the sometimes radical business of sociology. Arthur Raper, who worked on a study of rural poverty in Georgia, recalled: "Well, Howard Odum, bless his heart,

Howard Odum wanted some things said that he himself didn't want to say, but he wanted somebody else to say them and he would help get the money for us. And then he'd see what the response was."[162]

A decade earlier Communists had seen underpaid black workers and sharecroppers as a reserve proletariat shoring up capitalism; now New Dealers saw their exploitation as a cancer gnawing at capitalism. The black workforce toiled for substandard wages, which brought down southern wages as a whole and reduced consumer spending. Few denied that the poverty of the region's people was part of the national economic problem, even if they argued over how to fix it. Southerners who worked in the New Deal began to espouse a new explanation for white racism, one that slashed through folkways with a slightly Marxist edge: "Racial antagonism was fostered and fed by the low economic level of white as well as Negro people; . . . competition for jobs was increasing this already strong antagonism."[163] Here lay the exposed roots of a strategy that would begin to convince some southern whites that the path to their own economic betterment lay in improving conditions for southern blacks.

By working together on a common problem rather than simply discussing the tensions between them, southern white and African American liberals began to share a true mutual respect that had been too often missing in the approach of the CIC in the 1920s and early 1930s. For example, Will Alexander became a close friend and admirer of Robert C. Weaver, a black economist with a Harvard PhD. The two men worked together in the Farm Security Administration, ate together in the cafeteria, and traveled together. The relationship changed Alexander's life, and from about 1937 on he embraced integration and full civil rights for African Americans.[164]

Guy Johnson, who worked for Howard Odum, changed as well when he began working with Charles Johnson and black Atlanta University sociologist Ira De A. Reid on the Commission on the Study of the Participation of Negroes in Southern Life. Guy Johnson served on the Howard University board and spent a good deal of time touring the South, stopping at black colleges to gather "data." At Fisk, for example, he stayed up "very late" drinking beer with James Weldon Johnson and then set out for Tuskegee via Montgomery, where Olive Stone introduced him to her hospitable study group. Guy told his wife, Guion, "Miss Stone's friends—and they seem to be numerous and Jewish, tho much more entertaining than the gang she had at her house that time—have led us on a fast life."[165]

Until the late 1930s whites conceived of the interracial cooperation model as a sort of floodgate to contain southern racial violence and escalating oppression. In the 1920s that interracial dam stood between black Southerners and the deluge of oppression that disfranchisement, World War I, and the Great Migration had unstopped. Interracial cooperation commissions opened channels of communication, built mutual respect among individuals, and succeeded in condemning lynching and reducing its frequency. In the 1930s those structures continued to hold back the worst of white racial prejudice, but its most liberal practitioners deserted it for varieties of political action that might increase pressure on the system itself. For example, Will Alexander, Clark Foreman, and Guy Johnson turned to the New Deal to force change. Other white moderates, like Howard Odum, continued to believe in incrementalism. Since they saw themselves as more tolerant than other white Southerners, they acted as hydraulic engineers at Jim Crow's watershed. Let a little pressure off the Negro, they would shout to southern whites. Be patient, they would whisper to southern blacks; remember, we are all that stands between you and an ocean of hate. Many white southern moderates were unable to imagine an integrated future in which they would be carried forward with the flow of ideas.

Commission on Interracial Cooperation members had avoided forcing one another to declare their stand on segregation. A few of them—for example, Arthur Raper and Rupert Vance—were integrationists—always. "I can't remember when I thought segregation was good," Raper recalled, "I can't remember ever thinking it was going to last." By 1939 he believed that as long as white Southerners believed in innate differences between people, democracy would be impossible, and he began "working for integration." Others, who had been less certain about where they stood on segregation—for example, Guy and Guion Johnson—saw segregation's end when they went to work for a Swedish sociologist, Gunnar Myrdal, who was studying the "race problem." In 1936 Guy Johnson told participants in the Chapel Hill Institute on Regional Development that integration would be the "simplest and most economical solution."[166] In the late 1930s Will Alexander decided "that this segregation issue had arrived and had to be faced." The CIC was "quietly but definitely allowed to die." The South, as one black Atlantan put it, had spent long enough talking about "the good-will mess."[167] But Howard Odum stayed put, his finger in the dike, never finding it the right time to declare himself in favor of desegregation, as the waters rose.

Integration was born as interracial cooperation collapsed. In 1937 Olive Stone joined Junius Scales and Helen Bryan at the first meeting of the Southern Negro Youth Conference in Richmond, Virginia. The integrated meeting included Communists and liberals. The Communist Party openly promoted it and claimed that it was, "as everybody knows, . . . organized by us." Earl Browder proclaimed: "This in the South—is a new day." More than five hundred attendees called for "free and equal" education, "equal pay for equal work," "the right to vote, to serve on juries," and an end to lynching. [168] Within three months seven thousand had attended Southern Negro Youth Conference meetings across the South.[169]

Interracialism's International Crisis

As some white Southerners moved from interracial cooperation toward advocating black political equality and integration, white South Africans who espoused interracial cooperation moved toward more rigorous segregation. Max Yergan's experience in his adopted country proves that the tangible benefits of the interracial cooperation model depended on larger political and economic forces. The Popular Front in the United States opened new avenues for racial progress, but the same period in South Africa resulted in a white supremacy campaign reminiscent of the U.S. South in the 1890s.[170] Interracial cooperation in South Africa did not slow apartheid; indeed, some black contemporaries argued that it held out a false illusion of progress and thus dissuaded Africans from more radical political change, leaving the door open to apartheid. Although the U.S. South and the Union of South Africa were vastly different places, the comparison is fruitful because the interracial cooperation model shared individual practitioners.

In 1920, 1.5 million Europeans, 170,000 Indians, 500,000 multiracial "coloured" people, and 5 million Africans lived in South Africa. Africans and "Coloureds" voted—for all-white slates—in Natal and the Cape provinces until 1936. The 16 percent of Africans who lived in urban areas did so in strict segregation, initially imposed by executive regulations and then spread throughout the Union by legislation.[171] In 1926, J. B. M. Hertzog, the first Afrikaner nationalist prime minister, began a decade-long campaign to disfranchise, segregate, and control Africans. Europeans began to doubt that they could continue to rule over a growing African majority as it gained "in intellectual and economic power." [172] As in the U.S. South in the 1890s, black success, not black deficiency, helped push whites to solidify their grip on power and to disfranchise and segregate blacks.[173]

In 1921, Thomas Jesse Jones and James Emman Kwegyir Aggrey went to South Africa to establish joint councils modeled on the Commissions on Interracial Cooperation in the U.S. South.[174] Jones, a white man, worked for the U.S.-based Phelps Stokes Fund. Aggrey was an African-born graduate of North Carolina's Livingstone College. When Max Yergan first tried to enter South Africa to take up a position with the international YMCA, government officials had asked Jones if they should let him into the country.[175] Jones warned that African Americans working with the International Y were of two sorts, the "Pan-African Negro with a violent antipathy to cooperation with white people" and the "cooperative type." Certainly, the white YWCA head in Cape Town didn't want any "Martin Garvies" around, since he was already uncomfortable with the Cape Town Garvey chapter.[176] Aggrey finally convinced Jones that Yergan, whom he had known very well from student YMCA years together in North Carolina, was a "cooperative type," and the Union allowed Yergan to enter the county to work "under responsible European supervision."[177]

In December 1921 Yergan arrived in Cape Town, accompanied by his wife, Susie, and their baby son. After two years they moved to the South African Native College in Alice in the Eastern Cape, where Yergan became general secretary of the Bantu Department of the Student Christian Association of South Africa.[178] Most of the students were Xhosa people, whose missionary-educated farming fathers made up the bulk of enfranchised Africans in the Cape Province. Yergan and other black leaders, in keeping with white South African usage of the time, referred to them as "Bantu." The college, known as Fort Hare, was the first tertiary African educational institution below the equator, with a curriculum modeled on British public schools. African students studied under mostly white professors; thus Davidson Don Tengo Jabavu, one of the few African professors, greeted Yergan's arrival in 1922 with "delight."[179] The students saw Yergan as a prophet of modernity and as their diplomat to the Europeans. Because he operated successfully in both the African and European worlds, students called him "the Men of Me."[180]

Yergan used the interracial cooperation model to win European South Africans' respect. The white South Africans had "so much confidence in him that [they] . . . were willing to hear his criticism."[181] Fort Hare's white principal called him "a man of great commonsense, sound learning and real Christian character."[182] Through the leaders of the white Student Christian Movement at Stellenbosch, Yergan spoke to white college students on "the Christian approach to the racial question." The International YMCA characterized Yergan this way: "His cultured personality dispels any doubt that the African people can succeed to higher attainment when given opportunity. His Christian attitude bespeaks the patience of his aggrieved race. His faith in a Christian solution for Africa's distress wins the confidence of both races." [183]

As Yergan's fame grew, he returned to the United States in 1926 to accept the Harmon Award for religious and social service. His admirers exhorted young African American men: "Be like Max Yergan; God wants you to take up that cross and follow him."[184] Mary White Ovington of the NAACP compared Gandhi with Yergan: "Is there any man in that faraway land to emulate Max Yergan? We have heard of but one . . . and he, Gandhi, in old-time parlance would be called a heathen."[185]

Yet even as African Americans and their allies praised the value of uplift and interracial cooperation in Africa, they realized that a black-majority country presented a different kind of challenge from the U.S. South. "Something baneful, malignant, seems to overtake white Christians in those communities where white rules black," Ovington mused. "There is danger in the South African situation."[186] Mulling over his morning paper, James Weldon Johnson came to the same conclusion in 1932: "When India gains restoration of independence and sovereignty, and China has well established central government, the stranglehold which the White Race has held over the whole world will be broken. . . . The white government of South Africa will not be able to stand long."[187] Yergan too realized that he now lived in a black-majority country, where uplift, interracial cooperation, and politics might combust. At an international Y conference in Holland, he noted that "white people had been discussing for years, 'What shall be done with the Negro,' but . . . an African chief recently said, 'What are we to do with the white people?'"[188]

Yergan dreamed of training Africans at Fort Hare to return to their rural homes for "youth work, Christian education, and public health instruction." Until then he did that work himself, traveling at first on horseback and then by Ford throughout the country. As he drove, he began to link evangelization and economics. For example, he argued that if Africans did not get land, they would not become civilized Christians. Yergan established thirty-four YMCAs, with more than three thousand members, which he hoped trained African social workers could take over.[189] In 1929 Fort Hare donated land for a building where students would train in "social service," and John D. Rockefeller, Jr., and the Harlem YMCA provided funds to build a house for the Yergan family.[190]

To win white support for African uplift, Yergan held the Bantu-European Conference in June 1930. This was the interracial seminar that so inspired Helen Bryan as she planned the Swarthmore Institute. Yergan called together almost 300 "Dutch, British and Bantu, old and young, experienced leaders and College Freshmen," what one observer called "a motley crowd," to Fort Hare for a weeklong seminar on race relations.[191] Roughly equal numbers of European and African students filled the auditorium of the brand-new Christian Union Building, broke into small groups in the conference rooms, and worshiped together in the Fort Hare chapel.[192] To European South Africans, Yergan frankly reported it as an "inter-racial" conference, and he suggested it might cure South Africa's "growing spiritual poverty." He hoped it would convince the Europeans that they must reach out to "the whole of mankind" just as Christ had.[193]

The conference's purpose—"to make men know each other better" and "to make them love each other more"—mirrored the core mission of the interracial cooperation movement in the U.S. South.[194] A white conference speaker invoked "the simile of Dr. Aggrey" when he compared African and European students with black and white piano keys that play in harmony. Evening prayers came in four languages: Tamil, Afrikaans, Sesuto, and English. Finally Yergan's friend Dr. Alfred Bitini Xuma spoke on "Bridging the Gap between Black and White."[195] After two segregated meals, the "European students refused to be segregated" any-more.[196] Moreover, conference attendees "enjoyed sport on the playing field together, they sat at Holy Communion together." Yergan thought that the conference marked "the beginning of a new era in the great prob-lem of race relations in Southern Africa."[197] It had allowed participants "to realize that South Africa's all-shadowing problem is a section of a far wider human concern." One European student looked back at it as "the most liberating experience of my life."[198]

Most European South Africans wanted nothing to do with such "liber-ating" experiences or those who organized them. "Some of the criticism has been very adverse," Yergan confided to American benefactor Anson Phelps Stokes. Nonetheless, he added, "We expected this inasmuch as the conference was so extraordinary."[199] What mattered most was the "mere fact that it happened." The attendees were "pioneers" who were left "con-spicuous and exposed," who might be "set upon and pounded unmerci-fully." Yergan still hoped that a vigorous grassroots program might spring from the conference. "Study is not enough," he insisted. "There must be *Service*." He proposed a formal social work school at Fort Hare to train "settlement workers," who would act as uplifters among the Africans, ridding them of their "mass of primitive fears and taboos" but not making the African "dissatisfied with everything in his own back-ground."[200] Yergan foresaw that the social workers would work for the government and that the entire scheme would "raise up a new leadership among Africans."[201]

The last thing that the Union of South Africa wanted was to "raise up a new leadership among Africans." In 1934, after lobbying for the social work training and placement for two years, Yergan had gotten nowhere, and European attitudes toward him had gone from lukewarm to chilly to frosty.[202] When Anson Phelps Stokes gushed about Yergan to the new South African minister to the United States, the minister refused to say a word about Yergan. U.S. philanthropies deemed his social service project "too elaborate and ambitious," worried that its graduates would not get jobs, and refused to fund him. Moreover, Fort Hare officials implied that he had become too big for his britches there since they were "completely in the dark regarding Yergan's schemes."[203]

Worse, whites at Fort Hare began to suspect Yergan of radical political agitation. School officials found on campus a copy of the *Spark*, a Leninist-inspired Workers' Party newspaper. The Workers' Party was a sort of South African Lovestoneite faction, a Communist Party opposition unit. Informants told police that it was Yergan who secretly distributed the paper.[204] He may or may not have been the source of the *Spark* at Fort Hare, but he certainly was not a member of the Workers' Party or the Communist Party of South Africa (CPSA) at that time. The Communist Party of South Africa had been a predominantly white party since 1921 with a membership that rose and fell dramatically. After 1928, African Americans Harry Haywood and William Patterson tried to enforce adherence to the "Native republic" line, the South African equivalent of "self-determination for the black belt," with abysmal results.[205] African American (and Dutch-speaking) Otto Huiswoud visited South Africa on a Comintern mission in 1933 and described the Party there as "practically non-existent."[206] Despite their failure to draw more than a handful of educated Africans, white Communists never stopped trying. Edward Roux set up a tent on a hill above Fort Hare from which he lectured to students in 1934, but he drew no converts. Yergan missed Roux's visit, but about this time he began to read Marxist literature. For example, he once shared Lenin's *The State and Revolution* with a student who was a member of the African National Congress (ANC).[207]

In April 1933 Yergan was back in the United States to accept the NAACP's Spingarn Medal for furthering "interracial understanding among black and white students."[208] He attended the Swarthmore Institute of Race Relations, and he returned to the States the following year as well. That visit should have been a triumph. The NAACP board member Mary White Ovington called Yergan "my dearest friend" and told a large crowd that he represented "the voice of our idealism" abroad.[209] But by 1934 Yergan was no longer an idealist. "This European minority" in South Africa would, he told the NAACP, use "whatever force it has at its command" to retain power in "this hell which exists in South Africa," where race problems were "acute." When he returned to Fort Hare, one student noticed, "he was no longer the Max Yergan we had known—concerned only with church work."[210] Somehow, the student recalled, Yergan had lost his "faith in Christian Theology as a vehicle for social liberation."[211] Politics would become his new religion.

His loss of faith reflected a worsening political situation in South Africa. Hertzog's party maintained power by running on a "black peril" platform, which included pitting the "Coloured" population against the "Black Menace."[212] The Native Acts of 1936, also known as the Hertzog Bills, built on earlier proposals to disfranchise Africans, give them a limited number of "representatives," and increase the tribal "reserves."[213] In the two years leading up to the passage of the Native Acts, white South Africans launched a full-fledged assault on the nominal progress that Africans had made. Yergan had always considered the South African government repressive, but now he began to talk in "extreme terms" about politics.[214]

The proposed Native Acts drove Yergan's friends D. D. T. Jabavu, Dr. A. B. Xuma, and Zachary Matthews to found the All African Convention (AAC) in December 1935. All three had some association with African American education. Jabavu had made his pilgrimage to Tuskegee in 1913, and Xuma had begun in the Tuskegee preparatory school in 1916 and earned a medical degree from Northwestern before returning in 1926 to South Africa. There he served as the vice president of the Johannesburg Joint Council for interracial cooperation.[215] Yergan and Matthews were especially close. He had been Yergan's student at Fort Hare, and during the time that he earned his MA at Yale University in 1933–1934, Yergan was nearby in New York. When Matthews returned to South Africa from New Haven, he joined Yergan at Fort Hare.[216]

Yergan considered the 1936 Native Acts "the last straw" and readily denounced them to white South Africans who asked his opinion, but he also held other Europeans accountable for Africa's plight. The Italian invasion of Ethiopia, two months before the AAC meeting, merely underscored the importance of political rights for black South Africans. Yergan saw the invasion as "one of the clearest demonstrations of the nature and methods of capitalistic imperialism," and he recognized that Italy came late to the game that other European powers had already perfected. The invasion drove home to Yergan the fact that interracial cooperation and Christian uplift did not stop tanks. The battle for Ethiopia represented for him the "last stand in Africa against the octopus of imperialism which has fastened itself upon an entire continent."[217]

Many All African Convention members had been active in the interracial joint councils, but now they lost faith in talk and turned to politics.[218]

Photograph of James Weldon Johnson *(James Weldon Johnson Collection, Yale Collection of American Literature, Beinecke Rare Book and Manuscript Library, Yale University)*

Angelo Herndon *(Tamiment Library, New York University)*

Mollie Lewis Moon in 1956, after her marriage to Henry Lee Moon *(James Weldon Johnson Collection, Yale Collection of American Literature, Beinecke Rare Book and Manuscript Library, Yale University, with permission of the Carl Van Vechten Trust)*

CONTEMPO

*A Review of
Books and Personalities*

Volume 1. Number 13 • Dec. 1, 1931, Chapel Hill, N. C. Ten Cents a Copy

Lynching by Law or by Lustful Mob North and South: Red and Black

By LINCOLN STEFFENS

The first time I heard of the now famous Scottsboro case, the narrator told how those colored boys under sentence saw it. And they saw what they saw of it from a rear car. There was some sort of a row—a scrap—or a fight going on in a car so far ahead that they could get glimpses of it only as the train bent around the curves till, by and by, the train stopped. Then they saw a lot of the fighters jump off that front car and run away. They went up forward to hear more about it.

It was later, when the train arrived at its destination, that those witnesses of the incident, were arrested as the scrappers and—rapists. They were so dazed that they never quite recovered from their frightful astonishment.

But you don't have to go by this casual alibi. Take the record of the trials, the speed of them, the ages of the convicted and the circumstances, and one can realize for himself that there was no justice in these cases. There was the opposite. There was righteousness in it.

In Alabama and some parts of the South the more respectable people are yielding to the Northern clamor against lynching. There is lynching in the North, too, but it is not against blacks. It is against the Reds. And it is not by mobs. It is by the police, the courts and juries; and therefore legal, regular, righteous. The righteous people of the South have been gradually waking up to the idea that they can save their face by taking justice out of the rude hands of the mob and putting it in the delicate hands of the lawyers, and judges and a few representatives of the better people in a jury. That is to say, they can lynch their blacks the way the superior North, West and East get their Reds.

Well, now, you can see that the Alabama righteous must feel the Scottsboro case was a perfect example of the new ideal of justice modelled on the great (anti-) Red North. They had some blacks in a jam where the whites might have wreaked their fear of the colored folk by a

Christ in Alabama
By LANGSTON HUGHES

Christ is a Nigger,
Beaten and black—
O, bare your back.

Mary is His Mother—
Mammy of the South,
Silence your mouth.

God's His Father—
White Master above,
Grant us your love.

Most holy bastard
Of the bleeding mouth:
Nigger Christ
On the cross of the South.

Notes from Nowhere

Langston Hughes, prominent poet and novelist, is soon to be the guest of the editors of CONTEMPO * * * Phillips Russell, of historical and literary biography fame, recently married Cara Mae

Southern Gentlemen, White Prostitutes, Mill-Owners, and Negroes

By LANGSTON HUGHES

If the 9 Scottsboro boys die, the South ought to be ashamed of itself—but the 12 million Negroes in America ought to be more ashamed than the South. Maybe it's against the law to print the transcripts of trials from a State court. I don't know. If not, every Negro paper in this country ought to immediately publish the official records of the Scottsboro cases so that both whites and blacks might see at a glance to what absurd farces an Alabama court can descend. (Or should I say an American court?) . . . The 9 boys in Kilbee Prison are Americans. 12 million Negroes are Americans, too. (And many of them far too light in color to be called Negroes, except by liars.) The judge and the jury at Scottsboro, and the governor of Alabama, are Americans. Therefore, for the sake of American justice, (if there is any) and for the honor of Southern gentlemen, (if there ever were any) let the South rise up in press and pulpit, home and school, Senate Chambers and Rotary Clubs, and petition the freedom of the dumb young blacks—so indiscreet as to travel, unwittingly, on the same freight train with two white prostitutes . . . And, incidently, let the mill-owners of Huntsville begin to pay their women decent wages so they won't need to be prostitutes. And let the sensible citizens of Alabama (if there are any) supply schools for the black populace of their state, (and for the half-black, too—the mulatto children of the Southern gentlemen. [I reckon they're gentlemen.]) so the Negroes won't be so dumb again . . . But back to the dark millions—black and half-black, brown and yellow, with a gang of white fore-parents—like me. If these 12 million Negro Americans don't raise such a howl that the doors of Kilbee Prison shake until the 9 youngsters come out, (and I don't mean a police howl, either) then let Dixie justice (blind and syphilitic as it may be) take its course, and let Alabama's Southern gentlemen amuse themselves burning 9 young black boys till they're dead in the State's electric chair. And let the mill-own-

---

LEFT: Photograph of Frank Porter Graham in the 1940s by Bayard Wooten *(Frank Porter Graham Papers, Southern Historical Collection, University of North Carolina at Chapel Hill)*

BELOW: From left, unidentified, Milton Abernathy, Paul Green, and Anthony Buttitta, around 1932 *(Paul Green Papers, Southern Historical Collection, University of North Carolina at Chapel Hill)*

Howard Odum standing in front of a poor white folks' cabin beside a lonesome pine *(Howard Washington Odum Papers, Southern Historical Collection, University of North Carolina at Chapel Hill)*

Olive Stone picnicking on the
Dnieper River in Russia, 1931
*(Olive Matthews Stone Papers,
Southern Historical Collection,
University of North Carolina
at Chapel Hill)*

Will Alexander as a young man
*(Robert W. Woodruff Library,
Atlanta University Center, Archives
and Special Collections)*

Robert George Fitzgerald and Cornelia Smith Fitzgerald, Pauli Murray's grandparents
(The Schlesinger Library, Radcliffe Institute, Harvard University)

Pauline Dame and Pauli Murray in the late 1920s at home in Durham
(The Schlesinger Library, Radcliffe Institute, Harvard University)

Africans had been fooled by interracial cooperation, the AAC argued. "The stage seemed set for revolt against White domination, when Dr. Aggrey came in 1921 and advocated co-operation," the AAC recalled. Africans had followed the cooperation model, but "Bantu-European movements . . . to promote smooth race relations . . . [have] been offset by oft recurring repressive legislation and unjust Social acts."[219] First and foremost, the AAC would work to preserve and expand the right to vote and "protest against the principle of segregation implied in the . . . Natives Bill." In segregation's place, the AAC advocated African ownership, uplift, and political power. The interracial cooperation of the past fifteen years had amounted to nothing: "The pendulum has swung right back to where it stood in 1920,"[220] Xuma thought, "Politically, the cloud is heavy and dark. There is a storm ahead." The convention resolved to "sever all connection" with "European institutions, religiously, socially, culturally and economically," and to "refuse to submit to any laws, regulations or other legal authority inimical and opposed to the best interests" of Africans.[221]

As his closest friends entered politics, Yergan began to question his future. He had believed interracial cooperation would result in improvement of Africans' status, but now he realized that South Africa would always follow "the theory and practice of imperialism."[222] Since he was an alien, Yergan could be deported if he took a leadership role in the AAC. Xuma tried to convince Yergan to stay in South Africa, suggesting that he could still "be in the theatre, perhaps not as the star actor, but . . . as a coach or stage manager."[223] However, on Yergan's next visit to the United States, he openly condemned the government of South Africa and imperialism at the annual meeting of a new organization, the National Negro Congress. He had already decided to leave both South Africa and the YMCA, and he used the 1936 trip to find a new home in the United States.[224]

He may well have found a new intellectual home as well, the Communist Party. Six months earlier Yergan's growing radicalism had troubled Xuma, who had cautioned him against "extreme action" that might "victimize the African" and curtail African American travel to the Soviet Union.[225] Yergan understood. He resigned from the YMCA as he sailed out of New York in early March 1936. He resigned because "the Government of South Africa . . . is quite definitely committed to a policy which is destructive of any real growth among Africans." Yergan did not want to run "the risk of possibly embarrassing the [YMCA] International Committee" by speaking out on politics.[226]

As he cut his ties with the Christian Social Gospel, he sailed for Africa via Europe and the Soviet Union, where his contacts belied his characterization of himself as a "tourist." He took along the names of three African Americans in Moscow, William Patterson, Homer Smith, and Lovett Fort-Whiteman, who, unbeknownst to Yergan, was already in exile by then. He met with Red International Labor Union chief Solomon Abramovich Lozovsky, who had spent years tracking labor issues in Africa and the American South. Yergan found himself "naively amazed at his detailed grasp of facts about social and educational conditions in Rhodesia and the Union of South Africa." He finally arrived in South Africa in mid-April 1936.[227]

Eslanda Robeson, Paul Robeson's wife, visited six weeks later, as the Yergan family prepared to leave for the United States.[228] Eslanda Robeson and the Yergans stayed up many nights talking about "the political position of the Negro and the African, and what could be done to improve it." Yergan worried about the Fascist invasion of Ethiopia, the League of Nations' weak response, and the horrific possibility that Germany's African colonies might revert to the Nazis. Eslanda remembered that she and Max talked "big talk, challenging ideas, enthralling discussion. . . . The walls of our world moved outward, and we caught a glimpse of things in the large." They found hope in the Soviet Union, where, they believed, there was no racism.[229]

The Yergans sailed out of Africa in August 1936, just before the governor-general began an investigation into Max's activities. The South African police closed in on Fort Hare, and its principal proclaimed Yergan an agitator, possibly a Communist. The head of the Cape Town Institute for Race Relations, a white man who had torpedoed Yergan's social work school, called him embittered.[230] Yergan was more than embittered; he was radicalized, and he returned to New York to support the AAC as an outside agitator, "Secretary for External Relations for the All African Convention" and organizer of the International Committee on African Affairs. From New York he hoped to help Africans establish a counterpart to Gandhi's cooperative movement to send freedom fighters to South Africa.[231] Xuma loved the idea. For his part, Yergan sailed with "no regrets."[232]

Christian faith had lifted Max Yergan out of Raleigh, North Carolina, whisked him through Europe and India, and set him down in Africa. It inspired him to believe that Christian people could settle their differences peacefully, outside politics, among themselves, if only they came to know one another. Nestled within the interracial cooperation model for twenty years, Yergan had counted on the power of uplift, person-to-person contact, and Christian goodwill. Yet all the classes, the conferences, the evenings in the Y huts along the lines of four continents came to naught before white supremacy's relentless regeneration.

For Yergan, it was déjà vu all over again. What he had witnessed as a child—for example, the day when Pullen Park in Raleigh was suddenly closed to little black girls and boys, or the morning his grandfather went to the polls, as he had many times before, and came back distraught because the registrar prevented him from casting his vote, or the time white women quit ordering dresses from his mother, forcing her to start cleaning their houses—he saw happening again in South Africa in the mid-1930s. The last time he had escaped to Africa. This time he escaped to America.

On July 4, 1936, as Angelo Herndon addressed the American Youth Congress, as Jesse Owens made the U.S. Olympic team, and as Eslanda Robeson and Max Yergan enjoyed bracing conversations in the cool Fort Hare winter, folks in Charleston, South Carolina, sat on their verandas, listening to the whir of their ceiling fans straining against a muggy summer morning. If any white South Carolinians worried on this Fourth of July that the defenders of democracy had taken the day off, their fears must have been assuaged by an editorial in the morning newspaper, "The South and South Africa." The editor believed that South Carolina's 45 percent black population put the state's white people in a position "almost identical with that of the English and the Dutch in the South African Union."[233] South African democracy, readers learned, should serve as a model for South Carolina.

The editor argued that the northern Republicans or Democrats who demanded the enfranchisement of black southern voters courted disaster. Politics in the South bore no resemblance to politics in the North; rather, it resembled the South African political situation. If either party toyed with the southern black vote as a factor in national elections, it risked everything. "It is as if two political parties in England, in order to carry elections at home, tried to compel the white people in the South African Union, an English dominion, to admit a million Negroes to vote in South African elections—which, obviously, would be disastrous to the civilization of the white people, English and Dutch, in South Africa."[234] Max Yergan would have thought, "Exactly!" had he read the piece. By the following Fourth of July he was back in the States—back home—fighting to ensure that black people in South Africa and South Carolina won equality. "There is no longer any such place as 'far away,' " Yergan once wrote. "The world has become a neighborhood. . . . It must by the same token become a brotherhood."[235]

If Yergan had stayed on for three more years at Fort Hare, he would have encountered a new generation of activists. Oliver Tambo and Nelson Mandela, bright and energetic students, tried to form a student council at Fort Hare, encouraged by their favorite teacher, Yalie Zachary Matthews. They got expelled for their efforts. A. B. Xuma, by then president of the African National Congress, welcomed them into his organization and encouraged them to start a student group within it.[236] Theirs would be a struggle first for power. Understanding would follow.

An anti-Fascist Left moved the U.S. South from the status quo of interracial cooperation to more radical political action in the late 1930s. Even then, it took a nonviolent civil rights movement and twenty-five years to pass the Civil Rights Act of 1964. An antidemocratic Right moved South Africa away from interracial cooperation to the total political exclusion of Africans. In that case it took "armed struggle" and fifty-five years to elect Nelson Mandela, Fort Hare alumnus, president of South Africa.[237]

6

IMAGINING INTEGRATION

By the late 1930s some of the South's prodigal sons and daughters had begun to wish they were in Dixie. Away, where they had ventured to imbibe radical politics and searched for racial equality, just never felt like home. They had left under varying degrees of duress to find a safe space, to find a place where they, not Jim Crow, charted their futures. Since Jim Crow was crazy—the kind of madman who lynched black men and women; the kind of madman who dictated where people could or could not sit down—they searched for a politics that diagnosed the South's psychosis and prescribed remedies. For some, that remedy was Communism; for others, work in New Deal agencies; for still others, seminars on interracial cooperation; for many in the NAACP, it was litigation.

To this shifting Dixieland, southern expatriates returned to take their stand. Their calculus of change gave them hope that Dixie was dying, and their heartstrings, stretched, but never snapped, over years of exile, now contracted to draw them back to the heart's home. The South was changing. Popular Front projects, incremental legal victories, and a wave of tolerance born in anti-Fascism and nourished by Communist challenges to white supremacy all harmonized to sound a call to home. To expatriate radical Southerners like Pauli Murray, a native black North Carolinian, it seemed as if the time were right to demand full citizenship on her own ground.

Howard Odum must have felt like Job when Murray applied to enter the University of North Carolina in late 1938 to get an MA in social work in the department that he chaired. No one, he thought, had done more for the Negro than he had. Despite that, he was being challenged on his home ground only a year after becoming the secretary of the regional Commission on Interracial Cooperation.[1] No doubt he thought it would have been better if Murray had wanted a graduate degree in history. Then she would have had to contend with a real southern conservative like J. G. de Roulhac Hamilton, who might have told her that her mind had frozen at age twelve. At that point Odum could have rushed in, explained the conflict, lamented southern white folkways, and advised Murray that the time was not right. But Murray thought it was the right time. The late 1930s offered a propitious moment to challenge educational segregation, particularly at the graduate level, where the absence of black graduate programs and professional schools in many states defied *Plessy v. Ferguson*'s mandate for equal institutions.

Pauli Murray's attempt to desegregate UNC provides deep local context for the NAACP's national litigation campaign against educational inequality, the practical effects of anti-Fascist ideology, and the southern Left's influence on its home ground. African American comparisons of the U.S. South with Hitler's Germany became a wedge that Murray hammered into segregation's increasingly visible cracks. By challenging segregation at the most liberal of southern state universities, Murray held up the fearsome Fascist mirror to the fairest of them all. When we look forward, we see that her case demonstrates the strengths and weaknesses of the NAACP litigation strategy that culminated a decade and a half later in *Brown v. Board of Education*.

By 1939 Jim Crow had begun to totter before the bench, foreshadowing his fall in *Brown*. When the NAACP's challenge to segregation in the courts ultimately prevailed before the Supreme Court in 1954, it produced a backlash of massive resistance among white Southerners. There was an opportunity cost as well: The NAACP's incremental cautiousness in the 1930s meant that the association had to forgo grassroots organizing and campaigns for economic justice. Moreover, it had to proffer model plaintiffs, rather than argue more broadly for integration as a civil right.[2] The campaign to desegregate graduate and professional education was a formidable challenge to the status quo, but it was not the only challenge or the most comprehensive available. It limited participation on the local level, and it meant that only middle-class African Americans could participate at all.

Moreover, the association proceeded extremely slowly and carefully, confining itself to cherry-picked lawsuits that did not directly challenge *Plessy v. Ferguson* but rather would force southern states to live up to the "equal" part of segregation. It paced itself to nudge, rather than shove, the white public along because many Americans believed that people could not be forced by law to do something that betrayed their value system. If the NAACP moved too quickly and outdistanced moderate white southern opinion, there might be a race war, black and white Southerners cautioned. Nonetheless, the NAACP's emphasis on legal gradualism contained and limited protest, even as it made civil rights law.

This is not to blame the victim; it is to see the association's legal campaign as one of many civil rights campaigns at the time. The NAACP chose litigation as a practical allocation of resources; yet those who seek to understand the mechanisms of social change must evaluate that choice as historically contingent. The association opted to move against educational discrimination at the graduate level because of the expense that southern states would have to incur to make such specialized training equal and because the question of "social equality"—sex—was less charged with adult graduate students than with elementary school children. Moreover, it chose to litigate in the field of education, rather than housing, public accommodation, or economic opportunity, because the inequality proscribed by *Plessy* was most easily proved in that realm. It began their campaign in the border states because it planned to pick off the weakest among its opposition one by one.[3] The circumscribed and careful NAACP strategy makes clear that the association expected a decades-long struggle, of which educational litigation would be only a part.

World War II interrupted that strategy, so that instead of coming in the late 1930s at the high tide of a vibrant Left, *Brown v. Board of Education* came during the Cold War as that Left was under attack and in disarray. Its timing limited its effect. Without strong help on the ground from liberal Southerners, the case had to carry the weight of desegregating education as well as realizing the hopes of equality in many other facets of

American life. *Brown's* context was not the 1930s milieu of interracial unionism, interfaith organizing against discrimination, actions for economic empowerment, unprecedented federal influence on the workings of state governments, and an anti-Fascist climate. Instead, *Brown* was born in a period of anti-Communist hysteria and conformity that stunted its strength.

North Carolina's Daughter

When Pauli Murray launched a one-woman war against segregation at the University of North Carolina, she did not want to begin a decades-long struggle; she wanted to enter UNC at once. Aware of the historical moment and her place in it, she thought she would succeed. Combining the local and the global, she appealed to black and white power brokers on her home court, even as she threatened them with comparisons with Fascists and pressured them to conform to national and international discourses on tolerance. As a member of a radical new generation of African Americans trained as labor activists, Murray used the heat of the Popular Front to melt the gradualism of moderate whites and penetrate regional isolation. She recognized a spectrum of white opinion on segregation, and she planned to use it to her advantage.[4]

When she applied to the University of North Carolina in late 1938, Murray was twenty-eight years old, the great-great-granddaughter of James Strudwick Smith, one of antebellum North Carolina's foremost white men and a trustee of the University of North Carolina.[5] In the early 1840s his sons, Sidney, a lawyer, and Frank, a doctor, graduated from UNC and prepared to follow in his footsteps.[6] Then, one night, Sidney forced his way into their slave's cabin and raped her. Frank heard her screams, jumped on his brother, and beat him savagely, crippling him for life. Nine months later, in 1844, the slave, Harriet, gave birth to a light-skinned baby girl, Cornelia Smith.[7] If Frank acted out of outrage, he may also have acted out of jealousy. Harriet bore Frank three daughters in the decade that followed.

All this took place under James Smith's nose, and he seems to have done only one thing to protect Harriet and his four enslaved grandchildren. Around 1846 he sold them to his daughter Mary, thus voiding Frank or Sidney's claims to them upon his death.[8] And he moved the whole big messy family out into the country, three miles south of Chapel Hill.[9] Although Sidney ceded Frank's possession of Harriet and never touched her again, he flaunted the fact that Cornelia was his child. She played in his study and sat on his lap. He taught her to read. He practiced his legal arguments on her, and she lit his pipe for him. A lifetime later she referred to him as "my father, Lawyer Sidney Smith," and a "remembered joy shone in her eyes" when she talked about him. Harriet, Frank, and Mary hated Sidney; to them he was a cruel drunkard. The only person who ever loved him was his slave daughter.[10]

Mary assumed authority over Harriet and her children, and her northern governess stayed on to tutor the "black" Smiths, although that act violated the state law against teaching slaves to read or write. On Sunday mornings Mary gathered Harriet and the children into the family buggy and drove them to services at the Episcopalian Chapel of the Cross, on the campus of the University of North Carolina. There they sat in the slave balcony overlooking their white relatives, and there Harriet's children were baptized in 1854.[11]

When emancipation came at the end of the Civil War, the African American Smiths stayed put. In 1869 Cornelia married Robert George Fitzgerald, a young man of mixed racial background from Pennsylvania who had come south as a teacher. Mary Smith died in 1885, leaving most of her estate to the Episcopal Church and the University of North Carolina. She also left each niece $150 and deeded each of them one hundred acres. Thus Mary gave her black relatives a start in life, but not such a generous start that they might rise above their station. They were the only living Smiths, but they were not white Smiths, a fact that Mary's meager legacy reminded them of even from the grave.[12]

Cornelia and Robert Fitzgerald were Pauli Murray's grandparents. Born in 1910, she was young when her mother died, so she went to live with the Fitzgeralds and another of Cornelia's children, Pauline Fitzgerald Dame, in Durham, North Carolina. Pauli called Dame Mother, and Dame legally adopted her in 1919.[13] In the 1910s and 1920s Durham was a fast-growing town, home to a fledging black middle class and a large black working class in the tobacco industry. The Fitzgeralds and Dames were considered middle class, and Pauline Dame was a much-respected elementary school teacher. But Robert Fitzgerald had gone blind, and the family lived among those Murray termed the "respectable poor."[14]

While Dame bustled about between teaching and her beloved Episcopal church work, little Pauli rocked on the front porch, listening to her grandparents tell stories that made slavery, the Civil War, and emancipation seem close at hand. At night Cornelia barricaded the doors and yelled out her bedroom window at a ghost Klan that haunted her dreams. A new Klan, born in 1915 in Atlanta, haunted young Pauli. If Cornelia had witnessed violence, Pauli felt only the brush of its wings; "news of lynchings . . . , frequently unreported in the newspapers, traveled by word of mouth."[15] Cornelia may have sat on her white daddy's lap and lit his pipe, but segregation was ubiquitous for Pauli. She knew nothing else: "It's something you simply grow up with. It's not something that you suddenly experience." Black passengers were barred from city buses in Durham until 1930, when the Commission on Interracial Cooperation sued for the right for African Americans to ride, albeit at the back. Judge Maurice Victor Barnhill, who had presided over the trial of the Gastonia defendants, ruled in the CIC's favor.[16]

Murray protested even then; she walked all over Durham rather than take her seat at the rear of the bus.[17] Murray loathed Jim Crow as much for its repression of the soul as for its repression of the body. When she graduated from Hillside High School, her class prophecy predicted that she would study law.[18] But Murray was sure of only one thing: "I hated segregation so that all I wanted to do was to get away from segregation."[19] She left for New York, hoping to enter college, but was astonished to discover that northern states required twelve, not eleven, years of secondary school. Living with relatives in the city, Murray took another year at an integrated high school and then enrolled in Hunter College. Perhaps prompted by her poverty, Murray eloped with a young man, William Roy Wynn, while at Hunter. Before the honeymoon ended, they both realized the marriage had been a colossal mistake and separated at once.[20]

In the spring of 1932 a friend, probably Mildred Jones, urged Murray to take off for the USSR as a cast member in the movie *Black and White*. Murray simply couldn't afford to leave school or her part-time jobs, and she forever regretted that she didn't go. Graduating from Hunter in 1933, Murray emerged into a city in the grip of the Great Depression and into a

Harlem alive with radical politics and the arts.[21] When Mildred Jones returned from Moscow, she introduced Murray to fellow cast member Dorothy West, who had decided to start a magazine of the Harlem Renaissance, *Challenge*. Murray's poem, "Song," appeared in the first issue, along with West's account of her sojourn in Moscow, "A Room in Red Square."[22] Murray knew Langston Hughes and Countee Cullen, who encouraged her to write.[23] Her poems were not her best writing. She was to find her formidable literary voice much later in autobiography.

Hustling about, doing odd jobs while writing, Murray won a spot at the federally funded Camp TERA (Temporary Emergency Relief Administration) in 1934. Camp TERA, in beautiful Bear Mountain, New York, fifty miles from New York City, was a residential workers' camp. Eleanor Roosevelt's brainchild, the camps were her answer to the all-male Civilian Conservation Corps (CCC). The idea of women's worker camps unsettled some because of gender—they called them the She-She-She camps—and others because of class. For example, the American Legion accused Camp TERA of being a Communist breeding ground because campers sang "The Internationale."[24] Murray spent her time reading *Das Kapital* and helping her roommate fire off politically charged letters to Eleanor Roosevelt, who served on the camp's board. Then one day Roosevelt visited Camp TERA in person. As ER walked through the large hall, the campers stood up, but Murray, in an inchoate rebellious gesture, remain seated, reading a newspaper. Her direct action, coupled with the camp administration's discovery of *Kapital* in her room, earned her expulsion.[25]

Murray recalled that she "left Camp TERA, determined to educate myself on communism and find out why communists were so hated and feared." Not the first Communist who went out and became one because others accused her of being one, early in 1936 Murray joined Jay Lovestone's Communist Party (Opposition) (CPO), instead of the Communist Party (CPUSA), in part because she found the CP line of self-determination for the Black Belt a bizarre form of segregation. Despite its name, the CPO did not oppose Communism itself; rather, it opposed those in power in the CPUSA. Founded by Lovestone after Stalin had deposed him, the CPO saw itself as the "real" Communist Party. Murray took a workers' education course taught by Lovestone himself.[26]

In 1936 Murray landed a teaching job in the Works Progress Administration (WPA). She began by teaching reading to immigrant children but soon won a transfer to a workers' evening education project based in Harlem. There she found herself working under the direction of fellow North Carolinian Ella Baker, who also belonged to the CPO and who later became a renowned civil rights leader.[27] At YWCAs and union halls, Murray taught everything from "The Background of the Negro Problem" to "Fascism and Racial Prejudice," in which she discussed the "Nazi treatment of the Jews" and "The Negro and the Jew."[28]

The next year Murray took a leave from the WPA to attend the Brookwood Labor College in Katonah, New York.[29] Brookwood accepted leftist workers and union members and allotted two spots to CPO members. Brookwood aimed to turn out labor leaders well grounded in the history of oppression.[30] The school was a microcosm of organizing: Students joined a local picket line, and two men joined the Abraham Lincoln Brigade to fight against Fascism in the Spanish Civil War.[31] For her part, Murray argued for "a woman on the faculty." But being a student in remote Katonah did not suit Murray, and she went into the city as often as possible. The school, in its last months of operation, rippled with petty academic politics; ultimately Murray dropped out. Still, she regarded the experience as beneficial. Later, she recalled, "the study of economic oppression led me to realize that Negroes were not alone but were part of an unending struggle for human dignity the world over." [32]

By November 1938 Murray was standing at a crossroads. Although she returned to the WPA, terms of employment in the agency limited contracts to eighteen months, and the agency itself might close sooner. Moreover, she had come to see the Communist Party Opposition as dogmatic and ineffectual, and that month, prompted in part by a turn toward home, she resigned.[33] The CPO had no presence in the South, and her membership in it would impede her new plan. Pressed for money and homesick for her family, she decided to apply to the graduate program in social work at UNC, headed by Howard Odum. Despite the clear need for black social workers in the South, only Atlanta University trained African Americans for secular social work. UNC constituted North Carolina's sole graduate program in social work, and only whites could be admitted.

Disillusioned with Marxism, increasingly anti-Fascist, and homesick, Murray believed that the time was ripe to challenge segregation and that she had a historical role to play in the assault. She pointed to "the inescapable parallel between Nazi treatment of Jews in German and the repression of Negroes in the American South." Moreover, she "became convinced that the alternative to communism was a democracy that could be made to work for all its people, including Negroes." Murray mused: "It seems to me that the testing ground of democracy and Christianity in the United States is in the South." [34]

Storming the Ivory Tower

Three court challenges had already opened the way for Pauli Murray's application. In 1933 Thomas Raymond Hocutt, a friend of hers, sued North Carolina for admission to the UNC pharmacy school. [35] Then Donald Gaines Murray sued Maryland to be admitted into its law school, and finally Lloyd Lionel Gaines sued Missouri to enter its law school. Despite the profusion of Gaines and Murray surnames, the plaintiffs were not related to one another. At first, after the NAACP had won a hundred-thousand-dollar grant in 1930 to challenge segregation, it planned to file lawsuits simultaneously in several states. It even set out to enlist its white southern allies in the cause; for example, NAACP secretary Walter White asked Paul Green for support. But the litigation plan had languished, a victim of the Depression and NAACP infighting over priorities. [36]

Action meanwhile started at the local level. "A group of young Negroes in the city of Durham have been planning for some time to test the constitutionality of the practice of excluding colored youth from the professional schools of the University of North Carolina," attorneys Conrad Pearson and Cecil McCoy wrote to White in February 1933. Pearson had just returned to Durham from Howard Law School, where he studied under NAACP attorneys Charles Hamilton Houston and William Hastie. Pearson and McCoy wrote to ask White for permission to solicit the state's NAACP branches for funds and to get his suggestions on how to proceed. [37] White wrote back at once to congratulate them on their "initiative." They made plans for Thomas Hocutt, a graduate of the North Carolina College for Negroes (NCC), to apply to the pharmacy school at the University of North Carolina. [38]

To accomplish anything at all in Durham, they needed more than a collection and initiative; they needed the support of Charles Clinton "C. C." Spaulding, the president of the North Carolina Mutual Life Insurance Company and the wealthiest and most influential black man in the state. Initially Spaulding backed them 100 percent. He commended the young attorneys to White, promised to raise the money for the case, and quickly became deeply involved in case strategy.[39] But one NAACP chapter president warned: "As for C. C. Spaulding, he is not worth . . . a tinkers damn [sic] for fighting purposes."[40]

The black president of NCC, James Shepard, meanwhile sought to protect and increase state funding for his segregated college by thwarting the lawsuit. He leaked Hocutt's challenge to the press and produced a firestorm of reaction that caused Spaulding to beat a retreat. Spaulding urged Pearson and McCoy to drop the matter and forced the Durham NAACP branch to withdraw its support.[41] He undermined the suit behind the scenes but was careful to avoid speaking publicly against it because he knew that would cost him the support of the "younger element of Negroes . . . [who] think the older Negroes represent the servile type." Spaulding and Shepard turned the Hocutt threat into an opportunity to lobby the General Assembly to appropriate funds for a black graduate school at NCC.[42]

The NAACP stood up to Spaulding and Shepard: "Certain types of Negroes are doing all they can to hurt the case, as these types always do, by 'Uncle Tom-ing' and writing letters to the papers saying they are pleased with what the white folks are doing for them and that only the 'radical' young Negroes are for the case." But Pearson and McCoy found themselves cast out of the black Durham establishment. By the time that the NAACP dispatched William Hastie, a former Howard professor then earning his doctorate at Harvard Law School, the local lawyers were awfully glad to see him.[43]

Hocutt had been one of a handful of male students at Hillside High with Pauli Murray.[44] Southern African American men knew that few "black" jobs required a high school degree, and most had little chance of attending college. But with a high school diploma, Hillside women could work in the offices of Durham's black-owned businesses or land teaching positions. Hocutt did go to college and graduated from NCC with a B average. He wanted to become a pharmacist, but segregated UNC offered the only pharmacy program in the state. Moreover, pharmacy was an undergraduate program. If he had been a white man, he could have been admitted into it straight from high school. Louis Austin, editor of the *Carolina Times*, went with Pearson and McCoy to help Hocutt enroll at UNC, but the registrar refused him.[45]

Hastie traveled to North Carolina to help Pearson and McCoy try the case before Superior Court Judge Barnhill, who had presided over the Gastonia trial and ordered Durham buses to admit black riders.[46] The university's refusal to accept Hocutt violated his rights under the Fourteenth Amendment and the Constitution of North Carolina, the attorneys argued, and they sought a writ of mandamus ordering his admission. In keeping with the Supreme Court's *Plessy* decision, the North Carolina Constitution mandated a segregated public school system, even as it prohibited "discrimination in favor of, or to the prejudice of either race."[47]

The state's attorneys presented a phantasmagoria of precedents to prove that equal did not mean same; in fact, it did not even mean equal. No consolidated school for "colored children" in Mississippi? Well, that didn't mean there couldn't be one for white children.[48] Had it been all right to suspend that "colored" high school in Georgia in hard times but to continue funding the white one? Certainly, since the suspension was only temporary.[49] Was it constitutional to build a new school for white children in North Carolina while leaving black children in a shack? Sure, they had a building, didn't they?[50] Moreover, the state argued that the court could not order an individual to be admitted to the university; it could only order the university not to discriminate, as, of course, it was not doing, because the state did provide a "general and uniform system of public schools." In 1933 North Carolina could confidently argue that equal meant comparable only in the most expansive terms.

In a courtroom packed "like a sardine box," almost every black and white lawyer in town watched the March 1933 trial. Hastie's performance took everyone's breath away. Judge Barnhill kept sustaining his objections, and at one point a white lawyer in the audience jumped up, shook Hastie's hand, and congratulated him on his skill. Even the dean of the UNC law school commended Hastie's "brilliant presentation of the case" to UNC president Frank Graham.[51] On a courtroom break, Hastie cabled Walter White: "Getting money's worth. Town agog. Community less hostile than anticipated. . . . Incalculable good done whatever the outcome."[52] When the state attorney general argued, "I think there is a deep motive behind this suit and that that motive is that this 'Nigra' wants to associate with white people," the whites sat quiet and stony-faced, but the African Americans broke out in such "loud, derisive" laughter that Barnhill had to pound his gavel for order.[53]

Despite Hastie's skill, NCC's black president, James Shepard, proved an insurmountable obstacle. He simply refused to release Hocutt's college transcript to UNC, rendering his application incomplete. The only person willing to testify on Hocutt's qualifications was his high school principal, probably because he was attorney Pearson's uncle. But Hocutt had not done very well in high school.[54]

Judge Barnhill ruled that the plaintiff had sought improper relief. He could not order the university to *admit* an individual; he could only order the university to *consider* an applicant without regard to the fact that he "was of African descent."[55] Further, he found that Hocutt's application was incomplete without the transcript. But the judge admonished the state that the university had never considered Hocutt's application in "good faith" because he was a "person of African descent." Moreover, he stated flatly that "so long as the State fails to provide equal opportunity for training," it had a "duty" to "admit persons of African descent as students in the professional schools." Moreover, "if and when" another person of African descent applied, this case should not stand in the way.[56] "Person of African descent," "if and when," "duty to admit," "so long as the State fails": Even as he rejected Hocutt's claim, Barnhill lent it legitimacy. The judge privately told Walter White that Hastie had delivered "one of the most brilliantly argued trials in [my] . . . twenty-two years on the bench."[57]

White soon visited North Carolina, met with Frank Porter Graham, and revealed that the NAACP was considering filing another suit on Hocutt's behalf. White reported to James Weldon Johnson that *Hocutt* had had a "tremendous effect": "We have a golden opportunity right now to make progress hitherto impossible in the matter of education." The timing of Hocutt's fight was perfect, White said, because "the white people are afraid of the effect of Communist propaganda on the Negro. As a result, they are willing now more than ever to consider the program of the

N.A.A.C.P. and to make concessions for it if for no other reason than that in their opinion it is the lesser of two evils."[58]

Growing anti-Fascism gilded the NAACP's southern opportunity as well. A month after White's visit with him, Frank Porter Graham joined 142 other college presidents to issue an "appeal to common sense" to the presidents of all German universities. It pleaded "for recognition and respect of the rights of Jews and all minorities as essential to culture and civilization." The educators, including at least 12 white Southerners, told their German counterparts, "The world is too small for persecution. . . . A poverty-stricken world cannot afford bitter hostility and the denial of civil and religious rights." Needless to say, the black press had a field day with the presidents' appeal, exposing the southern institutions over which they presided: "Each of them is lily-white, despite the fact that it is supported . . . by public tax funds."[59] While Graham abolished the 10 percent admittance quota for Jews at UNC's medical school, he remained silent on Hocutt's challenge, bound by his oath as a state employee to uphold the state constitution and its separate but "equal" mandate.[60]

Graham's stand against German discrimination and tacit support for UNC's segregation aroused the New York Friends of Social Justice, who wrote to Graham: "It is a cheap courage which condemns in Poland the very injustice we, ourselves, practice at hand." Graham answered: "Every person living in America or in any other nation is at least indirectly a participant in some social injustice. . . . There has been only one person who ever lived on earth who had the moral freedom to take stands." He concluded: "I intend to continue to take my stands and join in statements regardless of their consistency with the economic, political, and social set-ups of which I am a part."[61]

As the NAACP considered whether to pursue Hocutt's admission, Mary White Ovington, its white treasurer, visited Howard Odum in Chapel Hill. She bought Odum's "go slow" argument and wrote to dissuade Hastie from pursuing the case. Instead, echoing Odum, she argued that they should hold an interracial conference to ask for funding of black schools.[62]

When the NAACP dropped its support of Hocutt, local radicals deplored the interracial cooperation model's capacity to thwart change.[63] One North Carolina man described the process to Walter White: " 'Call

Spaulding when the radicals are on the war path' is a Durham Racket. The technique is as follows: Stir up something. . . . [Attorney] Pearson jumps into the limelight. A conference with the best white people is called. The pseudo-liberals at Chapel Hill . . . sit in. . . . Then Durham Negroes take a big hand from the white folk for sitting on the lid and keeping the young Negroes quiet. . . . Call them interracial racketeers."[64] Newspaperman Louis Austin derisively referred to "Cap'n" Odum, thereby making fun of Howard Odum's racial paternalism by using the Reconstruction honorific required of all blacks addressing white men.[65]

The NAACP still believed that "with proper handling," it could send an African American graduate student to UNC. But to do so, it would have to have a perfect plaintiff, preferably one who did not live in Durham under Spaulding's and Shepard's noses. The very elements that made North Carolina famous for its "civility" made the NAACP fear alienating its moderate center.[66] Frank Porter Graham's sweet reasonableness, C. C. Spaulding's hard-earned wealth, and James Shepard's prominence as an educator all stymied radical action.

Nevertheless, the association applied what it learned from *Hocutt* elsewhere. In June 1935 young Thurgood Marshall and his mentor Charles Houston found a dream plaintiff in Amherst graduate Donald Gaines Murray, who had been denied admission to Maryland's segregated law school. No one could call Amherst a second-rate school, nor would its registrar withhold Murray's transcript. Moreover, as a border state Maryland fitted the NAACP's plan to attack legal segregation on its outermost perimeter. Bringing the case in Baltimore City Court put the drama before an urban area with a large black population and a nationally circulated black newspaper, a venue that would allow the NAACP to achieve its secondary goal of publicity.[67]

To bow to the equal part of *Plessy*, Maryland paid black residents who attended law schools elsewhere the difference between the in-state and out-of-state tuitions. But practicing law well in Maryland, Marshall and Houston argued, depended on studying state law, which was, the dean of the Maryland Law School testified, exactly what the white law students learned there. At the time sixteen states maintained segregated universities. Six paid the difference between in-state and out-of-state tuition to send away African Americans who wanted to pursue graduate studies, and ten did nothing. North Carolina was among the ten states that did nothing. Thus it used African Americans' taxes to fund white graduate schools without providing any graduate education for African Americans. If black North Carolinians went to out-of-state graduate or professional schools, they were on their own.[68]

In Donald Murray's case, the municipal judge, Eugene O'Dunne, issued a writ of mandamus ordering that he be admitted to the law school, an order that the Maryland Court of Appeals upheld six months later.[69] Maryland could integrate its law school or open a separate—and equal— law school for African Americans. Whichever choice it made, it had to choose *now*. Donald Murray enrolled in the University of Maryland's law school after O'Dunne's ruling.[70]

The judge who ruled in Murray's favor had lived his life as a grass-roots progressive in a society that had changed profoundly, except in the courts. As a crusading young deputy state's attorney in 1912, O'Dunne had chaired a governor's commission that exposed abuse of black prisoners at the state penitentiary. Back then pundit H. L. Mencken noted that O'Dunne possessed "an Irish frenzy to break heads . . . a kind of boyish delight in alarming sinners."[71] Moreover, in days just before O'Dunne ruled on Donald Murray's case, he had watched the U.S. Supreme Court eviscerate the New Deal, culminating in the decision that the National Recovery Administration was unconstitutional.[72] With his writ to admit Murray, O'Dunne reached out to a legacy of grassroots Progressive Era judicial activism that had not yet reached the Supreme Court. His decision taunted the Court's nineteenth-century mind-set. Perhaps he also heard the thunk of boxing gloves. On the very day that O'Dunne issued his writ, June 25, 1935, the "Brown Bomber," Joe Louis, toppled the "Ambling Alp," Primo Carnera, Mussolini's great white hope.[73]

It fell to H. L. Mencken to link the Murray case to Italian aggression, commenting that in the past Maryland might as well have sent black students to "Addis Ababa or Timbuctoo" for legal training. Now, he exclaimed, "There will be an Ethiop among the Aryans when the larval Blackstones assemble next Wednesday."[74] As whites protested the ruling, Baltimore's black-owned newspaper, the *Afro-American*, characterized them as "American Nazis" who were "Quite as Bestial as their German Brothers." Six weeks later Mussolini ordered the invasion of Ethiopia.[75]

The issue of how African Americans would pursue graduate or professional education represented a real weakness in the separate but equal dogma, and African Americans continued to call the question. For example, Louis Austin of the *Carolina Times* wrote to Frank Porter Graham early in 1934, asking, "Do you feel that Negroes in North Carolina are entitled to professional training; if so, how and to what extent should the state provide for the same?"[76] In August 1936 Walter White wrote to Guy Johnson, UNC professor of social work and Howard Odum's right-hand man, that perhaps he was being "too optimistic," but his contacts with southern white students make "me less pessimistic about the attitudes of Southern white students towards the admission of Negroes to Southern Colleges and universities." Johnson retorted: "Mr. White's point of view is indeed 'too optimistic.' " Southern white students did not represent the thinking of southern white legislatures, Johnson knew, and he recommended a stipend to send black students out of state. Even then he thought there should be a cap on it so that black students did not end up at Columbia (tuition $375) when white students' limited funds kept them at the state university. The other option, which both Johnson and Odum supported, would be to found a few regional black graduate schools supported by various states. In contrast, the North Carolina General Assembly eschewed out-of-state tuition and scrambled to upgrade graduate education for African Americans.[77] In 1936 the General Assembly granted James Shepard $333,000 to improve the campus of North Carolina College for Negroes, with an eye toward adding graduate education there if the courts forced it to do so. Black schools benefited from the attention. The aim of the upgrade, however, was to maintain segregation and to prevent access to the vastly superior resources at white institutions.

Maryland did not appeal *Murray* to the federal courts, but Lloyd Lionel Gaines's NAACP-backed attempt to attend the University of Missouri's law school went to the U.S. Supreme Court in 1938 as *Missouri ex rel Gaines v. Canada*. Charles Houston had targeted Missouri and engaged a local lawyer who quietly let it be known that a plaintiff would be welcome, while cautiously trying not to step over the line of fomenting litigation. Learning a lesson from James Shepard's obstruction in *Hocutt*, the attorney secured in advance the cooperation of the state's black college president.[78] Plaintiff Lloyd Gaines was a find: valedictorian of his high school class, a history major with a B average at Lincoln University, articulate, and thoughtful. One of eleven children of poor Mississippi sharecroppers, he had moved with his widowed mother to St. Louis, where he entered the fifth grade at fifteen. Eight and a half years later he graduated from college.[79] As controversy raged over the Nazi Olympics in the summer of 1936, a Missouri court quickly ruled against Gaines.[80] The next month black sprinter Jesse Owens took four gold medals in Berlin.

As the NAACP pressed on to make the equal playing field that Owens enjoyed in Germany a reality in Missouri, the shift in the Supreme Court's makeup put the finish line in sight for Gaines. As a result of Franklin Roosevelt's court-packing scheme, Justice Owen Roberts's switch from conservative to liberal, Hugo Black's appointment, and a vacant seat left by Benjamin Cardozo's death, the *Gaines* court was very different from that of two and a half years earlier, when Eugene O'Dunne had ruled in favor of Donald Murray.[81] Had Maryland decided to appeal *Murray* to the Supreme Court in 1936, it most probably would have been overturned. Now, in a breakthrough six to two decision on December 12, 1938, the Supreme Court ordered Missouri to provide equal graduate education for black residents.[82] The Court did not order integration; rather, it enforced *Plessy*'s equal imperative. States across the nation now had a choice of desegregating white graduate and professional schools or of opening new all-black graduate and professional schools equal to white facilities. The NAACP was ecstatic since the Court had stated, "in the plainest of English," that schools must be equal. That meant, the association believed, that teacher salaries must be equalized, that "transportation for rural pupils" must be provided, and that out-of-state graduate school tuition schemes were unconstitutional.[83]

The white Missouri student newspaper called the plaintiff "the inevitable Mr. Gaines" and argued that "our actions in accepting him will define our status as Americans." Referring to conversations among white law students threatening to treat Gaines badly, the editor observed: "One caught the scent of Nazi anti-semitism, saw a race magnified in its role of an underdog. Lincoln University for the Negro. The Ghetto for the Jew. For, wherein is there a basic difference?"[84] The state chose to establish an "equal" segregated law school, scheduled to open the next September. The

NAACP immediately charged that the instant law school would not meet the Court's order, and litigation continued through 1939.[85]

While *Gaines* made its way through the courts, the NAACP recruited other black college students to apply to graduate schools across the South; it knew that unless numerous applicants came forward quickly, law and graduate schools would not meaningfully desegregate before the states had time to open segregated graduate programs that might meet the equal standard.[86] Turning back to the University of North Carolina, the association focused on Walter Raleigh Goldston, a young black man from High Point, who had made As and Bs at Fisk University in Nashville and was currently working in Tennessee on a WPA project. He had applied to UNC's medical school and been summarily rejected. However, when the NAACP realized that Goldston had scored only 4 of a possible 100 on the national Medical Aptitude Test, they quickly dropped him.[87]

Pauli Murray, Applicant

Pauli Murray always claimed that she "knew nothing of the Lloyd Gaines' case" when she applied to UNC to do graduate work in sociology; indeed, she sent in her application a month before the Court ruling.[88] But her claim was disingenuous. First, she had known for years of the broad NAACP call for graduate school applicants, which included women graduate students. Three years earlier the association had helped a black Virginia woman apply to do graduate work in English at the University of Virginia; she had been refused and was given money to attend graduate school out of state. Second, the previous spring Murray had spoken with someone at NAACP headquarters, probably Walter White, about the desegregation campaign. Moreover, Charles Houston and William Hastie were Murray's "heroes"; surely she knew what they had been up to.[89] Perhaps most tellingly, it was on November 10, 1938, the day after the Supreme Court heard *Gaines*, that Pauli Murray first wrote to the University of North Carolina, requesting the graduate school catalog and an application. Murray would not have wanted her own case to seem too "fomented," and she was aware that folks back home would welcome an insider more quickly than an outsider inspired by a national campaign. A month later Murray wrote to Gaines himself, identifying herself as a "fellow pilgrim." She noted ruefully that "our own Southern Negro leaders may not be willing to support us in this battle for equality of human rights." Murray urged Gaines: "Accept your admission," no matter how "uncomfortable" whites might make it.[90]

She quickly realized that she had an uncomfortable fight on her own hands. The UNC dean who answered her letter replied to "Mr." Murray, signing it "cordially yours."[91] But when the application arrived a few days later, someone had typed on the printed form, "Race _____" and "Religion _____."[92] Murray proposed to earn an MA in public welfare social work, the applied sociology program under Odum, who had recently served with C. C. Spaulding on the North Carolina Commission on Interracial Cooperation.[93] Murray's application arrived just as Swedish economist Gunnar Myrdal visited UNC to seek advice on how to begin his monumental study on southern white supremacy and to recruit sociologist Guy Johnson and his historian wife, Guion, to work on the project later published as *An American Dilemma*.[94]

Murray saw herself as a perfect plaintiff for the NAACP. She had left North Carolina at seventeen "determined not to attend a segregated college."[95] Part of her goal had been to gain academic credentials that white people could not deny. Hocutt told Murray that his case had been hurt by his academic background; now Murray dared UNC to question the "academic standing of a Hunter College degree."[96] She applied in sociology, a discipline in which the state would be hard pressed to open an "instant" department at North Carolina College for Negroes. But perhaps most important, Murray was terrifically well connected in her hometown of Durham. When she was eleven, she had begun delivering Louis Austin's newspaper by bicycle. In the summers she had typed policies at C. C. Spaulding's life insurance company. In fact, when she took a semester away from Hunter to earn expenses, Spaulding lent her money to return to college.[97]

She also gambled that she could disarm James Shepard, the man who had sunk Hocutt, because Shepard was her mother's friend. Like a true Southerner, Murray wrote to Shepard, telling him just exactly *who* she was: "You will probably recall that my grandfather, Robert G. Fitzgerald, was one of the first educators in North Carolina after the Civil War and that my aunt and adopted mother, Mrs. Pauline F. Dame, has been a teacher in the Durham City Schools for some decades." Once she placed herself, Murray declared that she was "very anxious to get your opinion and advice concerning the higher education of Negroes in North Carolina." She knew full well that Shepard opposed integrating graduate schools but pretended that she did not: "My personal opinion is that . . . setting up separate graduate schools merely continues the double standard of education. . . . Students in the South [should] come together on a basis of equality to study the problems which affect both races."[98]

Even as she wrote, "I am not opposed to the establishment of Negro universities *per se*," Murray hinted that Shepard had a counterpart in Nazi Germany, the collaborator. "Each day the newspapers report further and more brutal injustices against our brothers and sisters in Germany, the Jews; ghettoes are being reopened, elementary human rights are being violated. . . . Can we then, as Americans and members of a minority group, collaborate on any policy which will stop short of equality?" She answered herself: "Our task" is to be "uncompromising . . . on the issue of equality guaranteed in our Constitution." By the time that Murray wrote to Shepard in 1938, Nazi persecution of the Jews had become so violent that most African Americans now saw Fascism as more horrific than Jim Crow, even as they pointed out that Jim Crow undercut the American response to Hitler.[99]

Without mentioning the fact she had already applied to UNC, Murray asked Shepard "what support" a student who tested the system could "expect from Negro educators and liberal forces." She closed by evoking "the traditional place of respect which you hold in my family." When Shepard did not answer for four weeks, Murray gave him tougher treatment: "May I expect an immediate answer from your office?" At the bottom Murray typed, "copy to the *Carolina Times*, Durham, North Carolina," but she crossed it out. Shepard took in the full import of her threat. Within a day of the second letter, he wrote a terse reply, pleading recent absence and declining to debate the issues with her.[100] The battle lines were drawn: Not only was Murray taking on North Carolina's white establishment, but she was taking on a powerful segment of its black establishment as well.

While James Shepard had been avoiding Pauli Murray, he had been scrambling to use the Missouri case to increase funding for the North Carolina College for Negroes. He sent North Carolina's governor, Clyde

Hoey, a copy of a telegram from a black newspaper that demanded Shepard comment on the *Gaines* case. Both Shepard and Hoey knew just how unequal North Carolina's schools really were, despite the nine new buildings the state had built at NCC the previous year and Frank Porter Graham's delivery of the keynote speech when they opened. Even though Graham told the crowd, "Equal opportunity for education should not depend upon the section of the country, nor of the race to which one belongs," no one took that as an endorsement of integration. Pauli Murray's initiative presented Shepard with the perfect opportunity to press for more money.[101]

UNC rejected Murray's application on December 12, the day *after* the *Gaines* decision, stating flatly that "members of your race are not admitted to the university."[102] At once Murray wrote to Graham, noting that the rejection was illegal since it had come after the Court announced the *Gaines* decision. "How much longer, Dr. Graham," Murray asked, "is the South going to withhold elementary human rights from its black citizens? How can Negroes, the economic backbone of the South for centuries, defend our institutions against the threats of Fascism and barbarism if we too are treated the same as the Jews of Germany?"[103]

As much as Murray wanted to represent her application as home-grown rather than federally inspired, she never hesitated to use the power of the federal courts as a threat. "It would be a victory for liberal thought in the South, if you were favorably disposed toward my application instead of forcing me to carry the issue to the courts." she told Graham, and she asked if she could meet with him over the upcoming Christmas holidays. Likewise, Murray informed the UNC administration, "I am thoroughly prepared to fight this case through to the Supreme Court, but would much prefer to do it another way."[104] For his part, Frank Porter Graham told Murray he would be out of town at Christmas and could not see her.[105]

Pauli Murray never made idle threats; as soon as she finished her letter to Graham, she picked up her pen to organize her legal strategy. "Listen, Lisha," she wrote to a high school friend in Durham, "I need your help." She enclosed a copy of her letter to Graham and asked her to take it to three black Durham lawyers, including Conrad "Pug" Pearson and Cecil McCoy, who had represented Hocutt. "We gotta work fast before the Supreme Court and the Southern legislatures stop us." Murray believed that if black applicants besieged southern white universities to enter a variety of graduate programs, instant segregated alternatives would be impossible, and some white schools would have to admit African American students, at least temporarily. Murray asked Lisha to take a copy of her letter to her mother, Pauline Dame, "so as not to shock her," when it appeared in the newspapers. "O.K. pal," she closed, "stick with me and this race of ours in North Carolina will go places."[106]

The NAACP could not enter Murray's case until UNC rejected her, and on January 2 she sent all her official correspondence in the case to Walter White. "I would like very much to know what is the next step in this case," Murray asked, promising that she was willing to "stick with it until the precedent of permitting Negro students to enter this school is established."[107] White referred her letter to Thurgood Marshall, who instructed Murray to order a transcript from Hunter sent to the NAACP and to charge the dollar transcript fee to the association. Murray implored Marshall: "When do we get going? I feel like a race-horse champing at the bit."[108]

Frank Porter Graham's Dilemma

Even as Murray set out to take UNC to court, she kept trying to convince Frank Porter Graham to support her. She wrote to him for a second time on January 17, suggesting that a mutual understanding would naturally result from any discussion between her and graduate students or university officials. She explained that she wanted to study "the social, economic, and racial problems of the South" with Professor Odum and his associate Guy Johnson, who "naturally attract serious-minded" students, such as her. While she appreciated the "psychological conflicts confronting any interracial undertaking south of the Mason and Dixon line," she could also "conceive of a give-and-take process where prejudices are openly aired and accounted for." Moreover, admitting "Negro students . . . would have a definite contribution to make to inter-racial understanding and good will." She suggested that Graham ask the graduate students if they thought they might "gain insight into social problems" by "admitting a Negro student to their classes."[109] If Graham's heart went out to Murray, he refused to comment on how the university would comply with the

Gaines decision, saying that this would be a matter for the state of North Carolina to decide.[110]

Murray's application arrived at a time when Odum and Graham were at odds over a new interracial group that threatened to supplant the Commission on Interracial Cooperation. Its name signified its commitment to equality: the Southern Conference for Human Welfare (SCHW).[111] Ten days after Murray had applied to his university, on November 21, 1938, Graham was in Birmingham, Alabama, giving a keynote speech to the SCHW. Olive Stone of UNC, Myles Horton and Jim Dombrowski of the Highlander Folk School, Charles Johnson of Fisk, Don West, lately of Kentucky, and C. Vann Woodward, now teaching in Florida, joined him.[112] Gunnar Myrdal attended and later characterized the meeting as a "point of departure" for the white South, in part because it left behind the moderate CIC.[113] Virginia Durr, a white Alabamian whose husband, Clifford, worked in the New Deal, remembered the initial meeting of the SCHW as "the New Deal come South."[114] Odum boycotted the meeting, in part because he couldn't run the organization, in part because he feared that the SCHW would compete with the CIC, of which he had become president. He wanted to turn the CIC into the Council on Southern Regional Development, an organization that would focus on economics and planning in the New Deal model.[115] He also worried that the SCHW would "label" the South if it did not "follow any ideology that comes up." It is unclear precisely what sort of label he expected to be applied to the South; perhaps it was "racist." The SCHW spotlight made Odum sweat. To him, the Southern Conference for Human Welfare seemed "hellbent to make the South show up its emotional and provincial qualities."[116]

Odum's primary fear, however, was that "the whole thing was initiated from a communistic source."[117] In this he was partially right. The conference came out of New Dealers' efforts to tie the South's economic problems to its history of racial discrimination, and it used the *Report on Economic Conditions of the South*, released under Graham's name, to point up the "social and economic problems" of the South. Addressing southern economic problems squarely was part of FDR's attempt to break the hammerlock that conservative southern Democrats held on Congress, which prevented the passage of New Deal legislation.[118]

The SCHW began when liberal politics joined Communist activism.

Joseph Gelders convinced Lucy Randolph Mason, the prominent Virginian and a CIO organizer, that the time was ripe for a southern conference on economic and race issues. Gelders, a physics professor at the University of Alabama, had joined Olive Stone and her friends to support unionists and the unemployed in Birmingham. For his troubles, three thugs kidnapped him and beat him to a pulp. Crippled for the rest of his life, he moved to the left. The 1935 All Southern Conference for Civil and Trade Union Rights, which the Communists and Christian Socialists had sponsored in Tennessee, had been a turning point for Gelders.[119] Mason facilitated Gelders's introduction to Eleanor Roosevelt, and ER introduced Gelders to her husband. Franklin Roosevelt met with Mason and Gelders and encouraged them to plan a southern conference to mark the release of the *Report on Economic Conditions of the South*.[120]

By 1937 Gelders was an underground member of the CP, working as a "critical link between the Communists and the liberals." He was southern representative for the National Committee for the Defense of Political Prisoners, the organization in which Paul Green was active.[121] The Popular Front had refocused Communist attention on the South, and it was looking for an organization that would draw in southern leftists.[122] Gelders put together the organizing committee that planned the first meeting of the SCHW in Birmingham.[123]

Very few people knew that Gelders was a Communist, but when the conference convened in November 1938, Frank Porter Graham recognized "a handful" of Communists among the twelve hundred delegates. Since being a member of the CP was legal, Graham remarked, "I do not object to the members of any political party, Democrats, Republicans, Socialists, Communists, or what-not coming into an open democratic meeting so long as it is open and above board."[124] Others disagreed. Howard Kester, the radical Socialist who headed the Southern Tenant Farmers' Union, complained that "the Birmingham conference was conceived and in the main executed by persons who were either members of the Communist Party and known as such, and well known and not so well known fellow-travelers."[125] Sociologist Arthur Raper attended, but he remained skeptical of the organization because he had always "found it nearly impossible to work with the Communists." But some had grown used to working with the CP in the Popular Front. For example, Lucy Randolph Mason told

Olive Stone that she was "willing to accept and tolerate Communists, because she wanted as many groups as possible to organize."[126]

The SCHW addressed issues ranging from public health to race relations to prison reform; in many ways, it took up the agenda of Olive Stone's Southern Committee for People's Rights. It boldly included "suffrage and constitutional rights" and the abolition of the poll tax and appointed Joseph Gelders secretary of the Civil Rights Committee. With the help of Virginia Durr, the committee initiated a "Free America First" campaign, but it did not explicitly call for an end to all segregation in the South at the first meeting. Instead, it practiced desegregation within its group.[127]

Sounding for all the world like Pauli Murray, Graham told those gathered for the SCHW: "In this day when democracy and freedom are in retreat everywhere in the face of totalitarian powers and their regimentation of youth and persecution of minorities, let us raise the flag of freedom and democracy where it counts most. . . . The black man is the primary test of American democracy and Christianity."[128] In Murray's case, however, Graham found himself powerless to pass his own test.

After the conference white supremacists condemned its flouting of Birmingham's strict segregation laws inside the auditorium and cursed Eleanor Roosevelt for her attendance along with twelve hundred white and black Southerners.[129] Graham's mailbox filled up with hate mail from North Carolinians, one of whom told him, "If I must favor social equality with the Negro, with all that that implies, in order to be called liberal and democratic, then I have no hesitation in renouncing liberality and democracy." From the Left, the Communists criticized the conference for its failure to challenge segregation outside the auditorium.[130]

Graham originally turned down the SCHW chairmanship, but in response to the firestorm that followed the meeting, he reversed himself and accepted it just to spite the anti-Communists and racists. "I propose not to run because some groups shout Communist or Negrophile," Graham vowed. Gelders became the conference's only full-time employee.[131] Had the liberals known him to be a Communist beforehand, it is likely that they would have rejected him for the job.

The outrage over the SCHW meeting underscored Graham's fear that southern racism might combine with domestic Fascism to thrust the

South back into the race wars of the 1890s. He warned Murray about the danger of trying to change the state constitution, which could be done only by popular vote. Frankly, he told her, "The Negro leaders in this state and the white leaders who have been friends of the Negroes in the struggle for justice are strongly of the opinion that the most unfortunate thing that could happen at this time would be a popular referendum on the race issue." Here he evoked the Fascist threat, but to a different end from Murray: "The possibilities of an interracial throback [sic] do not have to be emphasized in our present world."[132] He may have sympathized with Murray, but he disagreed with her about the limits of possibility in the South.

As evidenced by his support of FDR, his work in the SCHW, and his outspoken support of Jewish civil rights, Graham stood on the front lines of domestic anti-Fascism and liberal antiracism. He genuinely feared what might happen if European Fascists joined with southern racists. The same international events that gave Murray and other African Americans a powerful tool to argue for an end to southern white supremacy now underscored the familiar "The time is not right" refrain from white southern liberals.

Integration would blow the lid off things, Graham wrote to Murray, but perhaps the example of Fascism could be used to force whites to upgrade black education. Graham pointed out to her that white North Carolinians had been working since 1934 with James Shepard to improve North Carolina College for Negroes, even as he acknowledged, "I am aware of the inequities which you point out." He pledged that UNC would cooperate with NCC "toward a more adequate provision for . . . a substantial beginning in the provision for graduate and professional work. . . . This may seem to you to be an inadequate and minimum program, but it is going to take the cooperation and the struggle of us all to bring it to pass."[133]

Then he forthrightly assessed his own position: "I am under very bitter attack in some parts of North Carolina and the lower South for what little I have tried to do on behalf of the Negro people [at the Southern Conference for Human Welfare]. . . . I realize I am also subject to attack because I understand the limitations under which we must work in order to make the next possible advance."[134] He copied his letter to Murray to Walter White, Roy Wilkins (editor of *Crisis*), attorney Charles Houston, and Leon Ransom of Howard Law School. White answered him warmly.

Subsequently he forwarded copies of Graham's correspondence to another white educator with the comment "Dr. Graham . . . is certainly a magnificent and courageous person, isn't he?"[135] As a state employee Graham had sworn to uphold both the U.S. Constitution and the North Carolina Constitution. As a white liberal and a state employee Graham played his role at the outer limit of the politics of the possible.

But he also depended on people like Pauli Murray to point out that that limit was not nearly far enough. Murray thanked Graham for his "very fine letter" and peremptorily told him, "In fairness to those [who] . . . hold your point of view . . . am releasing it to the Negro press." His solution, however, just wouldn't do, since "we of the younger generation cannot compromise with our ideals of human equality." Moreover, Graham had cleared one thing up for Murray: "This much is certain . . . that the Constitution of North Carolina is inconsistent with the Constitution of the United States and should be changed to meet the ideals set forth by the first citizens of our country." Murray might be no closer to matriculating at UNC, but she had put its president on record as favoring equalization in black education at all levels, even as she told him that was not enough, not nearly enough. Black newspapers across the country printed the two letters with photographs of Murray and Graham side by side.[136]

Not Waiting for Roosevelt

After Murray tried to win over Shepard to reason with Graham and to line up her legal defense, she tried yet another tactic: to win national politicians to her side. She sent an open letter to President Franklin Delano Roosevelt, "pouring out the heart of 12,000,000 black citizens, 3,000,000 WPA workers and little Pauli."[137] She meant to hold him accountable for a speech that he had made at UNC the previous December 1938, a few weeks after she applied there.

FDR had accepted an honorary UNC degree as Graham, along with twelve thousand others, had packed into Woollen Gymnasium in a miserable downpour.[138] Although the undergraduate who headed the Carolina Political Union in December 1938 had announced that "everybody is invited, and that there will be no tickets—and no admission charge," everybody knew that he meant only white people could come. A WPA

choir from Durham, the only African Americans present, burst into spirituals that evoked slavery, but FDR had asked his white southern audience
to embrace change.[139]

What sort of change they were to embrace is not exactly clear. It had
something to do with labor and something to do with race. When FDR
began to speak, he was, in effect, speaking in tongues. Roosevelt used the
coded language that liberal northern white people spoke to bring out the
best in white Southerners without ever criticizing squarely the problems of
segregation and labor oppression. He began by quoting Justice Benjamin
Cardozo's observation "If a body of law were . . . adequate for the civilization of today, it could not meet the demands of tomorrow. Society is incon-
stant. . . . There is change whether we will it or not." In the last days of
1938, FDR warned that "many other democracies look to us for leadership
that world democracy may survive." Hope sprang from the way that the
United States solved problems "without bitterness and factionalism, by the
time-honored democratic methods of tolerance, self-restraint and compromise." His point was not to urge his audience to fight Fascism abroad;
rather, he wanted his listeners to fight inequities in the U.S. South. "I am
speaking not of the external policies of the United States," FDR made
clear; rather "I would emphasize the maintenance of successful democracy
at home. . . . Democracies all change through local processes . . . the kind of
change to meet new social and economic needs." Although his twenty-
minute exercise in circumlocution never included the words *labor union,
minimum wage, Negro, poll tax, lynching,* and *desegregation,* it could not have
been lost on his white audience that the president of the United States was
calling on them to extend the limits of southern democracy to serve as an
example to Europe. "That is why," FDR concluded, "I am happy and proud
to become an alumnus of the University of North Carolina, typifying as it
does American liberal thought through American action."[140]

"Everybody" might not be welcome in Woollen Gym, but the airwaves
proved more democratic. Pauli Murray listened to FDR's address by radio
in New York and realized that she was becoming weary of "waitin' on
Roosevelt." Langston Hughes explained:

> *And a lot o' other folks*
> *What's hungry and cold*

Done stopped believin'
What they been told
By Roosevelt,
Roosevelt, Roosevelt—[141]

The promises, the waitin', the plea for democracy before a segregated audience were not lost on Pauli Murray, who dashed off a letter to FDR when he concluded his speech.

"I am a Negro," she wrote, "the most oppressed, most misunderstood and most neglected section of your population." She informed FDR that although she knew UNC to be segregated, she deserved to go there because her grandfather Robert Fitzgerald and her mother, Pauline Dame, had devoted themselves to southern education. Could Roosevelt, in good conscience, "ask your young Negroes to return to the South? . . . Have you raised your voice loud enough against the burning of our people?" Murray asked. Did FDR mean it when he called UNC a place where "Americans [could] . . . support a liberal philosophy based on democracy"? If so, did "it mean that colored students in the South will be able to sit down and study problems which are fundamental and mutual to both groups"? Murray asked. "Or, does it mean that everything you said has no meaning for us as colored?" She told the president: "We are as much political refugees from the South as any of the Jews in Germany."[142]

By the time Murray confronted the president, domestic Fascists were constantly linking Jews and African Americans. The German American Bund fulminated that FDR had too many Jews in his administration; moreover, his wife, Eleanor, was a race traitor in thrall to African Americans. A popular rhyme from the time imagined FDR's telling Eleanor:

You kiss the Negroes,
I'll kiss the Jews,
We'll stay in the White House
As long as we choose.[143]

It might have been enough for most people to lecture the president of the United States and then distribute copies of the letter widely to the black press, but that wasn't enough for Pauli Murray. She sent a copy of her letter to Eleanor Roosevelt, along with a personal note. She introduced herself boldly: "You do not remember me, but I was the girl who did not stand up when you passed through the Social Hall of Camp Tera. . . . I thought you are the sort of person who prefers to be accepted as a human being and not a human paragon." Now she wanted the first lady to intervene with the president to help her desegregate UNC. Could ER "try to understand" her dilemma? While Murray got a form letter from FDR, Eleanor answered her personally, beginning a friendship and collaboration on civil rights issues that spanned decades. "I understand perfectly," ER told Murray. "But great changes come slowly," she said. "I think they are coming, however, and sometimes it is better to fight hard with conciliatory methods." She cautioned: "The South is changing, but don't push too fast."[144]

"Rah, Rah, Carolina . . . lina"

Murray's application had become public in Chapel Hill after the Christmas break. When they heard about it, the all-male, all-white undergraduate students moved in and out of the houses on fraternity row, talking big about what they would do if it proved to be true. Several vowed to "tar and feather any —— 'nigger' that tried to come in class." One declared, "I think the state would close the University before they'd let a Negro in. I've never committed murder yet but if a black boy tried to come into my home saying he was a 'University student . . .' "[145]

Those undergraduate bullies who predicted violence knew from the start that the applicant was a woman, yet they immediately deployed the argument that African American civil rights led inexorably to "social equality," a euphemism implying interracial fraternizing that would inevitably encourage black men to desire sex with white women. So, instead of Murray, they imagined a black man, one they could tar and feather, one they could shoot, one they could lynch, one they could use to prove their own manhood by protecting white women, whom the University of North Carolina would not admit to the undergraduate school except in limited special programs. That's how the system worked: The General Assembly funded the institution with taxpayers' dollars, guaranteeing white boys, many from wealthy families, a first-rate undergraduate education for minimal tuition at the expense of white women, black women, and black men.

When they learned of Murray's application, undergraduates debated what should be done in the context of the *Gaines* decision. The worst possible outcome, the undergraduate *Daily Tar Heel* maintained, would be to integrate UNC. The editor saw three options for the university: "close its doors to whites and Negroes alike, thereby 'equalizing' educational facilities; . . . allow Negroes to enroll, thus creating a dangerous situation; or . . . provide separate colored schools of a grade equal to similar white institutions."[146] Only the last statement reflected a state constitutional option.

The point was that the rarefied Supreme Court could not change much on the ground. One undergrad warned: "Prejudices in Southern minds can never be removed if they are suppressed and denied by external forces from without. For the roots of prejudice grow healthier when the branches are clipped." The student's statement reflected an understanding of human behavior consistent with Howard Odum's regional sociology: People could not be forced by law to do something that betrayed their folkways. After all, the student cautioned, white Southerners had proved this fact after Reconstruction, which brought on, he said, "seven decades of lynchings and close-mindedness." Others reported an "ante-bellum spirit" on campus.[147]

Local white newspapers struggled to give shape to the threat that Pauli Murray posed to the Carolina boys. Four headlines sorted it out: NEW YORK WOMAN SEEKS TO ENTER GRAD SCHOOL; ADMINISTRATION CONFRONTED WITH "LIBERALISM ISSUE"; NEGRESS APPLIES TO ENTER CAROLINA; and COLORED, TRIES TO ENTER CAROLINA U.[148] To translate: A brazen black Yankee woman (not from here) had decided to trap UNC president Frank Graham in a snare of his own foolish liberal making. Murray had an army of contacts sending her press clippings from back home, the student newspaper office at Columbia University held the latest exchange copy of the *Daily Tar Heel* for her, and recent UNC graduate George Stoney, who had been at the SCHW meeting, advised her in New York.[149] She learned, for example, that the white *Durham Morning Herald* responded with a call to found graduate schools at North Carolina College for Negroes; after all, "No one in his right mind favors trying to abandon" segregation.[150] When the *Daily Tar Heel* cabled the NAACP to ask for its stand on the case, staffer Roy Wilkins answered, "We have opposed separate schools for the races . . . [for] 30 years . . . because all surveys and statistics show conclusively that there does not exist in America a so-called equal school system."[151]

Most white liberals took the *Durham Morning Herald*'s position and called for increased funding for African American education. Eleanor Roosevelt made herself heard above the roar, probably with Murray's case in mind: "I would like to see the federal government take steps to equalize educational opportunities everywhere . . . every child . . . should have the opportunity to get education." Frank Graham publicly came out in support of building equal graduate schools at North Carolina College for Negroes and defended himself from charges of hypocrisy by pointing out that the SCHW had not passed resolutions opposing segregation.[152]

But a few whites also had the courage to support integration here and now. Jonathan Daniels, who had been on "both ends of the gun" regarding the Eston Ericson and James Ford dinner, put his experience to good use. This time he told UNC students, "I don't see how anybody can object to taking a graduate course at the University with a Negro." Ten graduate and professional school students wrote to the *Daily Tar Heel*, calling for immediate acceptance of Murray and deploring the idea of a separate graduate school at NCC. "It has taken over a hundred years to make this university what it is. The Negroes cannot and should not wait that long."[153] At nearby Duke University, Dean Elbert Russell told a Sunday morning church service, "As wise as has been the sympathy of the rest of the world with the plight of the Jews, it is doubtful if any section or race has sympathized more whole-heartedly and keenly than Negro Americans, for they have known the same type of persecution. . . . One wonders that white Americans can become so incensed over the ousting of Jews from German universities and yet not raise a whisper over the banning of Negroes from many American universities."[154]

A few UNC faculty members spoke up for integration as well. They included Howard K. Beale, the history professor, native Northerner, and Harvard graduate. Beale was one of only two northern-born men teaching history in the South, and as C. Vann Woodward recalled, he "didn't get along with the faculty very well . . . [he] found it hard as a fresh Northerner to adjust to the thing." The "thing" was segregation, and Beale pointed out that the Sociology Department taught theories of interracial cooperation that required interracial contact. "Are the theories wrong?

Then let's eliminate them." UNC, Beale asserted, was proud of its "tradition of liberalism that gives her prestige in the nation. This tradition has not been created by boasting of it in the abstract. . . . Liberalism cannot be pursued in all other categories and then denied whenever the Negro appears." Admit Pauli Murray forthwith, he demanded.[155] Paul Green, who had already told Howard Odum that the Commission on Interracial Cooperation would "never do anything," saw the moment as an opportunity to move beyond the gradualist approach.[156] "We learn that justice pays," Green stated simply as he argued in favor of desegregating the graduate school.[157] The brave voices of Odum's erstwhile allies made his silence all the more profound.

As UNC students began to debate Murray's application, it became clear that a substantial minority of them actually supported her matriculation. In a law school vote, eighteen voted to "admit Negroes to the University," sixty-five against.[158] In a similar straw poll, the graduate students voted eighty-two to thirty-eight to admit Murray, while ten wrote to the *Daily Tar Heel* to condemn as a "disgrace" the university's noncompliance with recent Supreme Court decisions. From New York the Communist *Daily Worker* called the election a "resounding rebuke" to "Jim Crow campus regulations."[159]

The Baptist students took up the matter at a discussion led by Guion Johnson, who was already working with Gunnar Myrdal. But she did not support admitting Murray. Rather, she used the occasion to point out the inequality in black education from first grade through college, and she also read papers written by black college freshmen elsewhere who opposed integration because they feared unjust treatment, certainly a possibility, and preferred to "build up their own schools."[160]

Murray disagreed. On January 12, in a characteristic move, she faced adversity squarely and wrote a letter to the *Daily Tar Heel*. Already she saw herself as a member of the student body through intimate bonds of place, affection, suffering, and blood. Saying that she was "never able to understand your definition of social equality," she reminded the undergraduate "mob" that they had most likely had a "colored nurse to whom they poured out all their childish woes. . . . Yet if that same colored nurse decides that she too is a human being and desires to study under the same group of professors and with the same equipment as you, you go into tantrums, organize 'lynching parties' and raise the old cry of Ku Klux Klan." Murray asked: "Why not be honest with yourselves?" Students went "wild" over black bands and loved spirituals, yet "if a young woman . . . as native as any of you, as aware of the deep emotional prejudices and misunderstandings on the part of both races . . . happens to feel that you have one of the best public welfare and social science departments of any university in the country . . . are you so intellectually ungenerous as to resent her desire to gain this information through normal channels—just because she is a Negro?"[161] Seven days later she wrote to Louis Austin at the *Carolina Times*, saying it was time to "let the cat out of the bag" and organize a press campaign.[162]

In mid-February 1939 the campus Young Men's Christian Association and the American Student Union (ASU) sponsored an interracial panel discussion on Murray's application and integration in general. The ASU was formed in 1935 in a merger between the "Communist-influenced" National Student League and the Socialist League for Industrial Democracy. In 1938 the national ASU adopted the goal of "equal participation of Negro students in every phase of college life," on the ground that discrimination undercut education in democracy for everyone.[163] ASU members included liberals, Socialists, and Communists, and it produced leaders as politically diverse as Joseph Lash, who advised Eleanor Roosevelt, and Intimate Bookshop devotee and Chapel Hill student Junius Scales. Scales joined the Chapel Hill ASU chapter early in 1939, when it began to champion Murray's admission. He quickly realized that within the ASU lay "a wheel within a wheel" run by Communists.[164]

The YMCA and the ASU came together to discuss the implications of Murray's application. They invited black students and professors from Bennett College, North Carolina College for Negroes, and Agricultural and Technical College (A&T). They also invited white women students from Woman's College, in nearby Greensboro. Among UNC professors, Guy Johnson attended from Sociology, Paul Green from Drama, and Eston Ericson from English.[165] One hundred students who attended the meeting drafted a resolution for the General Assembly, urging it to admit "carefully chosen Negro students . . . at the graduate and professional levels." It was too expensive, they argued, to set up separate schools for African Americans, and it would "deter the future progress . . . in race relations."[166]

Louis Harris, an undergraduate student and future pollster, covered the meeting for the *Daily Tar Heel*, and immediately some readers complained that he had made it sound as if the meeting had unanimously endorsed the resolution. It had not. The black dean dispatched by James Shepard opposed it, as did the white YMCA director, who feared that "social equality," code words for interracial sex, would spring from "the large amount of intramural activity."[167] One UNC professor, who had previously taught at Yale, sounded the outside agitator cry: The resolution had been pushed through by "those [students] from other states . . . trying to decide how North Carolina should run her institutions."[168] In the end, "division of opinion did not correspond either to geographical or racial lines. Negro professors were divided . . . though Negro students were overwhelmingly in favor of it. Southerners [meaning white Southerners] were very prominent on both sides."[169]

Finally, Howard Odum spoke out against Murray's admittance in the *Carolina Magazine*. He lectured that "it is not possible that the South can forever go on being different in many fundamental aspects of life," but for now, he said, "it is asking too much of a region to change over night the powerful folkways of long generations." Odum supported the principle of "the gradual admission of well-equipped Negro students, tested by the same standards of preparation and equipment as are the whites, into selected professional and graduate schools, followed by critical and progressive experimentation to the end that ultimate adjustments might be made." He just didn't support the application of that principle right now. Alas, said Odum, it would be illegal under state laws—he did not reconcile that with the recent Supreme Court decision—and "the facts of race relations and culture of the South" would not permit any such thing immediately. Instead he advocated setting up regional centers for black graduate education across the South.[170] The idea of regional centers was so perfectly Odum. It would buy time while upgrading black education; it would take a good deal of regional planning, happily supplied, no doubt, by Odum; and it would bring the society back into Odum's imagined equilibrium. When Howard Odum condemned graduate school integration at a time that it was endorsed by others, including the editor of the state's largest newspaper and the state's most beloved playwright, he compromised his usefulness to the interracial movement.

Murray had never expected Odum to support her application. Her own reading of his work led her to think that he had "grown more progressive," but he was still "too close to the Old South" to help her.[171] Murray pointed out the irony: "Sociologists who . . . realize the necessity for giving the Negro equal opportunity" could not accept Negroes in their own universities. Moreover, "Negro educators, whose prestige and influence depend upon the improvement of their own segregated institutions," found themselves in the position of defending "segregation with fervor." Even so, Europe's clouds threatened to rain on America's South. "White Southerners with a social conscience are beginning to squirm," Murray observed, "because they cannot howl against Hitler with self-righteous integrity" and hold African Americans in "social bondage" without endangering freedom. [172] How could the global onslaught of Fascism be turned back by temporizing?

The editor of the campus literary magazine discovered one of Murray's published poems, "Song of the Highway," and cabled to ask for permission to reprint it in the February issue.[173] He also wrote her an agonized letter. If the decision were his alone, the editor thought "that a Negro could be admitted without much fuss—if it were done quietly." He thought it would be good for the university and the students. Yet outrage prompted by Murray's application from "the semi-barbarous inhabitants of the Southland" dismayed him. Promising to let Murray know the reaction to her poem, he hoped that by his publishing it "others will feel— acutely just what sort of student we are missing by excluding Negroes from the University."[174]

Murray certainly believed that she would do the other students, and Howard Odum, good. She pushed Frank Porter Graham to solicit student opinion on ten questions, ranging from "Does the concept of democracy include equal rights for minority groups?" to "Would the white students be able to discuss Negroes frankly if a Negro student were present in their classes?" The *Daily Tar Heel* ran her questions under the banner headline NEGRO APPLICANT SEEKS STUDENT OPINION.[175]

She itched to tell white North Carolinians that she shared with them prominent white ancestors who had been university benefactors. "If you check back into the history of Cornelia Smith Fitzgerald, whose forebears donated some part of their wealth to the University of North Carolina, you will see that no one has any better right than her granddaughter to apply for entrance at this particular school," Murray wrote to the white Durham newspaper. "I did not create this problem," Murray continued. "The white south did." But Murray thought better of sending this letter. The "colored nurse" tactic that she had chosen represented a safer way to convert whites to her cause than invoking the legacy of raped slave women.[176]

Plaintiff Pauli Murray

Even when Murray restrained herself a bit, she exposed herself a lot. It hurt to be Pauli Murray. On her clippings of "Negress Applies to Enter Carolina" and "Colored, Tries to Enter Carolina U.," Murray wrote, "'Colored girl,' 'Negress.' Did it hurt? *Yes!!*" On another clipping, one referring to her as a "Negress," Murray simply wrote, "Ouch!" Still, it was worth it. Her application changed her life and freed her from "a lurking fear." She had been "terrified of the consequences of overt protest against racial segregation." She later remembered this moment, when she "confronted my fear and took a concrete step to battle for social justice," as pivotal in her life. Only then "the accumulated shame began to dissolve in a new sense of self-respect."[177]

Murray's mother, Pauline Dame, by now an elderly public school teacher, was terribly vulnerable to local reprisals. "Please be careful what you do about all of this for you can make it very uncomfortable for me," she told Pauli. But she was also incredibly proud of her headstrong daughter. When Murray went public, Dame reported without censure, "Everybody is talking about the open letter."[178] Throughout their lives Dame offered Murray advice, backed up Murray's decisions even when she disagreed with them, and loved her with a fierce pride that fueled Murray's activism.

As Murray had feared, James Shepard turned out to be a formidable opponent. Shepard, the *New York Times* reported, had a "simple argument for Negro education": "A trained anything is better than an untrained one."[179] Shepard assured the General Assembly that "Negroes could do their best work in their own schools." From Durham, Dame reported the political odds to Murray: "I think Dr. Shepherd [*sic*] is going to get the graduate school. Pharmacy and medicine."[180]

Indeed, in early January Governor Clyde Hoey had responded to *Gaines* and to Murray's application by calling for "courses" in law, medicine, and pharmacy at North Carolina College, with additional graduate courses in agriculture at the black agricultural and technical college, A&T. He asked the General Assembly to equalize the salaries of black and white teachers in the public schools; and it began, very gradually, to do that, at a pace that did not close the gap until 1945.[181] In addition, he asked the General Assembly to fund a twelfth year of high school for both white and black schools, North Carolina remaining one of only six states that did not provide it. Hoey's solution reflected the dual response of many southern states to the challenges of the late 1930s: They would never accept integration, but they would improve the conditions of segregation. He also used the formulation that became ubiquitous in the 1950s, as he linked school desegregation and interracial sex. "North Carolina does not believe in social equality . . . and will not tolerate mixed schools for the races," Hoey declared. Of course, he added, "we do believe in equality of opportunity." The *Afro-American* reported sardonically, "N.C. Governor Unearths 'Social Equality' Bogey."[182]

The bill, introduced a month later, testified to the hypocrisy of the education plan. It did not call for actual permanent graduate schools; rather, it authorized law and pharmacy courses at NCC and agriculture and technology courses at A&T. If fewer than ten students enrolled in "graduate classes," North Carolina would send them out of state to study.[183] Despite ordering Missouri to integrate or provide equal facilities, the federal courts had not yet explicitly rejected the out-of-state stipend as an alternative. Meanwhile the General Assembly appropriated no money specifically for the graduate courses; that would follow if and when students enrolled. And to their man Shepard's college, the legislators gave $128,000, a 400 percent increase over the allocation four years earlier, while slighting the other black colleges in the state. For his part, Shepard announced that he would open a law school the next fall.[184]

Carolina Times editor Louis Austin was furious at the collaboration among Shepard, Hoey, and the General Assembly, calling the bill a "villainous attempt to fool Negroes of this state, and at the same time make pretense at obeying the constitution of the United States." He wrote: "We have come to realize a majority of North Carolina white folks, regardless of their claim to superiority, are miserable and weak."[185] Austin dubbed Shepard a member of the " 'Old Guard' of Negro . . . leaders fighting . . . to preserve the supremacy of the white race," and he called most state-supported black colleges incubators for weaklings.[186] Pauli Murray concluded that "the State legislature was conveniently using . . . [Shepard] as the cat to pull its 'jim-crow' chestnuts out of a very hot fire."[187]

Despite all this action on the ground, the NAACP still had not formally agreed to represent Pauli Murray. After her "champing at the bit" letter to Thurgood Marshall remained unanswered for two weeks, Murray began to suspect that the association was dragging its feet. Pearson and McCoy stood by in Durham.[188] Actually, Roy Wilkins, editor of the association's magazine, *Crisis*, had decided to stop Pauli Murray by any means necessary. Wilkins and Murray knew each other, and she believed him to be on her side.[189] She was entirely mistaken.

Wilkins thought that Murray posed a terrible risk to the NAACP. When the Norfolk *Journal and Guide* telegraphed the association to ask the name of the UNC plaintiff, it was Wilkins who answered: "Our association not yet sponsoring her case only investigating and advising privately." When Thurgood Marshall asked Wilkins to cosign the one-dollar chit for Murray's transcript, Wilkins went out of control. He fired off a memo to Walter White, protesting that he had "signed the voucher under protest." He pointed out that the NAACP had not taken the case and that Murray "did not seek our advice before making her application (not that she had to), but I feel that since she has gone this far she should be allowed to proceed by herself." He objected to her "extensive correspondence" with university officials and observed that "in the present delicate situation following the University of Missouri decision, Miss Murray's letters are, to say the least, not diplomatic." He "strongly" opposed taking the case and thought that Murray's "letters to President Graham and other university officials have constituted a distinct setback to any hopes we might have had in that direction." Therefore, he argued, the NAACP should have no "record anywhere as having had anything to do with Miss Murray's application."[190]

White castigated Wilkins, pointing out that it was not in his "province to pass upon this case," since Wilkins's duties did not involve legal affairs. Nevertheless, White, and Marshall too, thought that Murray had used an "unfortunate tone" in her letter to Frank Graham. Apparently Marshall told Murray that the association disapproved of her bold interactions with North Carolinians and the press, but his warning seems not to have slowed her down one little bit. Likewise, White's reprimand of Wilkins did not stop the latter's criticism of Murray. Two weeks later Wilkins sent a rejoinder to White: "Any involvement of the Association in Miss Pauli Murray's application . . . is distinctly more than a subject for legal opinion." Moreover, he pointed out, if White thought Murray's first round of correspondence was "unfortunate," and if Marshall had warned her to stop it, she had only gotten worse. "I know you have noted her release of additional correspondence to the press, and this latter is much more unfortunate than the first letter," Wilkins told White. Unlike the NAACP administrators, Murray understood her correspondence with Graham to be the exchange of ideas between two intelligent people over a pressing issue; she saw herself as equal to Graham. She thought that "Dr. Graham was sympathetic to my position. And he was a friend from within." She continued to pressure him but believed him when he said that his hands were tied by the North Carolina Constitution.[191]

But the worst blow, and the strongest evidence of Wilkins's determination to sink Murray, came when he lobbied against her with Charles Houston. When Houston stopped by the office, the Murray case came up "quite by accident," Wilkins recalled, and he told Houston that the NAACP check for Murray's transcript would leave a record of their involvement. Houston, Wilkins reported to White, "agreed most emphatically . . . that the Association should not be connected in any way with Miss Murray's application."[192] Wilkins got to Houston in late January 1939, when Marshall and White remained open to taking on the case. On February 9, Marshall sent Houston and Leon Ransom, the Howard law professor, copies of Murray's "champing at the bit" letter and Graham's reply, the one in which Graham feared homegrown Fascists and argued for improving North Carolina College for Negroes.

Sometime between February 10 and 22 Marshall mentioned to Murray for the first time that her case suffered because she was not currently a resident of North Carolina. At some point between February 22 and March 6, he called her into his office and told her he could not take the case because of that issue. "I tried to argue with Mr. Marshall that if the state permitted nonresident white students to attend its educational institutions, it had a similar obligation under the Fourteenth Amendment to admit Negroes," Murray recalled.[193]

Marshall's explanation for refusing Murray fits the legal incrementalism that the NAACP embraced, but his reasoning is betrayed by the association's attempt to recruit Walter Raleigh Goldston as an applicant to UNC's medical school. Goldston had been attending college and working in Tennessee for several years, Murray's situation precisely. Anyway, how could Thurgood Marshall tell Pauli Murray that she was not a North Carolinian? Absurd! Murray protested that her "ancestral home was there" and that she was an heir to North Carolina property. Pauli Murray was the Ur-North Carolinian, descended from generations of white and black Tar Heels. As the NAACP worried about Murray's nonresidency, surely it was also worried about her Durham roots. Another plaintiff from James Shepard's and C. C. Spaulding's backyard was the last thing the association would have relished.

But there was more. Years later Murray admitted that in the interview, an event that she always called her worst disappointment, Marshall had hinted that she was "too maverick" and might not be "Simon-pure enough" to be an NAACP plaintiff.[194] Wilkins and White objected to her ferocious letter-writing campaign, her engagement with the black press, and her interaction with white North Carolinians, all of which made her "too maverick." The record might have been used by university counsel in court to impugn her motives, to argue that she did not want to study sociology but rather, wanted to desegregate the university. Since, under *Gaines*, equal facilities, not desegregation, were at stake, Murray had crossed a line when she argued that it would benefit white students to have Negroes present to discuss race relations. That said, NAACP officials and lawyers, especially Roy Wilkins, also thought she was "too maverick" because they could not make her shut up.

Then there was the "Simon-pure enough" problem. One might suspect that the NAACP did not want to accept Murray's case because she was a woman since female plaintiffs might be more vulnerable to attacks on their reputations than male plaintiffs. But even as Marshall turned down Murray, the association accepted the case of a woman in Missouri.[195] Marshall may have told Murray that her past membership in the Communist

Party Opposition would come out in court. The NAACP could never risk representing a Red, or even a pinkish, plaintiff, since it thought that much of its newfound acceptance in the South sprang from offering African Americans a moderate alternative to Communism.

But Marshall may have told Pauli Murray something far more personal, that the NAACP could not represent her because she did not conform to feminine standards. Murray was a tiny woman who often dressed as a man and lived with women. Her nicknames, Lennie and Pauli, were male. And there was something on the record. At the time she worked for the WPA, Murray had been arrested and taken to Bellevue Hospital when the police found her hysterical on the street in New York. Beside herself after a lover's quarrel with a woman, Murray had reached a sexual identity crisis. She transferred from Bellevue to a private psychiatric hospital, where she told doctors that she thought she was a "pseudo-hermaphrodite." Since she appeared to be a woman, she asked for an operation to find her male sex organs but was refused. In the late 1930s, two decades before the adjective existed, Murray thought that she was a transgendered person.[196]

Murray wanted to be heterosexual, and she approached her attraction to women with characteristic determination to fix the problem. She didn't understand homosexuality, and science didn't either. Her "deep religious nature" made her believe that it was wrong, and she found it odd that "homosexuals irritate me instead of causing . . . sympathy." She was attracted to "extremely feminine and heterosexual women." In the months after the NAACP refused to take her case, she sought help at a psychiatric clinic. Doctors there told her that her sexual problems resulted from an unwillingness to submit to authority and accept her natural role as a woman. But Murray had the great good sense to ignore such drivel. "If it is a question of race conflict, submission to authority, being hemmed in by restrictions, why is it I am proud of my Negro blood?" she asked in her diary. Anyway, she told herself, "I do submit to authority as far as I am able, until I am proven wrong, or my point of view is accepted." She was who she was, Murray finally decided. She never went back to the clinic "because psychiatric treatment is not what I need."[197]

Murray's decision to join the CPO and her sexual identity crisis, on the record because of her arrest and commitment to Bellevue, left trails like coiled snakes that hissed for the rest of her life. We cannot know what Thurgood Marshall knew or what he revealed to Murray, but she remembered the conversation as "galling." Conrad Pearson wanted to continue to pursue her case locally, but Murray thought that she could not defy the NAACP.[198]

What if the NAACP had taken her case? The timing was perfect. A few weeks after the NAACP turned Murray down, the Daughters of the American Revolution refused to allow Marian Anderson to sing in Constitution Hall, and the nation began its most robust debate on segregation thus far.[199] Murray's case would have been in the courts just as Hitler lauded the U.S. legal system of states' rights. Moreover, North Carolina would have been a good place for the fight. The judge in *Hocutt* had left the door open, and white North Carolinians prided themselves on their civility. Graham would have been a constructive influence. Here the association had a real chance to win a case in a real southern state, not a border state, such as Maryland or Missouri.

What if the NAACP had won? Murray would never have been intimidated; she would have enrolled if it had been the last thing she ever did. In fact, in a self-mandated test of her courage, she actually visited the UNC campus four months later, meeting students and faculty.[200] Moreover, as it turned out, the *Gaines* decision was a Pyrrhic victory. Lloyd Gaines disappeared and was never heard from again. He was probably murdered in Chicago.[201] Pauli Murray suspected that he was dead and blamed "his own Negro leaders," who had deserted him. "How many Negroes were prepared to stand there behind him every step of the way, with funds, meetings, letters, telegrams and mass demonstrations?" she asked. "We Negroes can throng the streets 300,000 strong . . . when Joe Louis knocks out a single white opponent . . . but when a Lloyd Gaines, single-handed, comes up against a whole region of the country, with its hidebound folkways of 'white supremacy,' . . . not a single mass demonstration is held anywhere in the country."[202] Claude Barnett of the Associated Negro Press told Murray that he heard "all along that Gaines is in Michigan. He has . . . a job there and had to establish residence in that state to get it." Moreover, Barnett alleged, "Certainly the NAACP knows where he is but I understand that organization does not regard Gaines as the ideal subject for the type case they are pressing."[203] NAACP leaders remained mute on Gaines's disappearance. If he was in fact alive, the

NAACP had simply deserted him, as they had Pauli Murray. If he had been murdered, he was a martyr.

The association did not win another higher education case for a decade, pushing the desegregation crisis that many Southerners recognized as inevitable in the late 1930s on into the 1950s. Had the NAACP been able to win desegregation decisions in World War II America, white Southerners would have had a more difficult time mounting massive resistance in the midst of a war against intolerance. Moreover, their weapon of choice in that struggle—that integrationists were Communists—would have lacked the power in 1942 that it had gained by 1952.

Even after Murray knew that the NAACP would never support her, she still maintained cordial relations with Marshall and threatened others who stood in her way with the association. Shepard's new law school at North Carolina College for Negroes found it rough going, and with only one student the first year, it suspended operations. Murray hit her type-writer, requested an application to the UNC's law school, and alerted Marshall to stand by. When UNC responded, telling her to apply to the law school at NCC, she replied that it was "for all practical purposes . . . non-existent." She continued: "I am referring your letter to the N.A.A.C.P. with the suggestion that they correspond with you further about it."[204] But Marshall refused Murray again, saying vaguely that North Carolina might have "a good defense since the school has actually opened."[205] In *Plessy's* house, the window of opportunity to desegregate opened only a crack. Murray kept pushing, but in time Marshall met her entreaties with silence. The diverse forces that combined to thwart Murray's homecoming had succeeded, if only for the time being. North Carolina lost a social worker, and the nation gained a social activist.

Fred and Red Come Home

Even as Dixie turned its black daughter away, it recaptured a couple of its missing white sons. A few months before Murray tried to enter UNC in 1938, Fred Beal, strike leader and one of the Gastonia defendants, entered the North Carolina prison system. He and Kelly Yale "Red" Hendricks had jumped bail and lived in the Soviet Union in the early 1930s. Hendricks came home first, in 1932. When he returned from Moscow, he dyed his red hair black and began organizing in New York City, where he was arrested on the outstanding Gastonia warrant. Soon he found himself in North Carolina's Central Prison, serving a term of five to seven years.[206]

While the Chapel Hill intellectuals and Communists reveled in the free speech in their charmed corner of North Carolina, forty miles away Red Hendricks sat in prison, serving out his term. The CP decided to let him sit there. Hendricks wrote to Beal back in the USSR: "Regardless of What happens to me, I am a Social Revolutionist and Will Continue on With the Struggle." Soon Beal heard disturbing news from Red: "I wint out for a hearin I was closed in a ware cage like a wild man and no wone has bin aloud to speak to me sinc I was caut. You must rite to me very often."[207] Beal organized an effort to rally support for Red within the Soviet Union and in the United States through the ACLU. The Comintern quickly informed Beal: "You are not to give the Hendricks case further consideration."[208] The next year Red wrote Fred again, this time begging for money. The Party had given him only ten dollars before it cut him off. Red complained that all the necessities of life had to be purchased in prison: "They do Not even Give You Soap to Wash With; Nothing to Smoke, No Tooth Paste, No brush, No Shaving Articles Not even a face Towel. One cannot live in here Without These Necessities. . . . There is Nothing being done for me Whatever. . . . I am Buried Alive in a Morgue and Forgotten by the Outside World, especially Those Who Are Supposed to look after me."[209] One person had not forgotten Hendricks; Paul Green visited him in prison. But Beal despaired. "If I was to help Hendricks," Beal recalled, "there was only one course open to me and that was to get out of Soviet Russia."[210]

Beal escaped from the USSR with forged documents and in December 1934 made his way back to New York, where he lived undercover for three years, surfacing occasionally to criticize the USSR in the press. Hiding from both the police and the Communists, who pronounced him "rotten and a maggot," Beal dared not contact Red. Hendricks won release early in 1936 and went to work as a CP organizer in High Point's cotton mills; the Highlander Folk School recruited him as a student in 1938. Despite his "mixed" feelings about the USSR and the Party's abandonment of him in prison, Hendricks still believed that there was "great hope for the future of the Revolution."[211]

By 1937 Beal had tired of his underground life. "I would like to see Red Hendricks more than anyone I know of but I do not dare look for him," Beal told a newspaperman. Beal had been to Kharkov and back—hence to hell and back. "I saw a man-made famine in which millions perished," Beal recalled. "I stood aghast at murder becoming a normal function of the state—the state of my dreams." Now he was "a man without a country and a man without a cause." Shaken by his experience with the Soviet famine and the Comintern's authoritarianism, Beal came to believe that the United States was a far better place than the USSR. "Virtually isolated," Beal had exasperated the Party by proclaiming that he would "rather be in jail in this country than free" in the USSR. Then, conversely, he vexed the ACLU, which had put up his bond in 1930, by proclaiming, "I don't want to be in jail." Beal particularly did not want to be in jail in North Carolina and therefore dependent on the mercy of Governor Hoey, who had been one of his prosecutors in the Gastonia trial.[212] In 1938 Beal was arrested in Massachusetts.

Out on bail, Beal waived extradition and wrote to Paul Green to orchestrate his surrender. Green took Frank Graham and Jonathan Daniels with him to the Sir Walter Raleigh Hotel, where they rented a room and waited for a knock on the door. When Green opened it, he saw "sort of a short fellow" with "sort of red hair." They all walked over to the governor's mansion, where Hoey greeted Beal with the words "Mr. Beal, you have done a noble thing." Beal asserted his "complete innocence" and that "my real 'crime'—[was] the organizing of one of the most under privileged groups of workers in the country." He argued: "Much of what we fought for in Gastonia in 1929 has by this time been accepted by public opinion and by the law of the land as indispensable to the welfare of the American people." "My championship of the workers in Gastonia won me the hatred of anti-labor forces in North Carolina," Beal said, just as "my denunciation of the Russian system has won me the hatred of the communists."[213] He faced seventeen to twenty years and was shipped off in 1938 to North Carolina's Caledonia Prison Farm, where he worked on the chain gang.[214]

One cold, sunny morning eight weeks later Fred Beal peered out of the darkness of Caledonia to see Paul Green striding toward him. As tirelessly as always, Green began working for Beal's release, first persuading Frank

Porter Graham and another UNC professor to organize a petition drive for his parole. The three recruited almost two hundred prominent signatories.[215] A New York group of liberals, labor leaders, and former Communists hired an attorney to plead with Hoey for a pardon.[216] Beal's anti-Communism stood him in good stead in his attempt to cut his time. For example, southern newspaperman Wilbur J. Cash argued that Beal "is now about as anti-Communist as a man can be" and that North Carolina did not need to create a martyr by keeping him imprisoned. Jonathan Daniels editorialized: "There are plenty of people in North Carolina as well as beyond . . . who seriously doubt that Beal was in any real sense guilty of any such crime as that for which he was convicted."[217]

Green originally "thought Fred would be out in thirty days," but something had stopped Hoey in his tracks. When Green visited Hoey on the eve of his departure from office, the governor astonished Green by vowing that Beal would serve every day of his sentence. "But, governor!" Green exclaimed. Hoey interrupted Green's plea for mercy: "You know what? He had syphilis. He had syphilis, I'm telling you. . . . When I found that out, I said, 'No, not one day.' "[218] Beal's preincarceration medical exam had sealed his fate.

Beal's experience did not replicate Angelo Herndon's in Fulton Tower or Shropshire's and Barnes's at that horrific Mecklenburg County prison farm. At Caledonia, prisoners made table scarves and listened to "hillbilly music." Beal read all the anti-Stalinist exposés he could get his hands on. The prisoners worked on the roads, and Beal reported, "We all laugh and try to be cheerful here." Indeed, they did. Caledonia Farm stationery instructed, "Please write cheerful letters."[219] In 1942 Paul Green convinced the new governor, Melville Broughton, to grant Fred Beal parole.[220] Fred still loved Red above all other men, but he never saw him again.[221]

For every errant son it incarcerated, Dixie begat another. A month after UNC's American Student Union endorsed graduate school desegregation and Pauli Murray's admittance, ASU member Junius Scales joined the Communist Party on his nineteenth birthday. He was a reluctant Communist over the spring and early summer of 1939, but that changed when Bart Logan, the new CP district organizer, came looking for him at The Intimate Bookshop. That day Logan brought Scales back to his hometown of Greensboro. No ideological lesson could have been more effective for Scales than visiting Logan's "run-down little house" across town from the thirty-six-room mansion that had sheltered Scales during his unhappy early childhood. Logan introduced Scales to his wife, Belle. After a dinner of beans, fatback, and cornbread, they drove to High Point. There Scales "met Red Hendricks and a whole bunch of workers. The first workers that I ever met in my life and it was a love affair that I hope never ends."[222] Scales described Red this way: "His face was deeply seamed with hard work (since childhood), a great deal of suffering, and too much heavy drinking." The two shared a house together as they organized High Point workers at the Highland Cotton Mill.[223]

Bart Logan and Red Hendricks personified for Scales what was right about the Communist Party. Scales joined the CP because it "opposed fascism, organized workers, projected a socialist future, and, alone, stood for the full economic, political, and social equality of blacks."[224] Much later Scales tried to convey what it meant for white people to live in a Jim Crow system. "You just can't imagine the feeling of guilt of anybody growing up in that time, for blacks. It was an absolute horror that you couldn't live with. It was so pervasive and so corrupting and so destructive to have people. . . . " He trailed off, then observed, "If they had been second class citizens, that would have been a major step up."[225] From Paul Crouch, up on Brushy Mountain thinking about Socialism in the 1910s, to Fred Beal, whom Crouch dispatched to Gastonia in the 1920s to bring Communism to poor white millworker Red Hendricks, to Junius Scales, privileged child of the state's elite, the search for a radical alternative to southern exploitation grew in native North Carolina red clay, nourished by the injustice that rained down on it.

PART THREE

REBELLION

7

EXPLOSIVES IN
DEMOCRACY'S ARSENAL

Pauli Murray met Max Yergan in New York on July 31, 1939, at her new office, a place that bore the awkward name The Negro Peoples Committee with the Medical Bureau and the North American Committee to Aid Spanish Democracy. Most often they called it the Negro Peoples Committee of the Spanish Refugee Relief Campaign, or simply, the NPC. These names sounded a bit tinny to Murray, the former Lovestoneite, whose ears pricked up at their slightly Soviet ring. She worried as well about some of the names on her new letterhead. William Patterson, the black Communist and former International Labor Defense head, served on the NPC board, and his new wife, Louise Thompson, *Black and White* alumna, was a committee sponsor.[1] Langston Hughes joined his old friend Thompson as a sponsor. Angelo Herndon's name appeared as well, but people said it was his personal heartbreak, not his Communism, that inscribed it. Two years earlier Langston Hughes had reported from the front lines of the Spanish Civil War that Angelo's brother Milton had died saving a white soldier's life. Thus Herndon sat on the board as "a man whose brother died in Spain and not as a representative of the C.P.," an insider told Murray.[2]

Even though Murray had lived from hand to mouth for most of the 1930s, her doubts about the NPC's Communist membership caused her to hesitate before accepting the temporary administrative position. But the

Negro Peoples Committee chairman, Urban Leaguer Lester Granger, assured her that Communists did not dominate the organization. He was right. A. Philip Randolph, Mary McLeod Bethune, and Max Yergan served on the board. Murray's fear of being associated with the CPUSA grew from her antipathy to it, nourished by her abiding and ill-founded faith that the NAACP would someday see the error of its ways and make her a plaintiff in a desegregation suit. She signed on but warned Granger that she would walk off the job if the Communists took control. Granger assured her that he would be hard on her heels if they did.[3]

Yergan harbored no such doubts about associating with Communists. In the two and a half years since he had returned to the United States, he had forged an intricate network of Communist friends. Abner Berry, a black Communist from Houston living in Harlem, recalled that shortly after Yergan's arrival he had asked to meet with Berry and James Ford. Lovett Fort-Whiteman had recruited Ford and Berry to the Party in the 1920s in Chicago. Berry had listened to Fort-Whiteman, wearing "one of them Russian hats," talk about Communism and his experiences in the USSR. After Berry "found out about these child care centers in the Soviet Union," he said, he "was for the Russian Revolution."[4]

Now Yergan poured out his heart to Berry and Ford. He spoke with bitterness about "the indignities he had to suffer in South Africa, how he couldn't teach the kids what he wanted," referring to his stillborn social work curriculum. He told them that "he wanted to put himself at the disposal of the Party." They marveled at what "a big fish we caught." It is unclear whether Yergan's putting himself at the "disposal of the Party" meant actually joining it. He functioned as an "influential" but does not seem to have joined a local Party unit. Paul Robeson served on the board of Yergan's International Committee on African Affairs, and Yergan traveled around the world, giving anti-imperialist and anti-Fascist speeches.[5] Since the committee operated on a shoestring, primarily the fifteen hundred dollars that Robeson donated, Yergan supported himself and his family by teaching "Negro History and Culture" at City College. CCNY students, backed by the teachers' union, had wrested the course from a reluctant administration. The only black professor in the four colleges that made up CCNY, Yergan loved his lectureship and was proud that the students had demanded it.[6]

Yergan's optimism about racial politics in the United States—"We Negroes in America are on the threshold of one of the greatest democratic movements in History," he thought—contrasted with his pessimism about South Africa. Just three weeks before Murray met Yergan, he attended the 1939 International Labor Defense conference that marked the crest of the Popular Front. There the NAACP lawyer and Howard University law professor Charles Hamilton Houston mingled with such Communists as Angelo Herndon and William Patterson. Yergan spoke to the group on the "problem of the political refugees" from "Nazi and Fascist Oppression," the same concern that now brought him to the Negro Peoples Committee and to Pauli Murray.[7] His remarks found favor with Patterson and Herndon, since Communist criticism of U.S. isolationism increased in the spring and summer of 1939. For example, James Allen, the former editor of the *Southern Worker*, wrote of U.S. "complicity in 'nonintervention' in Spain" and characterized it as "support of appeasement."[8]

The NPC wanted to rescue "thousands of neglected Ethiopian refugees," who had fled to Kenya to escape Mussolini's net. For her part, Murray coordinated fundraisers to underwrite the Negro Peoples Committee's operating expenses, which consisted primarily of her salary. After that, however, there was nothing left to donate to refugees. The NPC's parent organization, the North American Committee to Aid Spanish Democracy, had raised about three million dollars, but the Negro Peoples Committee simply tried to justify its own existence, made possible primarily from the proceeds of an annual Paul Robeson concert.[9] As Murray learned more about the ebb and flow of NPC revenue, she began to wonder why such a committee existed at all.

In the summer of 1939, as white Americans anxiously debated being drawn into war, black Americans attacked Jim Crow with renewed vigor. Their campaign to link the Nazis and Dixie had begun to pay off. Support for dismantling white supremacy was stronger than ever before, some of it coming from white Southerners themselves. The Southern Popular Front brought together liberals, Socialists, and Communists in such organizations as the Southern Conference for Human Welfare and the Southern Negro Youth Conference. The New Deal's attack on the southern economic structure had highlighted the costs of Jim Crow and created national movements to abolish the poll tax and eliminate sharecropping.

The Supreme Court's decision in *Gaines* six months earlier had opened the way for more lawsuits to desegregate southern education. When the Daughters of the American Revolution had barred black singer Marian Anderson from Constitution Hall in Washington the previous spring, northern public opinion swelled against segregation.[10]

Perhaps most important, as the nation debated mobilization, African Americans put to use the lessons that they had learned from World War I. The two hundred thousand African Americans who had fought in the Great War believed that they had sold their patriotism cheaply for an empty promise of full citizenship. The virulence of discrimination during the war and the racial violence afterward transformed African Americans' political consciousness. In the long run up to World War II they resolved that "when the battle is won the black patriot does not expect to be robbed of his fruition of victory as he was in the First World War." This time they would get their guarantees up front.[11]

International politics intervened to complicate the coalition that African Americans had put together when the German Joachim von Ribbentrop met the Russian Vyacheslav Mikhailovich Molotov in Moscow in August 1939. The Nazi-Soviet Nonaggression Pact that Molotov and Ribbentrop bound together split the Popular Front, particularly in the South. With black Communists suddenly opposed to U.S. entry into the war, the politics of patriotism and citizenship became more complicated. On the one hand, the pact devastated alliances on the Left over the issue of entry into the war. On the other, it made the patriotism of non-Communist African Americans more important. If, as Du Bois famously said at the end of World War I, "We return fighting," now black soldiers and civilians set out fighting on the home front before they ever left for World War II. As Franklin Roosevelt made the United States the arsenal of the democracies, black Americans exploded the myth of a democratic United States.[12]

Pauli Murray's experiences in the three years after she had applied to UNC in 1938 and before Pearl Harbor in 1941 illustrate the new immediacy and fresh radicalism of African American demands to desegregate inter-state transportation, to establish criminal rights in the southern justice system, eliminate sharecropping, and end the poll tax. By tracing the modern civil rights movement in 1939, we see its roots in the Popular Front.[13]

African Americans and the Nonaggression Pact

Even as Murray and Yergan worked with refugees from Fascism, Ribben-trop's meeting with Molotov suddenly reordered the world and reshuffled relationships among African Americans. The Nazi-Soviet Nonaggression Pact of August, 23, 1939, formally named the Molotov-Ribbentrop Pact, stopped Soviet anti-Fascist activity cold.[14] Before the pact, Communists faulted the United States for failing to intervene in the war against Fascism. After the pact, the Party condemned it for supporting an "imperialist" war against Germany and Italy.

Because the issue of black patriotism was central to civil rights strategy, the pact marked the end, at least for a time, of the black Popular Front in which such diverse activists as NAACP legal strategist Charles Houston and Communist organizer Angelo Herndon worked together. For the next twenty-two months Hitler and Stalin remained allies; whenever non-Communist African Americans tried to seize their rightful share of the opportunities that the U.S. defense machine churned out or spoke up for war preparation, they encountered black and white Communists who condemned them as pawns of an imperialistic war and citizens of an antidemocratic country.[15]

Moreover, the Nazi-Soviet Pact undercut the southern Left by undermining the strongest argument of non-Communist Southerners for associating with Communists: anti-Fascism.[16] The comparison of Jim Crow and Fascism had been the most powerful single weapon in the southern Left's arsenal. The Party's postpact substitution of enemies—imperialism for Fascism—meant that white and black Southerners could no longer justify their cooperation with Communists as being necessary in the fight against Fascism, which endangered the country from without, and the fight against racism, which endangered it from within.

White supremacists, whom African Americans had successfully compared with Fascists, now leaped to the moral high ground, even if they balanced precariously there. They quickly equated Fascism and Communism to convince Southerners that all "isms" were antidemocratic, while they blurred the differences between Fascism and Communism into a new specter called totalitarianism.[17] As anti-Communism gained ground, the glimmers of an illogical equation began to shine through. Communists supported black equality; therefore, any supporter of black equality might be a Communist. While the links among black equality, Communism, and anti-Americanism were at least as old as J. Edgar Hoover's pursuit of Lovett Fort-Whiteman, anti-Fascism and the Popular Front had strained them. Now the Nazi-Soviet Pact offered white supremacists what they considered positive proof that U.S. Communists held no anti-Fascist principles and blindly followed a foreign power.

Yet the aftermath of the Nazi-Soviet Pact proved that the southern Popular Front was not simply a Communist front. The nascent visions of equality, alliances with labor, and alternatives to incremental interracial cooperation that had built a southern coalition continued to come into focus from 1939 to 1941, even as the coalition itself began to fray. As the United States prepared for war, non-Communist civil rights demands became more immediate and far-reaching. The Carnegie Corporation's research mandate on race in America nourished those demands and included many who had become more liberal during the Popular Front. Recruited by the head of the Carnegie study, the Swede Gunnar Myrdal, liberal white Southerners and African Americans began to explore America's "race problem." The UNC sociology professor Guy Johnson became deputy director of Myrdal's study. Johnson left a skeptical Howard Odum behind in Chapel Hill and brought several of his coworkers into Myrdal's stable of researchers and writers. New Dealer Clark Foreman and UNC graduate George Stoney contributed as well. They joined African Americans Charles S. Johnson, Horace Cayton, and Ralph Bunche, among others, to investigate southern racism, to lend historical, sociological, and economic perspective to the problem, and to suggest new alternatives to white supremacy.[18]

If Pauli Murray had spent most of the 1930s prodding historical change down the pike, after 1939 events propelled her into the fast lane of social upheaval. She learned first of the Nazi-Soviet Pact on August 24 and then, on September 1, of the German invasion of Poland. It proved a dizzying week for U.S. Communists. Anti-Fascist books and films disappeared overnight in the Soviet Union, but Earl Browder and the CPUSA denied any change in Soviet policy against Fascism. The day after the Germans invaded Poland, the *Daily Worker* called for "every possible support of the heroic and beleaguered Polish people."[19] When Britain and

France declared war on Germany the next day, the CPUSA National Committee pledged to aid those who helped "Poland defend its national independence." Ben Davis, who had learned a thing or two about Fascism from Atlanta's Black Shirts, condemned the Nazis and praised FDR on September 12.[20] Then, on September 17, the Red Army invaded eastern Poland to claim the sphere of influence that the Molotov-Ribbentrop Pact had secretly afforded the USSR. Ten days later Stalin and Hitler signed the Friendship Pact. The new allies sealed the fall of Poland, called for a time out in the fighting, and blamed Britain and France "for any continuation of the war." Anti-Communist feeling ran high, and by October, Earl Browder was facing retrospective charges for having entered the United States from Moscow on a forged passport before U.S. recognition of the USSR.[21]

At ten on the morning following the Red Army invasion of Poland, Pauli Murray wrote a frantic letter to the permanent NPC staffer whose job she temporarily held. "Politics," Murray exclaimed, "has entered the job situation. . . . Undoubtedly, the Communists will lose support and the respect of the liberals in this country. . . . Those . . . who believe there is the possibility of communist-directed NPC will certainly disassociate themselves with this committee." Murray was one paycheck away from destitution, but she stuck to her guns. She did "not approve of the Soviet Union action" and thought that she would "have to resign in the interests of my own integrity and that of the Committee."[22]

Finally, at the end of the month, Moscow radioed the CPUSA: "Fascism is now secondary; the main and basic thing is the struggle against capitalism. . . . Must cease to trail in wake of FDR." A few days later another message ordered Browder to end his alliance with "Social Democracy." The message's last four words conveyed perhaps a touch of defensiveness: "Days change, so needs." Browder spun around and proclaimed the Polish, not the German, government to be Fascist.[23]

As Murray worried about looming conflict within the Negro Peoples Committee, A. Philip Randolph threw down the gauntlet to his fellow NPC members. "War is here!" he wrote after the Polish invasion. "Who can tell what nations may be drawn into the conflict tomorrow?" He pointed out that Poland was "not a Democracy, and has also been one of the worse persecutors of the Jewish people. Having sown the wind, Poland is reaping the whirlwind." But he saved his strongest invective for Germany and condemned the Soviet Union for "demanding its pound of 'flesh.' . . . The great and monumental moral and spiritual loss . . . in this conflict is the desertion of the fight against world Fascism by the Soviet Union," Randolph concluded.[24] Non-Communists, Pauli Murray among them, loathed the Party's decision to protect the Soviet Union by collaborating with Hitler.

But some Communists—Junius Scales, for example—worked too close to the ground to let international politics drive them out of the Party. When Scales heard about the pact over the radio in Greensboro, he exclaimed, "Fat chance! That's about as likely as a snowstorm in hell." When it became clear that the pact was fact, a confused and horrified Scales clung to the explanation that Stalin must have had to sign it to save the Soviet Union. Then he returned to organizing black and white college students in a "huge interracial meeting."[25] Scales thought that the CP furnished the only platform from which he might work to overthrow white supremacy. International events, disquieting as they might be, simply could not distract him from that mission. Don West seems to have felt differently. He became a minister of an Ohio church and, in the late fall of 1939, asked to be accepted in the liberal Fellowship of Southern Churchmen. He must have abandoned the Communists by then, and he sought membership "even with the inferior background of having had a few tastes of hell in the scarlet stream of the labor movement."[26]

The Negro Peoples Committee, dedicated to aiding victims of Fascism, collapsed quickly. If Murray was convinced that she would soon have to resign because she opposed the Soviet Union's actions, Communist members of the committee became convinced that they should no longer help Fascist victims. In early October Max Yergan declared in the pages of the *Daily Worker* that he "regard[ed] the Soviet-German non-aggression pact, and the subsequent action of the Soviet Union, as the one great contribution to world peace and democracy to come out of the conflict thus far."[27] Meanwhile Murray slogged on through October and into early November, toward the day of the committee's major fundraiser. The event was to feature Sylvia Chen, the West Indian–Chinese who had been Langston Hughes's great friend in Moscow, now dancing under the name Si-Lan Chen. But Chen did not show up for her November 5 performance, and Paul Robeson, who had promised the NPC the proceeds from one of his concerts, refused to return Murray's calls or letters seeking to schedule his performance. Since the NPC's goal was to "alleviate the distress of victims of fascist aggression," Communists who had formerly supported it now acted as if absence were the better part of valor.[28] NPC board members floundered as well, and Lester Granger called a meeting to discuss whether the committee should disband or "take a position regarding an international alliance and our national peace time policy."[29]

When the NPC meeting came, members exercised extreme caution as they danced around the topic of the Nazi-Soviet collaboration. Yergan's position straddled the new line: "I recognize the necessity of doing everything to stop and overthrow fascism. At the same time, I recognize the present governments of Britain and France as being imperialistic at heart. A victory for either side is not a victory for democracy."[30] For now he thought that the NPC should defer action until it received direction from its parent organization, the North American Committee to Aid Spanish Democracy. For her part, if Murray suspected that the Communist Party paid her salary, she didn't put it that way to the board. Rather, she simply reiterated that no money came into the organization from the public, and she thought that the committee should at least be able to finance itself, if not actually help refugees. Yergan commended her on "her concern over the dignity of the Negro Peoples Committee as such." Unmollified, Murray resigned. Despite the committee's tiptoeing around the Red elephant in the room, the headlines pointed directly toward it: COMMUNIST SQUABBLE SPLITS HARLEM GROUP.[31]

Was the Negro Peoples Committee a Communist-controlled organization, as some contemporary observers and later historians dubbed it? The NPC letterhead confirms that *non*-Communists were in the majority. After the pact, however, the Communists refused to permit a group that existed to aid victims of Fascism to issue a statement condemning Fascism. The absurdity of the NPC's postpact position provides a microcosm of the damage that Nazi-Soviet Pact did to the health and structure of Popular Front organizations that involved African Americans. The Negro Peoples Committee's membership also illustrates the inappropriateness of condemning Popular Front participants as "fellow travelers." On the contrary, many NPC members were resolutely opposed to Communism but shared social justice goals with them.[32] Most Popular Front organizations, many of those that worked for black civil rights, had Communist members. Murray had sworn when she joined the NPC that she would leave if the Communist minority came to dominate the board, and she did. Did that make her a fellow traveler or a civil rights supporter who worked alongside Communists for a greater good? One thing is sure: Her three-month stint at the NPC made her more vulnerable to later charges that she had been a Communist.[33]

For Yergan and others who had not declared themselves Communists, the pact turned a spotlight on them because they publicly had to support the new Communist line. Yergan's open friendship with Browder and the Robesons qualified him for extensive FBI surveillance as early as 1940. An anonymous informant identified Yergan as a "national representative of the Executive Committee of the Communist International of Moscow, looking after negro [sic] affairs in North and South America and the West Indies." It stretches credulity to believe that Yergan would have risen so quickly that Stalin would have invited him to join the ECCI, but he was active in almost every Communist and Communist-influenced organization.[34]

The CPUSA saw a 15 percent drop in membership in 1939, but remarkably few Jewish members abandoned it. No information exists on the number of black Communists who left the Party in the South, but in Harlem, as Abner Berry acknowledged, the Party began to lose its "base." Recruitment of new members plummeted across the country, and the earthquake of the Nazi-Soviet Pact caused the foundations of Popular Front organizations to crumble.[35]

After the 1939 pact most African Americans continued to consider Fascism a present danger to themselves and their country, in keeping with the critique they had been mounting since 1933. They wanted little to do with a Soviet Union allied with Hitler. In December the *Afro-American* devoted an entire page to "The 1939 Sepia Retreat from Moscow." If "hatred for Hitler and Mussolini drove liberals into the arms of Stalin," now "the violent Reds, the parlor pinks, the radicals of various degrees of sincerity and purpose and fellow travelers" had been "left defenseless on a limb." As the writer reviewed the past decade, he argued that the "persecution of Jews," the "rape of Ethiopia," and "the depths of economic chaos" of the Depression had convinced some African Americans that "the Reds

seemed to point the only way out." The Communist defense of the Scottsboro "Boys" and Angelo Herndon had helped the Communist cause, but
"the chief bugaboo of the period which drove many into the ranks . . . was
the fear of Nazism and Fascism." Now Stalin had "burned the ideology of
fair play by joining Hitler."[36] A Howard University historian put it this
way: "After the Soviet pact with Germany, not even a Sophist could
beguile an intelligent person into the belief that the dictatorship of the
proletariat is scheduled for the near future."[37]

Watching the Soviets explain themselves in the fall of 1939 is like
watching theater of the absurd. In November 1939 the anti-Fascist hero
Georgi Dimitrov, now secretary of the Comintern, followed the new line
when he argued that Germany, Italy, and Japan had been "aggressor
States" prior to 1939, but that now "the imperialists of Britain and France
have passed over to the offensive, have hurled their peoples into war
against Germany."[38] In the early days after the pact Paul Robeson
announced, "Hitler has delivered himself into the hands of Russia." By
continuing the war, Robeson warned, Britain and France fought to
"uphold Fascism and not to achieve democratic ends." The same day James
Ford told African Americans, "This is not a war against Fascism. It is a
war between two imperialist groups."[39] One columnist wrote in the *Nation*
of postpact Communist behavior, "If they had set out to prove themselves
scoundrels they could not have worked to better effect."[40]

Randolph, Yergan, and the National Negro Congress

The Nazi-Soviet alliance had dire consequences for the four-year-old
National Negro Congress (NNC) and for Pauli Murray's colleagues A.
Philip Randolph and Max Yergan. Both served in the NNC, which had
grown out of a Howard University meeting held in May 1935. John P.
Davis, a Harvard Law School graduate who worked on black labor
issues; Robert C. Weaver, Will Alexander's black colleague in the Farm
Security Administration; and Howard University Professor Ralph
Bunche called the conference on "The Position of the Negro in Our
National Economic Crisis," and its agenda fitted in nicely with New Deal
initiatives to dismantle the South's racialized capitalism.[41] Olive Stone
came from the University of North Carolina to attack sharecropping and

tenancy before the 250 black and white delegates. James Ford talked about "The Communist's Way Out for the Negro." A. Philip Randolph blasted organized labor for its exclusion of African Americans, and W. E. B. Du Bois pronounced himself skeptical of the value of any alliance with whites.[42] Afterward the organizers and a small group of attendees began to plan for the next year a national congress that would maintain the focus on black economics. Only a few days later the CPUSA and the Comintern signaled their interest in the National Negro Congress and began to promote it.[43] Sanhedrin veteran Kelly Miller, still teaching at Howard, alleged that the original meeting had brought to his campus "prominent Communists, Socialists, reds, and semi-reds of varying degrees of radicalism." His protest sparked a congressional investigation of his colleagues.[44]

The next year, when a "thousand fiery-eyed delegates" to the National Negro Congress convened in Chicago in February 1936, the NNC did not deny Communist participation.[45] In this Popular Front moment, its official statement concluded, "The Congress had no desire to exclude any group," but no group should be found "unduly influencing or dominating its activity."[46] The Communists were in but were warned that they should not try to take over the congress. Nevertheless, "some alleged the expenses of the Congress were underwritten by the Communist Party," one observer reported.[47] NNC organizer John P. Davis had been a Communist since at least the previous fall, although he remained underground.[48] The birth of the NNC coincided with the growth of black unionists organized by the CIO after the passage of the Wagner Act. From 1936 to 1940 the number of black union members in the United States increased from one hundred to five hundred thousand.[49]

Everyone noticed that unlike the Sanhedrin a decade earlier, when elder statesmen like Kelly Miller had kept a firm hold on the proceedings, "the Congress was seeking a new race leadership." A committee named John Davis secretary and Randolph president.[50] Communists involved in planning included Ben Davis, Angelo Herndon, and James Ford, but such non-Communists as Randolph, Helen Bryan and Crystal Bird Fauset of the Swarthmore Institute of Race Relations, and Ralph Bunche of Howard contributed in equal measure. Langston Hughes, who attended, must have thought that the National Executive Council meeting resembled a *Black and White* film reunion, with Matt Crawford and Henry Lee Moon in attendance.[51] Yergan, not yet resident in the United States, spoke against imperialism and set up a relief committee for Ethiopians. He also made valuable contacts for his upcoming trip the next month to the USSR. By the next conference Yergan would be living in the United States.[52]

A few months later in Moscow a "special discussion" on the "Negro Question" within the Comintern offered up the National Negro Congress as proof of Popular Front success. "It is a long way from the Arkansas peonage cases of 1923 . . . to the National Negro Congress of to-day, in which the Communist Party plays the leading role."[53] By 1938, the Comintern claimed, "throughout the Congress in its organization and activities, the role of the Communist Party as the guiding force was outstanding in every phase of its activities."[54]

President A. Philip Randolph did not see the CP as "the guiding force" in the NNC from 1936 to 1940, although he appreciated the advantages of a black Popular Front based on working-class participation. Throughout the 1920s and 1930s, as he headed the Brotherhood of Sleeping Car Porters, Randolph had pushed aside the more radical Socialist beliefs that had led him to start the *Messenger* twenty years earlier and emerged as a mainstream labor leader.[55] The Congress organized its delegates from the bottom up and incorporated among them working people and labor activists. The 817 delegates were overwhelmingly labor-oriented and secular. They came from local community meetings, such as one at the Harlem YMCA, in which Louise Thompson and Ella Baker, then Pauli Murray's WPA supervisor, both took leadership roles. In North Carolina, CP district organizer Paul Crouch tried to rouse some NNC delegates, but he failed.[56] Alabama, however, sent four delegates. Three were Communists, and the fourth was the president of Mobile's NAACP chapter.[57]

The NNC's success came from its blend of direct protest tactics, Popular Front alliances, working-class representation, and urgency. Many black people had had enough of the gradualism that ran first forward, then backward. "The issues should be obvious, clear and simple," Randolph told the delegates. The solutions should embody nonviolent direct action: "parades, picketing, boycotting, mass protest, the mass distribution of propaganda literature, as well as legal action. . . . Weakness or timidity" had vanished to be replaced by black power. Never again should the

"Negro peoples . . . place their problems for solution down at the feet of their white sympathetic allies."[58]

After such a promising start, the NNC's unity became a casualty of the Nazi-Soviet Nonaggression Pact. The showdown took place in April 1940, at the first congress following the pact. As delegate Pauli Murray listened from the floor, Randolph took the podium.[59] He knew that many in the audience were Communists, yet he minced no words in his speech, titled "The World Crisis and the Negro People Today." This was not, as the Communists had been telling everyone, your father's war, he argued. There were no "Hoenzollerns, Romanoffs and Hapsburgs"; instead the danger came from the totalitarian states of "Nazi Germany and Communist Russia and Fascist Italy." At that point many of the white delegates, who made up one-third of the audience, walked out. Randolph went on to review the congress's accomplishments over the past four years, and he condemned the United States for its antidemocratic treatment of African American citizens.[60]

But Randolph also condemned Hitler and Mussolini and stated flatly: "Nazi Germany and Communist Russia, where freedom of speech, press and assembly, the foundations of democracy, is suppressed, could not, and would not uphold and protect democratic traditions and institutions." The only "rational conclusion," he told the congress, "seems to be that the Negro and the other darker races must look to themselves for freedom. . . . Freedom is never granted, it is won." By the time Randolph called a spade a spade—"the Communist Party of America stems from Communist Russia, its policies and program tactics and strategy are as fitful, changeful and unpredictable as the foreign policy and line of Moscow"—two-thirds of his audience had left the hall.[61]

When the NNC Resolutions Committee passed a motion against U.S. involvement in the "imperialist war," Randolph refused to stand for reelection as president. He explained later that the congress had "brilliantly succeeded" in portraying itself as a "Transmission Belt for Communists' propaganda" and seemed to be controlled by white Communists. "Uproarious applause greeted every favorable reference . . . to Soviet Russia," Randolph recalled. He put it simply: "I quit the Congress because I was opposed to it, or its officials, expressing sympathy for the Soviet Union, which is the death prison where democracy and liberty have walked their 'last mile' and where shocking 'blood purges' wipe out any, and all persons who express any dissenting opinions from dictator Stalin."[62]

After Randolph resigned, Max Yergan ascended to the presidency. The NNC soldiered on, although it lost much of its legitimacy along with its non-Communist support. "There are those who quail before the strength of the oppressors," the decimated NNC argued. "Who would have believed that A. Philip Randolph would turn back? Black America is not yellow, Philip."[63]

With Yergan at the helm, the group equated winning civil rights at home with staying out of an imperialist war abroad, a less compelling comparison than the Nazi Germany-Dixie parallel, even though it spoke to the liberation of Africa. The NNC conceded that "the Negro people want nothing of Hitler." But if "the British warmakers hold Africa, India, the West Indies and other colonial areas in a cruel bondage often infinitely worse than oppression known by Negroes in America," the Negro could not fight on the side of the British either.[64]

Is This My People's War?

Many African Americans had a keen interest in anticolonialism, but they also understood Fascism and naturally wanted to save themselves first. Over the previous decade they had recognized the similarities between southern white supremacy and Fascism and thought that Dixie and Germany posed more immediate problems than did British colonialism. Yet they were no friends of empire. For example, in 1940 the normally prowar *Afro-American* published this argument: "Nothing Hitler could do to England would be any worse than what Britain's South Africa and Australia are doing to the natives."[65] The fear that they might have to fight on the side of the imperialists prompted some non-Communist African Americans to become more outspoken against colonialism. They were loath to enter a war that aided Britain and France, as Pan-Africanist and former Communist George Padmore put it, in "the preservation of their colonial empires and the monopoly which they enjoy in the exploitation of cheap colored labor."[66]

Events in Europe, however, began to take precedence over a generalized anticolonialism. Most African Americans had reacted to the German invasion of Poland with horror, and the *Afro-American* announced, "War has come. . . . Perhaps it would be better if we didn't delay our help so long." African Americans wondered: "What will Adolf Hitler Do to Us?" One man suggested that in addition to creating ghettos, segregation, and concentration camps for African Americans, Hitler would quickly ban "swing music," since it seemed to have a dissolute effect on whites.[67] When news from Poland revealed that the Germans had instituted "Jim Crow street cars" in Warsaw, "how much like our dear old Southland this sounds," one black writer pointed out.[68]

African American debate during the eight months that elapsed between the Nazi-Soviet Pact and the fall of France differed from debates among white Americans. African Americans asked what U.S. entry into a war between European Fascists and imperialists would mean to their place in the domestic polity. They aimed to avoid their mistake in World War I, when they had bargained their support away for a hypothetical reward that did not materialize. Rather than be "frozen in the status quo" for the duration of this war, they knew they must win concessions up front.[69] White contemporaries sometimes thought that African Americans opposed U.S. entry into the war; however, that was a misinterpretation of a complex situation. After the pact, black opinion leaders, such as Paul Robeson, who were pro-Communist opposed entry into the war, while other non-Communist African Americans—for example, W. E. B. Du Bois—agonized over the issue of fighting on the imperialist side and afforded themselves the luxury of trying to win advantages for the colonized.[70] On the other hand, some replied affirmatively to the question "Is it our business?" Yes, answered one black columnist: "When there is a mad man on the loose" in the neighborhood, we do not wait until we "wake up some night to hear his heavy tread on our porch . . . his blood stained hand on our door knob."[71]

French lessons convinced African Americans that European Fascism posed the most pressing threat to their own safety and that of people of color around the world. With the fall of France in June 1940, the Nazis captured some two million French soldiers, four hundred thousand of whom were "colored," specifically, Africans and "Arabs." A captured white French fighter reported that it seemed that "the Negroes were 'expected.'" The Germans immediately put them into a "special fenced enclosure" and executed many who they claimed refused to quit fighting. In one incident the Nazis randomly chose eighty black men for public execution. As the Nazis marched the French forces to prison camps, they refused to allow the African fighters to eat or drink. Upon arrival, "the Negroes were immediately isolated." Because they had not eaten, hundreds died as the Germans were "constantly standing around and taking pictures." Hitler called these camps "the laboratories of his future policy."[72] In October 1940 Nazi occupiers of Rheims blew up a monument to black troops who had served in World War I.[73] African Americans soon learned that a newspaper in occupied Paris had declared, "Negroes have no place in the new order of European civilization."[74]

Responding to the news from France, the *New York Age* announced that it was not "a white man's war" and only the "Garveyites and Communists" thought that it was.[75] The week after Paris fell, the *Afro-American* put it bluntly: "It isn't too late, we hope, but with our present crop of Communists, Nazists, Ku Kluxers and 100-per-centers still prating about peace and the color line, we are in dire danger. Hatred of the Jews, discrimination against colored people will have to go. We can't have race hate and patriotism at the same time." The author concluded, "Uncle Sam needs every citizen, not merely every white citizen, to do his duty."[76] At the same time, the black press argued, a strong national defense required unified citizens, and unity required a commitment to "democracy in its truest light." The editor of the *Chicago Defender* argued: "National defense means an unquestionable integration of black and white citizens in all the phases of governmental activities." Since the Revolution, black patriots' sacrifices had amounted to little more than "foot-notes in some obscure history book." This time, if the country demanded unity, it must first extend democracy.[77]

In the split between Yergan and Randolph, it was Randolph who probably spoke for more African Americans. One of Randolph's favorite expressions—"the leadership would have to catch up with the followership"—explains his emergence as a leader in 1940.[78] Others, for example, Ralph Bunche, who predicted a "return of slavery if Hitler wins," also became prominent during that year.[79] While the debate over African Americans' place in the European conflagration roared in the black press, Randolph deftly directed African Americans into the war column, even as he pressured Washington for better marching orders than ever before. For example, when FDR announced in January 1941 that the United States would become the arsenal of democracy for Britain and France by providing arms, one black columnist chided the president: "It was not enough merely to make us the arsenal of the democracies. He also should have set a goal that would make us the model of democracies by insisting that . . . we should also fortify ourselves with the spiritual armament of democracy."[80]

Black Communists meanwhile hurled themselves into preventing U.S. entry into the war. If Paul Robeson didn't return Pauli Murray's telephone calls from the Negro Peoples Committee, he certainly returned those from the American Peace Mobilization (APM). The organization arose from the American League for Peace and Democracy, which turned on a dime less than two weeks after the Nazi-Soviet Pact from fighting Fascism to promoting U.S. isolationism. The APM drew black Communists, those who questioned the African American stake in the war, pacifists, Socialists, and traditional isolationists.[81] Louise Thompson, Langston Hughes, and Richard Wright, a young black writer from Mississippi who had joined the CPUSA in 1933, served with Robeson on the APM National Council. The Peace Mobilization used civil rights as an antiwar tool: "Democracy begins at home. . . . All of us . . . must band together . . . to fight for the real Democracy that is our American heritage." The Comintern was delighted to learn from the *Daily Worker* that Wright, "famous Negro writer in America" had adopted the Communist cause since they had no record of his membership in Moscow.[82] Wright took a lead in the APM effort to organize Volunteers for Peace Clubs that urged members to "Vote Out Conscriptors."[83]

As the CPUSA sang the refrain "The Yanks Are Not Coming," the American Peace Mobilization threw up a picket line in front of the White House and announced its intention to remain "until peace comes." The Howard University professor and APM demonstrator William Alphaeus Hunton, Jr., recalled that they were assaulted by "soldiers, sailors, and marines."[84] Meanwhile the *Daily Worker* declared, "The war drive is a lynch drive" and "peace will break out." Richard Wright said in June 1941 that it was "Not My People's War," but by then most black Americans did not agree with him.[85]

Greyhounds, Guts, and Gandhi

As a delegate to the National Negro Congress, Pauli Murray had watched the drama unfold between Randolph and Yergan. After her ejection from the Negro Peoples Committee in the spring of 1940, she landed on her feet at the Socialist Workers Defense League, which she called "Norman Thomas' answer to the International Defense League." The WDL "defended poor workers and trade unionists" and formed a partnership with the Southern Tenant Farmers' Union. Since 1937 the organizations had jointly sponsored National Sharecroppers Week (NSW) to publicize the plight of black and white sharecroppers.[86] For Murray, who had made educating the public on discrimination a personal crusade, it was her dream job. When she left the Negro Peoples Committee for the Workers Defense League, she didn't change direction even though she had jumped from the platform of the Popular Front to the Christian Socialist side of the radical track. Her leap landed her among people who remained her allies for years to come, but she did not join the Socialist Party at that time.[87]

Less than a year after the NAACP had refused to take her case against the University of North Carolina, Murray savored the sweetness of seeing her name appear on the National Sharecroppers Week letterhead with board members UNC president Frank Porter Graham and NAACP staffer Roy Wilkins. Her new job kept her in touch with A. Philip Randolph, who cochaired the WDL Labor Committee. She planned community meetings across the country, including one in Chapel Hill, and asked New Dealer Will Alexander to speak at another in Washington, D.C.[88]

Murray dreamed up a student essay contest on "A Proposed Solution to the Sharecropper Problem" and convinced editors at the *Nation* to publish the winning essay.[89] With typical boldness, Murray wrote to Eleanor Roosevelt for an interview, met with her in Manhattan, and secured ER's promise to serve as contest judge and speaker at the NSW dinner and forum. Accomplishing all this in her first three weeks on the job, Murray recalled, "[m]ade my stock go high, very, very, high" at the office.[90]

For everyone except Pauli Murray, the National Sharecroppers Week dinner and forum in February 1940 turned out to be a smashing success. Five hundred and fifty contributors packed New York's Hotel Commodore. Roy Wilkins, Norman Thomas, and Eleanor Roosevelt spoke.[91] Will

Alexander, who had been waging war against tenancy since the mid-1930s as head of the Farm Security Administration, had taught ER everything she knew on the subject. That night Roosevelt termed sharecropping a national problem, and the event raised more than four thousand dollars.[92] But Pauli Murray didn't see any of it. She explained to ER, "When people overwork themselves, even for the best of causes, they must pay for it. And so I was in the Hospital on the night of the Annual Dinner-Forum." Organized as always, from her hospital bed she wrote a little essay for her doctors entitled "Patient's Analysis of Nervous Collapse." The problem had been sleeplessness, overwork, poor diet, money worries, anxiety over the sharecroppers' event, and "inability to integrate homosexual tendencies into a 'socially acceptable' pattern of living." For public consumption, she simply said that she suffered from exhaustion. Roosevelt responded at once by sending flowers, which Murray promptly handed out one by one to "patients, doctors, nurses, neighbors, and friends." That way, she told Roosevelt, "a great personality touches the lives and hearts of many people unknowingly." Of course, distributing Roosevelt's flowers stem by stem maximized Murray's bragging rights as well.[93]

Over the next few years Murray and Roosevelt cultivated a friendship based on their differences—"race," age, and temperament—rather than on their similarities. ER used Murray to hear what "Negroes" were thinking, and Murray used ER to tell the administration what "Negroes" were thinking. ER used Murray to divine the future, but Murray used ER to realize her future. ER warned Murray to slow down and criticized her methods; Murray warned ER to speed up and criticized her methods. Murray wrote the longer letters, but ER always responded and sometimes invited Murray to the White House. Pauli Murray adored Eleanor Roosevelt. Recalling her 1939 meeting with ER, Murray wrote that "she was positively beautiful in our interview—a glow such as I've never seen."[94] If Roy Wilkins saw danger in Pauli Murray, or Howard Odum saw annoyance, or Thurgood Marshall saw impurity, Eleanor Roosevelt found a kindred spirit. Each woman recognized and treasured the other's pilgrim soul.

When Murray left the hospital, she and her housemate, Adelene McBean, set out to spend Easter 1940 in Durham, North Carolina, with Murray's mother, Pauline Dame. Murray agonized over the price of a bus ticket from New York to Washington, where she hoped to borrow her sister's car to drive on to Durham. Murray described McBean, whom she called Mac, as "a peppery, self-assertive young woman of West Indian parentage." Mac simply "could not believe that there were such things as real segregation laws in the South." Instead she figured that "American Negroes were just too timid" and simply put up with being pushed around. Unable to borrow the car, Murray worried that McBean would raise a ruckus when the Greyhound turned segregated somewhere south of Washington.[95]

Murray had been studying Gandhian techniques of nonviolence, so she brought with her a chart she had drawn entitled "India . . . Am. Negro." She noted that Indians constituted a majority in their own country, while the "Am. Negro" constituted a minority "living side by side" with white people. She admired the Indians for a "willingness to sacrifice . . . to change heart of the enemy" and contrasted their activism with white people's criticism that African Americans "move too fast, upset friendly relations between the races." While the Indians made up a "well disciplined movement," Murray lamented that African Americans suffered from the lack of a grassroots movement. They counted instead on a "legalistic movement" headed by the "NAACP—through court tests."[96] In the weeks before Easter, Murray had met Gandhi follower Krshnalala Sridharani and read his *War without Violence.* She set out for home armed with nonviolent ideas, but they took her only as far as Virginia.[97]

"TO MRS. PAULINE DAME . . . EASTER GREETINGS. ARRESTED. PETERSBURG WARRANT GREYHOUND BUS. DON'T WORRY. CONTACT WALTER WHITE," read the (collect) telegram that Murray sent her mother on March 23, 1940. A year shy of seventy and still teaching elementary school, Dame had barely recovered from the intensity of Murray's campaign to integrate UNC, but she absorbed the shock quickly and wired back the next afternoon: "HOPE YOU OK DID AS REQUESTED WIRE ME YOUR NEEDS."[98] Compassionate, discreet, efficient, and selfless, Dame's message beamed like a ray of sunshine through the bars of the Petersburg, Virginia, city jail. Equally encouraging was the telegram that arrived from the Workers Defense League as a result of Dame's alert: "HAVE ASKED R A THOMPSON OF . . . PETERSBURG TO HELP YOU. ROY WILKINS ASKING LOCAL NAACP TO HELP. KEEP US FULLY INFORMED."[99] Both Dame and Murray's WDL coworkers wondered how the women had landed in this mess.

The ride from D.C. to Richmond had been fine, but in the latter city the regular bus was filled, and Mac and Murray toted their luggage—a typewriter, a hatbox, a briefcase, and a stack of books—over to a broken-down "relief bus."[100] They had to take seats in the back, where the rear wheel well pushed into their space. On the short ride from Richmond to Petersburg, Virginia, McBean complained that her side ached from being thrown against the wheel. Jim Crow's seating plan lacked place cards. Black passengers had to fill the bus from the back, stopping behind the last row of whites. In other words, the "front" of the bus and the "back" of the bus were relative concepts. Looking forward, Murray saw "several white passengers sitting alone on two-seat rows," and "two empty seats . . . just behind the driver's seat." If two white children, currently seated toward the middle of the bus, moved up to the empty row behind the driver, the demarcation line would advance, and Murray and McBean could move out of the row with the protruding wheel well. Murray went up to the front, explained their discomfort, and asked the driver if he would reseat the children. The driver "pushed Pauli Murray backward" and yelled, "Get out of my face and go back and take your seat."[101] She asked again. She then appealed to the mother of the children, explaining the situation. The mother refused to reseat her children.

In Petersburg, Jim Crow seating reshuffled as a large group of African Americans waited to board the bus. Trying to guess where the color line would fall, Murray and McBean moved up to the third row from the back, but that seat was broken. They moved up one more row, "behind all the white passengers," leaving the row with the broken seat empty behind them. The driver mounted the steps, spied them there, and "growled from the front, 'You'll have to move back!' "[102] It was then that Murray snapped.

Murray later vowed that the image of her grandfather, a black Union veteran who had fought at the Battle of Petersburg, appeared before her, and she "let go a machine gun fire of legal questions concerning the policies of the Greyhound Bus Lines." The driver, "disdaining any discussion with the two passengers," threatened to call the police. Murray threatened to call the NAACP and invoked "the 14th amendment, the Constitution and the Supreme Court of the United States." There! Murray thought. That would "fix him!" It didn't. When two "huge members of the Petersburg police" boarded the bus, McBean yelled, "If you're looking for me, here I am. But you needn't think that your big brass buttons and your shiny bullets are going to scare me, because I have rights, they're substantial, and I'm sitting on them." Murray described herself as honey-tongued, and she used her "legal mind" to query the police officers, who admitted that they couldn't act unless the driver swore out a warrant in the name of the Greyhound Lines.[103]

While the police lingered, Murray and McBean decided to use "Mahatma Gandhi's technique with the British Lion" and "just sat—and sat." A crowd of white men gathered outside the bus. Finally the bus driver returned with a warrant. Murray and McBean protested about the broken seat to their rear, and the bus driver fixed it. They moved back, but now McBean demanded an apology from the driver, who "mumbled something" suggesting he "wanted everybody to have a square deal." The women would not leave it there, however. When the driver distributed "witness cards" to the white passengers, but not to the African Americans, Murray protested. The driver alighted and returned with the officers, who finally arrested the women for "creating a disturbance."[104]

McBean became hysterical and fainted, so the police stopped at the hospital on the way to jail. When she arrived at the Petersburg City Jail, Murray demanded that she be allowed to contact someone. The jailer responded, "Don't come here trying to boss me. We're the boss now, and if you don't shut up, I'll beat your head." Murray kept protesting, whereupon he threatened: "Keep on talkin' and I'll set your ass in the dungeon." The women shut up and settled in for a stay that was to last three days.[105]

Murray's jailer finally allowed her to send telegrams, including the one to Dame and another to her sister in Washington, instructing her to contact Eleanor Roosevelt and the NAACP. Murray started writing a "prison diary" along with letters demanding that the jailer provide nicer soap and clean up her cell.[106] Writing her prison diary in the third person, she exclaimed, "To this situation the sensitive, intellectually aware Negro woman is brought—with a hodge-podge of training in various Negro and mixed public schools, a hatred for filth and uncleanness, a resentment against inequality, and an almost pathetic loyalty to her racial group. She is most astonished at the relation of the Negro prisoners among themselves." The black male prisoners were housed in a cell next to the women, separated by a locked door. They had perfected the art of lying "down outside the [adjoining] women's cell" and slipping under the door a "thin hand mirror at a certain angle to observe the female prisoners." Murray listened to the male prisoners go on and on about "sex, sex experiences, sexual gratification." Their "picturesque, earthy language" repelled her, yet, she predicted, "if they could express themselves creatively, a new poetry would spring up to enrich the soil of American literature." Once the male prisoners learned the nature of Murray and McBean's arrest and protest, however, they shut up about sex and asked for the women's help with their own cases.[107]

Murray spent one glum night waxing mordantly over her dim view of the Petersburg courthouse through the cell's narrow window—"this single romantic experience of jail life glimmers toward one's starved eyes"— but on Easter Sunday 1940 two of Charles Houston's former law students who practiced law in Petersburg arrived at the jail. Thurgood Marshall assured the lawyers that the NAACP would foot the bill.[108] After meeting with the Petersburg Two, they phoned Houston and told him that "the ladies DO NOT want bail." Their trial would be Tuesday morning.[109]

By now Murray and McBean saw themselves as political prisoners. Murray wrote her boss at the Workers Defense League that a "black Maria" had brought them to the jail, where they "now languish[ed] and meditate[d] upon the ways of Hitlerism and their American facsimile." She vowed that they would, as Pauline Dame might have predicted, "go all the way to and from the Supreme Court and back again, if necessary." When Pauli Murray had tried to volunteer as an NAACP plaintiff to desegregate UNC, Charles Houston had refused to take her. Now, when Murray's sister, a prominent Washingtonian, called Houston, he went to her house to discuss the Petersburg case with her.[110] Murray's New York friends peppered the NAACP with calls. "We have talked with . . . a Mr. Marshall at the N.A.A.C.P.," they reported. Thurgood Marshall assured them that "two of the N.A.A.C.P.'s best lawyers were in charge of the case." For her part, Eleanor Roosevelt contacted the governor of Virginia, who told the president's wife that "Miss Murray was unwise not to comply with the law."[111]

When Murray and McBean left for court three days later, a mixed group of thirteen black and white prisoners sat "indiscriminately" in the station wagon that took them to court, demonstrating to Murray the "glaring contradictions of Jim Crow." The judge found them guilty of "creating a disturbance, disorderly conduct, and violation of Virginia segregation law." He allowed that "this is not the worst case of its kind," but "the law, very wisely in my opinion, has granted to the driver widely discretionary powers, police powers." He fined Murray and McBean five dollars each plus costs. They appealed.[112]

Friends wrote quickly to urge Murray and McBean to forgo their appeal and go to jail to "make a test case" so that they could follow Gandhi's tactic of satyagraha. "The *real* purpose as Gandhi would see it . . . the only way you can vindicate the principle at stake . . . is to pay the full penalty by serving the jail sentence," a New York ally advised. But Murray and McBean chose Pauline Dame's front porch in Durham over another night in jail. After court they rushed to the bus station, boarded a "new-style" bus, and noticed two Greyhound guards wearing "Sam Browne Belts" aboard. Then they realized that the driver was the same man who had had them arrested. This time he was "the 'epitome' of courtesy."[113] They arrived in Durham by dark. As Murray sprang up the path laid with the bricks that her grandfather had made, the Carolina spring hit her in full force. The blossoming pear trees tossed like clouds, the wisteria vines that latticed the porch perfumed the air, and her grandfather's green rocker creaked its welcome as a breeze stirred. Home![114]

Their arrest made the news when Ted Poston, journalist and former *Black and White* cast member, announced in the *Pittsburgh Courier* Murray and McBean's intention to challenge Greyhound to provide "*equal* accommodations for Negroes."[115] From Durham, Louis Austin predicted that the women were "the beginning of a new type of leadership—a leadership that will not cringe and crawl on its belly merely because it happens to be faced with prison bars in its fight for the right."[116]

The WDL associated four white lawyers to work with the NAACP team on the appeal, and Murray felt "overwhelmed with joy" when she heard about their intent to push on. The appeal hinged upon the fact that the Virginia segregation statutes did not explicitly require that Negro passengers fill up the bus from back to front, just to segregate themselves, as Murray and McBean had actually done. Murray also hoped to complain about the unequal treatment: the wheel well, the broken seat, and the fact that McBean, as a sick passenger, was not treated as a white woman surely would have been.[117]

On the eve before the appeal was to be heard, Murray, McBean, and their Petersburg counsel plotted in Washington with Marshall, Hastie, and Ransom.[118] However, the next day their Washington NAACP lawyer's flight was delayed as his plane circled over Richmond, and when the trial commenced the argument fell to two white attorneys, one local, one with the WDL. The judge, aware that the NAACP would make this a test case, dismissed the charge of violating segregation statutes and convicted the women on the disorderly conduct charge. The NAACP attorney rushed into the courtroom late and argued that raising one's voice to defend one's civil rights did not constitute disorderly conduct.[119] The judge granted another hearing on that issue but upheld the conviction two weeks later. An appeal to the U.S. Supreme Court would cost three hundred dollars. Murray held her breath to see if this time the NAACP would stand by her, even though the issue on appeal was standing up for civil rights in a "disorderly" way, not violating the segregation statute.

As Murray waited to hear from the NAACP on the appeal, she opened her May issue of *Opportunity*, a widely circulated African American magazine published by the Urban League. One of the stories, "Color Trouble," began, oddly enough, with the sentence " 'It Can't Happen Here'—But it did, on a bus in Petersburg, Virginia. An eye-witness account. . . ."[120] Had someone else been arrested in a similar incident? Murray must have felt a stab of jealousy when she read that the author, Harold Garfinkel, was a white sociology student earning his MA in Howard Odum's UNC department, where she had hoped to be at that very moment. Garfinkel's "drama" had been staged on a "bus that traveled from Washington to Durham on Saturday afternoon, March 23, 1940." It was her story! A corroborating white witness, sympathetic enough to find his way into print in a black periodical, was about to tell their story to the world. His opening reference to *It Can't Happen Here*, the book on a Fascist takeover of the United States, suggested that his larger purpose would be to equate segregation with Fascism.[121]

Then she read a paragraph that shot through her like a molten comet: "A young colored girl and her youthful companion had slipped up behind the last white couple in the row. . . . She was perhaps twenty-four years old, high spirited, loud and infectious in her laughter. Slender, light colored, but not very good looking," Garfinkel wrote. He continued: "The young man with her was lighter than she, of slight build, thin shoulders, flat chest, sensitive, self-conscious in voice and manner. He carried with him a pile of books."[122]

"The young man with her" was Pauli Murray. Adelene McBean was the "not very good looking" "colored" girl. In Garfinkel's account, the bus driver exhibited the patience of Job when he first asked them to fill up the bus from back to front. "Say, who do you think you're talking to? . . . How dare you speak to me that way? . . . The young colored girl" challenged him as her "voice rose." She argued, "I have my rights, the seat is broken." McBean declared that the "boy" had previously complained to the driver about the seat. Next, a policeman boarded and asked what was wrong. McBean refused to answer. The "boy" answered: "Nothing's wrong officer. . . . We are simply sitting in these seats we paid to ride in. My friend here is ill. She can't ride over the wheel, and besides the seat back there is broken."[123]

Garfinkel described the white passengers' reaction to the "boy": "His voice was just a bit too loud and too clear, an arrogant adolescent repeating by rote. Clearly he was not the one to deal with. The whites were not attracted to him because he was neither white nor black, spoke like neither, and threatened to upset a good fight." A white passenger muttered, "Why doesn't that guy shut up and let her do the talking?"[124]

The writer's account of events roughly followed Murray's but portrayed McBean as abrasive, the "boy" as cringing, and the police as diplomatic. McBean, he reported, responded to the policeman by shouting, "Now *you* look, Mister . . . I think I'm as good as anybody on this bus." And, then after another round of arguments, McBean cried out, "Just what is it I *have* done? Is it the color of my skin, is that what it is? Well, can I help the color of my skin? Can I? CAN I?" The police officers asked for their names and addresses, and Garfinkel listened. "Alice McBean," the "not very good looking . . . colored girl," responded. Then the police officer "turned his attention to the boy" and asked: "Yours?" "Oliver Fleming, one-thirty-five West One Hundred and Fortieth Street," Pauli Murray answered, before she began to cry. She had given the police a man's name and a false address.[125]

Garfinkel, the white passengers, and the police all recognized Murray as the person she intended to be on the ride, a boy. Murray was cross-dressing. She had grown accustomed to presenting herself as a boy a decade earlier, when she rode the rails back home from California. At five feet one and one hundred pounds on a good day, she had discovered when she dressed in male clothes, "my boyish appearance was a protection" among hoboes. Murray later reflected that to her horror, "around the same time I was riding freights, nine boys were taken off a freight in Scottsboro . . . and charged with raping two white female hoboes." Those two white women had also been dressed as men. Even if Scottsboro had not crossed her mind at the moment of her own arrest on the Greyhound bus, she would have realized she was in a difficult position. Crossing state lines with a woman while dressed as a man violated morals statutes in many states and could be considered a violation of the federal Mann Act. On the spot, she had no choice other than to give the police a man's name.[126]

A master of self-presentation, Murray found in cross-dressing a respite from shouldering the cloak of middle-class female dignity that she had to wear as a black woman activist. It was fun, comfortable, and perhaps erotic to travel as a man with Mac. Even their accoutrements reinforced gender roles: Mac carried a hatbox with her Easter bonnet inside, and like a schoolboy, Murray carried a briefcase and some books held together with a strap. After their arrest Murray must have realized that she had to straighten out her sexual identity or she would be thrown in jail with men. She had ample time to sort this out when they stopped at the hospital, although we cannot know how she did it. In the end Murray had, after all, been booked under her own name and placed in the women's cell with Mac.

Since her Petersburg arrest had already been in the news, Pauli Murray realized anyone who read "Color Trouble" could easily identify her as Oliver Fleming. Harold Garfinkel had inadvertently outed Pauli Murray. The young sociology graduate student went on to become an illustrious scholar who founded the social science of ethnomethodology, which closely studies personal interactions. He published work about shaming rituals and transgendered people. But Garfinkel did not realize that his first published piece was about the shaming ritual of a transgendered person. When he recalled the incident over sixty years later, he still described the couple as a woman and a boy.[127]

Murray feared that the readers of "Color Trouble," including those at the NAACP, would connect the story with her. She put down the magazine and called Washington to ask for the NAACP's decision on her appeal, whereupon she learned that Hastie would not pursue it, ostensibly because the segregation statute was no longer at issue. Murray doubted Hastie's explanation for dropping the appeal and wrote to her Petersburg attorney: "We were wondering if this article had anything to do with a change of opinion on the part of Attorney Hastie?"[128] She apparently received no reply. McBean and Murray felt "particularly badly, because they [the NAACP lawyers] led us to believe that the case had such far-reaching implications they were going to see it through."[129] Crushed, they refused to pay the fine and packed their bags to report to the Petersburg City Jail to serve thirty-day sentences for disorderly conduct.[130]

Murray later maintained that "the incident attracted little attention outside Petersburg."[131] In fact "Color Trouble" attracted enormous attention—as fiction. Without asking Garfinkel, the editors of the *Best Short Stories of 1941* anthologized it, placing it just following a short story by William Faulkner. It apparently never occurred to them that black people might have *actually* challenged bus segregation in Petersburg, Virginia. Astonished at its new incarnation, Garfinkel never corrected the impression that his story was fictional, and his "fiction" writing took on a life of its own.[132] For her part, Murray never engaged the claim that she had been cross-dressing. She simply pronounced "Color Trouble" repetitious, "inaccurate," and "fictionary" and did not refer to it again.[133]

Public notice as a transgendered person might have cooked Murray's goose with the NAACP, but her sexuality was beginning to be a source of strength for her as well. Early in the 1930s she had tried first to deny it by marrying briefly, then to persuade a doctor to find the male sex organs that she imagined she possessed, but by 1940 she had begun to embrace her differences. After all, she was headed home to her mother that day dressed as a boy accompanied by a woman friend. Pauline Dame knew by now that Murray was attracted to women, and Dame referred to her cross-dressing as Murray's "little boy-girl personality."[134]

"Mother, you've been so understanding—both you and Aunt Sallie," Murray wrote to Dame, "but where you and a few people understand, the world does not understand nor accept my pattern of life." Her sexuality had limited her success because "this conflict rises up to knock me down at every apex I reach in my career." She had to remain constantly on guard since, she lamented, "I'm exposed to any enemy or person who may or may not want to hurt me."[135] Murray had struggled so hard to find a "cure" for her condition to protect her career.

In the end, however, the most important issue for Dame and Murray was not what other people thought but what God thought. Murray may have sought surgery to discover her male sex organs because she believed that if God had made her attracted to women, God had intended her to be a man. That explanation would have relieved her of any pain that she felt about the "sin" of being a lesbian. Dame walked through her life holding God's hand, and Murray's faith began to grow in the late 1930s. As it did, she became increasingly comfortable with herself and with the idea that she was a lesbian. Six months after the Petersburg incident, she wrote in her journal: "It is dangerous for you to think too much about your weakness. . . . The great secret, you see, is not to think of yourself, of your courage or of your despair, of your strength or your weakness, but of Him for whom you journey." She was without parents, yet she made parents of those who loved her. She was white and black, a materialist and a believer, a Northerner and a Southerner, in her own mind, a woman and a man. But Murray believed that God left nothing to chance. She told herself, "He cannot show you a task without making you capable of fulfilling it."[136] She came to believe that God had put her in the middle so that she would learn to stretch across the world's divisions.

After the NAACP refused to pursue their appeal, Murray and McBean used their time in the Petersburg City Jail to situate their experience within Gandhi's teachings. "Law is a tedious method of fighting social issues," Murray reflected, writing from jail to friends who shared her interest in Gandhi's technique of satyagraha, "the power of truth, love, and nonviolence . . . The fundamental issues themselves may be lost through quips and quirks of the judge or the way the case is filed," she said. From jail, Murray set about to retell their ordeal as a saga of her patient teaching through the Gandhian example. By their conduct during their arrests, their imprisonments, and their trial, she and McBean had educated those around them in satyagraha. Murray wrote to friends who were trying to start a satyagraha movement in New York that black newspaper editor Louis Austin had

urged her to remain in Durham to "help him fight this race battle by starting a Ghandi-type [she was still having trouble spelling it] movement
among Negroes." But Murray and McBean worried that they might not be
"strong enough or sacrificial enough to give up our freedom for the South."
Looking back at the events leading to the arrests, Murray remembered that
she and McBean had "applied what we knew of satyagraha ON THE
SPOT." Murray's behavior, as she recalled it, "tended toward *civil disobedience*," while McBean acted a bit more "instinctively." In Murray's estima-
tion, they used satyagraha when they protested that they would not
"accept uncomfortable seats," in their "cordial attitude toward the police
officers," and their "willingness to be arrested rather than submit to open
discrimination." Murray was most proud that their "intelligent and
restrained handling of our situation" brought "sympathy" from white passengers and that their conduct in jail won over their fellow inmates. Looking back on her court testimony, Murray stressed "our refusal to stand by
and see open discrimination of Negro passengers without protesting" to
the 250 people crowded into the courtroom. [137]

Moreover, the experience had taught Murray that African Americans
must mount a direct action movement alongside the NAACP's litigation
strategy. She argued that, "a Supreme Court ruling on segregation will
not be enforced . . . unless Civil Rights Laws are introduced into various
state legislatures." Since no African Americans served in any state legislatures, "it is hardly likely that such laws will be repealed unless some 'civil
disobedience' movement is started and catches the imagination of the
Negro masses."

Thus Murray became convinced that she should start an "American
Satyagraha movement." Her employers and friends at the WDL had tried
hard to make Murray a committed Socialist, but now she wrote to them: "I
want to stay out of politics long enough to study the whole question of
minority group struggle. . . . While very close to the Socialists, I'm particularly interested in Gandhi's movement and its possibilities for American
minority and labor action." She mused: "Negroes are not as mild as we
believe them to be," and she saw before her a "difficult task to transfer to
them the Indian's hatred for violence."[138]

In fact turning Pauli Murray, Fighter, into Pauli Murray, Cheek
Turner, would take some doing as well. She moved into a Harlem ashram

to begin that quest with an Indian spiritual teacher, who had already published two influential books on nonviolence and Gandhi. It seemed to Murray a "well-meaning but ill-assorted collection" of people, including James Farmer, who went on to found the Congress of Racial Equality. Her journey toward spiritual rebirth came to a screeching halt when the leader told her to quit smoking or to leave the ashram. Murray chose the latter.[139]

Murray's refusal to abide by segregation custom and law, her conscious practice of nonviolent direct action, her decision to serve her prison sentence, and her determination to link her individual oppression to that of her people all represent strategies that made Rosa Parks and Martin Luther King icons of the civil rights movement fifteen years later. Moreover, Murray's early challenge to segregation followed many others—that was why the judge pronounced it "not the worst case of its kind"—even as it heralded the patriotic call for immediate desegregation that emerged in the early days of World War II. By the time that the United States entered the war, a well-developed campaign in the black press had linked segregation, inefficiency, and antidemocratic practices. For example, an editorial cartoon in the *Chicago Defender*, titled "Sacrifice to Segregation," illustrated an empty Jim Crow car on an otherwise crowded train inscribed "equal but *separate* accommodations." A black passenger remarked, "It's funny how 'some' people will inconvenience themselves and others to keep democracy from working, isn't it?"[140] The cartoon's critique clearly rejects "separate but equal" as a goal because it depicts a Jim Crow car superior to the white ones and still complains about segregation. At a time when the NAACP argued against *Plessy* the only way that it legally could, by challenging the equality of accommodations, African Americans had already rejected segregation as inherently unequal. Moderate whites got on board too. In 1943, Virginius Dabney, the white editor of the *Richmond Times-Dispatch*, wrote an editorial urging Virginia to repeal its segregation ordinances for public transportation.[141]

The same year an apocryphal story bearing the title "A Soldier Takes a Ride" appeared in a race relations magazine. A black first lieutenant, "very straight and very young" entered a bus. He met a white officer of the same rank, "clean cut, slender and also very young." They sat down together and struck up a conversation. A white passenger complained. The motorman looked "very, very tired," but he asked them to move. "It's the law."

"What the hell . . ." the white officer exclaimed. "I understand," the black officer said quietly. The white officer blushed scarlet. He sprang up. "I feel like a goddamned fool! Maybe they'll let us *stand* together!" he blurted out. The motorman grinned: "You're right, sir!" "A sigh of relief rippled along the bus. . . . Everybody smiled happily at each other and the two soldiers."[142] The improbable story's purpose is to project to white people a world that African Americans believed was within their reach during World War II. Indeed, six years after McBean's and Murray's arrests, a Supreme Court ruling in an almost identical case proved that they had been right all along. In 1944 Irene Morgan of Baltimore refused to move to the back of a Greyhound bus after it crossed into Virginia. This time the only charge was violating the Virginia segregation statute, even though Morgan was an interstate passenger. There was a war on, and William H. Hastie argued that this was a matter of "national policy." In 1946, in *Morgan v. Virginia*, the U.S. Supreme Court found that forcing *interstate* passengers to abide by Virginia segregation law put an "unconstitutional burden on interstate commerce." Murray must have smiled as she clipped the judgment from the newspaper and put it carefully in her files.[143]

Sharecropping and Justice

Despite the fact that Murray had twice been a flawed plaintiff in the eyes of the NAACP, only months after her Petersburg arrest she transformed herself into an advocate for another black defendant in Virginia. By December 1940 Odell Waller was facing execution for the murder of his white landlord. The Waller case stands out in bold relief against the backdrop of an ever-whirling cyclorama of innocent black men lynched without trial or quickly found guilty by white jurors and summarily executed. Waller, a sharecropper, admitted that he had shot Oscar Davis, who died two days later. Unlike thousands of black men without counsel, or those who had bumbling, inattentive, or drunken lawyers, Waller was counseled by the accomplished Thomas H. Stone, a white Richmond lawyer who had visited Murray in the Petersburg City jail. In fact Stone had become involved in the case at the outset and advised Waller from the preliminary investigation onward.[144]

The factual issue at trial came down to whether the crime was manslaughter, not a capital crime, or premeditated murder, which could carry the death sentence. Odell Waller pleaded self-defense, which would have been manslaughter. The white jury found him guilty of premeditated murder and sentenced him to be executed. Pauli Murray became a special field agent on the case for the Workers Defense League, which publicized it and provided counsel on appeal. The WDL maintained that Waller's crime was manslaughter and employed a critique of sharecropping and discriminatory jury selection to protest his death sentence. If Waller had killed Davis without premeditation and thought that he was acting in self-defense, then his life should be spared. Moreover, because payment of the poll tax was a requirement for jury service, and Waller's jury was all white, he had been deprived of a jury of his peers.

The differences between the treatment of Waller and that of the thousands of black people who had preceded him through the southern criminal justice system illustrate just how rapidly the underlying concepts of black criminal rights changed in the South in the late 1930s and 1940s. Waller had not been wrongly accused of killing Davis. He had not been lynched but duly tried. However, his supporters contended that his rights had been violated because the all-white jury could not credit his version of the facts. From the Scottsboro "Boys" to Odell Waller, many white Southerners slowly realized that those accused of crimes had rights.[145] Although law enforcement and the courts continued to violate those rights as a routine matter, they could no longer be certain that their violations would go uncontested.

When Waller's case began, however, few white Southerners would have even suspected that his *rights* would be at issue: He had admitted that he had killed a white man, and he had had competent counsel and a more than perfunctory trial. What could possibly be wrong with that? Virginius Dabney, the white southern liberal who edited the *Richmond Times-Dispatch*, expressed his peers' incredulity when he called Waller's appeal "an unfortunate set of circumstances on which to base a fight in the courts." Dabney concluded: "There is no doubt in my mind that Waller is guilty of manslaughter or something worse, probably the latter." The issue was precisely "manslaughter or something worse," and Dabney's comments indicate that at the very least he was willing to sacrifice a controversial defendant rather than defend his right to a fair trial. But Pauli Murray and the Workers Defense League turned the case into a national cause through their portrayal of sharecropping as undemocratic, southern jury selections as discriminatory, and the poll tax as the "enemy of democracy."[146]

The particulars of the Waller case nestle within a discourse that Murray had helped craft during the Workers Defense League's National Sharecroppers Week a year earlier. Sharecropping was an undemocratic institution that ate away at the country's agrarian base. The exploitative nature of sharecropping might have seemed an esoteric exercise to the student competitors in Murray's contest who wrote, "Great Uncle Sam cannot allow such conditions" . . . or "Were the slaves really freed?" . . . or "By what right can men plunder and destroy others?" Now the cruelty of sharecropping had driven Odell Waller to shoot Oscar Davis. The case brought democracy, slavery, plunder, and destruction before the American public, and a man's life hung in the balance.[147]

Oscar Davis had degraded his sharecropper Odell Waller in the best of times, but in the spring and summer of 1940 he replaced degradation with depravity. The prosecution contested little of Waller's account of his life as Davis's cropper. Two years before the trouble began, Waller's foster father had died, and the family lost their mortgaged land. Odell, his new wife, Mollie, and his foster mother, Annie, moved into a drafty, unpainted, tin-roofed cabin near Gretna, Virginia, on land rented by Davis, a white tenant farmer. Thus the Wallers worked for a man too poor to own his own land. Gretna is in Pittsylvania County, in the middle of the state on the North Carolina line, and there the Davises and Wallers farmed corn, tobacco, and wheat.[148] Both families barely got by. To help out, Waller and Davis made some bootleg liquor from the corn and sold it locally. Waller had attended high school, but his landlord, Davis, probably had not. Waller had a healthy young wife. Davis had buried two wives before he married a sickly third one. All three women had been cousins. Waller worked with Davis and his sons to raise that family's crop, but Waller worked his own shares alone and gave Davis a fixed amount of the proceeds. Waller testified: "We got along all right, didn't have no trouble along during the year 1939—but Mr. Davis was mighty crabby anyway, didn't bother me none at all, but would jump on the boys [Davis's sons] for the least thing. He carried a pistol and his oldest son threatened to kill him."[149]

In 1940 federal Agricultural Adjustment Act agents cut Oscar Davis's tobacco allotment for the year. They paid him cash for the difference, and Davis was legally required to give Waller a proportionate share of the money.[150] But a sharecropper lived on a landlord's mercy, and the law rarely intervened in that relationship. Unless there was a crop lien with a local merchant, agreements on shares were verbal. No black man could impugn a white man's character by demanding that they write down their agreement. "It's easy for white men to string colored folk along," Pauli Murray observed. "Promises made are lightly broken; like promises to children or to animals, there's little honor in them."[151]

As the two men began to plant under the restricted allotment in 1940, Davis's promises to Waller became more and more begrudging. The AAA cash represented payment for the tobacco crop they would not plant. But Davis kept the cash and cut Waller's share of tobacco from planting seventy-five thousand hills to four thousand. Waller begged to plant more, but Davis refused. Despite the fact that Waller had already planted wheat and a garden, he said he couldn't support his family on less than an acre and a half of tobacco, the only cash crop.[152] He told Davis he would have to go to work for a while on a construction crew in Maryland. At that point Davis repossessed the cow that the Wallers had been using for milk. Then he told Waller to move his family off the land, even though it was too late in the season for the Wallers to become sharecroppers elsewhere, there was wheat in the ground, and Waller had helped Davis prepare the land to plant tobacco. Waller responded, "I can give you the house tomorrow. . . . You ought to pay me something for working, don't you think?" Davis said, "Naw, I aint going to pay you none," to which Waller replied, "Naw, I aint going to move either." Given this standoff, the family stayed in the house, and both men understood that Waller retained the right to his share of the wheat already growing.[153] That was where things stood when Waller left to work in Maryland.

Davis's hatefulness and Waller's feistiness hung in the air, but the two families needed each other. While Odell was away, Annie Waller nursed Mrs. Davis for the promise of pay, cooked for the Davises during wheat harvesting, and helped Davis put in tobacco. Then spiteful old Davis refused to pay her the $7.50 he owed her for nursing his wife. When he asked Annie Waller to help in the tobacco fields one more time, she responded, "I don't know, Mr. Davis, I bin workin' and workin' around here, and it seems like everything goes to Mr. Davis. It's all for Mr. Davis; I don't see nothin' in the ground for Annie."[154]

As bad as things were, Annie's resistance made them worse. Davis sent over the sheriff, who evicted Annie and Mollie. Their preacher let them live in a shack that he owned. When the women went back to the Davis farm to get produce from their garden, which Davis recognized as their right, they let their dog romp around the old place. Oscar Davis or his hired man castrated the dog, which ran back to them bloody and howling.[155]

When the wheat came in, Odell's cousin Robert Waller went over to help harvest it so that the Wallers could retain the right to their share. As the threshing machine spewed out the wheat, Robert bagged it, putting every fourth bag aside for Odell. Davis ordered him to stop setting aside Odell's share. "Everybody takes out the fourth at the thrash-box, don't they?" Robert asked Davis. All the bags stayed at the Davis place. The next week Odell returned from Maryland to find his destitute mother and wife temporarily sheltered in their preacher's cabin with the castrated dog but without the greens from their garden, the milk from their cow, or any of their wheat.[156]

After a calm weekend Waller borrowed a truck early on Monday morning to pick up his wheat from Davis. He asked Mollie to make his breakfast while he was gone since he expected to return shortly. Waller, Annie, and three friends drove to Davis's place. The dog stayed home. Out of view of the truck and out of earshot of its occupants, Waller went up to Davis and announced he had come to get his wheat. As a black hired hand who stood by overheard, Davis told Waller he wouldn't "carry it away from here." Davis proceeded to "use some dirty words, and from one word to another, and he usually carried a gun and run his hand into his pocket like he was trying to pull out something." But Waller was ready and quicker. He said, "I had my gun and out with it. I opened my pistol and commenced to shoot at him—I don't know how many times." Davis fell without returning fire. Waller took off on a Greyhound and made it to Columbus, Ohio, before he was apprehended. At the trial it was Waller's word against that of the black hired hand, who testified that Waller had shot Davis four times, twice in the back, and that Davis had not gone for his pistol. Davis's family members testified that the stricken man had no pistol on him. Defense attorney Thomas Stone argued for self-defense, but the all-white jury found Waller guilty of premeditated murder and sentenced him to death on December 27, 1940.[157]

Odell Waller's pathetic story signified for nine million other sharecroppers, according to the Workers Defense League. It pointed out that sharecroppers lived a "feudalistic" existence, "excluded from all social legislation," struggling with "malnutrition and disease." Evicted because of the AAA crop reduction program, sharecroppers moved to towns and cities, burdening the urban taxpayer, or became migrant workers, driving down the incomes of farm hands across the nation. It suffered from "political impotence" and "put no faith in the democratic process," making them a threat to democracy. As the United States watched Europe's people suffer from the displacement of war, the 1939 publication of John Steinbeck's *The Grapes of Wrath* heightened public awareness of the problem and caused many to draw international parallels.[158]

The rights of criminals, even guilty ones, furnished the second leitmotif of the Waller publicity campaign. Establishing criminal rights in the South was a highly local endeavor. The tangled issues in each criminal case, where truth was often partial at best, made it difficult to standardize criminal defendants' rights. Nonetheless, the federal courts executed great leaps forward as NAACP lawyers and others isolated common issues: presumptions of guilt, police brutality, coerced confessions, inadequate counsel, discriminatory jury selection, and "mob-dominated trials."[159]

Even as late as the 1930s African Americans themselves took up the problem of black criminal rights with a slight ambivalence because they continued to fight two more immediate battles. First, they had to contest the myth that all African Americans naturally possessed criminal natures; thus black leaders themselves believed that they had to be tough on crime to prevent all African Americans from being branded as criminals. Then they had to work hard to get black defendants into court at all. African Americans and their allies had become increasingly successful in turning potential black lynch victims into black defendants. There were three lynchings in the South in 1939, one of a white man, rather than the one hundred a year that the region had averaged from 1893 to 1903. But the decline of lynching went hand in hand with the rise of mob-dominated trials.[160] Waller's trial, however, was not mob-dominated, since everyone expected him to be found guilty. Thus it represents the next step in the evolution of injustice: from lynching to a mob-dominated trial to a perfunctory ritual.

Most white Southerners figured Waller should consider himself lucky that he had not been lynched. As Waller appealed his verdict, A. C. Williams, a twenty-two-year-old black man in Quincy, Florida, was lynched twice. On the eve of Williams's scheduled induction into the army, he was alleged to have broken into a white family's home, where he "stole two watches and $1.65" and choked a twelve-year-old girl who screamed. She did not allege rape. A group of men abducted him from the jail, "gave him a knife and attempted to force him to castrate himself." Then they hanged him from a tree, riddled him with bullets, and left. Miraculously, one of the bullets had frayed the noose, and Williams fell down and crawled to his mother's house. The sheriff called an ambulance, which the lynchers hijacked in short order. Then they lynched Williams again, this time successfully. The black press called it a "story of bestiality and stupidity that rivals crimes of Hitler," argued that the lynchers "stole a page from Nazi barbarism," and ran Williams's story beside an account of Nazis torturing Jews with the headline HERE'S THE WAY NAZIS LYNCH. The Williams murder followed that of a black soldier, lynched in uniform, in South Carolina.[161]

Despite this backdrop of heinous crimes, southern members of Congress regularly filibustered against federal antilynching bills.[162] When the Senate debated the matter in 1939, Josiah Bailey of North Carolina spoke for his southern peers when he warned northern and western Democrats: "In the hour that you come down to North Carolina and try to impose your will upon us about the Negro, so help me God, you are going to learn a lesson that no political party will ever again forget."[163] Even so, in 1940, an antilynching bill passed the House and cleared the Senate Judiciary Committee. Most observers thought that the "bill would pass the Senate also if it could be brought to a vote"—that is, if southern Senators did not filibuster.[164] But they did.

The criminal right at stake in Waller's case was that discriminatory jury selection robbed him of a jury of his peers. The argument had been made successfully eight years earlier in *Lee v. State*. Then a black man had been convicted of murdering a white family, but the Maryland Court of Appeals reversed his conviction on the basis that no African American had served as a juror in living memory. In addition, a 1933 Virginia case replicated Waller's circumstances: A black Virginia man fought extradition from Massachusetts, where he had fled after being indicted for murder by an all-white grand jury. A federal judge ordered the man released, but the appeals court reversed that decision. The upshot was a Virginia judges' conference at which they agreed for the first time that blacks should be entitled to serve on grand juries.[165] Shortly before the Waller case, the U.S. Supreme Court reversed a black Texan's rape conviction on the ground that the grand jury was made up only of "personal acquaintances" of the jury commissioners.[166] The wheels of justice ground exceedingly slow, and each particular method of jury discrimination had to be found unconstitutional.

The Poll Tax as a National Problem

The particular method of jury selection in Waller's case provided an opening for the Workers Defense League to campaign for a third reform, abolition of the poll tax. Virginia called jurors from rolls of voters, people who had paid their $1.50 poll taxes consecutively for three years, thus excluding most African Americans, many poor whites, and virtually all sharecroppers, black or white, since they lived an almost cashless existence. Only 10 percent of Pittsylvania County's adult residents qualified to vote under the consecutive three-year payment rule. Eight southern states required an annual poll tax to vote, and a Texas case had found use of poll tax rolls to choose jurors constitutional in 1928.[167] Nonetheless, by the time that Waller shot Davis, "white resistance to black jury service had slightly eroded in the peripheral South," as demonstrated by the presence of "a single black on an occasional jury," in "large cities."[168]

That erosion had not seeped far enough to help Waller. Since only poll tax payers sat on juries in agrarian Gretna, twenty-three white men made up the jury pool. Twenty of them were farmers, and nine "employed sharecroppers." In the end the jurors consisted of "eleven farmers, six of whom hired sharecroppers," and a carpenter.[169] This was not a jury of Odell Waller's peers. It was a jury of Oscar Davis's peers. According to Loren Miller, the former *Black and White* cast member who became a lawyer and ultimately a judge in California, "Southern jurors knew full well that they were selected on a racially discriminatory basis; it would have been more than a miracle if their verdicts had not reflected the discrimination exercised in their own selection."[170]

The Workers Defense League's condemnation of the poll tax fitted into an ongoing national liberal campaign to abolish it. Because the poll tax reduced voter registration, in 1940 only 24 percent of adults voted in poll tax states, compared with 66 percent of adults in the rest of the country. In several states the tax was cumulative as it was in Virginia: If you wanted to vote, you had to pay annually for the previous two or three years or, sometimes, cumulatively with interest. In some states payment had to be made nine months prior to the election.[171] Among whites, the poll tax particularly disfranchised poor white women, who had little cash of their own and could not convince their husbands to pay the tax for them. Black Southerners who lived in poverty could not pay the poll tax, but those who could afford it hesitated because they probably would be denied registration anyway. As one white election commissioner put it, "it's a little hard to make a Negro pay it when he doesn't get a chance to vote." Even if African Americans paid the poll tax and then succeeded in registering, in many states they still could not vote in the Democratic Party primary—the white primary—which nominated the only possible electoral victors. In 1940 the National Committee to Abolish the Poll-Tax estimated that the poll tax disfranchised almost eleven million people, 60 percent of whom were white.[172]

Moreover, the poll tax also saw to it that elite white Southerners had disproportionate representation in national affairs. Seventy-eight U.S. congressmen represented the poll tax states. The damper that the poll tax placed on voter participation meant that "a Representative of the tax-free states must be elected by nearly four times as many votes as a Representative of the tax-ridden states, yet in Congress their vote is equal." The venerable issue of disproportionate representation for the white Southerners dated back to the three-fifths compromise at the Constitutional Convention. After the Fifteenth Amendment, white Southerners preserved their congressional power by disfranchising the poor, and especially the black poor, in the 1890s. There had never been a time when the South was a democracy. Thus by 1941 the Georgian who chaired the House Rules Committee had been elected by only 5,187 voters, while a Washington

State congressman represented 147,061 voters. Rhode Island elected only *two* congressmen with 314,023 votes when four poll tax states elected *thirty-two* congressmen with only 264,429 votes.[173]

Restricting the southern electorate secured safe congressional seats and longevity for southern Democrats, ensured their seniority on congressional committees, and made trouble for liberal New Deal initiatives for black equality and labor. In 1943 poll tax state representatives headed seventeen of forty-seven standing committees in the House and ten of thirty-three in the Senate. The history of the Alien Registration Act, known as the Smith Act, illustrates the power that the poll tax gave entrenched southern congressmen in committees.[174] A month before the Nazi-Soviet Pact, unabashed white supremacist Howard Worth Smith, a Virginia congressman, introduced an "anti-alien and anti-radical" bill to target Nazis and Communists.[175] White Southerner Virginia Durr characterized Smith as "the worst man in all of Virginia." Although she reported that he "looked like an old buzzard," Smith was nonetheless "the most powerful man in the House." Only 5 percent of the adults in his district voted for him.[176] Capitalizing on fear of "saboteurs," Smith actually worried less about alien agents than about labor organizing. He used the international crisis to limit Communist participation in labor unions and to Red-bait members of the southern Popular Front. His bill, he later recalled, represented his "opposition to the threatened labor dictatorship."[177]

The Smith Act also represented southern Democrats' congressional power. When the Senate Judiciary Committee took it up in 1940, it went to a subcommittee of three, in which two Southerners, Tom Connally of Texas and John Miller of Arkansas, held power. Connally sharpened the bill's sanctions.[178] Then the Senate subcommittee met with a House subcommittee of three. Here again, two of the three were Southerners, poll tax congressmen from Alabama and Texas. The Smith Act's passage illustrates the fruits of a well-pruned electorate. The southern congressmen responsible for passage of the act had been elected in their home states by an average of less than one-fourth of those who would have been eligible to vote without the poll tax. The Texans on both subcommittees that considered it had won election from a voting base of only 26 percent of adult Texans. By the time the southern committeemen finished, only four congressmen voted against the bill.[179]

The Smith Act was a wolf in sheep's clothing. Many people thought that the act merely required the registration and fingerprinting of legal aliens for the purpose of recording their current addresses. Immigration authorities could then check criminal records and could deport anyone who had committed a crime. But the act also made it unlawful for native-born citizens to "knowingly or willfully advocate, abet, advise or teach the duty, necessity, desirability, or propriety of overthrowing or destroying any government in the United States by force or violence," to circulate literature that did so, or to organize or help any organization that did so.[180]

Thus the entire country came under an insurrection law that bore a remarkable resemblance to the Georgia sedition law under which Angelo Herndon had been convicted and to state syndicalism statutes enacted against labor organizations. At least the Smith Act substituted imprisonment and/or deportation for the death penalty. The ILD immediately began campaigning for its repeal.[181] The only people indicted and convicted under the Smith Act before the United States entered World War II belonged to a group of Trotskyites, but it was to have great significance after the war.[182]

Poll tax repeal campaigns brought together a coalition of interest groups.[183] White southern liberal editors began to condemn the poll tax in 1936, and in 1939 Richmond's Virginius Dabney dubbed it "a relic of Reconstruction" in the *New York Times*, while assuring readers that white supremacy would continue without it.[184] The Women's Division of the National Democratic Committee began working on the issue around 1938, but White House made it drop the issue after southern Democrats complained. Frank Porter Graham had called for abolition in his *Report on Economic Conditions of the South*, and the Southern Conference for Human Welfare began a legislative campaign to abolish it. In 1940, Graham pressed his attack in the strongest terms: "Denial of the right to vote on the grounds of property, race, and sex have given way before the advance of common men and women along the rough road toward democracy. Across this road the poll tax stands as a surviving barrier." SCHW secretary Joseph Gelders convinced a California congressman to introduce legislation to outlaw the poll tax, and Virginia Durr began working for its passage on Capitol Hill. In 1941 she helped establish the National Committee to Abolish the Poll-Tax (NCAPT).[185]

The anti–poll tax campaign demonstrates the influence of white southern liberals as it underscores the importance of black voting *outside* the South to black voting rights *inside* the South. While African Americans began voting in the cities of the upper South in increasing numbers in the late 1930s and 1940s, their votes made little difference on issues stretching past local boundaries. It was black voting outside the South that made the greatest difference in the period. The National Negro Congress predicted that "three million Negroes will vote in 1940. The Negro vote will be the decisive balance of power in 124 congressional districts. . . . The Negro vote also will be significant in the selection of 252 pledged delegates to the Democratic National Convention."[186] Actually close to two million voted, but many claimed that African Americans controlled "the balance of power in some seventeen of the Northern states."[187] Those northern black constituents pressured their congressmen to attack the poll tax, an issue that would be popular with white Northerners because of disproportionate elite southern representation in Congress.

Attacked from within and from without, with no possible way to reverse the larger trends that contributed to those attacks, southern representatives and senators knew that their careers depended on maintaining the poll tax. As their white constituents began to complain, they dug in. Typical was Mississippi Senator James Eastland's response when a group of white Mississippi Methodist women asked for his support to abolish the poll tax. As Virginia Durr took them into Eastland's office, she noted approvingly, "They looked very lovely, I thought—very Women's Society." She introduced the ladies to their senator, and "everything started off very pleasantly," Durr recalled. But when they mentioned the poll tax, Eastland "jumped up. His face turned red. He's got these heavy jowls like a turkey and they began to turn purple. And he screamed out, 'I know what you women want—black men laying on you!' "[188]

A federal anti–poll tax bill, the Geyer-Pepper Bill, went to the House nine months before Odell Waller shot Oscar Davis. It passed in October 1941, the same month that the Virginia Supreme Court affirmed the death sentence in Waller's case, but senators from poll tax states killed it in 1942.[189] The black *People's Voice*, a self-proclaimed "militant paper," of which Max Yergan was the treasurer and business manager, internationalized the defeat: "Sixteen poll tax senators turned traitor to their country." Defeating the poll tax sent an antidemocratic message to allies of color around the world: "They laid a bull whip across the backs of 160,000,000 Africans and 400,000,000 Indians. They betrayed our brave Chinese and Filipino allies."[190] Through the Committee on African Affairs, Yergan continued during the war to push the Union of South Africa to lift that whip. When the Union relaxed the pass laws a bit in 1942, Yergan wrote to praise the minister of native affairs in Pretoria for the "growing close relations between the American and South African peoples." For the moment Yergan was more demanding of the U.S. Congress than of the South Africans.[191]

The Soldiers Vote Bill of 1942, which simply waived the poll tax for those serving in the armed forces, turned out to be the "most volatile measure dropped in the hopper since Pearl Harbor." As members of the House debated the bill, senators from Texas and Alabama complained that it violated states' rights. Finally a "blue eyed, 21-year-old sailor" jumped up in the gallery and shouted, "These people are fighting the Civil War all over again. They should be spending their time fighting this war. Why should anybody in the great democracy have to pay a poll tax to vote?"[192] The Soldiers Vote Bill passed in August 1942. As Durr and others continued to push for eliminating the poll tax altogether, she lobbied a young Texas congressman, Lyndon Johnson. He would put his arm around her and say, "Honey, I know you're right. I'm for you. I know the poll tax ought to be abolished, but we haven't got the votes. As soon as we get the votes I'll see that we do it." At the end of World War II states began one by one to abolish the poll tax, but a constitutional amendment to outlaw the poll tax had to wait until 1964, when President Lyndon Johnson finally kept his promise to Virginia Durr.[193]

Exposing Sharecropping and the Poll Tax

If the poll tax evoked strong feelings nationally, abolishing it was a "life-and-death necessity" to poor black Southerners like Odell Waller.[194] When the poll tax deprived defendants of juries of their peers, it sometimes murdered them as well. Jonathan Daniels, of the *Raleigh News and Observer* and formerly of the Southern Committee for People's Rights, commented on the Waller case: "Once more our colored citizens, already deeply aroused over discrimination against them . . . have been presented with a grievance. . . . I can understand the contention that poor little Waller was the product . . . of a whole system of racial suppression, of racial fear."[195] Author Pearl Buck wrote, "Odell Waller has ceased to be an individual, he has become a personification of all those to whom democracy is denied in our country."[196]

Without Pauli Murray and the Workers Defense League, Odell Waller would have been executed long before he became the "personification" of the disfranchised.[197] In November 1940, six weeks after Waller's conviction, Murray and a white WDL representative visited Richmond to organize local support. She was thrilled when the black ministers' alliance allowed her to speak at its meeting, but to her horror, she found herself following silver-tongued Howard law professor Leon Ransom, appearing before the ministers to raise funds for an NAACP case. She described her stage fright this way: "I get out two words and then I just burst into tears and stand there and just utterly collapse in tears trying to tell the story of this young sharecropper." But the response was "like a miracle," Murray recalled. The ministers felt so sorry for her and Waller that they gave generously. Professor Ransom even invited her to apply to Howard Law School. Composure regained, Murray saucily replied to Ransom, "Give me a fellowship and I will."[198]

The WDL succeeded in associating John Finerty, who had represented Tom Mooney and Sacco and Vanzetti, to assist the defense pro bono. Finerty and Thomas Stone, Waller's original attorney, argued that Stone had committed an error when he failed to introduce evidence of the exclusion from the jury pool of those who had not paid their poll taxes. But the Virginia Supreme Court refused to recognize error. The attorneys twice appealed to the U.S. Supreme Court, which both times refused to hear the case. From November 1940 through June 1942 they won three stays of execution.[199]

Meanwhile Murray saw to it that the court of public opinion reheard the case. Two weeks after her trip to Virginia, she brought Odell's mother, Annie Waller, to New York to publicize her son's plight. Waller stayed in Murray's apartment for a month. Annie Waller commented, "This here's a new place, and I haven't never been up this far before. . . . But I had to come to help my boy."[200] Waller and Murray made an unlikely but effective pair.

"Annie Waller is an old woman . . . still the simple Negro woman of the tobacco hills; she speaks the unpracticed tongue of the people who work the white man's crop for shares. . . . Pauli Murray is the Negro of the new South, full of the problems of her people and an earnest student of their background," wrote journalist Murray Kempton. The WDL engaged Kempton, a former Communist turned Socialist, to publicize the *Waller* case, and Kempton applauded Murray: "The long, steady growth of the Negro race towards a full share of the benefits of emancipation is symbolized in the aspirations of young women like Pauli Murray."[201]

By the time that she became Waller's advocate, Murray was a spinmaster who had perfected her skills during her UNC desegregation attempt and Petersburg arrest. She garnered endorsements for Waller's defense from A. Philip Randolph, Mary White Ovington, John Dewey, and a score of other liberals. After several months of visits and letters to *Richmond Times-Dispatch* editor Virginius Dabney, she convinced him to reverse himself and sign Waller's clemency petition. Previously Dabney just couldn't see the difference between manslaughter and murder as far as "Negroes" were concerned. Now he wrote: "There is reasonable doubt in the case of Odell Waller's conviction of first degree murder."[202] For almost two years Waller's case made headlines around the world, in both the black and white press. Dabney pointed out that "Waller's fate has become a *cause célèbre*, with national, even international, implications." John Dewey and A. Philip Randolph argued: "In 1856, Dred Scott became a symbol for the abolition of slavery. Today another unknown Negro, Odell Waller, like that runaway slave, has in our time become the rallying point for those who would abolish the poll tax and the injustices of the sharecropper system."[203]

In the spring of 1941 Murray and "Mother Waller" toured the nation from Pittsburgh to Pasadena. Through meetings with mothers of imprisoned WPA strikers to lunches with Urban League secretaries to CIO union halls, the two raised money and their listeners' consciousness. Murray left her Oliver Fleming persona behind. A white reporter for the *Los Angeles Daily News* wrote: "I heard Pauli Murray, a slim, lissome and almost exquisitely pretty colored girl, talk to a handful of perspiring people about the conditions of sharecroppers, black and white in the South. It was one of the best addresses I had heard anywhere in recent years. . . .

Frankly, I thought of Joan of Arc as she spoke. . . . I pictured her not only as the champion of her own people . . . but as their emissary to the rest of us." Murray even collected contributions from the waiters and porters on the trains they took, and the tour "more than paid for itself." Murray bemoaned the lack of a pamphlet that recorded the facts of the case and exposed sharecropping and poll tax discrimination.[204] She spent the early part of the summer of 1941 working with Murray Kempton to craft one. It would be simply perfect if she could find a progressive white Southerner to write a preface for it.

Murray had the extraordinary knack of drawing in all her experiences, good and bad, and reweaving the past into a serviceable garment for the present. Now her mind turned to Carolina. "Miss Pauli Murray's pamphlet is both basic and timely," Frank Porter Graham wrote as he began the preface of "All for Mr. Davis." "It reveals and stirs intelligent interest in Negroes, white and Negro sharecroppers, the tenancy system, disposed human beings and emergent democratic hopes," he observed. Then Graham made the link between Fascism and black Southerners' civil rights that Murray had tried to get him to make in her own case two years earlier. "With Hitlerism dominant in Europe and with a threatened resurgence of Ku Kluxism, anti-Semitism, and demagoguism in America, she [America] should be sensitive and alert to the conditions, rights, and welfare of religious, political, and racial minorities and the disinherited and disfranchised millions who are a present test of freedom and a source of our democracy," Graham argued.[205] Just as she had wrung friendship from Eleanor Roosevelt, so too had Murray won the heart of her recent adversary Frank Graham. The two corresponded for the rest of the decade.

Now thirty years old, an exhausted Murray completed the Waller tour in the summer of 1941 with no idea what to do next. She bargained some speaking engagements on sharecropping for a cabin at a Socialist camp in the Catskills, where she wrote several short stories about "Bennie," a young black girl growing up in the South. She had applied to Howard Law School the preceding fall and even convinced Thurgood Marshall to write her a letter of recommendation. Marshall informed Dean Leon Ransom that Murray had "the courage and initiative, as well as the ability, to take an active part in the legal battles to secure full citizenship rights for Negroes." Finally a letter arrived at her cabin from Ransom: "You have been admitted to law school and awarded a scholarship." It was perfect. If she couldn't be a plaintiff, she would be a lawyer.[206]

Throughout her work on the *Waller* case, Murray had been telling herself, "If we lose this young man's life, I'm going to study law." Waller's case remained on appeal, but by now she had done all she could to publicize it. Early in September, Murray attended the latest Waller hearing before the Virginia Supreme Court, drove to Washington, and entered Howard Law School. The law professor and NAACP legal strategist Charles Houston had retired the year before, but William Hastie and Leon Ransom would be her teachers.[207] After a decade of her trying to find a place in the world, the perfect place had found her. Or so she thought.

Murray was one of two women in the class. She had not been there three days when one of her professors prefaced his assignment to her with the words "We don't know why women come to law school anyway, but since you're here . . ." Then all the "male members of the first year class" were invited—through a poster on the bulletin board—to a "smoker" at a dean's house. There in the bosom of Howard University "the racial factor was not the problem," but "immediately the sex factor was isolated," Murray recalled. If you have been fighting injustice alone and finally find yourself invited to a place where you are among like-minded friends, do you protest the way that they do things? Sure. Murray marched up to her professors and asked, "Well, if it is a legal fraternity, why am I not eligible?" They suggested she form a "legal sorority." This kind of "crude," "unvarnished" sexism, she came to believe, thrived in "minority groups." "It is not a smooth, kind thing," Murray learned. "It is a kind of straight out machismo."[208] She began to wonder if it might be a long three years.

8

GUERRILLAS IN THE
GOOD WAR

JIM CROW'S LAST STAND

Pearl Harbor put Jim Crow on the Run.
That Crow can't fight for Democracy
And be the same old Crow he used to be—
Although right now, even yet today,
He tries to act the same old way.
But India and China and Harlem, too,
Have made up their minds Jim Crow is through.

—LANGSTON HUGHES, "JIM CROW'S LAST STAND," 1943[1]

Thirteen days after the Japanese attack on Pearl Harbor on December 7, 1941, NAACP executive secretary Walter White told Americans, "Declarations of war do not lessen the obligation to preserve and extend civil liberties here." White averred: "Admittedly, this is not going to be easy to do." If the promise of World War I had been "after the war, democracy in full measure," this time there could be no waiting. The "lines are more sharply drawn," White pointed out; "the Nazi philosophy crystallizes all and every anti-colored, anti-Jewish, anti-liberal and anti-freedom principle." A movement for the full rights of citizenship must begin alongside the war against Fascism. When African Americans fought for their rights on the home front, they fought against the principles of Fascism.[2]

From 1941 to 1945 black Americans brought to bear a new litmus test for full citizenship: desegregation, which meant an end to discrimination in employment, education, and public accommodations. Moreover, *segregation* and *desegregation*, terms rarely used as nouns in the 1930s, functioned as powerful rhetorical symbols during World War II. Demanding an end to segregation worked as well in the North as it did in the South, whereas Jim Crow implied the southern *system* of oppression by law. In the first years of the war, condemnations of segregation were ubiquitous, but the use of the word *integration* remained rare. Ending segregation implied opening up opportunity; integration implied something else, a future that no one could quite see yet.

Now when African Americans referred to Jim Crow, he had a slightly antique sound about him. *Jim Crow* had always been bizarre shorthand to describe a wide range of oppressions, and as shorthand the term did not name them individually. Using the expression *Jim Crow* gave everyone a little wiggle room; African Americans could condemn Jim Crow without being specific. Demanding an end to segregation, however, was a different thing entirely: It was specific, immediate, and far-reaching. As the war continued, African Americans began to use the word *segregation* where they had formerly used *Jim Crow*. Desegregation meant opening jobs, hotels, restaurants, buses, schools, and neighborhoods to African Americans. Some did not cringe when they explained that it might mean opening hearts as well.

The demand for desegregation came from black people themselves, beginning in the North and in the armed forces, and they demanded it across party lines, without regard to organizational expediencies, and ahead of their various white allies. Americans had spent the 1930s analyzing, discussing, interrogating, and sometimes challenging white supremacy piecemeal. It had been complicated and exhausting, from self-determination to litigation for equal graduate education. Suddenly it seemed as if they had gone about the whole thing backward. They had fought segregation's consequences; now, as America fought the Fascists, they could fight segregation itself. The well was poisoned, yet African Americans had had to spend the interwar years trying to redirect its rivulets. All that exhausting work brought them to this moment when segregation must go. Many African Americans believed that it was now or never.

The CPUSA remained viable among African Americans in northern and western cities, even though its focus on the South was subsumed by its war effort. It flourished in Harlem, where Ben Davis ran as a Communist in 1943 for the New York City Council and won.[3] After finding their voice in the Popular Front and sustaining it in the face of Red Scares from 1939 to 1941, white liberal Southerners reached a critical mass. After carving out ideological affinities with the sharp edge of shared oppression, African American–Jewish alliances grew strong enough to stare discrimination in the face and pronounce it evil. After a hodgepodge of New Deal initiatives, failures, and partial successes, African Americans tunneled through to the heart of the Roosevelt administration so that their voices might be heard, if faintly.

All this recent history mattered, but it mattered less than the fact that African Americans no longer simply fought for themselves; they fought for their country. In the bright light generated by the battle between good and evil, they believed that their country needed to end segregation to win the war. If the United States defeated Fascism without defeating Jim Crow, it would be a hollow victory. New Fascisms, domestic and foreign, would sprout up after victory to threaten America. So if it seemed selfish, awkward, opportunistic, ill timed, or unpatriotic to demand an end to segregation during this war, African Americans knew that by doing so, they saved not only themselves but their country. *Crisis* urged African Americans to "speak out, not in disloyalty, but in the truest patriotism . . . about the breaches of democracy here in our own land."[4] The demand for desegregation, taken as a starting point and spoken aloud and unapologetically, united African Americans in a way that all the Sanhedrins and National Negro Congresses never had. If there is no power equal to that of an idea whose time has come, there is also no guarantee that its time will last. The fight was on; the enemy engaged. There could be no retreat, no surrender.

Pauli Murray characterized the movement for black liberation on the World War II home front as a "guerrilla-like warfare." The guerrilla warriors fought skirmishes, and sometimes battles, in many of the same minefields through which activists had tiptoed during the interwar years. The difference was that now they caught a glimpse of victory just over the next hill. Murray understood these protests as a war within a war, comparable to resistance in an occupied country. She saw herself as a member of the Free Southern Forces, temporarily a government-in-exile, waiting for the day when a multihued army would march triumphantly across the Mason-Dixon line. She wrote to "Dear Brother Randolph," who led the March on Washington Movement, "I've taken it upon myself to act as a 'little lieutenant' to the Commander of our new movement for Freedom."[5] Throughout the war African Americans fought "America's second foe," racism, in the streets and in the press, through direct action and through the power of ideas.[6]

Snatched from the Jaws of a Red Scare

In the months before the United States entered World War II, liberals and radicals of all stripes found themselves threatened by the anti-Communist undercurrent that swelled during the Nazi-Soviet Nonaggression Pact. By 1940 white supremacists had added new rhetoric to their old campaign against those who fought for the civil rights of labor and African Americans. Those who disputed the status quo were "subversives." North Carolina, for example, drew up "Anti-Subversion Plans" to stop "Fifth Column advancements" in the state. High on the list was the vow that "school systems be kept free of any foreign propaganda by constant vigilance and study."[7] The *Charlotte Observer* proposed that the state's Communists be put in "concentration camps," since they were "foreign agents." Bart Logan, the man who had plucked Junius Scales from The Intimate Bookshop and deposited him in the heart of the working class, reminded Charlotte readers that "concentration camps for Communists really mean concentration camps for all militant opponents of the war and the defenders of the civil rights and living standards of the people." Concentration camps could not destroy the Communist Party, he argued, but they could "destroy the peace and freedom of the American people."[8]

A chilly wind blew over Chapel Hill's liberals. Paul Green worried that the "fine forces of liberalism in the university and North Carolina generally are in danger of suffering a serious if not permanent setback." He urged Frank Porter Graham to run for governor to prevent more damage.[9] Green had no idea how serious or permanent that setback might be. In May 1940 he hoped to collaborate with Richard Wright, the black Communist writer, on turning Wright's novel *Native Son* into a play. Years earlier Wright had lost his job with the Works Progress Administration when he tried to stage Green's *Hymn to the Rising Sun*, so he was thrilled to hear from Green, whom he had never met. They spent two weeks in the summer of 1940 together in Chapel Hill, writing a script and flouting many of segregation's conventions. A gang of toughs threatened to run Wright out of town, and Green talked them out of it with the promise that Wright was leaving the next day. After many revisions, *Native Son: The Biography of a Young American* opened on Broadway in February 1941. The play met with "mixed success," but Green's collaboration with Wright attracted FBI attention. Bureau agents combed through every aspect of Green's life, followed him, and interviewed his friends and colleagues. After the Japanese attack on Pearl Harbor, Green gave up his pacifism and tended to avoid the Left-Wing groups, perhaps because of FBI pressure. He devoted himself to working for criminal rights.[10]

The Red Scare was a national phenomenon. "A dangerous alien-bred and alien-minded Fifth Column has invaded an unsuspecting Southland," the Constitutional Educational League reported. A Right-Wing and anti-Semitic organization, the New Haven, Connecticut-based league set up an office in Birmingham, Alabama. The pressure in Tennessee proved so intense that Highlander's Myles Horton appealed to Roger Baldwin of the ACLU for help.[11] In Memphis city authorities exploited fifth column fears to thwart Congress of Industrial Organizations' organizing among black and white workers.[12] In 1939 the New York legislature set up the Rapp-Coudert Committee to investigate "subversive activities" in public schools and called witnesses to testify about what went on in the College of the City of New York's classrooms, resulting in the suspension of fourteen teachers in 1941. One witness mentioned that Max Yergan's class in Negro history was "attended and made popular by Young Communist League students."[13] After the hearing the CCNY administration failed to renew Yergan's contract, citing the need for a change, lack of scholarship on Yergan's part, and a routine faculty housecleaning. Yergan, hurt and embarrassed by this attempt to "discredit" him, correctly blamed his plight on his political activities.[14] Paul Robeson, Franz Boas, and Mary White Ovington organized a publicity campaign to win his reappointment, many New Yorkers joined the hastily formed Committee for Defense of Public Education, and Yergan turned to the NAACP for help, all to no avail.[15]

A month later a House Un-American Activities Committee investigator branded Howard University professor and National Negro Congress board member William Alphaeus Hunton, Jr., a Communist because of his work with the American Peace Mobilization. Hunton responded by "asking why the Dies Committee does not devote just one-tenth of its time to investigating the subversive undermining of American democracy represented by the varied form of discrimination and oppression practiced against Negro citizens." He affirmed his participation in the American Peace Mobilization, "which is dedicated to the maintenance of peace and democracy in America." He said, "I see nothing subversive in that." His last retort could have been a requiem for the Popular Front: "You cannot make something bad by merely calling it a name."[16] Actually, Americans soon learned that you could, and that people would, make something bad by merely calling it a name.

Southern politicians capitalized on the antialien hysteria to further their own down-home racist agendas. Their new argument went like this: In totalitarian systems such as Germany and the USSR, the leaders told you how to think about minorities, for better or worse. The Nazis despicably tried to eliminate them; the Communists despicably tried to elevate them. In a democracy such as the U.S. South, local traditions and states' rights enabled people to make up their own minds about the place of minorities within their society. *Freedom* was just another word for the right to discriminate. White journalists had long used the example of Reconstruction to prove that governments could not compel people to change deeply held beliefs, and now they tacitly compared Hitler, Stalin, and Ulysses S. Grant.[17]

Following the Nazi-Soviet Pact, southern demagogues unleashed attacks on "subversives." Eugene Talmadge, back in the governor's office in Georgia after four years of sulking and criticizing FDR, went on a tear in 1941, abolishing the offices of the controller general and state treasurer, burning books, and announcing that he would fire any university professor who "dissents from the proposition that the white man is by nature the superior of the black man."[18] He got wind of a three-year-old funding proposal for interracial conferences that the dean of the College of Education at the University of Georgia and the president of the Georgia State Teachers College had sponsored and ordered them to resign. When they refused, he ordered the university board of regents to fire them. When it refused, he purged the board. Then a Talmadge ally in the Ku Klux Klan kidnapped the dean's black house servant and threatened to kill him if he did not steal or fabricate "letters from Negro teachers" from his boss's house. At a second trial before the newly stacked board of regents, the board voted ten to five to fire the two. The next day Talmadge fired eight more professors in the university system, including the vice-chancellor of the University of Georgia and the dean of women at the teachers' college. He also banned twenty-three books from the public schools of Georgia.[19]

Talmadge might have gotten away unscathed with all this, but the Southern University Conference expelled the University of Georgia from membership, and the Southern Association of Colleges and Secondary Schools, the accrediting body, threatened to withdraw its accreditation. That got the attention of the student body, whose degrees would suddenly be dramatically devalued. The road from Athens to Atlanta was just two lanes then, so the sight of 125 cars and seven hundred students snaking along its seventy-five miles drew enormous attention. The protesting students bore an effigy of Talmadge, and they knew just where they wanted to hang it, over the statue of Tom Watson at the state capitol. Tom had gone from Populist to bigot. Gene Talmadge had traveled a shorter route. The students carried "Pin the Blame on the Jackass" posters that showed Talmadge's face where the beast's posterior belonged. "Take Politics Out of Our University," they demanded.[20]

This time, it was the white press, not the black, that compared the Nazis with Dixie. "Hitler in Georgia," the magazine *America* declared. *Life* ran a photo spread, and *Collier's* dubbed Talmadge "The Fuehrer of Sugar Creek." Frank Porter Graham told the International Student Assembly, which was overwhelmingly white, that Talmadge was one of the "forces working on behalf of the Axis powers." Moreover, he was "anti-American and unrepresentative of progressive southern leadership."[21] All that criticism probably rolled off Talmadge, but he had to take notice when Georgia Bulldogs' fans booed him at a football game.[22]

Jonathan Daniels of Raleigh, formerly of the Southern Committee for

People's Rights and soon to serve in FDR's Office of Civilian Defense, argued that Talmadge was "no Hitler." Yet he was not simply representative of "the disagreeable dramatics of a politically comic South." Although he could not put his finger on exactly how a nation on the verge of war should deal with Talmadge, Daniels recognized his antics as something new, something that should fill Southerners with foreboding. As Daniels put it, "Here is a dirty sign in a dark Southern sky, and it is at least as big as Hitler's funny mustache looked ten years ago." That dirty sign in the dark southern sky lit the way for white supremacist politicians, already slouching toward a virulent anti-Communism. World War II interrupted, but did not derail, their journey.[23]

As Max Yergan tried to win back his teaching position, as Pauli Murray looked forward to attending Howard Law School, and as Odell Waller sat on death row, General Georgi Zhukov woke Joseph Stalin at 3:30 A.M. on June 22, 1941, to tell him that the Germans were at that moment bombing towns in Belorussia. That day Junius Scales had been organizing millworkers in High Point and decided to hitchhike over to Chapel Hill to visit his girlfriend. When he arrived, he found her glued to the radio, listening to news of the Nazi invasion. "We listened to the kitchen radio for hours till at last, to our relief, Churchill declared Britain's unequivocal support of the Soviet Union," Scales recalled. "Until then we had feared that the West would leave the Soviet Union to its fate." Sometime during those hours in the kitchen, the couple decided to marry. The next day they drove to South Carolina, where there was no matrimonial waiting period, and returned as man and wife. Then they heeded Robert Minor's call to an emergency conference in New York on marshaling domestic Communist troops for the new anti-Fascist war.[24]

Despite Foster's admonition that they should not forget the "imperialist character" or "imperialist aims" of the United States, the CPUSA quickly downplayed anti-imperialism and embraced anti-Fascism and war preparation once again. The time had come to renew the Popular Front, Max Yergan began to proclaim. Suddenly he urged African Americans to avoid the "fascist forces of appeasement" and "support the foreign policy of the National administration." He lectured anyone who would listen that Stalin had done the United States a favor by signing the nonaggression pact, since it had "held off attack for a while."[25]

Franklin Roosevelt pledged on June 24 to send "all the aid we possibly can to Russia."[26] Less than two weeks later, on the Fourth of July, a black columnist asked, "Who is a Communist now?" He went on to say, "Red this, Red that, is about all you have heard in the last three or four years." "But now look. . . . Now our great President shakes hands with the father of Communism." Franklin Roosevelt embraced Joseph Stalin because he had to, and so did non-Communist African Americans. Earl Browder won early release from prison in 1942 and emerged to find the Party "was opposing any mass activities for Negro rights." He recalled, "I immediately changed that position."[27]

Even though the Popular Front had been destroyed, the alliance between the United States and the USSR created an opportunity for discussions about race that sparked interaction between the Left and conservatives. For example, when Max Yergan visited Highlander in 1943, Myles Horton scrambled to bring up a "good representative group" for an "interracial conference." His invitations to spend a night at Highlander went out to such strange bedfellows as Don West, now an *ex*-Communist and James Shepard, president of North Carolina College for Negroes. The optimism and Americanism behind Horton's invitation papered over the fact that such wartime conversations across the political spectrum were strained at best, and many, West and Shepard included, declined to participate in them. The National Negro Congress, which had met biennially, did not meet in 1942 or 1944, in part to avoid factionalism.[28]

Nonetheless virulent, public anti-Communism returned during the war to the depths that had nurtured it and there waged a subterranean war against civil rights and civil liberties. J. Edgar Hoover believed those who pursued black civil rights were definitely subversive and probably Communists. In World War I, investigating African Americans who advocated integration and equality had meant shadowing a few black Communists like Lovett Fort-Whiteman and banning issues of the *Messenger* and the *Crusader*. In World War II, since virtually every black newspaper spoke out against segregation, it required an enormous commitment of resources and staff. Hoover rose to the occasion. Throughout the war the FBI chief dispatched agents to black newspapers to interrogate writers. From June 1942 until the war's end agents covered black political activity in most U.S. cities.[29] For example, a national network of agents followed

Max Yergan's every move, tapped his telephones, and broke into his apartment.[30] Hoover used World War II to establish an elaborate system of surveillance of African Americans that he was to use a decade later to subvert black leaders such as Martin Luther King.

But Hoover had limited success during the war, in part because black journalists, remembering the lesson of World War I, began calling for a free press immediately following Pearl Harbor. In the spring of 1942 Walter White assembled a conference of black newspaper editors to present a united front against "government agencies . . . [that would] crack down on Negro newspapers and organizations which are too outspoken in their criticism of discrimination in the war program."[31] Throughout the war the newly formed National Newspaper Publishers Association lobbied to convince Roosevelt of its loyalty and its right to speak out against discrimination.[32] Nonetheless, Hoover pursued the black press and vigorously sought to indict several newspapers for sedition and espionage.

The Roosevelt administration itself thwarted Hoover. Five times Hoover tried to convince the Justice Department to prosecute particular mainstream black newspapers; five times the department refused. In 1943 the FBI published the fruits of its surveillance, *Survey of Racial Conditions in the United States.* It alleged that Communists were on the staffs of thirteen black newspapers, including the *Chicago Defender*, where William Patterson was working as a reporter. However, despite the fact that Hoover continued to gather intelligence on African American activists, southern Communists, and the black press, a strong attorney general, the demands of the war, and the need for a united home front meant that he had to tread carefully.[33]

African Americans changed the tenor of the discussion from a question of black sedition to a question of black morale and held whites accountable for seeing that black spirits remained high. The federal government investigated black morale in 1942 and became "seriously concerned" that African Americans considered the war "a white man's conflict." In World War I "Negro morale" had barely registered on the public consciousness, but the term became ubiquitous during World War II.[34] Five weeks after Pearl Harbor the question came up at a Conference of National Organizations on Problems of Negroes in a World at War. The group was middle of the road and middle class, from the sorority Alpha

Kappa Alpha to the YWCA to the NAACP. Attorney William Hastie, serving as a civilian aide to the secretary of war, asked the delegates to vote on the question, Was the Negro "whole-heartedly and unreservedly for the all-out program in support of the war against Hitler, Japan and Italy? No, one delegate shouted, because "the Negro was being told that this war was for democracy while the morale of the Negro was drifting to a low ebb." In the end an overwhelming majority of delegates voted that "the Negro was not" ready to rescue democracy until democracy rescued African Americans from discrimination.[35] One writer pointed to the irony that "the one virtue which the South publicly bestows on the dark brethren [loyalty] is in grave jeopardy." The old unquestioning loyalty, also known as obedience, had vanished, and a new kind, a loyalty that allowed the patriot to question his or her country's policies, had emerged. As the war progressed, black servicemen and women demonstrated spectacular loyalty to their country on the battlefront, and the black civilian population rallied behind them.[36]

Taking It to the Streets

After his resignation from the National Negro Congress in 1940, A. Philip Randolph carried impeccable anti-Communist credentials and fire in his belly. Few people knew better than he the dialectic of war's promise and betrayal. As an idealistic young Socialist he had not wanted any part of World War I but soon discovered that war pervaded every aspect of domestic politics. He had seen the *Messenger* banned, his friends radicalized, and postwar racial violence kill the hopes of black progressives and drive some to Communism. "That war," he recalled, "neither won democracy abroad or at home." In wartime, Randolph now knew, African Americans must get guarantees up front, not vague promises that would surely end in betrayal. In 1940 he urgently endorsed the idea of the United States as the arsenal of democracy at the same time that he argued that the "American Government should resolutely refuse to curb the civil liberties of its citizens."[37] In the long rehearsal leading up to World War II, Randolph felt more and more certain that this was the time to press for desegregation, particularly in employment and the military.

Rayford Logan, a Howard University history professor, and Charles

Hamilton Houston, Howard law professor and NAACP legal strategist, took similar questions to Capitol Hill as Congress debated a proposed Selective Service Act late in 1940. Nearly four hundred thousand African Americans had served in World War I, half of those in France, where Logan and Houston had served. Yet no black officer (or reserve officer) had been in the regular army. The War Department discouraged black National Guard units, despite "a shortage of men," Logan and Houston told the House Subcommittee on Military Affairs. The army excluded African Americans from flight training.[38] From within the administration, black economist Robert Weaver and white Southerner and former CIC secretary Will Alexander recommended the appointment of African Americans to all selective service boards and as assistant secretaries in the War and Navy departments.[39] When the Selective Service Act took effect in September 1940, it included a prohibition against racial discrimination in its "interpretation or execution." But the reality was a different matter. In Charlotte, North Carolina, recruiting officers beat up a black teacher who sought to enlist.[40]

On that cue, Randolph, Walter White, and economist T. Arnold Hill of the National Urban League met with FDR and asked that he desegregate the military and war industries. The president equivocated, and in October the White House announced that the army would remain segregated. Worse, the announcement made it sound as if White and Randolph had agreed to segregation. The situation grew tenser as daily reports came back from black draftees who found themselves shipped to army bases in the South, where black soldiers clashed with police. Some predicted "another Houston riot"; during World War I in Houston black soldiers had marched on police in a suicidal last stand against maltreatment.[41]

FDR's refusal to desegregate the military gave "the green light to a complete segregated pattern for Negroes throughout American life." *Crisis* warned: "We may be forced to accept it, but we can never agree to it."[42] Upon even more vigorous protest by White and Randolph, the administration clarified its policies to the military: African Americans could serve in proportion to their population percentage, get flight, combatant, and officer training, and would enter an expanded variety of assignments within the branches. FDR refused, however, "to intermingle the colored and white enlisted personnel in the same regimental organizations."[43]

These concessions represented an improvement over conditions in World War I, but they fell far short of what the new dual patriots demanded. *Crisis* stated simply, "segregation must go."[44]

On January 6, 1941, the president devoted his annual congressional address to what he believed should be the birthright of all people, the Four Freedoms: freedom of speech and expression, freedom of worship, freedom from want, and freedom from fear. "Freedom," Roosevelt intoned, "means the supremacy of human rights everywhere."[45] A. Philip Randolph saw the Four Freedoms as an agenda on which he would hold FDR accountable. Just as African Americans had insisted that Woodrow Wilson's "safe for democracy" slogan should apply at home during World War I, so throughout World War II they seized on the Four Freedoms to illustrate their country's hypocrisy. For example, the *Chicago Defender* ran a cartoon, entitled "The Four Freedoms: Dixie Style," that depicted a lynch noose, a poll tax collection box, a ball labeled "peonage" on a chain, and Jim Crow himself, looking awfully out of sorts.[46]

African Americans joined other ethnic Americans in May 1941 to underscore their belief that the Four Freedoms should be practiced at home. I Am an American Day in Chicago brought together Ethel Waters, Pat O'Brien, Don Ameche, and Catholic, Jewish, and Protestant religious leaders. To ensure a mixed audience, the planners organized a South Side committee to turn out the black neighborhood. An audience of a hundred thousand packed Soldier Field, only to be greeted by eight young black men and two young black women silently marching and carrying signs reading, WE ARE AMERICANS, TOO, BUT WE ARE DENIED JOBS IN DEFENSE INDUSTRIES and WE ARE JIM-CROWED IN OR EXCLUDED FROM THE ARMED FORCES. WE OBJECT. The police arrested them.[47] The incident taught a near-perfect lesson on the dangers of invoking a shared citizenship in a country where some did not share equally in that citizenship. It represented a blueprint for the next three years as well. African Americans would be delighted to celebrate Americanism, but they would never forgo an opportunity to point out its shortcomings.

Will Alexander and Robert Weaver made plans in the Office of Production Management (OPM) to open up jobs in defense industries to black Americans. They had formerly written in a nondiscrimination clause in contracts for public housing construction with great success.

Now, with the support of Eleanor Roosevelt, they lobbied the heads of their agency to "include a non-discrimination clause in government defense contracts." In their scheme, the employer would be responsible for enforcement and subject to audits. But, Alexander recalled, the OPM "wouldn't touch it."[48] Aware of such setbacks, Randolph concluded that "Negroes are not getting anywhere with National Defense," and he pushed for African Americans "in responsible posts of every department of the Government." In public appearances throughout the South he began to talk about a march of ten thousand African Americans to Washington to demand an end to segregation in defense work and in the armed services. Going public with the plan on January 15, 1941, he announced that the ten thousand would march under the slogan "We loyal Negro-American Citizens demand the right to work and fight for our country." [49]

In a period of three months Randolph developed the March on Washington Movement (MOWM) into a national organization with grassroots units and planned a march for July 1, 1941. First of all, the march would be limited to African Americans because Randolph believed that it would be a radicalizing experience for the participants and that prohibiting whites would eliminate any Communist influence. He organized thirty-six MOWM chapters, including ten in the South. In Chicago he held a mass meeting built on the support he had already gained from labor leaders. Working through the churches, he set up steering committees, developed sponsors, many of them women, to recruit and organize the marchers. In turn, they organized young people and sold buttons to raise funds for the trip. Soon it looked as if a hundred thousand black people would rise up and march on Washington.[50] Randolph also had the NAACP's behind-the-scenes support. Across the country NAACP branches organized protests against plants that discriminated against African Americans. In the North the NAACP picketed such companies, carrying signs like HITLER MUST RUN THIS PLANT: THEY WON'T EMPLOY NEGROES and NO TAXATION WITHOUT INTEGRATION.[51]

In May, Randolph sent six proposals to President Roosevelt, demanding an executive order to forbid discrimination among government contractors, in defense training, in the federal government, and in the branches of the armed services. In addition, the president should ask Congress to pass a law excluding discriminatory unions from the National Labor Relations Act and order the federal Employment Services to supply workers "without regard to race, creed, or color." The black press kept up the pressure with articles such as "Roosevelt Gives Only 'Lip Service' to Aid Negroes."[52]

In hopes of stopping the march, FDR sent a memo to the Office of Production Management declaring, "Our government cannot countenance continued discrimination against American citizens in defense production." Alexander and Weaver had already tried to get the OPM to stop discrimination in defense industries, to no avail. Many African Americans recognized this presidential directive as more "lip service" and agreed with Randolph that Roosevelt's memo did not get "to the root of the problem."[53] Eleanor Roosevelt pleaded with Randolph to cancel the march because she expected violence. When she asked where the marchers would stay, Randolph assured her that they "would simply march into the hotels and restaurants, and order food and shelter." He told her he was looking forward to addressing the NAACP national conference on "employment in defense industries" just a week before the scheduled march.[54] All this exacerbated the administration's fears.

FDR met on June 18 with Walter White, A. Philip Randolph, and Layle Lane, a black woman who was a close associate of Pauli Murray's at the Workers Defense League and offered to call the heads of defense plants and tell them to give African Americans equal opportunity. Randolph countered by demanding an official executive order banning discrimination in defense industries and government. He also insisted on reviewing drafts of the order before Roosevelt issued it. FDR issued Executive Order 8802 on June 25, 1941, six days before the scheduled march, banning discrimination in "defense industries or government" and creating a temporary Fair Employment Practices Committee (FEPC) to review complaints. Randolph canceled the march.[55]

This all looked quite sudden to white Americans, and a debate arose over whether Roosevelt had jumped or been pushed into issuing the order. Most likely he jumped. FDR realized that he would have to desegregate defense industries, since on both coasts, plants building ships and aircraft "were being filled with boys of draft age," who would soon be called up. He knew better than anyone that if they were drafted, their absence would cripple the plants. If they obtained an exemption to work, their absence would cripple the military.[56] In June 1941 other Americans might still dream that the United States could stay out of World War II, but FDR was convinced that U.S. military intervention was inevitable.

Would Randolph have marched on Washington? He certainly would not have welcomed the chaos that might have resulted from the encounter in Washington, but he had built a grassroots organization that could have easily turned out ten thousand demonstrators, if not one hundred thousand. If FDR had stopped short of a resolution that had the force of law, it seems likely that Randolph would have marched. He had waited all his life to recover from the oppression of World War I, and he believed that a reprise of that wartime repression could set back civil rights for another generation. As it was, Randolph endured a great deal of criticism for canceling the march, especially from young people.[57]

Randolph's bargain with FDR was reciprocal. To obtain the executive order, he promised black support if and when the war came. He made good on that promise after Pearl Harbor when he wrote, "Japan has fired upon the United States, our country. We, all of us, black and white, Jew and Gentile, Protestant and Catholic, are at war.... What shall the Negro do? There is only one answer. He must fight."[58]

It would be hard to exaggerate how astonishing white Southerners found the executive order. First of all, many honestly believed that work fell into preordained categories: white work and "nigger work." Black Southerners were incapable of doing the work that white Southerners did, and if white Southerners worked alongside them, they degraded themselves. Above all, Jim Crow rested on two fundamental beliefs: maintaining the "integrity" of the white race and maintaining the southern labor system, which depended on a base of underpaid black labor to keep the wages down for all. All else—political repression, segregation, degradation, lynching, a poor educational system—existed to keep those two pillars in place. When the federal government condemned employment discrimination, it struck at the heart of white supremacy. When it put Milton Webster, Randolph's associate in the Brotherhood of Sleeping Car Porters, on the FEPC, it put a black man in the jury box at Jim Crow's trial. Eugene Talmadge "plastered Georgia with photographs of Webster sitting in judgment upon the white South." Since 17.6 percent of the national total spent on defense was spent in the South, the effect of the order was far-reaching.[59]

FDR issued an executive order, but he lacked the will to enforce it. He named a liberal white southern newspaper editor, Mark Ethridge of Louisville, to chair the FEPC. With a tiny staff and minuscule budget, the committee operated by conducting hearings across the country rather than by systematically enforcing the order. At the third hearing, in Birmingham, Alabama, in June 1942, Chairman Ethridge gave a most remarkable speech. He argued that "the committee has taken no position on the question of segregation" and that the order did not require desegregation; in fact, if it had, he would have considered that "in the Nazi dictatorial pattern." All in all, black Americans had "magnified its import and possibilities." He concluded, "There is no power in the world—not even in all the mechanized armies of the earth, Allied and Axis—which could now force the Southern white people to the abandonment of the principle of social segregation." Of course the FEPC was not about "social segregation"; it was about desegregating defense industries to win the war.[60] Ethridge did not discuss how the government, defense industries, and any organization receiving federal aid could "provide for the full and equitable participation of all workers in defense industries, without discrimination because of race, creed, color, or national origin," in training and on the job, while segregating them.[61]

Black leaders, including two FEPC members, condemned Ethridge's statement and called for him to resign. The committee moved forward with the inherently contradictory position that "segregation could be a cause for complaint and committee action only if it resulted in discrimination." Perhaps companies could build Jim Crow factories side by side to comply with separate but equal facilities.[62] Ethridge subsequently resigned from the committee, which went through several incarnations within the administration. Throughout its troubled history African Americans criticized the FEPC's effectiveness, arguing that companies simply did not comply with the order. "Nice work . . . if you can get it," the *Chicago Defender* commented on hypothetical defense employment.[63] With the FEPC in shambles, Roosevelt turned to Will Alexander to "take this FEPC thing and run it, get it straightened out. It's a mess." Alexander refused because the committee had no enforcement powers. Frank Porter Graham refused the chairmanship as well.[64]

In January 1943 the March on Washington Movement held a "Save

FEPC Conference" to keep pressure on the president, and Randolph termed the FEPC board a "meatless bone of appeasement to [the] Negro people."[65] Max Yergan, Walter White, and others beseeched FDR to make it an independent agency reporting directly to the president, and in May 1943 he did.[66] He persuaded a prominent Catholic monsignor to accept the chair, and Pauli Murray cabled Eleanor Roosevelt to urge the appointment of a woman to the committee to "balance tensions and help over tactless situations." When the board was reconstituted, it included a woman.[67]

The monsignor who headed the FEPC exhibited what Alexander described as "Christly patience" and succeeded in establishing field offices, including one for southeastern District VII in Atlanta in 1943. The office's director, a native white Virginian, was determined to run a desegregated office with an integrated staff. He battled to get office space, resolved a bathroom brouhaha, withstood a blast from Eugene Talmadge about the "flat-nosed mulatto secretary" he hired, and fought off a city council resolution to Georgia's congressional delegation to force the FEPC to leave the city. Whether defense contractors hired black Southerners within the South depended on a complicated mix of location, labor availability, and the ease with which the industry could practice job segregation within a single plant. Some black Southerners were willing to accept this job segregation because it meant jobs but also because they hoped to hold on to the well-paying jobs after the war, when they expected federal protection to evaporate. The FEPC was limited and confusing and ineffective at best. Nonetheless, in 1944, Smith Act sponsor Senator Howard W. Smith of Virginia began hearings to determine if it had reached beyond its powers. Smith never succeeded in proving that the committee had exceeded its authority; he simply tried to distract it so that it could not do its job.[68]

Nonetheless, the establishment of the FEPC by the president of the United States incarnated what had heretofore been only an allegation, that discrimination in employment was wrong. Despite the committee's vicissitudes, the fierce opposition that it drew, and its own ineffectiveness, the very idea that the government had decided that employment practices should be fair to African Americans represented an enormous departure from Jim Crow practice. The Atlanta City Council certainly saw it that way. Pauli Murray did too. Referring to the executive order and the

FEPC, she wrote: "This victory cannot be overestimated. It was the first national wedge in discrimination in employment and MOWM's greatest contribution to the goal of equal rights for all."[69]

If he could not foresee the future, Randolph knew that the status quo could not continue. He told African Americans, "Rather that we die standing upon our feet fighting for our rights than to exist upon our knees begging for life." One sarcastic white man commented: "Someone has talked him into the idea that he is a kind of Gandhi of the Negroes." But Will Alexander thought that Randolph actually resembled Gandhi or that at least half of him did. Alexander characterized Randolph as "sort of a combination John L. Lewis and Mohandas Karamchand Gandhi," with a "mystical streak that reminded you sometimes of Gandhi."[70] When Randolph maintained that he had not canceled but merely postponed the March on Washington, he spoke the truth. The postponement of the Washington march had won concessions, but in the summer of 1942 the march actually marched, albeit in New York City. Pauli Murray planned it.

Pauli Murray's March on Washington

Six weeks after Pearl Harbor a horrible lynching linked victory abroad and victory at home. A crowd of three hundred white people took a black man from jail in Sikeston, Missouri, dragged him behind a car throughout town, poured gasoline on him, and burned him alive. The *Chicago Defender* began running the slogan "Remember Pearl Harbor—and Sikeston Too." In February 1942 the *Pittsburgh Courier* initiated its Double V Campaign: "The first V is for victory over our enemies from without, the second V for victory over our enemies within." In Baltimore the *Afro-American* ran a closed fist, a precursor to the 1960s Black Power sign, as its signature. By closing Booker T. Washington's metaphorical separate fingers into a fist, the *Afro-American* argued, "Uncle Sam has two fists and ten fingers. One of those fingers is colored. . . . We can't go into a fight to the death with a sore finger, or one disabled from lack of use."[71] A December 1942 poll found that 65 percent of black Southerners thought that the war would "aid the Negro's fight for democracy at home."[72]

Then the *Afro-American*'s editors uttered the words spoken only by Reds in the previous decade: "The *Afro* believes in social equality if it is anything other citizens have. . . . If mixed schools involve social equality, we are for mixed schools. . . . If intermarriage is social equality, we are for it. . . . If removing the 'white only' signs from public conveyances, hotels, restaurants, and stores is social equality, we are for it. . . . If social equality means service on juries, holding public office, voting . . . , using public parks and libraries, we are for it. If social equality means equality in civil service or membership in mixed labor unions or equal pay for equal work in government or government-aided enterprises, we are for that."[73]

No one was more for it than Pauli Murray. Although busy in law school, she devoted much time to activism. During the war she became a public person, widely published and known to black leaders. In 1942 and 1943 she was devoted to A. Philip Randolph and the March on Washington Movement. When a black columnist in the *Pittsburgh Courier* criticized Randolph in July 1942, she took him to task. "Dear Mr. Schuyler: . . . You state that the March on Washington Movement is A. Philip Randolph. I cannot agree," Pauli Murray wrote. "I am only representative of an increasing number of militant young Negroes. . . . If A. Philip Randolph is a leader, it will be because these young Negroes make him a leader." The "yearlings" were ready to go to jail and ready to follow Randolph down "the path of Ghandi [*sic*] and Nehru."[74]

Murray saw the MOWM as the only available vehicle for mass protest. The NAACP focused on legal strategies before its great growth during the war, and the Urban League did not represent the masses but were merely their black middle-class spokespeople. Murray believed that ending segregation "demanded forceful action" and that the MOWM could provide it. During Murray's first year in law school, 1941–1942, racial incidents broke out all over the United States, and Randolph suggested a series of mass meetings "to protest . . . flagrant, outrageous and indefensible discriminations against the Negro." They would focus on reversing the Red Cross's decision to segregate the blood supply, desegregating the military, protecting black soldiers from southern mobs, and increasing black representation in federal government agencies.[75]

These strategies excited Murray, who grew increasingly angry in the first year of the war. She published "Negro Youth's Dilemma" to speak for herself, but also for many young black people. "I too want to be a loyal citizen," Murray wrote. "I want something to believe in." But she cataloged countless insults of the war that disillusioned young African Americans. Living in Washington, she especially felt the sting of discrimination against those African Americans serving their country in government jobs or the military. "Brown public servants are refused transportation by taxicabs and service in restaurants. Theatres and places of entertainment refuse to sell tickets to Negro government workers," she noted. "Is this the brand of democracy we are asked to die for?" Murray asked. In the South "a khaki uniform and a brown face are open invitations to cold-blooded murder." In Washington in the spring of 1942, Murray watched "a new hatred seep through a race of people who have marched with patience through the centuries." As reports of violence against black soldiers became commonplace, the black press connected "lynching and national security" and called lynching "treason."[76] At the same time, African Americans were "revolted at the monstrous atrocities Hitler is heaping upon the Jewish people." Nazi persecution of "the stricken Jewish people [would] strengthen the arm of every Negro soldier."[77]

During her first year at law school Murray also remained preoccupied with Odell Waller's case. She had watched Waller's lawyers appeal to the Supreme Court of Virginia in September 1941 and fail. She had felt hope ebb as the U.S. Supreme Court refused to grant a writ of certiorari and watched as his execution date of June 19, 1942, loomed closer.[78] Then the day before Waller's scheduled execution Virginia Governor Colgate W. Darden, Jr., granted him a two-week reprieve with a special commutation hearing on June 29. Murray read with amazement and not a little satisfaction Virginius Dabney's editorial in the *Richmond Times-Dispatch* calling for commutation of the death penalty.[79]

A. Philip Randolph took up Waller's cause as his lawyers ran out of options. He staged a mass rally at Madison Square Garden on June 16 to protest the sorts of things Murray had itemized in her April article, but he also used the rally to campaign to save Odell Waller.[80] Calling for Harlem's merchants to turn off their lights in a silent protest blackout, the MOWM organizers assembled eighteen to twenty thousand at Madison Square Garden, the largest black rally to date.[81] The meeting brought together a cross section of black leaders, including Mary McLeod Bethune, Walter White, and a relative newcomer, Harlem minister Adam Clayton Powell, Jr. As Murray watched in awe, Randolph entered the Garden in a cordon of one hundred Pullman porters and fifty Pullman maids in uniform. Banners crying SAVE ODELL WALLER decorated the arena, and Randolph introduced Annie Waller to the screaming crowd.[82] Thirteen days later, on June 30, after a long commutation hearing, Governor Darden failed to stay Waller's execution and set the date for July 2.[83]

Randolph called Pauli Murray, still in New York for the summer, and asked her to organize a delegation to meet with President Roosevelt. By the next morning the delegation, joined by Murray's law school dean, Leon Ransom, was in Washington. They were greeted by a full-page ad in the *Washington Star* asking FDR to investigate the case. It was signed by scores of national leaders, including Frank Porter Graham. Despite the boost that the ad gave them, the group had no appointment and was shuttled from office to office. No one at the White House would see them. Murray remembered the day as "one of unrelieved failure and humiliation." Finally they returned to NAACP headquarters to await a call from Eleanor Roosevelt, who had been working all day to stop the execution. When she called, her voice "trembled and almost broke." ER told them, "I have done everything I can possibly do. I have interrupted the President twice." FDR told his wife that the matter was "not of the heart" but of the law. He could not pardon Waller. Randolph told the group, "The President and the Government of the United States have failed us. Waller's death will 'stab in the back' a group of people who are asked to defend their country, but whom the leaders of their country will not defend."[84]

While Murray met with heartbreak in Washington, Waller wrote a dying statement. "Have you ever thought about how some people are allowed a chance over and over again, then there are others [who] are allowed little chance—some no chance at all?" he asked. Waller died the next morning.[85] Devastated, Murray returned to New York and wrote a two-part article, "He Has Not Died in Vain," for the Socialist paper the *Call*. Her anger spilled over in print. Reaction to Waller's death had proved that "even the most downtrodden Negroes are in a fighting mood." Whites should take this as a "danger signal" of an "explosion ahead." Murray was sick of fighting for "Negro rights"; she announced that henceforth she would fight for "human rights," a change that acknowledged the importance of civil rights to everyone and disavowed racial difference.[86] Randolph asked Murray to draft a letter to Roosevelt for the delegation.

She described the disrespect that members of the administration had shown the group, characterized abuses of African Americans as "fascist-like brutalities" and scored the "poll tax southern bloc which decides the fate of American citizens it does not represent."[87]

That letter was widely released to the press, but Murray also wrote a private letter to the president that she sent through Eleanor Roosevelt. Desperate, she begged him to order the evacuation of African Americans from the South just as he had ordered that of the Japanese on the West Coast. Furious, ER wrote back to Murray. She thought that Murray's evacuation idea was horrible. "How many of our colored people in the South would like to be evacuated and treated as though they were not as rightfully here as any other people?" she asked. "I am deeply concerned that we have had to do that to the Japanese who are American citizens, but we are at war with Japan and they have only been citizens for a short time," Roosevelt told Murray. "Your letter seems to me one of the most thoughtless I have ever read," ER added. Always one to press the advantage, Murray realized from this angry response that she had ER's "ear" and wrote back at once to point out ways that FDR could be more effective in his support of African Americans.[88] She also quickly realized that her Japanese analogy was sinister and destructive when she read a story, "Americans in Concentration Camps," in *Crisis* the following month. The author argued that the Japanese-Americans were there because authorities thought "they are not 'white.' They are 'not to be trusted.'"[89]

Meanwhile, under the auspices of the New York chapter of the March on Washington Movement and the Workers Defense League, Murray threw herself into organizing a "silent parade" scheduled for July 25 "to mourn the death of sharecropper Odell Waller and to protest the poll tax which killed him."[90] Murray had only two weeks to plan the only march that the March on Washington Movement ever made in the 1940s, and she threw herself into it. One participant remembered meeting her at a planning session: "I walked into this meeting . . . and heard this little small person with cropped hair, wearing these white sailor pants and standing on the table. She was on *fire*, talking about social injustice and Jim Crow."[91] Wearing black armbands in honor of Waller, five hundred people marched through midtown Manhattan to the sound of muffled drums. Young women, dressed in frilly white summer dresses, silently walked down

Fifty-sixth Street carrying signs that shouted: JUSTICE AND MANHOOD: THE POLL TAX MUST GO, FREE THE SOUTH: ABOLISH THE POLL TAX, and DEMOCRACY HERE IS OUR FIRST LINE OF DEFENSE. The march went off without a hitch.[92] Afterward Murray sank into depression as she remained in New York waiting to return to law school.

A letter from Eleanor Roosevelt's secretary interrupted Murray's torpor. She invited Murray to come to ER's New York apartment on August 27 to talk things over. Murray was terrified, but Roosevelt met her at the door with a big hug. They talked frankly, and Murray did not—of course she could not—curb her militancy as she spoke with the first lady. In the fall Murray returned to law school with the responsibility of organizing the NAACP's national annual student conference and serving as publicity chairman for the MOWM's policy conference.[93] In her spare time she would lead a sit-in movement to desegregate the nation's capital.

"The South" under Siege

In 1943 a rash of articles in the white press about the new black militancy led W. E. B. Du Bois to comment that "the white world has suddenly become conscious of the Negro press." White Southerner Thomas Sancton wrote "Something's Happened to the Negro," in the *New Republic*. He noted, "When a white man first reads a Negro newspaper, it is like getting a bucket of cold water in the face."[94] The Negro, said another white journalist, "is the great American democrat. He has taken our announced war aims seriously and he is in no mood to compromise on them with either Hitler or Talmadge."[95]

White Southerners reacted by calling an interracial conference, this time with a twist. Black Southerners would first meet separately and draw up a position paper; whites would meet separately and answer it; then both groups would meet together and determine a course of action. The idea for the meetings came from Jessie Daniel Ames, director of woman's work for the Commission on Interracial Cooperation, who had worked virtually alone to keep the CIC going for the past three years. Will Alexander had resigned in 1938, and Howard Odum had become president, but both men thought that the CIC should "be allowed to die." Ames joined a black Richmond educator, Gordon Blaine Hancock, to arrange a meeting of only *southern* black leaders in Durham, North Carolina, in October 1942. The planners excluded governmental employees as well. These exclusions pinpointed the engines of change: black expatriate Southerners, black Northerners, and anyone in the New Deal.[96] One of the conveners invited Du Bois, who found himself otherwise occupied when he heard about the exclusionary invitations. The fifty-eight black delegates to the African American conference held in Durham were a conservative lot, mostly ministers, state employees, or black educators. Only four women attended. The most nationally connected delegate was Fisk sociologist Charles S. Johnson.[97]

The Durham meeting nonetheless produced a New Charter of Race Relations in the South, known as the Durham Manifesto, that explicitly rejected the old "paternalistic and traditional" one that had licensed Jim Crow. While the black Southerners saw the need to speak for themselves, the conference was not "secessionist" from their union with black Northerners, Hancock argued, but he argued that it was necessary to influence "local measures." He deflected anticipated southern white criticism by arguing that the conference was not "seditionist" and tried to avoid northern black criticism by arguing the delegates would "not cringe and crawl, tremble or truckle or even tip-toe."[98]

In fact they didn't truckle. The Durham Manifesto demanded an end to the poll tax, the white primary, police brutality, voter intimidation, and exclusion from juries and unions. The black southern delegates gave Jim Crow his notice: "We are fundamentally opposed to the principle and practice of compulsory segregation in our American society, whether of races or classes or creeds." There, they had said it! They had named segregation and denounced it, although they had failed to include the word *now*. On the other hand, they made it clear that all the political, social, and economic issues they addressed sprang from "current problems of racial discrimination." "Problems" resulted from "racial discrimination," not from black degeneracy or unreadiness, from some fuzzy lack of understanding between the races, from a deplorable lack of information, or from a few misguided black Northerners, all explanations that had been tried-and-true obfuscations in the South. Moreover, they endorsed the "principles" of the Fair Employment Practices Committee, which, as no white Southerner needed to be reminded, actually came down to only one principle,

The Dude – 1931

Murray dressed as "The Dude" in 1931 *(The Schlesinger Library, Radcliffe Institute, Harvard University)*

Max Yergan in the 1940s *(Robert W. Woodruff Library, Atlanta University Center, Archives and Special Collections)*

Photograph of Walter White by Carl Van Vechten *(James Weldon Johnson Collection, Yale Collection of American Literature, Beinecke Rare Book and Manuscript Library, Yale University, with permission of the Carl Van Vechten Trust)*

Asa Philip Randolph *(Tamiment Library, New York University)*

Ad for *The Negro Quarterly*, edited by Angelo Herndon during World War II
*(Langston Hughes Papers, Yale Collection of American Literature, Beinecke Rare
Book and Manuscript Library, Yale University)*

50,000 NEGROES MUST ATTEND
MADISON SQUARE GARDEN RALLY
JUNE 16, 1942
RADIO, SCREEN, THEATRE, SPEAKERS
March - On - Washington Movement
"Winning Democracy for the Negro Is Winning the War for Democracy"

March on Washington Movement bumper sticker announcing the rally for Odell Waller
(Tamiment Library, New York University)

Pauli Murray in the 1940s *(The Schlesinger Library,*
Radcliffe Institute, Harvard University)

Murray and her own "embryonic United Nations" in San Francisco, 1945
(The Schlesinger Library, Radcliffe Institute, Harvard University)

Pauli Murray and Thelma Stevens consulting *States' Laws on Race and Color*
(The Schlesinger Library, Radcliffe Institute, Harvard University)

integration of the workforce.[99] *Crisis* read between the lines of the manifesto, which the editor called "carefully-worded." He concluded that "close study of it will reveal that southern Negro leaders want the same things . . . that Negroes want everywhere." Du Bois, however, thought it pandered to white Southerners and was glad he had had no part in it.[100]

When white Southerners responded from Atlanta in April 1943, it was they who cringed. Beginning by recognizing that "the Negro, as an American citizen, is entitled to his civil rights and economic opportunities," they argued that "the only justification" for segregation laws "is that they are intended to minister to the welfare and integrity of both races." That statement was both a threat and a promise. Racial "integrity"—in other words, no interracial sexual relations—trumped everything else. That integrity depended on segregation. If black Southerners wanted integration, then their "welfare" would suffer. Granted, the white Southerners continued, "there has been widespread and inexcusable discrimination in the administration of these laws." In other words, there had been discrimination in carrying out discriminatory laws. The Atlanta conference delegates couched everything in typical interracial cheer and reasonableness, but they naturalized segregation, even as they pledged once again to ameliorate its consequences.[101]

When the white and black delegates convened as one body in Richmond in June 1943, they came to praise interracial cooperation but stayed to bury it. Gordon Hancock, the black convener of the Durham meeting, cautioned against "the grave danger of going too slow," whereupon a white delegate "rebuked him for 'going too far.'"[102] The black delegates threatened a walkout, and Howard Odum pulled out his old plan to establish a southern regional council. Everyone agreed to a second meeting, which eventually issued a rueful "collaboration committee" report mostly written by Odum, with the help of Charles Johnson.[103] It acknowledged that the war presented "a rare challenge to the leadership of the South." "Two great peoples" were "caught up in the midst of transition between the powerful heritage of the past and the pull of the future." The black South needed "plenty of understanding and cooperation," but the white South was "suffering terribly too." As usual, the threat that such suffering white folk might erupt in violence emerged as the reason that the time was not right. The committee pointed out that the "opening up of the basic questions of racial segregation and discrimination" caused "racial tensions, fears, and aggressions." Talking about desegregation made whites unlikely to grant "even elementary improvements in Negro status." Then the committee abolished the Commission on Interracial Cooperation and established the Southern Regional Council (SRC), which did not endorse desegregation.[104] This is the way the Commission on Interracial Cooperation ended, "Not with a bang but a whimper."

After the Richmond meeting, Howard Odum published a book-length warning to all who pressured the South to abolish segregation. In *Race and Rumors of Race*, Odum assumed an almost intolerably smug parental tone as he lectured the nation on the harm done to the white South in only one year between July 1942 and July 1943. "Militant" black Northerners, "outside agitators," "northern white intelligentsia," "a small group of Negro agitators," and white Northerners with an attitude of "ignorant detachment" had been responsible for "extreme attacks by the Nation upon the South—those which inflamed the majority of the southern people." It would have been "a magnificent chapter in American history," if only, Odum maintained, the South had been able to reply to the North, "Sure we know you urge these things; we understand from your viewpoint why it is natural that you should. We will try to understand you and will try to show you why this is an impossibility. So what and what of it?"[105]

Odum lectured those he called "extremists." They were "willing to throw the Nation and the races into a war of brothers again just to satisfy their egoistic 'courage,' their new-found freedom." Prevented from brushing off civil rights by the contingencies of war, in one year—July 1942–July 1943—the formerly tranquil Southland had erupted with "continued growing animosities, conflicts, and approaching hate, and a wellnigh universal inflaming of Negroes against the whites and of whites against Negroes." Parts of the book implied that if desegregationists persisted in their demands, a race war would erupt. Other chapters indicated that the race war had already arrived. In "hundreds" of towns there had broken out "what appeared to be unreasonable acts of brutality on the part of whites against Negroes."[106]

Odum was right about the increasing racial violence. Many of these incidents occurred when whites beat up or lynched black men in uniform, and many black service people stationed in the South repeatedly challenged Jim Crow. The military had its own problems: structural segregation, abuse of black soldiers, and a failure to protect them off the base. In January 1943 William Hastie resigned as a civilian aide to the secretary of war, arguing that as discrimination after discrimination piled up in the services, he was powerless to stop them. He returned to Howard Law School to teach for Murray's final year.[107]

Outside the South, wartime pressures produced problems as well. In 1942 a housing riot in Detroit prompted the headline HITLER INVADES AMERICA.[108] In 1943 forty-seven cities experienced 240 racial incidents, with full-blown race riots in Detroit, Los Angeles, and Mobile. In Beaumont, Texas, several hundred whites burned and looted the black section and killed two men in a "week end of terror, worse than anything visited upon the Jews by Nazi fanatics at the height of their pogroms." Whites beat African Americans bloody in Detroit, and police "used the ultimate in force" against African Americans but "persuaded" whites, Thurgood Marshall, NAACP counsel, reported. He characterized police action as "the Gestapo in Detroit." Reporters captured the carnage in photographs run nationwide, yet little was done to punish the white bullies.[109]

Pauli Murray wrote a poem about the violence that appeared in the *Crisis* along with Marshall's report. She had hoped that FDR would speak out more forcefully and say something more than the statement he issued, which read: "I share your feeling that the recent outbreaks of violence in widely spread parts of the country endanger our national unity and comfort our enemies. I am sure that every true American regrets this." That sounded so "mealy-mouthed" that it made Murray furious, so she penned "Mr. Roosevelt Regrets."

> *What'd you get, black boy,*
> *When they knocked you down in the gutter,*
> *And they kicked your teeth out,*
> *And they broke your skull with clubs*
> *And they bashed your stomach in?*
> *What'd you get when the police shot you in the back,*
> *And they chained you to the beds*
> *While they wiped the blood off?*
> *What'd you get when you cried out to the Top Man?*

When you called on the man next to God, so you thought,
And you asked him to speak out to save you?
What'd the Top Man say, black boy?
"Mr. Roosevelt regrets . . ."

Murray sent a copy to Eleanor Roosevelt, who returned it with a note scribbled on top, "I'm sorry, but I understand."[110]

Next time the rioters would be African Americans. Murray's article "Negroes Are Fed Up" appeared in *Common Sense* in August 1943, just days before violence erupted in Harlem. When Harlemites heard the rumor that a black soldier had been shot by a white policeman, there was an outpouring of frustration, led by black soldiers and sailors, who were joined by others who rose up to protest abuse of black soldiers everywhere.[111] Murray watched the rioting and looting and "the little people—arguing, persuading, trying to explain to the police how the people of Harlem felt." She hated the senselessness of it all. "Why would they destroy the things they need?" a Jewish woman who owned a pharmacy asked her. Murray wondered, "How could I tell her that a mob moves without head or heart, and that when the last man down, who has felt the pressure for centuries and can find no scapegoat below himself, revolts, he strikes blindly and without discrimination." She understood it, but she could never condone it. "The shame was mine," Murray concluded.[112] A little over two months later Harlem voters elected Ben Davis their city council representative, casting over forty-four thousand votes for the Communist candidate.[113]

The sorts of false rumors that had set off the Harlem riot abounded in the South, but it was white Southerners who were enmeshed in their web. Odum determined to track them down and bring them to light as examples of white southern folkways in *Race and Rumors of Race*. His research method had been to send 102 white college professors, including Olive Stone, across the South to gather rumors from "common" white folk. Eighty-nine pages swelled with the two thousand rumors, and Odum did not interview African Americans. About half the professors who sent in rumors urged him not to print them, arguing that their publication would "do more harm than good."[114] Odum designed a research project that went looking for trouble among white people and found it. Then he published it and privileged it as the voice of "the South" without differentiating among the ignorant, the fantastic, the false, and the true. His hodgepodge of chapters would have been terrifying if he had not adopted such a universally disdainful narrative tone to the subject matter. Half of him wanted the reader to laugh at/with the ignorant white Southerner, and the other half wanted the reader to fear her.

Factual, serious incidents appeared alongside accounts such as that of the "Disappointment Clubs." White southern ladies believed that black Disappointment Club members were *required* to respond to ads in the classified section of the newspapers under "Colored Help" and to promise to come right over to start work. Then they never showed up. One could read this unlikely story as a "weapons of the weak" parable, in which black people organized to drive white people crazy, one by one. But it is more likely a way that white Southerners tried to make sense out of a world that no longer made sense to them. Previously, black Southerners applied for domestic jobs by knocking on the back door. Employment decision making went only one way: If the white woman wanted help, she put the African American to work on the spot. Now, in the middle of a wartime emergency and accompanying wartime prosperity, black Southerners finally had job choices as they went through the classified ads, and many also had telephones to call prospective employers. They could make their way through the ads by phone, choosing the employer who sounded the best or promised to pay the most. The Disappointment Club rumor provides a stunning evidence of changing labor markets during the war as well as the self-centered way in which a southern white woman thought about her right to domestic help. In the middle of a war against Fascism and the greatest civil rights campaign in U.S. history, she honestly thought that black people had organized clubs for the express purpose of disappointing her.[115]

The facts turned out to be worse than white Southerners knew at the time. Black labor had begun to desert the South as early as 1940. One black writer explained that "when we get enough money, we quit the South because we're safer in the North. One of these days we'll make it safe both North and South."[116] The longer black Southerners stayed in the armed services, the more determined they were to leave the South after the war. In 1944 more than half of those who had some high school education and had been in the service for more than a year planned to abandon the South upon their release. Moreover, five hundred thousand black southern civilians left during the war to work in industries in other regions. Among black women, there was a saying, "Lincoln freed the Negroes from cotton picking, but Hitler was the one that got us out of the white folks' kitchen."[117] Under the FEPC, black Southerners made some progress in southern war industries, but across the country, not just in the South, black progress sparked "hate strikes" and racial violence on the part of their white coworkers.[118]

If the Disappointment Clubs were fantasy, many of the "rumors" involved home front mobilization. Regularly crowded past normal standing room because of gas rationing, southern buses were battlefields. Black Southerners abandoned the custom of waiting to board the bus until all the white passengers had boarded. If they did, whites would fill up the bus, and black passengers would have to wait, sometimes for hours, as the experience repeated itself with each passing bus. Now, when the bus arrived, white and black Southerners alike pushed their way on board. Moreover, many black soldiers refused to be Jim Crowed, and countless black Southerners became inspired to challenge segregation in daily skirmishes. With gas rationing and the demands of war, it was "physically impossible to separate the races as the law requires in the southern states," Murray observed.[119] Riding the bus was a free-for-all that often erupted into violence, and it hampered the war effort because it delayed defense workers. In Murray's hometown of Durham, all her fears came true when a black soldier quarreled with a white bus driver who forced him to move to the back of the bus. As the soldier left the bus, he turned and called the driver a "lousy 4-fer," whereupon the driver shot him to death.[120] A cartoonist in the *Afro-American* offered a solution: "Disarm Dixie Bus Drivers or Give Soldiers a Gun Too."[121]

With a large population of black and white service people, Montgomery, Alabama, stood at the epicenter of the guerrilla war on buses. Early in the war police shot a black airman after a dispute with a bus driver. When a local black GI, home on leave, sat down in a front seat, the bus driver threw him off the bus and shot him in the leg. When a bus driver attempted to evict black passengers to reserve rear seats for whites on an overcrowded bus, a black army lieutenant refused to get up. She was an army nurse. Police "brutally" beat her, broke her nose, and threw her in jail for defying the driver.[122] Rosa Parks would have known each of these hometown stories—and more—by heart.

Odum used *Race and Rumors of Race* to warn those who supported desegregation that white Southerners would fight back. In an article in the NAACP's *Crisis*, he argued not that something must be done about segregation but that "something must be done about the [white] South." While pressure to eliminate segregation grew, so too did "an almost universal southern movement to resist." Black Southerners seemed determined "to fight it out," and white Southerners vowed to ignore federal laws. He deplored "a growing hatred on the part of many Negroes for the whites" and "relative retrogression in the South" on "emergency racial matters," an Odum-ism for lynching and racial massacres. All in all, there was "an unmeasurable and unbridgeable distance between the white South and the reasonable expectation of the Negro," he said. He exhibited "the South" as a giant white bear, powerful, grizzly, now sleeping, now growling. By publishing the rumors, he baited his bear so that the rest of the nation could hear it roar. Odum had purported to calm fears by dispelling rumors, but he ended up trying to foil integrationists by pronouncing their task impossible. He declared that "the South and the Negro are facing their greatest crisis since the 1840s."[123]

Odum praised the Durham-Atlanta-Richmond conferences and called on the rest of the nation to let the South take the lead in solving its own problems. There must be a way, he argued, "to give opportunity and freedom to all folk without destroying other folk of different cultural and physical heritage." It just wasn't fair that the white South had to conform to the rest of the country, since white Southerners bore "the unequal burden of the crisis." Odum argued that "national planning" might bring about opportunities that could be "offered to the Negro on a voluntary basis, in all the regions." The government should provide "facilities for the migration and education of Negroes, for their training and employment in areas where the people had constitutional provisions and the will to do the job." This would result in the "diffusion of those Negro people who wanted to move."[124]

Rather than have one nation, under the Constitution, with liberty and justice for all, Odum proposed to move black Southerners to places where the Constitution had not yet been suspended. The process would be entirely voluntary, but when is exile ever voluntary? It was a remarkable proposal, reminiscent of the Missouri Compromise and foreshadowing a possible national apartheid. If Odum had stopped to think, he would have realized that the "diffusion" of black Southerners had already occurred. Now those diffused—black expatriates who had become the northern "Negro agitators"—were returning to destroy segregation. In addition to the Negro diffusion proposal, Odum begged the nation for more time. Couldn't everyone just get together after the war, when things were calmer, and accomplish a "realistic working out of next steps?" he implored. Timing was always "Go Slow" Odum's weak point. In defiance of the fight against Fascism, he wanted to defer democracy to appease racism. He simply did not understand that rights, to exist at all, have to be unalienable. If deferred, circumscribed, incrementalized, or exercised only in certain areas of the country, they aren't rights. Critics called the "planned migration" that Odum proposed "loose thinking" and "unpalatable and impractical."[125]

What *Does* the Negro Want?

As Odum gathered and narrated his rumors, his publisher, William Terry Couch, the director of the University of North Carolina Press, decided to ask African Americans what *they* thought. He engaged Howard University history professor Rayford Logan to collect and edit articles written by African Americans to explain what the Negro wanted. At Couch's urging, Logan solicited authors who would contribute both conservative and "radical" views. The manuscript for *What the Negro Wants* arrived at the press in September 1943, just after Odum completed *Race and Rumors of Race*.[126]

Couch and his associates were horrified to discover that what the Negro wanted was integration. Every one of the fourteen authors demanded an end to segregation laws. Mary McLeod Bethune, recruited as a moderate, entitled her article "Certain Unalienable Rights" and stated flatly, "We must challenge everywhere the principle and practice of enforced racial segregation." A. Philip Randolph simply included the March on Washington's "Program for the Negro," which listed the "Aims of the Negro," including "economic, political and social equality."

Langston Hughes condemned segregation as well, but for him the central problem was "what to do about the South." Maybe it was educable. He proposed to test his premise by sending an interracial duo—Paul Robeson and Paul Green sprang to mind—on a tour of the South. He regretted it would be necessary to send some soldiers with them to "protect them from the fascist-minded among us." Couch did not see any humor in this suggestion. Even Gordon Blaine Hancock, wiser after his experience with the Durham-Atlanta-Richmond meetings, wrote that "spreading segregation in its ultimate implications means the extermination of the Negro."[127]

Worst of all, five contributors mentioned interracial marriage. Hancock argued that integration did not lead to intermarriage. Black poet and intellectual Sterling Brown assured readers that intermarriage wasn't a goal but that African Americans did "not want laws on the statute books branding them as outcasts."[128] More affirmatively, Logan and Du Bois acknowledged, in Du Bois's words, "the right to select one's own mates."[129] They did not expect interracial marriage to occur with frequency, but Logan added that if sometime in the future white and black people started marrying each other, it would be because "public opinion" had changed. "We shall all be dead in 2044 and the people will do what they wish," he said. "After all," he added, "most Southerners have accommodated themselves to the abolition of the 'divine institution' of slavery."[130]

After reading the manuscript, a stunned Couch wrote to Logan, "The things Negroes are represented as wanting seem to me far removed from those they ought to want. Most of the things they are represented as wanting can be summarized in the phrase: complete abolition of segregation."[131] He searched for a way to avoid publication, and he sent the manuscript out to white reviewers. One responded that these contributors could not possibly be representative Negroes. Some bizarre screening process must have been responsible for soliciting the opinions of these astonishing Negroes, who "talk of intermarriage and world congresses of Negroes as nonchalantly as Walrus and Carpenter might discuss cabbages and kings."[132] Another reviewer told Couch that many Southerners, especially politicians, might "not be moved to greater cooperation and a helpful attitude toward Negroes" by reading the book but that it was "important" and would ultimately do good. He did suggest that Langston

Hughes might want to eliminate his suggestion "that the Federal Government provide instructors to educate the South in the practice of democracy" and that the contributors drop their advocacy for the "repeal of laws forbidding intermarriage."[133] In a meanspirited move, the reviewer Howard Odum recommended publishing it, arguing that the essays would frighten white Southerners into action since their demands demonstrated precisely the kind of outside agitation he had been condemning. He reveled in what he saw as the book's weaknesses: "extreme statements, cynical references, misstatement of fact—all of those are a part of the value inherent in the book."[134]

After abortive tries to force the contributors to revise their articles, Couch told Logan that the UNC Press could not publish the book. When Logan threatened to sue, Couch backed down, and added a "Publisher's Introduction" that muttered darkly about sociologists' "zeal to reform the South." He asked if there was "any sanity in the view now often stated that no one but a Fascist or Nazi can believe one people or race superior to another." Then he quoted Abraham Lincoln—"We cannot make them equals"—and asked if Lincoln "was, after all, only a Fascist, a Nazi?"[135] Couch seized on the mention of intermarriage and argued that what these Negroes wanted was "biological integration." If they achieved that, they would "destroy all rights." Couch didn't care if twenty million people called for "amalgamation" and two resisted. The two resisters followed a "valid authority." Actually, not a single author had mentioned "amalgamation" as a way to solve the race problem by eliminating racial "differences." But Couch argued that what the Negro wanted was sex with white women. Finally, he eliminated the book's subtitle, *Fifteen Ask for Democracy*.[136]

The Agony of White Southern Liberals

If Odum's *Race and Rumors of Race* portrayed white Southerners as a beleaguered people shocked by what the Negro wanted, perhaps he did not reveal the full measure of conservative white Southerners' hatred. In the year during which Odum investigated rumors, a liberal northern magazine sent a white man undercover to gauge the mood of white Southerners. The reporter came away "feeling that the war the South is fighting isn't the same war that the rest of the country is fighting." In Birmingham he chatted with the secretary of the Chamber of Commerce and was shocked to hear him say, "There's one thing you can put in your pipe and smoke. There's no white man down here goin' to let his daughter sleep with a nigger, or sit at the same table with a nigger, or go walkin' with a nigger." The white man went on: "The war can go to hell, the world can go to hell, we can all be dead—but he ain't goin' to do it." Whenever the reporter explained that job opportunities did not equate to marrying his daughter, the Chamber of Commerce man returned time and time again to the same theme. [137]

By 1943 white Southerners who had been happy to be called moderate before the war were issuing ultimatums against integration. John Temple Graves informed the North that white Southerners "will not be forced . . . [that] they consider the problem delicately their own and not to be settled by analogy with conditions in India or Manhattan." Moreover, he predicted a realignment of white Southerners from the Democratic to the Republican Party, since "Northern Negroes may become more important than Southern whites" to the Democrats. He bluntly stated in *Negro Digest* that "right or wrong, segregation is not going to be abolished in the South, nor, apparently, in many other parts of the country where it exists informally but definitely. Meanwhile, insistence on abolition is robbing the Negro of other advancements for which he cares more and which he needs more."[138]

Virginius Dabney of Richmond condemned "extremist Negroes" who were "demanding an overnight revolution in race relations" and characterized the South as "Nearer and Nearer the Precipice." [139] Formerly "moderate" politicians felt it necessary to affirm segregation. When Georgia liberals supported Ellis Arnall against Eugene Talmadge in the Democratic primary for governor in 1942, they had to overlook his grandstanding capitulation to racism. Arnall beat Talmadge by putting his prosegregation credentials up front, announcing, "If a nigger ever tried to get into a white school in my part of the State, the sun would never set on his head." When asked about the political climate in the South during the war, one black Southerner just sighed and said, "We ain't even got promises."[140]

No law, no political party, no army, nothing could force white Southerners to abandon segregation, many declared. How could they be so confident of victory? White Southerners assumed that they would maintain segregation because they held ten million African Americans hostage, and if pressed, they would hurt them. Well, maybe not "they," the better class of white Southerners, but certainly poor, uneducated Southerners would. As shameless as it was in the midst of a war against the Nazis, the elite white Southerners who abjured integration and predicted racial violence implied that such violence was inevitable and they could stop it. The hostage analogy was ubiquitous. The Atlanta Conference had used it when it mentioned threats to the "welfare" of black Southerners. One white southern historian predicted "violent retaliation against the Negroes—themselves often innocent." FEPC head Mark Ethridge threatened that "cruel disillusionment" would give way to "strife and per-haps tragedy." Odum observed "relative retrogression in the South" on "emergency racial matters" and predicted that outside agitation would lead to "tragedy of the highest order . . . because it was the innocent Negroes who suffered." Another white Southerner predicted civil war and "irreparable harm of the Negro." Black poet Sterling Brown, a contributor to *What the Negro Wants*, characterized the hostage threat as "Watch out . . . or *Negroes* will get hurt. . . . For all their protesting of decency and good will, the intellectuals do not talk very differently from Gerald L. K. Smith," a domestic Fascist who advocated violence.[141]

Faced with an uproar in the South and concentrating on fighting the war, Franklin Roosevelt left race problems to his wife and his white south-ern aides, including North Carolinian Jonathan Daniels. In January 1942 Daniels took a position as assistant director of the Office of Civilian Defense for seven months, focusing on black morale, and then became an assistant to FDR as an adviser on race relations. He met with black lead-ers, urged the president to order investigations of racial violence, and tried to soothe racial tensions in governmental agencies. After racial vio-lence increased in 1943, black leaders called for a presidential council on race relations. Odum suggested to Daniels that the solution might be a "President's Committee on Race and Minority Groups," on which Odum would gladly serve. FDR rejected the idea.[142]

During the war Frank Porter Graham joined his old friend Daniels in Washington. His service on the War Labor Board thrust him into the limelight on difficult labor and racial issues. For example, on June 5, 1943,

Graham struck a harder blow against employment discrimination than did all the FEPC hearings. The case involved two separate job categories at a Texas oil company, "colored laborer" and "white laborer." Graham asked to write the board's opinion striking down the categories. He recounted the case briefly and urged that "America . . . must not in the days of its power become the stronghold of bigots." Not only was black cooperation important to winning the war, but antidiscrimination was "a test of our sincerity in the cause for which we are fighting." In his labor board decision, Graham dreamed of the world after the war: "With the victory of the democracies, the human destiny is toward freedom, hope, and equality of opportunity."[143]

Although Graham and Daniels did not explicitly call for an end to segregation, Will Alexander did. The formerly cautious head of the Commission on Interracial Cooperation finally answered the question that he had avoided in public for more than two decades when he announced in 1942 that segregation should end. He had been convinced by his close working relationship in the New Deal with the black economist Robert Weaver, whom Alexander had come to love. He called his friendship with Weaver "the most satisfactory relationship that I ever had with any human being."[144] Alexander was not alone. White Southerner Lillian Smith, who published *South Today* from the Georgia mountains, warned that Jim Crow must go at once, since he was "a greater menace to democracy than Hitler" and would have to be "conquered in our hearts before Hitler can be conquered in Germany."[145]

Some white Southerners who came of age in the 1930s thought that their generation was ready for desegregation. Thomas Sancton, a white New Orleanian who became managing editor of the *New Republic*, condemned the South's "pale, dishwater liberalism." He explained that people like Dabney, Ethridge, and Graves had contributed to the "growth of a liberal tradition in the South" but were trapped by "their fathers' shadow." To the older generation of white Southerners, "the Negro is a little less than human; he must always expect to be Jim Crowed. In varying degrees, they have spoken for years for better treatment of the Negro." These "Humanitarian Southerners" were certainly an improvement over the likes of Eugene Talmadge, "but their liberalism has always been the liberalism of yielding, not dynamic." Sancton doubted the ability of the "Humanitarian

Southerners" to change because they would resent independent black leadership that said, "The hell with you; I want democracy and I want it now."[146] Of course, the "Humanitarian Southerner" was better than the "cruel ignoramus" who could incite violence since "a minority is at the mercy of the bloodlust."[147]

To demonstrate the generational differences between white Southerners, Sancton shared a letter from his mother in New Orleans complaining that her black maid had quit. The "wide gulf" between "young Southerners, who see things as I do, and our parents" saddened Sancton. He wanted to ask his mother, "What God-given right do we white people have to expect them to be our servants?" He wanted to tell his mother that it would be a "patriotic" duty to give up their servants. Why did people like Lillian Smith and Thomas Sancton speak out against segregation in defiance of even their own family members? Arthur Raper once said of Smith that "she let herself feel this thing. . . . I think Lillian didn't protect herself." Most of white southern life was designed so that whites would not "feel this thing," so that they would never put themselves in a black Southerner's place or truly consider his or her humanity. When you felt the horror, you had no choice but to break with your friends and family. Sancton looked forward to the day when those who felt this thing could remain within their families and remain Southerners. He believed that his generation could save the South and "repair the wreckage which bigotry and blindness and ignorant leaders have strewn across the years."[148]

Pauli Murray's Sit-Ins

No one "felt" segregation more than Pauli Murray did. As she began her second year in law school in the fall of 1942, she attended a national planning conference to institutionalize the March on Washington Movement and helped produce an outline for mass protests using nonviolent direct action. After calling for an end to discrimination in employment, in the press, and in public accommodations, Murray's committee did something most unusual: It revealed a plan to seize, not simply to demand, those rights. A well-trained "Action Corps" would stage demonstrations, protests, street meetings, and poster walks (picketing), all orchestrated with an eye toward getting maximum publicity. The committee proposed "techniques for breaking down discrimination in Restaurants, hotels, buses, movies, etc." and argued that "too little careful attention" had been "given to the strategy of this problem." Currently many racial altercations erupted on the spot because of the anger of a black person's being moved, not seated, or refused entrance to an accommodation. Job discrimination was certainly important, but it was in these seething segregation encounters that "racial tensions reach a crescendo," often resulting in violence.[149]

Then, in three paragraphs, Murray and her associates laid out the strategy for the modern civil rights movement. First, one had to know the legal environment in which the discrimination had occurred. In a state with civil rights laws, one should first seek recourse through those laws. In states without civil rights laws or with mandatory segregation statutes, it would take "disciplined and trained leaders, students and young people" who "should use a carefully planned non-violent technique of refusal to accept such discriminations." They had to be prepared to go to jail and to court and then to go back out and do it all over again, "until the pattern is broken down, or public action is taken to eliminate such discriminations." In states with segregation statutes, they should start by desegregating "all public places of amusement or otherwise who [sic] can be proven to come within the interstate commerce act." Local boycotts, managed "through close knit community organization," would become national boycotts through "unfair lists" and picketing elsewhere.[150] It was simple, nonviolent, unceasing, and results-oriented.

The activism of Murray's committee echoed A. Philip Randolph's injunction to the delegates that "Negroes have a moral obligation to demand" their rights. At the polls the March on Washington Movement would develop plans "to secure mass registration of the Negro People." It would try to place black Southerners in bus driving jobs, starting during the war with black women. It would abolish the poll tax. "We are fighting for big stakes," Randolph told MOWM members. "This is the hour of the Negro. This is the hour of the common man. May we rise to the challenge to struggle for our rights." They would do all this by organizing people block to block across the nation.[151]

The March on Washington Movement believed in "mass action by Negroes—not in educating high government officials or in deals and horse-trading negotiations" or in "educating . . . white friends." This was a "mass movement rather than a pressure group." To make its demonstrations, sit-ins, and picketing effective, the MOWM adopted " 'non-violent direct action' on the Gandhi model." It acknowledged "there will be violence unleashed against MOW[M], as in India, but this will be met with passive resistance." In the draft statement of principles, that sentence originally read, "will be met with passive resistance so far as possible," but someone marked out the qualifier. Passive resistance must be endless, "matching one's ability to suffer against an opponent's ability to inflict the suffering." Passive resistance "is not resignation; it is not submission; it is bold, aggressive, and revolutionary. It invites attack, meeting it with a stubborn and non-violent resistance that seeks to recondition the mind and weaken the will of the oppressor." If this were to succeed, they would have to develop a "closely-knit unit of leadership, trained with "severe and exacting" discipline.[152] A "non-violent civil disobedience campaign" would be launched nationwide after the planning conference. For a specified period African Americans across the country would boycott Jim Crow accommodations and use those designated white. When arrested, they would meet "resistance with love instead of hate, simply going constantly until the world knows that the Negroes mean to be free."[153]

Murray contributed to the MOWM's formulation of nonviolent resistance, which sprang not simply from Gandhi but also from Socialist practitioners in the Fellowship of Reconciliation (FOR). The strategy resonated with her training at the Socialist Workers Defense League and the Harlem Ashram. J. Holmes Smith, a white founder of the ashram, with whom Murray had lived in Harlem before she went to law school, served as a resource member of the movement's National Advisory Board.[154] Murray's former boss at the Workers Defense League answered yes to the question "Civil Disobedience: Is It the Answer to Jim Crow?" The question was more than rhetorical since two black members of FOR, Bayard Rustin and James Farmer, who had also lived with Murray at the ashram, had started the Congress of Racial Equality the previous spring. For her part, Murray published an article in Lillian Smith's *South Today* that called for nonviolent direct action.[155] As African Americans heard more and more about nonviolent direct action in 1943, *Negro Digest* conducted a poll that asked, "Is civil disobedience practical to win full rights for Negroes?" Clearly, the MOWM and FOR had not yet succeeded in winning over their constituency, since 52 percent of the black respondents said no, 32 percent said yes, and 16 percent were undecided. Black Southerners remained more skeptical than African Americans in other regions: Only 27 percent thought that civil disobedience would work.[156]

MOWM organizers responded by telling black Southerners that nonviolent direct action was nothing new to them; they had always known how to "Jump Jim Crow." From mass migration to avoiding public transportation to passing for white if the occasion called for it—all qualified as nonviolent direct action. Those things had been hidden from whites' view. Now jumping Jim Crow would become performance, as "Negroes will consciously dramatize the problem before the whole nation by a mass demonstration of disobedience to jim crow laws and patterns." Moreover, "citizens are morally obligated to disobey an unjust law." The MOWM planned to "harness the flow of rising resentment" and "turn it into a deep spiritual force for constructive social action."[157]

As a member of the Washington MOWM chapter Pauli Murray set out to demonstrate the usefulness of civil disobedience in the segregated capital. As twenty-three of the thirty men at Howard Law School went to war, she felt a great responsibility to make sure that the soldiers did not return to "the same old intolerable" country that they left. She asked herself:

> . . . how can you make it easier for them to bear—
> Down there in the grim dark Southland
> Out there in the hell of battle
> Out on that stricken field of the dying.[158]

The South, the battlefield, the killing fields: They were all of a piece. The women of Howard would lead the first sit-ins in the South—and Washington was very much a southern city—in the spring of 1943 and 1944.[159]

First, there was one woman. Ruth Powell was a Howard undergraduate from Milton, Massachusetts. During 1942 and 1943 Powell went throughout Washington sitting in segregated restaurants—all by herself. No one ever served her. She simply sat and stared at the waiters and waitresses. She had come to her singular sit-ins innocently enough. In her first year at Howard she had realized that Washington restaurants were segregated, but she had no idea when she sat down at a drugstore counter that she would not be served. She sat for an eternity; then the manager came up and unscrewed the stool seats on either side of her and put up a sign, THIS SECTION CLOSED. As she continued to sit, immobilized by humiliation and rage, she realized what she had done. Out of confusion, she had just sat there and provoked a response. Engulfed by humiliation, she had remained and lived to tell the tale.[160]

Then there were three women. Everyone at Howard knew that going out with Ruth Powell could be dicey, but when two Howard students joined her for a cup of hot chocolate at a shop counter, they were served. Then they were charged twenty-five cents per ten-cent cup. They put down thirty cents. The manager called the police. The policeman who arrived told them he was taking them to jail because they might be "subversive agents." The arrests galvanized the Howard student body.[161]

Murray's experience in the March on Washington Movement's direct action planning, her interest in Bayard Rustin and James Farmer's new organization, and her legal training made her an ideal adviser for the Howard undergraduates who sought her out. But later she remembered that she did it for Bill Raines, drafted from Howard Law School even though he opposed fighting in a segregated army. Raines was a North Carolinian who had graduated from Shaw University in Raleigh. Murray recalled, "Raines came out of that North Carolina tradition of struggle . . . and for a long time he had been agitating for what he'd called the stool-sitting technique." Raines told Murray that "if the white people want to deny us service, let them pay for it. . . . We'll take a seat on a lunch stool, if they don't serve us, we'll just sit there and read our books."[162]

Murray assumed the role of adviser to the undergraduates, loosely organized in the student chapter of the NAACP. She immediately sent out a questionnaire to all students and faculty asking, "Am I a 'screwball,' or am I a pioneer? Do others think as I do on the perplexing problem of minority rights?" Should "the struggle for equal rights" be suspended until victory? Would the respondent "actively join a campaign to break down segregation in Washington?" On the question of whether they should suspend activities until after the war, 284 of 292 respondents answered no, while 80 percent answered that they would participate, and an additional 17 percent said they would not but would support those who did.[163]

Murray conducted a class on nonviolent direct action techniques, using FOR lesson plans that argued, "One reason why racial prejudice has flourished in the South has been the docile acceptance by Negroes of segregation in principle." Her lesson of course ignored the hundreds of black Southerners who had already challenged segregation during the war. The lesson instructed those who sat in to respond to an order to move by asking why. When the manager or bus driver explained that there were segregation laws or that the accommodation served only whites, the protester should ask again why.[164] All the students she trained had to sign an "oath of nonviolence." Murray reminded them that "a tactful man can pull the stingers from a bee without getting stung."[165] The students approached on another front as well. The Howard chapter of the NAACP set up a civil rights committee to encourage passage of bills pending in the House and Senate to "assure to all persons with the District of Columbia full and equal privileges" in public accommodations.[166]

They chose the Little Palace Cafeteria as their target. Owned by two Greek men, the restaurant was in a black neighborhood close to the Howard campus but did not serve African Americans. Murray scrupulously planned the sit-in for a Saturday afternoon in late April. The students were organized into teams of four. Three students would go in; one would stay outside to picket. After servers had refused four groups of students, they sat down with their empty trays at tables, pulled out books, and "assumed an attitude of concentrated study. Strict silence was maintained." Outside, the pickets began marching, carrying such signs as WE DIE TOGETHER—WHY CAN'T WE EAT TOGETHER? and THERE'S NO SEGREGATION LAW IN WASHINGTON, D.C. WHAT'S YOUR STORY, LITTLE PALACE?[167]

Murray had lined up the Washington bureau reporters for the nation's black newspapers, and they stood on the sidewalk interviewing confused whites who tried to enter the restaurant. Told what was happening inside, one white man from Charlotte, North Carolina, exclaimed, "Well, now isn't that something! I eat here regularly and I don't care who else eats here." He did not know that there was a black Charlottean seated inside. Neither of them would eat that evening. The owner called the police, who arrived led by the city's only black police lieutenant, who "ordered his men to keep distance and simply to be alert for any disorder." The owner closed early, explaining, "I'd rather close up than practice democracy this way."[168]

But the students returned the next day, and the next, and the next. Finally the owner declared that he was "licked and ready to serve anyone." Murray felt sympathy for him. "He's a little man. He's a Greek. He has no country, and sometimes I think I don't have a country, too," she wrote in the poem "Prayer of a Solitary Picket." When it was all over, Leon Ransom, dean of the law school, confirmed that he had helped the students organize and told the press that he was proud of them.[169]

One can only imagine how the sit-in would have rocked the rest of the segregated South . . . if it had heard about it. It did not. While the black press broadcast news of the sit-ins nationwide, the white press, even locally, ignored it. This would be the policy for most of the next decade, until television began to cover civil rights protests. The only surviving white response is from a man who wrote, "Who wants to sit down to a table to eat with a dirty, greasy, stinking nigger; no matter how many times he bathes, he still 'stinks'? Instead of wasting your time by picketing, start at the beginning and educate the NEGRO—not to steal, lie, rape and assault women." The students reprinted the letter in their newspaper, telling their peers, "THIS IS TO YOU!! What are you doing about it?" Murray wrote Eleanor Roosevelt a long letter describing the sit-ins and included a copy of the nasty letter. ER put down her copy of the letter with disgust and invited Pauli Murray over for tea. If she couldn't eat in most places in town, Roosevelt would make sure that she could eat at the White House. Murray wrote home: "Dear Mother, the tea with Mrs. Roosevelt was exquisite." Scheduled for thirty minutes, they talked for an hour and a half, and "you would have thought I was talking to either you or Aunt Sallie, the way she talked to me."[170]

Summer vacation put a stop to the Washington sit-ins, but not before Murray and three friends on the civil rights committee resolved to go "downtown" next time. That summer Pauli Murray attended a March on Washington Conference that debated launching a sit-in movement across the country. A white minister who attended as a resource person in nonviolent direct action came away converted and told a meeting of white religious leaders, "Brethren, it looks very much like the Revolution is upon us."[171] But because of the Detroit riot, the MOWM decided to "defer, for the time being," the planned sit-ins. The *New York Times* reported the postponement with palpable relief. Pauli Murray finally gave up on the

Democrats and joined the Socialist Party that summer and decided that she was a pacifist.[172]

Murray and her friends decided to press on in Washington after the racial tension ebbed nationally, and in April 1943 they were ready to start what they called a civil rights campaign. Students signed a pledge of commitment against discrimination, promised to execute their "patriotic duty," and went through nonviolent direct action training. They anticipated confrontation and were taught to ignore it, even as they were to try to engage sympathetic people around them. With the help of the law school librarian, the students discovered that not only was there no law enforcing segregation in the city, but there was on the books a 1890s law *prohibiting* race discrimination. For this "campaign of 'sitting' in restaurants," Murray secured the names and addresses of the parent companies of chain establishments and came up with ideas for picket signs. She disabused herself of some slogans—"We are the paratroopers–March on Washington"—but others—"Is this Hitler's Way or the American Way?"—stuck. As in the preceding year, most of the campaigners were women. Murray gave them this final advice: "No matter what happens to you temporarily, whether you are served in a restaurant, or go to prison, or get slapped down, the resources of human history are behind you and the future of human society is on your side, if there is to be any human society in the future. You have nothing to lose and everything to gain."[173]

The protesters targeted Thompson's Restaurant, headquartered in Chicago, with three locations in Washington, when it refused to serve two "scouts" sent earlier.[174] Forty-three Howard students and three sympathetic white adults entered Thompson's in small groups, each group leaving a designated picket on the sidewalk. Again, they sat reading at tables with empty trays. They were shocked when they were joined by nine black soldiers in uniform, sitting separately from the white soldiers and sailors in the restaurant. By now the police had arrived, and they called the MPs. Things got tense when the black soldiers refused the MPs' order to leave, and Murray brokered a deal through which the MPs escorted all the soldiers, white and black, out of Thompson's. Four and a half hours later the Chicago office ordered the restaurant to serve the protesters. "It is difficult to describe the exhilaration of that brief moment of victory," Murray recalled. The next day the students put up posters on campus that listed the protesters' names and asked, "Were you there when we all took a chair at dear old Thompson's?" They sent out press releases and gloried in headlines such as NEW TECHNIQUE and HOWARD STUDENTS BREAK COLOR BAR IN D.C. CAFÉ. Again the white press, except for journalist I. F. Stone at the newspaper *PM*, ignored them. Nonetheless, they believed that this was the first of many victories.[175]

It was the first of many victories for the country, but it was the last victory for the Howard students. When Thompson's again refused service to two scouts the following week, students planned another sit-in. Howard's president, Mordecai Johnson, had been widely criticized during the war for "militant" statements, so the students were stunned when he called them in and told them to stop. His prohibition covered all "officially recognized organizations" that were "now engaged in a program of direct action in the City of Washington, designed to accomplish social reform affecting institutions other than Howard University itself." They could not demonstrate as school-sponsored groups, only as individuals through other groups. The problem was that Howard's annual appropriation was then before the Senate's District of Columbia Committee, chaired by Mississippi Senator Theodore Bilbo. The protest's faculty sponsor, the law school dean Leon Ransom, had no choice but to back up Johnson.[176]

The radicalized students immediately formed a Howard free speech movement. They asked Johnson to define "direct action" and "social reform" and protested free speech infringement.[177] With the help of Howard Thurman, dean of the chapel and a supporter of nonviolent action, Murray articulated the students' position in a meeting with the administration. President Johnson reiterated that they should work with outside groups, not student groups, to protest. After a week they met with the entire faculty and administration and agreed to refrain from demonstrations, in exchange for the chance to appeal to the trustees the next month. Thus the students stood up for their rights, and Mordecai Johnson quietly encouraged them to demonstrate outside school-sponsored organizations.[178]

At the meeting with the faculty Murray realized that a new militancy had taken hold of the younger students. Scary as it was to protest against white supremacy, it was just as scary to stand up to president Mordecai Johnson, who held their futures in his hands. Henceforth Murray would have company as she went through the continuous protest that was her life. She had seen the future, and it was on her side. She thought that the contretemps ended "magnificently." As she had so many times in the past, she belatedly contacted the NAACP to notify it of the sit-ins, the "confrontation" with the administration, and the appeal to the trustees, adding weakly, "I hope we have done the wisest thing all along the line." Then she sat down to explain herself to someone else: "Dear Mother, We have had quite a controversy on the Howard campus, but part of it ended magnificently with a conference with President Johnson today. But oh, we've taken a terrific pounding today. We really had to stand up and meet our responsibilities as students." She closed, "My Love, A Very Tired Fighter—it's that old Smith Fitzgerald Murray spirit."[179]

"I Am an American, Too"

Alongside the civil rights action of World War II, a rhetorical campaign sought to win a victory for desegregation and tolerance. In the summer of 1943 A. Philip Randolph planned an "I Am an American, Too" Week. He would "focus national and world opinion upon the struggles of American Negroes for their democratic and civil rights. By summer the slogan had been changed to "We Are Americans—Too."[180] As 1944 began, the National Negro Newspaper Publishers Association wrote a letter to Franklin Roosevelt. It began: "We are Americans! Our allegiance . . . is unlimited and unsullied." It concluded with the "resolve to work" for equal opportunity in the workplace and public educational facilities, "unrestricted suffrage," desegregation of the armed forces, and the "principle that government shall not impose, enforce, or sanction patterns of racial segregation." Furthermore, when the war finally ended, they would work for an international institution to establish "world order" and "social justice."[181]

By 1944 African Americans had perfected the rhetoric of dual citizenship and helped convince many whites that antidiscrimination speech, acts, and laws were good for America. By denouncing discrimination while pledging their loyalty, they transformed their critique of U. S. democracy from sedition into patriotism. Only through perfecting democracy at home could the United States win the war, keep the postwar nation safe, and extend democratic principles abroad. They had accomplished this remarkable feat by maintaining a balance between protest and proclamations of loyalty. The United States Supreme Court could not have ignored the wartime Double V campaign and the successful mix of protest and patriotism when it heard arguments on the constitutionality of the white primary in early January 1944. Three months later, on April 3, the court ruled in *Smith v. Allwright* that a whites only primary was unconstitutional, opening the way for "a revolution in politics in the urban South."[182]

By the end of the war some white people, including some in the South, thought that eliminating racism was "a test of the moral integrity of white America." It did not matter so much that the country had not yet achieved a desegregated, equal society. What mattered was that Americans embraced such a vision as their "ideal." In addition to African American action, whites' own war experiences, ever-clearer concepts of the Nazis' racism, hopes of getting black votes, fears of racial violence, and premonitions that the postwar country would be vulnerable to Fascists meant that "racism had . . . lost its intellectual respectability outside the white South" by the end of the war.[183] A swing toward "positive policies of fairness and appreciation for all minorities" in the white press and the publication of Gunnar Myrdal's *An American Dilemma* in January 1944 crystallized these issues for many whites. Myrdal's "study to end all studies" argued that America's dilemma—African Americans' place in the polity—must be solved for democracy to survive. Black reviewers lauded it, and white liberals coalesced around its conclusions. Odum carped that Myrdal did not understand southern white folk, that therefore *Dilemma*'s recommendations were useless. Du Bois praised Myrdal for standing up to conservative white Southerners.[184]

By 1945, then, most white Americans outside the South had accepted tolerance for racial and ethnic minorities as a civic value, even if they still were perfecting its practice. This majoritarian ideal of tolerance was so at odds with southern white supremacy and segregation that like slave and free states, the two ideas could not survive side by side in one nation. If white supremacy won the battle, the country was finished. As a white man told the National Conference of Social Work in 1944, "the white race is doomed unless it grants equality to colored peoples."[185]

By 1943 Americans had begun to talk about "civil rights" and "human rights" and to refer to "minorities." Former and future Republican presidential candidate Wendell Willkie appeared in the popular white magazine *Saturday Evening Post* to make "The Case for Minorities." He pointed out that "the full recognition of the rights of minorities has been a gradual evolution in America" and named the Quakers as an early minority. He worked his way through the Indians, Mormons, Catholics, and Jews and called the Ku Klux Klan activity after World War I "the most pernicious assault on human rights that our country has known in our times." He said, "each of us," meaning each of us white persons, had better beware, since we might be the "unconscious carrier of the germ that will destroy our freedom." That germ was "prejudice," and it lurked within, planted there by "inheritances of age-long hatreds" and man had the "tendency to find cause for his own failures in some conspiracy of evil." Willkie's argument offered a facesaving measure for whites that drew from the growing psychological theories that prejudice originated deep in the unconscious. We all had it; we just had to prevent it from clouding our judgments. The *Afro-American* ran Willkie's article on July 4, 1942, under the headline QUAKERS, MORMONS, INDIANS, JEWS AND CATHOLICS ARE MINORITY GROUPS TOO.[186] Under the rubric of minority rights, the FEPC's failures became an impetus for ethnic union, since minority groups other than African Americans had a stake in the executive order as well. The Minorities Workshop organized in Washington to put pressure on the FEPC. As it sought to integrate defense industries, the black press remarked that employment discrimination "hits Jews, too."[187]

Those who believed that tolerance should be an American ideal used the latest propaganda tools to convince Americans not to discriminate. Appreciate America, Inc., a Chicago organization, put out pamphlets and cartoons designed to prove that people of different religions, ethnicities, and races could all be "100% Americans." In *I Know My Neighbors, Do You?* cartoon character Joe Doakes boasts, "When somebody knocks a neighbor of mine because he is a Protestant, a Catholic, or a Jew, I tell him he may not know it, but he is falling for Hitler's stuff." In "Santa Keeps Books," a happy Santa sits on a stool above a trash can filled with papers labeled "Racial Hatred," "Prejudice," and "Discrimination." His enormous open ledger has "Good Americans" on the left page and "Bad Americans" on the right, as he tells the viewer, "I don't judge by creed or color." The term *intercultural education* brought together these lessons of tolerance of ethnic and racial minorities.[188] Will Alexander helped found the American Council on Race Relations, headquartered in Chicago, which taught tolerance of minorities and focused on "human relations."[189]

In 1943, after the Detroit race riot, the USO commissioned two women anthropologists who had studied with Franz Boas, Ruth Benedict and Gene Weltfish, to write a pamphlet that would explain race to soldiers. The army used it for soldier orientation, and it was in every military library. Entitled *The Races of Mankind*, it used simple language and cartoons to explain that "the peoples of the earth are one family."[190] To illustrate, two unclad beige people stand at the base of a tree that flowers into four people, one black, one brown, one beige, and one white. We all came from the same ancestors, they explained; "when you list all the little bones and muscles and the joints of the toes, it is impossible to imagine that that would all have happened twice." The white press mostly celebrated *The Races of Mankind*, but that cartoon alone would have unhinged most white Southerners.[191]

But it wasn't simplified anthropology that ultimately unhinged them; it was the table in *The Races of Mankind* that compared the "Median Scores on A. E. F. Intelligence Tests" of "Southern Whites and Northern Blacks." In an attempt to explain that environment made a difference in intelligence, the anthropologists revealed a truth so awful no white supremacist dared speak it. Black Northerners from New York, Illinois, and Ohio scored higher on average on the military intelligence test than white Southerners from Mississippi, Kentucky, and Arkansas. As if to rub it in, on the facing page, a cartoon showed an avid little black girl beating two dull-looking white kids in a quiz show with the caption "Susie Brown knows all the answers." Despite its widespread distribution, white southern politicians succeeded in removing and banning *The Races of Mankind* from armed forces libraries.[192]

The campaign for tolerance reached schoolchildren through the Service Bureau for Intercultural Education. Begun in 1934 by faculty at Columbia University, the bureau trained teachers to teach about race and ethnicity in the public schools. Originally celebrating cultural differences, in World War II the bureau began emphasizing similarities among groups.[193] Its new theme became "Out of the Many—One," and its board of endorsers included W. E. B. Du Bois, Howard Odum, and Eleanor Roosevelt.[194] During the war the bureau dwelt on "the obstacle of segregation," "stereotyped ideas of Negroes," and "inequalities of economic opportunity" among African Americans. It argued that it was "the school's responsibility for changing race attitudes" and ran articles on school desegregation in the North and West.[195]

By 1944 racism had become un-American. The Office of War Information published a lavishly illustrated book, *The Negro and War*, which celebrated African American achievement. Opportunities abounded and optimism overflowed in its seventy pages. The only evidence of racism, prejudice, or discrimination came from Hitler, whom the book quoted at length. Joe Louis, posing in uniform with his rifle drawn and bayonet fixed, reassured everyone that "we'll win 'cause we're on God's side."[196] After the defeat of Germany, but before Japan's surrender, Bob "Fair Play" Hope took a moment to reflect on his wartime experiences. Recalling "300 one night stands," Hope said, "I didn't see any signs of race or religious prejudice anywhere." Perhaps it was because he spent all his time with the troops, he suggested, "decent intelligent fellows," among whom "prejudice has always been deader than mackerel." He observed: "They had a sense of fair play." In fact "they never had any more use for race prejudice than they had for poison or brass knuckles," he told the folks back on the home front. Servicemen had no prejudice, Hope figured, "because they didn't have any 'superior race' ideals." Bob "Fair Play" Hope stated flatly that after the Japanese, "the bigoted and prejudiced" were "America's second foe." Frank Sinatra agreed and confessed the pain that he had felt growing up when the school kids called him little Dago. Names like "nigger" and "stingy Jew," Sinatra warned, "*can* hurt you." He was on a "campaign against race prejudice among bobby soxers."[197]

Such tolerance talk only spread with victory. Beloved *Stars and Stripes* cartoonist Bill Mauldin became a hero to African Americans upon his discharge when he began to ridicule racism in his civilian cartoons. He declared that if "the persecution of minorities because of race, color or creed continued in America," all who had fallen in World War II would have died in vain. Albert Einstein told Americans that "the fall of Berlin does not mean the end of fascism . . . yes, there are fascists in America, too." He deplored African Americans' unequal status and argued that "the whole thing is more and more a question of integration."[198]

African Americans had made the right decision five years earlier, when they had decided to fight segregation as an undemocratic institution. Had they taken a different path, arguing for increased opportunity within a segregated society, they never would have succeeded in making someone who supported segregation into a racist and that racist into a traitor. They did not succeed in ending segregation as a fact, but they did succeed in making it un-American. Will Alexander, by now the aging veteran of an era of interracial cooperation and a decade of New Deal optimism, wrote an article entitled "Our Conflicting Racial Policies" for *Harper's Magazine* in January 1945. He surveyed the wreckage that segregation had made and concluded: "Segregation . . . is rooted in fear and in doubt as to whether our democratic principles will really work. It remains to be seen whether or not our faith in democracy is strong enough to overcome our fears."[199] On the basis of their wartime experiences, Americans, white and black, had every reason to believe that the postwar nation would choose democracy, quietly and quickly dismantle segregation, and begin to erase its stain from American life.

If some saw the March on Washington Movement as a failure because it did not march, they might have concluded otherwise if they had seen a glowing Pauli Murray graduate as valedictorian of her law school class a few weeks after the downtown sit-ins. Two months earlier A. Philip Randolph had gently reminded her that "a mass movement" didn't develop by recruiting leaders to join the movement; rather, "competency and conviction grow out of the movement. They are seldom brought to it," he told the impatient Murray. "The March on Washington Movement is seeking just the average person," he said, to transform into a leader.[200] After years of quixotic sparring with Jim Crow on her own, Murray became such a leader through the movement.

When Pauli Murray invited Eleanor and Franklin Roosevelt to her law school graduation in June 1944, ER wrote back quickly to say that they could not come, but she invited Murray and her mother, Pauline Dame, to tea at the White House. The day before commencement, the brash valedictorian and the seventy-three-year-old Dame, still an elementary school teacher, went. The next day as Dean William Hastie prepared to confer degrees, a huge bouquet of flowers, a gift from Eleanor to Pauli, arrived at President Mordecai Johnson's office. It ended up on the platform for all to see, as they listened to Johnson urge graduates to move to the South to organize labor and work for the NAACP. The *Afro-American* scoffed: "Go South, Commit Suicide."[201] But Murray wrote an open letter to the entire class, urging her classmates to take Johnson seriously. She proposed that all seven law graduates head to Mississippi and invited the Class of 1944 to come as well.[202]

As ecstatic as Pauli Murray was that day, one remaining battle nagged at her. Dean Hastie had suggested that she apply for a Rosenwald Fellowship to do graduate study in law. Howard Law School's valedictorian had traditionally attended Harvard Law School for graduate work.[203] She won the fellowship, but Harvard Law responded to Murray's application this way: "Your picture and the salutation on your college transcript indicate that you are not of the sex entitled to be admitted to Harvard Law School." She felt the blow as sharply as she had when the University of North Carolina told her, "Members of your race are not admitted to the University." Murray appealed the decision to the Harvard Law faculty, and her appeal was still pending on graduation day. As she shook Dean Hastie's hand and reached for her diploma, she already looked forward to her next campaign, against an evil she called Jane Crow.[204]

9

COLD WAR CASUALTIES

"An American Girl Works Out a Way of Life," Pauli Murray announced to *PM* newspaper readers in the summer of 1944. From now on, Murray declared, she would choose "dignity" over segregation. Her alternative—living "half-Negro" and "half-American"—would be "spiritual suicide." Thus she declared herself All Negro and All American, but another identity would have to wait for self-actualization. She was an American "girl," even though she was thirty-four years old. Murray's manifesto set out a "code" for African Americans. It was up to every individual to achieve a "position of equality and respect," even though it might come at a high personal cost. A "quieting of the spirit . . . a pause before the conflict," she advised, would provide "the courage you need to hold fast to your self-control." It was pointless to wait for "public machinery" to step in to win equality for you; rather, you must be ready from within. Murray concluded that "you have nothing to lose and everything to gain for yourself and mankind."[1]

Her summer had been dizzying. D-day arrived a few days before Howard graduation in June, and throughout the summer Americans grew more confident of Hitler's impending defeat. The same month Murray met Frank Porter Graham for the first time at a Washington radio station when they went on the air together. She described their meeting and joint broadcast as a "joy."[2] She had appealed her rejection from Harvard Law

School on the basis of her sex, but in the meantime she was admitted to Boalt Hall School of Law at the University of California at Berkeley for a master's degree in law. Her sister found a nursing position with the Veterans Administration in Los Angeles, and the two drove west in early July. It was tough to find a place to live in wartime Los Angeles, but they finally settled in an apartment on Crocker Street about six blocks from Central Avenue in South L.A. Murray worked as a reporter for Loren Miller, the former *Black and White* cast member, now an attorney and the copublisher of the *Los Angeles Sentinel*.[3]

On the day that her "American Girl" article appeared, she came home to find two letters in the mailbox. Eleanor Roosevelt wrote to encourage her to pursue her Harvard appeal. The other letter was from her neighbors. We "wish to inform you the flat you now occupy is restricted to the white or Caucasian race only," The "South Crocker Street Property Owners" wrote, "We are quite sure you did not know of this restriction or you would not have rented the flat." They warned, "We intend to uphold these restrictions," demanding that the Murray sisters "vacate . . . within 7 days."[4] Apparently, the sisters had moved into a building "one-half a block across the line where the whites had decided to take their stand," Murray deduced. She sent a copy of the hate letter to Eleanor Roosevelt with the note "I wish you could see this 'restricted' palace. Why, Mrs. Roosevelt, you wouldn't want to put Fala in here." ER responded that she was "perfectly furious" about the threat.[5]

Warnings similar to the one that Murray received went out in many different forms to African Americans in northern and western cities across the country in 1944, and housing riots struck urban areas. Murray did not know that the particular Los Angeles terrain into which she moved had been contested since the 1920s, but she had sworn to stand up for her rights. Her new boss, Loren Miller, had been fighting the restrictive deed covenants that caused residential segregation for years. He ran a story on the threatening letter in the *Sentinel* and secured police protection for the sisters. Murray reported the threat to the FBI and declared in the *Sentinel*: "One thing is clear—we do not intend to move."[6] They stayed put.

That summer Murray completed an overdue legal project entitled "Should the Civil Rights Cases and *Plessy v. Ferguson* Be Overruled?" She answered yes, of course, and sent it off to her professor, Leon Ransom. Harvard Law School denied her admittance a second time, but she looked forward to going to Berkeley in October.[7] She wrote "An American Credo" for the magazine *Common Ground*, in which she elaborated on her "code" and vowed that she would not "submit to segregation . . . as long as my physical strength endures." She would resist, go to prison, and even leave the country if she had to. "When my brothers try to draw a circle to exclude me," Murray vowed, "I shall draw a larger circle to include them."[8]

Lessons of the Holocaust

By the summer of 1944 those African Americans who committed themselves to winning civil rights had expanded the angle of their compassion to project their circle of tolerance around the nation. Individual action must continue, but most realized that confrontations in crowded wartime cities across the country called for federal action.[9] The Fair Employment Practices Committee must continue after the war, and black Americans hoped that total military desegregation would prove easier in peacetime. Recognition of the horror of Fascism might raise a groundswell of opinion at home that would lead to abolition of the poll tax and the integration of higher education and housing. Interstate transportation would have to be desegregated. Pauli Murray had been working on all those things for more than a decade.

Sticking a finger into the political winds, Murray felt a warm breeze portending double victories over Fascism and racism. FDR had proclaimed that *all* Americans had a right to a job, housing, medical care and a good education. Prominent Republican Wendell Willkie had made a convincing "Case for Minorities" in the *Saturday Evening Post*, even though his article appeared just days after he lost the Republican presidential nomination to Thomas Dewey, who had positioned himself farther to the right.[10] Gunnar Myrdal's *An American Dilemma* was collecting favorable reviews everywhere except in the South.[11]

It even seemed possible that the radical Left would become a full partner in peace after the war. Stalin had disbanded the Comintern a year earlier, and in late June 1944 Earl Browder happily directed the Communist Party convention to dissolve the CPUSA and form the Communist Political Association. "Partisanship," he alleged, was "a most costly luxury," and he plunged into Roosevelt's reelection campaign. FDR won a fourth term by his slimmest margin ever in November 1944.[12] Through the spring of 1945 Soviet troops approached Berlin from the east, while U.S. and British troops moved east from Normandy.

When Langston Hughes stepped off a "Jim Crow car in Oklahoma" on May 2, 1945, he heard a black cabby exclaim that Hitler was dead. Hughes marveled that Hitler, who had "lynched thousands of Jews" and "believed in Jim Crow for all the world," was gone. As for the Soviet Army advancing across Germany, he added, "It is most right and fitting that Moscow should take Berlin first," since segregation prevailed in "Paris, London, or Washington."[13] However, Horace Cayton, who had witnessed Jewish persecution from a German park bench in 1933, did not take time to breathe a sigh of relief when V-E Day finally arrived on May 8, 1945. A recent U.S. poll had predicted "greater racial tensions and even riots after the war," he noted; therefore the "real fight for democracy has only begun."[14] On May 19, 1945, two stories that made the fight for democracy an immediate imperative broke in the African American press.

What Vincent Tubbs saw at Dachau and what Chatwood Hall saw at Auschwitz horrified African Americans accustomed to reading of atrocities against their own people. The two black reporters spared them nothing. Tubbs, the war correspondent for the *Afro-American*, reported that he could smell Dachau before he saw it. "It was like burning brown sugar with a low, sour stench of unwashed bodies," he said. The Nazis had tried to burn the prisoners alive as the U.S. Twelfth Armored Division bore down. Inside he found "charred bodies of uncountable men,'" some still smoldering. The Nazis had tied some prisoners to logs, which they set on fire in the woods. A few survived, and one rose up and kissed Tubbs's hand. Tubbs put it simply: "The inmates, those dead and those surviving out of the 4,000 internees there, were Jews."[15]

As Tubbs approached from the west, Chatwood Hall approached from the east with Soviet troops. Chatwood Hall was the pen name of Homer Smith, the young post office worker who had gone to Moscow with the *Black and White* cast and stayed on as a journalist. When Hall arrived at Auschwitz after the German surrender in May, he reported that the camp had the capacity to kill 10,000 to 12,000 people daily. He saw bales of human hair that weighed 15,400 pounds, which, Soviets calculated, represented 140,000 recently murdered women. Investigators estimated that "between four and five million" people had died there.[16] Black readers understood horror. The NAACP and the black press had spoken the unspeakable for decades in an attempt to stop the hanging, burning alive, and dismemberment of African Americans. But this horror defied understanding. It was as if millions of lynchings had taken place, mechanically and on a vast scale, for the same reason that white Americans tortured and killed black Americans: because of their identity.

After the camps came to light, African Americans knew that their prewar jeremiads about the Fascist danger to the Jews had been vindicated. Whether or not white Americans realized it at the beginning, in the end, this *had* been a war against racism. Black reporter Vincent Tubbs recounted the story of Tuskegee Airman Lieutenant Kenneth Williams to prove it. Williams had been a UCLA student when he volunteered for the Army Air Corps. Shot down over Athens, Greece, on October 4, 1944, he was imprisoned in Stalag 7A with twelve other black airmen. Williams ended up twenty miles from Dachau as his guards forced the prisoners to retreat before Allied troops. Starved and crammed into boxcars, they licked the sides of garbage pails at railway stations. In Williams's hometown, white Angelenos had pronounced Murray's flat "restricted to the white or Caucasian race only" six weeks before he had been shot down fighting for them. Pauli Murray acted as Lieutenant Williams's proxy. She had not put up with segregation while he was away; he would not put up with it when he returned.[17]

"A number of people have been asking me to make a statement on segregation," Eleanor Roosevelt wrote to Murray the day before Williams was shot down. Roosevelt hesitated to do so "until we have achieved the four basic citizenship rights," equal opportunity in work, medical care, housing, and education. ER thought that if she spoke out against segregation, she might jeopardize postwar legislation to guarantee those rights. She predicted that "very soon after the war comes to an end . . . those of us who really care that this question should be settled without bloodshed, will have to stand up and be counted."[18]

Roosevelt's reasoning points to more than strategic differences among white and black liberals; it also illustrates the complexity of the relationship between desegregation and civil rights. African Americans saw desegregation as a means, not as an end. Desegregation—to be closer to white people—was not their goal; their goal was civil rights. However, black Americans decided early in the war that they must defeat "separate" to achieve "equal." The powerless could not grant civil rights to themselves; rather, they had to seize those rights through desegregation campaigns. On the other hand, those with power thought that white legislators could grant civil rights and that desegregation campaigns might be a deterrent to bestowing them. ER understood the dialectic between bestowing and seizing. After she had told Murray that she could not stand up for desegregation personally, she also said that she admired Murray's refusal to "submit" to it.[19]

The U.S. in the UN

When Murray got the news of Hitler's suicide, Germany's surrender, and the Nazi death camps, she was living with forty-four women from all over the world in San Francisco's International House. By the time that the international "parley" on the United Nations began there in late April 1945, Murray had already started her own "embryonic United Nations" with her housemates: a Japanese American woman who had been interned, a Jew who had fled Germany as a child, a Chinese woman, a Mexican American, and a white American whose parents had been Chinese missionaries. The women's last names—Murray, Takita, Schiff, Li, Garcia, and Tutell—reflected their diversity. They formed a panel to speak to Bay Area groups on "the interrelatedness of minority problems" and "Breaking Down Barriers." "I was learning to see the civil rights struggle within the wider context of all human rights," Murray recalled.[20]

Murray's widening vision reflected that of her fellow Americans as they watched three thousand delegates from forty-six countries assemble in San Francisco to hammer out the UN Charter. The conference opened on April 25 and lasted into the summer. Franklin Roosevelt's death thirteen days before it began increased its significance as a means to institutionalize his influence on the world stage. President Harry S. Truman spoke at the opening session.[21]

Domestic civil rights and the colonial situation headed the African American agenda in San Francisco. Many were troubled by the outcome of a series of meetings held the previous fall among U.S., Soviet, and British diplomats at Dumbarton Oaks in Washington. In that discussion on how to bring about a postwar world order, "the matter of the colonies has been passed over," W. E. B. Du Bois thought. Murray reported to ER that the residents of International House agreed. They were "very discouraged'" by the planning, which also failed to determine voting procedure on the Security Council.[22]

Eleanor Roosevelt saw to it that an NAACP delegation, including secretary Walter White, W. E. B. Du Bois, and Mary McLeod Bethune, would be seated in San Francisco. The main Soviet delegate, Vyacheslav Molotov, and the Chinese delegates called for colonial liberation, while the Indian delegation supported the African Americans by desegregating many of their social functions. The most visible black American at the conference was Ralph Bunche, who served with the State Department. Max Yergan and Eslanda Robeson acted as observers, representing the Council on African Affairs (CAA) and the National Negro Congress (NNC).[23] Murray wangled a visitors' ticket.

Murray's dream of a United Nations combined her anti-Communist resolve with her passion for international human rights. After Japan surrendered on August 14, 1945, Murray worried that the USSR might "take over the moral leadership of the world" if America did not solve its "internal problem of race and color." For their part, African Americans had a bigger job than ever before, since bearing "the scourge of injustice" peculiarly qualified them "to work for peace and justice." Murray observed, "The world is crying for peace, but there can be no peace anywhere without justice."[24]

In the fall of 1945 the Indian delegation challenged South African Prime Minister Jan C. Smuts's grab for South-West Africa. Eager to invalidate the League of Nations' mandate over South-West Africa, Smuts proposed that his country assume administration of the territory, which included German speakers. India fought the proposal by calling attention to South Africa's treatment of its citizens of South Asian heritage. In response, Smuts argued that South Africans and South-West Africans had not protested his power grab. Max Yergan sprang into action and helped his old friend A. B. Xuma, by now president-general of the African National Congress (ANC), organize a letter-writing campaign. The ANC showered the delegates with protests. Ultimately, the United Nations decided to maintain the League of Nations' mandate in South-West Africa.[25] For Yergan, the Indian action set a "precedent" for international intervention into U.S. discrimination because it broke "the barrier of national sovereignty—the international equivalent of the 'states rights' obstacle."[26]

As a result of lobbying by African Americans, Indians, and Jewish groups from around the world, the UN Charter provided for a Commission on Human Rights, formally established in February 1946. The commission drew up an international bill of rights, defined civil liberties, free speech, and women's rights and established a Subcommission on Prevention of Discrimination and Protection of Minorities.[27] The commission found its authority in the nondiscrimination clause in the UN Charter, which the U.S. delegation had approved, despite State Department official John Foster Dulles's worry that it would authorize UN scrutiny of the "Negro question in this country."[28]

Such scrutiny came quickly. The NAACP attorney and Howard Law School dean William H. Hastie evoked the UN Charter when he argued for the right to desegregate interstate transportation before the Court of Appeals in Virginia. When the United States had ratified the UN Charter, he argued, it "embedded in its national policy a prohibition against racism and pledged itself to respect fundamental freedoms for all without distinction as to race, sex, language or religion."[29] Hastie no longer had to argue that being forced to sit at the back of the bus constituted unequal treatment. Now he could argue that segregation was just plain wrong because it violated national policy.

On June 6, 1946, Max Yergan's National Negro Congress filed a petition with the United Nations on behalf of African Americans. Yergan argued that domestic racial oppression was "identical with the super-racism utilized by the Nazis" and comparable to South Africa's discrimination against Indians. American racism "disfigures our democracy and menaces the peace of the world," he argued.[30] The United Nations referred the petition to its Human Rights Commission. When Eleanor Roosevelt became chairman of the commission in January 1947, she faced more than a thousand similar petitions from around the world. She wondered how the commission would " 'enforce' the international bill of rights" that it was drafting.[31]

While Eleanor Roosevelt chaired the larger commission, Jonathan

Daniels of Raleigh served on its Subcommission on Prevention of Discrimination and Protection of Minorities. His experiences quickly convinced him that the United States must do something about civil rights within the South or appear to be a "nation of hypocrites."[32] Certainly W. E. B. Du Bois was ready to point out that hypocrisy. In October 1947 the NAACP filed a petition that he had written and entitled An Appeal to the World: A Statement on the Denial of Human Rights to Minorities in the Case of Citizens of Negro Descent in the United States of America and an Appeal to the United Nations for Redress. The title stated the case, and the petition's overwhelming evidence proved it. Yet Du Bois's petition had little impact, and it was his last major accomplishment under NAACP auspices. He became involved with a group of young Southerners, many of them Communists, in the Southern Negro Youth Conference in Columbia, South Carolina. At the same time, he started to take more seriously the Communists whom he already knew in the Northeast.[33]

By the end of 1947 it was crystal clear why a segregationist would want the "U.S. out of the U.N." For example, the American Jewish Committee had urged that the German and Japanese peace treaties include human rights provisions under UN oversight. The Subcommission on Prevention of Discrimination and Protection of Minorities had met in Geneva, Switzerland, where Jonathan Daniels argued with the Soviet delegate, who wanted to outlaw "the advocacy of discrimination against any group of people." Daniels fought the provision and won, but he left Geneva thoroughly convinced that the South itself must quickly eliminate discrimination, or the rest of the world would force it to.[34]

Early in December 1947 the American Association for the United Nations filed an amicus curiae brief with the U.S. Supreme Court to contest restrictive covenants in the "purchase and use of real estate." Loren Miller arrived from Los Angeles to join Thurgood Marshall of the NAACP in the argument before the Court. They proved convincing; the Court's decision in *Shelley v. Kraemer* "barred the judicial enforcement of racially restrictive covenants."[35] Pauli Murray had been right again when she refused to be cowed by the South Crocker Street property owners. For a bright shining moment between 1945 and 1947 the United Nations represented the hope of the world. Many African Americans hoped that it would be the savior of their country.

Presidential Civil Rights

In December 1946, eleven months after the creation of the UN Commission on Human Rights, President Truman established the President's Committee on Civil Rights. Truman responded to the international example, but he also reacted to Democratic congressional electoral setbacks a month earlier. The Roosevelt coalition of African Americans, working-class white Northerners, and the ever-solid Democratic white South seemed to be imploding on Truman's watch. He appointed fifteen people to the committee and charged them to develop recommendations for "the protection of civil rights."[36]

The committee's membership reflected the public's postwar grasp of what Pauli Murray called "the interrelatedness of minority problems." Walking into committee meetings must have felt like boarding Noah's Ark; members included two African Americans, two labor leaders, two white Southerners, two businessmen, two Jews, two Catholics, the odd Episcopalian bishop, and three white men with governmental experience. Only three had been born in the South: Dorothy R. Tilly, active in the Commission on Interracial Cooperation's Association of Southern Women for the Prevention of Lynching and then head of the Methodist Women's Society of Christian Service; Channing Tobias, a black man who had long worked in the North as senior secretary of the YMCA and was a close friend of Max Yergan's; and Frank Porter Graham, president of the University of North Carolina. The committee's overall diversity reflected the fact that civil rights were a concern for all Americans. One of the governmental representatives recalled that "on the broad issues . . . the committee was clear and united." The disagreements arose not from principle but from enforcement mechanisms. For example, should the federal government withdraw funds from hospitals that would not desegregate?[37]

The committee's work proceeded alongside congressional drama. Bills "to prohibit discrimination in employment because of race, creed, color, national origin or ancestry," along with "mandatory, compulsory" enforcement powers, had been stalled since V-J Day. On one side were minorities across the country, joined by liberal white Southerners, such as journalist Thomas Sancton, who got behind a permanent Fair Employment Practices Committee as "a first objective" in the war against segregation. On the other side stood southern members of Congress, such as Senator Richard Russell of Georgia, who had told the Senate in 1944: "I am disturbed as I have never been disturbed before, by the evil which portends for the people of my State, both black and white, in the ruthless drive being made by the Fair Employment Practice [*sic*] Committee . . . to enforce their racial views on the Nation." When the permanent FEPC bill made it onto the Senate floor for the first time in January 1946, Georgia's other senator exploded: "If that is all Harry Truman has to offer, God help the Democratic Party in 1946 and 1948." Southern senators filibustered and killed the bill that time.[38]

Not since Reconstruction had the white South looked so out of step with the rest of the nation. *Time* magazine called the bill for a permanent FEPC the "hottest political potato on the Congressional agenda" and depicted white Southerners as "boiling at the idea of giving a Negro a white man's wage." The response of one white Southerner, the journalist John Temple Graves, illustrates how the white South used civil liberties to create states' rights and thwart civil rights. *Time*, Graves declared, was mistaken in its assumption that "this region fights the bill because it doesn't want Negroes to have white men's wages." To assume so, he bloviated, "is to be illiterate of the facts, bigoted in determination upon a point of view without regard to facts, and backward against blessed new trends persuading the South to make right its own wrongs without federal interfering." In that convoluted sentence, he turned illiteracy, bigotry, and backwardness against the North. Sure, there might be a few Southerners who "don't want Negroes to have white men's wages," he conceded, but not enough to inspire their congressional leaders to filibuster. At stake here was something greater, something shining and noble, something that evoked the Founders, an "issue more important than any legislation . . . involving needs as precious as any protected for minorities." That issue was states' rights.[39]

In the hue and cry for civil rights that lasted until the spring of 1948, people like Graves seemed to belong to the nation's past. Supporters of equal employment opportunities made inroads with state legislatures, while the National Council for a Permanent FEPC, organized in 1943 by A. Philip Randolph, pressured Washington. In many ways the National Council for a Permanent FEPC was simply the incarnation of the March on Washington Movement. In 1945 Congress mandated the expiration of the wartime FEPC on June 30, 1946, and Randolph's group took the fight to state legislatures and Congress.[40] New York passed the "first state FEPC law in America" in March 1945 as fourteen other states considered similar bills. Murray was thrilled when her completed master's thesis, "The Right to Equal Opportunity in Employment," appeared in the *California Law Review* that fall.[41]

Randolph prevailed upon Maida Springer, with whom Pauli Murray had worked on the National Sharecroppers Week and in the MOWM, to plan a rally for a permanent FEPC in 1946. Eleanor Roosevelt served as honorary chairman of the event, which attracted 17,500 people to Madison Square Garden. African Americans in southern cities organized local Committees for a Permanent FEPC and began voter registration drives.[42]

Truman underscored the importance of the President's Committee on Civil Rights in his State of the Union Address in January 1947, when he called disfranchisement and denial of equal employment opportunity crimes. However, he was careful to point out, they were crimes only in the moral sense, since the federal government lacked the "power to protect the civil rights of the American people." He sought that power two days later by including a permanent Fair Employment Practices Commission in his congressional agenda.[43]

Meanwhile the president's committee concluded its work in October 1947. Its report, *To Secure These Rights*, began with the premise that the United States had fallen "short of the goal" of "freedom and equality" and asserted governmental responsibility to secure civil rights. Then it made a plethora of practical recommendations. Among them, the Civil Rights Section of the Department of Justice should be strengthened, the FBI should take on a unit trained to investigate civil rights violations and the states should create similar agencies, and there should be policy-making civil rights commissions at the federal and state levels. Congress must strengthen punishment for violations, pass a law against police brutality, update legislation against involuntary servitude, and pass antilynching legislation.[44]

African Americans found what they were looking for at the end of the long list of recommendations, an end to discrimination and segregation in the armed forces, in public accommodations, and in transportation, along with a permanent FEPC to ensure equal economic opportunity. But those legal measures would simply be a start since the report called for "the elimination of segregation . . . from American life." It concluded: "The future of our nation rests upon the character, the vision, the high principle of our people. Democracy, brotherhood, human rights—these are practical expressions of the eternal worth of every child of God."[45]

By the time that *To Secure These Rights* emerged, Stalin had declared that Communism could never make peace with capitalism, and British Prime Minister Winston Churchill had pronounced the borders of Soviet-occupied Eastern Europe to be an iron curtain. The chairman of the Republican National Committee cast the 1946 congressional elections as a choice between "Communism and Republicanism."[46] In March 1947, before the Republican-controlled Congress, Truman laid down as doctrine America's unwillingness to tolerate the expansion of Communism or to compromise with the Soviets. Then he issued an executive order establishing a Federal Employee Loyalty Program to find and fire Communists in the government.

There would be no return to Popular Front cooperation, and the Left began a sorting-out process, sometimes at its own behest, sometimes under agonizing pressure from loyalty boards, the House Un-American Activities Committee, or the press. The overall result was to splinter and weaken the Left into factions distinguished by degrees of anti-Communism. By the time that the President's Committee on Civil Rights issued *To Secure These Rights*, a wave of anti-Communism had threatened to submerge the high tide of civil rights and diverted the power of the Left to implement desegregation.[47]

The Civil Rights Committee realized that it was powerless to command the rising anti-Communist waters to recede and was determined that neither anti-Communism nor Communists be allowed to compromise the work of civil rights. It tried to equate American patriotism with anti-discrimination principles. American Communists might profess "belief in universal civil rights"; however, the ideology and practice of international Communism betrayed that belief time after time. The growing Red Scare troubled the committee members as well. They cautioned against the "state of near-hysteria [that] now threatens to inhibit the freedom of genuine democrats." They "unqualifiedly oppose[d] any attempt to impose *special* limitations" on Communists or Fascists but recommended "systematic registration procedures" for all groups, including requirements to publish a list of officers, identify funding sources and expenditures, and state the purpose of the organization. The committee also endorsed loyalty tests for government employees but urged that they incorporate "clear, specific standards."[48]

Truman used the report to link civil rights and anti-Communism. The United States must create "a world-wide moral order" to deter the Soviet Union, and *To Secure These Rights* would serve as "a new charter of human freedom."[49] Truman made it seem that fighting Communism required supporting civil rights and that supporting civil rights required fighting Communism. These false dichotomies were anathema to people like Frank Porter Graham, who had worked all his life to uphold both human dignity and free speech. He saw Communism as an ideology, something that people believed in, however misguidedly. If they wanted to hold foolish ideas, the Constitution guaranteed that they could do so. Graham was, after all, the man who supported Langston Hughes's right to speak at UNC, the man who refused to hunt for Communists in the Southern Conference for Human Welfare, and the boss who refused to fire Eston Ericson for dining with James Ford. Cold War anti-Communism swept away his abiding principle, that America's democracy was strong enough to allow everyone to speak his or her own mind without fear of reprisal.

Graham had missed the meeting in which the committee voted to make federal aid contingent on desegregation of the recipient's facility and to establish a commission that could hold hearings, issue cease-and-desist orders, and levy fines in the permanent FEPC. The majority of the committee realized that enforcement mechanisms were necessary. Graham wrote a dissenting opinion that eschewed coercion and substituted education for tolerance that would "inculcate both the teachings of religion regarding human brotherhood and the ideals of our democracy." *To Secure These Rights* duly noted that "a minority of the Committee favors the elimination of segregation as an ultimate goal, but opposes the imposition of a federal sanction."[50] But anti-Communists ignored his dissent and portrayed the two white Southerners as turncoats. Frank Porter Graham and Dorothy Tilly, the Atlanta Methodist, had "affiliations with Communist-front organizations," they argued.[51]

Civil Rights, Anti-Communism, and the Election of 1948

The politics of race and the politics of anti-Communism played out in the South by providing handy rhetorical tools for black voter registration drives at the local level, even as it increased white segregationists' power at the state and congressional levels.[52] International scrutiny of human rights and the lesson of Fascism held back some white opposition to black voter registration in urban areas in the upper South in the immediate postwar years. African Americans registered and voted in the name of patriotism and occasionally elected black municipal officials. Anti-Communism, however, did not create increased black voter registration; it simply reaffirmed initiatives that African Americans had put in place during World War II and that black veterans executed with renewed force when they returned home. On the other hand, anti-Communism and the coming of the Cold War did create a Red Scare that removed white liberal forces from southern politics at the very moment that they were crucial to the extension of meaningful political and civil rights to the vast majority of black Southerners.[53] The Cold War pressure cooker trapped rising African American expectations in a heated, oppressive political environment. Conservative white anti-Communists kept the lid on black Southerners' expectations by removing from power influential liberals and leftists who could have joined them to make real changes in politics, the economy, and the judiciary.

In 1946 and 1947 black World War II veterans formed impromptu regiments to assault the polls of southern cities. By the fall of 1946 six hundred thousand black Southerners were registered to vote. In Georgia one black veteran announced that the hundred thousand newly registered African Americans would go to the polls despite "the Ku Klux Klan, Talmadge, [or] any other un-Christian Georgia fascists." In Winston-Salem, North Carolina, the United Citizens Committee elected a black city councilman.[54] Part of the support for the black Southerners came from labor. In 1944 the Congress of Industrial Organizations' Political Action Committee (CIO-PAC) had hired a black organizer to register black Southerners. Its choice was Henry Lee Moon, the *Black and White* cast member who had joined Lovett Fort-Whiteman to challenge Stalin over the film's cancellation. Moon had married fellow cast member Mollie Lewis when she returned from Berlin, leaving her "Mona, the Indian Girl" costume behind.[55] The CIO-PAC energized African Americans who had not previously been affiliated with labor to register. CIO organizers argued that they did not "seek social equality—only economic equality." If the CIO-PAC increased black voter registration, that would help ensure economic equality and protect unions.[56] The Southern Negro Youth Congress registered voters across the South in a voter education project before the 1948 elections. The SNYC had many Communist members but also welcomed non-Communists. In fact, several African Americans who were avowed anti-Communists served on its advisory board.[57]

The black veterans' voter registration and election campaigns in Charlotte, North Carolina, provide a good example of postwar grassroots organizing. Funeral home owner Fred Alexander founded the Citizens Committee for Political Action to "promote the political, social and economic welfare," brought in CIO-PAC speakers, and coordinated registration drives. The Citizens Committee made it clear that it would support "Negro candidates" in local elections. "Come and learn the truth about politics in Charlotte," it announced. "This is your opportunity to elect Negroes to city government," it declared in 1949. It made common cause with the white liberals in the local chapter of the liberal Americans for Democratic Action, which endorsed the committee's candidates. The endorsed black city council candidate made the runoff, and its school board candidate came in third out of four. In 1950 alone, the Citizens Committee registered seven thousand new black voters. The evening paper owned by whites saw all this activity as a "mixed blessing" and worried that "many Negroes are not sufficiently educated to keep themselves informed on the candidates and their issues." If the black Citizens Committee simply told people whom to vote for, the "child will not learn to tie his shoes." But the day of such paternalism had passed, and the local black newspaper reprinted the white editorial to get black voters to the polls.[58]

Many moderate white Southerners welcomed the changes they saw around them. For example, the all-white delegates to the Southern Baptist Convention approved a wide-ranging civil rights program in May 1947 and reaffirmed it the next year. "Encouraging progress is being made," the convention reported. "The right of all men to vote in government . . . has been upheld again and again in the high courts of the South. . . . The right

of all American citizens to equal recognition in employment has been confirmed in recent significant cases. . . . The right to equal opportunity in
education has gained considerable support . . . the University of Arkansas
voluntarily opened the doors of its graduate school to qualified Negro students," the Baptists affirmed. This evidence pointed toward "the undeni-
able truth that the South, of its own volition, is moving in the direction of
the objectives which were recommended by the report of the President's
Committee on Civil Rights."[59]

The Southern Baptists' concerns paralleled those of the Women's
Division of Christian Service of the Methodist Church, which organized a
Committee to Study Racial Policies and Practices. Black and white southern women vowed to review first their own Methodist practices and then
"all of the segregation ordinances of all communities in which the
Women's Division has institutions." The Methodist women ran settlement houses, social service agencies, and health centers in cities across the
nation. They hoped to sort out "law or custom," to equip Methodist
women to stand up for desegregation in their own communities. It was the
same sort of political model that the Methodist women had used in the
Southern Association of Women for the Prevention of Lynching: getting
the facts out to prominent Methodist women to empower them to challenge local racial practices. The guiding lights behind the project were the
Women's Division manager, Thelma Stevens, a Georgia white woman,
and Susie Jones, the wife of the president of Bennett College, a North Carolina black woman. At division headquarters in New York City, the staff
worked with the United Nations and ran training programs for thirty-six
thousand local Methodist women's units.[60]

Gathering the legal data to sort out local segregation laws would be
an enormous job, but the Women's Division found the perfect person to do
it, Pauli Murray. After working for the state of California for a few months
on antidiscrimination issues, Murray returned to New York and took a job
with the American Jewish Congress. When the congress retrenched after
nine months, Murray took the small retainer from the Methodist women's
project and opened a law practice. She passed the New York bar but
refused to take the North Carolina bar because she would have had to
swear that she would uphold the laws of the state, including those supporting segregation. Rather than affirm them, she compiled them. Two

years and 746 pages later, Murray and the Women's Division published *States' Laws on Race and Color*. They presented one of the first copies to representatives of the United Nations.[61]

When Southern Baptist and Methodist white women committed themselves to desegregation, it seemed as if Eleanor Roosevelt's moment "to stand up and be counted" had arrived. But those who stood up were mowed down by the postwar Red Scare.[62] Masquerading as anti-Communist, the Cold War conservative domestic forces were actually antiliberal. They destroyed the southern Popular Front coalition, along with the groundwork that it had laid for civil rights. Southern anti-Communists fought furiously against the national push for desegregation that coalesced in 1948, and they did not fight fairly.

Anti-Communists began undercutting those Southerners who worked for civil rights. For example, in 1947 the Southern Conference for Human Welfare, of which Frank Graham served as honorary president, drew the fire of the House Committee on Un-American Activities. In a scathing report, HUAC named Communist SCHW members, even though the report admitted there had been few. Since there weren't many Communist members, HUAC had to endow them with incredible powers; indeed, the committee saw Communist influence behind every liberal stand that the SCHW had taken. The report concluded that the SCHW was a Communist front organization, but many white Southerners thought that HUAC had overreached when it portrayed Graham as a Communist dupe. The North Carolina SCHW committee feared that it faced "a wave of reaction, amounting almost to hysteria . . . from the fear and hatred left over from the war." It might "last a year or two more before the public sanity is restored." It resolved to "stand firm," since HUAC had found "no evidence of Communist control of the SCHW."[63]

The 1948 election became a referendum on civil rights and Communism, and the two issues fused in the minds of many southern segregationists in Henry Wallace's candidacy. Franklin Roosevelt had named Wallace secretary of agriculture in 1933, and Will Alexander had worked for him throughout the New Deal. Wallace was Roosevelt's choice as vice president in 1941, but in 1944 FDR allowed the Democratic National Convention to replace him with Harry Truman. When Roosevelt subsequently offered Wallace his pick of cabinet positions, he chose secretary of commerce. It was from that job that Wallace began to criticize U.S. occupation policies in Europe and to accuse the United States of hypocrisy in its dealings with the Soviet Union. In 1946 Truman told him to refrain from commenting on foreign policy or be fired. Wallace chose the latter course.[64]

Shortly after the release of *To Secure These Rights*, Wallace joined with the Southern Conference for Human Welfare to conduct a series of desegregated rallies in the South in November and December 1947. Wallace and twenty-five thousand black and white Southerners heroically ignored segregation in fifteen venues. Many of the meetings were broadcast over the radio. The triumph of the Wallace tour made it appear that the President's Committee on Civil Rights recommendations could be implemented in short order. Wallace returned to Washington and announced that he would run for president as the candidate of the new Progressive Party.[65]

In March 1948 A. Philip Randolph met with Harry S. Truman and told him flatly that African Americans would no longer tolerate segregation. Randolph had been a canny anti-Communist in the midst of international politics back when Truman was selling shirts in Kansas City, but now Randolph told Truman that African Americans would not fight Communism in a segregated army. "Negroes are in no mood to shoulder a gun for democracy abroad so long as they are denied democracy here at home," Randolph reported to the president. "I wish you hadn't made that statement," Truman responded. "I don't like it at all." Randolph shrugged and said, "I'm giving you the facts." Randolph and his allies were ready to use "civil disobedience as a last resort for Negroes and sympathetic whites" to desegregate the military forces, and they told the Senate Armed Services Committee so.[66]

In the 1948 presidential campaign the issue of desegregating the armed forces focused the broader campaign for civil rights and joined anti-Communism and desegregation. The Republicans nominated Thomas E. Dewey and announced their support for desegregation of the armed forces. Henry Wallace's Progressive Party drew strength from Left-leaning Democrats and agreed with the Republicans on that issue. Moreover, with the party conventions looming in July, Stalin made the Soviet Union a campaign issue when he cut off access to Berlin on June 23. Truman began the Berlin airlift on June 27. An actual confrontation with the Communists made Wallace's advocacy of cooperation with the Soviet Union seem to some naive at best, subversive at worst.[67] If Truman found himself in a tight spot on the Left, it was nothing compared with the squeeze that disaffected southern Democrats were initiating from the Right.

The Democratic convention in Philadelphia in early July was a civil rights war in a supercharged anti-Communist atmosphere. Black Southerners challenged seating the all-white delegations from Mississippi and South Carolina. After Hubert Humphrey told the delegates that it was time "for the Democratic party to get out of the shadow of states' rights and walk forthrightly into the bright sunshine of human rights," delegates defeated a states' rights resolution by two to one and approved a civil rights resolution by a small margin. Half of Alabama's white delegation and all of Mississippi's walked out that night.[68]

Then, on July 17, six thousand white Southerners met in Birmingham, Alabama, formed the States' Rights Democratic Party, and nominated South Carolinian Strom Thurmond as their candidate for president. Under a portrait of General Robert E. Lee, Thurmond told the country that "there's not enough troops in the Army to force the southern people to break down segregation." As if to prove him wrong, on July 26, 1948, President Truman issued an executive order to desegregate the armed forces, and the following day he blamed the nation's slow progress in civil rights on the Republican Congress.[69]

A month later Henry Wallace attempted to re-create his triumphant southern tour of the previous winter. Mary Price, a former SCHW staffer in North Carolina, was his campaign manager in the state and had just been named as a member of a Soviet spy ring in Washington. Her accuser said that when she was Walter Lippmann's secretary, she had leaked his personal files to Soviet spies. What the Soviets could possibly do with Lippmann's correspondence remained a mystery.[70] The anti-Communist organization was ready for Wallace this time. His second stop, in Durham, North Carolina, introduced him to a very different South. Hecklers with Confederate flags yelled, "We want Thurmond," and, "Communist! Communist!" and fights broke out. The African Americans in the audience, who included newspaper editor Louis Austin, watched in amazement as the white people slugged it out. Organizers did not know if they could get Wallace out of the auditorium alive. Aside from short stops in Chapel Hill and Asheville, the rest of the tour proved just as terrifying, in part because someone was paying the same gang of hecklers to follow Wallace around. He finally quit trying to speak at all and, on several occasions, just sat in the car, afraid to roll down the windows. Crowds called him "a Communist" and "a nigger lover" interchangeably. Even then, when Truman beat Dewey, Wallace, and Thurmond, few realized it was liberalism's last hurrah. It seemed at the time to be a slim victory for civil rights.[71]

Breaking Frank Graham

In 1948 Graham told Pauli Murray confidentially that he had recommended to the board of trustees that the University of North Carolina desegregate the graduate and professional schools. James Shepard of the North Carolina College for Negroes had died the previous year, and Graham judged the political climate right for the historic action. Howard Odum disagreed openly with Graham and tried to convince the governor to combine the state's black colleges into a separate system under the UNC board of trustees. Under Odum's plan, African Americans would attend white campuses if certain graduate courses were not offered at their colleges. Ever the gradualist, Odum argued that his plan would leave the white South, rather than the federal courts or the black radicals, in charge.[72] Odum noted "an increase in thought and talk about 'racism' . . . [and] increasing tension and conflict." It was "the Negro himself [who had] changed tremendously"; alas, the southern white people had not. "The net result," Odum concluded, "is a 'new' Negro facing the 'old' white man." Odum expressed sorrow over the scowling countenances of the black Southerners around him. They seemed suddenly to think that "courtesy or cheerfulness is an index of subservience to the white man." But he also interpreted Truman's victory as a "mandate from the American people for the application of the civil liberties principles to all Negro-white relationships," and he finally (finally!) urged the white South "to stop being afraid of democracy."[73]

When Graham proposed desegregating the university, he did not fully realize how forcefully segregationists would be able to use anti-Communism in the coming months. Heretofore obscure commentators began to attack Graham and accuse him of being a Communist tool. The attacks mattered little to those who knew him, for example, to North Carolina Governor W.

Kerr Scott. When one of the state's U.S. senators died in March 1949, Jonathan Daniels suggested to Scott that he appoint Graham to fill the seat. When Graham declined by telephone, Daniels and Scott went over to Chapel Hill and talked him into it. Then, the day after Graham's appointment to the Republican-dominated Eightieth Congress was announced, an Ohio senator challenged Graham's loyalty to the United States on the Senate floor, reading out allegations made by Paul Crouch.[74]

Crouch had renounced Communism in 1942 and taken up a new vocation as a professional witness. Testifying before HUAC, he implicated every North Carolina liberal with whom he had ever come into contact as either a Communist or a Communist dupe. The false grandiosity of his testimony portrayed him as the most popular and powerful man in the state. Of Graham, Crouch said, "His record of collaboration with the Communists should not be overlooked. . . . There are few liberals of his type, and the Communists usually take full advantage of them." In fact the opposite was true. Graham had worked alongside the few Communists in North Carolina and in the Southern Conference for Human Welfare, and he had never allowed them to take advantage of him. But now Crouch spoke a new language of Cold War intrigue. He confided to HUAC that Communists regarded people like Graham "with secret contempt to be used until the revolution and then cast aside or liquidated."[75]

When the Ohio senator finished reading aloud Crouch's characterization of Frank Graham, North Carolina's other senator, Clyde Hoey, jumped to his feet and demanded the floor. Hoey was no liberal. He had been the prosecutor in the Gastonia strikers' trial. Later, as governor, he had responded to the *Gaines* decision by channeling money to James Shepard's black college, and he had refused to pardon Fred Beal. Senator Hoey still wore cutaway coats and let his silver hair grow down his back; no one looked more like a caricature of a southern senator. "I cannot remain silent," Hoey thundered, "when these suggestions or insinuations are made against the loyalty of Dr. Frank Graham. . . . There has never been any suggestion that he is not loyal and no one who knows him would hesitate to trust him," Hoey declared.[76]

Hoey did not try to explain the last three decades of North Carolina politics to his fellow senators. That would have been impossible to do in the electrified atmosphere of Cold War hysteria. Had he tried, he could have pointed out that Paul Crouch had always been intemperate, even back when he worked for the *Fool-Killer* up on Brushy Mountain. Hoey could have described a state where one could dine one night with Socialists and the next night with millowners. He could have illustrated how and why some poor textile workers once thought that Communism would put screens on their windows and get rid of the hank clock. He could have talked about the fine line that he had walked as governor when Pauli Murray tried to exercise her newly won constitutional right to go to graduate school and, instead, how he had improved the segregated black college. He could have explained that he had refused to pardon Fred Beal because he had syphilis, even though by then the man was a virulent anti-Communist. He could have argued that North Carolina politics had a lot to do with poverty and segregation, but little, if anything, to do with a sinister international plot. Hoey had been on the opposite side of Frank Porter Graham on almost every issue for the past thirty years, but he knew very well that these were political disagreements, not Soviet intrigues. It was ludicrous to doubt Graham's loyalty to his country. Graham took his seat.

Graham had acknowledged from the start that he would not simply be a place holder but would stand for election to the seat he held in the Democratic primary in late May 1950. Two men challenged him. One, Robert Reynolds, from Asheville did not present much of a problem. He had been so far to the right that even his constituents doubted his patriotism in the years before World War II. The other man was Willis Smith, a former president of the American Bar Association. As a political cipher running against one of the most beloved men in North Carolina, Smith had to make a name for himself. He did so by Red-baiting Graham on three fronts: HUAC's identification of Graham with "Communist-front" organizations, his presidency of the Southern Conference for Human Welfare, and his membership on the President's Committee on Civil Rights. Smith kicked off his campaign with the statement "I do not now nor have I ever belonged to any subversive organizations, and, as United States Senator, I shall never allow myself to be duped into the use of my name . . . by those types of organizations."[77] Both Reynolds and Smith attacked Graham for being, at worst, a Communist sympathizer, at best, a tool of Communism. One detractor dubbed him "Frank the Front."[78]

The primary unfolded as the perennial filibuster against a permanent

Fair Employment Practices Commission droned on in the Senate. Senator Hoey called the bill "un-democratic," "un-American," and "unconstitutional."[79] Graham had demurred from federal compulsion for compliance in *To Secure These Rights*, and he now supported a "noncompulsory FEPC." But he was really on the spot. He remained vague about what that noncompulsory FEPC might look like, and Willis Smith managed to turn Graham's equivocal position into support for compulsory integration. The Southern States Industrial Council, a group of industrialists, typified the utility of anti-Communism when it argued that a permanent FEPC was "collectivist" and threatened "our free economy." It asked: "What is the next step? State Socialism? Totalitarianism?" The FEPC must be defeated "if America is to live."[80]

When the moment came for senators to vote to stop the filibuster and thereby permit a vote on the bill, Graham was ill in North Carolina. His campaign advisers urged him to authorize Hoey to enter into the record a message of support from him for the filibuster. But Graham opposed filibusters at the same time that he opposed a compulsory FEPC. He refused to let Hoey speak for him and left voters wondering where he stood. His advisers thought that his failure to speak up for the filibuster cost him fifty thousand votes.[81]

Dirty tricks swept the state. Photographs of interracial couples dancing appeared on posters that asked voters if they would trust their daughters to Graham. A staple of North Carolina politics, the forged letter, supposedly sent to Negroes but mailed to white voters instead, appeared from "W. Wite, National Society for the Advancement of Colored People," urging African Americans to vote for "Dr. Frank." The brilliant black high school student who came in third in the state in a merit examination for the service academies became the Negro whom Graham had appointed to West Point, even though Graham had actually appointed a white boy. For all that, Graham won 303,605 votes, 7,000 votes short of a clear majority over Smith, who earned 230,222 votes.[82] It looked as if Graham would win the runoff primary.

For strategic advice, Smith turned to Jesse Helms, a young radio commentator in Raleigh. In between belching forth conservative screeds on the air, Helms spent his time driving Senator Hoey back and forth to Washington. During the runoff primary between Graham and Smith, the

Supreme Court decided *Sweatt v. Painter* and *McLaurin v. Oklahoma State Regents*, cases that finally ended the sham of separate but equal graduate education. The decisions galvanized the Smith campaign, even as black newspaper editor Louis Austin endorsed Graham and the state NAACP mounted a black voter registration campaign on his behalf. In the state's most vicious election since disfranchisement at the turn of the century, Smith promised white voters to "uphold the traditions of the South" and asked, "Do you want Negroes going to white schools and white children going to Negro schools?"[83]

Jonathan Daniels quoted the Smith campaign strategy in the first primary: "We threw the communism at him, and it didn't do any harm." In the runoff, Smith's staff decided "to throw the nigger at him." In Jesse Helms, it found its heavy lifter.[84] Helms formed front organizations to give the Smith campaign maximum deniability. "White People Wake Up Before It's Too Late," one poster read. "Frank Graham favors mingling of the races. . . . He says so in the Report he signed," referring to *To Secure These Rights*. "Do you want Negroes to occupy the same hospital rooms with you and your wife and daughters? . . . Negroes using your toilet facilities?" The poster officially came from the Know the Truth Committee, not the Smith campaign, but no one was fooled. The nastiest little piece of work was a photograph of a black soldier dancing with a white woman. Instead of the original white woman's head, Frank Graham's wife's head was crudely imposed on the body. Jesse Helms denied for the first of many times to come that the campaign was racist, demonstrating early his mastery of the southern white circumlocution that substituted for truth. He argued that the flyers and circulars did not come directly from the campaign itself, and anyway, weren't African Americans being racist when they organized black voters for Graham? Despite the denials, Helms personally conceived of many of the dirty tricks and approved almost all of them. Graham lost the runoff primary by a little more than twenty thousand votes. One of his closest supporters blamed Graham's defeat on the fact that the Court's desegregation decisions had "made everyone realize that 'it can happen here.'"[85]

Pauli Murray mourned Graham's loss and thought that voters had "crucified him for his efforts" in civil rights. It had been just the kind of "horrible 'nigger-communist' campaign" that Jonathan Daniels had told

Eleanor Roosevelt he feared. Will Alexander called it the "most villainous use of race propaganda there ever was." The campaign was "so violent and so bitter," Alexander recalled, "that I knew that something would follow very bad, because it opened the flood gates." The defeat broke Graham's heart and ended his lifelong love affair with North Carolina's people. Truman appointed him to the United Nations, where he spent years trying to broker a peace between India and Pakistan in the Kashmir dispute. He took an apartment in New York and shuttled around the world, rarely visiting North Carolina.[86]

Finally, in 1967, a few months after his wife's death in New York, Frank Porter Graham wrote to a friend in Chapel Hill, "I am on my way home." He had been in exile almost two decades. His homecoming was quiet; he spent time with friends and grew increasingly feeble. He died in Chapel Hill in 1972. Several years earlier he and his wife had chosen the words for their joint headstone: "They had faith in youth and youth responded with their best."[87]

Tipping Junius Scales

Junius Scales described himself as "a Pearl Harbor patriot" because he enlisted two days after the Japanese attack. Once the army realized that he was a Communist, it sent him twice to "something like an American Concentration camp," where the ratio of detainees was "about six Nazis to one left-winger." When not in a holding camp for subversives, Scales excelled in a variety of jobs in out-of-the-way places on the home front. The brass never told his immediate superiors about his background, and they were amazed that such a good soldier was doing such menial work. Whenever his commanding officers put him up for promotion, their superiors kicked it back with record speed. Scales's main goal was to get to Europe to fight the Nazis, but he was thwarted at every turn. His mother finally wrote an outraged letter to the adjutant general in 1944, ordering him to send Junius overseas: "He is a thoroughly loyal American . . . there is not reason for him to be under constant surveillance . . . his family antecedents will show loyal participation in American wars as far back as the Indian Wars." Scales finally reached Italy just a week before V-E Day.[88]

Scales returned home to Chapel Hill in January 1946 and immediately tried to figure out why Earl Browder had been removed from leadership of the Communist Political Association the previous June. William Z. Foster replaced Browder and turned the CPA back into the CPUSA. When Scales had departed for Italy, sixty-three thousand people had belonged to the CPA, and 10 percent of them were African American. In February the Party expelled Earl Browder, charging him with abandoning Marxism for reformism and shilling for U.S. imperialism because he had predicted a smooth postwar global economy and "class peace."[89] Scales, an enthusiastic supporter of Browder's, had voted for the formation of the CPA. Now he could not understand how he had made such a mistake. He came to believe that his "big bourgeoisie/landed aristocracy/half-baked intellectual" judgment had "played [him] false." Instead of losing faith in the Party, Scales lost faith in himself. In the post-Browder days, he thought that the CP stood for civil rights, a better quality of life, and, above all, Stalin.[90]

Two events brought Scales back to his roots in the interracial work of the southern Party. A district meeting in Richmond in November 1945 resolved to support a permanent FEPC and reaffirmed the antidiscrimination goals that the Party had pursued for two decades. The highlight of Scales's postwar Communist career arrived in September 1946, when he attended the Southern Negro Youth Congress in Columbia, South Carolina. There Scales met W. E. B. Du Bois and gave a paper arguing that southern graduate schools should desegregate at once. Paul Robeson sang before the integrated audience of hundreds, and Scales got to talk with him afterward. When the Southern Negro Youth Congress elected Scales vice-president—its first white officer—he was humbled and energized. His nagging doubts about the Browder purge retreated, and he remembered why he had become a Communist. The SNYC meeting convinced him that the Party was still in the civil rights vanguard. He also became active in the state branch of the Southern Conference for Human Welfare and joined its executive committee.[91]

Communists had become accustomed to being more open during World War II, and that made it much easier for anti-Communists to find them after the war. In the South the CP continued to act like a political party after Browderism. For example, in 1946 the Virginia Communist Party's voters' guide to bills before the General Assembly would have served the League of Women Voters in good stead.[92] The Carolinas CP district ran an ad in Jonathan Daniels's *News and Observer* calling for "A Program to Win a Better Life for the People of North Carolina." Recruiting through the Daniels family newspaper was a new Communist tactic, one that had the effect of "scaring the pants off a majority of citizens."[93]

The openness of the Communist Party in the South did not mesh well with the growing wave of anti-Communism. While there were fewer Communists in North Carolina in 1946 than there had been in 1931, the Party's more public style made it seem as if suddenly Communists were everywhere.[94] "Angry North Carolina labor leaders . . . unanimously repudiated" the Communist endorsement of unionism. Black ministers in Raleigh disavowed the CP's "Better Life" program as well.[95] In May 1947 a HUAC committee went to Winston-Salem to investigate Communists in Local 22 of the United Tobacco Workers CIO union, which was striking against R. J. Reynolds. "Former union officials" charged that Local 22 was a Communist union, despite the union president's threatening to sue for libel.[96] By July things had reached a boiling point, and the former treasurer of Local 22 identified Junius Scales as a Communist and Chapel Hill as a Communist hotbed. It was one thing for Scales's professors to greet him as "You old Bolshevik!" and another to be named in the press as a Communist.[97]

Despite his mother's "frenzied objections," Scales announced publicly that he was a Communist on October 29, 1947. The CP National Committee had pressured him to do so, and he had already been so open that many in the state suspected that he was a Communist. His main reason for the declaration, however, was to lessen his fellow North Carolinians' fear of Communists. Those who knew him were impressed by his gentleness, and those who did not know him were impressed by his pedigree. "I have been associated with the Communist Party for a number of years," he said. "I hope that I may in a small way dispel some of the dangerous illusions and falsehoods about the Communists which are being used to distract us from the real problems we must solve. As a Southerner," Scales argued, "I am especially glad to belong to the only organization which fights for the full and complete equality of the Negro." He completely misjudged the effect of the declaration. His neighbors and friends, even those who had ribbed him for years about being a "left-winger," now reacted with shock and often outright hostility.[98]

Scales tried his best to continue as a Communist and as a North Carolinian after he became district chairman of the Carolinas in 1948. He went on a radio program to defend civil liberties, sponsored a black man who wanted to attend graduate school at UNC, and tried to organize around postwar inflation issues. He fought against a bill in the North Carolina General Assembly to outlaw the Communist Party by arguing to his fellow citizens that the bill was not "anticommunist"; it was "anti-you."[99]

Nationally, Party leaders faced federal prosecution. Ben Davis and ten other Communists went on trial in New York under a Smith Act provision forbidding "conspiracy to overthrow the Government by force and violence."[100] After he had defended Angelo Herndon and moved to Harlem, Davis had been an open Communist and community leader. He was elected to the New York City Council on the Communist ticket in 1943 and was still serving when he was indicted. Davis had another courtroom in mind when he told the jury in October 1949 why he had become a Communist. Long ago a different jury had turned its backs on Ben Davis and Angelo Herndon during Davis's closing argument. "This case was the turning point of my whole life," Davis testified, recalling how the judge, prosecutor, and jury had treated him. Under cross-examination, the prosecution tried to prove that Davis was lying about how badly he had been treated in Atlanta. Despite his lack of faith in the justice system, when Davis heard the foreman say "guilty," he gasped audibly. He received a five-year prison term and a ten-thousand-dollar fine. The next month, while the case was on appeal, he lost his council seat. Eleven Communists were convicted and went to prison when their bail was revoked in the summer of 1951.[101]

Against a national backdrop of prosecutions, the FBI followed Scales's every move and paid informers to infiltrate the Chapel Hill Party. It responded by ordering Scales to go underground, and he left Chapel Hill on October 6, 1951. Years of intrigue ensued as he shuttled about the South, doing little except conferring with Party leaders, while the FBI played cat and mouse with him. Once when he was visiting Greensboro, FBI agents endlessly circled his mother's house on the winding roads of Hamilton Lakes and cast spotlights across the Scales's front lawn every time they passed. The G-men may have hoped that Scales would crack and come to them, ready to testify against other Communists. They may have just wanted him to know that he was under surveillance. Shadowing Mrs. A. M. Scales was not terribly exciting work. As a courtesy, she began to toot the horn at the federal agent parked in front of her house to wake him up and let him know she was home when she returned from shopping. Junius slipped more deeply underground.[102]

Then, on November 19, 1954, all of his mother's fears came true in the front-page banner headline in her morning paper: FBI NABS JUNIUS SCALES; BAIL IS $100,000. The "Carolinas Red Chief Seized in Tennessee" wore a "flaming red tie" and spoke in a "firm, clear but soft voice" when he told the press that "my activities for the last number of years have been for the good of the United States and in the interests of a peaceful world and democratic country." He had been arrested under the membership clause of Smith Act, which carried a fine of ten thousand dollars and a maximum of ten years in prison for belonging to an organization that advocated the violent overthrow of the government. The case differed from Davis's because Scales was not charged with conspiring, simply with belonging. The trial was to be in Greensboro, Scales's hometown. Three days before Christmas his mother posted bond.[103]

To prove its case, the government had to prove that the Communist Party came under the provisions of the Smith Act as "an organization devoted to the [violent] overthrow of the government." Then it had to prove that Scales, as a member of that party, "was aware of those aims, and acted to expend those aims." Scales was a Communist, his lawyer readily admitted.[104] The prosecution's case rested on an FBI informant, Ralph Clontz, who had been a law student at Duke when Scales was in Chapel Hill. Scales remembered him as "repulsive" and a "phony" and had long suspected him to be an informant. Clontz testified that Scales had argued that a "small militant force had to bring about a change in government by revolution." The press hilariously identified Clontz as a "counterspy." Over two hundred spectators packed the trial each day, but the atmosphere was oddly calm. Scales sat quietly, and the prosecutors never raised their voices. It was all that anyone in town could talk about.[105]

The prosecution's third and last witness was Charles Benson Childs, a "slightly-built, bespectacled, mild-mannered youth," who was majoring in physics at UNC. He had become interested in Communism in high school through an English teacher who told him about the Gastonia strike.

Scales had never realized that Childs was an FBI informant. Childs described a weeklong camp at a member's farm, but it seemed more like a picnic, complete with a cake decorated with a big red star on top, than a training camp for insurgents. While Childs's depiction of his Party experience often did not sound like much fun, he offered no testimony that Scales advocated the overthrow of the government by violence. The prosecution rested.[106]

Her son's "whole idea in joining the Communist Party was to help his fellow man," Junius's mother testified. She said that she had once asked him if he believed that the Communists would violently overthrow the government and he had told her that "it would be just plain silly for a little minority group to try to overthrow the United States." What Junius cared about was not the revolution but the "underdog," she explained. Several witnesses who had promised to confirm that Scales had never advocated violence backed out on the eve of the trial. Two graduate students scheduled to testify for Scales were told by FBI agents that if they did so, the bureau would plant the rumor that they were homosexuals. They weren't homosexuals, but after the threat they weren't witnesses either. An expert on Marxism and two of Scales's UNC professors rounded out the defense, which rested on the day it began.[107]

That evening the jury found him guilty "of advocating violent revolution to overthrow the Government of the United States." The judge refused bail, and Scales was in jail by nine twenty-five the next morning. Scales made a statement at his sentencing the next day. He swore that he was innocent and said, "No jury is competent to convict a man for his ideas. . . . For all the world, this has been like a medieval heresy trial." He would never belong to an organization that advocated violence, he vowed, since "it is foreign to my upbringing by my father and mother, who educated me in a tradition of democracy, honor, and devotion to principle." As he sat down, his mother whispered that she was proud of him and "his father would have been too." Asked by the press why he did not testify on his own behalf, he said, "I was sorely tempted to," but he did not want to have to "name persons as Communists who would suffer as a result." Finally he said, "My party has never advocated force and violence. I have not advocated force and violence." He was truly astonished at his conviction, even more so at his six-year sentence. The editors of the *Greensboro*

Daily News asked rhetorically, "Why aren't all members of the Communist Party indicted?" They should be, if they understood what the Party stood for, the editors concluded. "Scales got what was coming to him."[108]

But one man who covered the trial thought that the reporters present scorned the government informers and that the Communist "conspiracy" in North Carolina resembled the Keystone Kops. It was one of the most "seedy, claptrap, inefficient, bumbling, ham-handed, rank-amateur conspiracies that ever allegedly threatened the peace and security of North Carolina," the reporter concluded. North Carolinians had taken the whole thing seriously, so "we must have been plenty scared. . . . Of what?" he demanded. Finally he posed one of the most important questions of the twentieth century. "Are we . . . taking up the weapons of totalitarianism in order to fight totalitarianism?"[109]

Scales's appeal went all the way to the Supreme Court. While awaiting its decision, he learned of Nikita Khrushchev's exposure of Stalin's crimes, and the news sickened him. Then the Soviets invaded Hungary. With no money and no job prospects, but with enormous legal bills, Scales quit the Party. The Supreme Court reversed his conviction, and he returned to Greensboro to stand trial for a second time in February 1958. His heroic local lawyer, John McNeill Smith, was a moderate community leader in a mainstream law firm.[110]

In his opening remarks, McNeill Smith told the jury that Karl Marx was not on trial. The defendant was Junius Scales, "this boy, one of *our* boys." He argued that they would hear nothing of "rifles, bayonets, bullets, [or] bombs," because Scales had never talked about them. The prosecution's case was very similar to that of the first trial, but this time there were defense witnesses who swore that Scales had never advocated violence. The jury was out eighty minutes before it returned with a guilty verdict and another six-year sentence. The verdict was incomprehensible to Scales and Smith. It is likely that Scales's prominent social position worked against him. Perhaps jurors resented the fact that someone like him, descended from one of the finest families in the state and rich beyond their wildest dreams, would throw away his privilege on Communism. The hometown newspaper approved: "American justice has once again gone its even-tempered way." Scales went to prison on October 2, 1961.[111]

Almost as soon as Scales was imprisoned, liberals began working to get him pardoned. He had repudiated Communism, and the Party hoped he would rot in jail. Within six months, hundreds signed a petition urging President John F. Kennedy to pardon Scales. Frank Porter Graham, C. Vann Woodward, and Paul Green signed, as did the historian John Hope Franklin. A. Philip Randolph and Martin Luther King, Jr., did too. On Christmas Eve 1962 Kennedy commuted Junius Scales's sentence but did not pardon him.[112] Scales got a job working at night as a proofreader for the *New York Times* and ventured back to North Carolina rarely and with great trepidation. In the end he remembered why he joined the Party. He never regretted embracing its goals as he saw them: the defeat of Fascism, workers' rights to organize, full equality for African Americans, and a more equitable economic structure.[113] This boy, one of *our* boys, fought for the underdog.

Turning Max Yergan

"Hello, Max?"

"Yeah."

"I don't know if you've been listening to the radio but the filibuster has stopped."

"It has?"

"Yes, and it stopped because of a secret strategy meeting in which the South poll taxers feel that they have enough votes to defeat the bill."

—FROM A TRANSCRIPT OF A WIRETAPPED
TELEPHONE CALL, MAX YERGAN'S FBI
FILE, JUNE 30, 1945.[114]

After October 19, 1944, FBI agents heard every word that Max Yergan spoke and listened to every breath he took. They stood beside him in men's rooms at railway stations and rode with him on trains and planes. They sauntered down sidewalks together. They relaxed in Reno and snapped photographs of him while he fulfilled his residency requirements and divorced Susie Yergan. They transformed his friends into informers and his trash into intelligence. As his personal and professional lives collided, the FBI was privy to every detail. Yergan had no idea that he was under such extensive surveillance.[115]

J. Edgar Hoover personally directed the spying mission. He had tried to arrest Yergan in March 1943 but been stopped, probably by Attorney General Francis Biddle.[116] The next year Hoover received permission for "technical surveillances on the residence and office of Max Yergan for the purpose of determining the extent of his activities on behalf of the Comintern Apparatus and for the additional purpose of determining the identities of espionage agents." Hoover bolstered his request by telling the attorney general that "estranged wife" Susie Yergan had taken Comintern documents from a lockbox and hidden them, and the "Comintern Apparatus is attempting to determine their location." Susie Yergan apparently threatened Earl Browder with release of the documents, and he tried to dissuade Max from the divorce. When Yergan went ahead, Susie Yergan gave the documents to a "Trotskyite attorney."[117]

FBI surveillance of Yergan yielded mostly trivial information, sometimes interspersed with bursts of nuts-and-bolts work on social activism. For example, after searching Yergan's hotel room in Denver, an agent sent "a lemon as well as a four ounce bottle approximately one-third full" to the lab for tests to determine if "this liquid could possibly be used in the preparation of secret inks." Just as suspicious was an over-the-counter remedy "for 'between the toes' use." The agent explained that "the possibility exists that some of the specimen forwarded may have been used for the same purpose"—that is, making "secret ink."[118] That valuable piece of intelligence went straight to Hoover, along with all of Yergan's telephone conversations with Paul Robeson. While Yergan watched Robeson perform in *Othello* in Detroit, an "informant," whom he apparently knew, remained in his hotel room and copied a "lengthy letter" from Susie Yergan. "Much information relative to their marital life is gained by the reading of this letter," the FBI agent advised Hoover. The agent also reported the results of the laboratory analysis of the liquid and creams he had sampled back in Denver. "Even when mixed with lemon juice," the liquid "was unfit for the preparation of secret ink." The lab did find another use for it, however: "the prevention of fungus infections of the extremities." The agent had sent Yergan's athlete's foot medicine to the lab for analysis.[119] The hundreds of pages that make up Yergan's FBI files read more like Maxwell Smart than like James Bond.

But the incompetence of the FBI agents did not make up for their omnipresence. They conducted around-the-clock surveillance on Yergan at home and away.[120] In 1945 Hoover tried to arrest him for mail fraud because he traveled on a discount railroad pass reserved for clergymen. The FBI could find no record of his ordination despite the fact that he had served as a chaplain in World War I. After a year of dogged pursuit, the agents confronted Yergan with their accusations, and he tried to convince them that he had been ordained in the Congregational Church in 1919, which was the truth.[121]

In addition to facing possible indictment, Yergan faced turmoil in his personal life and uncertainty in his professional life. He was eager to marry Lena Halpern Hedley, a young Jewish woman who was a Marxist and a distinguished physician. The daughter of immigrants from Poland and Russia, she became a chemist after college and then went back to medical school. When they met, she was in her thirties and a published researcher in the Department of Internal Medicine at Yale Medical School. Professionally Yergan had wholeheartedly embraced Browderism and the Communist Political Association. He watched in horror as Foster replaced Browder in June 1945.[122]

Things got a lot worse for Yergan in the next two years. At war's end he was involved in three ventures: publisher of the black newspaper *People's Voice*, director of the Council for African Affairs, and president of the National Negro Congress. In its post-Browder days the CPUSA tightened its discipline. Ever since Yergan had begun working with the Communists in the late 1930s, they had always treated him as a "big fish." During the war the Party gave him incredible latitude. For example, when Adam Clayton Powell's *People's Voice* faced bankruptcy, he went to Ben Davis for help. Davis turned to Yergan, and Yergan turned to the Party, which funneled thousands of dollars through him to keep the newspaper going during the war.[123] After the war and Browder's fall, when Yergan continued to make his own decisions, the CP pulled the rug out from under him.

When the National Negro Congress met in June 1946 for the first time since the war had begun, Yergan called for "unity within the ranks of the Negro people." The NNC had just filed its petition with the United Nations, and it seemed poised to lead the Left against segregation. However, Yergan had found himself marginalized six weeks earlier, when a group had met in Detroit to form the Congress on Civil Rights. Yergan attended, but he was not on the "initiating committee," nor did he become an officer in the organization. Paul Robeson, heretofore Yergan's biggest supporter, was on the initiating committee, along with a lot of liberals, black and white. There were a few Communists present at the planning meeting, but very few.[124]

Yergan wondered what the relationship would be between the Civil Rights Congress and the National Negro Congress, and very slowly he realized that the CPUSA had pulled its support from the NNC. For the next several months he began to find it impossible to get anything done since the NNC's paid staff contradicted his instructions and the board's directions. Yergan got a resolution from his board that ordered the staff to do as he directed. The staffers responded that the "Secretariat of the Communist Party had issued orders to them not to carry out the decisions of the Negro Congress's Board." By the summer of 1947 only the Communist members were showing up for NNC board meetings, and Yergan felt increasingly rebellious under their "dictatorial methods." He told them so. In a show of independence, he fired Doxey Wilkerson from the staff of the *People's Voice* in July, ostensibly for shirking work but probably to get the known Communist out of the office. Yergan seemed to believe that he could retain control of the newspaper that the CP had financed, but the *Daily Worker* began to attack the *People's Voice* and Yergan. Party representatives and their attorneys met with Yergan and told him that they owned the paper, and he responded by threatening to sue them.[125]

In the fall of 1947 the CPUSA tightened control on organizations in which it played a part, the FBI heightened surveillance on them, and HUAC increased its pressure. In September, HUAC reported that the Civil Rights Congress was a "Communist front organization" despite its relatively liberal constituency. In October the Communist Party stepped forward to support the CRC petition for the abolition of HUAC and decided to tie the CRC more closely to the Party. The CRC met the same month in Chicago and called on Truman to sponsor legislation to implement the recommendations advocated in *To Secure These Rights*.[126] The Party decided to merge the National Negro Congress into the Civil Rights Congress formally in November 1947.[127] Yergan left almost at once on a fundraising trip with Paul Robeson for the Council on African Affairs.

As he and Robeson toured North and South Carolina, Yergan let himself relax a little. Everything seemed all right with his hero, Paul, and they talked about the future of the council warmly. But when they returned to New York a few days before Christmas, Robeson told him that "he was troubled by orders he had been told to carry out . . . [that] would make it impossible for him to continue good relations" with Yergan. "I have to tell you, Max," Robeson said, "you will find me getting tougher and rougher but I have to do what I am told to do." Within four weeks Robeson accused Yergan of stealing funds from the Council on African Affairs. In February Yergan tried to get the CAA board to "disavow any Communist or Fascist ties." By March the Communist board members had changed the locks, seized the CAA office, and made Louise Thompson Patterson the director.[128]

Yergan tried to pick up the shards of his life, but every time he reached for them, they shattered further. He began a close relationship with the FBI and told the bureau about everyone he had known in the Communist Party, even as he claimed that he had never joined it himself.[129] Even the gullible FBI agents did not believe that, but they pretended to believe he had been "duped" and had come to them as soon as he realized it. Yergan may have thought that he could get even with his enemies and be done with it, but the FBI made sure that informants were completely in its grip, not simply cheerfully volunteering information when it suited them. "I hope we're not tiring you, Doctor," one agent murmured sympathetically early in the relationship. "No. I'm glad to be of service," Yergan replied. "I am convinced that they are a vicious crowd and that they are a menace to our country."[130]

As he began talking with the FBI, Yergan made the terrible, disgusting mistake of extorting money by mail from a former lover in return for keeping her letters to him private. She paid on two occasions, but when she realized that he would continue to ask for money, she went to the postal authorities, who went to the FBI. Beyond a doubt, Yergan had written the last extortion letter—he had not even bothered to type it—and now only the FBI stood between him and a prison term. The bureau made the charges disappear, and Yergan testified before the federal grand jury in the Whittaker Chambers–Alger Hiss trial.[131] The FBI then helped him get a visa to visit Africa. He also traveled to Berlin to attend the anti-

Communist Congress for Cultural Freedom, which became a sort of CIA speakers' bureau in the 1950s.[132]

It was never going to be over. For years FBI agents talked with Yergan regularly and asked him to testify against every Communist they indicted. In 1954 he appeared before another grand jury in Washington, named names, and, under oath, "denied membership in the Communist Party at any time." Finally, in March 1955, Yergan told the FBI that he no longer wanted to appear as a witness for the government but would continue as an informant. He began to get hazy in his interviews with them; he simply couldn't prove all the allegations he had made in previous interviews, so maybe he wasn't right. When they read his words back to him, he couldn't remember them. His main argument against being a witness was that it would render him ineffective in his new work, convincing Africans that Communism was bad. The FBI told him that he had no choice; he had to testify when they told him to or go to prison. Yergan had denied under oath that he had ever been a Communist, and the Justice Department was building a perjury case against him. Justice could not prosecute Yergan without the FBI's help, and the FBI would not help as long as Yergan continued to testify. The FBI owned Max Yergan.[133]

Yergan thought that representing himself as an African expert would be his best hope for a productive life. He traveled to Africa in 1949, in 1952, and again in 1953 "to warn and advise against communist activities." After his 1953 trip *U.S. News & World Report* conducted a long interview with him that appeared under the title "Africa: Next Goal of Communists." Yergan argued that "Communists exercise a powerful influence in the African National Congress," but they prevented "a workable solution" to the authorities' oppression. Yergan found the South African government "completely justified in its policy of suppressing Communist influence." His interviewer asked, "What is this 'apartheid'?" Yergan told him that it was "an Afrikaans word which means segregation." Yergan asked readers to have a "sympathetic and constructive approach" toward the South African government. "Certainly white South Africa lets itself in for criticism," he observed, "but any person in Europe or America who levels criticism against white South Africa has to ask himself what he would do under similar circumstances. The white population there is dominated by fear—fear of this immediately more numerous nonwhite population."

He proposed some sort of vague "interracial cooperation" that would lead to a "partnership" as a substitute for apartheid.[134]

In the decade after the founding of the United Nations, six hundred million people, almost one-fourth of the global population, gained their independence, and Yergan saw Communists behind every freedom fighter. He reported on Communists in the African National Congress to the State Department. How he identified them was a mystery since during his 1952 trip Nelson Mandela "was struck by the fact that Mr. Yergan made no attempt to meet the Non-European leaders."[135] ANC member Zachary Matthews, Yergan's former protégé who had earned a master's degree at Yale, was devastated by Yergan's behavior. "I resent the suggestion that the African people require Communists to teach them to defend their rights," Matthews said.[136]

If Matthews's criticism stung, Yergan gave no sign. He returned to Africa many times and joined with white U.S. conservatives William F. Buckley, Jr., and L. Brent Bozell to aid rebels against the new independent, pro-Soviet state in the Congo. He joined the American African Affairs Association, which shilled for "four unpopular African White minority regimes" by putting out conciliatory public relations information in the United States. He supported Portuguese rule in Angola.[137]

In 1964 he returned to South Africa, this time to apologize more fully for apartheid. The problem lay not with the South African government but with the "rest of the world," which must "understand separate development more fully than they do now." South Africa deserved "a more honest, objective, and fair judgment." The Union was "in every sense a bright spot on the continent of Africa." As the world came to understand "separate development" better, the light that South Africa shone on the rest of darkest Africa would only get "brighter."[138]

That light failed to penetrate the cell on Robben Island that caged Nelson Mandela. He had served five months of a life sentence when Yergan begged the world to understand apartheid. Yergan had stirred up the anti-Communist hysteria that contributed to Mandela's conviction. At his trial Mandela made it clear that he was not a Communist. "From my reading of Marxist literature and from conversations with Marxists, I have gained the impression that communists regard the parliamentary system of the West as undemocratic and reactionary. But, on the contrary, I am an admirer of such a system," Mandela told the court. "The Magna Carta, the Petition of Rights, and the Bill of Rights are documents which are held in veneration by democrats throughout the world," he said.[139] Mandela had lost everything, but he kept his soul. Yergan had sold his long ago.

Being Pauli Murray

Faced with two Supreme Court decisions ordering graduate schools to desegregate, on March 23, 1951, the Executive Committee of the University of North Carolina voted to consider applications to the graduate and medical schools "without regard to color or race." The trustees approved the resolution the next month, despite dissidents on the board shouting, "If you want to maintain white supremacy, this is your opportunity to do it." Even as the trustees voted to desegregate, they approved a "last-ditch attempt to keep Negroes out of . . . [the] law school," by authorizing an appeal to the Supreme Court of a ruling against the university in an ongoing NAACP case. The Court refused to hear the case, and five black students entered the medical and law schools that fall.[140]

When Pauli Murray heard about the trustees' decision, she phoned Frank Graham in New York to celebrate with him. Then she wrote to Louis Austin in Durham, "This is a great day for people like you, me, [and] Tommie Hocutt."[141] To W. Kerr Scott, the North Carolina governor who, according to Graham, had been a "tower of strength" in the integration fight, she cast herself as a veteran of the struggle: "We who lost the fight, salute you!" And she congratulated Gordon Gray, the university's president, on the decision. Then she claimed herself, her whole self. "You see," Murray told Gray, "my grandmother was Cornelia Smith Fitzgerald, the daughter of Sidney Smith, a product of the law school of the University. . . . She was born in slavery. . . . I rejoice that the people of North Carolina have at last reached the point where they recognize that the grandsons and granddaughters of slaves have a real contribution to make to the great traditions of the University."[142]

Then Murray wrote to the dean of the UNC Law School to ask, "Would you be kind enough to send me your latest catalogue?" Having earned her law degree at Howard and her master of laws at UCLA, Murray now proposed to earn a doctorate of laws at UNC. However, she had already surpassed the level of legal education that North Carolina could offer to anyone. The dean responded that the University of North Carolina did not offer graduate work in law.[143]

When the Supreme Court outlawed racial segregation in the public schools on May 17, 1954, Pauli Murray was deeply engaged in writing the family history that became *Proud Shoes*. The first person she thought of when she heard the news was her grandfather Robert Fitzgerald, who had come south to teach the freedpeople and stayed after he married her grandmother Cornelia Smith. Then she thought of her aunts, one of whom had become her adoptive mother, Pauline Dame. She remembered that they "had borne the brunt of enforced segregation in impoverished Negro Schools for more than half a century." Aunt Sally and Aunt Pauline now lived with her in Brooklyn.[144]

Murray realized that her application to UNC in 1938 had contributed to the desegregation of public education, even though the NAACP never accepted her case. She was "part of a tradition of continuous struggle, lasting nearly twenty years, to open the doors of the state university to Negroes." She saw her effort as one link in a chain that had proved stronger than the bounds of segregation. "Each new attempt was linked with a previous effort," Murray thought. "Once begun, this debate would not be silenced until the system of enforced segregation was outlawed everywhere in the land."[145]

Two weeks after the *Brown* decision, the *New York Times* printed a very long and eloquent letter. "We have read every word of the *Times* carrying news and comments on the recent Supreme Court decision outlawing segregation in the public schools," signatories "Pauline Fitzgerald Dame (Aged 83) and Sarah A. Fitzgerald Small (Aged 76)" wrote. "We have rejoiced to see this day come at last." Together they had "seventy-five years in the classroom in every type of Negro school," and they had some advice for the Supreme Court as it decided how to carry out desegregation. "Negro teachers will play a significant role in the integration of the Southern school systems," they declared. Without the help of the Negro teacher, the Supreme Court decision would fail. "She has had to impart knowledge and civic pride to the Negro child . . . she has had to give the child a sense of self-confidence and feeling of worth against almost overwhelming odds," they advised. They predicted that the "change-over" would be smooth and "that white citizens will be surprised and pleased at the readiness of Negro children for nonsegregated education." It had been their life's work and that of thousands of other black teachers. "There is no more devoted or dedicated citizen in the United States than the Negro teacher of the South," the Fitzgerald sisters wrote. Their day had come at last; now they could rest.[146]

Pauli Murray lived a life filled to the brim in the following decades, working at Adlai Stevenson's law firm and finding a loving partner. She became a law professor in Ghana and earned a doctorate of law at Yale. She served on the Committee on Civil and Political Rights of the President's Commission on Women in 1962 and was a founding member of the National Organization for Women. When the March on Washington finally marched in August 28, 1963, Murray was furious at her old friend A. Philip Randolph for accepting an invitation to speak at the all-male National Press Club. She marched, of course, and celebrated by going to a downtown restaurant with a friend who had been in the Howard sit-ins. Murray described the march as a cross between "a jubilee and Judgment Day."[147]

One can only imagine how Randolph felt, reflecting back on his life from the days of the *Messenger* in World War I to the Brotherhood of Sleeping Car Porters to the March on Washington Movement to his demand that Harry S. Truman desegregate the armed forces. Journalist Murray Kempton had written a few weeks earlier: "It is hard to make anyone who has never met him believe that A. Philip Randolph must be the greatest man who has lived in the U.S. in this century. But it is harder yet to make anyone who has ever known him believe anything else."[148]

The next year Congress passed the Civil Rights Act of 1964, which outlawed discrimination based on race, color, religion, national origin, or sex in public accommodations, public facilities, and public education and in programs that received federal aid. It established the Equal Employment Opportunity Commission (EEOC) as its enforcement arm. When the EEOC dragged its feet in pursuing sex discrimination claims, covered in Title VII of the act, Pauli Murray coauthored a law review article to urge them along, "Jane Crow and the Law: Sex Discrimination and the Law." She asserted that "the rights of women and the rights of Negroes are only different phases of the fundamental and indivisible issue of human rights."[149]

When Murray moved to Washington in 1966 to work as a consultant to the EEOC, it seemed as if she had finally reached a position of influence and power, after years of working from the margins. EEOC chairman Stephen N. Shulman became enthusiastic about the possibility of Pauli Murray's becoming general counsel of the organization in 1967. He told her that he was putting her name up to the White House, as required on all high-profile appointments. Shortly thereafter Shulman got a call from Marvin Watson, Lyndon Johnson's chief of staff. The White House could not approve Murray's appointment, Watson told Shulman, because she had been a Communist. If the fledgling EEOC appointed a general counsel who had been a Communist, it would be impossible to defend itself from segregationist charges that integration of the workforce was a Communist plot. Shulman had no choice. He withdrew her name and told Murray she could not have the job, but he did not tell her the reason.[150] Despite the fact that she had assiduously avoided Communists since 1939, her brief stint as a Lovestonite in the mid-1930s had cost her the job of her dreams.

The news devastated Murray, and she realized that something in her past would always stand in her way. She guessed that it was her membership in the Communist Party Opposition. "Any thought of a government career is finished," she rightly concluded, and she spent days in agony. "The immensity of my hurt almost overwhelms me," and she confessed to some "suppressed rage" mingled with that hurt. She tried to reconcile her past and her present: "When I was younger I made choices which were laden with emotion and in which I could not foresee the outcome. I had few expectations or hopes of ever overcoming the obstacles which surrounded me. A point in time came where I did have hope, and I tried to overcome past mistakes of judgment. It seems that I have gone as far as I could go." She couldn't start over because it seemed that "by now a new generation is almost completely in control." In her despair she felt "more and more like a has-been." She prayed that "something will come along to lift my spirits and make me feel creative once more."[151]

In June 1973 something extraordinary came along when she entered the General Theological Seminary in New York "as a special student." Murray joined the movement within the Episcopal Church to ordain women as priests, but she had no way of knowing if this, her final civil rights movement, would succeed. She was sixty-three years old when she took her leap of faith. During the three years that Murray attended seminary, the Episcopal General Convention thrice rejected the ordination of women. When the convention met in September 1976, she had just been graduated, and she was sixty-six years old, and she was tired. She did not think she could stand "the possibility of still another rejection in my life," so she stayed home in New York and prayed, rather than travel to Minneapolis to see the convention reject women's ordination once again. She was alone when she got the news that the General Convention had voted to ordain women.[152]

A few minutes later she got a phone call from Minneapolis from the Reverend Peter James Lee, the rector of the Chapel of the Cross in Chapel Hill, North Carolina. "I want to invite you to celebrate your first Holy Eucharist as a priest at the Chapel of the Cross," Lee told Murray. The Chapel of the Cross, on the campus of the University of North Carolina, was the church in which her black and white ancestors had worshiped. Murray was ordained on January 8, 1977, at the Washington Cathedral.[153]

Six weeks later Murray held her grandmother Cornelia Smith Fitzgerald's Bible as she stepped up to the front of the chapel. She marked her scripture reading with a bookmark of dried flowers from the bouquet that Eleanor Roosevelt had given her for her law school graduation. Murray took a long look at the balcony where her great-grandmother Harriet and her grandmother Cornelia had sat as slaves. As she began her sermon, she gripped a lectern engraved with her great-aunt Mary Smith's name. The congregation was riveted as Murray preached. Never one to miss an opportunity to score a political point, Murray told her white and black congregants to pressure the North Carolina General Assembly to ratify the pending Equal Rights Amendment. She concluded: "The good news today in our small corner of the planet is that the South is rising out of its own ashes, out of redemptive suffering and is becoming purified. Deep in our hearts, we believe that the American South will lead the way to the renewal of the moral and spiritual strength and to a sense of mission." To Murray, it was as if "all of the strands of my life had come together."[154]

When asked in the late 1970s about her struggles, Murray looked back on her one-woman civil rights movement with satisfaction. "In not a single one of these little campaigns was I victorious," she recalled. "In each case, I personally failed, but I have lived to see the thesis upon which I was operating vindicated," she said. She smiled. "I've lived to see my lost causes found."[155]

A century earlier Murray's grandfather Robert Fitzgerald had written in his diary, "The past is the key of the present and the mirror of the future."[156] Murray knew that Americans share an interracial past, filled with violence and hatred, balanced by brave action and love, a past where one person, determined and courageous enough to do what is right, could change the present. Her life suggests that we should analyze not simply the victories but also the failures that preceded them. In the past, individual protest worked alongside legal strategy, political ideology, and group mobilization to unlock the present. Those who defied Dixie proved that democracy is a debate, not a set of rules. Our responsibility to freedom is to challenge its limitations whenever and wherever we encounter them. Only then will we live to see our "lost causes found."

ACKNOWLEDGMENTS

I watched the aftermath of the 2000 election while trudging on a tread-mill in Moscow's beautiful Hotel National. In the early-morning hours that jet lag bequeaths, I divided my attention between the scene outside, spitting snow enveloping the Kremlin, and that on the screen, caustic confusion enveloping Florida. After watching an improbable series of political events unfold on CNN, in the archives I pored over the proof of an equally improbable series of political events that had taken place in the 1920s and 1930s. I tracked Communists entering the South and Southerners embracing Communism. Now, many miles later, not all by treadmill, all politics seem improbable.

It began over dinner in Melbourne, Australia, in 1997, when Robert W. Cherney told me that the Russian State Archive of Socio-Political History (RGASPI) was packed with information on the Communist Party in the South. John Earl Haynes at the Library of Congress, David Brandenberger, and J. Arch Getty were incredibly helpful as I planned my trip to Moscow. Sergei Zhuravlev graciously shared information on the first American-born black Communist, Lovett Fort-Whiteman. But it was an undergraduate student in my New South class, intrepid Yalie Laura Kennington from Durham, North Carolina, who dared me to go to Moscow, figured out how to get both of us there, and stiffened my resolve when countless obstacles arose. She and I worked together in RGASPI with the invaluable help of Ludmilla Selivanova, our translator and researcher, and our research assistant/punk rocker/menu reader/Russian speaker Darryl Kucera, whom Laura met at an airport bar in Florida and brought along. It was a great team in the archives, and we had a great time.

Defying Dixie uses material from four continents, twenty cities, thirty-nine interviews, and eighty-seven collections, some of it gathered with the help of research assistants. I wasn't lucky enough to visit South Africa, but Deborah Dinner and Dalia Hochman researched in Johannesburg and Cape Town when they were Yale undergraduates. Today both are completing their doctorates.

Indeed, most of my students, undergraduate and graduate, grew up with this book. Sarah Jane Mathieu helped on Haiti. Adriane Lentz-Smith, Katherine Charron, Caitlin Crowell, Tammy Ingram, Jason Ward, Alison Greene, Claire Nee Nelson, Quiana Robinson, and Gretchen Boger visited out-of-town archives and pieced together far-flung clues. Garry Reeder, Elizabeth Hardy, Linnea Duvall, Erin Wood, Jay Driskell, Kendra Mack, and Sarah Coleman worked with me in the fabulous African American collections at the Beinecke Library at Yale. Christopher Nichols, now finishing his doctorate at the University of Virginia, repeatedly found Lovett Fort-Whiteman's tracks, and Bruce Baker helped with the *Southern Worker*. Andy Horowitz ran the New Haven Oral History Project with a steady hand and graciously managed his work around mine. Samuel Schaffer is a marvelous editor and insightful scholar. He also redeemed my footnotes, thereby maintaining (or establishing) my sanity. Stephen Prince conducted the great photo search at Yale; Josie Rodberg joined him in New York and Boston, while Tammy Ingram covered Atlanta. Josie worked on *Defying Dixie* as an undergraduate, as a history teacher in New York, and finally in Boston as she began her graduate studies in history at Harvard. Robin Morris worked on my first book as an undergraduate student in North Carolina in 1995 and mopped up footnotes for *Defying Dixie* as a graduate student at Yale in 2006. Anita Seth translated Russian, Joshua Kronen translated German, and Emmerentia van Rensburg, in South Africa, translated Dutch. All along the way, research funding from Yale University expanded the scope of this project. I got by with more than a *little* help from my friends. My copying costs boggle the mind.

Fellow scholars supported me as well, often from their works in progress, a truly generous gesture. Katie Scharf allowed me to copy her research on Charles S. Johnson from the Fisk Archives. Robert Erik Bruce shared his thesis on the Smith Act. Kip Kosek gave me letters on Max Yergan from the Kirby Page Collection in California. John Salmond gave me a taped interview with Sophie Melvin Gerson and was gracious in many other ways. David Anthony, Max Yergan's biographer, was especially cordial and helpful. James Cobb shared enthusiasm and letters from the Glenn Rainey Collection. Anne Scott shared my absorption with Pauli Murray and saved me from numerous errors, while moving me forward. She is someone I cherish.

Those who read the book in draft contributed to argument, structure, and narrative. Some read chapters; others read the entire manuscript. The list of readers looks inordinately long, and each of them made it a better book. Thanks to Henry Turner, Eric Foner, Steve Forman, Jane Dailey, David Godshalk, Skip Stout, Bob Korstad, James Barrett, David Montgomery, William McKee Evans, Oscar Berland, Karen Leathem, Robert Korstad, Jed Shugerman, David Cecelksi, Anne Firor Scott, Stephen Kantrowitz, Ben Kiernan, Nell Irvin Painter, Jacquelyn Dowd Hall, Bryant Simon, Tim Tyson, Adriane Lentz-Smith, and Katherine Charron. A few of these people labored over every word; some, like Jim Barrett, were kind enough to read sections as specialists. Jacquelyn forced me to be fair, Bryant impressed upon me the importance of narrative thrust, and Steve Kantrowitz forced me to argue more clearly. Tim read last, lending me gorgeous turns of phrase, bucking me up, and tearing out paragraphs in a last, painful round of cuts. Tammy Ingram, Jane Dailey, Heather Williams, and Crystal Feimster stood behind me all the way. Kat and Adriane walk beside me, literally and metaphorically. Ben Kiernan edited gracefully and made me believe in the book's importance, chapter draft by chapter draft. These readers did not just shape the work; they shaped the author too. The standard academic conventions don't begin to describe their role in this project. *Collegiality* is too tepid a word to describe their largess, and *gratitude* doesn't begin to convey my recognition of their work.

My debt to other historians' works is staggering as well. I have tried to give credit in the notes, less discursively than I would have liked, given space considerations. I have leaned heavily on many existing historiographies—for example, of Communism, of southern labor history, of civil rights law—and I hope I have done them justice in my narrative. There are foundational books without which I could not have found a starting point for my own narrative and arguments: for example, Robin D. G. Kelley's *Hammer and Hoe* and Nell Irvin Painter's account of a black

Communist, *The Narrative of Hosea Hudson: His Life as a Negro Communist in the South.* Mark Solomon's *The Cry Was Unity,* the history of black Communists and Communism and blacks, is encyclopedic; without it, I could never have navigated RGASPI. Mark Naison's *Communists in Harlem during the Depression* furnished the background for black Southerners up north. Theodore Draper's *The Roots of American Communism* sorts out an incredibly complicated situation. Harvey Klehr and John Earl Haynes have written a helpful short history of the CPUSA, *The American Communist Party: Storming Heaven Itself.*

It would have been impossible to understand the Left in the South without the extensive work that exists on white southern liberals and others who challenged Jim Crow. Jacquelyn Dowd Hall's *Revolt against Chivalry* opened up the contested South for me. John Egerton's *Speak Now against the Day* brought to light the white Southerners who became liberal New Dealers, some of whom associated with the southern Popular Front. Patricia Sullivan's *Days of Hope* mapped connections between the federal government and many of the lesser-known activists who populate these pages. Gerald Horne's work on Ben Davis and black Communists was invaluable. Legal histories, especially Michael Klarman's *From Jim Crow to Civil Rights,* enabled me to sort out what the law was, even when white Southerners resolved not to follow it.

The burgeoning field of southern labor history, especially Robert Rogers Korstad's *Civil Rights Unionism,* provided a rich backdrop for the connections between labor rights and civil rights at the same time that it provided a compelling narrative from the workers' point of view. And of course the work of historians who have long been working on black civil rights before the 1950s, from Harvard Sitkoff to Steve Lawson to Timothy Tyson, repeatedly directed me to go hunting where the ducks were.

Strong books on certain key events enabled me to incorporate them into my narrative without additional years of research. John Salmond's account on the Gastonia strike and Dan Carter's and James Goodman's works on Scottsboro are invaluable. Charles H. Martin's *The Angelo Herndon Case and Southern Justice* and Richard B. Sherman's *The Case of Odell Waller and Virginia Justice* both are polished jewels.

I owe a debt of gratitude to audiences at the University of Pennsylvania, the Miller Center at the University of Virginia, Princeton University,

Columbia University, Yale University, and the National Humanities Center. A special thanks to John Mason of the University of Virginia, who listened well. Yale has been unbelievably generous to me, and my colleagues' support extraordinary. I owe them a great deal, especially Jon Butler and Robin Winks, who believed in this book. I wish he could have seen it. Charles Johnson deftly supplied the "defying" part of *Defying Dixie*. My ever-patient editor, Steve Forman, has borne with me for a decade, and this is a better, and shorter, book because of him. My agent, Andrew Wylie, is amazing, and I am grateful to be his client.

Yale University's Morse Fellowship enabled me to start this project, and Yale's Griswold Fellowship funded my Moscow research. Along the way I received a John Simon Guggenheim Fellowship, a fellowship from the Radcliffe Institute for Advanced Study at Harvard University, an Archie K. Davis Research Grant from the North Caroliniana Society, and a visiting fellowship from the University of Melbourne in Australia. I could not have completed the book without the great good fortune and enormous honor of holding the John Hope Franklin Senior Fellowship at the National Humanities Center in 2006–2007. Kent Mullikin and Lois Whittington were especially helpful. Karen Carroll taught me many tricks as she painstakingly abbreviated the notes, and she stiffened my spine as I drooped during the last mile.

Jacquelyn Hall's example teaches me to embrace the responsibility that comes with being a historian. *Defying Dixie* relies heavily on interviews that she conducted or facilitated in the 1970s. She has built an invaluable resource in the Southern Oral History Program that will shape the writing of southern history for generations to come. Her fairness and rigor, both as ferocious reader and as abstract inspiration, made this a much better book. From conception to execution, *Defying Dixie* has benefited from her articles and book in progress on Katherine and Grace Lumpkin and the Southern Left and her articulation of a long civil rights movement. We have approached from different directions to arrive on the common ground of a southern Popular Front. Hall's forthcoming book focuses on writers and intellectuals and emphasizes how labor and gender interacted with race among those who would reform the South, while I have focused on those who put the overthrow of segregation first. These categories are not clean-cut, and people in both books were in conversation with one another when they lived. Our complementary and contrasting approaches to the Left in the first half of the twentieth century demonstrate the vibrancy and complexity of the South and Southerners, at home and abroad.

Defying Dixie also reflects the lessons that Nell Painter taught me, the license she gave me, and the model she provided to turn southern history inside out and retell it with African American history at the core of the story. Her early glimpse of a radical South illuminated my quest.

I knew and loved two people who appear in these pages: C. Vann Woodward and Junius Scales. I talked with both of them many times about the 1930s and 1940s, but I made a decision not to interview them for this project. When I write about them, I rely on information available to every researcher. Certainly, my conversations with Vann Woodward helped shape *Defying Dixie*, but more important, we had a ball together. I loved his outrage and stubbornness as much as I loved his fierce intellect. He died in 1999. I came to know Junius Scales while I was writing *Gender and Jim Crow* and corresponded with, telephoned, and met him at conferences throughout most of the 1990s. By the time that I realized that I was writing about southern Communists, I had received a letter he had dictated to his daughter Barbara saying that he had Alzheimer's disease and would no longer be able to correspond or travel. He was one of the dearest and most idealistic people I have ever known. He died in 2002.

Now comes the point at which the author laments the extraordinary amount of time that it took to write the book and the hours spent away from his or her family. As you might surmise from the cast of thousands of research assistants, this book took a very long time to write. I began *Defying Dixie* the year that Ben Kiernan and I blended our families. Miles was five, Derry was ten, and Mia-lia was thirteen. In the fall of 2007, Miles was fifteen, Derry twenty, and Mia-lia twenty-three. On the one hand, if I recall that decade through the haze of twenty-five hundred footnotes, it seems like a very long time. On the other hand, it seems very short when I remember it through the haze of boys running up and down countless playing fields, or through the glow of ten sweet potato casseroles with marshmallows ablaze. When I recall weaving together its narrative strands, it feels like forever, but when I recall weaving together our families, it feels like yesterday.

When I think of my family, the very long time that it took to write this book could never have been long enough. Beautiful and funny Mia-lia has become my wise rock. Writer Derry keeps me going with cooking and humor, and we became comrades over our last, phat summer. Miles is a great gift, a leap of faith rewarded a million times over. I can't imagine how impoverished life would be without his wry humor and sweet temperament. And every day Ben makes me better than I ever hoped to be.

Glenda Gilmore
Chapel Hill, N.C.
November 2006

NOTES

Unless otherwise indicated or made apparent by context or speaker citations, the source of a quotation is listed first in a note with multiple sources. The titles of newspaper articles and the titles of many individual archival documents have been shortened.

INTRODUCTION

1. Hughes, "Sunset in Dixie."
2. Lawson, *Civil Rights Crossroads*, 11. Extensive historiography follows in chapter notes.
3. De Jong, *Different Day*, 1.
4. Kluger, *Simple Justice*.
5. J. D. Hall, "Long Civil Rights Movement"; Chafe et al., ed., *Remembering*.
6. Scales and Nickson, *Cause at Heart*, 66–67.
7. The term *insurgent South* is Lawrence Goodwyn's, by way of Timothy Tyson to Katherine Charron to me.
8. Pfeffer, *Randolph*; Kornweibel, *No Crystal Stair*.
9. J. D. Hall, "Long Civil Rights Movement," 1251.
10. For example, Dudziak, *Cold War Civil Rights*.
11. J. A. Miller, S. D. Pennybacker, and E. Rosenhaft, "Mother Ada Wright."
12. Marable, *Race, Reform, and Rebellion*, 18, 13–39; Sullivan, *Days of Hope*; Korstad, *Civil Rights Unionism*; Horne, "Who Lost?"; Von Eschen, "Challenging"; J. D. Hall, " 'You Must Remember This' "; J. D. Hall, "Open Secrets."
13. "Awakenings," episode 2, *Eyes on the Prize*. On *Brown*, see Balkin, ed.,*"Brown vs. Board of Education"*; Klarman, *"Brown."*
14. P. Murray, *Song*, 128.
15. IPM/Mc, 3.

CHAPTER 1: JIM CROW MEETS KARL MARX

1. Woodward, *Strange Career*; Kousser, *Shaping*; Perman, *Struggle for Mastery*; Gilmore, *Gender and Jim Crow*; Feldman, *Disfranchisement Myth*.

2. Grossman, *Land of Hope*; Marks, *Farewell*; Harrison, ed., *Black Exodus*.

3. Du Bois, "Propaganda," 397; Tindall, *Emergence*, 143–50; Colson, "Confederate-Americanism," 10; McWilliams, *New South Faces*, 89.

4. Colson, "Confederate-Americanism," 10. See McWilliams, *New South Faces*, 92–93; Williamson, *Crucible of Race*, 364–65; Schaffer, "Avoiding Friction," 45–52; Cooper, *Warrior and the Priest*, 210–11, 230–32; Neu, "Woodrow Wilson," 248–55.

5. J. S. Rosenberg, "For Democracy," 592–625; Keith, *Rich Man's War*; Du Bois, "Propaganda," 403; Lentz-Smith, "Great War for Civil Rights."

6. "American Attempt to Plant Race-Poison," 559; "League for Defence of the Negro Race," Sept. 29, 1930, fond 495, opis 155, delo 87, RGASPI. A fond is a record group, an opis is a sub-record group, and a delo is a file. Hereafter I use the system adopted by American researchers in RGASPI—for example, 495/155/87. I include page numbers in notes when available and clear.

7. Briggs, "Fighting Savage Hun," 3; Du Bois, "We Return Fighting," 14; J. S. Rosenberg, *How Far?*, 70–71.

8. Dykeman and Stokely, *Seeds*, 56–57.

9. Tuttle, *Race Riot*; "What the South Thinks," 17–18; On Elaine, see Woodruff, *American Congo*, 83–109; Stockley, *Blood in Their Eyes*; Cortner, *Mob Intent*; K. Taylor, "'We Have Just Begun,'" 265–84.

10. Sen. James K. Vardaman of Mississippi, quoted in M. Ellis, *Race, War, and Surveillance*, 222; Tindall, *Emergence*, 151.

11. Sosna, *In Search*, 20–27, quot. 26; "Southwide Movement," *N&O*, March 6, 1921; Dykeman and Stokely, *Seeds*, 52–76; J. D. Hall, *Revolt against Chivalry*; Godshalk, *Veiled Visions*.

12. P. E. Baker, *Negro-White Adjustment*; "Repairers of the Breach," ser. 1, f7, b9, SEPC; "Some Recent Trends," r4, 61, CIC.

13. "Will W. Alexander and the South," 164–65; Tindall, *Emergence*, 175–82.

14. IAR/S, 61–62; Sosna, *In Search*, 24–26.

15. Tindall, "Significance," 285–307; Kneebone, *Southern Liberal Journalists*, 86–88; M. O'Brien, *Idea*, 32–36; Brazil, *Odum*, 72–123; Sosna, *In Search*, 43.

16. Brazil, *Odum*, 183; G. B. Johnson and G. G. Johnson, *Research in Service*, 3–5; Tindall, *Emergence*, 283; Singal, *War Within*, 151; Dykeman and Stokely, *Seeds*, 282; Sosna, *In Search*, 29, 51.

17. IRV, 65; M. O'Brien, *Idea*, 40–44; Singal, *War Within*, 115–52. On Odum and the primitive, see Sanders, *Folklore Odyssey*, x.

18. Quoted in P. Murray, *Song*, 8.

19. Odum, *Social and Mental Traits of the Negro*, quoted in Brazil, *Odum*, 141; Sosna, *In Search*, 44–45.

20. The Nazi appropriation of *Volkerpsychologie* is debated. M. O'Brien, *Idea*, 34–35; Brock, "Was Wundt a 'Nazi'?" 205–23. Brazil, *Odum*, 123, discounts Wundt's influence on Odum; IRV, 66, upholds it.

21. Odum, "Epic," 419–21; Odum, "Notes," f652, ser. 2.2, HWO; M. O'Brien, *Idea*, 65–69.

22. Stoddard, *Rising Tide*.

23. "Harding at Birmingham"; "Klan Views Avowed," both in *NYT*, Apr. 13, 1923, 20; Tindall, *Emergence*, 167.

24. "No Segregation!" *NYAN*, March 28, 1928, in Scrapbook, Political Campaign, 1928, JWJ.

25. Redpath, *L'Ouverture*, iii, vi, 364; D. B. Davis, *Slavery*, 115–16.

26. Schmidt, *United States Occupation*, 48; Logan, *Haiti and the Dominican Republic*; Nicholls, *From Dessalines to Duvalier*; Adams, "Intervention," 45–56; Maclean, "'They Didn't Speak,'" 44–55; Suggs, "African American Press," 33–45; Plummer, *Haiti and the Great Powers*; Renda, *Taking Haiti*, 10–181.

27. "Haitian Memorial"; Du Bois, "Haiti," 466; "Giving Daniels the Lie." On Daniels, see Gilmore, *Gender and Jim Crow*, ch. 3; Morrison, *Josephus Daniels*.

28. Daniels, *Cabinet Diaries*, 331.

29. Gruening, "Haiti," 836–45; Douglas, "Occupation of Haiti I," 228–58; Douglas, "Occupation of Haiti II," 368–96; Renda, *Taking Haiti*.

30. Hughes, "White Shadows," 157; Seligmann, "Conquest of Haiti," 35–36; "American Kultur," 12–14; Daniels, *Cabinet Diaries*, 332.

31. Quoted in Schmidt, *United States Occupation*, 111; Douglas, "Occupation of Haiti II," 380–82, 388.

32. Typescript, Haiti [n.d., 1924?], 495/155/43, RGASPI; Douglas, "Occupation of Haiti II," 376–77.

33. Jean G. Lamothe to Editor, *CD*, May 10, 1923, in f5, b3, RSC; G. W. Brown, "Haiti," 134–52; Pamphile, "Policy-Making," 102–05; Don Glassman, "Our Marines," *NYW*(?), March 1930, in Scrapbook Haiti, 1930—Sept.–March, JWJ.

34. "Haiti's Masses," in Scrapbook 1930—Sept.–March, JWJ.

35. "L'Américain et Nos Ecoles," March 14, 1928, 1, and "Notre Lycée," July 9, 1928, 6, both in *Le Petit Impartial*; "Organe officiel de la Ligue de la Jeunesse Patriote Haïtienne," *Le Petit Impartial*, Apr. 18, 1928.

36. "Haiti's Masses," in Scrapbook 1930—Sept.–March, JWJ; Pamphile, "Policy-Making," 102–05; "Economic and Social Background," March 24, 1930, 495/155/87, 73, RGASPI; "Meeting of the National Negro Department," June 11, 1929, f515, r130, d1685, 31, and letter from Haiti, Nov. 10, 1929, f515, r130, d1688, 29, both in CPUSA; Fort-Whiteman to Comrade Lozovsky, Dec. 23, 1929, 524/7/485, and Anglo-American Secretariat, Jan. 1, 1930, 1, 495/72/91, 52, both in RGASPI; Fowler, *Knot in the Thread*, 141–56, 175.

37. "Haiti," [*Messenger*]; "Haiti Is America's India," 418; "Haitian Memorial," 209; "Haiti," *Crisis*; "Haiti: What We Are Really Doing There," 125–27; J. M. Turner, *Caribbean Crusaders*, 222–23.

38. Pamphile, "NAACP," 91–100; Gibbs, "James Weldon Johnson," 329–47; Plummer, "Afro-American Response," 135–43; Logan, "James Weldon Johnson," 396–402. See Haitian/Johnson correspondence, f180–87, b8, JWJ; J. W. Johnson, "Self-Determining Haiti."

39. Du Bois, review of Balch, *Occupied Haiti*, *NYAN*, Aug. 24, 1927, r84, WEBDB; Balch, ed., *Occupied Haiti*.

40. Owen, "South's Triumph!" 386. See also Briggs, "Klu [*sic*] Klux Klan," 971; Tindall, *Emergence*, 186–96.

41. "Canada Also Stirred," *NYT*, Apr. 6, 1924, 20; "Klan Organizers," *NYT*, May 4, 1924, pt. 2, 7; Mathieu, "Jim Crow Rides."

42. The would-be coup leader was Gen. Carlos García Vélez. "Cubans Here Assist," *NYT*, Apr. 2, 1924, 32; "Race Riot at Havana," *CNC*, Jan. 4, 1910; Urrutia, "Racial Prejudice," 473–82; "Mexico City Editor Seized," *NYT*, Aug. 28, 1923, 19; "Report 1,000 in New Zealand Klan," *NYT*, Aug. 28, 1923, 19.

43. "Japan on American Lynching."

44. "India Speaks."

45. Chalmers, *Hooded Americanism* dismisses foreign chapters as inconsequential (279–80). See also Rice, *Ku Klux Klan*, 4–84; Goldberg, "Unmasking," 32–48; Rhomberg, "White Nativism," 39–55; Lay, *Invisible Empire*; Sher, *White Hoods*; Blee, *Women of the Klan.*

46. Mathieu, "Jim Crow Rides"; Lentz-Smith, "Great War for Civil Rights"; "American Attempt to Plant Race-Poison in France," 559.

47. Rogers, "Negro's Reception," 320.

48. Cunard, "Colour Bar," 342–45; Ademola, "Colour Bar Notoriety," 346–47.

49. "London Is Aroused," *NYT*, Nov. 17, 1929; "London Hotels," in Scrapbook 1929–1930, JWJ.

50. White, "Color Line," 331.

51. G. Hutchinson, *Harlem Renaissance*, 184–85, 193–248; Smethurst, *New Red Negro*; Favor, *Authentic Blackness*; D. L. Lewis, *When Harlem Was in Vogue*; Huggins, *Harlem Renaissance*; A. Douglas, *Terrible Honesty*. On performance, see Rogin, " 'Democracy and Burnt Cork' "; Lott, *Love and Theft.*

52. J. T. Kirby, *Media-Made Dixie*, 66–70.

53. Paul Green to Nell Battle Lewis, March 16, 1927, repr. in Avery, ed., *Southern Life*, 135–36; Paul Green to Jay Broadus Hubbell, Nov. 15, 1924, f Go-L, b4, JBH; Edmonds, "Some Reflections," 303–05; J. W. Johnson, *Black Manhattan*, 207–08; J. H. Roper, *Green*, 93–109; Tindall, *Emergence*, 305.

54. Hughes, *I Wonder*, 70; "Pulitizer Laurels," in f83A, b1B; "Paul Green's Thoughtful Plays," f30, b1B, both in PG; Joyner, "Julia Peterkin," *Encyclopedia of Southern Culture*, 1585–86; Tindall, *Emergence*, 306–09; Peterkin/Green correspondence in f46, b1B, PG. On southern literature, see Singal, *War Within*; R. H. King, *Southern Renaissance*; R. Gray, *Literature of Memory*; A. G. Jones, *Tomorrow*; M. O'Brien, *Idea.*

55. "Negro Mystery," *NYT*, Oct. 16, 1927, in Scrapbook, Music-Art, Sept. 1927–July 1928, JWJ; "Porgy"; Playbill, f51, b3, DW/HU.

56. Renda, *Taking Haiti*, 184–88, 196–212; Carby, *Race Men*, 78–80; "Riots Feared," *NYAm*, March 18, 1924, in Scrapbook, "Theatre Clippings, 1925–1930," JWJ.

57. I. Fisher, "Negro," 65; "Green Pastures," 35–37; Nolan, "Marc Connelly's 'Divine Comedy,' " 216–24.

58. Heywood Broun, "It Seems to Me," *NYTel*, Feb. 28, 1930, Robert Benchley, *New Yorker*, March 8, 1930, and Alexander Woollcott, "Shouts and Murmurs," *New Yorker*, March 22, 1930, all in Scrapbook "Green Pastures," JWJ.

59. Edmonds, "Some Reflections," 304; R. Matthews, "Negro Theatre," 312.

60. S. A. Brown, "Negro Character," 179.

61. S. Young, "Negro Material," 331; Pilkington, "Stark Young," 903–04.

62. "Nigger Heaven—Not in Harlem," *NYW*, March 23, 1930, in Scrapbook "Green Pastures," JWJ. Emphasis added.

63. "Exodus from Dixie," in North, *Minor*, 161.

64. Fry, "Negro in the United States," 26–35.

65. Best overviews of black Communists include Solomon, *Cry Was Unity*; Naison, *Communists in Harlem*; E. Hutchinson, *Blacks and Reds*; Record, *Negro and the Communist Party*; H. Williams, *Black Response*; Kelley, " 'Afric's Sons' "; James, *Holding Aloft*. On Fort-Whiteman at the KUTV, see "Central Executive Committee," Oct. 13, 1928, LFWD, 495/261/1476, RGASPI; "Lovett Fort White-man," 22. On Tuskegee, see B. T. Washington, ed., *Tuskegee*; Norrell, *Reaping the Whirlwind*, 1–30.

66. Claude McKay, "Soviet Russia," [January], 114, found Russians "curious with me . . . in a friendly refreshing manner." On black Muscovites, see Haywood, *Black Bolshevik*, 167–69; Du Bois, "Russia, 1926," 8; Blakely, *Russia and the Negro*, esp. 81–104.

67. Haywood, *Black Bolshevik*, 143–44; Klehr, Haynes, and Anderson, *Soviet World*, 218; Minor, "First Negro Workers' Congress," 70. Shaved heads represented futurist style. See "Trade Union Students," 62.

68. R. Robinson, *Black on Red*, 68; Haywood, *Black Bolshevik*, 170–71; Glazer, *Social Basis*, 171.

69. Brandenberger, *National Bolshevism*.

70. Naison, *Communists in Harlem*, 18–19; "Russia in 1924"; C. J. Robinson, *Black Marxism*.

71. "Draft Manifesto," 495/155/ 4, RGASPI; Solomon, *Cry Was Unity*, 40–41; Maxwell, *New Negro*, 90.

72. Haywood, *Black Bolshevik*, 186; Khanga, *Soul to Soul*.

73. For the opposite view, that of African Americans as pawns of Moscow, see Record, *Negro and the Communist Party*, 105–06; Glazer, *Social Basis*, 173–74; Klehr, *Communist Cadre*, 54; Sworakowski, *Communist International*, 8.

74. The only other contender for the first *American-born* black Communist is Otto Hall, who joined in 1922, but Fort-Whiteman claimed membership from 1919. "To the Central Executive Committee, Oct.13, 1928," 495/261/1476/34, RGASPI; Haywood, *Black Bolshevik*, 129; "Black and Red," 8; J. M. Turner, *Caribbean Crusaders*, 87.

75. "Bolsheviki Movement," Oct. 15, 1919, r12, *FSAA*. His birth date was Dec. 3, 1889, *Twelfth Census, 1900*, Dallas, TX, r1625, Dist. 6, Enumeration Dist. 118, p. 105. *Morrison and Fourmy's*, 1888–89, 400; *Morrison and Fourmy's*, 1891–92, 589; *Morrison and Fourmy's*, 1893–94, 523; *Morrison and Fourmy's*, 1894–95, 321; *Evans and Worley*, 464; *Twelfth Census, 1900*, Dallas, TX, r1625, Dist. 6, Enumeration Dist. 118, p. 105. The family lived at 408 Flora St., Dallas, TX. L. J. Geeman, "Lee Fort Whiteman," Oct. 14, 1919, r12, *FSAA*.

76. Notes on Interview with W. A. Domingo, f3, b21, TDRF; *Evans and Worley*, 51.

77. *Thirteenth Census,1910*, New York City, Dist. 1, Ward 12, 24 W. 135th St., accessed at http://www.ancestry.com; Blossom, "Rand School," 22; Loebl, "Lovett Fort-Whiteman," Oct. 22, 1919, r12, *FSAA*.

78. The date of 1914 is based on verifiable points in Fort-Whiteman's life. For

African Americans in Mexico, see Jacoby, "Between North and South," 333–85; Kornweibel, *No Crystal Stair*, 4–10; Folsom, ed., *Mike Gold*, 49; Katz, *Secret*, and Horne, *Black and Brown*; Kornweibel, *"Investigate Everything,"* 76–117; Ellis, *Race, War, and Surveillance*, 22–23; La Botz, "American 'Slackers' in the Mexican Revolution," 563–90.

79. Nash and Loebl, Fort Whiteman Statement, Oct. 11, 1919, r12, *FSAA*.

80. Ibid. LFW claimed to have been a Socialist for "about four years, I first joined in Mexico." To the question "Are you a Syndacalist [*sic*]," he answered, "I am a member of the party." On Casa del Obrero Mundial, see Joseph, *Revolution from Without*, 93, 111–12.

81. Nash and Loebl, Fort Whiteman Statement, Oct. 11, 1919; "Bolsheviki Movement," Oct. 15, 1919, both on r12, *FSAA*.

82. *DW*, Feb. 9, 1924 and March 24, 1924; E. Hutchinson, *Blacks and Reds*, 15–16. On the draft, see Kornweibel, *"Investigate Everything,"* 86–87. World War I draft card, Lovette Huey Whiteman, 24 W. 135th St., New York, June 6, 1917, accessed at http://www.ancestry.com.

83. Blossom, "Rand School," 22; Kornweibel, *No Crystal Stair*, 30. A. Philip Randolph was also a Shakespearean actor, Pfeffer, *Randolph*, 8.

84. Foner, *American Socialism*, 265–336, esp. 270–71. Solomon, *Cry Was Unity*, 4, dates the founding of the Socialist 21st A.D. Branch (in Harlem) 1918, but Lovett Fort-Whiteman's membership card is dated Oct. 1, 1917. "Bolsheviki Movement," Oct. 15, 1919, r12, *FSAA*; S. M. Miller, "Socialist Party"; Kornweibel, *No Crystal Stair*, 22–27.

85. "Southern Bourbons Ignorant"; J. S. Rosenberg, *How Far?* 47–48.

86. Blossom, "Rand School," 22; J. M. Turner, *Caribbean Crusaders*, 19–22, 24.

87. A. L. Harris, "Negro Problem," 413; "Bolsheviki Movement," Oct. 15, 1919; W. C. Samuels, "Fort-Whiteman IWW," both on r12, *FSAA*; "I.W.W. Raid," *SLS*, Oct. 11, 1919, 2.

88. Notes on Interview with W. A. Domingo, Jan. 18, 1958, f3, b21, TDRF; Fort-Whiteman, "Untitled," 29–30.

89. Fort-Whiteman, "Nemesis," 25; Fort-Whiteman, "Wild Flowers," 603–07.

90. Draper, *Roots*, 159–61; "Call for a Third International," (Jan. 1919), and "Socialist Party Faction Manifesto," (Feb. 1919), both in *Documentary History*, ed. Johnpoll, 1:36–52; Draper, *Roots*, 144–47, 156–59; Howe and Coser, *American Communist Party*, 41–42.

91. "Weekly Situation Survey," Jan. 16, 1920, f Government Investigations, b2; "Radicalism in St. Louis," Oct. 3, 1919, f Government Investigations, b2, both in MSRK; Draper, *Roots*, 161–63.

92. "Left Wing Manifesto," (June 21–24, 1919), and A. Pauly, "Historical Review," both in *Documentary History*, ed. Johnpoll, 1:137–61, 1:197–217; Draper, *Roots*, 168–69, 176–81; Howe and Coser, *American Communist Party*, 43–52. Eighty-two went to the CLP, and 128 to the CPA.

93. James, *Holding Aloft*, 156–60. Draper argues that no blacks were present, but Hill and Solomon put Huiswoud and Hendricks, West Indian immigrants, there. See "Re: Otto Eduard Huiswoud," b2, MSRK; Draper, *American Communism and*

Soviet Russia, 325–26; Solomon, *Cry Was Unity*, 3, 4; R. A. Hill, "Introduction," xxvi; "Otto Huiswoud," *DW*, Dec. 31, 1961, 8; T. R. Taylor, "Cyril Briggs," 164; Griffler, "Black Radical Intellectual," 53–62; Solomon, *Cry Was Unity*, 10–11, and 316 n. 1; J. M. Turner and W. B. Turner, ed., *Richard B. Moore*, 19–108; J. M. Turner, *Caribbean Crusaders*, 83–90.

94. American Party Representative to Central Executive Committee, CPSU, Oct. 13, 1928, 495/261/1476/34, RGASPI. Cyril Briggs to Theodore Draper, March 17, 1958, falsely claimed that Fort-Whiteman joined the CP through the ABB, f Briggs Correspondence, b1, and "Radicalism in St. Louis," Oct. 7, 1919, f Government Investigations, b2, both in MSRK. Fort-Whiteman identified himself as a Communist in Oct. 1919, according to investigators, "Lovett Fort Whiteman," Loebl Interrogation, Oct. 15, 1919; W. C. Samuels, *United States vs. Lovett Fort-Whiteman*, Oct. 22, 1919, Exhibit C; Loebl, Confidential Informant, Oct. 2, 1919; F. A. Blossom to Comrade Whiteman, Exhibit E; "Bolsheviki Movement," Oct. 15, 1919, all on r12, *FSAA*. See also H. Williams, *Black Response*, 7–13; Draper, *Roots*, 186, 197–69.

95. Horne, "Race from Power," 437–61; Powers, *Not without Honor*, 27–31.

96. "Has the Negro Gone Bolshevik?," 12–13; "Mob Fury and Race Hatred"; Kornwiebel, *Seeing Red*, 64–65, 168; Tuttle, *Race Riot*; Jaffee, *Crusade against Radicalism*.

97. "A Reply to Congressman James F. Byrnes," 11–14; Cyril Briggs to Theodore Draper, March 17, 1958, in f Briggs Correspondence, b1, MSRK; Kornwiebel, *No Crystal Stair*, 73; J. S. Rosenberg, *How Far?*, 64–66; M. Ellis, *Race, War, and Surveillance*, 101–13; Jordan, *Black Newspapers*.

98. "Programme," 449–54; Richard J [*sic*] Moore, Jan. 15, 1958, f3, b21, and ABB typescript, f2, b21, both in TDRF; Cyril Briggs to Theodore Draper, March 17, 1958, estimates less than 3,000 members, in f Briggs Correspondence, b1, MSRK; T. R. Taylor, "Cyril Briggs," 112; Robinson, *Black Marxism*, 216–18; James, *Holding Aloft*, 155–73; Solomon, *Cry Was Unity*, 1–11.

99. "Worm Turns"; "Congress, the Lusk Committee," 505–06.

100. W. C. Samuels, *United States vs. Lovett Fort-Whiteman*, Oct. 22, 1919, r12, *FSAA*.

101. Fitch, Introduction to Foster, *Great Steel Strike*, 205–12; Barrett, *Foster*, 96; Foster, *Bryan to Stalin*, 125–31; Foster, *Pages*, 171–72.

102. Robert Minor, son of Robert Berkeley Minor and Routez Houston, born July 14, 1884, San Antonio, TX, *International Geneaological Index*, www.familysearch .com; Minor, "How I Became a Rebel," 25–26; North, *Minor*; "Terms of the Third International"; Draper, *Roots*, 121–26, 418 n. 13; Solomon, *Cry Was Unity*, 44; McKay, *Long Way from Home*, 193, 106. Haywood, *Black Bolshevik*, 139–410, 143–47, quote on 146 argues that Minor "groomed" Fort-Whiteman. See also M. Bird, "Robert Minor," in *Encyclopedia of the American Left*, ed. M. J. Buhle, P. Buhle, and Georgakas, 475.

103. The St. Louis Communists joined the CPA but switched to the CLP, "Radicalism in St. Louis," Oct. 1, 1919, and "Radicalism in St. Louis," Sept. 25, 1919, both in f Government Investigations, b2, MSRK. L. J. Geeman, "Lee Fort Whitman," Oct. 14, 1919; Loebl, Confidential Informant, Oct. 6, 1919; Loebl,

"Fort Whiteman Negro Radical"; Loebl, "Fort Whiteman, Negro I.W.W.," "Bolsheviki Movement," Oct. 15, 1919; W. C. Samuels, "Lovett Fort White," all on r12, *FSAA*; "Two More Arrested," *SLGD*, Oct. 12, 1919, 6; "I.W.W. Raid," *SLS*, Oct. 11, 1919, 1; Kornweibel, *Seeing Red*, 168–71; Whitney, *Reds in America*, 95.

104. "Memo. on Lovett Fort Whiteman," Nov. 3, 1919, r12, *FSAA*. The police reported that Whiteman called for the "overthrow of capitalism and the present form of government" and "Soviet Control, and Dictatorship of the Proletariat," Speed and Doherty to Chief of Detectives, Oct. 14, 1919, in f Government Investigations, b2, MSRK. See also Draper, *Roots*, 147.

105. Loebl, Confidential Informant, Oct. 6, 1919, and "Report of Meeting October 10," both on r12, *FSAA*; "U.S. Agents Here Arrest Negro IWW," *SLPD*, Oct. 11, 1919, 1; "Negro Active as IWW," *SLPD*, Oct. 12, 1919, 1; "Two More Arrested," *SLGD*, Oct. 12, 1919, 1; "I.W.W. Raid," *SLS*, Oct. 11, 1919, 1. On IWW, see Kornweibel, *Seeing Red*, 162; "Bolsheviki Movement," Oct. 15, 1919, r12, *FSAA*.

106. "I.W.W. Raid," *SLS*, Oct. 11, 1919, 1; Nash and Loebl, Fort Whiteman Statement, Oct. 11, 1919, r12, *FSAA*.

107. "Radicalism in St. Louis," Oct. 13, 1919, f Government Investigations, b2, MSRK; "I.W.W. Raid," *SLS*, Oct. 11, 1919, 1, 2; "Two More Arrested," *SLGD*, Oct. 12, 1919, 6; Nash and Loebl, Fort Whiteman Statement, Oct. 11, 1919, r12, *FSAA*; Klehr and Haynes, *American Communist Movement*, 20–21.

108. "I.W.W. Raid," *SLS*, Oct. 11, 1919, 1; Ellis, *Race, War, and Surveillance*, 33–38.

109. "Negro I.W.W. Leader Held," *SLS*, Oct. 15, 1919, 3; "Memo. on Lovett Fort Whiteman," Nov. 3, 1919, and W. C. Samuels, *United States vs. Lovett Fort-Whiteman*, Oct. 22, 1919, both on r12, *FSAA*.

110. Nash and Loebl, Fort Whiteman Statement, Oct. 11, 1919, r12, *FSAA*.

111. L. J. Geeman, "Lee Fort Whiteman," Oct. 14, 1919, r12, *FSAA*.

112. Exhibit A, Item 6, letter from sister, W. C. Samuels, "Lovett Fort-Whiteman," Oct. 21, 1919, r12, *FSAA*. The *Messenger*'s second-class mailing permit had been revoked, Kornweibel, *No Crystal Stair*, 53.

113. Kornweibel, *Seeing Red*, 171, says that he jumped bail, but the Jan. 13, 1920, census enumerates him in jail, *Fourteenth Census, 1920*, St. Louis, Dist. 183, Enumeration Dist. 115, Ward 6, accessed at www.ancestry.com; Draper, *Roots*, 203; Howe and Coser, *American Communist Party*, 52.

114. American Labor Alliance, "Workers! Unite!," in *Documentary History*, ed. Johnpoll, 1:353–55; Klehr and Haynes, *American Communist Movement*, 35–37; Whitney, *Reds in America*, 19–38; Draper, *Roots*, 282–375.

115. American Party Representative to Central Executive Committee, CPSU, Oct. 13, 1928, 495/261/1476/34, RGASPI; Draper, *Roots*, 205–07; Cannon, *First Ten Years*, 43–46, and *Cannon and the Early Years*; P. Buhle, *Marxism*, 121–55. J. Anderson, *Randolph*, 87, 133, dates Fort-Whiteman's membership to 1921without documentation. See also Kornweibel, *No Crystal Stair*, 66–99.

116. "Editorials," "Bolsheviki," *Messenger*, 7. The Comintern read the *Messenger*, "Messenger," 495/155/18, RGASPI. See also Powers, *Not without Honor*, 58–59.

117. "Federated Farmer-Labor Party," 782; Draper, *Roots*, 331–32, 341–55, 388–90; Kornweibel, *No Crystal Stair*, 98, 224–28; J. Anderson, *Randolph*, 205; J. S. Rosenberg, *How Far?*, 85–87.

118. Lovett Fort-Whiteman, "Negro in Politics," *DW*, Jan. 13, 1924, sec. 3, n.p.; "January 29, 1924," LFWP; Naison, *Communists in Harlem*, 5.

119. "Resolutions," f Negro-Sanhedrin, 1924, b13, RM; Foner and Allen, eds., *American Communism and Black Americans*, 53. "Sanhedrin Idea Draws Approval of Jewish Race," *CD*, Jan. 19, 1924, 3. Five WP members attended, Jan. 29, 1924, 495/261/1476, 39, RGASPI.

120. Kelly Miller, "Sanhedrin," *NYAN*, Jan. 31, 1923, 2; "Sanhedrin Conference," *NYAN*, March 28, 1923, 1; Kelly Miller, "Radicalism," 33–37, and *Negro Sanhedrin*; J. O. Young, *Black Writers*, 6–13. For a contrasting account, see Cyril Briggs to Theodore Draper, March 17, 1958, and Briggs to Mr. Johns, June 7, 1961, both in f Briggs Correspondence, b1, MSRK. See also James, *Holding Aloft*, 190; J. M. Turner, *Caribbean Crusaders*, 113–14.

121. "Sanhedrin Conference," *NYAN*, March 28, 1923, 1; Harry Heywood [*sic*], Otto Hall, William Wilson, Roy Farmer, to Comrades, [1928], 495/155/66, and ABB letterhead, 1923, 495/155/11, both in RGASPI; "Programme," 449–54; R. A. Hill, "Introduction"; Solomon, *Cry Was Unity*, 3–21; Kornweibel, *Seeing Red*, 132–54.

122. "Programme," 449–54; R. A. Hill, "Introduction," xlvi; Berland, "Emergence of the Communist Perspective, Part One," 418–19; Whitney, *Reds in America*, 190–94; James, *Holding Aloft*, 177–78; Haywood, *Black Bolshevik*, 122–26.

123. "Programme," 451–52; "Report on Individuals," [1924?], 495/155/43, RGASPI; "African Blood Brotherhood," 22; Cyril Briggs, " 'Angry Blond Negro,' " in Hill, "Introduction," xlix; Kelley, " 'Afric's Sons,' " 37–39; Schwarz, "Cyril Briggs"; T. R. Taylor, "Cyril Briggs"; Notes on Interview with W. A. Domingo, Jan. 18, 1958, f3, b21, TDRF.

124. E. Hutchinson, *Blacks and Reds*, 16–21; Berland, "Emergence of the Communist Perspective, Part One," 423; "Dean Kelly Miller's All Race Conference," *PC*, June 23, 1923, 16; "Sanhedrin to Meet," *CD*, Feb. 9, 1924, 1. Photograph, see "Representative Group," *CD*, Feb. 16, 1924, 12; "Great All-Race Negro Congress," *DW*, Feb. 11, 1924, 1; "Radical Negro," (LFW) *DW*, Feb. 11, 1924, 2; "Greets All-Race Negro Congress," *DW*, Feb. 11, 1924, 6; "Harassed Negro Turns on Foes," Apr. 8, 1923, and "Minutes to the 4th Meeting," July 19, 1923, both in 495/155/11, RGASPI. Marcus Garvey's UNIA was not invited.

125. "Prejudice Is Not Inherent," *CD*, Feb. 2, 1924, 2; Fort-Whiteman, "Negro in the Industries," *DW*, Jan. 29, 1924, 6; Fort-Whiteman, "Negro Petty Bourgeoisie," *DW*, Jan. 31, 1924, 6; Fort-Whiteman, "Negro Leadership," *DW*, Feb. 1, 1924, 6; "Negro and American Race Prejudice," *DW*, Feb. 9, 1924, 3; "Negro Organizations Forming United Front," *DW*, Feb. 8, 1924, 3.

126. "Sanhedrin Launches," *PC*, Feb. 23, 1924, 9; "January 29, 1924," LFWP; "Delegates Lovett Fort-Whiteman (James Jackson), Eugene Burton, Miss Ethel Hall, Gordon Owens, S.[H]V. Phillips," Feb. 12, 1924, 495/155/23, RGASPI; Duplicates in f Negro-Sanhedrin, 1924, b13, RM; "Radical Negro," *DW*, Feb. 11, 1924, 2.

127. "Sanhedrin Launches," *PC*, Feb. 23, 1924, 9.

128. Hutchinson, *Blacks and Reds*, 19; "Delegates Lovett Fort-Whiteman . . . ," Feb. 12, 1924, 495/155/23, RGASPI; "Negroes at All-Race Congress," *DW*, Feb. 13, 1924, 1; "Negro Workingmen," *DW*, Feb. 14, 1924, 1. On race and the AFL, see Karson and Radosh, "American Federation of Labor," 155–87.

129. W. H. A. Moore, "Reflections," *DW*, Feb. 23, 1924, sec. 2, n.p.; "Winning," *DW*, March 20, 1924, 3.

130. "Labor Fights," *DW*, Feb. 15, 1924, 3; "Negro Workingmen," *DW*, Feb. 14, 1924, 1; E. Hutchinson, *Blacks and Reds*, 20.

131. "Negro Race Movement," *DW*, Feb. 19, 1924, 2; "Labor Fights," and "Labor, Lynching," both in *DW*, Feb. 15, 1924, 3, 1; "Negro Workers," *DW*, Feb. 16, 1924, 1; "Sanhedrin Ends," *DW*, Feb. 18, 1924, 1; "Sanhedrin Capitalists," *DW*, Feb. 18, 1924, 3; "Negro Race Movement," *DW*, Feb. 19, 1924, 2.

132. Minor, "Black Ten Millions"; "Negro Bourgeois Leader," *DW*, May 16, 1924, 3.

133. "Negro Tenants Will Hit Rent Hogs," "Chicago, Forgetting," and "*Daily Worker* Exposing," all in *DW*, May 14, 1924, 1, 2; "Southside Workers," *DW*, March 18, 1924, 2; "Chicago Negro Tenants," *DW*, March 19, 1924, 3; "Negro Juniors Win Boy Scouts to Communism," *DW*, June 10, 1924, 4.

134. "Seeing Black as Red," *State*, May 6, 1924.

135. "Negro Audience Joins Tenants League," *DW*, Apr. 2, 1924, 2.

136. *Fifth Congress*, 5; Foster, "Russia in 1924"; Heller, "U.S.S.R., 1921–1925," pts. 1 and 2.

137. Executive Secretary, June 2, 1924, 38, LFWP; Degras, ed., *Communist International*, 1:117; *Fifth Congress*, 196, 198, 200–01.

138. *Fifth Congress*, 200–01; Draper, *American Communism and Soviet Russia*, 329–30; Solomon, *Cry Was Unity*, 46–48; Berland, "Emergence of the Communist Perspective, Part One," 427–28.

139. Trotsky, "Extracts from a Manifesto," in Degras, *Communist International*, 2:112; *Fifth Congress*, 283.

140. To the Central Executive Committee, Oct. 13, 1928, and July 2, 1924, delegate list, LFWP; Foner and Allen, eds., *American Communism and Black Americans*, 41; Degras, *Communist International*, 2:94. After Fort-Whiteman attended, it was renamed Stalin Communist University of Toilers of the East, Universitet Trudiashchikhnsia Vostoka Imeni Stalin.

141. Fort-Whiteman, "Racial Question," 495/155/18, 95–97, RGASPI; Pipes, *Russia*, 362–67.

142. Fort-Whiteman, "Racial Question," 495/155/18, 95–97, RGASPI; Hughes, *I Wonder*, 172; Khanga, *Soul to Soul*, 81, and photographs following 128.

143. "Russia Solves Race Problem Says Whiteman," *AA*, March 14, 1925, 1; Briggs, "Bolshevism"; J. S. Rosenberg, *How Far?*, 88.

144. James Jackson to William Dubois [sic], July 15, 1924, Misc. 932, r13, 1–2, WEBDB; J. S. Rosenberg, *How Far?*, 79.

145. Fort-Whiteman, "Negro and American Race Prejudice," *DW*, Feb. 9, 1924, quoted in Foner and Allen, eds. *American Communists and Black Americans*, 42.

146. Fort-Whiteman, "Racial Question," 97; "Russia Solves Race Problem Says Whiteman," *AA*, March 14, 1925, 1.

147. Fonville, "South as I Saw It"; Katayama, *International Press Correspondence*, Aug. 13, 1928, in Foner and Allen, eds., *American Communism and Black Americans*, 188–89. The official history of the school does not say that black students attended, S. T. Wilson, *Century*.

148. Claude McKay's description of Katayama, *Long Way from Home*, 164. See also photographs in Cehatopob, *Sen Katayama*, and Sen Katayama, photographs nos. 162, 198, 199, r7, RPS/YU.

149. Sen Katayama, "My Life," July 22, 1924, 521/1/1, list 16, RGASPI. Foner and Allen, eds., *American Communism and Black Americans*, 188, misidentify the school as Fisk, probably following McKay, *Long Way from Home*, 164. See Horne, "Race from Power."

150. Kublin, *Asian Revolutionary*, 240, 243, 248; Solomon, *Cry Was Unity*, 11; [Hermie Huiswoud], "Re: Otto Eduard Huiswoud," b20, Office M.I.B., to Director, MID, Nov. 20, 1918, "Bolsheviki Activities," Nov. 19, 1918, Harvey W. Miller to The Director, MID, March 23, 1921, all in f Communist Party-Gestation, b1, MSRK.

151. Katayama, *International Press Correspondence*, Aug. 13, 1928, in Foner and Allen, eds., *American Communism and Black Americans*, 188.

152. Haywood, *Black Bolshevik*, 656, n. 5.

153. McKay, "Soviet Russia," 64; McKay, *Long Way from Home*, 165.

154. Draper, *Roots*, 268–70; Kublin, *Asian Revolutionary*, 261–80; McKay, *Long Way from Home*, 164–65; Degras, *Communist International*, 2:101, 119; "Extracts from the Theses," "Correct Attitude to the Peasantry," in Degras, *Communist International*, 2:149.

155. Berland, "Emergence of the Communist Perspective, Part One," 414–22; "Theses of the Fourth Comintern Congress," in Degras, *Communist International*, Nov. 30, 1922, 1:398–401; D. Ivon Jones, South Africa, 1923, "Call a Negro Congress at Moscow," 495/155/3, RGASPI.

156. White Tulsans accused the ABB of starting the rioting, something that Briggs and the commander of the Tulsa ABB vehemently denied. "Tulsa Riot," 1173; "Denies Negroes Started Tulsa Riot," *NYT*, June 5, 1921, 21. A white New Yorker was arrested a few days later with printed appeals for victims of "The Tulsa Massacre," signed by the CP, "Communists Champion Negro," 1212.

157. Sen Katayama, "Action for the Negro Movement," May 22, 1923, and "Negro Race as a Factor," July 14, 1923, both in 495/155/17, RGASPI.

158. Notes on Interview with W. A. Domingo, f3, b21, TDRF; Haywood, *Black Bolshevik*, 166; Khanga, *Soul to Soul*, 50; Garb, *They Came to Stay*, 36–40; Solomon, *Cry Was Unity*, 51.

159. E. Hutchinson, *Blacks and Reds*, 21–22; Khanga, *Soul to Soul*, 47.

160. Khanga, *Soul to Soul*, 41, 46–51; "International Trade Union Committee of Negro Workers," in Foner and Allen, eds., *American Communism and Black Americanism*, 151; Berry, introduction, 13.

161. Khanga, *Soul to Soul*, 47–49; "Communists Boring," *NYT*, Jan. 17, 1926, E1; "Black and Red," *Time* 6 (Nov. 9, 1925): 8; Haywood, *Black Bolshevik*, 160–68.

162. Warren, *Liberals and Communism*, 63–64, 8. On the English-language *Moscow News*, see Gitlow, *Whole of Their Lives*, 174; J. Fineberg, *Moscow News*, 495/72/41, RGASPI.

464 | NOTES TO PAGES 49-51

163. Du Bois, "Russia, 1926"; Lewis, *W. E. B. Du Bois*, 2:194–204; Du Bois, *Autobiography*, 289–91; "Americans to See Soviet Fete," *NYCP*, Sept. 23, 1927, in Scrapbook, Music-Art, Sept. 1927–July 1928, JWJ Papers; McKay, "Soviet Russia"; McKay, *Long Way from Home*, 7–8, 167; Gitlow, *Whole of Their Lives*, 171–73.

164. H. Smith, *Black Man in Red Russia*, 64; Khanga, *Soul to Soul*, 71–80.

165. H. Smith, *Black Man in Red Russia*, 56.

166. Quoted in J. S. Rosenberg, *How Far?*, 84.

167. William L. Patterson to Comrade Brigadier, Feb. 8, 1936, 495/14/36, 1–2, RGASPI.

168. Haywood, *Black Bolshevik*, 170.

169. Ibid., 154; Robinson, *Black on Red*.

170. McClellan, "Africans and Black Americans," 372; Berland, "Emergence of the Communist Perspective, Part One," 414–22; "Theses of the Fourth Comintern Congress," in Degras, *Communist International*, Nov. 30, 1922, 1:398–401; Solomon, *Cry Was Unity*, 42–43.

171. List and explanation are from Haywood, noting that Japan was not a colonial country. Haywood, *Black Bolshevik*, 155–57, 164; Berland, "Emergence of the Communist Perspective, Part Two," 197.

172. Degras, *Communist International*, 2:124–25; McClellan, "Africans and Black Americans," 375.

173. "Vaughn Mise, Louise Rivers, Denmark Vesey, Wilson [Patterson], to American Political Bureau," n.d., "Bittelman, Engdahl, Weinstone, to the Political Secretariat," [1928?], and "Having been requested," Feb. 2, 1928, all in 495/155/65; "Meeting of the Negro Section," Jan. 8, 1930, 495/155/83, all in RGASPI.

174. "Meeting of the Negro Section," Jan. 8, 1930, 495/155/83, RGASPI; W. L. Patterson, *Man Who Cried Genocide*, 102–06; Solomon, *Cry Was Unity*, 89–91; "International Trade Union Committee of Negro Workers," July 3, 1936, 495/14/36, 19–27, and "International Trade Union Negro Committee," Aug. 19, 1935, 495/14/60, both in RGASPI. George Padmore also signed, Hooker, *Black Revolutionary*, 4–6, 14–15.

175. James Jackson (Fort-Whiteman), "I wish an interview with Comrade Cinarchowsky," n.d. [1924], 495/155/27, RGASPI.

176. "Communists Boring," *NYT*, Jan. 17, 1926, E1; "Black and Red," 8, "Bolshevizing the American Negro," 631, Comrade Petrovsky [Max Goldfarb], Secretary, Anglo-American Secretariat, June 18, 1928, 495/155/66, "Policies on Work among the Negroes," May 26, 1928, 495/155/ 64, "Directions for the Party Fraction," 495/155/39, all in RGASPI; Solomon, *Cry Was Unity*, 58.

177. "Soviet Trains Negroes Here," *HT*, June 29, 1927, 1; "Soviet Stupidity," *HT*, June 30, 1927, 20; "White Paper Warns Nation of Soviet Scheme," *NW*, July 9, 1927, 2; "American Negro Labor Congress Radicals," *NW*, July 16, 1927, 4; "Moscow Seeking to Doom Negroes," *NW*, Aug. 13, 1927, 5; "To Turn Negroes into 'Reds'!"; "Negroes Trained by Soviets," *NYA*, July 9, 1927, 1; "Bolshevist Bogey Again," *NYA*, July 9, 1927, 4.

178. "Bolshevizing the American Negro," *Independent* (Dec. 5, 1925): 631.

179. James Jackson [LFW], 1924, "Suggested Agenda," 495/155/25, RGASPI.

180. "American Organizer of Negro Labor Here," *NYAN*, May 20, 1925, 2; Minor, "Negro Finds His Place"; Record, *Negro and the Communist Party*, 31–33; Entz, "American Negro Labor Congress," 54–56; Solomon, *Cry Was Unity*, 50–51.

181. James Jackson [LFW], [1924], "Suggested Agenda," 495/155/25, and "Notes from the Preamble," 495/155/87, 108–09, both in RGASPI; "A.N.L.C. Takes Stand," *DW*, Oct. 31, 1925, 1; James Jackson [LFW], "Negro in America," 51.

182. Agenda for Fort-Whiteman, [Feb. 1925], f Negro 1924–25, b12, RM; James Jackson [LFW] to John Pepper, n.d. [spring 1924], 495/155/102, RGASPI. John Pepper was Joseph Pogany, a Hungarian Communist. Whitney, *Reds in America*, following 44.

183. James Jackson [LFW], June 2, 1925, 495/155/27, RGASPI; D. L. Lewis, *W. E. B. Du Bois*, 2:196; Solomon, *Cry Was Unity*, 52–56.

184. "Preparation for the American Negro Workers Congress," Eastern Department of the ECCI, Oct. 25, 1925, 495/155/34, RGASPI. For the "from below" strategy, see Draper, *Roots*, 329–30.

185. "Communists Boring," *NYT*, Jan. 17, 1926, E1; "American Negro Labor Congress," *AA*, Apr. 18, 1925, 18; "Call to Action," in Foner and Allen, eds., *American Communism and Black Americans*, 109–12; Record, *Negro and the Communist Party*, 43–44.

186. Randolph, "Case of the Pullman Porter"; Randolph, "Pullman Porters Need Own Union."

187. "Black Man and Labor."

188. On the CP and the BSCP, see "Statement to the American Commission on Trade Union Work amongst Negro Workers from the International Trade Union Committee of Negro Workers of the RILW," Draft-Heywood [*sic*], 495/155/77, 87, RGASPI; Moore, "An Open Letter," in *Richard B. Moore*, ed. W. B. Turner and J. M. Turner, 147; "A. F. of L. and the Negro Worker." For BSCP suspicion of the CP, see J. Anderson, *Randolph*, 205.

189. Randolph, quot. in J. Anderson, *Randolph*, 205; "Randolph's Reply"; Pfeffer, *Randolph*, 25–29. Fort-Whiteman's last *Messenger* byline was in 1923. When Draper asked Randolph about Fort-Whiteman, Randolph replied that he had "got completely out of touch with me and apparently the country." Randolph to Draper, May 27, 1958, f2, b21, TDRF.

190. A. L. Harris, "Negro Labor's Quarrel." Wesley, *Negro Labor*, 271, in error states that more than 100 accepted blacks. Brazeal, *Brotherhood*, 130–33; J. Anderson, *Randolph*, 204–05; W. H. Harris, *A. Philip Randolph*, 23–25.

191. Pfeffer, *Randolph*, 25–26; Kornweibel, *No Crystal Stair*, 186; Nelson, *Divided We Stand*.

192. Green, quoted in Foner and Allen, eds., *American Communism and Black Americans*, 116; "U.S. Is on Alert," *CHE*, Oct. 15, 1925, in f Negro 1924–25, b12, RM; "Communists Boring," *NYT*, Jan. 17, 1926, E1; K. Miller, "Negro as a Working-man."

193. W. Green, "Our Negro Worker."

194. Untitled typescript, f Negro 1924–25, b12, RM; William N. Jones, "Day by Day," *AA*, Aug. 15, 1925, 9.

195. Letterhead, Jackson [LFW] to John Pepper, n.d. [spring 1924], 495/155/102,

RGASPI. Otto Hall is listed on the "Provisional" committee letterhead, but he left for KUTV, and Harry Haywood served with organizers Howell V. Phillips, Edward L. Doty, and Otto Huiswoud. Haywood, *Black Bolshevik*, 143.

196. Quoted in Haywood, *Black Bolshevik*, 144–45, description 142–47; Poster, Metropolitan Community Center, 3118 Giles Ave., with a dance at Vincennes Hall, 36th and Vincennes Ave.; "Grand Opening," f Negro 1924–25, b12, RM; " 'Reds' in Chicago," *AA*, Oct. 31, 1925, 1; Record, *Race and Radicalism*, 33–34; Solomon, *Cry Was Unity*, 67; E. Hutchinson, *Blacks and Reds*, 29–42; J. W. Ford, *Negro and the Democratic Front*, 81–83; Draper, *American Communism and Soviet Russia*, 331–32.

197. Lovett Fort-Whiteman, "Proceedings," *DW*, Oct. 28, 1925, in Foner and Allen, eds., *American Communism and Black Americans*, 112.

198. Minor, "First Negro Workers' Conference," 71; "Report of Radical Activities," Nov. 2, 1925, f Government Investigations, b2, MSRK.

199. "American Negro Labor Meet Opens," *DW*, Oct. 26, 1925,1; Haywood, *Black Bolshevik*, 145; Fort-Whiteman claimed 49 delegates, "Statement," Sept. 27, 1925 [date incorrect], 495/155/34, RAGSPI.

200. "Extract from Decision of the Organizational Bureau of the ECCI on September 14, 1925 on the A.N.L.C.," 495/155/87, RGASPI.

201. "Committees," List of delegates, 495/155/33, RGASPI; ANLC press release, Oct. 1925, f ANLC, b3, MSRK.

202. Minor, "First Negro Workers' Congress," 68–71; "Warns Negro Labor," *NYT*, Aug. 10, 1925, 14; "Negroes and Labor," *NYT*, Aug. 13, 1925, 18.

203. ANLC press release, Oct. 1925, in f ANLC, b3, MSRK; "Radicals Urge Removal of the Color Line," *AA*, Nov. 7, 1925, 3; " 'Reds' in Chicago," *AA*, Oct. 31, 1925, 1.

204. Minor, "First Negro Workers' Congress," 73. See also "Struggle for Advancement of Negro Labor," *DW*, Oct. 27, 1925; "A.N.L.C. Gives Entire Session to Trade Unions," *DW*, Oct. 28, 1925; 1; "A.N.L.C. Takes Rap at Green," *DW*, Oct. 29, 1925, 1.

205. ANLC press release, Oct. 28, 1925, f ANLC, b3, MSRK; "Negro Labor Meet Attacks Ku Klux Klan," *DW*, Oct. 30, 1925, 1. The speaker was black nationalist George Wells Parker. See Schwarz, "Cyril Briggs," 43–44; Stephens, "Black Transnationalism," 592–608.

206. ANLC press release, f ANLC, b3; MSRK; "Radicals Urge Removal of Color Line," *AA*, Nov. 7, 1925, 3; "Full Equality," *DW*, Oct. 18, 1925, and "Resolutions," in Foner and Allen, eds., *American Communism and Black Americans*, 118, 120–22; "Constitution," f ANLC, b1, MSRK.

207. "Imperialism and the American Negro," *DW*, Nov. 14, 1925, in Foner and Allen, eds., *American Communism and Black Americans*, 122–24.

208. "Grand Opening," f Negro 1924–45, b12, RM.

209. Minor, "First Negro Workers' Congress," 68–69.

210. A. L. Harris, "Lenin Casts His Shadow," 275.

211. Fort-Whiteman, "Statement," 495/155/34, RGASPI.

212. Draper, *American Communism and Soviet Russia*, 331–32.

213. James Ford spoke at the 1926 NAACP convention. E. Hutchinson, *Blacks and Reds*, 21–23; Record, *Race and Radicalism*, 40; Dunne, "N.A.A.C.P. Takes a Step

Backward," 460–61; "Outline for Party Speakers," f Negro 1924–25, b12, RM; J. W. Ford, *Negro and the Democratic Front*, 82.

214. "Fort-Whiteman" and "Fort-Whiteman Is He a 'Red?,' " both in *AA*, March 13, 1926, 13.

215. "Editorial," *Opportunity* (Dec. 1925): 354.

216. "Black and Red"; "Bolshevizing the American Negro"; "Communists Boring," *NYT*, Jan. 17, 1926, E1.

217. "Plot to Make Our Blacks Red."

218. Fort-Whiteman, "Statement," 495/155/34, RGASPI; Fort-Whiteman, "Proceedings," *DW*, Oct. 28, 1925, in Foner and Allen, eds., *American Communism and Black Americans*, 113.

219. "Black Man and Labor." Fort-Whiteman asked to meet Du Bois in Apr. 1928, D. L. Lewis, *W. E. B. Du Bois*, 2:256. See also Griffler, "Black Radical Intellectual," 81–105.

220. Entz, "American Negro Labor Congress," 54; Masthead, *NC*, June 1926; T. R. Taylor, "Cyril Briggs," 112–13; W. B. Turner and J. M. Turner, eds., *Richard B. Moore*, 52.

221. "Colored Workers in N.J. Fight," *NC*, June 1926, 1.

222. Perhaps "Dolson," Alabama, was Dothan, and perhaps Thomas Lane was a figment of Fort-Whiteman's imagination. Thomas Lane to the editor, *NC*, June 1926, 3.

223. Fort-Whiteman to Robert Minor, Aug. 6, 1925, 495/155/27, RGASPI.

224. Lovestone, "Great Negro Migration," 179; "National Platform of the Workers (Communist) Party, 1928," in Foner and Allen, eds., *American Communism and Black Americans*, 146; Ware, "From Cotton Fields"; Dunne, "Negroes in American Industry"; A. L. Harris, "Negro Labor's Quarrel"; Griffler, *What Price Alliance?*; A. L. Harris and S. D. Spero, *Black Worker*.

225. Entz, "American Negro Labor Conference," 55. Hutchinson quotes these figures, substantiated only by Fort-Whiteman's claims. E. Hutchinson, *Blacks and Reds*, 35; Solomon, *Cry Was Unity*, 56–57.

226. "Directions for the Party Fraction," 495/155/39, RGASPI.

227. Solomon, *Cry Was Unity*, 58–59. In 1958 Richard Moore ended his interview when asked about LFW: "Richard J. Moore," f3, b21, TDRF; W. B. Turner and J. M. Turner, eds., *Richard B. Moore*, 51–52, 219; E. Hutchinson, *Blacks and Reds*, 35–36; J. M. Turner, *Caribbean Crusaders*, 133–34.

228. W. B. Turner and J. M. Turner, eds., *Richard B. Moore*, 51–52, 219; E. Hutchinson, *Blacks and Reds*, 35–36.

229. Solomon, *Cry Was Unity*, 330 n. 18.

230. J. W. Ford, *Negro and the Democratic Front*, 82; Haywood, *Black Bolshevik*, 146–47.

231. Mary Adams, July 3, 1928, letter, 495/155/64, RGASPI.

232. J. M. Turner, quoting Richard Moore, *Caribbean Crusaders*, 168.

233. "Robert Harry Lowie," www.anthrobase.com; "Robert Harry Lowie," www.mnsu.edu/museum/information/biography, accessed on May 31, 2004; Murphy, *Lowie*, 5, 11–14; Lowie, *Are We Civilized?*, ch. 4; Fort-Whiteman to Franz Boas, Nov. 7, 1927, and Boas to Fort-Whiteman, Nov. 9. 1927, both in ser. 1, box Fischer E. to Frachtenberg, L., FB.

234. Boas, quoted in Melville J. Herskovits, foreword to Boas, *Mind of Primitive Man*, 8; Boas, *Mind of Primitive Man*, rev. ed., 178–79.

235. "Thesis for a New Negro Policy," May 28, 1928, 495/155/64, 2, RGASPI; Solomon, *Cry Was Unity*, 64, 331, n. 36. Black Communist Howell Phillips also signed. Patterson later disavowed this position.

236. Lovestone, "Great Negro Migration," 182–84; Berland, "Emergence of the Communist Perspective, Part One," 427–28; R. J. Alexander, *Right Opposition*, esp. intro. and ch. 1; Draper, *American Communism and Soviet Russia*, 248–314; Cannon, *First Ten Years*, 138–89, 201–04.

237. Draper, *American Communism and Soviet Russia*, 341.

238. Barrett, *Foster*, 155–56; Draper, *American Communism and Soviet Russia*, 268–99; R. J. Alexander, *Right Opposition*, 15–27; Harrison George, "Basis of the Right Danger," 534/7/489, 46–49, RGASPI.

239. T. Morgan, *Covert Life*, 69–74.

240. Solomon, *Cry Was Unity*, 63–67; Draper, *American Communism and Soviet Russia*, 267, 300–14; Jay Lovestone, "Party's Shortcomings," *DW*, Sept. 22, 1927, 4; R. J. Alexander, *Right Opposition*, 13–28; Commission of the Central Committee of the C.P.S.U. (B.), *History of the Communist Party*, 293–95.

241. H. Smith, *Black Man in Red Russia*, 81; Gitlow, *Whole of Their Lives*, 154–57.

242. Berland, "Emergence of the Communist Perspective, Part Two," 196. American Party Representative to the ECCI, June 18, 1928, and American Party Representative to the Militia, Nov. 22, 1928, 29, 37, LFWP.

243. Howell V. Phillips was the other black Lovestone delegate; Roy Mahoney and Harold Williams were in Moscow. Moore to K/2, Feb. 28, 1928, telegram, 495/155/66, and Comrade Petrovsky, Secretary, Anglo-American Secretariat, June 28, 1928, 495/155/66, both in RGASPI. Haywood, *Black Bolshevik*, 253, 260. Solomon, *Cry Was Unity*, 64–65. A full Foster delegation was present, T. Morgan, *Covert Life*, 72.

244. Naison, *Communists in Harlem*, 30, n. 69; Record, *Negro and the Communist Party*, 54–69.

245. Foster, *Great Steel Strike*, 205; Berland, "Emergence of the Communist Perspective, Part One," 429. Undated, unsigned note in Lovett Fort-Whiteman's (beautiful) handwriting, 495/155/43, RGASPI. On Foster, see Barrett, *Foster*.

246. Harry Haywood and N. Nasanov, "Task of the American Communist Party Regarding Negro Work," Aug. 2, 1928, 495/155/56, RGASPI; Solomon, *Cry Was Unity*, 68–81.

247. Haywood, *Black Bolshevik*, 45–53.

248. Haywood recounts that Katayama introduced the black KUTV students to Lenin's writings on the South; *Black Bolshevik*, 218, 656 n. 5. Quotation from verbatim account of the debate, "Minutes of the Negro Commission," Aug. 2, 1928, 495/155/56, RGASPI; Katayama, *International Press Correspondence*, Oct. 30, 1928, 1392–93, quoted in Foner and Allen, eds., *American Communism and Black Americans*, 188; Solomon, *Cry Was Unity*, 40; Agrarian program, reprinted in Whitney, *Reds in America*, 112.

249. Stalin, *Marxism and the National Question*, 182–92; Stalin, quoted in Foster,

Negro People, 464; Draper, *American Communism and Soviet Russia,* 334; Haywood, *Black Bolshevik,* 134–35; Klehr and Tompson, "Self-Determination," 358.

250. Nasanov was the YCI representative to the United States from 1924 to 1926, Joseph Z. Kornfeder to Theodore Draper, Apr. 18, 1958, and Sam Darcy to Mark Solomon, June 27, 1974, both in f Communist Party-Gestation, b1, MSRK. Haywood, *Black Bolshevik,* 218–27; Berland, "Nasanov"; Solomon, *Cry Was Unity,* 70–71, 332, n. 3; J. M. Turner, *Caribbean Crusaders,* 156.

251. "Minutes of the Negro Commission," n.d., 495/155/30, RGASPI.

252. Lenin, "Right of Nations to Self-Determination," in *Lenin Anthology,* ed. R. C. Tucker, ed., 153–80; Lenin, *Collected Works,* 31:144–51, quot. 148, misquoted in Haywood, *Black Bolshevik,* 223; Solomon, *Cry Was Unity,* 38–40; Record, "Development of the Communist Position"; Foster, *Negro People,* 462–78; Kelley, "Communist Party USA," 492. Berland, in "Emergence of the Communist Perspective, Part One," 416 n. 6, argues that Lenin meant to include African Americans as a *nation.*

253. Stalin, quoted in Foster, *Negro People,* 463–64; Draper, *American Communism and Soviet Russia,* 321, 349; Stalin, *Marxism and the National Question,"* 182–92; Agarwal, *Soviet Nationalities Policy;* Roucek, "Soviet Treatment of Minorities"; Conner, *National Question;* H. B. Davis, *Toward a Marxist Theory.*

254. Draper, *American Communism and Soviet Russia,* 341–53; Haywood, *Black Bolshevik,* 218–80; Foster, *Negro People,* 461–78, 557–65; P. Buhle, *Marxism;* Record, "Development of the Communist Position," 306–26; Van Zanten, "Communist Theory"; Klehr and Tompson, "Self-Determination," 354–66; R. C. Tucker, *Stalin in Power,* 148–49; Berland, "Emergence of the Communist Perspective, Part One" and "Part Two."

255. The transcript proves more black involvement than indicated by Klehr and Tompson, "Self-Determination," 354–66, or Draper, *American Communism and Soviet Russia,* 344. See also Theodore Draper to Dear Jim, Feb. 21, 1958, f2, b21, TDRF. Berland notes the influence of the Far East policy at KUTV, Berland, "Emergence of the Communist Perspective, Part One," and refutes Draper in "Part Two," 212–13. Solomon notes that Draper argued that *Stalin* had imposed self-determination but proved "the opposite," Solomon, *Cry Was Unity,* 335 n. 48. J. M. Turner, *Caribbean Crusaders,* 157–61.

256. Haywood, *Black Bolshevik,* 218; quot. from "Minutes of the Negro Commission," Aug. 2, 1928, 495/155/56, RGASPI; Solomon, *Cry Was Unity,* 68–91.

257. "Report to the Polcom," Feb. 4, 1930, f515, r41, d2024, 3, CPUSA.

258. Haywood, *Negro Liberation,* 136–67, 205; Haywood, *Black Bolshevik,* 228–30. Hall quot., Unsigned [Carl Jones–Otto Hall] B1/CJ, "Comrade Jones report," "Is There a Basis for a Nationalist or Separatist Movement in the United States?," June 14, 1928 (routed to Nasanov), 495/155/56, 8, RGASPI. Darcy opposed it as well, Sam Darcy to Mark Solomon, June 2, 1974, f Correspondence, b1, MSRK. Record, *Race and Radicalism,* 57; Berland, "Emergence of the Communist Perspective, Part Two," 197–98.

259. Part of the Colonial Commission, I. Amter, "Negro and the World Revolution," 495/155/17; "Supp. Papers No. 1," 495/155/43; "Historical Summary," [1924],

495/155/42, 43; "To the Negroes of the United States," 495/155/44, 37–39; Harry Haywood, "Industrialisation of the South," Nov. 27, 1929, 495/155/77; Haywood, "Negro Liberation Movement," 495/155/78, all in RGASPI. Berland, "Emergence of the Communist Perspective, Part Two," 200–20; Klehr and Tompson, "Self-Determination," 359; Foner and Allen, eds., *American Communism and Black Americans*, 189; *International Press Correspondence*, Oct. 30, 1928, 1393. Solomon and Turner used RGASPI and offer the best accounts. Solomon, *Cry Was Unity*, 82–84; J. M. Turner, *Caribbean Crusaders*, 159–62.

260. African Americans Roy Mahoney and Howell V. Phillips attended the meeting. In addition to those mentioned in the text, other attendees included Sam Adams Darcy, Bertram D. Wolfe, Charles Shipman [Manuel Gomez], J. Louis Engdahl, William Dunne, Alexander Bittleman, William F. Kruse, Clarence Hathaway, Herbert Zam, James Cannon, Jay Lovestone, Carl Reeve, Max Goldfarb [Petrovsky], John Pepper, Harry M. Wicks, "Charlie" Nasanov, and "Zack and Skripnik," whom I cannot identify. All identifications using Solomon, *Cry Was Unity*, Draper, *American Communism and Soviet Russia*, and RGASPI documents listed in other notes.

261. Draper, *American Communism and Soviet Russia*, 347–53; Lovett Fort-Whiteman, *International Press Correspondence*, July 25, 1928, 708; Ford, *International Press Correspondence*, Oct. 25, 1928, 1345–47. Solomon writes that Fort-Whiteman was "present but did not participate in the discussion of the national question," but I did not find evidence of his attendance, *Cry Was Unity*, 69. RTsKhIDNI is now RGASPI.

262. "Tasks of the American Communist Party," Aug. 2, 1928, 495/155/56, RGASPI.

263. "Minutes of the Negro Commission," Aug. 2, 1928, and "John Pepper," both in 495/155/56, RGASPI.

264. "Minutes of the Negro Commission," Aug. 3, 1928, 495/155/56, RGASPI; for Patterson's (selective) memories, see W. L. Patterson, *Man Who Cried Genocide*, 108–09.

265. Best summary is Berland, "Emergence of the Communist Perspective, Part Two," 214, n. 16.

266. Johns, *Raising the Red Flag*, 219–29, quot. 224, 222; "Minutes of the Negro Commission," Aug. 4, 1928, 495/155/43, RGASPI; "Communists Are for a Black Republic!," *DW*, Nov. 12, 1928, 6; Haywood, *Black Bolshevik*, 235–40.

267. Carl Jones [Otto Hall], "Nationalism among American Negroes," Aug. 10, 1928, f515, r91, d1233, 30–53, CPUSA; Solomon, *Cry Was Unity*, 80. Hall's position on culture ran counter to that developing in the Harlem Renaissance; see Smethurst, *New Red Negro*, 24–27.

268. Debate of Aug. 18, 1928, Jones, *International Press Correspondence*, Oct. 30, 1928, 1392–93; Solomon, *Cry Was Unity*, 80.

269. "Minutes of the Negro Commission," Aug. 11, 1928, 495/155/43, RGASPI. On amendments and drafts, see Solomon, *Cry Was Unity*, 77–81; "Communist International Resolution on the Negro Question in the U.S.," in Foner and Allen, eds., *American Communism and Black Americans*, 189–98.

270. Katayama, *International Press Correspondence*, Aug. 13, 1928, 856–57, in Foner

and Allen, eds., *American Communism and Black Americans*, 188–89. The debate over self-determination was made public in a series of articles published by Andre Shiek, James Ford and William Wilson [Patterson], Harry Haywood, Otto Hall, and Sen Katayama, in August, reprinted in Foner and Allen, eds., *American Communism and Black Americans*, 163–89.

271. "Workers Party Will Invade the South," *AA*, Nov. 10, 1928, 11.

272. "Roosevelt Gets 25,564 Plurality," *NYT*, Dec. 12, 1928, 33.

273. Maxwell, *New Negro, Old Left*, uses the term *Home to Moscow*, 63–93. Solomon, *Cry Was Unity*, 96; H. Smith, *Black Man in Red Russia*, 77; American Party Representative to the ECCI, Oct. 4, 1928, and American Party Representative to the ECCI, Oct. 14, 1928, 35, 36, both in LFWP.

CHAPTER 2: RAISING THE RED FLAG IN THE SOUTH

1. Haywood, *Black Bolshevik*, 5–55; quot. 7.

2. Ibid., 26.

3. Nalty, *Strength*, 112, 116; Williams, *Sidelights*, 141–42. For discrimination, see Lentz-Smith, "Great War for Civil Rights." Haywood, *Black Bolshevik*, 79–83, puts Otto at Camp Stewart, but it may have been Camp Hill.

4. J. D. Hall et al., *Like a Family*, 227; Salmond, *Gastonia*, 36, 52, 66–67. Pope, *Millhands*, 244–45, discounts firsthand testimony on black workers' involvement. See also Haessley, "Mill Mother's Lament"; J. D. Hall, "Women Writers"; Draper, "Gastonia Revisited"; Solomon, *Cry Was Unity*, 108–11.

5. ISAD.

6. Draper, *American Communism and Soviet Russia*, 350–54, 386–91, 398–401; T. Morgan, *Covert Life*, 78–83; Klehr and Haynes, *American Communist Movement*, 49–50; R. J. Alexander, *Right Opposition*, 20–21; Graziosi, *New Peculiar State*, 28–29.

7. "Meeting of the Negro Commission," Jan. 3, 1929, f515, r130, d1685, 1, CPUSA; "Huiswoud Makes Report," *DW*, March 9, 1929, 1; Huiswoud, "Report," 203–08. After reorganization in 1929, Huiswoud claimed 12 branches and 159 members. See Stachel, "Organization Report" (Apr.): 184, and Stachel, "Organization Report" (May): 246. Briggs, "Our Negro Work," 495; Solomon, *Cry Was Unity*, 97–98; Klehr and Haynes, *American Communist Movement*, 55–56; J. M. Turner, *Caribbean Crusaders*, 162–64, 171; Naison, *Communists in Harlem*, 19.

8. "Minutes of the Negro Department, Central Committee," Feb. 12, 1929, f515, r130, d1685, 12, CPUSA; "Huiswoud Makes Report," *DW*, March 9, 1929, 1; Huiswoud, "Report," 207.

9. "Meeting Negro Department," March 11, 1929, f515, r130, d1685, 17, CPUSA; "Huiswoud Tells Convention," *DW*, March 11, 1929, 1; Puro, "Tasks."

10. Klehr and Haynes, *American Communist Movement*, 45–47.

11. Ibid., 45–47, 64–66. Dual unionism was to be international. On the RILU (Profintern), see Swain, "Was the Profintern?"; Barrett, *Foster*, 160; Draper, *American Communism and Soviet Russia*, 284–90.

12. "Trade Union Programme," March 11, 1929, 495/155/74, RGASPI; Huiswoud, "World Aspects."

13. Ibid.; Griffler, "Black Radical Intellectual," 56.

14. Draper, *American Communism and Soviet Russia*, 287–90. Crouch, *Testimony*, 183.

15. Thirteenth Census, North Carolina, r1135, Moravian Falls Township, 5601; Turner and Philbeck, comp., "Wilkes County"; Absher, ed., *Heritage*, vol. 1, and Simpson, ed., *Heritage*, vol. 2; Crouch, *Historical Sketches*, 115, 315; "No 'Nigger Equality' Eh?" *YJ*, Oct. 1924.

16. *FK*, June 1925; Alice McFarland, "James Larkin Pearson," reprinted from *CO*, June 9, 1929, NCCCF.

17. Klansman's Creed," *YJ*, Oct. 1924; "Ku Klux Klucks," *PP*, March 1923; "James Larkin Pearson," *WSJS*, Feb. 17, 1963, NCCCF; "Upton Sinclair Praises," *WSJ*, Apr. 22, 1929, NCCCF.

18. Associate Editor, "Joycrafter Ideals," *PP*, May 1923, 3.

19. Paul Crouch, "Thoughts," *PP*, June 1923, 3; "Turn Soldiers into Reds," *NYT*, Apr. 24, 1926, 19.

20. PCT; Crouch, *Testimony*, 181–83; "Turn Soldiers into Reds," *NYT*, Apr. 24, 1926, 19; "Army 'Red' Sentenced," *NYT*, Apr. 5, 1925, E16; "Army 'Reds' Terms," *NYT*, May 13, 1925, 34; "To Aid Convicted," *NYT*, May 21, 1925, 15; "Army 'Reds' Ordered," *NYT*, Aug. 2, 1925, 8.

21. PCT; Crouch, *Testimony*, 181–82. Crouch became an FBI informer and HUAC witness. When his testimony involves others, I do not credit it without corroborating evidence.

22. "V. The Strike," Nov. 10, 1929, 534/7/482, 161, RGASPI; "Cases," Dec. 29–31, 16, rl, 0023-52, ILD.

23. Beal, *Proletarian Journey*, 48, 54, 88–106. Beal gives the date of his arrival as January 1929, but Supreme Court of North Carolina, Spring Term, 1930, No. 456—*State v. Fred Erwin Beal, et al.*, gives the date as December 1928, f4521, b125, PG.

24. PCT. Crouch chose Beal as the "most suitable organizer." See Salmond, *Gastonia*, 17–19; Beal *Proletarian Journey*, 110–11.

25. Beal, *Proletarian Journey*, 131; Reeve, "Gastonia Textile," 37–40; quot. 39; Lloyd, *Gastonia*, quot. 8.

26. Weisbord, *Radical Life*, 177; Salmond, *Gastonia*, xii; Myers, "Field Notes."

27. Quote in ISG/S; Myers, "Field Notes"; "Widely Known Agitator," *N&O*, Apr. 9, 1929, 2; Dunne, *Gastonia*, 58. A semiskilled woman made $14 per week, Lloyd, *Gastonia*, 7–8.

28. J. D. Hall et al., *Like a Family*, 183; Weisbord, *Radical Life*, 180; Lloyd, *Gastonia*, 10; Pope, *Millhands*.

29. J. D. Hall, "Private Eyes," 24–39; Fink, *Fulton Bag*; Kuhn, *Contesting*; Salmond, *Gastonia*, 14–16.

30. Weisbord, *Radical Life*, 179; Dunne, *Gastonia*, 19–20.

31. Pope, *Millhands*, 234. Pope concedes the story might have been apocryphal.

32. "Embryo Strike," *GDG*, Apr. 2, 1929, 1; "Report to CEC," NTWU, Feb. 1929, 532/7/489, 21–22, "Special Report to the CEC," NTWU, 534/7/489, 148, "Report on the Gastonia Strike," May 8, 1929, 534/7/489, 102, all in RGASPI. Draper, "Gastonia Revisited," 13; Beal, *Proletarian Journey*, 124–29; Salmond, *Gastonia*, 24. With 1,100 workers per shift, management claimed 50% of the day

shift remained on the job. Night shift workers were more prounion, so 1,000 total strikers is a reasonable estimate. The second day, Beal reported 95% out, and the mill reported 50% of the night shift and 25% of the day shift out, "Call Out the Militia," *GDG*, Apr. 3, 1929, 1.

33. "Labor Federation," *N&O*, Apr. 12, 1929, 2; "Report on the Gastonia Strike," May 8, 1929, 534/7/489, 102, RGASPI; "Reds Are Threatening Southwide," *GDG*, Apr. 5, 1929, 1; "General View," *GDG*, Apr. 8, 1929, 1; "Widely Known Agitator," *N&O*, Apr. 9, 1929, 2; "End of Strike Trouble," *N&O*, Apr. 11, 1929, 1; "Strike Status," *N&O*, Apr. 13, 1929, 1; Salmond, *Gastonia*, 9. Concurrent strikes in Elizabethton, TN, and Union and Greenville, SC, were non-Communist, Myers, "Field Notes." Pineville millowners had recently replaced some white workers with black workers, Beal, *Proletarian Journey*, 120.

34. ISG/S; Beal, *Proletarian Journey*, 130, 140; Clarence Miller and Jack Johnstone also went.

35. Crouch, "Testimony," 187; "Developments," *N&O*, Apr. 7, 1929, 2; Beal, *Proletarian Journey*, 130; Morray, *Project Kuzbas*, 126; "Who Are the Gastonia Prisoners?," 171.

36. Weisbord, *Radical Life*, 115–16; Weisbord, "Passaic."

37. Pope, *Millhands*, x; Jack Johnstone to Comrade Lozovsky, May 10, 1929, 534/7/485, 91, RGASPI; Salmond, *Gastonia*, 52.

38. Jack Johnstone to Comrade Lozovsky, May 10, 1929, 534/7/485, 91, RGASPI; Draper, "Gastonia Revisited," 20–23.

39. "5 De New York YM3 138 Nil Bia Northern=WLT Profintern Lozovsky Moscow," 29 IV 29 (Apr. 29, 1929), 534/7/485, RGASPI. On Lozovsky, see Draper, *American Communism and Soviet Russia*, 284; Draper, *Roots of American Communism*, 319.

40. "Meeting of Negro Department," Apr. 12, 1929, f515, r130, d1685, 23, CPUSA.

41. "Weisbord Urges National Guard to Meeting," *GDG*, Apr. 8, 1929, 2.

42. John Owens, "Analysis," Apr. 13, 1929, 534/7/489, 61, RGASPI; "Meeting of the National Negro Department," Apr. 15, 1929, f515, r155, d1685, 24, CPUSA.

43. John Owens, "Analysis," Apr. 13, 1929, 534/7/489, 61, RGASPI; Owens, "Strike Vignettes," 101; Salmond, *Gastonia*, 24; Myers, "Field Notes."

44. "Meeting of National Negro Department," Apr. 15, 1929, f515, r155, d1685, 24, CPUSA; Garrison, *Vorse*, 220.

45. "Fifty-Five Hour Week," *N&O*, Apr. 13, 1929, 2.

46. Beal, *Proletarian Journey*, 141–42; Weisbord, *Radical Life*, 179.

47. Weisbord, *Radical Life*, 175. Beal, *Proletarian Journey*, 139, says he "disregarded" Weisbord's orders.

48. Briggs, "Negro Question," 326; Jack Johnstone to Comrade Lozovsky, May 10, 1929, 534/7/485, 91, RGASPI; Solomon, *Cry Was Unity*, 145.

49. "Call Out the Militia," *GDG*, Apr. 3, 1929, 1; "Weisbord Urges National Guard," *GDG*, Apr. 8, 1929, 2; "Troops Sent to Gastonia," *N&O*, Apr. 4, 1929, 1.

50. "Sermon on the Strike," *FK*, May 1929.

51. "Gardner Denounces," *N&O*, Apr. 21, 1929, 1; "Demands Prosecution," *N&O*, Apr. 23, 1929, 1; Myers, "Field Notes"; Beal, *Proletarian Journey*, 149–50; Salmond, *Gastonia*, 37–38, 41–43.

52. "Gardner Denounces," and "Draws Dynamite," *N&O*, Apr. 21, 1929, 1; "Officers Use Bayonets and Blackjacks, *N&O*, Apr. 23, 1929, 1; Reeve, "Gastonia," 23; Salmond, *Gastonia*, 45–46, 74–75.

53. "Worker's Friend," *GDG*, Apr. 4, 1929, 1.

54. "Ad," Apr. 3, 1929, 8, and "Viper!" Apr. 11, 1929, 1, both in *GDG*; Salmond, *Gastonia*, 26, 29, 35.

55. "If the Leaders Were Gone," *GDG*, Apr. 13, 1929, 4; "Waving the Red Flag," *GDG*, Apr. 13, 1929, 4.

56. Dunne, *Gastonia*, 29.

57. "Red Russianism Lifts Its Gory Hands," *GDG*, Apr. 5, 1929, 12. On interracial dancing, see Maxwell, *New Negro, Old Left*, 95–96.

58. David Clark, *GDG*, Apr. 6, 1929, 1.

59. "Becky Ann, for Many Years Was a Mill Worker," *GDG*, Apr. 12, 1929, 2.

60. AFL rep. quoted in Salmond, *Gastonia*, 55; Heywood Broun, *Nation*, Sept. 25, 1929, quoted in Reeve, "Gastonia Textile," 38.

61. "Meeting OG Group," May 12, 1929, 495/155/77, 2, and Harold Williams, May 11, 1929, 495/155/80, both in RGASPI; Salmond, *Gastonia*, 41.

62. "Pineville Repudiates Beal and Pershing," *GDG*, Apr. 18, 1929, 5; "Draws Dynamite," *N&O*, Apr. 21, 1929, 1; "Wennonah Mill," *N&O*, Apr. 23, 1929, 2.

63. "Women Playing Big Part," *GDG*, Apr. 4, 1929, 2; "City Passes an Ordinance," *GDG*, Apr. 20, 1929; Weisbord, *Radical Life*, 195; Salmond, *Gastonia*, 48, points out many male pickets arrested, but Gerson remembers "a larger number of women," ISG/S.

64. Weisbord, *Radical Life*, 195.

65. "Report on the Gastonia Strike," May 8, 1929, 534/7/489, 102, RGASPI; Salmond, *Gastonia*, 46–47.

66. "Meeting National Negro Department," June 11, 1929, f515, r130, d1685, 32, CPUSA.

67. Briggs, "Negro Question," 326; "Leadership of the Struggles," f515, r130, d1687, 52–54, CPUSA; Salmond, *Gastonia*, 36, 66–67; ISG/S.

68. Photograph, *LD* 4 (Aug. 1929): 100; Salmond, *Gastonia*, 21.

69. "Pershing and Beal Strive," *GDG*, Apr. 6, 1929, 1; "More Evictions," *N&O*, May 24, 1929, 6; "Success of Strike Hangs," *GDG*, Apr. 11, 1929, 1; "1,000 Operatives Back," *GDG*, Apr. 12, 1929; "Strikers Build Tent Town," *GDG*, May 23, 1929, 1; Weisbord, *Radical Life*, 176, 180, 203; Salmond, *Gastonia*, 54.

70. Obituary of Mrs. Daisy Davis McDonald, Apr. 18, 1977, obituary notice, James Elmer McDonald, "abt. 2004," all on www.roots.web.com, accessed May 18, 2006; ISG/S. Elmer returned by January 1930, J. Louis Engdahl, "Six Months in the South," *LD* (Jan. 1930), in 534/8/135, RGASPI.

71. Weisbord, *Radical Life*, 206.

72. John Owens to Isbell, May 22, 1929, 495/155/80, and A. L. Isbell, Elizabeth L. Griffin, C. Henry, E. L. Doty to Central Executive Committee, May 24, 1929, 534/7/485, both in RGASPI; Cyril Briggs to Comrades Isbell, Henry, Griffin, Doty, June 12, 1929, f515, r1, d1689, CPUSA; Solomon, *Cry Was Unity*, 129; Weisbord, *Radical Life*, 193, attributes the shortage of funds to party factionalism.

73. Beal, *Proletarian Journey*, 156.

74. Earl Browder to Comrade Lozovsky, Apr. 29, 1929, 534/4/485, 84, RGASPI; Salmond, *Gastonia*, 23.

75. "Call Out the Militia," Apr. 3, 1929, *GDG*, 1; Beal, *Proletarian Journey*, 136.

76. T. Morgan, *Covert Life*, 84; R. J. Alexander, *Right Opposition*, 16–28; Gitlow, *I Confess*, 532–35.

77. J. M. Turner, *Caribbean Crusaders*, 173–76; quoted in Draper, *American Communism and Soviet Russia*, 422–23; Gitlow, *Whole of Their Lives*, 160–61; Haywood, *Black Bolshevik*, 291–304. T. Morgan, *Covert Life*, 99, relates the Welsh quote "What the hell does this bastard single me out for?"

78. T. Morgan, *Covert Life*, 94–96; Draper, *American Communism and Soviet Russia*, ch. 18, quot. 422; Klehr and Haynes, *American Communist Movement*, 46–50; R. J. Alexander, *Right Opposition*, 22–28. See also Gitlow, *I Confess*, chs. 14, 15.

79. Benjamin Gitlow, Jay Lovestone, William Miller, Tom Mycouch, Edward Welsh, William J. White, Bertram D. Wolfe, "Appeal to the Comintern," in f23, b20, and Gitlow, Lovestone, White, Wolfe, to Every Party Member, Aug. 27, 1929, f2, b6, both in TDRF.

80. "Minutes for the Negro Bureau," June 8, 1929, 495/155/67, RGASPI; 125 families (500 people) had been evicted by May 13, 1929; "More Eviction Papers," *GDG*, May 13, 1929, 1; "Fifteen Strikers Are Reinstated," *N&O*, May 23, 1929, 3.

81. F515, r1, d1688, 34, CPUSA; Kennington, "African-American Organizing," 40–41.

82. The Negro Department censured Johnstone, Reeve, and Pershing for "retreating on the Party's Negro policy." They then condemned Hall's formation of a separate ANLC, but ANLC members were not textile workers. See Draper, "Gastonia Revisited," 22; Griffler, "Black Radical Intellectual," 170. For Hall's organizing of black textile workers, see "Meeting of the National Negro Department," June 11, 1929, f515, r130, d1685, 32, CPUSA; Harold Williams [?] to ?, May 11, 1929, 495/155/80, and "Report on the Gastonia Strike," May 8, 1929, 534/7/489, 109, both in RGASPI; Briggs, "Negro Question," 326; Briggs, "Further Notes," 391–94; O. Hall, "Note"; "Negroes Invited," *GDG*, May 11, 1929, 1.

83. F515, r1, d1688, 12, CPUSA; Briggs, "Our Negro Work"; Naison, *Communists in Harlem*, 19; "Race Question Raised," *N&O*, May 12, 1929, 2; Salmond, *Gastonia*, 65.

84. "Negroes Invited," *GDG*, May 11, 1929, 1; "N.T.W.U. an Outlaw," *GDG*, May 14, 1929, 4; "Strike in Gaston County," *GDG*, May 17, 1929, 1.

85. Historians have referred to May as Wiggins, even though she had resumed using her maiden name, May. Only one of her children used Wiggins. Vincent Lee Payne, son of Charlotte (Chalady) May and grandson of Ella May to author, July 10, 2001. "Strike Situation," *GDG*, Apr. 16, 1929, 1; "Three Additional Strikes," *N&O*, Apr. 25, 1929, 1, 2; "Partial Walkout at Another Mill," *N&O*, Apr. 27, 1929, 1, 2. The American Mills used black labor. The Osage Mill employed white labor, except in the preparation and cleaning.

86. Tippett, *When Southern Labor Stirs*, 83–88.

87. Dunne, *Gastonia*, 58.

88. Weisbord, *Radical Life*, 208, 260; Pope, *Millhands*, 245–46.

89. Paul Crouch, [1931], f515, r173, d2284, CPUSA; Crouch, *Testimony*, 219; Salmond, *Gastonia*, 185; Beal, *Proletarian Journey*, 148; "Pioneers Return from Soviet Union," f Blacks and Soviet Russia, b1, MSRK; IMHV, 1:28.

90. "Race Question Is Raised," *N&O*, May 12, 1929, 2; Reeve, "Gastonia," 27–28; "12 Gastonia Textile Strikers Pay Visit," *GDG*, May 11, 1929, 9; Salmond, *Gastonia*, 60.

91. Supreme Court of North Carolina, Spring Term, 1930, No. 456—*State v. Fred Erwin Beal, et al.*, f4521, b125, PG; "Strikers' Guard Fires," *N&O*, June 8, 1929, 1; Weisbord, *Radical Life*, 220–24; Beal, *Proletarian Journey*, 161–71; Dunne, *Gastonia*, 36; Salmond, *Gastonia*, 70–76.

92. "Long Song about a Strong Wrong," *FK*, June 1929; Cash, "War in the South," 163; Salmond, *Gastonia*, 146–50.

93. Salmond, *Gastonia*, 66–68, 80, follows Sophie Melvin Gerson's interview to argue that Hall left well before the shoot-out. On the event, see "Redouble Effort to Apprehend," *GDG*, June 8, 1929, 1; "24 Are Released," *GDG*, June 13, 1929, 3. Evidence on Hall's presence includes *DW*, Oct. 4, 1929; Briggs, "Results of National Negro Week," *DW*, June 8, 1929, 6, and June 12, 1929, 2; "Meeting of National Negro Department," June 11, 1929, f515, r130, d1685, 32, and Cyril Briggs, "Leadership," f515, r130, d1687, 52–54, 73–74, both in CPUSA; "White Workers Help Negro to Escape Bosses' Thugs," *NM* 1 (July 1929), 495/155/80, RGASPI; O. Hall, "Gastonia and the Negro," 153, 164. Briggs to Comrades Isbell, Henry, Griffin, Doty, June 12, 1929, reports Hall "just returned from Gastonia after having been in great personal danger," in f515, r1, d1689, CPUSA. Weisbord, *Radical Life*, 206, 226; Haywood, *Black Bolshevik*, 317–19.

94. "Their Blood Cries Out," *GDG*, June 8, 1929, 4.

95. "Nat Turner," Nov. 11, 1929, 495/155/82, 24, RGASPI; "Race Workers Frown," *AA*, Aug. 3, 1929, 3.

96. "White Workers Help Negro to Escape Bosses' Thugs," *NM* 1 (July 1929), 495/155/80, RGASPI.

97. Page, "Inter-Racial Relations," and Page, *Gathering Storm*.

98. Quoted in Herndon, *Let Me Live*, 81. Quoted differently by C. A. Hathaway in a speech reprinted in Foner and Shapiro, eds., *American Communism and Black Americans*, 157.

99. Page, "Inter-Racial Relations."

100. "Negro Trade Union Work," f515, r130, d1687, 74, CPUSA; Denning, *Cultural Front*, 262.

101. "Meeting of National Negro Department," June 11, 1929, f515, r130, d1685, 32, CPUSA.

102. "Report of Comrade Lozovsky," *International Press Correspondence*, Oct. 4, 1929, 1197; Weisbord, *Radical Life*, 293; Draper, *American Communism and Soviet Russia*, 434; Haywood, "Report on the Negro Work," Nov. 11, 1929, 494/155/177, 219, RGASPI.

103. "Beal Was Not Threatened," *GDG*, June 9, 1929, 1; "Beal Says," *GDG*, June 10, 1929, 2; "Friday Night's Tragedy," *N&O*, June 9, 1929, 1, 2.

104. Dunne, "Gastonia"; Dunne, "Resolution and Report," [summer 1929], 534/7/90, 48, RGASPI. Seventy-one arrested, in ISG/S. Charges were made and dropped: CP records say 13 charged with murder, 10 with assault. Salmond, *Gastonia*, 87–88, gives 15 and 8; Beal, *Proletarian Journey*, 177, says 16 charged with murder. The ILD reported 16 charged with murder and 7 with assault, "Cases," Dec. 29–31, 1929, r1, 0023-52, ILD.

105. Beal, *Proletarian Journey*, 180–82; Salmond, *Gastonia*, 99–103; ISG/S.

106. Dunne, Gerson, Oehler, Melvin, Oak, "Thesis on Work among Negroes in the South," Oct. 8, 1929, 495/155/67, and Dunne, Gerson, Oak, [fall 1929?], 534/7/90, 35–36, both in RGASPI; Salmond, *Gastonia*, 30.

107. Dunne, Gerson, Oak, [fall 1929?], 534/7/90, 36, RGASPI.

108. C. L. Baker and W. J. Baker, "Shaking All Corners."

109. Jessie Lloyd, "Gastonia Sidelights," Aug. 27, 1929, f11, b93, JLO. Salmond, *Gastonia*, 113, quotes Margaret Larkin that the lines ended with an "odd sort of yip," characteristic of Appalachian folk singing and lining out hymns. Ella May, "Song Ballet," f11, b93, JLO.

110. Weisbord, *Radical Life*, 245; "To All Workers!" f11, b93, JLO; Salmond, *Gastonia*, 113–24. Judge Barnhill thought the jurors hopelessly split and saw the juror's psychotic break as a "godsend," "Barnhill Talks," *N&O*, [date obscured], f12, b93, JLO.

111. Margaret Larkin, [Sept. 16, 1929], and Mary Heaton Vorse, "Songs Live on, Ella May Dies," [*The Graphic*], Sept. 16, 1929, f12, b93, JLO; "Gastonia Mob Slays Woman," *N&O*, Sept. 15, 1929, 1; Salmond, *Gastonia*, 128, 157–59, 163; Tippett, *When Southern Labor Stirs*, 106, reports, "My God, they have shot me!"

112. Weisbord, *Radical Life*, 260.

113. "The Rope as Well as the Electric Chair," *DW*, [Sept. 20, 1929], "Hit Mill Terror," *DW*, [Sept. 20, 1929], "Tend [*sic*] Huge Meets," *DW*, [Sept. 20, 1929], "Jury Probes Slaying," *CO*, [Oct. 24, 1929]; "Gaston Jury Declines to Indict," *CO*, [Oct. 25, 1929], "Gastonia Frees 9," *NYT*, [Oct. 24, 1929], all clippings in f12, b93, JLO; Salmond, *Gastonia*, 155.

114. "Governor Declares Law," *N&O*, Sept. 15, 1929; ISG/K; Morrison, *O. Max Gardner*, 55–64, quot. 58, 61, 63; Weisbord, *Radical Life*, 260; Salmond, *Gastonia*, 128, 158–66.

115. Beal, *Proletarian Journey*, 195; CEC Minutes, Oct. 6, 1929, f515, r128, d1654, 59, and Hugo Oehler to Dear Comrades, Oct. 7, 1929, f515, r128, d1654, 53, both in CPUSA; Haywood Speech, Jan. 1, 1930, 495/155/83, RGASPI; typescript in f NY Negro-1–3, b12, RM; "Cases," 18, Dec. 29–31, 1929, r1, 0023-52, ILD; Salmond, *Gastonia*, 128, 140–41.

116. "Barnhill Talks," *N&O*, [date obscured], f12, b93, JLO; prosecutor quoted in Salmond, *Gastonia*, 142; Beal, *Proletarian Journey*, 175–76, 198–99.

117. "Gastonia Verdict," f12, b93, JLO; Salmond, *Gastonia*, 147–48.

118. Salmond, *Gastonia*, 148.

119. "Red Hendryx [*sic*] Goes Right Back to Gastonia," *Labor's News*, Nov. 16, 1929, 6, f11, b93, JLO.

120. Beal, *Proletarian Journey*, 209–10; Lloyd, *Gastonia*, 30–31; "Workers Trial," n.d., and "10,000 Reds at Rally," [*NYT*], Nov. 4 [?], both in f13, b2, SAD.

121. "Resolution on March 16," Dist. 16, f515, r162, d2147, 8, CPUSA; "Organization Conference Minutes," March 31–Apr. 4, 1930, f19, b6, TDRF; Huiswoud,
"October Plenum"; Kelley, *Hammer and Hoe*, 14.

122. ISG/S. Organizing began during the Gastonia strike, Reeve, "Gastonia," 25.

123. J. Louis Engdahl, "Six Months in the South," and photograph in 534/8/135,
RGASPI; Hugo Oehler to Dear Comrades, Dec. 11, 1929, f515, r128, d1564, 61,
CPUSA.

124. Tom Johnson and Harry Jackson were the first organizers in Birmingham, Kelley, *Hammer and Hoe*, 14, J. S. Allen, *Organizing*, 22–25.

125. Salmond, *Gastonia*, 154; Sol Harper to Dear Comrades, 1929, f515, r155, d2024,
16, "Communist Party of the USA," Dec. 22, 1929, f515, 137, d1807, 22, Hugo
Oehler to Dear Comrades, Dec. 11, 1929, f515, r128, d1654, 61, and "Meeting of
the Provisional," Dec. 29, 1929, f515, r137, d1807, all in CPUSA; Naison, *Communists in Harlem*, 25.

126. "Workers Come," f515, r162, d2148, 25, CPUSA.

127. "White Workers/Negro Workers," f515, r317, d1807, 29, CPUSA.

128. "A New Line," f515, r155, d2024, 39, CPUSA.

129. Otto Kuusinen, "Directives for the Thesis on the Negro Question," Sept. 29,
1929, 495/155/94, 203, RGASPI.

130. "Ladies Hold Nice Conference," *SW*, Nov. 8, 1930, f515, r162, d2150, 1, Dear
Comrade, n.d. [12/30?], f515, r162, d2148, 21, and "Meeting of the Secretariat
of Dist. 16," Feb. 3, 1930, f515, r162, d2147, 31, all in CPUSA.

131. Feimster, " 'Ladies and Lynching.' "

132. "Negro Department Minutes," May 12, 1929, 495/155/77, 125–32, and "Negro
Department CPUSA, Part Two," (n.d.), 495/155/43, both in RGASPI.

133. "Minutes of Subcommittee," f515, r130, d1685, 18, CPUSA; "Negro Question in
the U.S.A.," f515, r130, d1687, CPUSA; Darcy, "Fight on Lynching," 251.

134. Solomon, *Cry Was Unity*, 108; Lewis, *In Their Own Interests*, 131–32.

135. Irving Keith, "Organizing in Virginia," *DW*, May 6, 1929, in Foner and Allen,
eds., *American Communism and Black Americans*, 209–10; "Report of Negro
Department," June 19, 1929, 495/155/80, RGASPI; Harry Haywood, "Report
on Negro Work," Nov. 11, 1929, and "Report of Acting Negro Director," June
19, 1929, both in f515, r139, d1687, 2, "Meeting of the Secretariat of Dist. 16,"
Feb. 3, 1930, f515, r162, d2147, 42, all in CPUSA; Briggs, "Our Negro Work,"
494–501; Solomon, *Cry Was Unity*, 132–33.

136. "Memorandum for Mr. Mumford," Oct. 6, 1942, FBI, f LSNR, b3, MSRK;
"Report of Earl Browder," *DW*, Apr. 14, 1934, reprinted in Foner and Shapiro,
eds., *American Communism and Black Americans*, xv, xvi, 117–22; "League of
Struggle for Negro Rights," in *FBI's RACON*, ed. and comp. R. A. Hill, 586; J.
M. Turner, *Caribbean Crusaders*, 183–84.

137. Klehr and Haynes, *American Communist Movement*, 75–76; Otto Hall, "On
Underestimation of Negro Work," f Negro 1931, b12, RM; Browder, "For
National Liberation."

138. "Resolution of the Central Committee," March 16, 1931, f Negro 1931, b12,
RM.

139. "C.I. Resolution," 49, and William Wilson [Patterson], "Alliance of the Negro

and White," Aug. 9, 1930, 286, both in 495/155/87, RGASPI. Patterson/Wilson in Hans Thogersen to Comrade [?], May 13, 1930, 495/155/90, 68, RGASPI.

140. "Excerpts from Comrade Browder's Report," f515, r167, d2222, 42-5, CPUSA; Kuusinen, "Directives for the Thesis on the Negro Question," Sept. 29, 1930, 495/155/94, RGASPI; Barrett, *Foster*, 179.

141. "Report of Comrade Tom Johnson to Politburo," May 14, 1931, f515, r167, d2222, 53, CPUSA.

142. "Negro Department Meeting," Sept. 10, 1929, f515, r130, d1685, 36, and "National Negro Department," Nov. 22, 1929, f515, r130, d1685, 42, both in CPUSA.

143. "C.I. Resolution," 48–55. The final text appeared in English in 1931. See "Resolution on the Negro Question," 153–67; Lovestone, "Some Issues"; Pepper, "American Negro Problems"; Rubinstein, "Industrialization of the South"; *Thesis and Resolutions*, in *Documentary History*, ed. Johnpoll, 2:24–27; untitled, Aug. 19, 1935, 495/14/60, RGASPI; Haywood, *Black Bolshevik*, 321–27; Solomon, *Cry Was Unity*, 81–89, 164–84; Draper, *Rediscovery*, 64–65; Draper, *American Communism and Soviet Russia*, 350–53; J. M. Turner, *Caribbean Crusader*, 181–85; Klehr and Tompson, "Self-Determination," 354–66; Kanet, "Comintern"; R. J. Alexander, *Right Opposition*, 17–19; Berland, "Emergence of the Communist Perspective, Part One," 411–32, and Berland, "Emergence of the Communist Perspective, Part Two."

144. Beal, *Proletarian Journey*, 247; Solomon, *Cry Was Unity*, 85–89.

145. Solomon, *Cry Was Unity*, 84.

146. Haywood, "Against Bourgeois-Liberal," 694–712; Nasanov, "Against Liberalism," 296–308; Haywood, "Theoretical Defenders," 497–508; Haywood, *Black Bolshevik*, 331–38; Griffler, "Black Radical Intellectual," 110–21.

147. "Resolution on the Negro Question," 153–67. Gastonia organizer Amy Schechter wrote the draft, "Bureau Meeting," Jan. 21, 1931, 495/72/94, 1, and "Minutes," Oct. 10, 1929, 495/155/67, both in RGASPI. Schechter, "Proposals," Oct. 11, 1931, f515, r167, d2222, CPUSA; Solomon, *Cry Was Unity*, 83. Trotskyites ridiculed self-determination, Shachtman, *Race and Revolution*, 67–88.

148. W. W. Ball to W. J. Thackston, Oct. 15, 1929, b19, WWB.

149. Sol Harper to Dear Comrades, 1929, f515, r155, d2024, 16, CPUSA.

150. "Communist Party Organization Conference," March 31–Apr. 4, 1930, 7, f19, b6, TDRF.

151. "Report of Comrade Tom Johnson to Politburo," May 14, 1931, f515, r167, d2222, 52; J. S. Allen, *Organizing*, 51; J. S. Allen, *Negro Question*, 169–203.

152. "Report on Tour of Comrade Ford," Jan. 19–Feb. 19, 1930, f515, r163, d2174, 8, CPUSA; "Third Session of the National Executive Board," March 19, 1930, "Report of Ford on Negro Work," 534/7/494, RGASPI.

153. Beal, *Proletarian Journey*, 208–16.

154. Weisbord, *Radical Life*, 284; Salmond, *Gastonia*, 141–53, quot., 142, and ch. 6, "Aftermath"; Beal, *Proletarian Journey*, 209–21. Clarence Miller was the only organizer who happily stayed in the USSR. Clarence Isadore Miller Dossier, 1938, "Form for International Work," 495/261/1633, "Spies," 515/1/2/772,

91, "Secret. Party Committee, Administration, MOPR" (in Russian), Apr. 23, 1935, 495/72/282, all in RGASPI.

155. Beal, *Proletarian Journey*, 217–18, 226.

156. Ibid., 245.

157. "Won't Give Up Reds," [*NYT*], Aug. 22, 1930 (handwritten), "Hunt Gastonia Reds," [*NYT*], Aug. 22, 1930 (handwritten), both in f14, b2, SAD; William Z. Foster to Gentlemen, [n.d.], 515, r162, d2174, 51, and [Roger Baldwin] to Foster, on ACLU letterhead, Nov. 13, 1930, f515, r163, d2174, 60, both in CPUSA; Baldwin to Editor, *DW*, June 20, 1929, f15, b1, SAD; Salmond, *Gastonia*, 167.

158. American Party Representative to ECCI to Central Executive Committee, Oct. 13, 1928, 495/261/1476, 34, RGASPI. H. Smith, *Black Man in Red Russia*, 77–83, remarks that Fort-Whiteman often offered to introduce him to Bukharin, even after Stalin denounced Bukharin.

159. Fragment of the poem in a Moscow newspaper, in the possession of Sergei Zhuravlev. Transliteration Zhuravlev; translation Anita Seth.

160. Ashkhabad, Turkmenistan, cotton mill, 1933, Diary No. I, f12438, b492, LH.

CHAPTER 3: FROM THE GREAT DEPRESSION
TO THE GREAT TERROR

1. "Grand Rally!" *BS*, Aug. 22, 1930, r2, 20, CIC; "Fascists Open War," *AG* (extra ed.), July 18, 1930, 13; *AJ*, July 28, 1930, quoted in J. H. Moore, "Communists and Fascists"; Tribble, "Black Shirts"; C. H. Martin, "White Supremacy"; D. L. Smith, *New Deal*, 27–28. The full name was the American Fascisti Association and Order of Black Shirts.

2. "Grand Rally!" *BS*, Aug. 22, 1930, 1, r2, 20, CIC.

3. Quoted in J. H. Moore, "Communists and Fascists," 447–48; Tribble, "Black Shirts," 205.

4. "Black Shirts Meet Defeat," [1930], r4, 70, CIC.

5. "Black Shirts Versus Night Shirts," 758; Engdahl, "Storm over the U.S.," 118.

6. "Depression and the Race Problem," r4, 72, 6, CIC.

7. "What Is the American Fascisti?," *BS*, Aug. 22, 1930, 1, r2, 20, CIC.

8. Tribble, "Black Shirts," 204–06; C. H. Martin, "White Supremacy."

9. "Black Shirts Meet Defeat," r4, 70, 1, CIC; Tribble, "Black Shirts," 205; quoted in J. H. Moore, "Communists and Fascists," 371–72, 378, 445. According to Moore, they had 1,700 members.

10. "Depression and the Race Problem," r4, 72, 2, CIC; Ferguson, *Black Politics.*

11. Mordecai Johnson, May 8, 1931, 12, CSPA; Biles, *South and the New Deal*, 16–35.

12. "Depression and the Race Problem," r4, 72, 4, CIC; E. C. Green, ed., *Before the New Deal*; E. C. Green, ed., *New Deal and Beyond.*

13. "Depression Emphasizes Race Discrimination," 2.

14. "Aid the Needy," *BS*, Aug. 22, 1930, 1, r2, CIC.

15. "Wanted," *BS*, Aug. 22, 1930, 4, r2, 20, CIC; Cell, *Highest Stage*, 131–44.

16. C. H. Martin, "White Supremacy," 370, 378. African Americans made up 10% of the U.S. population. Jews made up 1% of the German. D. B. Dodd and W. S. Dodd, *Historical Statistics*, 19.

17. "May Face Indictment," *AI*, n.d. [Sept. 1930], 1, 2, r2, 20, CIC; "Fascisti Waits Court Action," *AG* (home ed.), Sept. 6, 1930, 5; "Grand Jury Raps," *AJ*, Sept. 5, 1930, 1.

18. "Decatur and Macon Pastors," *AJ*, Sept. 1, 1930, 3.

19. "Black Shirts Meet Defeat," r4, 70, 4, CIC. For the riot, see Godshalk, *Veiled Visions*.

20. "Mayor A. G. Dudley," *BS*, Sept. 5, 1930, 1, and "Injunction," *BS*, Sept. 5, 1930, 1, both on r2, 20, CIC; "Black Shirts' [*sic*] Enjoined," *AG* (mkts. ed.), Sept. 1, 1930, 3.

21. R. B. Eleazer to Clarence Bowden, Jr., Nov. 7, 1930, Eleazer to Walter B. Hill, Nov. 14, 1930, Hill to Eleazer, Nov. 12, 1930, "Injunction," *BS*, Sept. 5, 1930, 1, "Attempt to Steal," *BS*, Sept. 26, 1930, 1, and "Jury Condemns," *ADW*, Sept. 26, 1930, 1, all on r2, 20, CIC.

22. "Decatur and Macon Pastors," *AJ*, Sept. 1, 1930, 3; "End of the Black Shirts," *AC*, Sept. 19, 1930, 10; "Black Shirts Get Florida," *AC*, Sept. 26, 1930, 1, 9; "Black Shirt Fascism Not Needed," *AJ*, Sept. 2, 1930, 10; "Grand Jury Raps," *AJ*, Sept. 5, 1930, 1; "Grand Jury Urges Denial," *AJ*, Sept. 7, 1930, 7; J. H. Moore, "Communists and Fascists," 450; C. H. Martin, "White Supremacy," 373.

23. "Appeal to Reason," *AC*, Aug. 31, 1930, 18.

24. "Blackshirts Balked," *SW*, Oct. 25, 1930, 2.

25. "After Hoover, the Blackshirts," *SW*, Oct. 19, 1930, 1. The attorney was Marvin Ritch.

26. M. L. McNeill to ?, Aug. 31, 1930, f515, r162, d2148, 10, CPUSA.

27. "Blackshirts Balked," *SW*, Oct. 25, 1930, 2.

28. "Rep. Bulwinkle," *ACT*, June 18, 1950, "Bulwinkle Ready," *N&O*, June 23, 1950, and "Man Who Gets Things Done," *DMH*, July 16, 1950, all in NCCCF; "Resolution on the Results of the Election Campaign [NC]," f515, r162, d2147, 29, CPUSA; "After Hoover, the Black Shirts," *SW*, Oct. 18, 1930, 1. On the CP ticket, Dewey Martin ran for U.S. Senate; J. A. Rogers and W. G. Binkley for the House. "Vote Communist," f515, r162, d2148, 17, CPUSA; "Our Candidates," *SW*, Nov. 1, 1930, 1.

29. "Resolution on the Results of the Election Campaign [NC]," f515, r162, d2147, 27, CPUSA.

30. "Economic and Political Situation," [1930?], f515, r162, d2147, 23–6, and "Dist. Meeting," Feb. 8, 1930, f515, r162, d2147, 1, both in CPUSA; C. A. Hathaway, "Failure to Organize," 786–94; Benjamin, "Unemployment Movement," 528–47; J. A. Williams, "Struggles of the Thirties," 166–78; Leab, " 'United We Eat.' " The Unemployed Councils became the Workers Alliance of America in 1935, C. A. Goldberg, "Haunted," 725–73. Solomon, *Cry Was Unity*, 147–63; F. Folsom, *Impatient Armies*; Rosenzweig, "Organizing the Unemployed."

31. "Starvation Faces Unemployed," f515, r298, d3882, 5, CPUSA; "Fight against the Plunder Program," Dec. 24, 1931, f History 1931, 1940s, 1950, 1951, b3, RM. Central Committee, "Employed and Unemployed Workers!" f19, b6, "Questions for Darcy," f3, b9, "Main Demand," f3, b9, and Jack Stachel, "March 6," *Worker* (March 7, 1965), f16, b17, all in TDRF. Herbert Benjamin coordinated the CP hunger marches, interview notes and Benjamin/Draper corre-

spondence in f15, b17, TDRF. Lorence, "Mobilizing," 66; Leab, " 'United We Eat,' " 310; Theodore Draper, *American Communism and Soviet Russia*, 175–76; Solomon, *Cry Was Unity*, 149.

32. Leab, " 'United We Eat,' " 305; Skotnes, "Communist Party, Anti-Racism"; Cyril Briggs, "Decline of the Garvey Movement," *International Press Correspondence* (Apr. 23, 1931): 407–08.

33. "Next Steps," n.d. [Dec. 1931], f Negro 1932, b12, and in f Negro 1932, b12, both in RM; "Resolution on March 6," Dist. 16, f515, r162, d2147, 8, and "Report of March 6th," f515, r162, d2148, 1, both in CPUSA; Leab, " 'United We Eat,' " 305–07.

34. "Special Meeting of Negro Department," Apr. 5, 1930, f515, r155, d2023, 7, and "Secretariat of Dist. 16," Feb. 3, 1930, f515, r162, d2147, 35, both in CPUSA; Korstad, *Civil Rights Unionism*, 125–26; Solomon, *Cry Was Unity*, 150.

35. "Fight against the Plunder Program," f History 1931, 1940s, 1950, 1951, b3, RM; Leab, " 'United We Eat' "; "Communist Party Organization Conference," March 31–Apr. 4, 1930, f19, b6, TDRF.

36. "Report of March 6th," f515, r162, d2148, 1–8, Tom Johnson to Rudy Baker, f515, r176, d2322, 198, Johnson to Sam Darcy, July 27, 1930, f515, r162, d2150, 7, all in CPUSA; Kelley, *Hammer and Hoe*, 14–18; Kelley, "New War."

37. "Report of Comrade Tom Johnson," May 14, 1931, f515, r167, d2222, 46, 42–43, CPUSA; Kelley, "New War"; Kelley, *Hammer and Hoe*; Painter, *Narrative*.

38. "London International Conference," Apr. 9, 1930, 495/155/89, RGASPI; Tom Johnson to Dear Comrades, Apr. 23, 1930, f515, r155, d1960, 9, Johnson to Max Bedacht, May 15, 1930, f515, r155, d1960, 11, Johnson to Comrade Campbell, July 28, 1930, f515, r151, d1960, 34, all in CPUSA. On money shortage, see P. Buhle, *Marxism*, 143–44. On violence, see Hy Gordon to Comrade Browder, [1930] f515, r151, d1960, 72–75, and Johnson to Browder, f515, r151, d1960, 76–79, both in CPUSA.

39. Tom Johnson to Rudy Baker, f515, r176, d2322, 198, CPUSA; "Police Squads," *AG* (home ed.), March 6, 1930, 1. For recent account that uses CPUSA papers, see Lorence, "Mobilizing," 61.

40. "Atlanta Reds," *AG* (extra ed.), March 7, 1930, 1; Tom Johnson to Max Bedacht, May 24, 1930, f515, r151, d1960, 13, CPUSA; "May Quash Six Reds' Case," *ADW*, March 24, 1932, 1; C. H. Martin, *Herndon Case*, 19.

41. " 'Reds' Adjourn in Haste," *AC*, March 10, 1930, 1; Engdahl, "Storm across the U.S.," 115–18.

42. Myra Page, "Body Wracked, Head Unbowed," *DW*, Apr. 27, 1934, reprinted in Foner and Shapiro, eds. *American Communism and Black Americans*, 340–45; "It Happened in 1933," r1, 675–96, ILD; Herndon Petition, f351, b5, PG; E. England, "Angelo Herndon," NTL; "Georgia Imprisons Negro Red," *NYT*, Jan. 19, 1933, 1; "Twenty Years!"; Brief for the Plaintiff-in-Error, in the Supreme Court of the State of Georgia, October Term, 1935, no. 11,226. *Angelo Herndon v. J. I. Lowry, Sheriff*, W. A. Sutherland, Whitney North Seymour, Counsel for Plaintiff-in-Error, 42–50, AH.

43. Acts of the General Assembly, Act No. 215, 153; "Two 'Reds' Indicted," *AJ*, Apr. 4, 1930, 2; " 'Communist' Meet," *MT*, March 10, 1930, 2; "Tear Gas Ends," *AC*,

March 10, 1930, sec. 2, 14; " 'Red' Organizers Held," *AC*, March 12, 1930, 2; "Trying to Incite Insurrection," *AC*, Apr. 5, 1930, 7; "Georgia Lawyer," *MT*, June 5, 1930, 4; "Hancock to Appeal," *AJ*, Nov. 23, 1932, 17; C. H. Martin, "Angelo Herndon Case," 6–10; C. H. Martin, *Herndon Case*, 19, 20; J. H. Moore, "Communists and Fascists"; Solomon, *Cry Was Unity*, 126.

44. "Communism and the Police," *MT*, March 12, 1930, 4.

45. "Down with Lynch Law!," f515, r137, d1897, 26, CPUSA; "Nation Searched," *AG* (eve. ed.), Apr. 5, 1930, 1; J. D. Hall, *Revolt against Chivalry*, 129–30.

46. O'Flaherty, "I.L.D."; "Lawyer Says Clients," *AG* (eve. ed.), Apr. 14, 1930, 3; "Two Reds," *AG* (eve. ed.), Apr. 21, 1930, 1; "State Wins First Step," *AG* (extra spts. ed.), Apr. 23, 1930, 1; Tom Johnson to Dear Comrades, Apr. 23, 1930, f515, r151, d1960, 9–10, and Johnson to Max Bedacht, May 15, 1930, f515, r151, d1960, 11, both in CPUSA; "Reds Threaten Reprisal," *AG* (eve. ed.), Apr. 28, 1930, sec. 2, 9.

47. "Atlanta Reds Defy Mayor," *AG*, May 1, 1930, 18; "Reds Are Warned," *AJ*, Apr. 29, 1930, 35; C. H. Martin, "Angelo Herndon Case," 2.

48. "Police Department Wins," *AJ*, May 2, 1930, 8; C. H. Martin, "Angelo Herndon Case," 13.

49. Tom Johnson to Max Bedacht, May 24, 1930, f515, r151, d1960, 14, CPUSA; " 'Reds' Plan May Day Rally," *AC*, Apr. 29, 1930; "Beavers to Prevent," *AC*, Apr. 30, 1930; "No Communism," *AC*, May 1, 1930, 10; "Death Threats," *AG* (mkts. ed.), May 1, 1930, 1, 4; C. H. Martin, "Angelo Herndon Case," 12.

50. "Carr and Powers," *AC*, May 6, 1930, 14; "Reds Threaten," *AG* (eve. ed.), Apr. 28, 1930, sec. 2, 9; "Mother Pleads," *AG* (eve. ed.), May 7, 1930, 3. ILD secretary was Louis Engdahl.

51. "Bail of $33,000," *AG* (eve. ed.), June 18, 1930, 3; "Six Alleged Reds," *AC*, May 22, 1930, 28; "Reds Held," *NYT*, March 12, 1930, 3; J. H. Moore, "Communists and Fascists," 441; C. H. Martin, "Angelo Herndon Case," 19–20. On Burlak, see Salmond, *General Textile Strike*, 89–90.

52. The printer was Henry Storey, and the organizer Herbert Newton, using the name Gilmer Brady. "Stop These 9 Scottsboro Murders," f515, r137, d1807, 41, and "Report of Comrade Tom Johnson," May 14, 1931, f515, r167, d2222, 46, both in CPUSA; "Six Are Seized," *AG*, May 22, 1930, 14; " 'Insurrection' Farce in Georgia," *AA*, 1932, reprinted in Cunard, *Negro Anthology*, 193; "Atlanta Woolen Mill Workers," [1931], f515, r137, d1897, 17, CPUSA; "Atlanta Six," [*LD?*] in f Gastonia, b3, MSRK; C. H. Martin, *Herndon Case*, 22, 45. Communist sources put an *e* in Storey. C. H. Martin, *Herndon Case*, 45; Solomon, *Cry Was Unity*, 126.

53. The couple was Julius and Lizette Klarin. "Six Are Arrested," *AJ*, May 22, 1930, 21; "Four Alleged Reds," *AC*, May 23, 1930, 5; "Save Them from the Electric Chair," broadside in f15, b2, SAD; Edwards and Kitchens, "Georgia's Anti-Insurrection Law"; "Atlanta Six," *SW*, Oct. 25, 1930, 1; C. H. Martin, *Herndon Case*, 22, 45. On Dalton in Chattanooga, see J. S. Allen, *Organizing*, 57.

54. "Two Girl 'Reds,' " *AG* (eve. ed.), May 23, 1930, 1.

55. Tom Johnson to Max Bedacht, May 24, 1930, 14, and Johnson to Bedacht, 16, f515, r151, d1960, both in CPUSA; "Carr and Powers," *AC*, May 6, 1930, 14.

56. Louis Engdahl, Tom Johnson to Max Bedacht, June 4, 1930, f515, r151, d1960, 17, CPUSA.

57. J. S. Allen, *Organizing*, 127–28; Kelley, *Hammer and Hoe*, 16, 25; T. Johnson, *Reds in Dixie*; Kelley, *Hammer and Hoe*, 31; Painter, *Narrative*, 110–68.

58. "For the Secretariat" to Tom Johnson, June 6, 1930, and Johnson to Comrade Darcy, Sept. 15, 1930, both in f515, r151, d1960, 18–19, 50–52, CPUSA; "Insurrection Case Coming," *SW*, Sept. 27, 1930, 1.

59. Tom Johnson to Comrade Darcy, Sept. 15, 1930, f515, r151, d1960, 50–52, CPUSA; "Bonds Are Fixed," *AC*, June 18, 1930, 1; "Bonds for Alleged," *AC*, July 5, 1930, 14; "Reds Freed," *NYT*, July 9, 1930, 3; C. H. Martin, "Angelo Herndon Case," 29; C. H. Martin, *Herndon Case*, 24–26; [?] to Harry Jackson, Sept. 18, 1931, f515, r173, d2285, 77, and [?] to Harry Jackson, Oct. 13, 1931, f515, r173, d2285, 80, both in CPUSA; "Dist. Bureau—Dist. 17," Mar. 13, 1932, f3, b7, TDRF; "Hancock to Appeal," *AJ*, Nov. 23, 1932, 14; Edwards and Kitchens, "Georgia's Anti-Insurrection Law," 124.

60. C. H. Martin, "White Supremacy," 374–75; C. H. Martin, *Herndon Case*, 36; "Interview between Kuusinen and Gastonia Comrades," 495/72/94, 109–21, RGASPI.

61. "Protect Rights of 'Reds,'" *AJ*, Aug. 3, 1930, sec. A6; "Ask Free Speech," *NYT*, Aug. 4, 1930, 4; C. H. Martin, *Herndon Case*, 24; J. H. Moore, "Communists and Fascists," 443.

62. Walter Wilson to ACLU, quoted in C. H. Martin, "Herndon Case," 30; C. H. Martin, *Herndon Case*, 24; Lorence, "Mobilizing," 63.

63. R. C. Miller, *Testimony*; Fish, "Menace"; T. A. Hill, "Communism." The NAACP included Kentucky, Missouri, Oklahoma, and West Virginia, "Memorandum to the Directors of the American Fund for Public Service" [1931?], f14, b1, JWJ.

64. Minor, "Negro and His Judases"; "DePriest Raves," *SW*, Oct. 3, 1931, 2.

65. Quote in J. A. Miller, S. D. Pennybacker, and E. Rosenhaft, "Mother Ada Wright," 388. Two of southern history's best books are Dan T. Carter, *Scottsboro: A Tragedy of the American South* and James E. Goodman, *Stories of Scottsboro*.

66. "Among the numerous tasks . . . ," and "Mr. Thomas," both in f37, b5, JSA; "Wave Red Flag," *CT*, Feb. 2, 1930, and "Local Reds Aided by Moscow," *CT*, Feb. 5, 1930, both in CPL.

67. SA to Comrade Browder, July 27, 1930, f515, r151, d1960, 21–22, CPUSA; J. S. Allen, *Organizing*, 21–46. Auerbach also used the name Biglow. A. M. Wald, *Exiles*, 386 n. 49; Goodman, *Stories*, 24. For Allen in the USSR, see "Comrades, We Welcome You," f20, b4, and military intelligence file, f6, b1, both in JSA.

68. Biglow to Comrade Browder, July 27, 1930, f515, r151, d1960, 21, CPUSA; Kleagle quote in J. S. Allen, *Organizing*, 36.

69. Date in Kelley, *Hammer and Hoe*, 16; SA to Comrade Browder, July 27, 1930, f515, r151, d1960, 21, Biglow to C.C., Aug. 4, 1930, f515, r151, d1960, 35, and Jim Allen to Dear Comrades, Oct. 4, 1930, f515, r151, d1960, 54, all in CPUSA. Allen exaggerates in *Organizing*, 43.

70. [HTW/Harry Wicks] to Isabel [Auerbach], Aug. 28, 1931, f515, r173, d2285, 64, CPUSA; unsigned to Comrade Jim [Weinstone], 1932, f3, b7, 4, TDRF. On finances, see Jim Allen to Earl Browder, Dec. 17, 1930, f515, r151, d1960, 65,

Allen to Browder, f515, r173, d2285, 54, HMW to Secretariat, Oct. 13, 1931, f515, r173, d2285, 84, all in CPUSA. Allen recounts this breezily in *Organizing*, 42, 128, but he was desperate.

71. James Allen to Earl Browder, Dec. 17, 1930, f515, r151, d1960, 66, and Allen to Browder, Apr. 17, 1931, f515, r173, d2285, 54, both in CPUSA.

72. J. S. Allen, *Organizing*, 80. Isabelle's alias was Helen Marcy. Trial notes, f7, b4, JSA.

73. "Whip Up Lynch," *SW*, Apr. 4, 1931, 1; Goodman, *Stories*, 24–31; J. S. Allen, *Organizing*, 79–95; Miller, Pennybaker, and Rosenhaft, "Mother Ada Wright," 390–91.

74. Naison, *Communists in Harlem*, 46–48, quot. 46; Solomon, *Cry Was Unity*, 139–40; Klehr and Haynes, *American Communist Movement*, 76.

75. H. Newton, Cyril Briggs, Harry Heywood [*sic*], "Statement," Apr. 23, 1931, 495/155/96, RGASPI; "Plenum of the CPUSA," f515, r167, d2222, 13, CPUSA; J. S. Allen, *Organizing*, 83–84.

76. Tom [Johnson] to Earl [Browder], Apr. 14, 1931, f515, r173, d2285, 22, CPUSA; Carter, *Scottsboro*, 3–10, quot. 5; Goodman, *Stories*, 3–23; H. Patterson and E. Conrad, *Scottsboro Boy*, 6.

77. "Copy of Confession," 539/3/1096, 78, RGASPI; Goodman, *Stories*, 12–21; D. T. Carter, *Scottsboro*, 13–16.

78. D. T. Carter, *Scottsboro*, 27–28; Goodman, *Stories*, 14; Tom [Johnson] to Earl [Browder], Apr. 14, 1931, f515, r173, d2285, 22, CPUSA; White, "Negro and the Communists."

79. Quote in "Whip Up Lynch," *SW*, Apr. 4, 1931, 1, 2; D. T. Carter, *Scottsboro*, 80–85; Goodman, *Stories*, 19–23.

80. White, "Negro and the Communists," 64–65; "Whip Up Lynch," *SW*, Apr. 4, 1931, 1, 2; Tom Johnson to Dear Hathaway, Apr. 15, 1931, f515, r173, d2285, 26, CPUSA. The ILD investigator was Lowell Wakefield, and the LSNR organizer was Douglas McKenzie. Miller, Pennybacker, and Rosenhaft, "Mother Ada Wright," 390; "Plenum of the CPUSA," f515, r167, d2222, 13, 16, 24, 33–35, 38–39, CPUSA; D. T. Carter, *Scottsboro*, 49; Solomon, *Cry Was Unity*, 192–203.

81. The "Boys" disavowed the ILD for a brief moment and asked that the NAACP represent them, but their parents convinced them to stay with the ILD. Naison, *Communists in Harlem*, 58–60; Goodman, *Stories*, 23–48; D. T. Carter, *Scottsboro*, 51–103; "Scottsboro Boys, Parents," *SW*, May 2, 1931, 1; Tom Johnson to Dear Earl, Apr. 14, 1931, f515, r173, d2285, 22, and "Plenum of the CPUSA," f515, r167, d2222, 32–33, both in CPUSA. "Statement by the N.A.A.C.P." denies that the ILD was involved in the case first. See also Janken, *White*, 148–60. On Communist arguments about the trial, see Lowell [Wakefield] to George [?], Apr. 14, 1931, f515, r173, d2285, 34, [Hathaway?] to Tom [Johnson], Apr. 21, 1931, f515, r173, d2285, 39, The Secretariat to Lowell Wakefield, Apr. 21, 1931, f515, r173, d2283, 41, all in CPUSA.

82. "Copy of Confession," 539/3/1096, 78, RGASPI; Goodman, *Stories*, 130–46; D. T. Carter, *Scottsboro*, 186–242. The boyfriend, Lester Carter, went on tour for the Scottsboro defense; see D. T. Carter, *Scottsboro*, 228–321, and Langston

Hughes to Carl Van Vechten, Sept. 22, 1933, in *Remember Me*, ed. E. Bernard, 107.

83. Goodman, "Pathology of Women," *Stories*, 163–72.

84. Goodman, *Stories*, 289–91, 393–97; D. T. Carter, *Scottsboro*, 369–98.

85. Chronology of the cases in Goodman, *Stories*, 393–97; Will Alexander to Eleanor Copenhaver, May 6, 1931, and Alexander to Louise Young, May 21, 1931, both on r8, 183, CIC; Kneebone, *Southern Liberal Journalists*, 80–81; D. T. Carter, *Scottsboro*, 302.

86. Foster Eaton (UPI) to Miss Johnson, Dictated for Mr. Eaton, Clarence Pickett to Will Alexander, July 21, 1931, Alexander to Carter Taylor, Aug. 5, 1931, Howard Kester to Dear Friend, Aug. 15, 1931, and Alexander to George Fort Milton, Aug. 10, 1931, all on r8, 183, CIC.

87. Walter White to Will Alexander, May 19, 1931, r8, 183, CIC; Darrow, "Scottsboro"; "No Illusions about Darrow," *SW*, Sept. 26, 1931, 4.

88. Walter White to James Weldon Johnson, Jan. 6, 1932, and Jan. 15, 1932, both in f541, b24, JWJ; Wilkins with Mathews, *Standing Fast*, 159.

89. Janken, *White*, 155–57; Walter White to Simon Guggenheim, Oct. 26, 1931, f540, b24, JWJ. See also White, "Negro and the Communists." J. W. Johnson, ACLU National Committee member, opposed outlawing the CP. Signatory, ACLU letter, Feb. 11, 1931, f13, b4, JWJ.

90. Du Bois, "Negro and Communism," 313–14.

91. Haywood, "Road to Negro Liberation," reprinted in Foner and Shapiro, eds., *American Communism and Black Americans*, 127. "Draft Resolution," f Negro 1931, b12, RM. On the "united front from below," see "Scottsboro Struggle."

92. Theodore Dreiser to Dear Friend, June 1931, r8, 183, CIC; White, "Negro and the Communists," 67–68; "Plenum of the CPUSA," f515, r167, d2222, 14, unsigned to Dear Comrades, Nov. 5, 1931, f515, r173, d2285, 116, both in CPUSA; "Expose NAACP Scottsboro Tricks," *SW*, May 23, 1931, 1; "NAACP Joins Southern Lynchers," *SW*, June 13, 1931, 1; "League of Struggle for Negro Rights," f Negro 1930s, b12, RM.

93. Paul Green to Theodore Dreiser, Apr. 11, 1932, Green to John Dos Passos, Oct. 26, 1932, Green to Langston Hughes, Nov. 13, 1933, all in *Southern Life*, ed. L. G. Avery, 202, 209–10, 226; NCDPP letterhead listing board members, including Paul Green, n.d. [1931], f 181, b2, ser. 1, PG; Goodman, *Stories*, 29–30.

94. Painter, *Narrative*, 83. For Scottsboro as an attraction to the CP, see Pettis Perry, quoted in "Man of the People," 8. Kelley, *Hammer and Hoe*, 78–91; Charney, *Long Journey*, 26.

95. D. T. Carter, *Scottsboro*, 147; quote in Mike Gold, "William L. Patterson," 39; "International Labor Defense," *PT*, March 2, 1933, 2; W. L. Patterson, *Man Who Cried Genocide*, 126–38.

96. J. D. Hall, *Revolt against Chivalry*, 145–57; Gilmore, *Gender and Jim Crow*; D. T. Carter, *Scottsboro*, 210–13. Sommerville, *Rape and Race*, esp. 256–57, and Dorr, *White Women*, esp. 2–3, argue that white women's reputations mattered to white juries in black rape trials. On other gender issues in the case, see Miller, Pennybaker, and Rosenhaft, "Mother Ada Wright," 410–13.

97. As quoted in Foner and Allen, eds., *American Communism and Black Americans*, xix.

98. J. D. Hall, " 'Mind That Burns in Each Body,' " and J. D. Hall, *Revolt against Chivalry*, 159–91.

99. "Meeting of the Buro of the Negro Department," f Negro 1932, b12, and "Draft Resolution," 2, f Negro 1931, b12, both in RM. Ames quoted in Hall, *Revolt against Chivalry*, 200.

100. "Minutes, August 5, 1931," 495/72/94, RGASPI; Miller, Pennybacker, and Rosenhaft, "Mother Ada Wright"; "Scottsboro Campaign in Europe"; Engdahl, "Scottsboro Campaign in England"; "Demonstrations round World," *SW*, May 9, 1931, 1; "Scottsboro Protest Grows," *SW*, July 18, 1931, 1; "Scottsboro Interrupts Show in Moscow," *SW*, Aug. 1, 1931, 2; "March on Capitol," *SW*, May 20, 1933, 1; "Mass Protests," *SW*, July 12, 1933, 1; "Proposed Scottsboro Protest," f Government Investigation, b2, MSRK; Solomon, *Cry Was Unity*, 203; Naison, *Communists in Harlem*, 57–94. For a contrary view, see H. T. Murray, "NAACP vs. the Communist Party" and D. T. Carter, *Scottsboro*, 137–73.

101. "Jacques Romain [*sic*]."

102. "Mass Protests," *SW*, July 12, 1933, 1; "Plenum of the CPUSA," f515, r167, d2222, 13, 14, CPUSA.

103. Patterson and Conrad, *Scottsboro Boy*, 232.

104. Barrett, *Foster*, 181; C. A. Hathaway, "Speech," and "James W. Ford Accepts," *DW*, May 31, 1932, both reprinted in Cunard, *Negro Anthology*, 275–79.

105. "Plenum of the CPUSA," f515, r167, d2222, 24, and Paul Crouch to Earl Browder, Oct. 15, 1934, f515, r281, d3625, 82, both in CPUSA; J. S. Allen, *Organizing*, 86.

106. Wexley, *They Shall Not Die*, 7, 76, 191; Thomas Cripps, intro. to Connelly, *Green Pastures*, ed. Cripps. On the genre, see Denning, *Cultural Front*, 262–63, 362–75.

107. Carl Van Vechten to Langston Hughes, Feb. 21, 1934, in *Remember Me*, ed. E. Bernard, 119; Van Vechten to James Weldon Johnson, Feb. 25, 1934, f501, b21, JWJ.

108. Hughes, "Justice."

109. Kelley, *Hammer and Hoe*, 21–49; Solomon, *Cry Was Unity*, 120–24.

110. "500 at Charlotte," *SW*, July 25, 1931, 2.

111. It is possible that this data set underrepresents CP members in Dist. 16 in 1931. The file is labeled "Dist. 16 New Members 1931," f 515, r311, d4122, CPUSA, but it contains a few members who joined in previous years. Since African Americans joined in greater numbers after Scottsboro in 1931, it may overrepresent them.

112. "Dist. 16 New Members 1931," f515, r311, d4133, CPUSA. On Norfolk, see E. Lewis, *In Their Own Interests*, 132–35.

113. Ibid. Of the applicants, 30 identified themselves as women, 60 as men, and 5 failed to indicate their sex. The figures of 32 women and 63 men are derived from the names of the 5 applicants. Nine left "Section/Unit locations" blank or wrote "Section 1, Unit 1," with no city and are not counted in the urban distribution that I discuss here.

114. Mary Adams, "New/Negro Women in Industry," 405/155/87, 458, RGASPI; "Negro Women Most Militant," in f Communist Party, b1, MSRK; Kelley, *Hammer and Hoe*, 21–22.

115. "N.T.W.U. a Fighting Union," f515, r138, d1832, 148, "Dist. 16 New Members 1931," f515, r311, d4133, and "Motion," f515, r162, d2147, 4, all in CPUSA. On the AFL strike, see Francis J. Gorman, "Labor Organization and Southern Industry," CSPA; J. D. Hall et al., *Like a Family*, 217, 219.

116. "Dist. 16 New Members 1931," f515, r311, d4133, and "[illegible] Chamber of Commerce," f515, r138, d1832, 147, both in CPUSA; E. D. Hoffman, "Genesis."

117. "Report of Comrade Clara Holden," Apr. 7, 1931, 534/7/500, RGASPI, contradicts Solomon, *Cry Was Unity*, 133.

118. "Hooded Klansmen Invade," *SW*, Apr. 8, 1931, 1, 4; E. D. Hoffman, "Genesis," 205.

119. "Mill Thugs" and "KKK Beat Two Negroes," both in *SW*, Sept. 12, 1931, 1, 2.

120. "Report of Comrade Clara Holden," Apr. 7, 1931, 534/7/500, RGASPI; unsigned letter to Secretariat, Oct. 28, 1931, f3, b7, TDRF.

121. "Dist. 16 New Members 1931," f515, r311, d4133, CPUSA. "Draft Resolution," [fall 1931], f Negro 1931, b12, RM, reports "sharper attention . . . toward Negro work during the spring and summer." Solomon, *Cry Was Unity*, 127.

122. M. H. Powers to Comrade Badacht, Sept. 19, 1930, f515, r151, d1960, 7, and "September First Report," f515, r162, d2148, 14, both in CPUSA; "Demand State Jobless Fund," *SW*, Dec. 13, 1930, 1.

123. "Charlotte Gives Bats for Bread," *SW*, Jan. 3, 1931, 1; "DEMONSTRATE FEB. 25," f140, r138, d1832 (end of reel), CPUSA.

124. "Dist. 16 New Members 1931," f515, r311, d4133, CPUSA. Two of the 23 black women omitted their location.

125. "YCL Holds Dance," *SW*, July 4, 1931, 2. On other interracial dances, see Skotnes, "Communist Party, Anti-Racism," and Pedersen, *Communist Party in Maryland*, 5.

126. "Women Organize," f146, r146, d1832, (end of reel), CPUSA.

127. "What's for Men Is for Women," f New York Negro-#1–3, b12, RM; Solomon, *Cry Was Unity*, 208–09.

128. "Form Body to Fight Lynch," *SW*, Nov. 8, 1930, 1; "What Is the A.N.L.C.?," *SW*, Oct. 11, 1930, 4.

129. "Communists in City Elections," *SW*, Apr. 25, 1931, 1.

130. "Seven Negro Editors," 117–19. On the *Afro-American* and Communism, see Farrar, "Afro-American," 148–53.

131. Sullivan, *Days of Hope*, 25–39; Torrence, *John Hope*, 335–36; Villard, "Our Attitude."

132. C. Vann Woodward to Glenn Rainey, Aug. 11 [1932], f4, b7, GWR.

133. ICVW; Roper, *C. Vann Woodward*, 54–55; J. R. Green, "Rewriting"; J. R. Green, "Past and Present"; IGR, 5–6.

134. El-Hai, "Black and White and Red"; Solomon, *Cry Was Unity*, 174–77; D. L. Lewis, *When Harlem Was in Vogue*, 288–93; C. N. Nelson, "Black and White" and "Patterson"; F. Berry, *Hughes*, 150–71; Blakely, *Russia and the Negro*, 93–96;

Rampersad, *Life of Langston Hughes*, 1:242–51; Baldwin, *Beyond the Color Line*, 95–102. Several memoirs discuss the trip; all benefit from hindsight based on the memorists' more mature politics. Hughes's *I Wonder* comes closest to depicting actual events but leaves much unsaid. Homer Smith's *Black Man in Red Russia* is bizarre because he pretends he was not a cast member and tells intimate stories about himself in the third person. Most useful, yet also biased, is Louise Thompson Patterson, unpublished MS, LTP, hereafter cited as LTP MS.

135. The background of the script(s) is confusing. A "committee of three"—a Russian, a German, and Lovett Fort-Whiteman—had written the first script, according to Henry Lee Moon to *NYAN*, June 11, 1932, f5, b12, LTP; F. Berry, *Hughes*, 160; H. Smith, *Black Man in Red Russia*, 26.

136. Grebner's 1929 film was *Salamander*, and his last film was *Snezhnaya Koroleva*, or *The Snow Queen*, released in 1957, with Sandra Dee as the voice of Gerda, www.gorkystudio.hypermart.net/English/. Junghans's experience included *Lenin* and *Such Is Life*, a model for *Black and White*. His African film was *Fleeting Shadows*, www.pragueonfilm.co.uk/pages/programme/theme_20s_30s.html. Hughes, *I Wonder*, 76, 79.

137. Louise Thompson to Meschrabpom Film Company, May 18, 1932, f19, b9, LTP; C. N. Nelson, "Louise Thompson Patterson" and "Patterson and the Southern Roots"; Jennings, "Louise Thompson." Thompson had reported sympathetically (and anonymously) on the strike. "An Onlooker," 345; "Hampton Strike," 346; Maxwell, *New Negro*, 141–51.

138. LTP MS, "Harlem in the 1920s," 5, LTP.

139. On Thompson's sad account of her marriage, see LTP MS, "Harlem in the 1920s," 9 (quote 11), LTP; Jennings, "Louise Thompson," 1134. On Thurman and Thompson, see D. West, *The Richer, the Poorer*, 215–17.

140. LTP MS, "Harlem in the 1920s," 23–24, LTP; Rampersad, *Life of Langston Hughes*, 1:193–200; Jennings, "Louise Thompson," 1135; Hughes and Hurston, *Mule Bone*, 157–280.

141. Thompson and Hughes were very close. He sends valentines; she calls him "darling." She is never possessive but always ready to see him. See Louise Thompson to Langston Hughes, Oct. 4, 1930, Oct. 24, 1930, March 10, 1932, May 9, 1932, May 16, 1932, May 27, 1932, all in f2872, b115, LH.

142. Louise Thompson to Langston Hughes, Oct. 4, 1930, f2872, b115, LH. ILTP, and LTP MS, "Trip to Russia," 7, both in the LTP; M. B. Wilkerson, "Excavating Our History"; Kellner, "Patterson."

143. Naison, *Communists in Harlem*, 67–68; LTP MS, "Trip to Russia," 1–2; Howe and Coser, *American Communist Party*, 94; Lewy, *Cause that Failed*, 26.

144. P. Murray, "Notes on San Francisco," Apr. 27, 1945, f1271, b73, PM. Roy Wilkins also regretted not going. Wilkins with Mathews, *Standing Fast*, 147.

145. Louise Thompson to E. Franklin Frazier, May 18, 1932, and Frazier to Thompson, May 26, 1932, both in f3, b12, LTP.

146. W. A. Domingo, Co-Operating Committee for Production of a Soviet Film on Negro Life, f6, b12, LTP; Louise Thompson to Loren Miller, Apr. 12, 1932, and Thompson to Langston Hughes, May 10, 1932, both in f2872, b115, LH.

147. LTP MS, "Trip to Russia," 4–5; Meschrabpom Film to James Ford, May 3, 1932, f19, b9, and Louise Thompson to Meschrabpom Film Company, May 18, 1932, f19, b9, both in LTP.

148. H. Smith, *Black Man in Red Russia*, 2. Lloyd Patterson became a set designer, and Rudd became an actor. LTP MS, "Trip to Russia," 6, 48, cast list, f5, b12, James Ford to Homer Smith, Apr. 24, 1932, f27, b16, Homer Smith to James Ford, Apr. 28, 1932, f3, b12, all in LTP; "A Negro Worker," f Blacks and Soviet Russia, b1, MSRK.

149. "Porgy," f51, b3, DW/HU. West was a resident of Catfish Row. West gave various birth dates, most reliably 1910; Elwanda D. Ingram, "Dorothy West" (1907); obituary in the *NYT*, Aug. 19, 1998, 29 (1907); McDowell, "Conversations" (1912), 265–81; DW/HU lists her birth date as June 2, 1910.

150. Inexplicably, Blakely, *Russia and the Negro*, 93, writes of "one white member, who was also a Communist."

151. Theodore R. Poston wrote for the *Pittsburgh Courier*, C. N. Nelson, "Black and White" and "Patterson." Other cast members included Fordham law student George Sample, Howard University student Frank Curle Montero, aspiring social worker Constance White, insurance clerk Matt Crawford, social workers Leonard Hill and Katherine Jenkins, and Laurence Alberga, a West Indian farm worker acquainted with W. A. Domingo. Juanita Lewis sang with the Hall Johnson Choir, Thurston McNairy Lewis had appeared in *Ham's Daughters*, and Taylor Gordon was a singer. LTP MS, "Trip to Russia," 6–7, LTP.

152. Moon, "Scottsboro and Its Implications," 23–24.

153. F. Berry, *Hughes*, 161; Louise Thompson to Langston Hughes, telegram, March 10, 1932; letters Mar. 10, 1932, May 10, 1932, May 16, 1932, May 27, 1932, and Thompson to Loren Miller, Apr. 12, 1932, all in f2872, b115, LH. On *Scottsboro Limited*, see Thurston, "Black Christ, Red Flag."

154. Louise Thompson to Langston Hughes, March 10, 1932, Thompson to Loren Miller, Apr. 12, 1932, and Thompson to Hughes, May 10, 1932, all in f2872, b115, LH.

155. Langston Hughes to Louise Thompson, June 6, 1932, f7, b12, cast list, f5, b12; [Louise Thompson?] to Meschrabpom Film, June 18, 1932, f19, b9, LTP MS, "Trip to Russia," 5–6, all in LTP; El-Hai, "Black and White and Red"; Hughes, *I Wonder*, 69–70.

156. Thurman, *Infants of the Spring*, 233–35, quoted in J. O. Young, *Black Writers*, 143.

157. Zora Neale Hurston to James Weldon Johnson, n.d. [summer 1934?], f223, b10, JWJ.

158. F. Berry, *Hughes*, 154–57; LTP MS, "Trip to Russia," 9–10, LTP.

159. R. Robinson, *Black on Red*, 320.

160. Louise Thompson to Mother, July 5, 1932, f23, b1, and James Ford to Homer Smith, Apr. 24, 1934, f27, b16, both in LTP; Dorothy West to My Darlings, July 13 [1932], b1, DW/BU; R. Robinson, *Black on Red*, 361; H. Smith, *Black Man in Red Russia*, 78; LFWD and ISZ. Fort-Whiteman's wife's name was Levitina.

161. Hughes, "Moscow and Me," 67.

162. I. D. W. Talmadge, "Mother Emma," *Opportunity* (Aug. 1933), in f Blacks and Soviet Russia, b1, MSRK; Haywood, *Black Bolshevik*, 67–69; H. Smith, *Black Man*

in Red Russia, 34–39; Hughes, *I Wonder*, 82–86. Two other black Muscovites included the singer Madam Arle-Titz and Robert Robinson, recruited from Detroit to work as a machinist.

163. H. Smith, *Black Man in Red Russia*, 25.

164. Louise Thompson to Mother, July 4, 1932, f23, b1, LTP; Haywood, *Black Bolshevik*, 385.

165. Hughes, *I Wonder*, 83–84.

166. CPT meant "colored people's time"—i.e., late. Louise Thompson to Mother Dear, July 14, 1932, f23, b1, LTP.

167. H. Smith, *Black Man in Red Russia*, 26. L. T. Patterson, "With Langston Hughes," 155–56.

168. Cullen to Dot, March 17, 1933, and Cullen to Dot, June 7, 1933, both in f6, b1, DW/HU.

169. Mother to Dot, Dec. 3, 1932, and Mother to Dot, Feb. 10, 1933, both in f2, b1, and Helene Johnson to Dorothy West, [Aug. 4, 1932], f9, b1, all in DW/HU.

170. Hughes, "Moscow and Me," in *Good Morning Revolution*, ed. F. Berry, 71; Louise Thompson to Mother Dear, July 14, 1932, f23, b1, LTP.

171. Hughes, *I Wonder*, 76. I have a version of the Fort-Whiteman script, entitled "Blacks and Whites," that differs from the draft that Hughes depicts and from the one in LTP. There may have been three or four versions of the script. Many thanks to Sandra Dickson and Churchill L. Roberts, codirectors of the Documentary Institute, University of Florida, for putting me in touch with JoAnne Van Tuyl.

172. Hughes, *I Wonder*, 78–79.

173. This in the version "Blacks and Whites," 9.

174. Haywood, *Black Bolshevik*, 144.

175. H. Smith, *Black Man in Red Russia*, 26.

176. W. A. Domingo, Co-operating Committee for Production of a Soviet Film on Negro Life, n.d., f6, b12, LTP.

177. Hughes, *I Wonder*, 77–79; F. Berry, *Hughes*, 159. Thompson writes: "Langston was offered the job of revising the script, but he refused it b/c the script was impossible." Elsewhere she says that Hughes's "assistance included only the English dialogue." LTP MS, "Trip to Russia," marginal notes, 27, 35. See also R. Robinson, *Black on Red*, 320.

178. Script, b2, LTP.

179. LTP MS, "Trip to Russia," 18, 19, 24–25, 33, 54, LTP. Haywood returned to Moscow in August 1932 after two years in the U.S. Haywood, *Black Bolshevik*, 382–83.

180. Elaine Woo, "Louise Patterson," *CST*, Sept. 20, 1999, 54; Richard Goldstein, "Louise Patterson, 97," *NYT*, Sept. 2, 1999, sec. C20.

181. Dorothy West to My Darlings, July 13 [1932], DW/BU; West to Dearest Mummy, June 29, West to Mums, and West to Dollie, Apr. 16, all in f1, b1, DW/HU.

182. Hughes to Van Vechten, March 1, 1933, in *Remember Me*, ed. E. Bernard, 102; Dorothy West to Dearest Mums, n.d., f1, b1, DW/HU; Hughes to Dottie, Dec. 5, 1933, DW/BU; West, "Adventure in Moscow," in *The Richer, the Poorer*,

205–09. On her marriage proposal to Hughes, see "Dorothy West . . . Dies at 91," *NYT*, Aug. 19, 1998, sec. A29. Under a pseudonym, West later published letters written to a lover in Central Asia in September 1932, Christopher, "Russian Correspondence," 14–19.

183. The Russian functionary is identified as Constantine Oumansky by H. Smith, *Black Man in Red Russia*, 28–29 and by Hughes in *I Wonder*, 103. But the suitor signed his name Boris to Dorothy, June 24, f14, b1, and Dorothy identified him as Boris Pilnyak (an alias?) and reported that he proposed marriage to Jones, West to Dearest Darling, March 5, f1, b1, both in DW/HU. See S. J. Taylor, *Stalin's Apologist*, 178.

184. West to Dearest Mums, n.d., f1, b1, DW/HU.

185. Garner was the daughter of A. C. Garner, pastor of the Grace Congregational Church in New York. "Sylvia Garner Engrossed in Study Abroad," *PT*, Aug. 17, 1933, 11. The cast member was social worker Connie White. Naison, *Communists in Harlem*, 61; Sylvia Garner to Langston Hughes, March 25, 1933, f1273, b66, LH; Hughes, *I Wonder*, 88.

186. Thompson to Mother, Sept. 4, 1932, f23, b1, LTP; Hughes, *I Wonder*, 210; Torrence, *John Hope*, 335–36.

187. LTP MS, "Trip to Russia," 22, LTP; H. Smith, *Black Man in Red Russia*, 25; Hughes, *I Wonder*, 98; Louise Thompson to Mother, July 14, 1932, f23, b1, 1932, LTP.

188. Hughes, *I Wonder*, 82.

189. Marginal notes on W. A. Slaughter to Louise Thompson, May 26, 1932, f3, b12, LTP.

190. H. Smith, *Black Man in Red Russia*, 25, 28–29.

191. Hughes, *I Wonder*, 91–92.

192. LTP MS, "Trip to Russia," 28, 33, LTP.

193. Moon, "Woman under the Soviets"; D. L. Hoffman, *Stalinist Values*, 88–117; Naiman, *Sex in Public*; Goldman, *Women, the State*.

194. Healey, "Sexual and Gender Dissent," quot. 150, 152, 153, 162; Naiman, *Sex in Public*.

195. Sylvia Garner to Langston Hughes, March 25, 1933, f1273, b66, LH.

196. F. Berry, *Hughes*, 160; H. Smith, *Black Man in Red Russia*, 28; Moon, "Woman under the Soviets." On Hughes's relationships with men, see F. Berry, *Hughes*, 150; E. Bernard, ed., *Remember Me*, xxiii. On his heterosexuality, see Hughes's hilarious "Tartar Rendezvous," 155–65, and "Natasha's Big Scene," 212, 223–26, 231, in *I Wonder*.

197. Haywood, *Black Bolshevik*, 139, 146–47; H. Smith, *Black Man in Red Russia*, 81.

198. Hughes, *I Wonder*, 98.

199. Ralph W. Barnes, "Negroes Adrift in 'Uncle Tom's Russian Cabin,'" *HT*, Aug. 12, 1932, 5.

200. Louise Thompson to Mother, Aug. 24, 1932, f23, b1, LTP; Hughes, *I Wonder*, 94–95.

201. Loren Miller, f3, b2, Dorothy Thompson to Mother, Aug. 24, 1932, f23, b1, LTP MS, "Trip to Russia," 27–29, quot., 29, all in LTP.

202. Miller states that "two bourgeois newspaper correspondents" (Moon and Pos-

ton) and a "member of the American Communist Party" (Fort-Whiteman) appeared before Meschrabpom, and the only member of the cast who was a Communist was Alan MacKenzie, who was in the opposing faction, Loren Miller, f3, b2, LTP.

203. Laurence Alberga, Henry Lee Moon, Ted Poston, and [Thurston] McNairy Lewis, Aug. 22, 1932, f2, b2, LTP. Henry Moon also signed, according to "Negro Worker," f Blacks and Soviet Russia, b1, MRSK; Hughes, *I Wonder*, 98.

204. LTP MS, "Trip to Russia," 30, and Louise Thompson to Dear Mother, Aug. 24, 1932, f23, b1, LTP.

205. Hughes, *I Wonder*, 96. Cast members were Moon and Poston. See also Hard, *Raymond Robins'*.

206. Hughes, *I Wonder*, 97; Felix Cole to the Honorable Secretary of State, July 8, 1932, f Blacks and Soviet Russia, b1, MSRK.

207. "Soviet Calls Off Film," Aug. 12, 1932 [newspaper unknown], and United Press News Letter, Mailed Aug. 9, both in f3, b2, LTP.

208. Alberga, Moon, Poston, Lewis, Aug. 22, 1932, f2, b2, LTP.

209. Loren Miller, f3, b2, LTP MS, "Trip to Russia," 30, Dorothy Thompson to Mother, Aug. 24, 1932, f23, b1, and "We, the undersigned," f1, b2, all in LTP.

210. Louise Thompson to Mother, Aug. 24, 1932, f23, b1, LTP.

211. "Negro Worker," f Blacks and Soviet Russia, b1, MRSK.

212. Ibid.

213. F. Berry, *Hughes*, 168–69. Felix Cole to the Honorable Secretary of State, July 8, 1932, f Blacks and Soviet Russia, b1, MSRK.

214. Taylor, *Stalin's Apologist*, 191.

215. LTP MS, "Trip to Russia," 33, and Thompson to Mother, Sept. 4, 1932, f23, b1, both in LTP. Emphasis added.

216. Marginal note, "Ted and Thurston left voluntarily in August," LTP MS, "Trip to Russia," 32, and Thompson to Mother, Sept. 4, 1932, f23, b1, both in LTP.

217. Dorothy Thompson to the *PC*, Sept. 19, 1932, and W. A. Domingo to Thompson, Oct. 6, 1932, both in f21, b1, LTP.

218. Dopomie to Dearest Marie, Jan. 7, DW/BU. West later implied that the money she brought back from Moscow was a payout to force her out of the country. See McDowell, "Conversations," 271. On Jones, see LTP MS, "Trip to Russia," 44, LTP.

219. LTP MS, "Trip to Russia," 52–53; Baldwin, *Beyond the Color Line*, 106–24.

220. Hughes, "Going South," 162–63.

221. Hughes, *I Wonder*, 179–80; Haywood, *Black Bolshevik*, 386–87.

222. Loren Miller to Langston Hughes, n.d., gives the date of her departure as Nov. 8, f21, b1, LH; Louise Thompson to W. E. B. Du Bois, Dec. 29, 1932, and W. A. Domingo to Thompson, both in f21, b1, LTP; L. Thompson, "Soviet Film," 37, 46.

223. P. Murray, "Notes on San Francisco," Apr. 27, 1945, f1271, b73, PM; Hughes, "Moscow and Me," 74.

224. Hughes, *I Wonder*, 85. West apparently saw more of the famine the next spring. See Christopher, "Room in Red Square," 11. The American Embassy helped

Emma Harris return to the United States in 1934. See H. Smith, *Black Man in Red Russia*, 39; Beal, *Proletarian Journey*, 276.

225. Graziosi, *Great Soviet Peasant War*, 46–70. For contrasting views on the famine, see Conquest, *Harvest*, and Davies and Wheatcroft, *Years of Hunger*, 423, who reported much cannibalism (441).

226. Torrence, *John Hope*, 339; ICVW.

227. Sullivan, *Days of Hope*, 38; Dalrymple, "Great Famine."

228. ISAD.

229. Ralph W. Barnes, "Grain Shortage," *HT*, Jan. 15, 1933, pt. 2, 5; interview with Gareth Jones, "Famine in Russia," *Manchester Guardian*, March 30, 1933, 12; Taylor, *Stalin's Apologist*, 193–223; Johnson, *Soviet Power*, 173–79; Foster, *Page*, 311–13. Haywood, *Black Bolshevik*, 388, denied that there was a famine.

230. "Interview between Kuusinen and Gastonia Comrades," 495/72/94, 109–21, RGASPI; Beal, *Proletarian Journey*, 225.

231. "Interview between Kuusinen and Gastonia Comrades," 495/72/94, 113, 119–20, RGASPI; William Z. Foster to Gentlemen, n.d., f515, r162, d2174, 51, CPUSA.

232. Beal, *Proletarian Journey*, 280–97, quot. 293, also quoted in Conquest, *Harvest*, 231.

233. Graziosi, *New Peculiar State*, 227, 240, 248, 252; Tucker, *Stalin*, 91–145.

234. Beal, *Proletarian Journey*, 303–08.

235. Lovett Fort-Whiteman to Dear Comrade, Oct. 27, 1933, 495/261/1476, 28, typed version with note dated 31/X/33 (Oct. 31, 1933), 495/261/1476, 27, RGASPI.

236. American Party Representative to the ECCI, Oct. 1928, 495/261/1476, 34, 35, 36, RGASPI, documents Fort-Whiteman's transfer to the CPSU.

237. [James Jackson], 495/155/33, RGASPI.

238. H. Smith, *Black Man in Red Russia*, 80.

239. Ibid., Haywood, *Black Bolshevik*, 253.

240. Haywood, *Black Bolshevik*, 384; Davis, "Rise and Fall of George Padmore," 15–17.

241. Blakely, *Russia and the Negro*, 92.

242. Shachtman, *Race and Revolution*, 66–102.

243. H. Smith, *Black Man in Red Russia*, 81.

244. Dates of Fort-Whiteman's banishment are clouded. Hughes returned from the USSR in August 1933, Hughes to Carl Van Vechten, Dec. 6, 1933, in *Remember Me*, ed. E. Bernard, 113–14. Baldwin, *Beyond the Color Line*, 126–48. Robinson places Fort-Whiteman in Moscow until around 1936 and describes the incident at the Foreign Club in *Black on Red*, 361. "Sub-Committee CPUSA Meeting on Organisational Questions," Aug. 25, 1935, RTsKhIDNI, in Klehr, Haynes, and Anderson, *Soviet World*, 223–24, called for a meeting to decide LFW's fate. LFW taught at the American School until at least mid-1935. The incident at the Foreign Club took place about three weeks before the NKVD told him he had to move and that "a black Lawyer from the upper echelon of the Communist Party USA" had called LFW's criticism "counter-revolutionary." Since the "disposition" subcommittee took place at the end of August, the meeting of the black delegates for the Seventh Congress must have taken place in September, and

LFW probably knew of his internal exile by the end of September 1935. He may have been given until the beginning of 1936 to move; this matches Robinson's recollection. Evidence in H. Smith, *Black Man in Red Russia*, suggests that during his exile of 1936–37, he may have returned on occasion to Moscow. For Klehr and Haynes's analysis, see *Soviet World*, 218–22.

245. Clay, "Negro in Recent American Literature," 148, quoted in Young, *Black Writers*, 158. See N. Grant, "Hughes/Lawrence/Douglass"; Denning, *Cultural Front*, 218.

246. Hughes, *Ways of White Folks*; Baldwin, *Beyond the Color Line*, 129–48.

247. Van Vechten quoted in *Remember Me*, ed. E. Bernard, 115 n. 2.

248. R. Robinson, *Black on Red*, 361. Patterson had been in school in Moscow from 1927 to 1930 and 1934–1936 (a period omitted from his autobiography); "To the Small Commission," Aug. 26, 1929, 495/155/80, RGASPI; Gold, "William L. Patterson," 40; LTP MS, ch. 5, 9, LTP.

249. "Strictly Confidential," Jan. 28, 1936, William Patterson, 495/14/10, RGASPI.

250. "Sub-Committee CPUSA Meeting," in Klehr, Haynes, and Anderson, *Soviet World*, 223–24.

251. Klehr and Haynes, *American Communist Movement*, 79. The congress opened July 25, 1935, Haywood, *Black Bolshevik*, 447.

252. H. Smith, *Black Man in Red Russia*, 81.

253. "Sub-Committee CPUSA Meeting," in Klehr, Haynes, and Anderson, *Soviet World*, 223. The new Communists were Ben Careathers, Claude Lightfoot, and Al Murphy, who probably joined Patterson and Ford. Haywood, *Black Bolshevik*, 447–51.

254. R. Robinson, *Black on Red*, 361.

255. Hughes, *I Wonder*, 104, relates that Tashkent, about the same distance from Moscow, was a five-day trip by rail. According to information gathered by Sergei Zhuravlev and in the author's possession, Fort-Whiteman lived in Alma-Ata.

256. H. Smith, *Black Man in Red Russia*, 82–83. It was in Alma-Ata that Alan Cullison, Moscow bureau chief of the Associated Press, and Dr. Sergei Zhuravlev found LFW's police file in the late 1990s, Cullison, "Secret Revealed." Information on teaching and boxing from ISZ.

257. Tucker, *Stalin*, 374–403; Hughes, *I Wonder*, 196. For an eyewitness account of Radek's trial, see ISAD.

258. H. Smith, *Black Man in Red Russia*, 81; Tucker, *Stalin*, 422; Getty and Naumov, *Road to Terror*, 364–419.

259. Getty and Naumov, *Road to Terror*, 456, 471–79.

260. LFWD; Zhuravlev electronic communication with author, Apr. 15, 2004. Under questioning about his relatives in the United States, Fort-Whiteman listed four siblings, all much younger than he, omitted his sister, Hazel, and said that his parents were dead. I have been unable to find the four siblings in the census, and they may have been half brothers and sisters from a possible second marriage of his mother. "Death Certificate," in Haynes, Klehr, and Anderson, *Soviet World*, 224–27; Young, "Stalin's Political Pilgrims"; Applebaum, *Gulag*, 94–95; Dallin and Nicolaevsky, *Forced Labor*, 259–61.

261. Applebaum, *Gulag*, 87–91. For a firsthand account of the camps in 1939, see Sgovio, *Dear America*, 181–91.

262. R. Robinson, *Black on Red*, 361. Another informer told Smith that he had seen in Kolyma Africans speaking with "British or foreign accents," including some who could not speak English well. H. Smith, *Black Man in Red Russia*, 176; "Death Certificate," in Klehr, Haynes, Anderson, *Soviet World*, 224.
263. Applebaum, *Gulag*, 111–12.
264. This follows Robinson, based on eyewitness testimony, *Black on Red*, 361.
265. "Death Certificate," in Klehr, Haynes, and Anderson, *Soviet World*, 224–27.

CHAPTER 4: THE NAZIS AND DIXIE

1. Cast list, f5, b12, LTP; Dorothy West to Dearest Mums, n.d., f1, b1, DW/HU.
2. Sylvia Garner to Langston Hughes, March 25, 1933, f1273, b66, LH.
3. Mollie Lewis to Dorothy West, Jan. 1, 1933, and Lewis to West, June 26, 1933, both in f14, b1, DW/HU.
4. Mollie Lewis to Dorothy West, Jan. 1, 1933, and Lewis to West, June 26, 1933, both in f14, b1, DW/HU; Craig, *Germany*; H. A. Turner, ed., *Nazism*; A. J. P. Taylor, *Origins*; J. A. S. Grenville, *History of the World*. On sex and Lewis's cohort, see N. Miller, *Making Love Modern*, 144–79.
5. Cayton, *Long Old Road*, 229–30.
6. Lipstadt, *Beyond Belief* argues that "the persecution of the Jews constituted only one small segment of the story of Nazi Germany and was never the central theme of the reports about the new regime," but she did not consult any African American newspapers. *Beyond Belief*, 15. See also Dawidowicz, *War against the Jews*; Wyman, *Abandonment of the Jews*; Novick, *Holocaust in American Life*.
7. My findings are contrary to those of Wedlock, "Comparisons by Negro Publications," 427–33. See also Von Eschen, *Race against Empire*, 1–23; Robin D. G. Kelley, " 'But a Local Phase,' " 1045–77; Kouhl, *Nazi Connection*; Diner, *Almost Promised Land*; Salzman and West, eds., *Struggles in the Promised Land*; S. Forman, *Blacks in the Jewish Mind*; V. P. Franklin et al., eds., *African Americans and Jews*.
8. Strong, *Organized Anti-Semitism*, 1, 2; Lipset and Raab, *Politics of Unreason*, 2d ed., 152–57; Amann, "Vigilante Fascism," 492; Payne, *History of Fascism*; H. A. Turner, ed., *Reappraisals of Fascism*, esp. Nolte, "Problem of Fascism," 35.
9. J. S. Rosenberg, *How Far?*, 111–19.
10. Grill and Jenkins, "Nazis and the American South"; Painter, "Shoah and Southern History"; Degler, *In Search of Human Nature*; Klinkner and Smith, *Unsteady March*; Kouhl, *Nazi Connection*. For arguments that Fascism encompassed racism but did not depend on it, see Sternhell, *Birth of Fascist Ideology*, 4–5, and Laqueur, *Fascism*, 24–25.
11. Naison, "Remaking America," 54–56; Foster, *Your Questions*; Kelley, *Hammer and Hoe*, 119–20.
12. C. H. Martin, *Herndon Case* is the definitive account.
13. K. Thomas, "*Rouge et Noir* Reread," 465–94; J. H. Moore, "Angelo Herndon Case"; Edwards and Kitchens, "Georgia's Anti-Insurrection Law"; C. H. Martin, "Communists and Blacks"; Street, *Look Away!*, 143–52; Solomon, *Cry Was Unity*, 219–21.

14. Gilmore, *Gender and Jim Crow*, 122, 275, n. 15; poster, "Be One of the 2,000,000, Sign Your Name!" f351, b5, PG.

15. Harris Gilbert to Tom Johnson, Sept. 21, 1931, f515, r176, d2322, CPUSA; Herndon, *Let Me Live*, 39–102; C. H. Martin, *Herndon Case*, 10; Herndon, "You Cannot Kill," 9; Kelley, *Hammer and Hoe*, 15.

16. Herndon, *Let Me Live*, 81; Tom Johnson to Comrade Amis, Sept. 16, 1930, f515, d150, d162, 20, and Harris Gilbert to Tom Johnson, Sept. 21, 1931, f515, d2322, r176, both in CPUSA; Lorence, "Mobilizing," 68.

17. Herndon, "In Memory of Harry Simms," r1, 696, ILD; Solomon, *Cry Was Unity*, 125.

18. IJJ, 5–6.

19. Nellie Bryant quoted in Georgina Hickey, *Hope and Danger*, 205; broadsides, f515, d1897, r137, 39–44, and "Demands for Immediate Relief," f515, d1832, r138, 157, both in CPUSA; minutes quoted in J. H. Moore, "Angelo Herndon Case," 63.

20. "Minutes of Meeting," March 13, 1932, f3, b7, TDRF.

21. Herndon, "You Cannot Kill," 22.

22. Herndon, *Let Me Live*, 188–89; C. H. Martin, *Herndon Case*, 3–6.

23. D. L. Smith, *New Deal*, 63.

24. Herndon, *Let Me Live*, 193; *Twenty Years*; C. H. Martin, *Herndon Case*, 7, 8; Lorence, "Mobilizing," 70–71.

25. Hall appeared on the July membership list seized by the police. He remained in Atlanta until at least mid-August, Clarina Michelson to Secretariat, Aug. 19, 1932, f13, b1, CM; C. H. Martin, *Herndon Case*, 45, 124–25; Kelley, *Hammer and Hoe*, 85.

26. Howard Kester to Dear Friend, Aug. 15, 1931, r8, 183, CIC.

27. "Death Penalty Asked," *NYS*, March 23, 1932, and Will Alexander to Walter White, March 29, 1932, both on r7, 143, CIC.

28. " 'Reds' Win Victory," *AC*, Apr. 2, 1932, 1; "1868 Law," *NYT*, Apr. 3, 1932, sec. E5; C. H. Martin, *Herndon Case*, 27. Some states fought unions with sedition laws that did not carry the death penalty. The Six forfeited their bonds, "Bonds Forfeited," *AC*, June 14, 1932, 3; "1868 Law Arouses Protest," *NYT*, Apr. 3, 1932, sec. E5.

29. Roger Baldwin to Will Alexander, July 25, 1932, Alexander to Baldwin, July 30, 1932, Baldwin to Alexander, Aug. 1, 1932, and Baldwin to Alexander, Aug. 8, 1932, all on r7, 143, CIC.

30. D. T. Carter, *Scottsboro*, 147; *Twenty Years*; C. H. Martin, *Herndon Case*, 79–81.

31. Torrence, *John Hope*, 238–39; Horne, *Black Liberation*, 17–26, 32, quot. 21; C. H. Martin, *Herndon Case*; Street, *Look Away!*; Herndon, *Let Me Live*; Ben Davis, "Why I Am a Communist"; Howard Fast, Re-Elect Ben Davis Leaflet, f Ben Davis, b5, RM; Horwitz, "Benjamin Davis," 93.

32. According to *Twenty Years*, 600 blacks and whites attended. B. J. Davis, "Why I Am a Communist," 108; C. H. Martin, *Herndon Case*, 36–61; Horne, *Black Liberation*, 31, 38; B. J. Davis, *Councilman*; "Death Penalty Asked," *AJ*, Jan. 17, 1933, 5.

33. *Twenty Years*.

34. "Death Penalty Asked," *AJ*, Jan. 17, 1933, 5; C. H. Martin, *Herndon Case*, 36, 39–43.

35. "Penalty of Death," *AJ*, Jan. 18, 1933, 22; Will Alexander to Roger Baldwin, Jan. 24, 1933, r7, 165–66, CIC.

36. "Herndon Gets 18 to 20 Years" and "Attorneys to Seek New Trial," both in *MT*, Jan. 19, 1933, 1.

37. *Twenty Years*; C. H. Martin, *Herndon Case*, 47, 48, 53.

38. B. J. Davis quoted in *Councilman*, 75–76; "Why I Am a Communist," 105–16. Robert Minor met Davis during the trial, "In Atlanta," f NY Negro, #1–3, b12, RM. Judge Wyatt was from La Grange, GA.

39. B. J. Davis, "Summary for Angelo Herndon Defendant," 351–54.

40. C. H. Martin, *Herndon Case*, 59; "Death of Herndon Is Asked," *AC*, Jan. 18, 1933, 1.

41. "New Trial Plea," *AJ*, Jan. 19, 1933, 9; "Herndon Found Guilty," *AC*, Jan. 19, 1933, 1; "Communist Seeks Freedom," *AJ*, Feb. 2, 1933, 4; "Herndon Is Refused Bond," *AJ*, Feb. 4, 1933, 14; Herndon, *Let Me Live*, 297; C. H. Martin, *Herndon Case*, 62–82.

42. "Carr's Indictment," *AJ*, March 19, 1933, 5.

43. "Klan Is Reorganized," *AJ*, May 7, 1933, 9.

44. "Armed Guards Posted," *AJ*, June 13, 1933, 1; "Georgia Capitol Guarded," *NYT*, June 14, 1933, 6; "Herndon Attorney," *SW*, June 10, 1933, 4.

45. "Communism Kills Itself," *AW*, March 4, 1934, 4. See also K. Miller, "Should Black Turn Red?," 328–32, 350; J. S. Rosenberg, *How Far?*, 126–27.

46. J. W. Johnson, *Negro Americans*, 7–12. See also "Communism and the Negro," July 21, 1935, *This Week*, Scrapbooks, 1936, JWJ; J. W. Johnson, *Along This Way*, 411.

47. Quoted in C. H. Martin, *Herndon Case*, 69. See H. T. Murray, review of *Herndon Case*, by C. H. Martin, 92.

48. "Herndon Committee," *NYA*, Dec. 21, 1935, 1; Horne, *Black Liberation*, 39–40.

49. J. W. Johnson, *Negro Americans*, 7–12, quote 11.

50. Du Bois, *Darkwater*, 16; "Paul Robeson," [n.p.], June 10, 1930, and Richard Reagan, "Be Yourselves, Robeson's Advice," *HT*, Jan. 11, 1930, both in Scrapbook, The Stage, 1931, JWJ.

51. Du Bois, "Postscript," 117, commenting as Hitler purged Jews from the civil service.

52. "Fascist Terror against Negroes," 1–3, 5; Lusane, *Hitler's Black Victims*; "Another Klansman," *PT*, Apr. 6, 1933, 3.

53. "Paris Paper Compares Hitlerism with Race Hate," *AA*, Sept. 28, 1933, 19.

54. "Jews in Germany vs. Negroes in America," *PT*, Oct.12, 1933, 4.

55. Bernard Lecache to the Editor, "Hand of Hitler," "300 Families Affected by Hitler Ban," all in *AA*, Dec. 30, 1933, 1. See Semples, "African Germans."

56. "Heil Hitler!" *AA*, Apr. 9, 1938, 4.

57. "ADOLPH HITLER, K.K.K.," *AA*, Sept. 9, 1933, 16.

58. Kelly Miller, "Hitler—The German Klu [*sic*] Klux," *JG*, Apr. 1, 1933, 6.

59. K. Miller, "Race Prejudice in Germany and America," 105.

60. J. A. Rogers, "American Fascism," *PC*, Oct. 17, 1936, sec. 2, 2.

61. "Plea for the Jews," *AA*, Feb. 3, 1934, 16; Ralph Matthews, "Watching a Big Parade," *AA*, June 17, 1933, 6.

62. Rauschning, *Voice of Destruction*, 69, 71; H. A. Turner, Jr., ed., *Hitler—Memoirs of a Confidant*, 289.

FILL

63. Quoted in "German Scores Treatment of Negro in U.S.," *JG*, Aug. 24, 1935, 3; "Hitlerism and the Negro," *NYAN*, Aug. 24, 1935, 10. Streicher also compared marriage laws, business opportunities, segregation, and education.

64. Preece, "Fascism and the Negro," 355–36. See also D. H. Pierce, "Fascism and the Negro."

65. Quoted in Strong, *Organized Anti-Semitism*, 126; Lavine, *Fifth Column*, 74–78.

66. High, "Star-Spangled Fascists," 240; Strong, *Organized Anti-Semitism*, 16, 21–39; L. V. Bell, *In Hitler's Shadow*, 14, 55; Diamond, *Nazi Movement*; Canedy, *America's Nazis*. Dickstein became a spy for the USSR, Weinstein and Vassiviev, *Haunted Wood*, 140–50.

67. V. Smith, "America's Black Legion."

68. "Fascism," 165; N. MacLean, *Behind the Mask*, 177–88.

69. Amann, "Vigilante Fascism," 501; V. Smith, "America's Black Legion," 915.

70. Lipset and Raab, *Politics of Unreason*, 157–59; Chalmers, *Hooded Americanism*, 309–10; Amann, "Vigilante Fascism," 508–09.

71. Amann, " 'Dog in the Nighttime,' " 566; Amann, "Vigilante Fascism"; Payne, *Fascism*; Seldes, *Facts and Fascism*.

72. Chalmers, *Hooded Americanism*, 305–18; Irwin, "Klan Kicks Up Again"; S. Kennedy, *Southern Exposure*, 170; Lavine, *Fifth Column*, 196–98; Carlson, *Under Cover*, 152–53. For Klan–Silver Shirt connections, Strong, *Organized Anti-Semitism*, 52; Randel, *Ku Klux Klan*, 222; G. S. Smith, *To Save a Nation*, 63; Ledeboer, "Man Who Would Be Hitler."

73. "Fascism," 165; N. Thomas, "Can America Go Fascist?"; Winner, "Fascism at the Door."

74. "Fight against Jim-Crowism," *LD*, r7, 745–46, ILD.

75. Herndon, *Let Me Live*, 294.

76. G. Dimitroff, "Let the Thunder," f Angelo Herndon, b2, MSRK; Blagoeva, *Dimitrov*, 64–66; World Committee, *Reichstag Fire Trial*; quote in J. H. Moore, "Angelo Herndon Case," 60.

77. Benjamin Davis to Will Alexander, Sept. 9, 1933, r7, 165–66, CIC.

78. C. Vann Woodward to Glen Rainey, Aug. 11, 1932, f3, b7, GWR; ICVW, 3–5; Roper, *C. Vann Woodward*, 54–55; J. R. Green, "Rewriting" and "Past and Present"; C. H. Martin, *Herndon Case*, 79–84; Ferguson, *Black Politics*, 64.

79. Benjamin Davis to Will Alexander, Sept. 9, 1933, and Alexander to Davis, Sept. 28, 1933, both on r7, 165–66, CIC; ICVW, 3. He says he sent it to "the lawyer for the Communists." Dykeman and Stokely, *Seeds*, 155–56.

80. Georgia State laid off "about thirty," but Woodward considered his firing a result of his participation in the Herndon case. ICVW, 3. The incident haunted Woodward in his FBI files, James C. Cobb, FOIPA Request No. 0942010-000/190-HQ-1340919, Nov. 10, 1964.

81. Don West acknowledged that he had joined the CP after he left Atlanta, "Georgia Wanted Me," 30–33, statement 32.

82. IGR, 5.

83. IDW, 2–6.

84. Jesse Stuart, "Portrait of a Mountain Boy," 35–38, in f14, b76, HERC; S. James, "Radical"; IDW, 7–8; Biggers and Brosi, "Introduction," xiv–xvii.

85. Don West, "Georgia Wanted Me," 31–32, Stuart, "Portrait of a Mountain Boy," f14, b76, F. A. Behymer, "Georgia Poet," *SLPD*, [n.d.], f14, b76, and Mabel West, "Southern Folk School and Libraries," f14, b76, all in HERC; Biggers and Brosi, "Introduction," xvi–ix.

86. Horton, *Highlander Folk School*, 11–27; Dunbar, *Against the Grain*, 39–40; Egerton, *Speak Now*, 77–78, 126.

87. Myles Horton, notes, "Folk School," f2, b54, HERC.

88. Myles Horton, "Discussion with Fjerland," Feb. 3, 1932, f2, b54, HERC.

89. Myles Horton, "Highlander Folk School Idea," [1933], f2, b54, HERC; F. Adams, *Unearthing*, 1–53.

90. ILY, 64–65.

91. Myles Horton, "Pre-Highlander Notes," f2, b54, HERC; Horton, *Highlander Folk School*, 29–42; IDW, 26.

92. IDW, 34–35.

93. IDW, 29. West left on April 1. "Don West," staff biography, f8, b3, and West to Myles Horton, Apr. 3, 1933, f21, b29, both in HERC; Horton, *Highlander Folk School*, 84; Dunbar, *Against the Grain*, 52.

94. Don West, "Georgia Wanted Me," 32; IDW, 29.

95. Don West to Myles Horton, Dec. 16, 1933, f21, b29, HERC.

96. Painter, *Narrative*, 204–06.

97. "Protest Injustice to Berry Students!" f21, b29, HERC.

98. "Attempt by Reds," *AJ*, Oct. 8, 1933, D8; IDW, 11, 42. The NSL sent Clyde Johnson, Dunbar, *Against the Grain*, 53–56. Kelley, *Hammer and Hoe*, 63.

99. Solomon, *Cry Was Unity*, 248. West later denied membership in the CP, IDW, 45, 68, and S. James, "Radical," but he claimed it in *New Masses* (July 1934), and CPUSA records confirm. Dunbar, *Against the Grain*, 54–59, and Egerton, *Speak Now*, 159–60, 167–72, did not have access to CPUSA records.

100. Don West, "Angelo Herndon Dreams," March 17, 1934, f Angelo Herndon, b2, MSRK.

101. IRNB; "Bail Forced," *SW*, July 1934, 4; "Negro Red Out," *NYT*, Aug. 5, 1934; Herndon, *Let Me Live*, 286–301; "Herndon Released" and "Down the Big Road," *CC*, Sept. 22, 1934, both on r7, 164–65, CIC; C. H. Martin, *Herndon Case*, 79.

102. "20 Mills in South Reopen," *NYT*, Sept. 18, 1934, 15; "Call 10,000 Troops," *NYT*, Sept. 16, 1934, 32; Irons, *Testing*, 3; Salmond, *General Textile Strike*; J. D. Hall et al., *Like a Family*, 289–357; Simon, *Fabric of Defeat*, 90–122; Stoney et al., *Uprising of '34*; Tindall, *Emergence*, 510–12.

103. Pickard, "Burlington Dynamite Plot," 4–5.

104. Quoted in Irons, *Testing*, 3, 191 n. 2; Salmond, *General Textile Strike*, 143–97; photograph in J. D. Hall et al., *Like a Family*, 333, also 329–43.

105. "Condemns Communism," *CO*, Sept. 15, 1934, 4.

106. Dist. 16 had 93 members in early 1934, "Report on Recruiting," f515, r281, d3625, 16–19, and Dear Comrades, July 10, 1934, f515, r281, d3625, 51, both in CPUSA. By Nov. 1934 there were 75 members, and by Feb. 1935 over 150, "Membership in District," f515, r298, d3882, CPUSA; Jack Stachel, "Report on Textiles," Sept. 17, 1934, 534/7/520, RGASPI.

107. "Crowd Threatens Red," *NYT*, Sept. 18, 1934, 15; Salmond, *General Textile Strike*, 155.

108. Quoted in Hickey, *Hope and Danger*, 190; C. H. Martin, *Herndon Case*, 45, 124–25. Over 70, Nannie Leah Young Washburn marched with Martin Luther King in the Poor People's March on Washington. She was arrested and dragged, kicking and screaming, to jail, IDW, 33.

109. "Industrial Fears," *AJ*, July 9, 1933, sec. 8B; "Mill Conditions," *AJ*, July 15, 1933, 3; "Mill Workers Study," *AJ*, July 13, 1933, 24; Simon, *Fabric of Defeat*, 93; Tindall, *Emergence*, 505–09.

110. "Labor Federation Roll," *AJ*, Aug. 7, 1933, 7; Irons, *Testing*, 63–78.

111. "Pay Rolls Gain Half Million," *AJ*, Aug. 2, 1933, 1; "Labor Official Moves," *AJ*, Sept. 5, 1933, 24; "Union Workers Here," *AJ*, Oct. 12, 1933, 15; "Atlanta to Get Labor Peace Board," *AJ*, Oct. 5, 1933, 30.

112. Quoted and analysis in J. D. Hall et al., *Like a Family*, 323–24; Irons, *Testing*, 63–78; Pickard, "Burlington Dynamite Plot," 10; D. L. Smith, *New Deal*, 45–61, esp. 57–58.

113. Sitkoff, *New Deal for Blacks*, 55; Amis, "National Recovery Act"; Solomon, *Cry Was Unity*, 234; Holmes, "Blue Eagle."

114. Salmond, *General Textile Strike*, 180–85; J. D. Hall et al., *Like a Family*, 338–40.

115. "Troops in Georgia," *NYT*, Sept. 18, 1934, 1; Simon, *Fabric of Defeat*, 111–19.

116. "Bayonet Wound Fatal" and "Women Held in Concentration Camp," *NYT*, Sept. 20, 1934, 1; "Record of Terror," *LD* (Oct. 1934), r1, 825–48, ILD; C. H. Martin, *Herndon Case*, 122; Irons, *Testing*, 147–50, 137; Salmond, *General Textile Strike*, 186–87; J. D. Hall et al., *Like a Family*, 332–34; Salmond, *General Textile Strike*, 189; Fraser, *Labor Will Rule*, 306–07.

117. "Emergency Detention Camp," *AJ*, Sept. 18, 1934, 1; "Pickets Having a Good Time in Internment Camp Here," *AJ*, Sept. 19, 1934, 2.

118. "Hays Plans Suit Here," *AJ*, Sept. 20, 1934, 7; "Week," 197.

119. "Nazis Stress Our Strike," *NYT*, Sept. 20, 1934, 1.

120. C. H. Martin, *Herndon Case*, 90, 125–30; J. H. Moore, "Angelo Herndon Case," 67; "Communists Will Seek Freedom" and quoted in "Thomas Discusses 'Red' Raid," both in *ADW*, Oct. 17, 1934; "As We Go Marching thru Georgia," *LD*, Nov. 1934, r1, 849–72, ILD; "Case of Angelo Herndon."

121. Quoted in Horne, *Black Liberation*, 42; C. H. Martin, *Herndon Case*, 135–37.

122. "Case of Angelo Herndon."

123. W. Wilson, "Georgia Suppresses Insurrection."

124. Haynes and Khler, *American Communist Movement*, 67; Langston Hughes to Carl Van Vechten, Nov. 1, 1933, in *Remember Me*, ed. E. Bernard, 110.

125. Quote in Herndon, *Let Me Live*, 294–96; Langston Hughes to Carl Van Vechten, Nov. 1, 1933, in *Remember Me*, ed. E. Bernard, 110; Haynes and Klehr, *American Communist Movement*, 67.

126. "Developing Educational Work," March 10, 1934, f "Negro 1930," b12, RM; Langston Hughes to Paul Green, Oct. 31, 1933, f282, b3, and Elliot E. Cohen to Paul Green, July 21, 1932, f225, b3, both in PG; S. Small, "Hell in Georgia," E. Lawson, "20 Years on the Chain Gang?," "Be One of the 2,000,000," and Angelo

Herndon to Paul Green, Sept. 26, 1935, all in f351, b5, PG; Hughes to Van Vechten, Dec. 6, 1933, and Dec. 26, 1933, in *Remember Me*, ed. E. Bernard, 113, 116–17; "Case of Angelo Herndon"; Dunbar, *Against the Grain*, 50; Glen, *Highlander*; Edgerton, *Speak Now*, 158–62.

127. Fowler, *Knot in the Thread*, 157.

128. "New Yorkers Give Herndon a Big Ovation," *ADW*, Aug. 23, 1934, 1, 2; C. H. Martin, *Herndon Case*, 115–19; Naison, *Communists in Harlem*, 75–89.

129. "New Yorkers Give Herndon a Big Ovation," *ADW*, Aug. 23, 1934, 1, 2; C. H. Martin, *Herndon Case*, 115–19.

130. http://www.spartacus.schoolnet.co.uk/GERthalmann.htm, accessed Oct. 29, 2003; World Committee, *Reichstag Fire Trial*, 273–75; Don West, "Georgia Officials Ape Hitler Terror," *LD* (July 1934): 6, r1, 777–800, ILD.

131. Nerouy, "Tutankh-Amen and Ras Tafari." "Italy and Abyssinia,"62–63, predicted the conflict in 1926. "Editorials," *Opportunity*, 230; W. E. B. Du Bois, "Inter-Racial"; Plummer, *Rising Wind*, 37–57; J. E. Harris, *Reactions*; J. S. Rosenberg, *How Far?*, 103–10; R. S. Young, "Ethiopia Awakens"; Diggins, *Mussolini*, 312; Von Eschen, *Race against Empire*, 11; J. E. Harris, *Reactions*, 1–18.

132. W. R. Scott, "Black Nationalism," 118–34; "Dr. W. N. Huggins," *NYT*, Oct. 6, 1935, 29; "Ethiopian Diplomat," *NYT*, Dec. 21, 1935, 8; "Ethiopians Continue Successful," *NYA*, Jan. 4, 1936, 1; "Report Zaphiro Was Sent Out," *PC*, Apr. 18, 1936, 9; J. E. Harris, *Reactions*, 81–84.

133. R. Wright, "Joe Louis Uncovers Dynamite," 397; Diggins, *Mussolini*, 306, 310–11; W. R. Scott, "Black Nationalism, 118–34; Naison, "Communism and Harlem," 2.

134. Walter White to Joel Spingarn, Oct. 22, 1935, and White to James Weldon Johnson, Nov. 8, 1935, both in f545, b24, JWJ.

135. Du Bois, "Inter-Racial," 86. On Mussolini's motivations, see Coon, "Realist Looks at Ethiopia"; J. S. Rosenberg, *How Far?*, 104–05.

136. W. R. Scott, "Black Nationalism," 129; "N.Y. Body Claims 17,500," *AA*, July 20, 1935, 1; "Courier Scoops Country," *PC*, July 13, 1935, 2. Some African Americans fought for Ethiopia, and others tried to enlist. See "Here's Why U.S. Citizens," *PC*, July 20, 1935, 1; "Julian Back Home, War Career Ended," *NYT*, Dec.14, 1935, 8; Stoddard, "Men of Color Aroused."

137. C. H. Martin, *Herndon Case*, frontispiece.

138. P. Robeson, *Here I Stand*, 51. "Joint Meeting," 145–46.

139. Du Bois, "Inter-Racial," 87; Plummer, *Rising Wind*, 40, 49. On the USSR, see Lyons, "Communist False Fronts," 18; "League Conclusion," *NYT*, Oct. 6, 1935, 29; "State Department," *NYT*, July 19, 1935, 2; Verich, *European Powers*.

140. Du Bois, "Inter-Racial," 92; Carter J. Woodson, "Abyssinia," *NYA*, Dec. 28, 1935, 12; W. R. Scott, "Black Nationalism," 122.

141. "James Weldon Johnson Resents," *Tribune* [Philadelphia?], Feb. 25, 1936, Scrapbook, 1936 Miscellaneous, JWJ.

142. Quoted in W. R. Scott, "Black Nationalism, 122.

143. "Lynch Rule in Addis," *AA*, May 23, 1936; "Machine Gun Trained," *CD*, June 20, 1936, 12; "Activities of the I.T.U.C.," [1936?], 495/14/60, RGASPI.

144. Quotes in "Support for Abyssinia," Aug. 28, 1935, 495/14/60, and "Report of

the I.T.U.C.," Oct. 16, 1935, 495/14/60, both in RGASPI. See also "District Buro (Dist. 16) September 16, 1935," f515, r298, d3882, 9, CPUSA; "International Negro Liberation Committee," [1935?], 495/14/60, RGASPI; "Ethiopia Drives Back," *SW*, Jan. 1936, 1; Ford, *Negro and the Democratic Front*, 70–72.

145. "Negro Red Loses," *NYT*, May 21, 1935, 5; "Masses Demand Re-Hearing," *SW*, June 1935, 1, 2; C. H. Martin, *Herndon Case*, 146–54; Horne, *Black Liberation*, 48, identifies the NAACP lawyer as Houston.

146. Dimitrov, "Future Is the Workers"; Charney, *Long Journey*, 37, 59, 62–65, 77; Warren, *Liberals and Communism*, 89–122.

147. Klehr and Haynes, *American Communist Movement*, 77–81; Naison, "Communism and Harlem," 1–25; Naison, "Remaking America," 44–73, figs. 45.

148. Naison, "Communism and Harlem," 1.

149. "Reds Launch New Drive,'" n.d., f "History, 1931, 1940s, 1950, 1951," b3, RM. Figures in J. L. Moore, Preimesberger, Tarr, eds., *Congressional Quarterly's Guide*, 671.

150. Ted Wellman [Sid Benson] to Dear Comrades, Jan. 30, 1936, f515, r306, d4029, 17, CPUSA. Some feared that the alliance with Socialists might reduce African Americans' power in the CP; see Bill [Marlow?] to Dear Comrade Brown, Feb. 13, 1936, f515, r306, d4029, 30, CPUSA.

151. Roger Baldwin to Will Alexander, Feb. 2, 1933, Apr. 19, 1933, and "Fund Appeal, ILD/ACLU," all on r7, 165–66, CIC.

152. "Unite the Negro People," f Negro 1931, b12, RM; Naison, "Remaking America," 48–50; Warren, *Alternative Vision*, 148–52.

153. J. H. Moore, "Angelo Herndon Case," 68; Herndon, *Let Me Live*, 318–19.

154. Herndon, *Let Me Live*, 332; "Students Ask Red's Freedom," *NYT*, Oct. 17, 1935, 11; "Herndon Cheered," *NYT*, Oct. 22, 1935, 15.

155. E. England, "Angelo Herndon," NTL; Denning, *Cultural Front*, 262–63.

156. North, "Angelo Herndon Back"; "Negro Red Seeks Release," *NYT*, Nov. 10, 1935, 2. Will Alexander convinced the ILD to hire a local white lawyer, Will Alexander to Mrs. Wells Harrington, Oct. 26, 1935, and R. B. Eleazer to A. O. French, Nov. 20, 1935, both on r7, 165–66, CIC. On North, see Denning, *Cultural Front*, 205.

157. Herndon, *Let Me Live*, 285; North, "Chain Gang Governor."

158. North, "Chain Gang Governor."

159. K. Miller, "Race Prejudice in Germany and America."

160. "Negro Republic," *AJ*, Nov. 13, 1935, on r7, 165–66, CIC; "Judge Upsets Georgia Revolt Law," *NYT*, Dec. 8, 1935, 1; "Herndon Appeal," *NYT*, Dec. 15, 1935, 2; "'Vagueness' Aids Herndon," *NYT*, Dec. 15, 1935, sec. E11; "Old Herndon Law," *AC*, Dec. 8, 1935, 1; C. H. Martin, *Herndon Case*, 161–64.

161. C. H. Martin, *Herndon Case*, 168; "List of Books," f 648, ser. 2.2, HWO.

162. "Herndon Committee Plans Mass Meeting," *NYA*, Dec. 21, 1935.

163. Ottanelli, *Communist*, 62–63; Lewy, *Cause that Failed*, 30–32.

164. "Warns of Danger," *NYT*, July 4, 1936, 13; Record, *Negro and the Communist Party*, 126.

165. "Negro Commission Meeting," Feb. 24, 1937, and Apr. 15, 1937, 495/14/60, RGASPI.

166. C. H. Martin, *Herndon Case*, 175; "Roosevelt in Court Poll," *NYT*, Feb. 23, 1937, 1.

167. Distinguished attorney Whitney North Seymour and the local white attorney William A. Sutherland represented Herndon, C. H. Martin, *Herndon Case*, 149. W. A. Sutherland to Will Alexander, Oct. 28, 1935, r7, 165–66; quoted from "Brief for the Appellant," Supreme Court of the United States, October Term, 1936, Nos. 474 and 475, Angelo Herndon, Appellant, J. I. Lowry, Sheriff of Fulton County, AH; "Communist's Conviction Upheld," *NYT*, June 14, 1936, 1; Damon, "Fresh Misdeeds," 915; "Communist Raid Appeal," *AJ*, July 10, 1936, 19; "New High Court Plea," *NYT*, Oct. 21, 1936; "High Court Review," *NYT*, Nov. 24, 1936, sec. L19.

168. Damon, "Fresh Misdeeds." The charge was later reduced to disorderly conduct.

169. Horne, *Black Liberation*, 30. Davis remembers it as a protest against himself, but Charles Drew was the black star of Amherst's team. See G. Ware, *Hastie*, 17; W. J. Baker, *Owens*, 35.

170. Wiggins, "1936 Olympic Games"; Kass, "Issue of Racism"; "Olympic Games, 1936"; "Owens, Peacock, Metcalfe," *CD*, Dec. 7, 1935, pt. 2, 15; Guttman, *Games*, 70.

171. "Johnson, Columbia University Track Star," *NYAN*, Oct. 26, 1935, 12.

172. "Brundage Scores 'Alien Agitators,'" *NYT*, Dec. 4, 1935, 26.

173. "Trials and Tryouts."

174. "Olympians All." Sources conflict on the number of black Olympians. *Opportunity* counts 11. D. L. Lewis, *W. E. B. Du Bois*, 2:402–03, mentions 13 black men, but Ben Johnson had to drop out. Two black women made the team: Tydie Pickett from Chicago and Louise Stokes from Boston. "Two Race Girls Win Olympic Berths," *CD*, July 11, 1936, 13.

175. "Spec Towns and Packard Win," *AJ*, July 5, 1936, sec. B1; "Towns Wins Heat in 14.3; Walker Loses in 100 Meters," *AJ*, July 12, 1936, sec. B1; "Towns and Packard Go to Olympics," *AJ*, July 13, 1936, sec. B9; "South Doubles Its Entries," *AJ*, July 14, 1935, 12. Eight white Southerners qualified.

176. Baker, *Owens*, 82, 84; "Maxie Mobbed," *AJ*, July 29, 1936, 13.

177. Baldur von Schirach, *Ich glaubte an Hitler* (Hamburg: Mosaik, 1967), 217–18, quoted in Mandell, *Nazi Olympics*, 236, 228–29; Heinrich Krieger, "How to Whip Out the American Negroes," *Die Tat* (Feb., 1936), pt. 3, ser. 5, r9, b97, frames 0307–0309, NNC.

178. "110,000 See Owens," *NYT*, Aug. 3, 1936, 1; "Owens Captures," *NYT*, Aug. 4, 1936; "U.S. Captures 4 Events," *NYT*, Aug. 5, 1936, 1; Quote from "While Hitler Retired," *NYP*, Aug. 7, 1936. Much of the press confused Johnson with Owens. See also W. J. Baker, *Owens*, 90–91; Kieran and Daley, *Story of the Olympic Games*, 162; Guttman, *Games*, 78; Kieran, *Story of the Olympic Games*, 240–44.

179. "Proud I'm an American," Scrapbook V:1–4, JWJ.

180. "Color Line Fades," *CD*, Aug. 15, 1936, 17; "Owens 'Shaky,'" *NYT*, Aug. 9, 1936, sports, 25; Geisen, *Nazi Propaganda*, 31; Guttman, *Games*, 80.

181. "Owens and Metcalfe," *AJ*, Aug. 3, 1936, 11; Guttman, *Games*, 80. For a "darky" example, see "Marietta Negro Groom Forgets Bride's Name," *AJ*, July 25, 1936,

5. Coverage in the *Constitution* was more gracious; see Alan Gould, "Historic Olympiad," *AC*, Aug. 17, 1936, 12.

182. Baldur von Schirach, *Ich glaubte an Hitler*, 217-18, quoted in Mandell, *Nazi Olympics*, 236.

183. "Three First Places," *CD*, Aug. 8, 1936, 1; W. E. B. Du Bois, "Forum," *PC*, Sept. 9, 1936, 11; Sollors, "W. E. B. Du Bois"; D. L. Lewis, *W. E. B. Du Bois*, 2:395–406.

184. "Hitler Praised above Roosevelt," *PT*, Oct. 19, 1936, 1.

185. J. A. Rogers, "American Fascism," *PC*, Oct. 17, 1936, sec. 2, 2; "Nazis and Dixie," *AA*, Feb. 22, 1936, 4; Kloss, *Das Volksgruppenrecht*.

186. Diamond, *Nazi Movement*, 69. The title means "Ethnic Group Law in the United States of America."

187. Rauschning, *Voice of Destruction*, 68–69, also quoted in Weinberg, "Hitler's Image," 1011; Weinberg, ed., *Hitler's Second Book*, 108–18. Hitler's belief in the imminent collapse of the U.S. was reinforced by his frequent viewing of *Grapes of Wrath*, L. V. Bell, *In Hitler's Shadow*, 9.

188. "White Racialism," 308.

189. Herndon v. Lowry, Sheriff, nos. 474, 475, Supreme Court of the United States, 301 U.S. 242; S. Ct. 732; 1937 U.S. Lexis 290; 81 L. Ed. 1066, quotes [3] 1, [4] 2.

190. "Herndon Set Free," *NYT*, Apr. 27, 1937, 1, 10; "Herndon Is Released," *AJ*, Apr. 26, 1937, 1; "Court Frees," *ADW*, Apr. 27, 1937, 1; "Herndon's Conviction Set Aside," 572; L. Patterson, "Angelo Herndon Is Free!" 3; C. H. Martin, *Herndon Case*, 182, 191–212. The state dropped indictments against the Atlanta Six and Nannie Leah Young and Annie Mae Young Leathers in 1939. Herndon went to work for the party on ILD issues and youth work and became president of the Young Communist League, "Negro Commission," Aug. 3, 1936, f "Negro 1931," b12, RM.

191. C. H. Martin, *Herndon Case*, 181.

192. "Mass War Urged to End Fascism," *NYT*, May 3, 1937, 6. Herndon died Dec. 9, 1997, in Sweet Home, AR.

193. "Draft Program," June, 1937, r1, 54–57, ILD; "National Conference," r1, 172–73, ILD.

194. "Negro Commission Meeting," Feb. 24, 1937, and Apr. 15, 1937, 495/14/60, RGASPI.

195. "Lily White Democracy"; "'A Rose by Any Name,'" *PT*, Aug. 22, 1935, 4; "Don't Kill Jews," *PT*, Aug. 22, 1935, 5; "American Practice of Lynching Forms Basis for Defense of Nazi Persecutions," *JG*, Feb. 2, 1935, 9.

196. Du Bois, "Forum," *PC*, Dec. 5, 1936, 13; quoted in D. L. Lewis, *W. E. B. Du Bois*, 2:398; analyzed in J. S. Rosenberg, *How Far?*, 116–17.

197. "Hitler Far Ahead of Simon Legree," *NYP*, Jan. 27, 1937, 16.

198. *Der Stürmer*'s publisher was Julius Streicher. W. E. B. Du Bois, "Forum," *PC*, Dec. 19, 1936, 11, and sec. 2, 3; McGovern, *Anatomy of a Lynching*. On the Florida lynching and German press, see *JG*, Aug. 10, 1935, 9; Chalmers, *Hooded Americanism*, 311.

199. W. E. B. Du Bois, "Forum," *PC*, Dec. 19, 1936, 11, sec. 2, 3.

200. On the black/Jewish relationship to 1933, see D. L. Lewis, "Parallels and Divergences," N. MacLean, "Leo Frank Case Reconsidered," and Dinnerstein, *Leo Frank Case.*

201. Wise, "Parallel between Hitlerism and the Persecution of Negroes," 128.

202. Everett R. Clinchy to James Weldon Johnson, Mar. 22, 1935, f346, b14, and Clinchy to Johnson, June 27, 1935, f346, b14, both in JWJ; "Institute of Human Relations," Williams College, r2, 12, CIC.

203. "Nazis, Negroes, Jews and Catholics"; Randolph, "Propaganda against Jews"; D. B. Davis, "Jews and Blacks." Wedlock, "Comparisons by Negro Publications" takes evidence out of chronological context.

204. A little-known anti-Semite, perhaps white, published *Dynamite* in Chicago, which *Opportunity* called a "scurrilous anti-Semitic sheet," L. D. Reddick, "What Hitler Says," 108. See also Carlson, *Under Cover*, 154–59. For late 1930s comparisons, see "Charity Begins" and "Refugees and Citizens."

205. Israel, "Jew Hatred among Negroes." Weisbord and Stein, "Negro Perceptions of Jews"; Plummer, *Rising Wind*, 67–69.

206. Israel, "Jew Hatred among Negroes"; Robert Bagnall, "Should Shun Jew-Baiting," *PC*, Aug. 4, 1938, 4; Ottley, "*New World a-Coming*," 122–36.

207. Klinkner and Smith, *Unsteady March*, 137.

208. James Weldon Johnson to Walter White, March 18, 1938, f547, b24, and Johnson to M. B. Schnapper, March 9, 1938, f415, b17, both in JWJ.

209. Robert W. Bagnall, "Fascism, Nazism Bad for Negro," *PC*, March 31, 1938.

210. "White Racialism," 308.

211. "We Must Stand Together."

212. *AJ*, Feb. 5, 1939, sec. B6, reprinted in Logan, ed., *Attitude*, 31–32.

213. "White Racialism," 308.

CHAPTER 5: MOVING LEFT FROM CHAPEL HILL TO CAPE TOWN

1. J. D. Hall et al., *Like a Family*, 343–44; Pickard, "Burlington Dynamite Plot," 4.

2. L. Alexander, "Durham Streets"; Weare, *Black Business*, 253–55.

3. L. Austin to My Dear Friend [Jim Weaver/Don West], March 12, 1935, f515, r298, d3882, 14, CPUSA; Warren, *Liberals and Communism.*

4. Tindall, "Significance," 287; Kneebone, *Southern Liberal Journalists*, 86–88.

5. C. Vann Woodward to Glenn Rainey, Sept. 24, 1934, f3, b7, GWR; ICVW; Woodward, *Thinking Back*, 20–21; Cobb, *Away down South*, 121–26.

6. Dykeman and Stokely, *Seeds*; J. D. Hall, *Revolt against Chivalry.*

7. Sosna, *In Search*, 38–39; Rose, "Putting the South."

8. Anthony, *Max Yergan*. Like Anthony, I was denied access to Yergan's papers, but in the summer of 2006 my research assistant Caitlin Crowell was allowed access.

9. Athas, " 'He Lived to Live.' "

10. Ashby, *Graham*, 4–5, 28, 21–22; quote from IPG, 26.

11. Ralph Miliband, "Harold Laski," quoted at www.spartacus.schoolnet.co.uk; biography from FPG; IGJ; Ashby, *Graham*, 42–62.

12. Frank Graham to Nell Battle Lewis, [Sept. 23, 1929?], f25, b1, and "Dean Gra-

ham's Picture of Ella May Wiggins," *Southern Textile Bulletin*, Apr. 10, 1930, 22, f51, b1, both in FPG; Ashby, *Graham*, 73–81.

13. Frank Graham to Roland Beasley, Dec. 23, 1929, f25, b1, "To the People," f48, b1, [Dec. 1929], both in FPG. The figure 300 comes from Harriet Herring to Gertrude Weil, Feb. 5, 1930, f50, b1, FPG. "A Statement by Some North Carolina Citizens" and "The Motives behind the Demand," both in f51, b1, FPG; Ashby, *Graham*, 77. See also S. Wilkerson-Freeman, "Women and the Transformation of American Politics."

14. "Motives behind the Demand," 31, f51, b11, H. W. Chase to J. A. Baugh, Sept. 21, 1929, f25, b1, and Clyde R. Hoey to Frank Graham, Dec. 30, 1929, f25, b1, all in FPG.

15. David Clark to Dear Sir, Jan. 31, 1930, f49, b1, and "Dean Graham's Picture of Ella May Wiggins," f51, b1, both in FPG.

16. Ashby, *Graham*, 83–86, 105–06; Woodward, *Thinking Back*, 19; IGR, 7.

17. Scales and Nickson, *Cause at Heart*, 45.

18. Athas, " 'He Lived to Live.' "

19. Roper interview notes with Bennett H. Wall, Apr. 11, 1979, 7, f9, b1, JHR.

20. Athas, " 'He Lived to Live' "; *Contempo* (June 1931); Scales and Nickson, *Cause at Heart*, 45–46, 63.

21. One of their favorite targets was the Nashville Agrarians. Knickerbocker, "Dilemma of the Fugitives"; Kneebone, *Southern Liberal Journalists*, 56–73; Winchell, *Where No Flag Flies*, 209–10.

22. Langston Hughes to Paul Green, Oct. 13, 1931, f178, b2, and "We Nominate," *Vanity Fair* (Apr. 1932): 54, in f208, b3, PG; IGJ, pt. 3, 20–21. Green invited Hughes, but Guy Johnson and the *Contempo* editors all later claimed to have done it. See G. B. Johnson and G. G. Johnson, *Research in Service*, 37–38; Roper, *Green*, 143, 187–89; Langston Hughes to Carl Van Vechten, Feb. 10, 1932, in *Remember Me*, ed. E. Bernard, 93; *Contempo* (Dec. 1, 1931); Rampersad, *Life of Langston Hughes*, 1:223.

23. "Negro Poet Will Deliver Talk," *DTH*, Nov. 19, 1939.

24. Hughes, "Christ in Alabama."

25. "Palmetto Publisher," "Not a University Responsibility," "University Disclaims Magazine," and "Hounds of Prejudice Unleashed," all in f13486, b563, LH; quoted in Rampersad, *Life of Langston Hughes*, 1:225; Hughes, *I Wonder*, 76–77; K. J. Ford, "Making Poetry Pay"; Maxwell, *New Negro*, 140–41; Cobb, *Away down South*, 155. My interpretation follows Thurston, "Black Christ, Red Flag."

26. Hughes, "Southern Gentlemen"; Hughes, *I Wonder*, 45; *Contempo* (Dec. 1, 1931); Rampersad, *Life of Langston Hughes*, 1:224.

27. Paul Green to Barrett H. Clark, Dec. 8, 1931, in *Southern Life*, ed. Avery, 191–93.

28. "Negro Poet Will Deliver Talk," *DTH*, Nov. 19, 1931; "Fifteen Hundred," *DTH*, Nov. 24, 1931.

29. Paul Green to Barrett H. Clark, Dec. 8, 1931, in *Southern Life*, ed. Avery, 193; Langston Hughes to Carl Van Vechten, Feb. 10, 1932, in *Remember Me*, ed. E. Bernard, 93.

30. Quotes in Buttitta, "Note on *Contempo*"; Hughes, *I Wonder*, 47; "J. Langston Hughes," *DTH*, Nov. 21, 1931.

31. Hughes, *I Wonder*, 47; editorial, *Southern Textile Bulletin*, 11; editorial, *Southern Textile Bulletin*, 19.

32. IGJ, pt. 3, 20–21; Guy Johnson to Paul Green, Nov. 14, 1931, f179, b2, PG; Ashby, *Graham*, 125–27.

33. *Contempo* (Oct. 25, 1932). Buttitta disappeared from the masthead Apr. 4, 1933, and published one issue of a rival *Contempo* from Durham Apr. 5, 1933. Meador, "History and Index of *Contempo*," 14.

34. Allen Johnson to Org. Commission, C.C., Aug. 15 [1934], f505, r298, d3882, 68, CPUSA; C. Vann Woodward to Glenn Rainey, Sept. 24, 1934, f7, b3, GWR; IGR, 5; IDW; Don West, "Georgia Wanted Me," 30–33.

35. Paul Crouch to Org Com CC, Aug. 19, 1934, f515, r281, d3625, 69, CPUSA; "Call 10,000 Troops," *NYT*, Sept. 16, 1934, 32.

36. Jim Weaver to Comrade Brown, [1934], f515, r298, d3882, 36, and Jim [Weaver] to Paul, Feb. 18 [1935], f515, r281, d3625, 21, both in CPUSA; PCT. West later believed that Crouch had become an FBI informant in 1935, IDW, 73.

37. JW to Dear Jim, Apr. 12, 1935, f515, r298, d3882, 22, CPUSA; IGR, 5, 10. Woodward carefully distanced himself from the CP after 1935.

38. Salmond, *General Textile Strike*, 213, 223–28. For "assistant chairman," see J. A. Weaver, "Leonard J. Green Helps Mill Owners," f4519, b125, PG.

39. Paul Green to David Cobb, June 2, 1952, f4508a, b118a, "Help Save Six Innocent Workers from the Penitentiary," f4519, b125, Jim Weaver, "Burlington Six 'Dynamite' Case: A Summary," f4519, b125, and FBI File, f4508a, b118a, all in PG; Roper, *Green*, 152–54; Jim [Weaver] to Dear Paul, Feb. 18 [1935], f515, r281, d3625, 21, CPUSA.

40. Klehr and Haynes, *American Communist Movement*, 77–78, point out that cooperation predated the new line. See also Denning, *Cultural Front*, 4–21.

41. Paul Crouch disagreed with Don West's united front strategies, Crouch to Comrade Stachel, Dec. 25, 1936, f515, r281, d3625, 105, CPUSA; Salmond, *General Textile Strike*, 214.

42. Paul Green to David Cobb, June 2, 1952, f4508a, b118a, and FBI File, f4508a, b118a, both in PG.

43. James Weaver to Jim Crews, Apr. 12, 1935, f515, r298, d3882, 22, CPUSA.

44. Jim Weaver to Earl Browder, March 14, 1935, f515, r298, d3882, 15, CPUSA; Crouch, *Testimony*, 208; IPG, 21; Roper, *Green*, 153. Ultimately, the defendants were found guilty. Salmond, *General Textile Strike*, 230–32.

45. Re Burlington Dynamite Case, Dec. 31, 1934, IDW; E to Dear Jim, [1935], f515, r298, d3882, CPUSA; PCT, 4; Crouch, *Testimony*; quote in IPG, 19.

46. Jim Weaver to Paul [Crouch], Feb. 18 [1935], f515, r281, d3625, 21, and Paul Crouch to CC, Oct. 30, 1934, f515, r281, f3625, 84, both in CPUSA.

47. Paul Crouch to Comrade Stachel, Dec. 25, 1934, f515, r281, d3625, 106, CPUSA; Norman Thomas in 1932 garnered 883,990 votes, of which 17,457 came from former Confederate states, *Presidential Elections since 1789*, 118–22.

48. "Conference of Younger Churchmen," May 27–29, 1934, f328, b9, Frances A. Henson, "Christian Attitude towards the Marxist Strategy," f336, b9, "Southern Socialist Conference," Apr. 7, 8, 9, 1939, f350, b10, "Annual Report," f314, b9, all in HK; Dunbar, *Against the Grain*, 39–40; Egerton, *Speak Now*, 77–78, 126,

158–62; Fannin, *Labor's Promised Land*, 71–129. On Dombrowski, see "Dombrowski Correspondence," f25, b22, HERC.

49. Reinhold Niebuhr to Myles Horton, Aug. 18, 1933, and Horton to Niebuhr, July 6, 1966, both in f1, b22, HERC; "Staff Meeting Minutes," Sept. 18, 1934, f4, b2, and [Myles Horton] to Norman Thomas, Apr. 24, 1933, f24, b27, both in HERC; "Conference of Younger Churchmen of the South," May 27–29, 1934, f328, b9, HK; Dunbar, *Against the Grain*, 50, 52–53; Egerton, *Speak Now*, 158–59.

50. "Annual Report," f314, b9, HK.

51. "Minutes-Soviet," Jan. 6, 1935, and "Letter from Jim Weaver re: students," June 17, 1935, both in f5, b2, HERC; Kelley, *Hammer and Hoe*, 126.

52. Dear Friend, Feb. 4, 1935, Mercer Evans to James Dombrowsky [*sic*], Feb. 9, 1935, [Dombrowski] to Evans, Feb. 11, 1935, all in f7, b31, HERC.

53. "Call for the All-Southern Conference," f15, b7, JBM.

54. Ibid., [Dombrowski] to Dear Friend, Feb. 1935, f7, b31, HERC; T [Ted Wellman/Sid Benson] to Dear Friend, [1935], f515, r298, d3882, 33, CPUSA; ILY, 64–65. On the CYC, see "Howard Kester Correspondence," f21, b17, HERC; Kelley, *Hammer and Hoe*, 120–21; Dunbar, *Against the Grain*, 137–38; Grubbs, *Cry from the Cotton*; H. L. Mitchell, *Mean Things Happening*, 166–70; Lichtenstein, intro. to *Revolt among the Sharecroppers*.

55. "Sprinkle Case" and "The charge has been made," both in f7, b31, HERC.

56. L. Austin to My Dear Friend [Jim Weaver], f515, r298, d3882, 14, and Jim Weaver to Earl Browder, Mar. 14, 1935, f515, r298, d3882, 15, both in CPUSA. Crouch later claimed that Austin and black Durham attorney Conrad Pearson became Communists in 1936, but there is no supporting evidence, PCT, 6–7.

57. "Membership in District," f515, r298, d3882, 43, 53, CPUSA.

58. C.C. Org. Dept., [Allen Johnson?], [spring 1935], f515, r298, d3882, Allen Johnson to Org. Commission, C.C., Aug. 15 [1935], f515, r298, d3882, 68, Paul Crouch and Fred Gray to Polburo, Aug. 1, 1935, f515, r298, d3882, 57, and Beth [Kathleen O'Shaughnessy] to Comrade Brown, [1935], f515, r298, d3882, 139, all in CPUSA.

59. Allen Johnson to Org. Com., C.C., [Sept. 1935], f515, r298, 3882, 94, CPUSA. Crouch later said that Alton Lawrence purchased the press, but Crouch was not involved in purchasing the press, PCT, 5.

60. C.C. Org. Dept., Johnson, [spring 1935], f515, r298, d3882, 146, The first issue that I located is *SW*, Feb. 1936. Johnson to C.C. Org. Dept., [spring 1935], f515, r298, d3882, 146, CPUSA; *SW* 5 (May 1937).

61. PCT, 5.

62. Athas, " 'He Lived to Live' "; Meador, "History and Index of *Contempo*," 35.

63. IOMS, pt. 2, 2, 29–47, and pt. 3, 2. Later renamed Huntington College.

64. IOMS, pt. 1, 10–13.

65. IOMS, pt. 3, n.p.; Kelley, *Hammer and Hoe*, 48–49.

66. Their guests included Nat Ross, Myra Page, and Sid Benson. IOMS, pt. 3; Virginia Durr to Olive Stone, Jan. 5, 1975, f13, b1, Mrs. Harry Schneiderman to Dearest Polly, Nov. 8, 1975, f13, b1, Stone to Paul Green, June 13, 1976, f14, b1, all in OMS. In addition, Olive Stone remembered George Stoney, IOMS, pt. 3, n.p. Haywood, *Black Bolshevik*, 391–415.

67. IOMS, pt. 3. The organizer was Al Murphy, Kelley, *Hammer and Hoe*, 44–45, 48.

68. "Annual Report," f314, b9, HK; IOMS, pt. 2, 26, 31, and IOMS, pt. 4, 31. She went to India in 1934.

69. J. Williams, "Struggles of the Thirties," 167–69; Kelley, *Hammer and Hoe*, 33.

70. Painter, *Narrative*, 142–45; "Southern White Girl," *DW*, May 20, 1933, "Jane Speed Trial," *Montgomery Advertiser*, May 19, 1933, "Jane Speed Is Serving in Jail," *Montgomery Advertiser*, May 26, 1933, all on r9, 195, CIC.

71. Will Alexander to James S. Childers, June 7, 1933, and Childers to Alexander, June 12, 1933, both on r9, 195, CIC; "Harlem Hails a Craik Exile," *NYAN*, Aug. 30, 1933, 1, 3.

72. "Officers and National Council," Oct. 29, 1933, fLSNR, b2, MSRK.

73. "Harlem Hails a Craik Exile," *NYAN*, Aug. 30, 1933, 1, 3; Allen, *Organizing*, 30, 31 n. 10.

74. IOMS, pt. 2, 23.

75. Institute of Race Relations, Schedule, f237, b11, JWJ; Helen R. Bryan to James Weldon Johnson, March 29, 1930, f70, b4, and Walter White to James Weldon Johnson, Jan. 30, 1934, f543, b24, both in JWJ.

76. Dykeman and Stokely, *Seeds*, 182; frontispiece to *Twenty Year Report*; *Beyond White Supremacy*.

77. "Dr. Thomas Jesse Jones," r15, 312, CIC; Cobley, *Class and Consciousness*, 89; *Twenty Year Report*, 27, 62.

78. "Conference on the Present Status of the Negro," r14, 281, CIC; Jan C. Smuts, "White Man's Task," quoted in Cell, *Highest Stage*, 224–25; Marx, *Making Race*, 99–100.

79. W. W. Alexander, "South's Opportunity"; IJDA; *Twenty Year Report*, 67; Edgar H. Brookes, "Memo to Committee Members," May 1, 1929, r15, 312, CIC.

80. Helen Bryan to James Weldon Johnson, Jan. 28, 1933, and extensive correspondence planning the conference in f70, b4, JWJ; Helen R. Bryan to Max Yergan, Jan. 13, 1934, f14, b206-3, MY. Bird married sociologist Arthur Huff Fauset, and she won election to the Pennsylvania House in 1938. The institute continued until at least 1936, Myles Horton to Ralph Bunche, Apr. 25, 1939, f32, b7, HERC.

81. Ulrich B. Phillips was also involved the first year. "Program for the Institute of Race Relations," July 1–30, 1933, in JWJ, 1931, Scrapbook, JWJ; Helen R. Bryan to Franz Boas, Dec. 21, 1932, and List of Persons, March 25, 1935, both in f Helen Bryan, b B61, FB; Kneebone, *Southern Liberal Journalists*, 92–94.

82. A. E. Talken to the Commissioner, Dec. 2, 1937, 29, SNA/NTS f7/328, NAR; K. J. King, "American Negro as Missionary."

83. J. J. Coetzee to Commissioner for Immigration and Asiatic Affairs, Apr. 14, 1938, 30, SNA/NTS f7/328, NAR; Anthony, *Max Yergan*, 5–8; Steuart, ed., *North Carolina 1870 Census Index*; *Students of Shaw University*; Anthony, "Max Yergan and South Africa," 185; Anthony, "Max Yergan in South Africa," 47, n. 1.

84. *Twelfth Census, 1900, North Carolina*, vol. 66, Wake County, Raleigh, r1221, 623, Enumeration Dist. 144, 98A; *Thirteenth Census, 1910, North Carolina*, vol. 83, Wake County, Raleigh, r1136, 624, Enumeration Dist. 120, 14B.

85. *Raleigh, N.C., 1909–1910*, 419; *Raleigh, N.C., 1915–1916*, 459.

86. W. A. Carter, *Shaw's Universe*, 58–59, 182, 224; Tobias, "Work of the Young

Men's"; "Career of Dr. Max Yergan," "c.v.," and "Max Yergan, Schools," all in ser. B, pt. 3, r4, frame 1466, NAACPM; Moorland, "Young Men's Christian Association"; Addie W. Hunton to Walter White, June 3, 1933, pt. 1, r6, frame 0698, NAACPM; Anthony, *Max Yergan*, 15–18.

87. Kirby Page to Dearest Folks, June 11–July 20th, 1916, KP; Ovington, "Max Yergan," 32–35; A. T. Schorn to Chief Native Commissioner, June 25, 1929, 20, and J. J. Coetzee to Commissioner for Immigration and Asiatic Affairs, Apr. 14, 1938, 30, both in SNA/NTS f7/328, NAR; Bullock, *In Spite of Handicaps*, 111–19, 114; Lynch, *Black American Radicals*, 17–18; K. J. King, "American Negro as Missionary," 8; Anthony, "Max Yergan and South Africa," 186; Anthony, *Max Yergan*, 5–8, 19–31.

88. E. G. Robeson, *African Journey*, 80; Max Yergan, "Y.M.C.A. Secretary in Africa"; Moorland, "Young Men's Christian Association," 68.

89. Ovington, "Max Yergan," 36, 37; Col. W. F. Creary, quoted in E. J. Scott, *Negro in the World War*, 405; K. J. King, "American Negro as Missionary," 8–9; E. J. Scott, *Negro in the World War*, 482; Bullock, *In Spite of Handicaps*, 115; Tobias, "Max Yergan," 155.

90. Saunders, "Forward Move in Africa," 83–85; K. J. King, *Pan-Africanism*, 79–94, quote 81.

91. "Bantu-European Student Conference Edition," *South African Outlook* (Aug. 1, 1930), in f286, b27, RG 2, RFA.

92. Bryan, "Max Yergan"; Shedd, *World's Alliance*, 152.

93. Helen Bryan to Mordecai Johnson, Jan. 6, 1933, f70, b4, JWJ.

94. Helen R. Bryan and Crystal Bird Fauset to Franz Boas, Dec. 21, 1932, f Helen Bryan, b61, FB.

95. Charles S. Johnson, "Approach to Race Relations," 1, in f20, b157, CSJ; C. S. Johnson, Review of *A World View of Race*, by Ralph Bunche.

96. "Program for the Institute of Race Relations," July 1–30, 1933, in JWJ, 1931, Scrapbook, JWJ; "Evaluation," [summer 1934], f6, b1, OMS.

97. The Carnegie Foundation and the Phelps Stokes Fund funded white South African C. T. Loram's Institute on Race Relations at Yale. Helen R. Bryan to Franz Boas, Apr. 3, 1933, f Helen Bryan, b61, FB; Crystal Bird Fauset to Franz Boas, Nov. 23, 1933, Boas to Fauset, Nov. 28, 1933, and Fauset to Boas, Dec. 12, 1933, all in f Crystal Fauset, b61, FB; Cell, *Highest Stage*, 221. Alexander and Odum do not appear after the first year.

98. "Evaluation," [summer 1934], f6, b1, OMS. Stone attended the second institute. Charles Johnson to James Weldon Johnson, June 7, 1934, f237, b11, JWJ; IOMS, pt. 4, 22.

99. IOMS, pt. 4, 22–23; Park, "Bases of Race Prejudice," 15; "Robert Park"; Robbins, "Charles S. Johnson."

100. Seminar on Segregation, Jan. 26, 1934, f14, b206-3, MY.

101. "Delegates to the Negro-White Conference," Nov. 30–Dec. 2, 1934, f6, b1, OMS; [Dombrowski] to Reinhold Niebuhr, Dec. 8, 1934, f1, b22, HERC.

102. Frances Henson, letter read into IOMS, pt. 4, 33.

103. Re. Burlington Dynamite Case, Dec. 31, 1934, copy of Jim Weaver letter to CO in IDW; IOMS, pt. 2, 25, and pt. 4, 3.

104. Olive Stone to Bruce Crawford, Feb. 6, 1976, and Stone to Crawford, May 13, 1976, both in f14, b1, OMS. The original name was the Southern League for People's Rights, IOMS, pt. 4, 21. For connections between the Burlington Defense Committee and the SCPR, see F. J. Gorman to Elizabeth Winston Malcombre, Oct. 21, 1936, and Secretary, SCPR to National Executive Board, U.T.W., Oct. 6, 1936, both in f62, b2, CPR.

105. "Southern Committee for People's Rights," f27, b2, OMS; IOMS, pt. 4, 1–4. Bruce Crawford was Atlanta chair. Salmond overlooks SCPR's Atlanta roots, *General Textile Strike*, 223, 225.

106. Olive Stone to Bruce Crawford, Feb. 6, 1976, f14, b1, Olive Stone to Professor and Mrs. C. Vann Woodward, Oct. 10, 1957, with note, f13, b1, Crawford to Stone, Feb. 11, 1976, f14, b1, all in OMS; IOMS, pt. 3, 21, 22. Woodward did not recall the SCPR. Crawford recalled that he visited one Atlanta meeting, and Stone remembered Woodward as a regular in Chapel Hill. In 1938 Woodward asked CP dist. organizer Rob Hall about Stone, Rob Hall to C. Vann Woodward, June 4, 1938, uncataloged, CVW. English professors J. O. Bailey, Phillips Russell, and George McKie and William Couch, director of UNC Press, joined the SCPR.

107. Eagles, *Jonathan Daniels*, 4, 10–16, 27–31.

108. O. M. Stone, "Civil Rights in the South," f27, b2, and "Alling Case," *People's Rights Bulletin*, March 1937, 3, f29, b2, both in OMS; IOMS, pt. 4, 7–12.

109. IOMS, pt. 2, 25, and pt. 4, 3.

110. "Negro Commission Meeting, February 24, 1937," [dated Apr. 15, 1937], 495/14/60, RGASPI; Scales and Nickson, *Cause at Heart*, 50–52, 59–60.

111. Fred Smethurst, *N&O*, Oct. 23, 1936, quoted in Eagles, *Jonathan Daniels*, 45–46.

112. "To Speak," *SW* 5 (Oct. 1936); "Professor Ericson Silent," [*CO?*], Oct. 29, 1936, NCCCF; Egerton, *Speak Now*, 134.

113. "Professor Ericson Upheld by Liberals," [*CO?*], Nov. 7, 1936, NCCCF.

114. IRV; Singal, *War Within*, 305–15.

115. "Letter Reopens Ericson's Case," *N&O*, Nov. 6, 1936, NCCCF.

116. Elizabeth Stevens to Frank Graham, Nov. 2, 1936, f468, b7, FPG; ICVW; Novick, *That Noble Dream*, 77–78, 181, 226–27.

117. Jonathan Daniels, "At Both Ends of the Gun," *N&O*, Nov. 7, 1936, NCCCF.

118. Kneebone, *Southern Liberal Journalists*, 74; Sosna, *In Search*, 20–42; Eagles, *Jonathan Daniels*, 51.

119. Olive Stone to Paul Green, June 13, 1976, f14, b1, OMS; quotes in "Southern Chain Gang," *People's Rights Bulletin*, Jan. 1936, 1, 2, in f29, b2, OMS. Eventually Shropshire and Barnes received state jobs and artificial limbs, IPG, 52–54.

120. John Dos Passos and Roger Baldwin to Dear Friend, Oct. 6, 1933, f Baldwin, Roger, b4, FB.

121. "Spice Bittings," f284, b4, PG; Paul Green to J. C. B. Eringhaus, May 20, 1934, in *Southern Life*, ed. Avery, 233–35.

122. Roper, *Green*, 163–73; Avery, "Paul Green," and *Green Reader*, ed. Avery, 10; P. Green, *Hymn*; Wilde, *Contemporary One-Act Plays*, 7–37.

123. Olive Stone to Nancy Rich, July 29, 1976, and Nancy B. Rich, "'Ironic Parable of Fascism' in *The Heart Is a Lonely Hunter*," both in f14, b1, OMS.

124. IOMS, pt. 5, 19.

125. Stone, "Civil Rights in the South," f27, b2, OMS; Olive Stone to Paul Green, June 13, 1976, f14, b1, OMS.

126. IOMS, pt. 4, 22, 33–35; Tindall, "Significance," 285–307; Brazil, *Odum*; Singal, *War Within*, 115–52; Sosna, *In Search*, 42–59.

127. Page from Graduate School Catalogue, f381, b15, PM; quote in IRV, 30; Howard Odum letter to editor, f652, ser. 2.2, HWO.

128. Odum, *Southern Regions*, 479; Challen, *Sociological Analysis*, 4; Singal, *War Within*, 135, 151; Dykeman and Stokely, *Seeds*, 282; Sosna, *In Search*, 29, 51.

129. Woodward, *Thinking Back*, 20; IRV, 91.

130. G. B. Johnson and G. G. Johnson, *Research in Service*, 5.

131. Howard Odum to Mark Ethridge, Dec. 6, 1938, f701, b10, FPG; Sosna, *In Search*, 46–47, 52–53, 55; Singal, *War Within*, 146–47.

132. Odum, "Presidential Address," f642, ser. 2.2, HWO; Odum, "Lynchings, Fears, and Folkways," 719.

133. "Changing Structure," f652, ser. 2.2, HWO; Tindall, *Emergence*, 582–88;Tindall, "Significance"; M. O'Brien, *Idea*, 47–48; Singal, *War Within*, 149; Simon, "Introduction," xv–ix; Rodgers, "Regionalism."

134. Locke and Odum, "Race Relations," 483; IOMS, pt. 5, 24.

135. Singal observes that Odum possessed "ahistorical innocence," Singal, *War Within*, 139; IRV, 69.

136. Odum, "Sociological Approach to National Social Planning," f642, Odum, "Sociological Aspects of Regionalism," f643, Odum, "Schematic Line-Breeding Concept of Progress," f648, all in ser. 2.2, HWO.

137. IRV, 67; Singal, *War Within*, 150–51.

138. Hankins, *Racial Basis*; Brazil, *Odum*, 207; Boas, "Race"; Boas, *Mind of Primitive Man*; Boas, "Problem of the American Negro"; di Leonardo, *Exotics*.

139. Description of the Records, CPSA; W. W. Alexander, "Negro in the New South," 152; Will Alexander to Walter White, March 25, 1926, f9, b4, JWJ.

140. G. B. Johnson and G. G. Johnson, *Research in Service*, 36, do not identify Hamilton. IGJ, pt. 3, 12, identifies Hamilton, but says the black guest was *Charles* Johnson. It is unlikely, but possible, that Hamilton stalked out in front of two Mr. Johnsons.

141. IGJ, pt. 3, 12.

142. J. W. Johnson, *Along This Way*, 388; Will Alexander to James Weldon Johnson, June 9, 1927, f9, b4, and "Negro Praises Spirit in State," *GR*, March 20, 1928, in "Music, Art, Sept. 1927–July 1928," Scrapbook, both in JWJ.

143. Robbins, *Sidelines Activist*, 58, 69–77; Odum, "New Southern Attitude," f626, ser. 2.2, HWO; IMOS; IRV, 78.

144. G. B. Johnson and G. G. Johnson, *Research in Service*, 188–89; IRV, 82–85, 88; M. O'Brien, *Idea*, 59–60; Biles, *South and the New Deal*, 49.

145. Ashby, *Graham*, 143–48; "CIC, 1933–1938," r4, 63, CIC.

146. Sullivan, *Days of Hope*, 25–40; Dykeman and Stokely, *Seeds*, 195–97; Egerton, *Speak Now*, 92–93; Sosna, *In Search*, 60–87.

147. Dykeman and Stokely, *Seeds*, 197, 199; Ashby, *Graham*, 143–48.

148. IAR/S, 58; Grubbs, *Cry from the Cotton*, 30–61; G. B. Johnson, "Does the South Owe the Negro a New Deal?," r29, CIC.

149. Charles S. Johnson to W. W. Alexander, Apr. 10, 1934, f11, b78, CSJ; Biles, *South and the New Deal*, 48–52; Sullivan, *Days of Hope*, 58; Dykeman and Stokely, *Seeds*, 199–200; Egerton, *Speak Now*, 96; C. S. Johnson, E. E. Embree, and W. W. Alexander, *Collapse*.

150. Dykeman and Stokely, *Seeds*, 226, 238–39; Biles, *South and the New Deal*, 119–20; Sullivan, *Days of Hope*, 125–27.

151. Will Alexander to James Weldon Johnson, March 16, 1934, and Alexander to Johnson, Apr. 12, 1934, both in f9, b4, JWJ; Sosna, *In Search*, 64–66.

152. Guy Johnson to James Weldon Johnson, Dec. 5, 1934, f240, b11, and James Weldon Johnson to Charles Johnson, March 29, 1937, f237, b11, both in JWJ; Jefferson, "Ira De Augustine Reid"; Charles S. Johnson, "Notes on a Conference," Jan. 5, 1935, f14, b78, and Charles S. Johnson to W. W. Alexander, Apr. 10, 1934, f11, b78, both in CSJ.

153. Sullivan, *Days of Hope*, 58–67, quote 59; Culver and Hyde, *American Dreamer*, 169–71.

154. FDR to the Advisory Committee, July 5, 1938, quoted in Ashby, *Graham*, 151; Tindall, *Emergence*, 598–99; *Report on Economic Conditions of the South*, f644, ser. 2.2, HWO; Ashby, *Graham*, 152–54.

155. Paul Kellogg to Sidney Hillman, June 14, 1937, r62, LRM/OD.

156. Mason, *To Win These Rights*, 195–96; J. D. Smith, *Managing White Supremacy*, 297–99; Storrs, *Civilizing Capitalism*, 125–52; Korstad, *Civil Rights Unionism*, for the CIO and tobacco workers; Tindall, *Emergence*, 515–18; Griffith, *Crisis of American Labor*; Zieger, *CIO*.

157. For example, Lucy Mason to Franklin Roosevelt, Aug. 12, 1937, LSM; Egerton, *Speak Now*, 180–81.

158. Quoted in Lucy Mason to [Donald Comer?], March 28, 1938, LSM. See also Biles, *South and the New Deal*, 137–47; McMahon, *Reconsidering Roosevelt*, 56–60, 79–86.

159. Sullivan, *Days of Hope*, 64–65; Honey, *Southern Labor*, 13–116; B. Davis, "Negro People in the Elections."

160. Richard Hail Brown to *CNC*, Feb. 14, 1940, b33, WWB.

161. IRV, 46–47.

162. IAR/OHS.

163. "CIC, 1933–1938," r4, 63, CIC.

164. Dykeman and Stokely, *Seeds*, 196, 258.

165. Guy Johnson to James Weldon Johnson, Dec. 5, 1934, f240, b11, and James Weldon Johnson to Charles Johnson, March 29, 1937, f237, b11, both in JWJ; Guy Johnson to Guion Johnson, March 22, 1936, March 25, 1936, and Guy Johnson to Guion Johnson, March 31, 1936, all in f16, b2, GGJ.

166. IAR/S, 23, 39; Buell Gallagher, "Notes on the Blue Ridge Conference," July 8–10, 1939," f335, b9, HK; Singal, *War Within*, 325.

167. IWWA, 655–58. J. D. Hall, *Revolt against Chivalry*, 257. Odum was president of the CIC when it disbanded. M. O'Brien, *Idea*, 72–73; Kneebone, *Southern Liberal Journalists*, xv, xvi; Sosna, *In Search*, 115–17; Sitkoff, *New Deal for Blacks*, 73–74. Quote "good will mess" in Ira De A. Reid to W. E. B. Du Bois, Feb. 15, 1940, reprinted in *Correspondence of W. E. B. Du Bois*, ed. Herbert Aptheker, 2:219–20.

168. "Third All-Southern Negro Youth Conference," Apr. 1939, "Proclamation of Southern Negro Youth," and "Draft Announcement," all in f30, b2, OMS; "Southern Negro, White Youth," *SW* (Jan. 1937): 3; "Negro Commission Meeting," dated Apr. 15, 1937, 495/14/60, RGASPI; Scales and Nickson, *Cause at Heart*, 119; Kelley, *Hammer and Hoe*, 200–02, 212–19; Egerton, *Speak Now*, 458–59.

169. "Negro Youth Conference," *SW* 5 (May 1937): 12.

170. Cell, *Highest Stage*; L. Thompson and H. Lamar, eds., *Frontier in History*; Gaston, "Black Liberation"; Fredrickson, *White Supremacy*; Fredrickson, *Black Liberation*; Marx, *Making Race*; Cuthbertson, " 'From White Supremacy to Black Liberation.' "

171. Buell, "Black and White," 302, 299.

172. Quote in Buell, "Black and White," 304; Hertzog, "Revolution in South Africa," 248; Cell, *Highest Stage*, 215–17; Marx, *Making Race*, 100–04; S. Marks and S. Trapido, "Politics of Race," 9–10; Walshe, *Rise of African Nationalism*, 111; Beinart, *Twentieth-Century South Africa*, 76–78; Dubow, *Racial Segregation*, 131–70.

173. Gilmore, *Gender and Jim Crow*, chs. 1–4.

174. Stokes, *Report*, 28–32, 54; "Dr. Thomas Jesse Jones," n.d., r15, 312, CIC; Bryan, "Max Yergan," 375–76.

175. H. A. Payne, letter to the editor, *Crisis* 21 (Nov. 1920): 20; Anthony, *Max Yergan*, 41–43.

176. K. J. King, *Pan-Africanism*, 81–85. On Garveyism in Africa, see T. Martin, *Race First*, 44; Cobley, *Class and Consciousness*, 184–88; Vinson, "See Kaffirs"; Anthony, "Max Yergan in South Africa," 28–29.

177. Quote in E. R. Garthorne to Secretary for the Interior, Feb. 12, 1921, 2, SNA/NTS f7/328, NAR; Max Yergan to J. J. Rhoads, Apr. 22, 1921, 13, Woodson, *History of the Negro Church*, 309, and Thomas Jesse Jones, 12, all quoted in K. J. King, "American Negro as Missionary"; Anthony, "Max Yergan in South Africa," 30; Carter Woodson to Benjamin Brawley, Jan. 7, 1932, f561, b25, JWJ; William A. Hunton to Kwegyir Aggrey, May 19, 1913, f4, b147-2, and Kwegyir Aggrey to Rose Aggrey, May 22, 1924, f14, b147-2, both in JEKA; E. W. Smith, *Aggrey*; "Executive Committee, North Carolina CIC" and "Six Regional Conferences," both on r53, 182, CIC; IAAL; *Twenty Year Report*, 20, 21–22; K. J. King, *Pan-Africanism*, 26; Kwegyir Aggrey, Rose D. Aggrey, and Max Yergan correspondence, f8, b206-3, MY.

178. Max Yergan to Honourable H. T. Andrews, March 30, 1949, 44–47, James Henderson to The Act. Magistrate, Alice, May 11, 1936, 8, A. T. Schorn to Chief Native Commissioner, June 25, 1929, 20, "Native Social Life," *Native Opinion*, Kingwilliamstown, March 28, 1922, *Die Burger* to Secretary of Bantu Administration, June 4, 1929, 13, all in SNA/NTS f7/328, NAR; K. J. King, "American Negro as Missionary," 5–22; Ovington, "Max Yergan," 38–39; Edward A. Johnson, "Y.M.C.A. Work in Africa," Jan. 17, 1941, f286, b27, RG 2, RFA; Anthony, "Max Yergan in South Africa," 31. On Fort Hare, see J. T. Campbell, *Songs of Zion*, 248.

179. "Bantu" grouped Africans in an artificial category considered offensive today.

Max Yergan, "Native Students of South Africa," *Student World* (Apr. 1923), f13, b147–3, JEKA; Stokes, *Report*, 54; Mabel Carney, *African Letters* (printed privately), 16, in f286, b27, RG2, RFA; Anthony, "Max Yergan in South Africa," 32; Cobley, *Class and Consciousness*, 127; Walshe, *Rise of African Nationalism*, 159; Robeson, *African Journey*, 59; "Men of Me," f3, b37, ser. 1, SEP; A. T. Schorn to Chief Native Commissioner, June 25, 1929, 20, SNA/NTS f7/328, NAR; Burrows, *Short Pictorial History*, 79; "News from Max Yergan," #1, f286, b27, RG2, RFA; "Native Social Life," *Native Opinion*, Kingwilliamstown, March 28, 1922, in SNA/NTS f7/328, NAR; Edgar Brookes, "Memo to Committee Members," May 1, 1929, r15, 312, CIC; Stauffer, ed., introduction to *Thinking with Africa*, vii–viii.

180. "Men of Me," [1927], f3, b37, ser. 1, SEP; Kerr, *Fort Hare*, 11–12; Anthony, *Max Yergan*, 45–77.

181. Mary White Ovington, pamphlet, f19, b206-1, MY; [indecipherable], July 7, 1922, 4, SNA/NTS f7/328, NAR; Anthony, "Max Yergan and South Africa," 204 n. 13.

182. Alexander Kerr to Magistrate, Alice, May 7, 1925, 7, James Henderson to The Act. Magistrate, May 11, 1925, 8, A. T. Schorn to Chief Native Commissioner, June 25, 1929, 20, all in SNA/NTS f7/328, NAR.

183. Quote in "Men of Me," f3, b37, ser. 1, SEP; Max Yergan to H. T. Andrews, March 30, 1949, 47, SNA/NTS f7/328, NAR.

184. J. W. Arthur, quoted in K. J. King, *Pan-Africanism*, 195; G. E. Haynes, "Harmon Awards in 1926"; "Men of Me," f3, b37, ser. 1, SEP; "Max Yergan," *CD*, Nov. 27, 1926; "Negro Artist," *NYT*, Dec. 8, 1926, 11; "Guests at Dinner," f174, b8, CTL.

185. Ovington, "Max Yergan," 42.

186. Ibid.

187. "Gandhi's Freedom Program Adopted," *NYT*, n.d. [12/31/32?], Du Bois, V:1–4, Scrapbook, JWJ; Meier and Rudwick, "Origins of Nonviolent Direct Action," 307–404.

188. "Mrs. Pickens and Miss Derricotte," *PT*, Aug. 30, 1924, 7.

189. "Men of Me," f3, b37, ser. 1, SEP; Ovington, "Max Yergan," 39; "Note from Africa," f2, b206-5, MY; Anthony, "Max Yergan in South Africa," 38; Higgs, *Ghost of Equality*, 66.

190. A. T. Schorn to Chief Native Commissioner, June 25, 1929, 20, SNA/NTS f7/328, NAR. Extensive correspondence on Rockefeller aid in f286, b27, RG 2, RFA.

191. Yergan, *Christian Students*; "Bantu-European Students' Christian Conference," 146; Max Yergan, "Training Africans," 2, f1593, b98, ser. 1, APS; Anthony, *Max Yergan*, 106–10.

192. Max Yergan to Thomas B. Appleget, Aug. 27, 1930, f286, b27, "From Max Yergan," Apr. 15, 1929, f286, b27, both in RG 2, RFA; Edgar Brookes, "Memo to Committee," May 1, 1929, r15, 312, CIC; Anson Phelps Stokes to Yergan, Sept. 8, 1930, f1592, b98, APS.

193. Yergan, "Bantu-European Student," 52; Yergan, "S.C.A. Conference."

194. Yergan, "S.C.A. Conference."

195. "Bantu-European Students' Christian Conference"; Yergan, *Christian Students*, 189; Gish, *Xuma*, 82; A. B. Xuma to Max Yergan, June 7, 1928, and extensive correspondence in f27, b206-4, MY.

196. News from Max Yergan, Aug. 15, 1930, f286, b27, RG 2, RFA.

197. Max Yergan to Thomas Appleget, Aug. 27, 1930, f286, b27, RG 2, RFA.

198. Yergan, *Christian Students*, 218, 221; Bryan, "Max Yergan," 375–76.

199. Max Yergan to Anson Phelps Stokes, Oct. 22, 1930, f1592, b98, APS; Anthony, *Max Yergan*, 110–12.

200. Yergan, *Christian Students*, 218, 221, 227–28; Yergan, "Training Africans," 2, 8, f1593, b98, ser. 1, APS.

201. Quote in Max Yergan, "Factors in the Racial Problem," pt. 1, r9, frame 0528, NAACPM; Stokes, *Report*, 54; Max Yergan to Anson Phelps Stokes, July 6, 1932, and Phelps Stokes to Yergan, Aug. 9, 1932, both in f1593, b98, APS; "It has become commonplace," f13, b206-5, MY.

202. Max Yergan to Anson Phelps Stokes, Feb. 8, 1934, f1593, b98, APS. For criticism from African students, see Ntantala, *Life's Mosaic*, 69–70.

203. "To elaborate" in J. D. Rheinallt Jones, "Memorandum by the Rev. Max Yergan," March 3, 1934; "In the dark" in Patrick Duncan to Jones, Feb. 26, 1934, Jones to Duncan, March 12, 1934, all in Aas.3, pt. 3, SAIRR; Anson Phelps Stokes to Max Yergan, Feb. 9, 1934, f1593, b98, APS.

204. A. E. Talken to Commissioner, Dec. 2, 1937, and Talken to Commissioner, Dec. 4, 1937, both in SNA/NTS f7/328, NAR; Workers' Party of South Africa to N. J. Barclay, Feb. 21, 1936, reprinted in *South Africa's Radical Tradition*, ed. Drew, 2:160–61.

205. D. G. Wolton to Roux, quoted in Walshe, *Rise of African Nationalism*, 177; "Report of Comrade X," Sept. 28, 1929, 495/155/77, "International Conference of Negro Workers," July 23, 1930, 495/155/87, 249, "Sending Instructors to the Negro Colonies," Feb. 6, 1930, 495/155/87, 43, "S. African Delegates Report to Negro Sub-Commission," 495/155/43, and D. Ivon Jones, "Gap in Our Front—the Negro," 495/155/17, all in RGASPI. On self-determination, see "Meeting of Negro Section," January 12, 1930, and Harry Haywood, George Padmore, and William Wilson [Patterson] to CPSA complaining that white Communists have not been "holding to a Native Republic," both in 495/155/83, RGASPI. See also "South Africa"; Haywood, *Black Bolshevik*, 235–40, 269–72; Kanet, "Comintern"; Benson, *African Patriots*, 73–74; S. Ellis and T. Sechaba, *Comrades against Apartheid*, 21–25; Cobley, *Class and Consciousness*, 196–97; Johns, *Raising the Red Flag*, 291–92; Kelley, "Third International."

206. J. M. Turner and W. B. Turner, *Caribbean Crusaders*, 204–08.

207. Anthony, "Max Yergan in South Africa," 41–42, dates Yergan's interest in Communism to a visit to London in 1931. Anthony, "Max Yergan and South Africa," 189–90, and Anthony, *Max Yergan*, 132–34, 139. The student was Govan Mbeki, a 1937 Fort Hare graduate, Drew, ed., *South Africa's Radical Tradition*, 2:390 n. 3. I could find no mention of Yergan in CPSA records; see, for example, Edward [Roux], "Report," Jan. 1937, 495/14/87, RGASPI.

208. "Yergan Awarded Spingarn Medal," *JG*, March 25, 1933, 1; "Max Yergan," Apr. 1, 1933, *PT*.

209. Mary White Ovington to Mr. White, March 24, 1933, pt. 2, r6, 0397, and "Remarks," pt. 1, r9, 0506, both in NAACPM.

210. "Address of Max Yergan," July 1, 1933, pt. 1, r9, 0514, NAACPM; "Race Prob-

lems Acute," Federal Council of Churches, May 26, [1934?], 97.9.2, SAIRR. Student quoted in Anthony, *Max Yergan*, 139.

211. Anthony, "Max Yergan and South Africa," 189–90.

212. S. Marks, *Ambiguities*, 81–82; Anthony, "Max Yergan in South Africa," 38.

213. Johns, *Raising the Red Flag*, 292; Drew, ed., *South Africa's Radical Tradition*, 1:120, n. 4.

214. Yergan, "Youth's Challenge," 164; quote in Max Yergan to A. B. Xuma, June 18, 1935, f27, b206-4, MY.

215. Ralston, "American Episodes"; Walshe, *Rise of African Nationalism*, 189; Gish, *Xuma*, 62–63; Higgs, *Ghost of Equality*, 129; Anthony, *Max Yergan*, 146–50. I am grateful to Emily Wilson for giving me Dr. A. B. Xuma's business card, given to her by Madie Hall Xuma.

216. Correspondence, Zachary Matthews and Max Yergan, f2, b206-4, MY; Anthony, *Max Yergan*, 100.

217. Max Yergan to Channing Tobias, Sept. 17, 1935, f22, b206-4, and A. B. Xuma to Yergan, Dec. 5, 1935, f27, b206-4, both in MY; "Imperialism and the Negro Peoples" and "Present Gallant Struggle of Ethiopia," both in f26, b206-5, both in MY.

218. Quote in Max Yergan to A. B. Xuma, June 18, 1935, 350618, box b, ABX; Kelley, "Religious Odyssey," 13; Higgs, *Ghost of Equality*, 115–17; Anthony, *Max Yergan*, 152–54.

219. Kabane, "All African Convention"; Cobley, *Class and Consciousness*, 80–81, 89, photograph following 100, 197–98; Anthony, "Max Yergan in South Africa," 45; Walshe, *Rise of African Nationalism*, 114–23, 190–91; Gish, *Xuma*, 83–84.

220. Kabane, "All African Convention," 187; Deputy Commissioner to the Secretary for Native Affairs, Apr. 14, 1938, SNA/NTS f7/328, NAR; A. B. Xuma to Max Yergan, Nov. 27, 1936, 361127C, box b, and Yergan to Xuma, Feb. 4, 1937, 370204, box b, both in ABX; Benson, *African Patriots*, 81–83; Gish, *Xuma*, 80–89; S. Marks and S. Trapido, *Politics of Race*; Hirson, *Yours for the Union*; Higgs, *Ghost of Equality*, 119; Anthony, "Max Yergan in South Africa," 45.

221. A. B. Xuma to Max Yergan, Dec. 5, 1935, f27, b206-4, MY; "Programme of Action," f31, b206-8, MY.

222. Quote in Max Yergan to Frank V. Slack, March 6, 1936, SNA/NTS f7/328, NAR, quoted from YMCA records in Anthony, "Max Yergan in South Africa," 45.

223. A. B. Xuma to Max Yergan, June 21, 1935, f27, b206-4, MY.

224. "Excerpts from Speech of Max Yergan," *Official Proceedings*, Feb. 14, 15, 16, 1936, f NNC 1941–1942, WAH; John P. Davis to Max Yergan, Jan. 31, 1936, frame 0646, and Davis to Yergan, May 23, 1936, frame 0654, both in b8, r8, ser. 2, pt. 1, NNC.

225. A. B. Xuma to Max Yergan, June 21, 1936, f27, b206-4, MY.

226. Quotes in Max Yergan to Frank V. Slack, March 6, 1936, SNA/NTS f7/328, NAR; Yergan to Channing Tobias, July 10, 1936, f22, b206-4, Yergan to A. B. Xuma, Apr. 22, 1936, and Xuma to Yergan, May 2, 1936, f27, b206-4, all in MY.

227. Yergan, "[Notes] Visit to Russia," f26, b206-5, MY; "Communist Party— U.S.A.," Nov. 5, 1948, f:100-26011, pt. 4, MY/FBI; Anthony, *Max Yergan*, 157–62; Yergan, "Communist Threat," 263; Max Yergan to A. B. Xuma, f27, b206-4, MY.

228. Max Yergan to A. B. Xuma, telegram, June 7, 1936, 3360706d, box b, ABX; Anthony, *Max Yergan*, 162.
229. Robeson, *African Journey*, 16–17, 47.
230. Anthony, *Max Yergan*, 172; A. B. Xuma to Max Yergan, Nov. 27, 1936, 361127C, box b, ABX; quote in Deputy Commissioner to the Secretary for Native Affairs, May 4, 1938, and [South African Police to Native Affairs], Feb. 5, 1949, both in SNA/NTS f7/328, NAR.
231. Max Yergan to A. B. Xuma, Feb. 4, 1937, 370204, box b, ABX; Yergan to Xuma, July 27, 1936, f27, b106-4, MY; Edgar, ed., *African American in South Africa*, 267; Lynch, *Black American Radicals*, 18–19.
232. Max Yergan to A. B. Xuma, July 27, 1936, f27, b206-4, MY. The two men maintained a close relationship. Xuma to Yergan, March 5, 1937, 370305C, box b, Xuma to Yergan, Apr. 2, 1937, 370402B, box b, Yergan to Xuma, Sept. 3, 1937, 370903, box b, all in ABX. Yergan introduced Xuma to North Carolinian Madie Hall, whom he married. E.Wilson, *Hope and Dignity*, 141–49; Gish, *Xuma*, 89–100; J. T. Campbell, *Songs of Zion*, 276.
233. "South and South Africa," *CNC*, July 4, 1936; [William Watts Ball] to Seth Low Pierrepont, Aug. 15, 1936, b27, WWB.
234. "South and South Africa," *CNC*, July 4, 1936.
235. Yergan, "Youth's Challenge," 171.
236. www.anc.org.za; Benson, *African Patriots*, 102–12.
237. "Unity in Action," www.anc.org.za/ancdocs/history/unity.html#ch8.

CHAPTER 6: IMAGINING INTEGRATION

1. Will Alexander to Friends, Oct. 22, 1937, f59, b8, FPG.
2. The NAACP chose its litigation offensive in 1933 and eschewed direct organizing among the masses. Holloway, *Confronting*, 8–16, 90–92; Janken, *White*, 181–85.
3. Kluger, *Simple Justice*; Juan Williams, *Marshall*; Tushnett, *Making Civil Rights Law*; Tushnett, *NAACP's Legal Strategy*; J. Greenberg, *Crusaders in the Courts*; G. Ware, *Hastie*; McNeil, *Groundwork*.
4. Works that capture the synergy among the NAACP challenges, individual plaintiffs, and local and global politics include Klarman, *From Jim Crow to Civil Rights* and Kluger, *Simple Justice*. On the courts and social change, see G. N. Rosenberg, *Hollow Hope*; Schultz and Gottlieb, "Legal Functionalism."
5. James Strudwick Smith (1787–1852) was a member of the 1835 Constitutional Convention that disfranchised free black North Carolinians. P. Murray, *Proud Shoes*, 35; P. Murray, *Song*; Boger, "Pushing the Envelope"; R. Rosenberg, "Pauli Murray," 279–85; Gilmore, "Admitting Pauli Murray"; A. Scott, "Introduction," 12–22.
6. Perry Young, "Pauli Murray," *CHH*, June 15, 1996, 4; "Legacy in Black and White," *New Carolinian* (March 1976): 19.
7. P. Murray, *Proud Shoes*, 34–54; P. Murray, *Song*, 4; P. Young, "Pauli Murray," *CHH*, June 15, 1996, 4.
8. P. Young, "Pauli Murray," *CHH*, June 15, 1996, 4.

9. Cornelia was born in 1844. Harriet's boy Julius Casar was "about three" when Cornelia was "about one year," according to the bill of sale from James Smith to his daughter Mary Ruffin Smith sometime before his death in 1852; quoted in P. Young, "Pauli Murray," *CHH*, June 15, 1996, 4.

10. P. Murray, *Proud Shoes*, 35, 49–50.

11. Ibid., 52; P. Murray, *Song*, 433.

12. P. Murray, *Proud Shoes*, ch. 5; Pauli Murray to Franklin Delano Roosevelt, f380, b15, PM; P. Young, "Pauli Murray," *CHH*, June 15, 1996, 4.

13. Her baptismal certificate shows her name to be Annie, not Anna. Murray's adoption papers (Sept. 17, 1919) show that her name was legally changed to Anna Pauline Dame. From her marriage in 1930 until its annulment in 1949, her name was Anna Pauline Dame Wynn. Yet all her life, she used the name Anna Pauline Murray. Adoption Papers, f249, b9, PM.

14. IPM/Mc, 12; Weare, *Black Business*.

15. P. Murray, *Song*, 35–36. North Carolina was 14th of 44 regions in the number of lynchings from 1922 to 1927, according to Ware, *Hastie*, 47.

16. IPM/Mc, 10; Beal, *Proletarian Journey*, 184.

17. Gershenhorn, "*Hocutt v. Wilson*," 279; Murray, *Song*, 60–61.

18. Hillside High Yearbook 1926, f367, b15, PM.

19. IPM/Mc,14; Hillside High Yearbook 1926, f367, b15, PM.

20. Murray and Wynn annulled the marriage in 1949. Passport application, f6, b1, Pauli Murray to Dear Billy, May 26, 1943, William Wynn to Murray, Apr. 15, 1948, and Murray to William, Sept. 10, 1948, all in f70, b3, PM.

21. P. Murray, "Notes on San Francisco Conference," Ap. 27, 1945, f1271, b73, and worksheet for application to bar, March 1948, f552, b28, PM.

22. Pauli Murray to Dorothy West, n.d. [Oct. 1933], f11, b1, DW/BU; P. Murray, "Song"; [Dorothy West], "Mary Christopher"; P. Murray, "Inquietude."

23. U. T. Summers, "Pauli Murray's 'Proud Shoes,' " *CN*, June 18, 1987; Bell-Scott, "To Write like Never Before"; IPM/Mc, 35.

24. "Events," f2, b1, PM; Kornbluh, *New Deal*, 75–90.

25. Pauli Murray to Mrs. Roosevelt, Dec. 6, 1938, r14, frames 0245–0375, ER.

26. P. Murray, *Song*, quote 97, 102–03. "Deposition," f554, b28, PM, shows that she joined in 1936. Draft Application and Application for Admission to the New York Bar, March 1948, f552, b28, PM. She left in 1937 or 1938, P. Murray, *Proud Shoes*, vii–viii.

27. Ella Baker, Dec. 12, 1938, f1236, b72, PM; Ransby, *Ella Baker*, 72, 91–98; Kornbluh, *New Deal*, 100–07.

28. YWCA Class, f1239, b72, class list, f1236, b72, and First Evaluation, Oct. 19, 1938–Jan.18, 1939, f1237, b72, all in PM.

29. P. Murray, *Song*, 105–07; Course Note, f379, b15, PM. A. J. Muste, the school's Socialist founder, had left before Murray arrived. See T. L. Dabney, "Brookwood Labor College"; Cummins, "Workers' Education"; Altenbaugh, *Education for Struggle*.

30. Bloom, "Brookwood Labor College," 37–39.

31. IPM/Mc, 44; Bloom, "Brookwood Labor College," 37; A. Levine, "Brookwood Remembered"; and Howlett, *Brookwood Labor College*.

32. P. Murray, *Song*, 107; Howlett, *Brookwood Labor College*, 326; Altenbaugh, *Education for Struggle*, 229. Murray's class, spring of 1937, was Brookwood's last.

33. Kornbluh, *New Deal*, 103; Application for Admission to the New York Bar, March 1948, f552, b28, and "Deposition," f552, b28, both in PM.

34. P. Murray, *Song*, 107–08.

35. Gershenhorn, "*Hocutt v. Wilson*," 275–308; Burns, "Graduate Education for Blacks"; Tushnett, *NAACP's Legal Strategy*, 52–54; Kluger, *Simple Justice*, 155–58; Klarman, *From Jim Crow to Civil Rights*, 149; Janken, *White*, 179–87.

36. McNeil, *Groundwork*, 113–14; Janken, *White*, 181–85; Walter White to Paul Green, Sept. 2, 1930, f155, b2, PG.

37. Gershenhorn, "*Hocutt v. Wilson*," 286; Burns, "Graduate Education for Blacks"; Kluger, *Simple Justice*, 155–58; Weare, *Black Business*, 232–37; G. Ware, "*Hocutt*"; Jankin, *White*, 184–85; Ware, *Hastie*, 46–54; Conrad O. Pearson and Cecil A. McCoy to Walter F. White, Feb. 6, 1933, pt. 3, ser. A, r15, NAACPM.

38. Walter White to Pearson and McCoy, Feb. 8, 1933, pt. 3, ser. A, r15, NAACPM.

39. C.C. Spaulding to Walter White, Feb. 6, 1933, and Cecil McCoy and Conrad Pearson to White, Feb. 11, 1933, both in pt. 3, ser. A, r15, NAACPM; G. Ware, *Hastie*, 47.

40. George Streator to Walter White, n.d., pt. 3, ser. A, r17, NAACPM.

41. Burns, "North Carolina and the Negro Dilemma," 125. My analysis follows Weare, *Black Business*, 233–39. On Shepard, see "Dr. Jas. E. Shepard," *WB*, July 21, 1906, 1.

42. Quoted in Gershenhorn, "*Hocutt v. Wilson*," 297.

43. Gershenhorn, "*Hocutt v. Wilson*," 292; Cecil McCoy and Conrad Pearson to Walter White, telegram, March 19, 1933, and McCoy to White, March 21, 1933, both in pt. 3, ser. A, r15, NAACPM; "N.A.A.C.P. Sends Attorney," Press Service NAACP, r4, 87, CIC.

44. P. Murray, *Song*, 64; Hillside High School Yearbook 1926, f367, b15, PM, records 3 men in Murray's class of 40.

45. Pearson and McCoy to White, Feb. 11, 1933, pt. 3, ser. A, r15, NAACPM; Louis Austin to Frank Graham, Jan. 6, 1934, f252, b4, and James Shepard to Graham, Jan. 26, 1934, f252, b4, both in FPG.

46. Cecil McCoy to Walter White, March 18, 1933, pt. 3, ser. A, r15, NAACPM. Barnhill had presided over the trial of the Gastonia strikers, and Clyde Hoey, the governor of the state when Hocutt applied to pharmacy school, had prosecuted. See "Barnhill, Maurice Victor."

47. *Complaint, Thomas R. Hocutt v. Thomas J. Wilson*, Memorandum of Authorities for Defendants in *Hocutt v. Wilson and University of North Carolina*, pt. 3, ser. A, r15, NAACPM.

48. *Barrett v. Cedar Hill Consol. School Dist.*, 85 So. 125 (1920), cited in "Memorandum of Authorities for Defendants in *Hocutt v. Wilson and University of North Carolina*," pt. 3, ser. A, r15, NAACPM.

49. *Cumming v. Richmond Board of Education*, 175 U.S. 528 (1899), cited in "Memorandum of Authorities for Defendants in *Hocutt v. Wilson and University of North Carolina*," pt. 3, ser. A, r15, NAACPM.

50. *Lowery v. Board of Graded School Trustees*, 52 S.X. 267 (1905), cited in "Memo-

randum of Authorities for Defendants in *Hocutt v. Wilson and the University of North Carolina,*" pt. 3, ser. A, r15, NAACPM.

51. Quote in "Mandamus in North Carolina 'U' Case Denied," NAACP, r4, 87, CIC; Conrad Pearson to Walter White, March 31, 1933, and Frank P. Graham to White, Apr. 10, 1933, pt. 3, ser. A, r15, NAACPM.

52. William Hastie to Walter White, telegram, March 25, 1933, pt. 3, ser. A, r15, NAACPM.

53. Quote in "Mandamus in North Carolina 'U' Case Denied," Press Service of the NAACP, r4, 87, CIC.

54. G. Ware, "Hocutt," 232; "Negro Youth Loses First Round," *NYA*, Apr. 8, 1933, 1.

55. G. Ware, "Hocutt," 232.

56. Judgment, *Thomas R. Hocutt v. Thomas J. Wilson*, pt. 3, ser. A, r15, NAACPM; Gershenhorn, "Hocutt v. Wilson," 301; P. Murray, *Song*, 110; Burns, "Graduate Education for Blacks," 196; Pauli Murray to Frank Graham, Jan. 17, 1939, f381, b15, PM; White, *Man Called White*, 156–60; Kluger, *Simple Justice*, 155–58; G. Ware, *Hastie*, 50–53.

57. White, *Man Called White*, 158.

58. Frank Graham to Walter White, May 13, 1933, pt. 3, ser. A, r15, NAACPM; Walter White to James Weldon Johnson, n.d. [June 1933], f 542, b24, JWJ.

59. "Appeal for Negroes and Appeal for Jews," *AA*, July 15, 1933, 5, and Friends of Social Justice to Frank Graham, Dec. 22, 1937, f566, b8, both in FPG.

60. The state constitution read, "[T]he children of the white race and the children of the colored race shall be taught in separate public schools," but did not mention universities. Gershenhorn, "Stalling Integration," 157; Ashby, *Graham*, 128; "North Carolina Lie," *AA*, July 14, 1933, 16.

61. Friends of Social Justice to Frank Graham, Dec. 22, 1937, f566, b8, and Graham to H. M. Smith, Jan. 1, 1938 [9], f566, b10, FPG.

62. Mary White Ovington to William Hastie, Apr. 18, 1934, Ovington to Walter White, Apr. 30, 1934, and Hastie to Ovington, May 24, 1934, all in pt. 3, ser. A, r15, NAACPM; Ovington, "Students Eager."

63. Gershenhorn, "Hocutt v. Wilson," 303–04.

64. George Streator to Walter White, n.d., pt. 3, ser. A, r17, NAACPM.

65. Quoted in Gershenhorn, "Hocutt v. Wilson," 289.

66. Chafe, *Civilities and Civil Rights.*

67. On the suitability of Maryland, see Tushnett, *NAACP's Legal Strategy*, 56–58.

68. "Court Backs Negro," *NYT*, Dec. 13, 1938, 1.

69. Kluger, *Simple Justice*, 193; *University of Maryland v. Donald G. Murray*, 169 Md. 478 (1936); Burns, "Graduate Education for Blacks," 200; Kuebler, "Desegregation"; Seawright, "Desegregation at Maryland"; Juan Williams, *Marshall*, 76–79; Sitkoff, *New Deal for Blacks*, 222–24; Klarman, *From Jim Crow to Civil Rights*, 149–51.

70. Kluger, *Simple Justice*, 187–94; McNeil, *Groundwork*, 138–39.

71. O'Dunne, *Report*; Mencken quoted at www.mdhs.org/shipping/publications/shugg/abusesofpower.

72. *Schechter Poultry v. United States*, 295 U.S. 495 (1935).

73. "Primo Carnera" and "Joe Louis," www.cyberboxingzone.com; Diggins, *Mus-*

solini, 306; W. R. Scott, "Black Nationalism"; J. E. Harris, *Reactions*; R. S. Young, "Ethiopia Awakens"; "Editorials," *Opportunity* 13 (Aug. 1935): 230.

74. Mencken, "Murray Case," *BaS*, Sept. 23, 1935, f344, b14, JWJ.

75. "American Nazis Quite as Bestial as Their German Brothers," *AA*, Aug. 24, 1935, 6; W. R. Scott, "Black Nationalism," 130.

76. Louis Austin to Frank Graham, Jan. 6, 1934, f252, b4, FPG.

77. Guy B. Johnson, "Graduate Study for Southern Negro Students," in f174, b8, CTL; "Report," Dec. 9–10, 1936, cited in Burns, "Graduate Education for Blacks," 201; Glenn Hutchinson, "Jim Crow Challenged." Graham had helped Shepard lobby the legislature since at least 1931. James E. Shepard to Graham, July 3, 1931, f82, b2, FPG.

78. Charles Houston to Sidney R. Redmond, July 15, 1935, Houston, "Memorandum," July 15, 1935, and Redmond to Houston, Aug. 27, 1935, all in pt. 3, ser. A, r14, NAACPM.

79. Lloyd Gaines to N.A.A.C.P. Legal Department, Sept. 27, 1935, Deposition of Lloyd L. Gaines, [May 26, 1936], Official Transcript, and Gaines, "Mississippi to St. Louis," all in pt. 3, ser. A, r14, NAACPM.

80. Prior to 1936 the state paid the entire out-of-state tuition for African Americans to attend law school elsewhere, but that year it began paying only the in-state/out-of-state difference. Charles Houston, Memorandum to Office, June 5, 1936, and Walter White to Houston, June 8, 1936, both in pt. 3, ser. A, r14, NAACPM.

81. Kluger, *Simple Justice*, 209–12. On FDR's strategies, see McMahon, *Reconsidering Roosevelt*, 97–143.

82. See McNeil, *Groundwork*, 143–45. The decision came down on December 12, 1938. "Court Rules Missouri U. Must Admit," *NYT*, Dec. 13, 1938, f382, b15, PM; "University of Missouri Case Won."

83. "Court Rules Missouri U. Must Admit," *NYT*, Dec. 13, 1938, f382, b15, PM; "University of Missouri Case Won"; McNeil, *Groundwork*, 143–45.

84. "Inevitable Mr. Gaines," *Missouri Student*, Dec. 14, 1938, in pt. 3, ser. A, r15, NAACPM.

85. Bluford, "Lloyd Gaines Story."

86. "To the Greek Letter Societies," Dec. 15, 1937, pt. 3, ser. A, r14, NAACPM.

87. Walter R. Goldston to Charles Houston, Sept. 13, 1936, [Houston?] to Goldston, Sept. 17, 1936, Charlie [Houston] to Leon A. Ransom, Sept. 17, 1936, Official Transcript Walter Raleigh Goldston, Ransom, Confidential Report re: Walter R. Goldston, Sept. 20, 1936, and Houston to Goldston, Sept. 26, 1936, all in pt. 3, ser. A, r15, NAACPM.

88. "To Times Letter Written to President Frank Graham," *CT*, [Jan. 1939]; P. Murray, *Song*, 114.

89. "School Honors Legacy of Black Woman"; Pauli Murray to ?, Jan. 19, 1939, pt. 3, ser. A, r18, NAACPM; IPM/M.

90. Pauli Murray to Lloyd Gaines, Dec. 18, 1938, f380, b15, PM.

91. For the Nov. 10 date, see Pauli Murray to George T. Guernsey, Feb. 6, 1939, f381, b15, and W. W. Pierson to Mr. Murray, Nov. 16, 1938, f381, b15, both in PM.

92. P. Murray, *Song*, 110; "To the Editor," *DMH*, Jan. 14, 1939, f380, b15, PM.

93. Will Alexander to Friends, Oct. 22, 1937, f59, b8, FPG; W. S. Powell, *First State University*, 210; Weare, *Black Business*, 253–55; copy of page of *Catalogue, Issue 1937–1938*, Graduate School Division of Public Welfare Social Work, f381, b15, PM.

94. W. A. Jackson, *Myrdal*, 90.

95. P. Murray, *Song*, 65.

96. Ibid., 110.

97. Handwritten notes on Lin Holloway, "Around the Town," *CT*, n.d., f90, b4, PM; P. Murray, *Song*, 22, 23, 63; worksheet for application to bar, March 1948, f552, b28, PM. She worked for Spaulding's North Carolina Mutual and for Austin's *Carolina Times* in the summer of 1927.

98. Pauli Murray to James Shepard, Dec. 6, 1938, f380, b15, PM.

99. Ibid.; "Negro Educator Condemns Nazis," *NYT*, Jan. 12, 1939, f381, b15, PM.

100. Pauli Murray to James Shepard, Dec. 6, 1938, Murray to Shepard, Dec. 31, 1938, and Shepard to Murray, Jan. 4, 1939, all in f380, b15, PM.

101. "Dedicate Nine New Buildings," Dec. 6, 1937, f566, b8, FPG; James Shepard to Clyde Hoey, Dec. 15, 1938, Graham quoted in Burns, "Graduate Education for Blacks," 204; Burns, "North Carolina and the Negro Dilemma," 124–25; Gershenhorn, "Stalling Integration," 157.

102. "Court Backs Negro on Full Education," *NYT*, Dec. 13, 1938; "For Human Rights," *NYT*, Dec. 13, 1938; P. Murray, "To the Oppressors," in *Dark Testament*, 31; quote in P. Murray, *Song*, 115; Murray to P. B. Young, Jan. 13, 1939, f381, b15, PM.

103. Pauli Murray to Frank Graham, Dec. 17, 1938, f380, b15, PM.

104. Ibid. and Murray to Dean W. W. Pierson, Dec. 31, 1938, both in f380, b15, PM.

105. Frank Graham to Pauli Murray, Feb. 5 [3? 8?], 1939, pt. 3, ser. A, r18, NAACPM.

106. Lennie [a Murray nickname] to Lisha [Felicia Miller], Dec. 17, 1938, f380, b15, and Pauli Murray to Louis Austin, Jan. 18, 1939, f381, b15, both in PM.

107. Pauli Murray to Walter White, Jan. 2, 1939, pt. 3, ser. A, r18, NAACPM.

108. Ibid., Murray to Thurgood Marshall, Feb. 8 [6?], 1939, Secretary to Mr. White to Murray, Jan. 3, 1939, Marshall to Hunter College, Jan. 26, 1939, all in pt. 3, ser. A, r18, NAACPM.

109. "To Times Letter Written to President Frank Graham," *CT*, n.d. [Jan. 1939], and Pauli Murray to Graham, Jan. 17, 1939, pt. 3, ser. A, r18, NAACPM.

110. Frank Graham to Pauli Murray, Feb. 5 [3? 8?], 1939, pt. 3, ser. A, r18, NAACPM; "Graham Discusses Negro Application," *DMH*, Jan. 10, 1939, f381, b15, PM.

111. Ashby, *Graham*, 154–68, 227–28; Egerton, *Speak Now*, 191, 232–33, 294. On the SCHW, see L. Reed, *Simple Decency*; Sosna, *In Search*, 88–104.

112. IOMS, pt. 6, 9; "Southern Conference for Human Welfare," f20, b2, OMS; Staff Meeting—Oct. 3, 1938, f5, b2, HERC; IDW, 72; Ashby, *Graham*, 154–68.

113. IAR/S, 25.

114. Durr, *Outside the Magic Circle*, 127.

115. Krueger, *And Promises*, 24–25; Ashby, *Graham*, 159; Egerton, *Speak Now*, 191; Sosna, *In Search*, 90–91; M. O'Brien, *Idea*, 76.

116. Tindall, "Significance," 301.

117. Ibid.

118. Krueger, *And Promises*, 11–17; Sullivan, *Days of Hope*, 5–6; L. Reed, *Simple Decency*, 4–10; Dunbar, *Against the Grain*, 187–93.

119. [Jim Dombrowski] and Myles Horton, "Comments on Henry Sprinkle Case," f7, b31, HERC.

120. Kruger, *And Promises*, 16–17; Kelley, *Hammer and Hoe*, 184–92; Sullivan, *Days of Hope*, 96–98; Egerton, *Speak Now*, 180–82; L. Reed, *Simple Decency*, 12–13; Foreman, "Decade of Hope."

121. Sosna, *In Search*, 89; "Dynamite Frameup," f420, PGM; Kelley, *Hammer and Hoe*, 128–31; Crouch, *Testimony*, 189–91. Egerton, *Speak Now*, 178–79, did not know Gelders was a member of the party.

122. Crouch, *Testimony*, 189.

123. Krueger, *And Promises*, 20–21; see Robert Hall, quoted in *Report on Southern Conference for Human Welfare*, 2.

124. Ashby, *Graham*, 161–64; Egerton, *Speak Now*, 187–88; Sosna, *In Search*, 92.

125. Howard Kester to Francis P. Miller, March 19, 1939, f866, b12, FPG; "Southern Conference for Human Welfare," f20, b2, OMS; Dunbar, *Against the Grain*, 193–95.

126. IAR/S, 28; IOMS, pt. 5, 10.

127. Press Release, Southern Conference for Human Welfare, Oct. 15, 1938, f697, b10, FPG; Joseph Gelders to Dear Friend, Oct. 12, 1939, f29, b2, OMS.

128. Quoted in Egerton, *Speak Now*, 188; draft speech, f704, b10, FPG.

129. The vice chairman resigned when he learned that the organization allowed Communists to be members. Francis P. Miller to Frank Graham, Dec. 21, 1938, f703, b10, Herbert Baughn to Graham, Nov. 26, 1938, f699, b10, Lucy Randolph Mason to Graham, Dec. 6, 1938, f700, b10, and Meeting of Executive Board, Feb. 7, 1939, f864, b12, all in FPG; "Graham Discusses Negro Application," *DMH*, Jan. 10, 1939, f381, b15, PM; C. S. Johnson, "Southern Welfare Conference," 14–15; Egerton, *Speak Now*, 177–97, 289–301; Sosna, *In Search*, 94–95; Krueger, *And Promises*, 20–59.

130. L. A. Crowell, Jr., to Frank Graham, Dec. 1, 1938, f700, b10, and O. L. Browne to Graham, Nov. 25, 1938, f699, b10, both in FPG; Kelley, *Hammer and Hoe*, 186.

131. Ashby, *Graham*, 158–64; Krueger, *And Promises*, 41.

132. Frank Graham to Pauli Murray, Feb. 5 [3? 8?], 1939, pt. 3, ser. A, r18, NAACPM.

133. Frank Graham to Pauli Murray, Feb. 6, 1936, pt. 3, ser. A, r18, NAACPM; J. C. B. Ehringhaus to Graham, Nov. 3, 1934, and James Shepard to Graham, Nov. 9, 1934, both in f253, b4, FPG; Ashby, *Graham*, 227.

134. Frank Graham to Pauli Murray, Feb. 3, 1939, f381, b15, and "North Carolina University," *NYAN*, Feb. 11, 1939, f383, b15, both in PM; J. C. B. Ehringhaus to Graham, Nov. 3, 1934, and James Shepard to Graham, Nov. 9, 1934, both in f253, b4, FPG; Ashby, *Graham*, 157–59; Krueger, *And Promises*, 37–39.

135. Walter White to Jackson Davis, Feb. 11, 1939, pt. 3, ser. A, r18, NAACPM.

136. Pauli Murray to Frank Graham, Feb. 6, 1939, f381, b15, and "North Carolina University Head," *JG*, Feb. 18, 1939, f383, b15, both in PM.

137. Dear Lisha from Lennie, Dec. 17, 1938, f380, b15, PM.

138. W. S. Powell, *First State University*, 202; "Roosevelt Urges New Deal," *NYT*, Dec. 6, 1938, f383, b15, PM; Walter Stokes, Dec. 5, 1938, f70, b10, FPG; "President States Faith in Liberalism," *N&O*, Dec. 6, 1938, 1; Egerton, *Speak Now*, 231–33.

139. "Arrangements Completed," *N&O*, Dec. 2, 1938, 2; "Roosevelt Urges New Deal Continue," *NYT*, Dec. 6, 1938, f383, b15, PM; "All in Readiness," *N&O*, Dec. 5, 1938, 2.

140. "Roosevelt's Address at Chapel Hill, N.C.," *NYT*, Dec. 6, 1938, and "Doctor of Democracy," *N&O*, Dec. 6, 1938, both in f383, b15, PM. Governor Clyde Hoey told the president that "his address was very appropriate to the occasion," quoted in "Views and Observations," *N&O*, Dec. 6, 1938, 14.

141. Hughes, "Ballad of Roosevelt."

142. Pauli Murray to President Roosevelt, Dec. 6, 1938, f15, b380, and "Did F.D.R. Mean It?" *AA*, Jan. 19, 1939, f382, b15, both in PM.

143. Schlesinger, *Coming of the New Deal*, 568.

144. Pauli Murray to Mrs. Roosevelt, Dec. 6, 1938, Roosevelt to Murray, Dec. 19, 1938, and Hilda Smith to Murray, Jan. 23, 1939, all in f380, b15, PM.

145. *DTH*, Jan. 5, 1939, f382, b15, PM.

146. "Officials Faced by Negro Entrance Application," *DTH*, Jan. 5, 1939, f382, b15, PM.

147. "Mills of the Gods," *DTH*, Jan. 7, 1939, f381, b15, and "Officials Faced by Negro Entrance Application," *DTH*, Jan. 5, 1939, both in f382, b15, PM.

148. "Officials Faced by Negro Entrance Application," *DTH*, Jan. 5, 1939, "Negress Applies to Enter Carolina," *DMH*, Jan. 6, 1939, and "Colored, Tries to Enter Carolina U.," *Daily News* [New York], Jan. 6, 1939, all in f382, b15, PM.

149. Krueger, *And Promises*, 27; Murray to Dear George, Dec. 6, 1939, f381, b15, and Murray to Carl De Vane, March 6, 1939, f381, b15, both in PM.

150. "Negro Education," *DMH*, Jan. 6, 1939, f382, b15, PM.

151. "Students Favor Negroes," *CT*, Jan. 21, 1939, f383, b15, PM.

152. "First Lady in Favor of U.S. Law," *JG*, Jan. 21, 1939, f382, b15, and "Graham Discusses Negro Application," *DMH*, Jan. 10, 1939, f381, b15, both in PM.

153. "Daniels Has No Objection to Entrance," *DTH*, Jan. 20, 1939, f382, b15, PM; To the Editor, *DTH*, Jan. 12, 1939, 2.

154. "Long Live Dean Russell," *CT*, Feb. 25, 1939, f383, b15, PM.

155. ICVW; Howard K. Beale, "Letter to the Editor," *DTH*, Jan. 11, 1939, f381, b15, PM.

156. Paul Green to Howard W. Odum, Dec. 18, 1934, quoted in Burns, "North Carolina and the Negro Dilemma," 257.

157. "Lethargy Is Relative," *DTH*, Feb. 19, 1939, f383, b15, PM.

158. "U.N.C. Law Students against Admitting Negroes to School," in f381, b15, PM.

159. "Carolina Poll Favors Admission," *JG*, Jan. 21, 1939, f382, b15, "Only One Negro Pressing," *DTH*, Jan. 10, 1939, f381, b15, "To the Editor," *DTH*, Jan. 12,

1939, 2, f382, b15, and "N.C. University Graduate Students Vote," *DW*, Jan. 12, 1939, f382, b15, all in PM.

160. "Negro Entrance to UNC," *DTH*, Jan. 26, 1939, f382, b15, PM.

161. Pauli Murray, "To the Editorial Board," Jan. 12, 1939, f380, b15, "Carolina U. Applicant Upbraids Mob Spirit," *AA*, Jan. 21, 1939, f382, b15, both in PM. The original letter reads "Negro," but some presses substituted "Colored" for Negro. "Negro Applicant Sends New Letter," *DTH*, (marked by hand Feb. 17, 1939), f383, b15, PM.

162. Pauli Murray to Louis Austin, Jan. 18, 1939, and Murray to P. B. Young, Jan. 13, 1939, both in f381, b15, PM.

163. Ruth Jaffe, "Report of the Negro Commission," ASUC, Dec. 28, 1938, f18, b206–7, MY; Eagan, *Class, Culture, and the Classroom*; "True Color."

164. Cohen, *When the Old Left*, 34, Murray case, 216–17; Scales and Nickson, *Cause at Heart*, 268–69; Ottanelli, *Communist*, 49–61; Scales and Nickson, *Cause at Heart*, 60–61. Scales's chronology may be wrong, since he dates the 1936 Ericson/Ford incident at 1938.

165. "Negro College Students to Be Here," *DTH*, Feb. 15, 1939, f383, b15, PM.

166. "Inter-Racial Discussion Group Adopts Resolution," *DTH*, Feb. 15, 1939, and "Phi against Negro Admission," *DTH*, Jan. 18, 1939, both in f383, b15, PM.

167. "Negro Applicant Sends New Letter," *DTH*, (marked by hand Feb. 17, 1939), f383, b15, PM.

168. Edward J. Woodhouse, "To the Editor," *DTH*, Feb. 17, 1939, f383, b15, PM. Woodhouse, a Virginian, had taught at Yale College from 1913 to 1917 and in 1919, Yale University, *Historical Register of Yale University*. "Threats of Reaction," *DTH*, Feb. 17, 1939, "In All Modesty," *DTH*, Feb. 21, 1939, "No Discrimination," *DTH*, Feb. 22, 1939, all in f383, b15, PM.

169. William L. Borders, Letter to the Editor, *DTH*, Feb. 23, 1939, f383, b15, PM.

170. Odum, "What Is the Answer?," 5–8; Glenn Hutchinson, "Jim Crow Challenged."

171. P. Murray, *Song*, 8–9, 110; IMOS; quote in Pauli Murray to John Allen Creedy, March 6, 1939, f381, b15, PM.

172. Pauli Murray, Letter to the Editor [unpublished?], f381, b15, PM.

173. John Creedy to Pauli Murray, n.d., f381, b15, PM; see also "Three Thousand Miles on a Dime in Ten Days" and "Song of the Highway," in Cunard, *Negro Anthology*.

174. John Creedy to Pauli Murray, n.d., and Creedy to Murray, March 2, 1939, f381, b15, PM; Pauli Murray, "Three Thousand Miles" and "Song of the Highway," in Cunard, *Negro Anthology*.

175. Pauli Murray to Frank Graham, Jan. 17, 1939, f381, b15, and "Negro Applicant Seeks Student Opinion," *DTH*, Feb. 5, 1939, f383, b15, PM.

176. "To the Editor," *DMH*, Jan. 15, 1939, and "To the Editor," *DMH*, Jan. 14, 1939, marked "Not Sent," both in f380, b15, PM.

177. Handwritten notes, "Negro Applicant Seeks Student Opinion," *DTH*, Feb. 5, 1939, f383, b15, PM; quote in P. Murray, *Song*, 128.

178. Pauline Dame to Pauli Murray, Jan. 6, 1939, and Mother to Lennie, Jan. 30, 1939, both in f380, b15, PM.

179. "Graduate School for Negroes Urged," *NYT*, Jan. 8, 1939, f381, b15, PM.

180. "Students Favor Negroes," *CT*, Jan. 21, 1939, f383, b15, and Mother to Lennie, Jan. 30, 1939, f380, b15, PM.

181. "Hoey Asks for N.C. Graduate Schools," *JG*, Jan. 14, 1939, f382, b15, PM; Burns, "Graduate Education for Blacks," 204–05; Burns, "North Carolina and the Negro Dilemma," 77–80.

182. Quoted in Glenn Hutchinson, "Jim Crow Challenged"; "Hoey Asks for N.C. Graduate Schools," *JG*, Jan. 14, 1939, and "N.C. Governor Unearths 'Social Equality' Bogey," *AA*, Jan. 14, 1939, both in f382, b15, PM.

183. "Solution for Negro Problem Put to House," *DTH*, Feb. 13, 1939, f383, b15, PM.

184. The General Assembly appropriated $128,000 to NCC in 1939–1940. Burns, "Graduate Education for Blacks," 204–06; Burns, "North Carolina and the Negro Dilemma," 132–33; Ashby, *Graham*, 228; Gavins, "Within the Shadow," 78–79.

185. Untitled, *JG*, Mar. 4, 1939, quotes in "Editorially Speaking," *CT*, Feb. 25, 1939, both in f383, b15, PM.

186. Louis Austin, *CT*, July 1, 1939, quoted in Burns, "Graduate Education for Blacks," 206, and "Equal Education for Negroes," *CT*, Jan. 21, 1939, both in f382, b15, PM.

187. Murray, "Who Is to Blame for the Disappearance of Gaines?," *Black Dispatch*, [1939?], f383, b15, PM.

188. C. O. Pearson to Pauli Murray, Dec. 27, 1938, Murray to Pearson, Dec. 30, 1938, Murray to Walter White, Jan. 1939, and Catherine Frand to Murray, Jan. 3, 1939, f380, b15, all in PM.

189. Pauli Murray to Thurgood Marshall, Feb. 6 [8?], 1939, pt. 3, ser. A, r18, NAACPM.

190. Roy Wilkins to *JG*, telegram, Jan. 19, 1939, Mr. Wilkins to Mr. White, Jan. 21, 1939, and Roy W[ilkins] to W[alter] W[hite], Jan. 21, 1939, all in pt. 3, ser. A, r18, NAACPM.

191. Mr. White to Mr. Wilkins, Jan. 23, 1939, pt. 3, ser. A, r18, NAACPM; IPM/M.

192. Mr. Wilkins to Mr. White, Feb. 2, 1939, pt. 3, ser. A, r18, NAACPM.

193. Pauli Murray to Carl DeVane, March 6, 1939, f381, b15, PM; quote in P. Murray, *Song*, 126.

194. Murray, *Song*, 126; IPM/Mc, 48.

195. Tushnett, *NAACP Legal Strategy*, 83–86. The plaintiff was Lucile Bluford, a friend of Lloyd Gaines's. See Bluford, "Lloyd Gaines Story," 242–46.

196. Murray preserved and annotated her medical treatment notes. Medical notes, Dec. 14, 16, 17, 1937, Pauli Murray to Dr. Richards, Nov. 4, 1939, with hand-written note, "For your information, I never came back to the Payne Whitney Clinic, because psychiatric treatment is not what I needed," all in f71, b4, PM.

197. Pauli Murray to Dr. Richards, Nov. 4, 1939, f71, b4, "Questions prepared for Dr. Titley," Dec. 17, 1937, f71, b4, and Pauli Murray to Bellevue, May 5, 1948, f554, b28, all in PM; Meyerowitz, *How Sex Changed*, 36–37.

198. P. Murray, *Song*, 128; IPM/Mc, 49.

199. John P. Davis to Frank Graham, Apr. 7, 1939, pt. 1, ser. 2, b16, r16, NNC; "D.A.R. Defends the Indefensible," *AA*, Apr. 22, 1939, 14.

200. IPM/M.

201. Gaines left his Chicago fraternity house for stamps and never returned. Pauli Murray, "Who Is to Blame for the Disappearance of Gaines?," *Black Dispatch*, [1939?], f383, b15, PM; Bluford, "Lloyd Gaines Story"; "Lloyd Gaines Still Missing Despite Years," *AA*, June 14, 1941, 2. There is no record of his Social Security death claim, www.ancestry.com.

202. Murray, "Who Is to Blame for the Disappearance of Gaines?," *Black Dispatch*, [1939], f383, b15, PM.

203. Claude Barnett to Pauli Murray, Feb. 13, 1940, f85, b4, PM.

204. Pauli Murray to W. W. Pierson, Oct. 19, 1939, Murray to Thurgood Marshall, Oct. 19, 1939, M. T. Van Hecke to Murray, Oct. 24, 1939, Murray to Marshall, Oct. 19, 1939, Murray to Van Hecke, Oct. 29, 1939, all in f381, b15, PM; Murray to Marshall, Apr. 13, 1940, f87, b4, "North Carolina Law School Closes," *Black Dispatch*, Oct. 14, 1939, f383, b15, and "N.C. State Law School Folds," *AA*, Oct. 14, 1939, f383, b15, all in PM; Gershenhorn, "Stalling Integration," 160. It reopened the next year with three students and three professors. IPG, 42.

205. Pauli Murray to Thurgood Marshall, Oct. 29, 1939, Marshall to Murray, Oct. 30, 1939, and Murray to Marshall, Dec. 6, 1939, all in pt. 3, ser. A, r18, NAACPM.

206. Salmond, *Gastonia*, 169–73.

207. Beal, *Proletarian Journey*, 338, 331, 333.

208. Quote ibid., 333–34 and 329–34.

209. Quote ibid., 337–38.

210. Anna Damon to Paul Green, May 31, 1935, f4519, b125, PG, and quote in Beal, *Proletarian Journey*, 338.

211. "Gastonia Leader Scorns Hearst," *SW*, Feb. 1936, 4; Clarence Miller, "Party Committee, Administration, MOPR," Secret (in Russian, trans. Ludmilla Selivanova), Apr. 23, 1935, 495/72/282, RGASPI; "Fred Beal May Surrender," *N&O*, Sept. 23, 1937, 1, 10; Graziosi, "Visitors from Other Times," 248, 252; Scales and Nickson, *Cause at Heart*, 71, quote 72; Staff Minutes, Nov. 28, 1938, HERC; Don Sweany to Frank J. McNamara, Aug. 7, 1962, f29, b440, JBM.

212. "Fred Beal May Surrender," *N&O*, Sept. 23, 1937, 1–10.

213. IPG, 47–48; "Fred E. Beal on surrendering . . . Wednesday, February 16, made the following statement," f3, b64, JBM. Eugene Lyons, former Moscow correspondent, accompanied Beal to Raleigh, "Fred Erwin Beal Gains Freedom," *N&O*, Jan. 9, 1942, 1.

214. Don Sweany to Frank J. McNamara, Aug. 7, 1962, f29, b440, JBM; "Scholarly Brief Asking Pardon," *GR*, June 9, 1939, f3, b64, JBM.

215. Avery, ed., *Southern Life*, 317 n. 9; "U.N.C. Leaders Urge Gov. Hoey to Parole Beal," *CO*, June 3, 1939, f3, b64, JBM.

216. Hugo Pollack to Dear Member, June 11, 1938, f29, b440, JBM; Hugo Pollack to Paul Green, Apr. 22, 1938, f431, PGM; "Attorney Pleads for Beal Pardon," *Raleigh Times*, June 8, 1939, f3, b64, JBM.

217. W. J. Cash, "Beal Case," *CN*, July 14, 1940, at www.wjcash.org; "Time for Justice"; Daniels in *N&O*, June 8, 1938, f3, b64, JBM; "Review of the Case of Fred E. Beal."

218. IPG, 48–49.

219. Fred E. Beal to Louis Nelson, Apr. 7, 1940, Beal to Nelson, June 30, 1940, Beal to Nelson, n.d., Nelson to Eugene Lyons, Oct. 11, 1941, all in f12, b1, ILGWU; "Beal," and Beal to Paul Green, Apr. 16, 1940, both in f4521, b125, PG.

220. "Fred Erwin Beal Gains Freedom," *N&O*, Jan. 9, 1942, 1; Avery, ed., *Southern Life*, 317 n. 9.

221. He later renounced Red as an illiterate alcoholic, after Red had denounced him as an anti-Communist. See Beal, *Red Fraud*, 57–62.

222. Scales and Nickson, *Cause at Heart*, 62–64, 68–71; IJS, 24; Bart Hunter Logan, Application for Social Security Number, May 1, 1942, SSA, www.ancestry.com.

223. Scales and Nickson, *Cause at Heart*, 71; Junius Scales to John Salmond, recounted by Salmond in ISGS.

224. "Junius Scales, 82, Communist Party Spokesman Jailed, Then Freed in '62," *Los Angeles Times*, Aug. 9, 2002, B13.

225. IJS, 31.

CHAPTER 7: EXPLOSIVES IN DEMOCRACY'S ARSENAL

1. News Release, July 31, 1939, f1244, b72, and Pauli Murray to Stephen N. Shulman, Apr. 18, 1967, f1246, b72, both in PM; W. L. Patterson, *Man Who Cried Genocide*, 139–40.

2. Rampersad, *Life of Langston Hughes*, 1:353; letterhead of the NPC, July 27, 1939, f1244, b72, and quote in Thyra Edwards to Pauli Murray, Oct. [2?], 1939, f1245, b72, both in PM.

3. Pauli Murray to Stephen N. Shulman, Apr. 18, 1967, f1246, b72, and letterhead of the NPC, July 27, 1939, f1244, b72, both in PM; Sitkoff, *New Deal for Blacks*, 248–49.

4. "Max Yergan, Progressive Leader," *DW*, July 26, 1938, 7; quote in Berry, *Little Closer*, 7–8.

5. Quoted in Naison, *Communists in Harlem*, 293; Yergan, *Gold and Poverty*; Max Yergan to Anson Phelps Stokes, Aug. 26, 1941, f2301, b128, ser. 1, APS; "Danger of Fascism Outlined by Yergan," *PC*, Oct. 22, 1938, 11; Lynch, *Black American Radicals*; Anthony, *Max Yergan*, 183–84; Von Eschen, *Race against Empire*, 17–21.

6. "Max Yergan, Schools," May 3, 1941, r4, pt. 3, ser. B, NAACPM; Anthony, *Max Yergan*, 184–86; Naison, *Communists in Harlem*, 293–94; Duberman, *Robeson*, 210.

7. "Danger of Fascism Outlined by Yergan," *PC*, Oct. 22, 1938, 11; *I. L. D. National Conference Proceedings*, 16, 19–22, and Program of the Biennial National Conference International Labor Defense, July 8 and 9, 1939, both at frames 218–41, r1, ILD.

8. Allen, "America and Neutrality," 14.

9. The parent committee relocated over 4,000 Spanish refugees. "Ethiopian

Refugees," July 2, 1939, News Release, July 31, 1939, Pauli Murray to Jack Sherman, Aug. 3, 1939, and Minutes Sub-Committee Meeting, Aug. 23, 1939, all in f1244, b72, PM; Thyra Edwards to Pauli Murray, Oct. [2?], 1939, f1245, b72, PM.

10. Janken, *White*, 246–49.

11. Quote in Kelly Miller, "Negro Faces the Second World War," *NYAN*, Sept. 23, 1939, 6; Lentz-Smith, "Great War for Civil Rights"; J. S. Rosenberg, *How Far?*, 143–44; Plummer, *Rising Wind*, 73–84.

12. J. S. Rosenberg, *How Far?*, 71; D. L. Lewis, *W. E. B. Du Bois*, 2:58.

13. Sitkoff, *New Deal for Blacks*, 298; Sullivan, *Days of Hope*; J. D. Hall, "Long Civil Rights Movement"; Korstad, *Civil Rights Unionism*; Klarman, *From Jim Crow to Civil Rights*, 173–96.

14. Read and Fisher, *Deadly Embrace*; Naison, *Communists in Harlem*, 287–314.

15. Record, *Negro and the Communist Party*, 184–242.

16. Naison, *Communists in Harlem*, 287–88. Biondi, *To Stand and Fight*, 1–16, argues that it did not have much effect in Harlem.

17. Kirchwey, "Red Totalitarianism"; Rainey, "America's Relation to the War," 21; Kneebone, *Southern Liberal Journalists*, 180.

18. Others included Thomas Woofter, Guion Johnson, Arthur Raper. W. A. Jackson, *Myrdal*, 109–14; Southern, *Gunnar Myrdal*; Egerton, *Speak Now*, 274.

19. Read and Fisher, *Deadly Embrace*, 266–79; Ryan, *Browder*, 159–62; Isserman, *Which Side?*, 32–35; Browder, "Second Imperialist War"; *DW*, Sept. 2, 1939, quoted in Ottanelli, *Communist Party*, 185, 182–94.

20. Quoted in Ottanelli, *Communist Party*, 185; Naison, *Communists in Harlem*, 290.

21. Ottanelli, *Communist Party*, 197; Read and Fisher, *Deadly Embrace*, 333–34; Lewy, *Cause that Failed*, 60–61. Browder went to prison and emerged in May 1942, Ryan, *Browder*, 175, 205.

22. Pauli Murray to Thyra Edwards, Sept. 28, 1939, f1244, b72, PM.

23. Quoted in Jaffe, *Rise and Fall*, 44–47; Ottanelli, *Communist Party*, 185–86; Klehr and Haynes, *American Communist Movement*, 92–93; Read and Fisher, *Deadly Embrace*, 292–93, 298.

24. Randolph, "War."

25. Scales and Nickson, *Cause at Heart*, 75–77.

26. Don West to Howard Kester, quoted in Dunbar, *Against the Grain*, 197.

27. "Negro Leader Calls Present Conflict Imperialist War," *DW*, Oct. 9, 1939, 2.

28. Thyra Edwards to Pauli Murray, Oct. 3, 1939, "Two Great Artists," Nov. 5, 1939, and Murray to Edwards, Nov. 8, 1939, all in f1245, b72, PM. Robeson had returned to New York in October, Duberman, *Robeson*, 233.

29. Lester Granger to Melva Price, Nov. 1, 1939, f1245, b72, PM.

30. "Escape War Zone," *AA*, Oct. 7, 1939, 1.

31. Granger ultimately resigned. Minutes, Nov. 19, 1939, "Communist Squabble Splits Harlem Group," [Nov. 18, 1939], and Lester Granger to Eslande Robeson, Dec. 14, 1939, all in f1245, b72, PM. Murray to Stephen N. Shulman, Apr. 18, 1967, f1246, b72, PM.

32. Record, *Negro and the Communist Party*, 182; Warren, *Liberals and Communism*, 216–34; Lewy, *Cause that Failed*, 28–29.

33. P. Murray, *Song*, 133–34, calls it a "liberal" organization.

34. March 19, 1942, Re: Dr. Max Yergan, f100–210026, pt. 1, MY/FBI; Naison, *Communists in Harlem*, 293, calls Yergan "an influential rather than a disciplined Party member."

35. Quoted in Naison, *Communists in Harlem*, 291; Isserman, *Which Side?*, 36–38. Ottanelli, *Communist Party*, 198–202; Lewy, *Cause that Failed*, 64; Warren, *Liberals and Communism*, 197–209.

36. Ralph Matthews, "1939 Sepia Retreat from Moscow," *AA*, Dec. 30, 1939, 12.

37. Rayford W. Logan, "New War Will Help Race," *NYAN*, Sept. 9, 1939, 1.

38. Dimitrov, "Tasks of the Working Class in the War," 450.

39. "Robeson Warns of Nazism," *NYAN*, Oct. 21, 1939, 1; "Ford Urges Negroes," *NYAN*, Oct. 21, 1931, 12.

40. Kirchwey, "Communists and Democracy," 399.

41. L. E. Martin, "National Negro Congress"; Holloway, *Confronting*, 66–75. On Davis, see Griffler, "Black Radical Intellectual," 246–49.

42. "National Conference on the Economic Crisis and the Negro," 1, 2; J. P. Davis, "Problems of the Negro," 3–12; O. Stone, "Negro Farm Population," 20–21; Randolph, "Trade Union Movement," 54–58; Ralph Bunche, "Critique of New Deal Social Planning," 59–65; J. W. Ford, "Communists' Way Out," 88–99; N. Thomas, "Socialists' Way Out"; Du Bois, "Social Planning"; Du Bois quoted in Griffler, "Black Radical Intellectual," 230, also 219–33; J. W. Ford, *Negro and the Democratic Front*, 66–67; Holloway, *Confronting*, 67–75; Sullivan, *Days of Hope*, 90–91; Record, *Negro and the Communist Party*, 153–62; Sitkoff, *New Deal for Blacks*, 258–60.

43. [?] to Earl Browder, May 31, 1935, f515, r301, d3943, 5, CPUSA. The CP claimed to have founded the NNC. See *American Negro in the Communist Party*, 10–11; "National Negro Congress," f1, b419, JBM; J. W. Ford, "National Negro Congress," 316–26; J. W. Ford, "Political Highlights," 437–64; J. W. Ford, "Building the National Negro Congress," 552–61; W. L. Patterson, "National Negro Congress," 194–95; Cruse, *Crisis of the Negro Intellectual*, 171–73; Holloway, *Confronting*, 76–79; Solomon, *Cry Was Unity*, 301–07.

44. Holloway, *Confronting*, 77.

45. L. E. Martin, "National Negro Congress."

46. *Official Proceedings*, Feb. 14, 15, 16, 1936, p. 3, in f NNC 1941–42, WAH; Howe and Coser, *American Communist Party*, 356–57; Wittner, "National Negro Congress," 883.

47. L. E. Martin, "National Negro Congress," 31; "National Negro Congress in U.S.A."; Janken, *White*, 119. On financing, see Haywood, *Black Bolshevik*, 494–95.

48. Griffler, "Black Radical Intellectual," 360 n. 40, states that Davis joined the CP and gives his party name. Solomon, *Cry Was Unity*, 303; "Minutes," July 15, 1940, f New York Negro #1–3, b12, RM.

49. John P. Davis to John L. Lewis, Oct. 19, 1937, f2, b1, MEGC; Wittner, "National Negro Congress," 892–97; Griffler, "Black Radical Intellectual," 256, ch. 7; Sitkoff, *New Deal for Blacks*, 187–89; Korstad and Lichtenstein, "Opportunities"; Korstad, *Civil Rights Unionism*, 130–41; B. Nelson, *Divided We Stand*.

50. L. E. Martin, "National Negro Congress," 32; quote in Holloway, *Confronting*, 75–80; Pfeffer, *Randolph*, 35–43.

51. *Official Proceedings*, Feb. 14, 15, 16, pp. 4–5, 40, f NNC 1941–1942, WAH.

52. "Speech of Max Yergan," *Official Proceedings*, Feb. 14, 15, 16, 1936, f NNC 1941–1942, WAH; John P. Davis to Max Yergan, Jan. 31, 1936, frame 0646, and Davis to Yergan, May 23, 1936, frame 0654, both in b8, r8, pt. 1, ser. 2, NNC; H. Newton, "National Negro Congress (U.S.A.)"; Anthony, *Max Yergan*, 168–70.

53. "Special Discussion Material," July 10, 1936, and "International Trade Union," July 3, 1936, both in 495/14/36, 9, 5, RGASPI.

54. "Second National Negro Congress," Jan. 3, 1938 [?], 495/14/113, RGASPI; J. W. Ford, *Negro and the Democratic Front*, 62–85; "National Negro Congress," in *FBI's RACON*, comp. and ed. R. A. Hill, 582–611.

55. Pfeffer, *Randolph*, 19–34, 39–40; Tye, *Rising from the Rails*, 131–67.

56. L. E. Martin, "National Negro Congress"; Griffler, "Black Radical Intellectual," 246–49. On Harlem, see "National Negro Congress," *NYA*, Dec. 28, 1935, 12; Record, *Negro and Communist Party*, 155–57; Naison, "Communism and Harlem Intellectuals," 5–6; Naison, *Communists in Harlem*, 199–200. Oakland, California, elected delegates, "Mass Meeting," Jan. 26, 1936, f12, b13; MEGC; *Negro Congress News* 1, no. 6 and no. 7, in f8, b1, MEGC; "National Negro Congress," *NYA*, Dec. 28, 1935, 12; Crouch to Organizational Committee, Jan. 6, 1936, f515, r304, d4028, 5, CPUSA.

57. Bill [Moseley] to Comrade Brown, Feb. 25, 1936, and Moseley to Brown, both in f515, r306, d4029, 9, 41, CPUSA.

58. "Keynote Address of President A. Philip Randolph," *Official Proceedings*, Feb. 14, 15, 16, 1936, p. 11, in f NNC 1941–1942, WAH.

59. Pauli Murray to Morris Milgram, Apr. 29, 1940, f85, b4, and Murray to Dear Mother, Apr. 25, 1940, f253, b9, both in PM.

60. Randolph, "World Crisis," 2, 8, frames 279–310, b21, r21, pt. 1, ser. b, NNC; Record, *Negro and the Communist Party*, 191–99; J. Anderson, *Randolph*, 234–35.

61. Randolph, "World Crisis," 14, 19, 25, frames 279–310, b21, r21, pt. 1, ser. b, NNC; J. Anderson, *Randolph*, 235; Wittner, "National Negro Congress," 899.

62. Randolph, "Why I Would Not Stand for Re-Election"; J. Anderson, *Randolph*, 237; Naison, *Communists in Harlem*, 295–97.

63. "Max Yergan, Progressive Leader," *DW*, July 16, 1938, 7; "Natchez Mississippi!" frames 0462–0466, b29, r29, pt. 1, ser. 2, NNC.

64. "Negro People Speak Out against Jim Crow," [spring 1941]), frames 0008–0010, b19, r20, pt. 1, ser. 2, NNC.

65. "Who Mourns for England?," *AA*, Aug. 3, 1940, 4; "Hitler like Bilbo," *AA*, Aug. 10, 1940, 1; "Cole Sees British Bias Equal," *AA*, Aug. 17, 1940, 3. Aldridge, "War for the Colored Races" argues that the *Afro-American* was prointervention, and the *Crisis, Pittsburgh Courier, Chicago Defender*, and *New York Amsterdam News* were "strongly anti-interventionist." See also Finkle, *Forum for Protest*, 51–62, 91.

66. Padmore, "Second World War and the Darker Races," 327.

67. "War Has Come," and "What Will Adolf Hitler Do to Us?," both in *AA*, Sept. 9, 1939, 3, 4.

68. "German Jim Crow," *AA*, Jan. 27, 1940, 4; "Our Own Nazism," *AA*, Feb. 17, 1940, 4.

69. Dalfiume, " 'Forgotten Years,' " 93–96; J. S. Rosenberg, *How Far?*, 132–40; Aldridge, "War for the Colored Races." In 1940 black newspapers' circulation was at 1,276,000, Finkle, *Forum for Protest*, 52, 61.

70. Aldridge, "War for the Colored Races," 330; D. L. Lewis, *W. E. B. Du Bois*, 2:461–65.

71. Ralph Matthews, "Watching the Big Parade," *AA*, Oct. 14, 1939, 4.

72. Dalfiume, " 'Forgotten Years,' " 93–96; J. S. Rosenberg, *How Far?*, 132–40.

73. Habe, "Nazi Plan for Negroes"; Aldridge, "War for the Colored Races," 342; "Monument to Black Frenchmen Blasted," *AA*, Oct. 19, 1940, 2.

74. "Sentence Four for Betraying Vichy France," *CD*, May 31, 1941, 3.

75. Quoted in Finkle, *Forum for Protest*," 91.

76. "Not Merely Every White Citizen," *AA*, June 22, 1940, 4.

77. "Defender Publisher Outlines Role of Democracy," *CD*, Oct. 12, 1940, 8.

78. Point made, and Randolph quoted in Finkle, *Forum for Protest*, 91. On Randolph's emergence as a leader, see Pfeffer, *Randolph*, 41–43.

79. "Bunche Sees Return of Slavery," *AA*, Feb. 22, 1941, 5.

80. Ralph Matthews, "Watching the Big Parade," *AA*, Jan. 18, 1941, 4.

81. "What Is APM?," f14, b3, JIS; "Are You Prepared?" f9, b4, ser. 1, SEP; Ottanelli, *Communist Party*, 174–75; P. J. Jaffe, *Rise and Fall*, 47; Lewy, *Cause that Failed*, 64; Isserman, *Which Side?*, 64.

82. "Are You Prepared?," f9, b4, ser. 1, SEP; Webb, *Wright*, 149–51. "Information. Secret. Richard Wright," Dec. 2, 1940, Personnel Files, 495/261/530, RGASPI, in Russian, trans. Ludmilla Selivanova.

83. APM to Local Peace Council, Oct. 15, 1940, frame 0444, b18, r18, pt. 1, ser. 2, NNC; *Youth Defends America*, July 3–7, 1940, ser. 1, f2, b5, SEP.

84. Isserman, *Which Side?*, 62–67; "Pickets to March," "Soldiers, Sailors Charge Pickets," and "Colonel Steps in to Protect Peace Pickets," all in f NNC 1941–42, WAH; "Yanks Are Not Coming," "Demonstrate on May Day," in "Communism," NCCCF.

85. "A.P.M. Delegates on Way Home," *DW*, Apr. 8, 1941, 1; Wright quoted in Webb, *Wright*, 150–51.

86. IPM/S; letterhead, Layla Lane and Candace Stone, Feb. 29, 1940, frames 0245–0375, r14, ER. National Sharecroppers Week began in 1937, "National Sharecroppers Week, March 6–13, 1938," f345, b10, and "Southern Tenant Farmers' Union," Jan. 3, 4, 5, 1936, f352, b10, both in HK; P. Murray, *Song*, 135.

87. Pauli Murray to Morris Milgram, Apr. 9, 1940, f1261, b72, PM.

88. Letterhead, National Sharecroppers Week, f399, b18, PM; Ashby, *Frank Porter Graham*, 316; "National Sharecroppers Week," Secretary Pauli Murray, f345, b10, HK.

89. "Contest for College Students," "Contest for High School Students," flyers on r14, ER; "National Sharecroppers Week," Secretary Pauli Murray, f345, b10, HK.

90. IPM/S, 21–22; Mrs. Raymond V. Ingersoll to Mrs. Roosevelt, Jan. 15, 1940, Pauli Murray to Malvina C. Thompson, Jan. 23, 1930, Thompson to Murray,

Jan. 25, 1940, Thompson to Murray, Jan. 29, 1940, Murray to Thompson, Jan. 31, 1940, and Candace Stone to Mrs. Franklin D. Roosevelt, Feb. 2, 1940, all on r14, ER; P. Murray, *Song*, 135.

91. Pauli Murray to Malvina Thompson, Feb. 16, 1940, and "Data on High School Contest," and "Invitation," all on r14, ER.

92. "First Lady Urges Sharecropper Aid," *NYT*, March 6, 1940, f399, b18, PM; Kneebone, *Southern Liberal Journalists*, 134–37.

93. "Patient's Analysis of Nervous Collapse," f71, b4, PM; Pauli Murray to Eleanor Roosevelt, March 7, 1940, and E. Roosevelt to Murray, March 9, 1940, both on r14, ER; Murray to E. Roosevelt, Mar. 15, 1940, f85, b4, PM.

94. Pauli Murray to George Stoney, Jan. 16, 1940, f85, b4, PM.

95. P. Murray, *Song*, 138; IPM/Mc, 51; notes on Harlem Bus Terminal pad, Western Union receipt, and Money Order Message, all in f85, b4, PM.

96. "Notes taken by P.M. on Non-Violence, March 1940," f86, b4, PM; Meier and Rudwick, "Origins of Nonviolent Direct Action," 313–88.

97. Pauli Murray to Jean and Pan, Apr. 9, 1940, f87, b4, PM; P. Murray, *Song*, 138–49; J. S. Rosenberg, *How Far?*, 89–94; Du Bois, "Gandhi."

98. Telegram, Pauli Murray to Mrs. Pauline F. Dame, and Pauline Dames [*sic*] to Perrie [*sic*] Murray, March 25, 1940, both in f86, b4, PM.

99. David L. Clendenin to Pauli Murray, March 25, 1940, f86, b4, PM.

100. "Summary of Facts Leading up to Arrest," f85, b4, PM; P. Murray, *Song*, 138.

101. Virginia Codes, Motor Vehicles—Segregation of Races, f85, b4, "Summary of Facts Leading up to Arrest," f85, b4, and "Jailed in Virginia," *CT*, [n.d.], f88, b4, all in PM.

102. "Jailed in Virginia," *CT*, f88, b4, PM.

103. Ibid.

104. Ibid., "Summary of Facts Leading Up to Arrest," f85, b4, and "Diagram of Bus," f85, b4, all in PM.

105. Quote in "Summary of Facts Leading Up to Arrest," f85, b4, PM; P. Murray, *Song*, 143.

106. P. Murray, *Song*, 144–45; Malvina Thompson to Mrs. Fearing, Apr. 10, 1940, f87, b4, and "Requests Made," f85, b4, both in PM.

107. "Requests Made," f85, b4, "Petersburg, Virginia, Bus Incident," f85, b4, and "Notes from Negro Male Prisoners," f86, b4, all in PM; P. Murray, *Song*, 144–45.

108. "Petersburg, Virginia, Bus Incident," f85, b4, and Murray to David L. Clendenin, March 25, 1940, f86, b4, both in PM. The attorneys were Raymond J. Valentine and Robert H. Cooley, Jr. Robert H. Cooley to Thurgood Marshall, Apr. 3, 1940, frame 613, and Thurgood Marshall to Robert H. Cooley, Apr. 5, 1940, frame 616, both on r17, pt. 15, ser. A, NAACPM; P. Murray, *Song*, 146.

109. Raymond Valentine and Robert Cooley to Charles Houston, f86, b4, and Pauli Murray to David L. Clendenin, March 25, 1940, f86, b4, both in PM.

110. Pauli Murray to David L. Clendenin, March 25, 1940, and Mildred Fearing to Aunt Pauline, [March 27, 1940], both in f86, b4, PM; Walter White to Thurgood Marshall, Apr. 6, 1940, frame 626, r17, pt. 15, ser. A, NAACPM.

111. Candace Stone to Pauli Murray, March 26, 1940, f86, b4, and Malvina Thomp-

son to Mrs. Fearing, Apr. 10, 1940, f87, b4, both in PM; "Unwise" quote in P. Murray, *Song*, 147.

112. "City Court House," and Pauli Murray to Jean and Pan, Apr. 2, 1940, both in f86, b4, PM; Judge Clemens's Opinion, March 26, 1940, f552, b28, PM.

113. Candace Stone to Pauli Murray, March 26, 1949, and Pauli Murray to Robert Cooley, Apr. 2, 1940, both in f86, b4, PM.

114. The description of Murray's house in spring (and March 26 is spring in Durham) comes from P. Murray, *Proud Shoes*, 2.

115. "Two New Yorkers Ready for Appeal," *PC*, marked Apr. 13, 1940, f87, b4, PM.

116. Quoted in P. Murray, *Song*, 147.

117. Robert Cooley to Pauli Murray and Adelene MacBean, Apr. 8, 1940, Murray and MacBean to Attorneys Valentine and Cooley, and "Two New Yorkers Ready for Appeal," *PC*, marked Apr. 13, 1940, all in f87, b4, PM.

118. Thurgood Marshall to William H. Hastie, Apr. 22, 1940, frame 648, r17, pt. 15, ser. A, NAACPM; P. Murray, *Song*, 147–48.

119. Pauli Murray to Morris Milgram, Apr. 29, 1940, f86, b4, and Murray to Milgram, May 14, 1940, f88, b4, PM.

120. Harold Garfinkel, "Color Trouble." Garfinkel earned his MA in sociology at UNC in 1942, a PhD from Harvard in 1952, and is professor emeritus at UCLA. Professor Garfinkel was surprised to learn in 2004 that the person about whom he had written was a woman, IHG.

121. Ibid., 144.

122. Ibid.

123. Ibid., 144–45.

124. Ibid., 145–46.

125. Ibid., 147, 149. Murray's address at the time was 35 Mount Morris Park West.

126. P. Murray, *Song*, 79, 80–81; E. L. Kennedy and M. D. Davis, *Boots of Leather*, 32–38.

127. Harold Garfinkel, *Studies in Ethnomethodology*, ch. 5, and Armitage, "Truth, Falsity, and Schemas of Presentation."

128. Pauli Murray and Adelene McBean to Robert Cooley, n.d., [mid-May 1940], Pauli Murray and Adelene McBean to Thomas Stone, May 14, 1940, and telegram, Milgram to Murray and McBean, all in f88, b4, PM.

129. Lennie to Mother, May 17, 1940, f88, b4, PM. Correspondence at frame 0607, r7, pt, 15, ser. A, NAACPM, shows the NAACP's avid support for the case.

130. Pauli Murray to Pan and Jean, May 16, 1940, f88, b4, PM.

131. P. Murray, *Song*, 147.

132. IHG; Harold Garfinkel, "Color Trouble," in *Best Short Stories of 1941*, ed. Edward J. O'Brien, 97–119.

133. Pauli Murray and Adelene McBean to Robert Cooley, n.d., f88, b4, PM. P. Murray, *Song*, 147.

134. Pauli Murray to Dear Mother, June 2, 1943, f253, b9, PM.

135. Ibid.

136. Journal entry, Jan. 2, 1941, f26, b1, PM.

137. Dalton, *Mahatma Gandhi*, 249; Pauli Murray to Jean and Pan, Apr. 2, 1940, f88, b4, PM.

138. Pauli Murray to Jean and Pan, Apr. 2, 1940, f88, b4, and Murray to Morris Milgram, April 9, 1940, f1261, b72, both in PM.

139. Pauli Murray to Stephen N. Shulman, Apr. 18, 1967, f1246, b72, and Journal entry, Jan. 6, 1941, f26, b1, both in PM; Muzumdar, *India's Non-Violent Revolution*; Muzumdar, *Gandhi.*

140. "Sacrifice to Segregation," *CD*, May 10, 1941, 3; Kelley, " 'We Are Not What We Seem.' "

141. Egerton, *Speak Now*, 256; Sosna, *In Search*, 121–39; Kneebone, *Southern Liberal Journalists*, 210–12; J. D. Smith, *Managing White Supremacy*, 280–84.

142. Shirley Graham, "Soldier Takes a Ride," f5, b55, ser. 1, SEP; Horne, *Race Woman*, 81–108.

143. "Hastie Seeking Court Reversal," *WT*, n.d., f1699, b96, and "Morgan vs. State of Virginia," *AA*, n.d., f4, b90, both in PM; Klarman, *From Jim Crow to Civil Rights*, 173, 220–24.

144. Sherman, *Waller* is the authority. See also Klarman, *From Jim Crow to Civil Rights*, 279–80.

145. In 1939 and 1940 NAACP lawyers successfully argued three coerced confession cases before the Supreme Court. J. Greenberg, *Race Relations*, 313–42; Tushnett, *Making Civil Rights Law*, 50–51; Klarman, *From Jim Crow to Civil Rights*, 117, 156; Goluboff, " 'We Live's in a Free House.' "

146. Dabney quoted in Sherman, *Waller*, 49–50. On Dabney's politics, see Egerton, *Speak Now*, 254–56; R. Smith, "Poll Tax—Enemy of Democracy," 106.

147. "Data on High School Contest," March 1, 1940, r14, ER; Raper, *Preface*; Daniel, *Shadow*; Klarman, *From Jim Crow to Civil Rights*, 286–88.

148. Sherman, *Waller*, 2–4, 5–10; Pauli Murray to Elmer Carter and Edward Lawson, Dec. 2, 1940, f1251, b72, PM.

149. Murray and Kempton, " 'All for Mr. Davis,' " 28; Sherman, *Waller*, 7.

150. Murray and Kempton, " 'All for Mr. Davis,' " 27–28; Sherman, *Waller*, 10; Bunche, *Political Status*, 610; Sitkoff, *New Deal for Blacks*, 52–54. Goluboff, "We Live's in a Free House" notes that the NAACP did not take up landlords' thefts of AAA checks.

151. Murray and Kempton, " 'All for Mr. Davis,' " 32. The coauthors wrote each paragraph together rather than divide the task into halves.

152. Pauli Murray to Elmer Carter and Edward Lawson, Dec. 2, 1940, f1251, b72, and Murray Kempton, "Odell Waller's Mother," f1255, b72, both in PM.

153. Murray and Kempton, " 'All for Mr. Davis,' " 30; Sherman, *Waller*, 11.

154. Murray and Kempton, " 'All for Mr. Davis,' " 31–32.

155. Sherman, *Waller*, 11.

156. Murray and Kempton, " 'All for Mr. Davis,' " 34; Sherman, *Waller*, 11–12.

157. Murray and Kempton, " 'All for Mr. Davis,' " 35–36; Sherman, *Waller*, 12, 25–32.

158. Denning, *Cultural Front*, 260–69.

159. Klarman, *From Jim Crow to Civil Rights*, 118–23, 267–86. Dorr, *White Women* found juries in Virginia occasionally acquitted black men charged with raping white women.

160. Sitkoff, *New Deal for Blacks*, 268–97. Figures in Hall, *Revolt against Chivalry*, 134. Sosna, *In Search*, 34; Klarman, *From Jim Crow to Civil Rights*, 120.

161. "Denmark Vesey," "Florida Lynchers Forced Victim to Castrate Himself," and "Here's the Way the Nazis Lynch," all in *AA*, May 24, 1941, 1–2; Ralph Matthews, "Big Parade," *AA*, May 31, 1941, 2.

162. Klarman, *From Jim Crow to Civil Rights*, 111–12; Sitkoff, *New Deal for Blacks*, 287–88. On federal antilynching legislation, see Zangrando, *NAACP Crusade*.

163. Quoted in "Lynching Democracy," NNC Anti-Lynching Conference, March 19, 1938, in f10, b13, MEGC.

164. "Anti-Lynching Bill," *Washington Relay*, March 27, 1940, 2.

165. J. Greenberg, *Race Relations*, 323–29; Klarman, *From Jim Crow to Civil Rights*, 126–27, 281–85; L. Miller, *Petitioners*, 238–39; R. Kennedy, *Race, Crime, and the Law*, 168–80.

166. "Supreme Court Frees Negro," marked "*Herald-Tribune*, November 26, 1940," f Negro-Lynching Record, b13, RM; Klarman, *From Jim Crow to Civil Rights*, 226.

167. Alabama, Arkansas, Florida, Georgia, Mississippi, South Carolina, Tennessee, Texas, and Virginia required the poll tax, but South Carolina did not require it to vote in the white primary. The Virginia law required that jurors must be "entitled to vote" to serve on a grand jury. "Waller Case and the Poll Tax," f1255, b72, PM; Ogden, *Poll Tax*, 33; Bunche, *Political Status*, 188, 357; Mangum, *Legal Status*, 318, citing *Ross v. State*, 110 Tex. Cr. Rep. 260, 7 S. W.(2nd) 1078 (1928); S. Kennedy, *Southern Exposure*, 95.

168. Kneebone, *Southern Liberal Journalists*, 142–43; quotes in Klarman, *From Jim Crow to Civil Rights*, 127, 154–55; Mangum, *Legal Status*, 308–35.

169. Murray Kempton, "Odell Waller's Mother," f1255, b72, PM. Murray characterized the jury as "ten planters, a carpenter, and a business man," Pauli Murray to Elmer Carter and Edward Lawson, Dec. 2, 1940, f1251, b72, PM. Sherman names 11 farmers and the carpenter, Sherman, *Waller*, 25. On juries, see J. Greenberg, *Race Relations*, 324, and R. Kennedy, *Race, Crime, and the Law*.

170. Miller, *Petitioners*, 240.

171. Ogden, *Poll Tax*, 33–36.

172. "Waller Case and the Poll Tax," f1255, b72, PM; Wilkerson-Freeman, "Second Battle for Woman Suffrage," 333–74; Bunche, "Racial Minorities," 572–73; Bunche, *Political Status*, 342, quotes 359, 363; Brewer, "Poll Tax and the Poll Taxers," 265; George Stoney to William Buttrick, Oct. 19, 1939, f6, b27, HERC; Stoney, "Suffrage in the South, Part I" and "Suffrage in the South, Part II"; Tindall, *Emergence*, 639–42.

173. Quoted in "Waller Case and the Poll Tax," f1255, b72, PM, stating that only 14% of adults voted in Texas. Bunche, *Political Status*, 330, lists Mississippi at 16%, Arkansas at 18%, and Georgia at 20%. See also Brewer, "Poll Tax and the Poll Taxers," 268; Konvitz, "Nation within a Nation," 75.

174. Brewer, "Poll Tax and the Poll Taxers," 278. On the power of southern congressmen, see Katznelson, Geiger, and Kryder, "Limiting Liberalism." Bruce, "Dangerous World"; Belknap, *Cold War Political Justice*.

175. Bruce, "Dangerous World," 14; *NYT*, Apr. 13, 1939, quoted in Belknap, *Cold War Political Justice*, 20; Dierenfield, *Keeper of the Rules*.

176. Durr, *Outside the Magic Circle*, 170; Brewer, "Poll Tax and the Poll Taxers," 272.

177. Dierenfield, *Keeper of the Rules*, 76–79.

178. Sitkoff, *New Deal for Blacks*, 287–88.

179. Bunche, *Political Status*, 330; "Waller Case and the Poll Tax," f1255, b72, PM, states that only 14% of adults voted in the 1940 election. Belknap, *Cold War Political Justice*, 24–26.

180. Alien and Registration Act, U.S. Code, vol. 18, pt. 1, ch. 115, sec. 2381 et seq.; Bruce, "Dangerous World," 9.

181. Belknap, *Cold War Political Justice*, 11–12; Dierenfield, *Keeper of the Rules*, 76–77; Bruce, "Dangerous World," 16, 54–55.

182. Klehr and Haynes, *American Communist Movement*, 126–27; Isserman, *Which Side?*, 123; Sherman, *Waller*, 16–17.

183. On Communist opposition, see R. Hall, "New Forces in the South," 699.

184. Virginius Dabney, "Shall the South's Poll Tax Go?," *NYT Magazine*, Feb. 12, 1939, 9, 20; Kneebone, *Southern Liberal Journalists*, 141–43.

185. Durr, *Outside the Magic Circle*, 152–57, 111–14, 118–20; R. Smith, "Poll Tax— Enemy of Democracy," 106; Joseph Gelders to Frank Graham, Sept. 20, 1939, frames 0596–0601, Gelders to Members, frame 589, both in b16, r16, pt. 1, ser. 2, NNC; "Speech of Joseph S. Gelders," Apr. 27, 1940, frames 0653–0667, b21, r21, pt. 1, ser. 2, and "Minutes [SHCW]," frame 0939, b28, r28, pt. 1, ser. 2, both in NNC; L. Reed, *Simple Decency*, 65–76; Kruger, *And Promises*, 42–51; Sosna, *In Search*, 98–104; Sullivan, *Days of Hope*, 98, 106–20; Eagles, *Jonathan Daniels*, 59–60; Bunche, *Political Status*, 331; Brewer, "Poll Tax and the Poll Taxers," 285.

186. Press release, J. P. Davis's speech, [1939], f NNC 1941–1942, WAH.

187. Bunche, "Racial Minorities," 580.

188. Durr, *Outside the Magic Circle*, 171–72.

189. Sullivan, *Days of Hope*, 120; Sosna, *In Search*, 100–01. Durr recalled that the National Committee to Abolish the Poll-Tax lost Mrs. Roosevelt's open support late in 1942 because FDR "needed Southern senators so badly for his foreign policy." Durr, *Outside the Magic Circle*, 158.

190. "We Are Not Alone!," *PV*, Nov. 28, 1942, 2. *People's Voice* had Communist and non-Communist staffers, and Yergan had invested $3,000 in it, Washburn, *Question of Sedition*, 182–83.

191. Max Yergan to Colonel Deneys Reitz, July 1, 1942, box E, 420701D, ABX.

192. Quote from *NYT*, Sept. 6, 1942, in Sullivan, *Days of Hope*, 116; "House Passes Antipoll Tax Bill," f1251, b72, PM.

193. Sosna, *In Search*, 103; Durr, *Outside the Magic Circle*, 173.

194. "Case of Sharecropper Waller," Feb. 4, 1941, f1257, b72, PM.

195. Jonathan Daniels quoted in "Case of Sharecropper Waller," data sheet f1251, b72, PM; Eagles, *Jonathan Daniels*, 59–63; Jonathan Daniels, "Native at Large."

196. "Defend Democracy at Home," f1251, b72, PM.

197. Sherman, *Waller*, 32.

198. Quote in IPM/Mc, 61; P. Murray, *Song*, 161–62.

199. "Funds Needed at Once"; "Cropper's Aged Mother"; Sherman, *Waller*, 37–38, 55–89; "Case of Sharecropper Waller," "Funds Raised," Nov. 12, 1940, and Murray Kempton, "Mother Waller and Pauli Murray," Apr. 3, [1942], all in f1251, b72, PM.

200. Sherman, *Waller*, 44–45; "Cropper's Aged Mother"; Murray Kempton, "Mother Waller and Pauli Murray," Apr. 3, 1941, f1251, b72, and Murray Kempton, "Waller's Mother," f1255, b72, both in PM; P. Murray, *Song*, 164–70.

201. Murray Kempton, "Mother Waller and Pauli Murray," f1251, b72, PM; on Kempton's radical youth, see Kempton, *Part of Our Time.*

202. "Case of Sharecropper Waller" and "To Vindicate Virginia Justice," *RTD*, [June 1942], both in f1251, b72, PM; Sherman, *Waller*, 141.

203. Dabney, "To Vindicate Virginia Justice," *RTD*, [June 1942], and Alfred Bingham, John Dewey, A. J. Muste, George S. Counts, Paul Kellogg, A. Philip Randolph to Dear Friend, Apr. 7, 1941, both in f1251, b72, PM.

204. "This Man Must Die! Unless," "Pasadena to Hear Annie Waller," May 22, 1941, National Administrative Committee, WDL, June 4, 1941, 2, "He Shall Not Die," Ted LeBerthon, "Night and Day," *Daily News*, May 24, 1941, all in f1251, b72, PM; Murray Diary, f26, b1, PM. See newspaper coverage in "Waller," frame 80, r4, pt. 3, ser. B, NAACPM.

205. Morris Milgram to Pauli Murray, Sept. 25, 1941, f1261, b72, and quotes in "All for Mr. Davis," f1250, b72, both in PM.

206. IPM/Mc, 61; Pauli Murray to Leon Ransom, Nov. 30, 1940, Murray to Thurgood Marshall, Feb. 13, 1941, and Marshall to Ransom, Feb. 26, 1941, all in f384, b15, PM; P. Murray, *Song*, 180–81.

207. IPM/M; IPM/Mc, 61, 63; P. Murray, *Song*, 182.

208. IPM/Mc, 65–66; P. Murray, *Song*, 182–84.

CHAPTER 8: GUERRILLAS IN THE GOOD WAR

1. Hughes, *Jim Crow's Last Stand.*

2. "War Cannot Halt Fight for Rights," *AA*, Dec. 20, 1941, 1; Dalfiume, " 'Forgotten Years' "; Kellogg, "Civil Rights Consciousness"; Klarman, *From Jim Crow to Civil Rights*, 173–96; Klarman, "*Brown.*"

3. Horne, *Black Liberation/Red Scare*, 97–118; Klehr and Haynes, *American Communist Movement*, 96–100.

4. "Now Is the Time Not to Be Silent"; P. J. Johnson, "Limits of Interracial Compromise"; Biondi, *To Stand and Fight*, 3.

5. P. Murray, "Negroes Are Fed Up," 274; Murray to A. Philip Randolph, July 24, 1942, f1265, b72, PM.

6. Quote in "This Is Bob 'Fair Play' Hope Speaking," f5, b7, SEPC.

7. "Anti-Subversion Plans," *N&O*, Aug. 7, 1940, in "Communism," NCCCF; Lavine, *Fifth Column*, 3–4.

8. Bart Logan, Letter to the Editor, *CO*, Apr. 9, 1940, in "Communism," NCCCF.

9. Paul Green to Frank Porter Graham, March 7, 1939, f484, PGM.

10. Paul Green to Constance Webb, May 9, 1967, in Avery, ed., *Southern Life*, 311, 322–24, 644–52; Webb, *Richard Wright*, 189, 297; Roper, *Green*, 187–92, 194–203. Green's FBI file is in f4508b, b118a, PG.

11. Kamp, *Fifth Column*; Kahn, *Treason*; Myles Horton to Roger Baldwin, Aug. 24, 1940, and Louise Dichman to Roger Baldwin, Nov. 30, 1940, both in f4, b6, HERC.

12. Honey, *Southern Labor*, 143–49.

13. *Flash*, March 19, 1942, in f:100-21026, MY/FBI; Ottanelli, *Communist Party*, 204; Schrecker, *No Ivory Tower*, 74–82.

14. "Statement by Dr. Max Yergan," May 16, 1941, frame 1466, r4, pt. 3, ser. B, NAACPM; Case, 2/16/43, NY, f:100-36011, pp. 13–14, MY/FBI; Anthony, *Max Yergan*, 200–01.

15. "Campaign for Education," May 3, 1941, and "Conference for the Reappointment," both at frame 1466, r4, pt. 3, ser. B, NAACPM.

16. Hunton was a Communist. *National Negro Congress News*, May 22, 1941, quote in Statement of Dr. W. A. Hunton, "Howard Prof Called 'Red,'" Arthur B. McLean to William A. Hunton, Nov. 10, 1942, all in f NNC 1941–1942, WAH.

17. Kneebone, *Southern Liberal Journalists*, 180–81.

18. "Hitler in Georgia"; Kneebone, *Southern Liberal Journalists*, 193.

19. Davenport, "Fuehrer of Sugar Creek," 17, 71–73; Kneebone, *Southern Liberal Journalists*, 193.

20. "Georgia Students 'Burn'"; Davenport, "Fuehrer of Sugar Creek," 73.

21. "Hitler in Georgia"; "Georgia Students 'Burn'"; Davenport, "Fuehrer of Sugar Creek"; W. Anderson, *Wild Man*, 195–204; "U of NC President Raps Dixie," *PV*, Sept. 12, 1942, 14.

22. Louis E. Burnham, "From the Public Platform," *Cavalcade* 1 (Nov. 1941): 1, 7, frames 0049–0056, b28, r29, pt. 1, ser. 2, NNC.

23. Jonathan Daniels, in *Nation*, quoted in Du Bois, "Chronicle of Race Relations," 404; Jonathan Daniels, *White House Witness*, 5; Isserman, *Which Side?*, 44, 67–71.

24. Scales and Nickson, *Cause at Heart*, 122–23; Read and Fisher, *Deadly Embrace*, 636. 106.

25. Max Yergan, "Address on Founder's Day," 10–11, f49, b206-6, and Yergan, "Some Problems of the Negro," n.d., f26, b206-5, MY; Eschen, *Race against Empire*, 22–43.

26. Isserman, *Which Side?*, 105.

27. Roscoe Conkling Simmons, "Week," *CD*, July 5, 1941, 15; IEB/S.

28. Correspondence on Max Yergan Conference, f9, b76, HERC.

29. "Pressure on Race Press," *CE*, May 28, 1942, 1; Washburn, *Question of Sedition*, 41–65, 81–85, 166–202; Finkle, *Forum for Protest*, 62–77; R. A. Hill, *FBI's RACON*.

30. The FBI suspected that Yergan was not a minister and spent years putting together a fraud case against him for buying a discounted clergy railroad pass. When confronted, he proved that he was ordained in the Congregational Church. The FBI tapped his telephone, followed him everywhere, bugged his apartment, and stole his diaries. Anthony lists 13 volumes of FBI files, *Max Yergan*, 334. My own FOIA request yielded 6 files and hundreds of pages, Dr. Max Yergan, f:100-26011, pts. 1–5, and Dr. Max Yergan, f 71-1978, MY/FBI.

31. "Pressure on Race Press," *CE*, May 28, 1942, 1; Washburn, *Question of Sedition*, 146–8; "Freedom of Negro Press," *CD*, Dec. 20, 1941, 1.

32. "Text of Publishers' Statement," f399, b18, PM; Marjorie McKenzie, "Pursuit of Democracy," *PC*, Jan. 24, 1942; "We are Accused"; Finkle, *Forum for Protest*, 60.

33. Washburn, *Question of Sedition*, 178–80, 183, 187–89, 203–08, credits Attorney

General Francis Biddle with stopping Hoover. For FBI reports on black Southerners, see R. A. Hill, *FBI's RACON*, 254–356.

34. Quoted in Gallicchio, *African American Encounter*, 137; L. E. Martin, "Fifth Column among Negroes"; Cayton, "Negro Morale"; Bond, "Should the Negro Care?"; Seligmann, "War for Common Humanity," 73–75; K. B. Clark, "Morale of the Negro"; Dalfiume, " 'Forgotten Years,' " 102; Dalfiume, *Desegregation*, 105–31.

35. "Declare War Effort Lacks Full Support," *CD*, Jan. 17, 1942, 5; Gallicchio, *African American Encounter*, 122–38.

36. L. E. Martin, "Fifth Column among Negroes," 360.

37. Randolph, "Editorial"; Randolph, "England's Fight Our Cause," *PC*, Feb. 8, 1941, 13.

38. On Logan and Houston in World War I, see Lentz-Smith, "Great War for Civil Rights"; quote in Nalty, *Strength*, 112, 132–33, 136.

39. Robert C. Weaver, "Negro and National Defense," in f7, b9, ser. 1, SEPC; "How Can Intelligent Southerners Best Help?"

40. "Conscription Bill"; Nalty, *Strength*, 136–37; Dalfiume, *Desegregation*; Wynn, *Afro-American*, 21–38.

41. Lentz-Smith, "Great War for Civil Rights"; "White House Blesses Jim Crow"; Herbert Garfinkel, *When Negroes March*, 34; Brooks, *Walls Come Tumbling Down*, 10–11; Dalfiume, *Desegregation*, 31–40; "Army Can Have Jim Crow"; Redding, "Byrnes"; Pfeffer, *Randolph*, 46; Janken, *White*, 253.

42. "Army Can Have Jim Crow"; Redding, "Byrnes," 115.

43. Nalty, *Strength*, 139–40; Sitkoff, *New Deal for Blacks*, 306–22.

44. "Army Can Have Jim Crow," "No Negro Draft Board Members," "Discrimination in the Draft"; J. Anderson, *Randolph*, 244–46.

45. Franklin Delano Roosevelt, Jan. 6, 1941, "Four Freedoms," at www.libertynet .org; Doenecke, *Storm on the Horizon*, 43.

46. "Four Freedoms: Dixie Style," *CD*, May 8, 1943, 16; J. S. Rosenberg, *How Far?*, 150.

47. " 'I Am an American Fête to Feature Ethel Waters," *CD*, May 10, 1941, 2; "Quash Youth Message," *CD*, May 18, 1941, 14.

48. Their bosses were Sidney Hillman and William K. Knudsen, quote in IWWA, 666–76; Weaver, "Defense Program and the Negro."

49. Herbert Garfinkel, *When Negroes March* uses "Discrimination in the Arsenal of Democracy," which suggested the title of ch. 7. Bracey and Meier, "Allies or Adversaries?"; Kesselman, *Social Politics*, 3–22; J. Anderson, *Randolph*, 248–49; " 'Defense Rotten'—Randolph," *PC*, Jan. 25, 1941, 13; [Randolph], "Let the Negro Masses Speak"; Kempton, *Part of Our Time*, 250–52; Dalfiume, *Desegregation*, 42; Pfeffer, *Randolph*, 47.

50. "Negroes Ban Whites in Fight," *NYT*, July 18, 1943, 20; "Chicagoans Join March," *CD*, June 7, 1941, 5; "Randolph Here Sunday," *CD*, June 21, 1941, 5; "March on Washington Rally," *PV*, June 13, 1942, 37; "Crusade for Democracy," *CD*, June 21, 1941, editorial page; "March on Washington Movement," r30, APR; Herbert Garfinkel, *When Negroes March*, 42–60; Pfeffer, *Randolph*, 48–49; J. Anderson, *Randolph*, 249–54; Sitkoff, *New Deal for Blacks*, 314–35; Klinkner

and Smith, *Unsteady March*, 149–60; Brooks, *Walls Come Tumbling Down*, 20–28; Bracy and Meier, "Allies or Adversaries?"

51. "47 Branches Picket"; "Voice Job Demands," *AA*, May 3, 1941, 6; Brooks, *Walls Come Tumbling Down*, 19–20.

52. "Proposals of the Negro March-on-Washington Committee," May, 1941, r22, APR; Lucius C. Harper, "Roosevelt Gives Only 'Lip Service,'" *CD*, June 21, 1941, 1.

53. Randolph, "President Roosevelt's Statement"; Ruchames, *Race, Jobs, and Politics*, 18–19.

54. Charley Cherokee, "National Grapevine," *CD*, June 28, 1941, 15; Pfeffer, *Randolph*, 48–49; J. Anderson, *Randolph*, 251–53, quote 255; A. Philip Randolph, "Employment in Defense Industries," June 25, 1941, r28, APR; "Negro in National Defense."

55. Frank R. Crosswaith was also present, E. P. Myers, *March on Washington Movement*, 3; "Roosevelt Orders End," *CD*, June 28, 1941, 1; Herbert Garfinkel, *When Negroes March*, 60–62; Dalfiume, *Desegregation*, 119–20; J. Anderson, *Randolph*, 257–59; Brooks, *Walls Come Tumbling Down*, 29–32; Egerton, *Speak Now*, 216; Janken, *White*, 253–57.

56. Officials at the Office of War Production supported more diversified hiring, IWWA, 681–85; Wynn, *Afro-American*, 41–42. Dalfiume, *Desegregation*, 120, argues that FDR welcomed the chance to issue the order and to blame it on coercion.

57. Dalfiume, *Desegregation*, 117–21; M. E. Reed, *Seedtime*; Hope Williams et al. to National Executive Committee, July 1941, b24, r20, APR; J. Anderson, *Randolph*, 265–66.

58. A. Philip Randolph, "Negro and the War," *PC*, Dec. 20, 1941, 12.

59. Kempton, *Part of Our Time*, 258; Tindall, *Emergence*, 699.

60. Mark Ethridge, quoted in Ruchames, *Race, Jobs, and Politics*, 28–29, Graves, "Solid South Is Cracking", and S. A. Brown, "Count Us In," 324; White, "Decline of Southern Liberals"; Sullivan, *Days of Hope*, 157–58.

61. Ruchames, *Race, Jobs, and Politics*, 22; M. E. Reed, *Seedtime*, 1–46; Brooks, *Walls Come Tumbling Down*, 36–40.

62. "Editor Mark Ethridge," *CD*, Oct. 25, 1941, 16; Ruchames, *Race, Jobs, and Politics*, 41–42.

63. "Nice Work," *CD*, Oct. 11, 1941, 6; "President's Executive Order," 296; "Defense Job Front," 327; "McNutt and the FEPC"; "Jimcro," *PV*, March 20, 1943, 31; Rush, "Fair Employment Practice Committee"; W. H. Harris, "Federal Intervention"; Collins, "Race, Roosevelt, and Wartime Production:"; M. E. Reed, "FEPC, the Black Worker"; Nuechterlein, "Politics of Civil Rights"; Winifred Raushenbush, "Jobs without Creed or Color," [1945]), frames 0163–0179, b99, r10, pt. 3, ser. 5, NNC.

64. IWWA, 688–92; Daniels, *White House Witness*, 95–98; Dykeman and Stokely, *Seeds*, 255–59; Weaver, *Negro Labor*.

65. "Save FEPC Conference," Jan. 30, 1943, and "Randolph Says Paid FEPC Board Meatless Bone of Appeasement to Negro People," Feb. 4, 1943, both on r22, APR.

66. "FDR 'Revives' Fading FEPC," *PV*, Feb. 13, 1943, 5; Max Yergan to Mr. Presi-

dent, Apr. 30, 1943, frames 0126, b32, r2, pt. 2, ser. 2, NNC; Ruchames, *Race, Jobs, and Politics*, 46; Anthony, *Max Yergan*, 209–10.

67. Pauli Murray to Eleanor Roosevelt, May 29, 1943, r14, ER. Sara Elizabeth Southall joined the committee, Ruchames, *Race, Jobs, and Politics*, 56–57.

68. IWWA, 692–93; Ruchames, *Race, Jobs, and Politics*, 73–86, quote 75; M. E. Reed, *Seedtime*, 223–25; Chamberlain, *Victory at Home*, 50–52, 125–53; Sullivan, *Days of Hope*, 157.

69. Pauli Murray, "Answers to Questionnaire," 10, f1269, b73, PM.

70. Sancton, "Something's Happened," 177; IWWA, 676. Gandhi monitored discrimination in the U.S.; see Chandrasekhar, "I Meet the Mahatma." A. C. Powell, Jr., *Marching Blacks*, 129.

71. "Negro Is Lynched," *NYT*, Jan. 26, 1942, 17; "Sikeston Disgraces Itself," *NYT*, Jan. 27, 1942, 20; advertisement, *CD*, March 21, 1942, 32; "Remember Pearl Harbor . . . and Sikeston Too!" *CD*, Mar. 14, 1942, 1; James G. Thompson to the *PC*, Jan. 31, 1942, quoted in Washburn, *Question of Sedition*, 55; "Courier's Double 'V'," *PC*, Feb. 14, 1942, 1; "What the Afro's Closed Fist Means," *AA*, July 18, 1942, 1, 4.

72. Lee, "Will Our War for Democracy Aid the Negro's Fight?"

73. "What the Afro's Closed Fist Means," *AA*, July 18, 1942, 1, 4; Farrar, *"Afro-American,"* 167–72.

74. Pauli Murray to George S. Schuyler, July 31, 1942, f1752, b98, PM.

75. "A. P. Randolph Suggests Mass Meet," *CD*, Feb. 28, 1942, 14; "March on D.C. Group Plans," *CD*, March 21, 1942, 10; "Conference Plans Mass Protest," *CD*, March 28, 1942, 9.

76. P. Murray, "Negro Youth's Dilemma," 8, 10, 11; P. Murray, *Song*, 185; "Lynching and National Security" and "Struggle for Democracy," both in *CD*, July 18, 1942, 16.

77. "Nazi Butchers," *CD*, Dec. 26, 1942, 16.

78. Pauli Murray to John F. Finerty, March 28, 1948, f553, b28, PM; "Waller Verdict Upheld"; "Waller Case"; Sherman, *Waller*, 74–87, 106–07.

79. "Reprieve Odell Waller," *NYA*, June 27, 1942, 1; Sherman, *Waller*, 122–23, 126, 142.

80. "Address by A. Philip Randolph, June 26, 1941," r28, and March on Washington Movement to Dear Friends, Apr. 29, 1942, r20, both in APR; Randolph, "Odell Waller Must Not Die"; Sherman, *Waller*, 126–27; P. Murray, *Song*, 171.

81. A. Philip Randolph to Pauli Murray, Apr. 16, 1943, f1265, b72, PM; "Blackout Harlem"; Kempton, *Part of Our Time*, 252.

82. "Program," f1251, b72, PM; J. Anderson, *Randolph*, 264–65; Sherman, *Waller*, 131–32.

83. Pauli Murray to George S. Schuyler, July 31, 1942, f1752, b98, PM; "Gov. Darden Refuses to Stay Waller's Death," *HT*, July 1, 1942, 19; Sherman, *Waller*, 163–67.

84. Quotes in P. Murray, *Song*, 172, 173, Sherman, *Waller*, 161–62; "Their Pleas Failed," "Week of July 2–9, 1942," "Last Minute Efforts Fail," and "Negro Delegation Meets Rebuff," all in f1250, b72, PM; Randolph quote in "Randolph Tells F.D.R. He Let Us Down," *AA*, July 25, 1942, on r14, ER.

85. "Odell Waller's Dying Statement," f1250, b72, PM; Sherman, *Waller*, 164; "Virginia Negro Dies," *HT*, July 3, 1942, 30; "Waller Executed," *NYA*, July 11, 1942, 1.

86. Pauli Murray, "He Has Not Died in Vain," f89, b4, and "Danger Signal: Explosion Ahead?" f90, b4, both in PM.

87. Pauli Murray, Albert Hamilton, Leon A. Ransom, Layle Lane, Anna Arnold Hedgeman, Rev. William Lloyd Imes, Frank R. Crosswaith, A. Philip Randolph, to Mr. President, July 17, 1942, f1251, b72, and "draft prepared by P.M.," f1267, b72, both in PM; P. Murray, *Song*, 174–75.

88. Eleanor Roosevelt to Pauli Murray, Aug. 3, 1942, r14, ER; P. Murray, *Song*, 189–92.

89. Howard, "Americans in Concentration Camps."

90. "Silent Parade to Mourn Waller Set for July 25," f1250, b72, PM.

91. "Things to Be Done—Parade" and "To Parade Committee," July 17, 1942, both in f1267, b72, PM; quote in Richards, *Springer*, 75–76.

92. "Join Us," "New York Parade to Protest Legal Murder," *Militant*, July 25, 1942, "March Special," "March on Washington Staging Silent Parade," *PV*, July 25, 1942, "New Yorkers Join Hands," *PC*, Aug. 1, 1942, and "Silent Parade," *LAT*, Aug. 10, 1942, all in f1267, b72, PM.

93. P. Murray, *Song*, 193; *MOWM: Proceedings, September 26–27, 1942*, 13, f1752, b98, PM.

94. Du Bois, "Race Pulse Reflected," *CD*, Feb. 20, 1943, 15; Sancton, "Something's Happened"; Sancton, "Negro Press," 558; Egerton, *Speak Now*, 263–64.

95. L. E. Martin, "Fifth Column among Negroes," 360.

96. J. D. Hall, *Revolt against Chivalry*, 258; Sullivan, *Days of Hope*, 165; Egerton, *Speak Now*, 302–12; Gordon B. Hancock, "Statement of Purpose," 3, f31, b30, ser. 1, SEPC.

97. "In Attendance," Southern Conference on Race Relations, 12, 13, f31, b30, ser. 1, SEPC; Egerton, *Speak Now*, 303–05; Kneebone, *Southern Liberal Journalists*, 203–07; Robbins, *Sidelines Activist*, 131–34; D. L. Lewis, *W. E. B. Du Bois*, 2:488–90.

98. Gordon B. Hancock, "Statement of Purpose," 4, f31, b30, ser. 1, SEPC.

99. J. D. Hall, *Revolt against Chivalry*, 258; quotes in "Basis for Inter-Racial Cooperation and Development," 6–7, SCRR, f31, b30, ser. 1, SEPC; W. A. Jackson, *Myrdal*, 236; Sullivan, *Days of Hope*, 165.

100. "Southern Whites Speak"; Lewis, *W. E. B. Du Bois*, 2:490.

101. CIC, *The Durham Statement, October 20, 1942, The Atlanta Statement, April 8, 1943, The Richmond Statement, June 16, 1943*, 10; "Southern Whites Speak"; Egerton, *Speak Now*, 307.

102. Quoted in J. D. Hall, *Revolt against Chivalry*, 259; Sullivan, *Days of Hope*, 165–66.

103. Jackson Davis to N. C. Newbold, July 6, 1943, f1041, b115, subser. 1, ser. 1, GEB; Egerton, *Speak Now*, 308–09; Robbins, *Sidelines Activist*, 133–34.

104. CIC, *The Durham Statement, October 20, 1942, The Atlanta Statement, April 8, 1943, The Richmond Statement, June 16, 1943*, 15; Stokes, "American Race Relations"; Robbins, *Sidelines Activist*, 134–35; Rodgers, "Regionalism."

105. Odum, *Race and Rumors*, 47, 143, 145–47, 151.

106. Ibid., 152, 143, 242.

107. "Judge Hastie Quits"; McGuire, *He, Too*, 52–97; Ware, *Hastie*, 97–143, 148–49; Sullivan, *Days of Hope*, 136–37; Sitkoff, "Racial Militancy," 668–70.

108. "Hitler Invades America," *PV*, Mar. 7, 1942, 1; "Sojourner Truth Homes"; L. E. Martin, "Truth about Sojourner Truth," 112–13.

109. "Detroit Riot Toll 25" and "Nazi Pogroms Tame to Texas Rioters," both *AA*, June 26, 1943, 1; Wynn, " 'Good War,' " 472; Marshall, "Gestapo in Detroit."

110. "Mr. Roosevelt Regrets," 252; "Mr. Roosevelt Regrets," July 22, 1943, r14, ER; ER quote in P. Murray, *Song*, 212.

111. P. Murray, "Negroes Are Fed Up," 274; P. Murray, *Song*, 212–13; Wynn, *Afro-American*, 69–70; A. C. Powell, Jr., *Marching Blacks*, 166–67.

112. Pauli Murray, "And the Riots Came," *Call* (Aug. 13, 1943): 1.

113. Horne, *Black Liberation / Red Scare*, 114–15; Biondi, *To Stand and Fight*, 6, 7, 11.

114. Odum, *Race and Rumors*, 232–34, 230, 231; Simon, "Introduction," xxvi.

115. Odum, *Race and Rumors*, 242; Odum, "Crisis in the Making." White Southerners also thought that the black servants whom they retained belonged to "Eleanor Clubs" to resist Jim Crow. See Simon, "Race Reactions," 239–59; Simon, "Introduction," is the best discussion of *Race and Rumors*.

116. "Viewing with Alarm," *AA*, May 11, 1940, 4.

117. Modell, Goulden, and Magnusson, "World War II in the Lives of Black Americans," quoted in Wynn, " 'Good War,' " 472.

118. The worst instances were in Texas, Mobile, Alabama, and Detroit, according to Sitkoff, "Racial Militancy," 672, and N. Lichtenstein, *Labor's War at Home*," 124–26.

119. P. Murray, "Negroes Are Fed Up," 274–75; Simon, "Race Reactions," 244–45. Trains were overcrowded as well, but black conductors kept better order.

120. "Tuskegee Aide in Army Slain by White Bus Driver," *CD*, July 22, 1944, 1.

121. "Disarm Dixie Bus Drivers or Give Soldiers a Gun Too," *AA*, July 22, 1944, 4.

122. Ware, *Hastie*, 116; W. P. Newton, *Montgomery*, 122–24; Odum, *Race and Rumors*, 118–35; Sitkoff, "Racial Militancy," 669, 671; Kelley, " 'We Are Not What We Seem.' "

123. Odum, "Crisis in the Making," 360; "Dr. Odum Speaks," *N&O*, July 5, 1943, in "Negroes," NCCCF.

124. Odum, *Race and Rumors*, 206, 212, 215–16.

125. Ibid., 221–22; "No Call for Planned Migration," *NYT* [June 1947], and Dumas Malone in *HT*, n.d., both in "Howard Odum," NCCCF.

126. Janken, "African-American Intellectuals"; Simon, "Introduction," xxv.

127. Bethune, "Certain Unalienable Rights," 256–57; Randolph, "March on Washington Movement," 133–62; Hughes, "My America," 305; Hancock, "Race Relations," 217–47.

128. Hancock, "Race Relations," 226–27; S. A. Brown, "Count Us In," 328.

129. Du Bois, "My Evolving Program," 65–66.

130. Logan, "Negro Wants First-Class Citizenship," 28; Janken, "African-American Intellectuals"; Egerton, *Speak Now*, 272–74. On interracial marriage, see A. C. Powell, Sr., *Riots and Ruins*, 163–65.

131. W. T. Couch to Rayford W. Logan, Nov. 9, 1943, quoted in Janken, intro., xix.

132. O. J. Coffin quoted in Janken, intro., xvii.

133. N. C. Newbold to W. T. Couch, Oct. 20, 1943, Newbold, "Comments, *What the Negro Wants: Fifteen Ask for Democracy*," Jackson Davis to Newbold, Oct. 15, 1943, and Newbold to Couch, Oct. 16, 1943, all in f104, b115, subser. 1, ser. 1, GEB.

134. Howard Odum to W. T. Couch, Sept. 17, 1943, quoted in Janken, intro., xvii.

135. Couch, "Publisher's Introduction," xi–xii.

136. Ibid., xxii; N. C. Newbold, "Comments, *What the Negro Wants: Fifteen Ask for Democracy*," in f104, b115, subser. 1, ser. 1, GEB.

137. Bernstein, "Deep South Fights," 17.

138. Graves, "Solid South Is Cracking," 402; Graves, "Should Negroes Accept Segregation?" 31.

139. V. Dabney, "Nearer and Nearer," 48; Kneebone, *Southern Liberal Journalists*, 198.

140. Bernstein, "Deep South Fights."

141. Frank L. Owsley, Mark Ethridge, Howard Odum, and David Cohn, quoted in Brown, "Count Us In," 324–27.

142. Daniels, *White House Witness*; Dalfiume, " 'Forgotten Years,' " 105–06; Eagles, *Jonathan Daniels*, 86–120.

143. Quoted in Ashby, *Graham*, 185–87.

144. IWWA, 679.

145. L. Smith, "Winning the World."

146. Sancton, "Southern View," all quotes, 198–99. See also Sancton, "South and the North."

147. Sancton, "Southern View," 201.

148. Ibid., 202, 205–06; IAR/S, 41–42.

149. *MOWM: Proceedings, September, 26–27, 1942*, 33–36, f1752, b98, PM.

150. Ibid., 37, f1752, b98, PM.

151. Ibid., 10–11, 30, f1752, b98, PM.

152. "Outline for Pamphlet?" r22, APR; E. P. Myers, "Non-Violent, Goodwill, Direct Action," 9, f400, b18, PM.

153. E. P. Myers, "Program of Non-Violent Direct Action" and "March on Washington Movement and Non-Violent Civil Disobedience," Feb. 23, 1943, both on r22, APR. See Meier and Rudwick, "Origins of Nonviolent Direct Action," 307–89.

154. Press release, Aug. 19, 1943, MOWM, r22, and [J. Holmes Smith], "March on Washington Movement," r30, both in APR; Dekar, "Harlem Ashram"; Kosek, "Richard Gregg, Mohandas Gandhi."

155. Morris Milgram and Haridas T. Muzumdar, "Civil Disobedience," *Non-Violent Action Newsbulletin*, n.d., nos. 2 and 3, pp. 7, 12–13, f400, b18, PM; P. Murray and Babcock, "Alternative Weapon," 57; Dekar, "Harlem Ashram," 2; Meier and Rudwick, *CORE*, 3–19; Wynn, *Afro-American*, 47.

156. Lee, "Is Civil Disobedience Practical?" The *Pittsburgh Courier* conducted another poll that found 70.6% opposed, 25.3% in approval, and 4.1% undecided, according to P. Murray, *Song*, 203.

157. E. P. Meyers, "March on Washington Movement and Non-Violent Civil Disobedience," r22, APR.

158. P. Murray, "You Saw Them Go," March 1943, and "65 Howard Men Have Gone to War," both in f397, b18, PM; IPM/S.

159. Lautier, "Jim Crow in the Nation's Capital."
160. IPM/S; P. Murray, *Song*, 204; F. B. Brown, "NAACP Sponsored Sit-Ins"; Meier and Rudwick, "Origins of Nonviolent Direct Action."
161. P. Murray, "Blueprint"; quote in P. Murray, *Song*, 203.
162. IPM/S; P. Murray, *Song*, 203.
163. "To the Howard Student," f395, b18, PM; IPM/S.
164. "Lesson Plan on Non-Violent Direct Action," f397, b18, PM.
165. IPM/M; "Sit-ins," f397, b18, PM.
166. Juanita Morrow to James T. Wright, March 16, 1943, 78th Congress, H.R. 1995, and "Campaign on 'Equal Rights Bill for the District of Columbia,' " [March 1943], all in f395, b18, PM.
167. IPM/S; P. Murray, *Song*, 207.
168. The black Charlottean was Thomas Wyche. Harry McAlpin, "Howard Students Picket," *CD*, Apr. 24, 1943 [handwritten], f399, b18, "Students Force Jim Crow Case," f90, b4, "H.U. Student Pickets Force Restaurant to Drop Color Bar," *AA*, Apr. 24, 1943, f399, b18, all in PM; P. Murray, *Song*, 208.
169. "H.U. Student Pickets Force Restaurant to Drop Color Bar," Apr. 24, 1943, f399, b18, PM; Pauli Murray, "Prayer of a Solitary Picket," fM, b21, BFC.
170. Pauli Murray to Mrs. Roosevelt, May 4, 1943, and *The Forty-Six*, May 4, 1943, both on r14, ER; P. Murray, *Song*, 195–97; Murray to Dear Mother, June 4, 1943, f253, b9, PM.
171. "Minutes Civil Rights Committee," May 3, 1943, f395, b18, and A. Philip Randolph to Pauli Murray, Apr. 15, 1943, f265, b72, both in PM; quote in [J. Holmes Smith], "March on Washington Movement," r30, and press release, Aug. 19, 1943, r22, both in APR; Herbert Garfinkel, *When Negroes March*, 133–38, 144–45; Pfeffer, *Randolph*, 82.
172. "Decides against March on Capital," *NYT*, July 4, 1943, 12; Pauli Murray to Eleanor Roosevelt, June 4, 1944, r14, ER. (She joined a year earlier.)
173. P. Murray, *Song*, 230–31; "Pledge, Civil Rights Campaign," Apr. 13, 1944, f395, b18, "Civil Rights Campaign," f397, b18, notebook, f395, b18, and quote in "Suggested Instructions," f396, b18, all in PM.
174. Notebook, and "What Took Place on 11th and Pennsylvania," Apr. 23, 1944, both in f395, b18, PM; P. Murray, *Song*, 223–25.
175. Press release, "Howard University Students Demonstrate New Technique in Securing Equal Rights," "Were You There?," "What Took Place on 11th and Pennsylvania," Apr. 23, 1944, all in f395, b18, PM; I. F. Stone, "One Elementary Step," *PM*, Apr. 29, 1944, f400, b18, and Horace Cayton, "New Technique," *PC*, Apr. 30, 1944, both in f400, b18, PM; "Howard Students Break Color Bar in D.C. Café," *PC*, Apr. 30, 1944, f399, b18, in PM.
176. Ruth B. Powell and Marianne E. Musgrave to Dr. Johnson, Apr. 30, 1944, f395, b18, Howard University Chapter, NAACP to Professor Ransom, May 2, 1944, f396, b18, "We Just Ain't Ready Dept.," *PC*, Apr. 30, 1944, f400, b18, Mordecai W. Johnson to Professor Ransom, May 2, 1944, f396, b18, all in PM.
177. "Among Howard University Students When President Bans Café Action," *Black Dispatch*, May 13, 1944, f400, b18, PM.
178. "Await Conference with President Johnson," *PC*, May 20, 1944, f400, b18,

Report of Emergency Meeting, May 1, 1944, f396, b18, and *Non-Violent Action Newsbulletin*, n.d., nos. 2 and 3, f400, b18, all in PM. Dean of the chapel Howard Thurman counseled Murray and later advised Martin Luther King, Jr., "Thurman-Murray Conference, May 5, 1944, Formulation of Principles on NAACP Student Controversy," f396, b18, PM. IPM/S, 65–67; P. Murray, *Song*, 225–28; Murray, "Blueprint," 358–59.

179. Press release, Civil Rights Committee, May 10, 1944, Conference with President Johnson, May 10, 1944, Pauli Murray, Confidential Report on Howard Chapter NAACP, and Civil Rights Committee, all in f396, b18, PM. Murray to Dear Mother, May 20, 1944, f253, b18, PM.

180. "Randolph Suggests 'I Am an American, Too,' Week," Dec. 30, 1942, and "MOWM Conference Will Ponder Program," Dec. 30, 1942, both on r22, APR; "Why Should We March?," [summer 1943], f22, b21, ser. 1, SEPC.

181. "Text of Publishers' Statement," f399, b18, PM.

182. C. W. Wesley, "Texans"; Klarman, *From Jim Crow to Civil Rights*, 454; Sullivan, *Days of Hope*, 169–70; Jackson, *Myrdal*, 234–35.

183. Kellogg, "Civil Rights Consciousness," 30, 35, 36.

184. Embree, *Rosenwald Fund*; Jackson, *Myrdal*, 231–71; Kneebone, *Southern Liberal Journalists*, 199–202; King, *Race, Culture*, 39.

185. Embree, "Warning to Western Civilization," *PV*, June 3, 1944, 16; Embree, *Brown Americans*.

186. Wendell Willkie, "Quakers, Mormons, Indians, Jews, and Catholics Are Minority Groups Too"; Jackson, *Myrdal*, 232.

187. Minorities Workshop to A. Philip Randolph, Jan. 1, 1943, r20, APR; "Discrimination Hits Jews, Too," *AA*, March 8, 1941, 2.

188. "Joe Doakes," *I Know My Neighbors, Do You?*, [1940–1941?], and "Santa Keeps Books," both in f7, b5, SEPC; William C. Beyer, "Creating 'Common Ground,'" 54; Denning, *Cultural Front*, 445–54; Jackson, *Myrdal*, 279–93.

189. Dykeman and Stokely, *Seeds*, 263.

190. Ruth Benedict and Gene Weltfish, *Races*, f1, b30, ser. 1, SEPC; "Gene Weltfish," at www.webster.edu/~woolflm/weltfish; R. A. Pathe, "Gene Weltfish," 372–81.

191. Benedict and Weltfish, *Races*, 4, f1, b30, ser. 1, SEPC; M. Taylor, "Through the Editor's Window," 9.

192. Benedict and Weltfish, *Races*, 4, f1, b30, ser. 1, SEPC; Pathe, "Gene Weltfish," 3.

193. Lal, "1930s Multiculturalism."

194. Ibid., *Out of the Many—One: A Plan for Intercultural Education*, f5, b6, ser. 1, SEPC.

195. "Leaders Identify the Obstacles Impeding Democratic Race Practices," *Intercultural Education News* (Jan. 1942): 3, "Issue of Race in War and Peace," *Intercultural Education News* (Oct. 1942): 3, and James H. Tipton, "Negro Enters the All-White School, *Intercultural Education News* (Fall 1946): 4–5, all in f5, b6, ser. 1, SEPC.

196. OWI, *Negroes and War*, n.p.

197. "This Is Bob 'Fair Play' Hope Speaking," poster distributed by Appreciate America, Chicago, in f7, b5, ser. 1, SEPC; Sinatra, "This Thing Called Prejudice."

198. "Bill Mauldin, Cartoonist," *CD*, Dec. 8, 1945, 13; " 'Negro Problem Vital Issue in Our Country'—Einstein," *CD*, May 19, 1945, 1.

199. W. W. Alexander, "Our Conflicting Racial Policies," 179; Dykeman and Stokely, *Seeds*, 272–73.

200. A. Philip Randolph to Pauli Murray, Apr. 16, 1943, f265, b72, PM.

201. Commencement at Howard, f81, b4, PM; Pauli Murray to Dear Mrs. Roosevelt, June 4, 1944, r14, ER.; P. Murray, *Song*, 244–45; "Go South, Commit Suicide," *AA*, June 24, 1944, f18, b400, PM.

202. Pauli Murray, Open Letter to the Graduating Class of 1944, Howard University, Washington, D.C., May 29, 1944, f18, b396, PM.

203. Ware, *Hastie*, 149–50.

204. Pauli Murray to Mrs. Roosevelt, June 24, 1944, r14, ER; P. Murray, *Song*, 239–44.

CHAPTER 9: COLD WAR CASUALTIES

1. Murray, "American Girl Works Out a Way of Life," *PM*, Aug. 20, 1944, 11, in f1301, b74, PM.

2. Pauli Murray to Frank Porter Graham, June 20, 1944, quoted in Ashby, *Graham*, 230.

3. Pauli Murray to Eleanor Roosevelt, Aug. 23, 1944, r14, ER.

4. South Crocker Street Property Owners to Mrs. Mildred M. Fearing, Pauli Murray, Aug. 20, 1944, r14, ER; Flamming, *Bound for Freedom*, 259–95, 350–55.

5. Pauli Murray to Eleanor Roosevelt, Aug. 23, 1944, r14, ER; IPM/S, 37.

6. "Pauli Murray Will Not Move," *AA*, Sept. 2, 1944, f12, b1, PM; IPM/Mc, 71; P. Murray, *Song*, 252–55; Sugrue, *Origins of the Urban Crisis*, 17–55; Klarman, *From Jim Crow to Civil Rights*, 212–17; Bates, " 'Double V for Victory' "; Marable, *Race, Reform, and Rebellion*, 15–19.

7. Pauli Murray, "Should the Civil Rights Cases and Plessy v. Ferguson Be Overruled?" f4167, b84, and "Harvard Won't Admit Women," *AA*, Aug. 2, 1944, in f12, b1, both in PM.

8. Murray to Roosevelt, July 11, 1944, r14, ER; Pauli Murray, "American Credo," *Common Ground* (Winter 1945), f400, b18, PM.

9. Korstad and Lichtenstein, "Opportunities Found and Lost."

10. Willkie, "Quakers, Mormons, Indians, Jews, and Catholics Are Minority Groups Too"; Sullivan, *Days of Hope*, 167–68.

11. W. A. Jackson, *Gunnar Myrdal*, 241–61; Sullivan, *Days of Hope*, 167–68.

12. Earl Browder, "A Great Ordeal . . . A Great Opportunity," *PV*, July 8, 1944, 14; Klehr and Haynes, *American Communist Movement*, 96–98; Ryan, *Browder*, 217–32; Isserman, *Which Side?*, 187–97.

13. Langston Hughes, "Here to Yonder," *CD*, May 12, 1945, 12.

14. Ibid.; Horace Cayton, "Hitlerism," *PC*, May 19, 1945, 7.

15. Vincent Tubbs, "Inside View of a Nazi Horror Camp," *AA*, May 19, 1945, 14.

16. Chatwood Hall, "Atrocities at Nazi Death Camp," *AA*, May 19, 1945, 20.

17. Vincent Tubbs, "Story of Life inside Nazi Prison Camps," *AA*, June 9, 1945, 5;

Nalty, *Strength for the Fight*, 147–52. The 13 airmen were shot down from mid-1944 onward, when black pilots began bombing runs into Germany, www .diversityinbusiness.com; A. Jefferson and L. H. Carlson, *Red Tail Captured*; J. E. Brooks, *Defining the Peace*, 13–36.

18. Eleanor Roosevelt to Pauli Murray, Oct. 3, 1944, r14, ER.

19. Ibid., Murray, "Social Equality Needs Definition," *LS*, [Sept. 14, 1944?], and Eleanor Roosevelt to Pauli Murray, March 23, 1945, all on r14, ER.

20. L. S. Horne, "Aims of Security Conference," *NYT*, Apr. 1, 1945, B6; Anne O'Hare McCormick, "Road to Berlin Crosses the Road to San Francisco," *NYT*, Apr. 2, 1945, 18; P. Murray, *Song*, 258–61; IPM/S, 36–37; Murray to Eleanor Roosevelt, March 30, 1945, r14, ER.

21. IPM/S, 36; Eleanor Roosevelt to Pauli Murray, Apr. 5, 1945, r14, ER; John H. Crider, "Blaze of Lights Limns the Scene," *NYT*, Apr. 26, 1945, 4.

22. C. Anderson, "From Hope to Disillusion," 525–26; C. Anderson, *Eyes off the Prize*, 36–40; P. Kennedy, *Parliament of Man*, 28–47; D. L. Lewis, *W. E. B. Du Bois*, 2:503–05; Pauli Murray to Eleanor Roosevelt, March 30, 1945, r14, ER; Hoopes and Brinkley, *FDR and the Creation of the U.N.*, 133–57.

23. Plummer, *Rising Wind*, 133–45; D. L. Lewis, *W. E. B. Du Bois*, 2:505–10; Janken, *White*, 297–301; J. S. Rosenberg, *How Far?*, 156–66; Anthony, *Max Yergan*, 221; C. Anderson, *Eyes off the Prize*, 41–57.

24. Diary, May 3, 1945, f253, b9, PM; "To All Who Are Interested in Interracial Peace," cover.

25. Alphaeus Hunton to A. B. Xuma, Oct. 4, 1946, 461004, D. [?] to Xuma, Oct. 25, 1946, 461025, R. V. Selope Thema to Xuma, Nov. 18, 1946, 461118, all in box k, ABX; C. Anderson, "From Hope to Disillusion," 548–51; Von Eschen, *Race against Empire*, 84–95.

26. Plummer, *Rising Wind*, 153–58; International Court of Justice case summaries, www.icj-cij.org/icjwww/idecisions/isummaries/ilsaesasummary621221.htm; Edward E. Strong to W. E. B. Du Bois, Jan. 9, 1946, frame 218, and Max Yergan to [NNC members], [Jan. 1946], frames 1097–98, both in b62, r28, ser. 2, pt. 2, NNC; "African Affairs Council Protests, [*DW*, Oct. 30, 1947], f:100-26011, pt. 4, MY/FBI.

27. John H. Crider, "Commissions Begin Drafting," *NYT*, May 4, 1945, 13; "Social Plan Vague," *NYT*, May 6, 1945, 30; Plummer, *Rising Wind*, 133–45; D. L. Lewis, *W. E. B. Du Bois*, 2:505–10; Janken, *White*, 297–301; J. S. Rosenberg, *How Far?*, 156–66; Pratt, *Influence of Domestic Controversy*, 36–54; Dudziak, *Cold War Civil Rights*, 43; Layton, *International Politics*, 49–50.

28. Borstelmann, *Cold War*, 41; Dudziak, *Cold War Civil Rights*, 43–45; Plummer, *Rising Wind*, 145, C. Anderson, *Eyes off the Prize*, 74–79.

29. "Hastie Seeking Court Reversal," *WT*, Apr. 2, 1946, f1699, b96, PM.

30. Max Yergan to [UN Delegates], [June 1946], frame 0233, Minutes, Feb. 8 [1946], frames 0199–208, "Petition to the United Nations on Behalf of 13 Million Oppressed Negro Citizens of the United States of America," frames 0159–0167, Andrew W. Cordier to Max Yergan, June 11, 1946, frame 1072, Max Yergan and Revels Cayton to Harry S. Truman, June 1, 1946, frame 1093,

all in b62, r28, NNC; IPM/S; C. Anderson, "From Hope to Disillusion," 552–63; C. Anderson, *Eyes off the Prize*, 79–93; Layton, *International Politics*, 49; Plummer, *Rising Wind*, 171–75.

31. Arthur Massolo, "Anti-Bias Resolution Is Adopted," *NYP*, Nov. 19, 1946, and "Mrs. Roosevelt Is Elected Chairman," *NYT*, Jan. 28, 1947, both in f90, b4, PM.

32. Eagles, *Jonathan Daniels*, 127–28; Pratt, *Influence of Domestic Controversy*, 35–80.

33. C. Anderson, "From Hope to Disillusion," 553–56; C. Anderson, *Eyes off the Prize*, 94–112; D. L. Lewis, *W. E. B. Du Bois*, 2:521–30; Janken, *White*, 308–09; Dudziak, *Cold War Civil Rights*, 44–45; Layton, *International Politics*, 51–57; Plummer, *Rising Wind*, 178–84.

34. "Jews Urge Treaties that Enforce Rights," *NYT*, July 27, 1946, 6; Eagles, *Jonathan Daniels*, 131–33.

35. The AAUN included Alger Hiss, who was later accused of being a CP member. "U.N. Charter Cited to High Court," *NYT*, Dec. 5, 1947; Klarman, *From Jim Crow to Civil Rights*, 212–17, 261–62; Flamming, *Bound for Freedom*, 369.

36. Berman, *Politics of Civil Rights*, 53–55; McMahon, *Reconsidering Roosevelt*, 184–86; Layton, *International Politics*, 53; Borstelmann, *Cold War*, 47–61.

37. IJD; Berman, *Politics of Civil Rights*, 56; J. D. Hall, *Revolt against Chivalry*, 217.

38. Sancton, "Segregation," 11; "Should Congress Pass a Law Prohibiting Employment Discrimination?," *Congressional Record* 24 (June 1945): 163, 173; "Congress," 22; "Birth of a Filibuster," 23; T. R. Brooks, *Walls Come Tumbling Down*, 58–59.

39. John Temple Graves, "This Morning," Jan. 29, 1946, in f Alabama, b2, RM; Kneebone, *Southern Liberal Journalists*, 196–220, esp. 216–17.

40. Kesselman, *Social Politics*, 29–46; Pfeffer, *Randolph*, 97–102; Chamberlain, *Victory at Home*, 177–80; Ruchames, *Race, Jobs, and Politics*, 122–36.

41. "N.Y. FEPC Adopted," *PV*, March 10, 1945, 32; Biondi, *To Stand and Fight*, 55; Augusta Strong, "Fair Employment Laws Pending in 14 States," *PV*, March 24, 1945, 10; P. Murray, *Song*, 262–63.

42. Affidavit, Maida Springer, f554, b28, PM; "Editorial"; I. F. Stone, "Swastika over the Senate"; "Rally for the F. E. P. C.," f90, b4, PM; Richards, *Springer*, 88–91; Chamberlain, *Victory at Home*, 177–80; Marable, *Race, Reform, and Rebellion*, 20–21; Lawson, *Black Ballots*.

43. Berman, *Politics of Civil Rights*, 57–58.

44. President's Committee, *To Secure These Rights*, table of contents, 151–62; Anthony Leviero, "35 Ideas Offered," *NYT*, Oct. 30, 1947, 1; Berman, *Politics of Civil Rights*, 68–72; Dudziak, *Cold War Civil Rights*, 79–82.

45. President's Committee, *To Secure These Rights*, 162–67, 175.

46. Caute, *Great Fear*, 26.

47. Leffler, *Specter*, 40–63; Sullivan, *Days of Hope*, 229–42; Powers, *Not without Honor*, 203–08; Korstad, *Civil Rights Unionism*, 415–19; Kellogg, "Civil Rights Consciousness," 36–41; J. Bell, *Liberal State*, 33–45, 78–79; Latham, *Communist Controversy*, 365–67; Heale, *American Anticommunism*, 134–38; Caute, *Great Fear*, 25–31.

48. President's Committee, *To Secure These Rights*, 48, 164–65; "Urges Registering Subversive Bodies," *NYT*, Oct. 30, 1947, 15.

49. "Statement by President," *NYT*, Oct. 30, 1947, 14.
50. President's Committee, *To Secure These Rights*, 166–67; Ashby, *Graham*, 225–26.
51. "President's Committee," f20, b458, JBM.
52. Biondi, *To Stand and Fight*, 164; Egerton, *Speak Now*, 448–71; Woods, *Black Struggle*, G. Lewis, *White South*.
53. In this assessment of the Cold War as an overall negative force for civil rights, I differ from Dudziak, *Cold War Civil Rights*, esp. 11–13, and agree with Marable, who argues that but for the Cold War, "The democratic upsurge of black people which characterized the late 1950s could have happened ten years earlier," Marable, *Race, Reform, and Rebellion*, 18; Sullivan, *Days of Hope*, 274–75; J. E. Brooks, *Defining the Peace*, 9–12; Korstad, *Civil Rights Unionism*, 415–19; G. Horne, "Who Lost?"; Von Eschen, "Challenging."
54. Sullivan, *Days of Hope*, 229; J. E. Brooks, *Defining the Peace*, 16, 27–36; Korstad, *Civil Rights Unionism*, 304–10.
55. Sullivan, *Days of Hope*, 173, 209, 193–220.
56. Chamberlain, *Victory at Home*, 181–82. In Winston-Salem, where there were tensions over a biracial strike, CIO-PAC did not come out openly for a black candidate, Korstad, *Civil Rights Unionism*, 307.
57. "Register!-Pay Your Poll Tax!-Vote in '48," "SNYC Clubs Action," *Young South*, Feb. 1948, 1, 6, and Edward K. Weaver to Dear Board Member, May 1, 1947, all in f8, b2, JIS.
58. Articles of Organization, "Citizens Committee for Political Action Presents Miss Anne E. Mason, CIO Political Action Committee," "Group to Support Negro Candidates," *CO*, Feb. 22, 1949, "Big Political Mass Meeting," "Voters Spurn Baxter's Try," *CN*, Apr. 26, 1949, "Everybody Is Mad about Taft-Hartley," "Mixed Blessing," *CN*, [1950], reprinted in *CP*, March 18, 1954, all in f19, b52, FDA; David Wallas to Dear ADA Member, Apr. 29, 1949, f20, b52, FDA.
59. "Report and Recommendations of the Social Service Commission," Southern Baptist Convention, May 21, 1948, "Race Relations: A Charter of Principles," Southern Baptist Convention, May 1947, St. Louis, Mo., reaffirmed, May 1948, Memphis, Tenn., both in f28, b30, ser. 1, SEPC.
60. P. Murray, *Song*, 283–89; Women's Division to Dear Friends, Dec. 29, 1947, Pauli Murray to Mrs. M. E. Tilly, Dec. 27, 1948, Tilly to Murray, Jan. 5, 1949, all in f1322, b75, PM; Murray to Governor Hastie, f556, b28, PM.
61. "50 Years Marked by Jewish Group," *NYT*, Apr. 7, 1947, 12; P. Murray, *Song*, 283–89; IPM/Mc, 71; Thelma Stevens to Pauli Murray, Feb. 1, 1950, and Murray to Stevens, Feb. 2, 1950, both in f1324, b75, PM; ITS, 74, 82–84; P. Murray, "Historical Development."
62. Eleanor Roosevelt to Pauli Murray, Oct. 3, 1944, r14, ER.
63. "Report on Southern Conference for Human Welfare," 2–3, and "Minutes," Apr. 23, 1947, f8, b2, JIS; Sullivan, *Days of Hope*, 240–41; Krueger, *And Promises*, 25–31; Klibaner, "Travail," 179–202.
64. Sullivan, *Days of Hope*, 174–86, 226–27; McCullough, *Truman*, 304–24, 513–17; Culver and Hyde, *American Dreamer*, 425–26.
65. Sullivan, *Days of Hope*, 244–47; Durr, *Outside the Magic Circle*, 195–201.
66. "Commission of Inquiry into the Effect of Discrimination and Segregation on

the Morale and Development of Negro Soldiers," f8, b9, ser. 1, SEPC; Pfeffer, *Randolph*, 138; J. Anderson, *Randolph*, 276–77; Berman, *Politics of Civil Rights*, 117; T. R. Brooks, *Walls Come Tumbling Down*, 70–72; Layton, *International Politics*, 58–64; Nalty, *Strength for the Fight*, 218–28, 238–39.

67. Yarnell, *Democrats and Progressives*, 76–77; Leffler, *Specter*, 82–85; Culver and Hyde, *American Dreamer*, 472–80.

68. Frederickson, *Dixiecrat Revolt*, 125–33.

69. Ibid., 139–40; Nalty, *Strength for the Fight*, 241–42; Dudziak, *Cold War Civil Rights*, 86; Berman, *Politics of Civil Rights*, 119–21; Marable, *Race, Reform, and Rebellion*, 23–24; Sancton, "Big Brass."

70. Scales and Nickson, *Cause at Heart*, 196; Klehr and Haynes, *Venona*, 99–108.

71. Sullivan, *Days of Hope*, 249–70; Scales and Nickson, *Cause at Heart*, 198; Krueger, *And Promises*, 185–86; Heale, *American Anticommunism*, 142–43; Bell, *Liberal State*, 150–59; Culver and Hyde, *American Dreamer*, 493–96.

72. Shepard died in October 1947. Burns, "North Carolina and the Negro Dilemma," 139; Howard W. Odum to W. Kerr Scott, Aug. 22, 1949, quoted in Burns, "North Carolina and the Negro Dilemma," 142–43.

73. Odum, "Social Change in the South"; Odum, "This Is Worth Our Best," f653, ser. 2.2, HWO.

74. Ashby, *Graham*, 237–39, 243–44; Egerton, *Speak Now*, 531–52.

75. Ashby, *Graham*, 244–45; "Absurd," *Time*, July 19, 1954; A. H. Belmont to L. V. Boardman, Apr. 1, 1954, re "Espionage in the White House, 1934–1948," f9, b1, VFD.

76. Ashby, *Graham*, 245.

77. Pleasants, *Buncombe Bob*; Chafe, *Never Stop Running*, 87–92; Furgurson, *Hard Right*, 49–55; Ashby, *Graham*, 257–58; Billingsley, *Communists on Campus*, xi–xiii.

78. Robert Thompson, quoted in Pleasants and Burns, *Frank Porter Graham*, 99.

79. Quoted in Hatcher, "Senatorial Career," 114.

80. "Revolt in the South," Feb. 18, 1948, f5, b31, ser. 1, SEPC.

81. Ashby, *Graham*, 260–61; Berman, *Politics of Civil Rights*, 173–76.

82. Ashby, *Graham*, 262–63. Ashby says that 11,000 was a clear majority; Eagles, *Jonathan Daniels*, 150, states that the majority would have been 7,000; Egerton, *Speak Now*, 531, gives 5,000; Chafe, *Never Stop Running*, 11,000.

83. Pleasants and Burns, *Frank Porter Graham*, 223, 238–41, 96; Hatcher, "Senatorial Career," 114–17, 176–77; Furgurson, *Hard Right*, 45–47.

84. IJD, 274.

85. "White People Wake Up," f3, b54, FDA; Pleasants and Burns, *Frank Porter Graham*, 268–69, 238; Roper, *Green*, 219–21.

86. Murray quoted in Burns, "Graduate Education for Blacks," 212; Daniels quoted in Eagles, *Jonathan Daniels*, 147; Alexander quote in IWWA, 726; Ashby, *Graham*, 288–302.

87. Ashby, *Graham*, 323–30, quote 330.

88. IJS, 27–9; Scales and Nickson, *Cause at Heart*, 131–42; Mrs. A. M. Scales to Adjutant General, July 30, 1944, f38, b5, JIS.

89. Ryan, *Browder*, 246–61; Isserman, *Which Side*, 214–43; Scales and Nickson, *Cause at Heart*, 149; Klehr and Haynes, *American Communist Movement*, 100–03.

90. Scales and Nickson, *Cause at Heart*, 151–53, 161–62.

91. "Resolution on: The Struggle for Negro Rights," November 25, 1945, f12, b2, JIS. The state SCHW branch was the Committee for North Carolina, Scales and Nickson, *Cause at Heart*, 162–69.

92. "Legislative Bulletin," Jan. 31, 1946, f7, b2, JIS.

93. "Communists Little but Loud in N.C.," *N&O*, "Communism," NCCCF.

94. There were 53 members in 1946 and 95 in 1931. Scales and Nickson, *Cause at Heart*, 152, and membership records, ch. 3.

95. "Labor, Negroes Angered by Communists' Program," *N&O*, Feb. 16, 1947, "Communism," NCCCF.

96. "Winston-Salem Red Probe Challenged by Local 22," *N&O*, May 30, 1947, "Communism," NCCCF; Korstad, *Civil Rights Unionism*, 322–33.

97. "Decline to Tell House Body," *N&O*, July 24, 1947, "Communism," NCCCF; Scales and Nickson, *Cause at Heart*, 184.

98. Junius Scales, "Statement to the Press, October 29, 1947," f38, b5, JIS; Sullivan, *Days of Hope*, 242–43; Scales and Nickson, *Cause at Heart*, 186–94.

99. "Broadcast by the Carolina District of the Communist Party," Oct. 2, 1948, and "Defeat Shreve-Regan Bill," both in "Communism," NCCCF; "Statement to Press by Sam Hall," f18, b3, Junius Scales on Shreve-Regan Bill, Feb. 16, 1949, f8, b2, and House Bill No. 342, Session 1949, f19, b3, all in JIS.

100. Belknap, *Cold War Political Justice*, 69–73, 77–116; Biondi, *To Stand and Fight*, 153–55.

101. Russell Porter, "Davis Joined Reds," *NYT*, July 8, 1949, 3; Russell Porter, "Davis Admits Lies," *NYT*, July 13, 1949, 19; G. Horne, *Black Liberation*, 210–44; Belknap, *Cold War Political Justice*, 99; Caute, *Great Fear*, 187–206.

102. Scales and Nickson, *Cause at Heart*, 229–52.

103. "FBI Nabs Junius Scales," *GDN*, Nov. 19, 1954, 1; "Scales Proclaims Innocence," *GDN*, Apr. 11, 1955, 1; Scales and Nickson, *Cause at Heart*, 255–58; Caute, *Great Fear*, 206–09.

104. "Scales' Lawyer Admits Client Was Communist," *GDN*, Apr. 13, 1955, 3; Belknap, *Cold War Political Justice*, 262–70.

105. "Clontz Tells Scales' View," *GDN*, Apr. 15, 1955, 1; "Counterspy Clontz to Testify," *GDN*, Apr. 18, 1955, 10; Scales and Nickson, *Cause at Heart*, 238–39.

106. David S. Greene, "UNC Student Appears," *GDN*, Apr. 19, 1955, 1; Jacob Hay, "Defense Unready," *GDN*, Apr. 20, 1955, 1; Scales and Nickson, *Cause at Heart*, 276–77.

107. "Scales Sought to Help Underdog, Mother Says," *GDN*, Apr. 21, 1955, 1.

108. "Scales Conviction," *GDN*, Apr. 23, 1955, 4; Scales and Nickson, *Cause at Heart*, 262–76, 282–84.

109. Jacob Hay, "People, Places, and Things," *GDN*, Apr. 24, 1955, sports sect., 1.

110. Scales and Nickson, *Cause at Heart*, 301–18, 322–28.

111. "Former Red Testifies," *GDN*, Feb. 5, 1958, 1; "Scales Trial," *GDN*, Feb. 23, 1958, 4; Scales and Nickson, *Cause at Heart*, 328–41.

112. Signatories, Apr. 5, 1962, in f1, b488, JBM; "Kennedy Frees Scales," *GDN*, Dec. 26, 1962, 1.

113. "Junius Scales," *NYT*, C23; obituary, *LAT*, Aug. 9, 2002.

114. 6/30/45, 2:35 p.m., INCOMING, TO: Max Yergan, f:100-26011, pt. 2, MY/FBI.

115. Teletype, Director—Urgent, 8:32 P.M., Oct. 19, 1944, E. E. Conroy to Director FBI, Oct. 31, 1944, and SAC, Salt Lake City, to J. Edgar Hoover, Nov. 7, 1944, all in f:100-210026, pt.1, MY/FBI; Anthony, *Max Yergan*, 215–16.

116. Memo for Lawrence M. Smith, cc to Wendell Berge, Assistant Attorney General, March 13, 1943, f:100-210026, pt. 1, MY/FBI.

117. J. Edgar Hoover, Memo for the Attorney General, Oct. 9, 1944, and E. E. Conroy to Director, FBI, Dec. 13, 1944, both in f:100-210026, pt. 1, MY/FBI.

118. R. A. Guerin to Director, Oct. 17, 1944, f:100-210026, pt. 1, MY/FBI

119. Max Yergan to Paul Robeson, Nov. 23, 1944, and quotes in report, Detroit, Nov. 19, 1944, both in f:100-210026, pt. 1, MY/FBI.

120. Surveillance Logs, f:100-26011, pt. 5, MY/FBI.

121. SAC, New York, to Director, FBI, July 28, 1947, and Assistant U.S. Attorney refusal, f:100-26011, pt. 4, MY/FBI.

122. Halpern, "Transfer of Inorganic Phosphorus," 747–70; *Fifteenth Census*, 1930, New York, NYC, Enumeration Dist. 8-670, sheet 11, Bronx; Communist Party—U.S.A., Nov. 5, 1948, f:100-26011, pt. 4, MY/FBI. Anthony and Lynch both depict Halpern as a socialite, but she was a respected research scientist. Anthony, *Max Yergan*, 215, 218; Lynch, *Black American Radicals*, 36.

123. Naison, *Communists in Harlem*, 293; Max Yergan, "You Cannot Do Business with Communists," f:100-26011, pt. 4, MY/FBI.

124. "Congress on Civil Rights, Detroit, Mich., April 27 and 28, 1946," f17, b90, JBM; Anthony, *Max Yergan*, 222–24.

125. Max Yergan, "You Cannot Do Business with Communists," f:100-26011, pt. 4, MY/FBI; Anthony, *Max Yergan*, 226–29; Patterson, *Man Who Cried Genocide*, 156–84.

126. HUAC, *Report on Civil Rights Congress*; Henry Winston to Dear Comrades, Oct. 10, 1947, f17, b90, JBM; "Civil Rights Laws Asked," *NYT*, Nov. 23, 1947, 21; Woods, *Black Struggle*, 31–33; Schrecker, *Many Are the Crimes*, 391.

127. Anderson, *Eyes off the Prize*, 92.

128. Max Yergan, "You Cannot Do Business with Communists," New York, Feb. 3, 1948, Bureau—Urgent, all in f:100-26011, pt. 4, MY/FBI; John Latouche, Mary Church Terrell, Henry Arthur Callis to Paul Robeson, May 15, 1948, f17, b1, WAH; Yergan to Anson Phelps Stokes, May 16, 1949, f2304, b128, and W. A. Hunton to Members of the Council, July 7, 1948, f2303, b128, both in APS; Janken, *Logan*, 191–92; Lynch, *Black American Radicals*, 35–38; Von Eschen, *Race against Empire*, 114–18, 134–42; Plummer, *Rising Wind*, 191–93.

129. Edward Scheidt to Director, FBI, May 27, 1948, Memo: Re: Max Yergan Internal Security, July 9, 1948, New York, Aug. 23, 1948, and New York, Aug. 30, 1948, all in f:100-26011, pt. 4, MY/FBI.

130. Communist Party—U.S.A., Nov. 5, 1948, in f:100-26011, pt. 4, MY/FBI.

131. New York, Dec. 1, 1948, Max Yergan Security Matter-C, Nov. 2, 1948, Max Yer-

gan Internal Security-C, Jan. 10, 1949, and SAC, New York, to SAC, New Haven, Apr. 29, 1949, all in f:100-26011, pt. 4, MY/FBI; Anthony, *Max Yergan*, 231–32.

132. Yergan promised to name South African Communists, R. Webster, March 25, 1949, SNA/NTS f7/328, NAR. On the visa, see Max Yergan to Honourable H. T. Andrews, March 30, 1949, Ambassador H. T. Andrews to Secretary for External Affairs, Apr. 6, 1949, Secretary for Native Affairs, Apr. 25, 1949, May 16, 1949, July 20, 1949, and Secretary for the Interior, Aug. 5, 1949, and Secretary for Native Affairs, May 12, 1949, all in SNA/NTS f7/328, NAR; Anthony, *Max Yergan*, 233–38. On the Congress for Cultural Freedom, see Powers, *Not without Honor*, 209–12.

133. SAC, New York, to Director, FBI, June 12, 1957, Bureau Urgent, Nov. 6, 1953, New York, Nov. 16, 1953, SAC, New York, Dec. 17, 1953, SAC, New York, to Director FBI, July 15, 1954, SAC, Philadelphia, to SAC, New York, May 18, 1955, Dr. Max Yergan, SM-C, Perjury, "Justice Dept. Threatens Group for Aid to Africa," [*DW*, Oct. 21, 1954], SAC, New York, to [?], Aug. 29, 1955, and SAC, New York, to [?], Oct. 26, 1955, all in f:100-26011, pt. 5, MY/FBI.

134. "Interview with Dr. Max Yergan"; Lynch, *Black American Radicals*, 51; Yergan, "Communist Threat," Aug. 1954, f17, b206-5, MY; Von Eschen, *Race against Empire*, 172–73.

135. Eichelberger, *U.N.*, 3; Ambassador G. P. Jooste to Secretary for External Affairs, May 29, 1952, SNA/NTS f7/328, NAR; Anthony, *Max Yergan*, 238–45; Mandela quote in "South African Leaders Blast Max Yergan," *Freedom*, Oct. 1952, f24, b206-1, MY; Anthony, *Max Yergan*, 245.

136. Matthews in the *NYP*, Sept. 28, 1952, quoted in Abner W. Berry, "On the Way," *DW*, May 12, 1953, in f100–26011, pt. 5, MY/FBI; Anthony, *Max Yergan*, 245–48.

137. Anthony, *Max Yergan*, 256–62; Max Yergan to Dear Friend, Dec. 29, 1961, American Committee for Aid to Katanga Freedom Fighters, f:100-26011, pt. 5, MY/FBI. See also Max Yergan, intro. *Shattered Illusion*, 1–2.

138. Anthony, *Max Yergan*, 263.

139. Nelson Mandela, "I Am Prepared to Die," Apr. 20, 1964, at www.historyplace .com/index.

140. Gordon Gray to Pauli Murray, Mar. 30, 1951, f381, b15, and Trustee quoted in Edward Joyner, United Press, Raleigh, N.C., Apr. 4, 1951, f383, b15, both in PM; Burns, "Graduate Education for Blacks," 216–17. Floyd McKissick, future leader of CORE, was one of the students, IEMM.

141. Pauli Murray to Louis Austin, March 24, 1951, f381, b15, PM.

142. Ibid., and Murray to Gordon Gray, March 23, 1951, both in f381, b15, PM.

143. Pauli Murray to Dean of the Law School, May 17, 1951, and Henry Brandis, Jr., to Murray, June 6, 1951, both in f381, b15, PM.

144. P. Murray, *Song*, 302–03.

145. Ibid., 128.

146. Pauline Fitzgerald Dame and Sarah A. Fitzgerald Small, "Role of Negro Teachers," *NYT*, May 30, 1954, E6.

147. P. Murray, *Song*, 318–48, quote on 353.

148. Quoted in J. Anderson, *Randolph*, 317, 327–32.

149. P. Murray, *Song*, 362, 367–68; Mayeri, "Reasoning from Race."

150. ISS.

151. Apr. 8, 1967–May 11, 1967, diary entries, f28, b1, PM.

152. P. Murray, *Song*, 432.

153. Ibid., 432–33.

154. "Pauli Murray Biography," *CHH*, June 15, 1996, and Sherry Shanklin, "Old Friends Turn Out," *CHH*, [Feb. 21, 1977?], clippings in the author's possession. P. Murray, *Song*, 432–35.

155. IPM/Mc, 77.

156. Ibid., 3.

WORKS CITED

Note on Abbreviations and Citations

Archival collections, oral interviews, names of all newspapers, and a few magazines and journals are abbreviated as shown below.

PRIMARY SOURCES

MANUSCRIPT COLLECTIONS

JEKA   J. E. Kwegyir Aggrey Papers. Mooreland-Spingarn Research Center, Howard University, Washington, DC.

FDA   Frederick Douglas Alexander Papers. Special Collections, Atkins Library, University of North Carolina at Charlotte, Charlotte, NC.

JSA   James S. Allen Papers. Tamiment Library and Robert F. Wagner Labor Archives, Elmer Holmes Bobst Library, New York University, New York, NY.

ACLU   American Civil Liberties Union Archives on microfilm.

AFPS   American Fund for Public Service Records on microfilm.

WWB   William Watts Ball Papers. Rare Books, Manuscripts, and Special Collections, Duke University, Durham, NC.

BFC   Benet Family Correspondence. Yale Collection of American Literature, Beinecke Rare Book and Manuscript Library, New Haven, CT.

MMB   Mary McLeod Bethune Papers on microfilm.

FB   Franz Boas Papers. American Philosophical Society Library, Philadelphia, PA.

CSPA   Carolina Symposium on Public Affairs Records. University Archives and Records Services, Wilson Library, University of North Carolina at Chapel Hill, Chapel Hill, NC.

CIC   Commission on Interracial Cooperation Papers on microfilm.

CPUSA   Papers of the Communist Party, United States of America. Manuscripts Division, Library of Congress, Washington, DC.

CPL   "Communists," clipping file. Historical Collection, Chattanooga Public Library, Chattanooga, TN.

CC   *Contempo* Collection. Harry Ransom Humanities Research Center, University of Texas, Austin, TX.

MEGC   Matt N. and Evelyn Graves Crawford Papers. Special Collections Department, Robert W. Woodruff Library, Emory University, Atlanta, GA.

PCT   Paul Crouch Typescript, "Brief History of the Communist Movement in North and South Carolina." North Carolina Collection, Wilson Library, University of North Carolina at Chapel Hill, Chapel Hill, NC.

SAD   Sam Adams Darcy Papers. Tamiment Library and Robert F. Wagner Labor Archives, Elmer Holmes Bobst Library, New York University, New York, NY.

TDRF   Theodore Draper Research Files. Special Collections Department, Robert W. Woodruff Library, Emory University, Atlanta, GA.

WEBDB   W. E. B. Du Bois Papers on microfilm.

VFD   Virginia Foster Durr Papers. Arthur and Elizabeth Schlesinger Library, Radcliffe Institute for Advanced Studies, Harvard University, Cambridge, MA.

FSAA   *Federal Surveillance of Afro-Americans (1917–1925): The First World War, the Red Scare, and the Garvey Movement* on microfilm. Lovett Fort-Whiteman File, RG65, Bureau of Investigation, Department of Justice, National Archives, USA.

FSCR   Fellowship of Southern Churchmen Records. Southern Historical Collection, Wilson Library, University of North Carolina at Chapel Hill, Chapel Hill, NC.

GEB   General Education Board Archives. Rockefeller Archive Center, Sleepy Hollow, NY.

FPG   Frank Porter Graham Papers. Southern Historical Collection, Wilson Library, University of North Carolina at Chapel Hill, Chapel Hill, NC.

PG   Paul Green Papers. Southern Historical Collection, Wilson Library, University of North Carolina at Chapel Hill, Chapel Hill, NC.

PGM   Paul Green Papers on microfilm.

AH   Angelo Herndon Collection. Schomburg Center for Research in Black Culture, New York Public Library, New York, NY.

HERC   Highlander Education and Research Center Records. Wisconsin Historical Society, Madison, WI.

JAH   James Allen Hoyt Papers. South Caroliniana Library, University of South Carolina, Columbia, SC.

JBH   Jay B. Hubbell Papers. Rare Books, Manuscripts, and Special Collections, Duke University, Durham, NC.

LH   Langston Hughes Papers. James Weldon Johnson Collection. Yale Collection of American Literature, Beinecke Rare Book and Manuscript Library, Yale University, New Haven, CT.

WAH   William Alphaeus Hunton Papers. Schomburg Center for Research in Black Culture, New York Public Library, New York, NY.

ILD   International Labor Defense Papers on microfilm.

ILGWU   International Ladies' Garment Workers' Union Records, Local 155. Kheel Center for Labor-Management Documentation and Archives, Martin P. Catherwood Library, Cornell University, Ithaca, NY.

CSJ   Charles Spurgeon Johnson Collection. Special Collections, Fisk University, Nashville, TN.

GGJ   Guion Griffis Johnson Papers. Southern Historical Collection, Wilson Library, University of North Carolina at Chapel Hill, Chapel Hill, NC.

GBJ   Guy Benton Johnson Papers. Southern Historical Collection, Wilson Library, University of North Carolina at Chapel Hill, Chapel Hill, NC.

JWJ   James Weldon Johnson Papers. James Weldon Johnson Collection. Yale Collection of American Literature, Beinecke Rare Book and Manuscript Library, Yale University, New Haven, CT.

TEJ   Thomas Elsa Jones Collection. Special Collections, Franklin Library, Fisk University, Nashville, TN.

HK   Howard Kester Papers. Southern Historical Collection, Wilson Library, University of North Carolina at Chapel Hill, Chapel Hill, NC.

MSRK   Mark Solomon and Robert Kaufman Research Files on African Americans and Communism. Tamiment Library and Robert F. Wagner Labor Archives, Elmer Holmes Bobst Library, New York University, New York, NY.

CTL   Charles Templeman Loram Papers. Manuscripts and Archives, Sterling Memorial Library, Yale University, New Haven, CT.

LRM   Lucy Randolph Mason Papers. Kheel Center for Labor-Management Documentation and Archives, Martin P. Catherwood Library, Cornell University, Ithaca, NY.

LRM/OD   Lucy Randolph Mason Papers. *Operation Dixie: The C.I.O. Organizing Committee Papers* on microfilm.

JBM   J. B. Matthews Papers. Rare Books, Manuscripts, and Special Collections, Duke University, Durham, NC.

CM   Clarina Michelson Papers. Tamiment Library and Robert F. Wagner Labor Archives, Elmer Holmes Bobst Library, New York University, New York, NY.

RM   Robert Minor Papers. Rare Book and Manuscript Library, Columbia University, New York, NY.

PM   Pauli Murray Papers. Arthur and Elizabeth Schlesinger Library, Radcliffe Institute for Advanced Study, Harvard University, Cambridge, MA.

NAR   National Archives Repository (Public Records of Central Government since 1910). National Archives of South Africa, Pretoria, South Africa. See SNA/NTS.

NAACP   National Association for the Advancement of Colored People Papers. Manuscripts Division, Library of Congress, Washington, DC.

NAACPM   National Association for the Advancement of Colored People Papers on microfilm.

NNC   National Negro Congress Papers on microfilm.

NTL   New Theatre League Collection. Rare Books and Manuscripts, Perkins Library, Duke University, Durham, NC.

NCCCF   North Carolina Collection, Clipping File. Wilson Library, University of North Carolina at Chapel Hill, Chapel Hill, NC.

JLO   Jessie Lloyd O'Connor Papers. Sophia Smith Collection, Smith College, Northampton, MA.

HWO   Howard Washington Odum Papers. Southern Historical Collection, Wilson Library, University of North Carolina at Chapel Hill, Chapel Hill, NC.

KP   Kirby Page Papers. Claremont School of Theology, Claremont, CA.

LTP   Louise Thompson Patterson Papers. Special Collections Department, Robert W. Woodruff Library, Emory University, Atlanta, GA.

GWR   Glenn W. Rainey Papers. Special Collections Department, Robert W. Woodruff Library, Emory University, Atlanta, GA.

APR   A. Philip Randolph Papers on microfilm.

JHR   James Henry Rice Papers. Rare Books, Manuscripts, and Special Collections, Duke University, Durham, NC.

PR   Paul Robeson Collection. Schomburg Center for Research in Black Culture, New York Public Library, New York, NY.

RFA   Rockefeller Family Archives. Rockefeller Archive Center, Sleepy Hollow, NY.

ER   Eleanor Roosevelt Papers on microfilm.

JHR   John Herbert Roper Papers. Southern Historical Collection, Wilson Library, University of North Carolina at Chapel Hill, Chapel Hill, NC.

RGASPI   Papers of the Anglo-American Secretariat of the Communist International. Russian State Archive of Socio-Political History, Moscow, Russia.

CPR   Charles Phillips Russell Papers. Southern Historical Collection, Wilson Library, University of North Carolina at Chapel Hill, Chapel Hill, NC.

JIS   Junius Irving Scales Papers. Southern Historical Collection, Wilson Library, University of North Carolina at Chapel Hill, Chapel Hill, NC.

SNA/NTS   Secretary of Native Affairs (NTS), Public Records of the Central Government since 1910. National Archives Repository (NAR), National Archives of South Africa, Pretoria, South Africa.

MS   Mildred Seydell Papers. Special Collections Department, Robert W. Woodruff Library, Emory University, Atlanta, GA.

RCS   Roscoe Conkling Simmons Papers. Harvard University Archives, Cambridge, MA.

SEPC   Social Ethics Pamphlets Collection. Special Collections, Yale Divinity School Library, Yale University, New Haven, CT.

SAIRR   Records of the South African Institute on Race Relations, Part II. Division of Historical Papers, William Cullen Library, University of the Witswatersrand, Johannesburg, South Africa.

APS   Anson Phelps Stokes Family Papers. Manuscripts and Archives, Sterling Memorial Library, Yale University, New Haven, CT.

RPS/YU   Rose Pastor Stokes Papers. Manuscripts and Archives, Sterling Memorial Library, Yale University, New Haven, CT.

RPS/NYU Rose Pastor Stokes Papers. Tamiment Library and Robert F. Wagner Labor Archives, Elmer Holmes Bobst Library, New York University, New York, NY.

OMS Olive Matthews Stone Papers. Southern Historical Collection, Wilson Library, University of North Carolina at Chapel Hill, Chapel Hill, NC.

STFN *Southern Tenant Farmers in the News: A Collection of News Stories, 1934–1973* on microfilm. Southern Historical Collection, Wilson Library, University of North Carolina at Chapel Hill, Chapel Hill, NC.

STFU Southern Tenant Farmers' Union Records. Southern Historical Collection, Wilson Library, University of North Carolina at Chapel Hill, Chapel Hill, NC.

WT Wallace Thurman Papers. James Weldon Johnson Collection. Yale Collection of American Literature, Beinecke Rare Book and Manuscript Library, Yale University, New Haven, CT.

DW/BU Dorothy West Collection. Howard Gotlieb Archival Research Center, Boston University, Boston, MA.

DW/HU Dorothy West Papers. Arthur and Elizabeth Schlesinger Library, Radcliffe Institute for Advanced Study, Harvard University, Cambridge, MA.

LFWD Lovett Fort-Whiteman Dossier from the NKWD. In possession of Sergei Zhuravlev, Institute of Russian History, Russian Academy of Sciences, Moscow, Russia.

LFWP Lovett Fort-Whiteman Personnel File, 495/261/1476. Russian State Archive of Socio-Political History, Moscow, Russia.

CVW C. Vann Woodward Papers. Manuscripts and Archives, Sterling Memorial Library, Yale University, New Haven, CT.

ABX A. B. Xuma Papers. Division of Historical Papers, William Cullen Library, University of the Witswatersrand, Johannesburg, South Africa.

MY Max Yergan Papers. Mooreland-Spingarn Research Center, Howard University, Washington, DC.

MY/FBI Dr. Max Yergan, Federal Bureau of Investigation, Department of Justice, Files 71-1978 and 100-26011, obtained through FOIA request.

ORAL INTERVIEWS

IWWA Alexander, Will Winton. Interview by Dean Albertson, Aug. 9, 1952. Oral History Collection, Columbia University.

IJDA Ames, Jessie Daniel. Interview by Pat Watters, [1965–1966?] (G-003). Southern Oral History Program Collection (#4007), Southern Historical Collection, Wilson Library, University of North Carolina at Chapel Hill.

IRNB Baldwin, Roger Nash. Interview by Harlan B. Phillips, 1954. Oral History Collection, Columbia University.

IEB/JS Browder, Earl. Interview by Joseph Starobin, 1964. Oral History Collection, Columbia University.

IEB/SMP Browder, Earl. Socialist Movement Project, Oral History Collection, Columbia University.

IABT Burlak-Timson, Anne. Interview, Dec. 18, 1980 (#351). Oral History of the American Left: Radical Histories. Tamiment Library and Robert F. Wagner Labor Archives, Elmer Holmes Bobst Library, New York University.

IJD   Daniels, Jonathan. Interview by Charles Eagles, March 9–11, 1977 (A-313-3). Southern Oral History Program Collection (#4007), Southern Historical Collection, Wilson Library, University of North Carolina at Chapel Hill.

ISAD   Darcy, Sam Adams. Interview by Ron Filipelli, March 23, 1971. In f32, b3, Sam Adams Darcy Papers, Tamiment Library and Robert F. Wagner Labor Archives, Elmer Holmes Bobst Library, New York University.

IJD   Dickey, John S. Interview by Richard D. McKinzie, July 19, 1974. www.trumanlibrary.org/oralhist/dickeyjs.htm.

IHG   Garfinkel, Harold. Telephone interview by author, Aug. 3, 2004.

ISG/S   Gerson, Sophie Melvin. Interview by John Salmond. In the author's possession.

ISG/K   Gerson, Sophie Melvin. Interview by Laura Kennington, March 30, 2001. In the author's possession.

IPG   Green, Paul. Interview by Jacquelyn Hall, May 30, 1975 (B-005-3). Southern Oral History Program Collection (#4007), Southern Historical Collection, Wilson Library, University of North Carolina at Chapel Hill.

IJJ   Jacobs, Joseph. Interview by Clifford Kuhn, Aug. 15, 1990. Oral History Collection, Georgia Government Documentation Project, Special Collections and Archives, Georgia State University Library.

IGJ   Johnson, Guion. Interview by Mary Frederickson, May 28, 1974 (G-029-4). Southern Oral History Program Collection (#4007), Southern Historical Collection, Wilson Library, University of North Carolina at Chapel Hill.

IHK/J   Kester, Howard. Interview by David Jones, March 5, 1976 (F-027). Southern Oral History Program Collection (#4007), Southern Historical Collection, Wilson Library, University of North Carolina at Chapel Hill.

IHK/H   Kester, Howard. Interview by Jacquelyn Hall and William Finger, July 22, 1974 (B-007-1). Southern Oral History Program Collection (#4007), Southern Historical Collection, Wilson Library, University of North Carolina at Chapel Hill.

IHK/F   Kester, Howard. Interview by Mary Frederickson, Aug. 25, 1974 (B-007-2). Southern Oral History Program Collection (#4007), Southern Historical Collection, Wilson Library, University of North Carolina at Chapel Hill.

IAAL   Lancaster, Abna Aggrey. Interview notes by author, June 25, 1991, and July 13, 1993, Salisbury, NC. In author's possession.

IEMM   McKissick, Ernest, and Magnolia Thompson McKissick. Interview by Louis D. Silveri [1998]. Louis D. Silveri Oral History Collection, D. H. Ramsey Library Special Collections, University of North Carolina at Asheville.

IPM/Mc Murray, Pauli. Interview by Genna Rae McNeil, Feb. 13, 1976 (G-044). Southern Oral History Program Collection (#4007), Southern Historical Collection, Wilson Library, University of North Carolina at Chapel Hill.

IPM/M   Murray, Pauli. Interview by Robert Martin, Aug. 1968. Pauli Murray

Papers. The Arthur and Elizabeth Schlesinger Library on the History of Women in America, Radcliffe Institute for Advanced Study, Harvard University.

IPM/S   Murray, Pauli. Interview by Thomas F. Soapes, Feb. 3, 1978. Pauli Murray Papers. The Arthur and Elizabeth Schlesinger Library on the History of Women in America, Radcliffe Institute for Advanced Study, Harvard University.

IRBN   Roger Baldwin Nash. Interview, n.d. Columbia Oral History Project, Columbia University.

ILTP   Patterson, Louise Thompson. Interview, Nov. 16–30, 1981 (#185). Oral History of the American Left: Radical Histories, Tamiment Library and Robert F. Wagner Labor Archives, Elmer Holmes Bobst Library, New York University.

IGR   Rainey, Glenn. Interview by John Herbert Roper, March 25 and 27, 1980. John Herbert Roper Papers. Southern Historical Collection, Wilson Library, University of North Carolina at Chapel Hill.

IAR/S   Raper, Arthur. Interview by Morton Sosna, Apr. 23, 1971 (B-009-3). Southern Oral History Program Collection (#4007), Southern Historical Collection, Wilson Library, University of North Carolina at Chapel Hill.

IAR/OHS   Raper, Arthur. Interview by the Oral History Seminar, Jan. 29, 1974 (B-009-1). Southern Oral History Program Collection (#4007), Southern Historical Collection, Wilson Library, University of North Carolina at Chapel Hill.

IJS   Scales, Junius. Interview by Mark Pinsky, Oct. 6, 1976 (B-052). Southern Oral History Program Collection (#4007), Southern Historical Collection, Wilson Library, University of North Carolina at Chapel Hill.

IMOS   Schinhan, Mary Frances Odum. Interview by author, Chapel Hill, NC, July 2000.

ISS   Shulman, Stephen N. Telephone interview by author, July 17, 2006.

ITS   Stevens, Thelma. Interview by Jacquelyn Hall, Feb. 13, 1972 (G-58). Southern Oral History Program Collection (#4007), Southern Historical Collection, Wilson Library, University of North Carolina at Chapel Hill.

IOMS   Stone, Olive Matthews. Interview by Sherna Gluck, March–Nov. 1975 (G-059-1 to 8). Southern Oral History Program Collection (#4007), Southern Historical Collection, Wilson Library, University of North Carolina at Chapel Hill.

IRV   Vance, Rupert. Interview by Daniel Singal, Sept. 3, 1970 (B-030-1). Southern Oral History Program Collection (#4007), Southern Historical Collection, Wilson Library, University of North Carolina at Chapel Hill.

IMHV   Vorse, Mary Heaton. Interview by Donald F. Shaughnessy, 1957. Oral History Collection, Columbia University.

IDW   West, Don. Interview by Jacquelyn Hall and Ray Faherty, Jan. 22, 1975 (E-016). Southern Oral History Program Collection (#4007), Southern Historical Collection, Wilson Library, University of North Carolina at Chapel Hill.

ICVW   Woodward, C. Vann. Interview by John Herbert Roper, July 18, 1978, and

      Apr. 13, 1979. John Herbert Roper Papers. Southern Historical Collec-
      tion, Wilson Library, University of North Carolina at Chapel Hill.
ILY   Young, Louise. Interview by Jacquelyn Hall, Feb. 14, 1972 (G-066).
      Southern Oral History Program Collection (#4007), Southern Historical
      Collection, Wilson Library, University of North Carolina at Chapel Hill.
ISZ   Zhuravlev, Sergei. Interview by author, New Haven, CT, Apr. 13, 2005.

NEWSPAPERS

AA	*Afro-American* (Baltimore)
AC	*Asheville Citizen*
AC	*Atlanta Constitution*
ADW	*Atlanta Daily World*
AG	*Atlanta Georgian*
AJ	*Atlanta Journal*
AI	*Atlanta Independent*
BaS	*Baltimore Sun*
BD	*Black Dispatch* (Oklahoma City)
BS	*Black Shirt* (Atlanta)
BW	*Black Worker*
CE	*California Eagle*
CT	*Carolina Times* (Durham, NC)
	Challenger (Columbus, OH)
CHH	*Chapel Hill Herald*
CN	*Charlotte News*
CO	*Charlotte Observer*
CP	*Charlotte Post*
CT	*Chattanooga Times*
CD	*Chicago Defender*
CSM	*Christian Science Monitor* (Boston)
CN	*City Newspaper* (Rochester, NY)
CC	*Cleveland Call and Post*
CR	*Columbia Record*
DTH	*Daily Tar Heel* (Chapel Hill)
DW	*Daily Worker* (Chicago)
DMH	*Durham Morning Herald*
	Flash
	Freedom
FK	*Fool-Killer* (Pores Knob, NC)
GDG	*Gastonia Daily Gazette*
GDN	*Greensboro Daily News*
GR	*Greensboro Record*
HT	*Herald Tribune*
JG	*Journal and Guide* (Norfolk, VA)
LS	*Los Angeles Sentinel*
LTi	*Los Angeles Times*

LAT	Los Angeles Tribune
MT	Macon Telegraph
	Messenger (New York)
MS	Missouri Student
N&O	News and Observer (Raleigh, NC)
NC	Negro Champion (New York)
NM	Negro Militant (Boston)
NW	Negro World
NC	New Carolinian
NYA	New York Age
NYAm	New York American
NYAN	New York Amsterdam News
NYCP	New York City Post
NYP	New York Post
NYS	New York Sun
NYTel	New York Telegram
NYT	New York Times
NYW	New York World
CNC	News and Courier (Charleston)
PP	Pearson's Paper (Pores Knob, NC)
PRB	People's Rights Bulletin (Chapel Hill)
PV	People's Voice
	Le Petit Impartial (Port-au-Prince, Haiti)
PC	Philadelphia Courier
PT	Philadelphia Tribune
PC	Pittsburgh Courier
PM	PM
RTD	Richmond Times-Dispatch
SW	Southern Worker (Chattanooga, Birmingham, Chapel Hill)
SLGD	St. Louis Globe-Democrat
SLPD	St. Louis Post-Dispatch
SLS	St. Louis Star
	State (Columbia)
WB	Washington Bee
WP	Washington Post
WT	Washington Tribune
WSJS	Winston-Salem Journal and Sentinel
YJ	Yellow Jacket

ABBREVIATIONS FOR SELECTED MAGAZINES AND JOURNALS

AHR	American Historical Review
AAAPSS	Annals of the American Academy of Political and Social Science
JAH	Journal of American History
JNE	Journal of Negro Education
JNH	Journal of Negro History

JSH   *Journal of Southern History*
LD   *Labor Defender*

PRIMARY SOURCES: MAGAZINES AND JOURNALS

America
American Mercury
Annals of the American Academy of Political and Social Science
Collier's
Common Ground
Common Sense
Communist
Competitor
Contempo
Crisis
Crusader
Harper's Magazine
International Worker's Review
Journal of Negro Education
Journal of Negro History
Labor Age
Labor Defender
Labor Herald
Life
Literary Digest
Nation
Negro Digest
Negro Quarterly
Negro Worker (*International Negro Workers' Review* in 1931)
New Leader
New Masses
New Republic
North Georgia Review
Opportunity
Phylon
Social Forces
South African Outlook
South Today
Southern Textile Bulletin
Southern Workman
Survey Graphic
Threshold
Time
Washington Relay
Workers Defense Bulletin
Workers Monthly

PUBLISHED PRIMARY SOURCES

"47 Branches Picket Defense Industries." *Crisis* 48 (May 1941): 164.

"The A. F. of L. and the Negro Worker." *Messenger* 7 (Sept. 1925): 324–25.

Absher, Mrs. W. O., ed. *The Heritage of Wilkes County*, vol. 1. North Wilkesboro, NC: Wilkes Genealogical Society with Hunter Publishing, Winston-Salem, NC, 1982.

"Absurd." *Time* (July 19, 1954), at www.times.com/time/magazine/article.

Acts of the General Assembly of the State of Georgia Passed in Milledgeville, at an Annual Session, in November and December, 1866. Macon, GA: J. W. Burke, 1867.

Ademola, A. Ade. "Colour Bar Notoriety in Great Britain." In Cunard, *Negro Anthology*, 346–47. New York: Frederick Ungar, 1970.

"African Blood Brotherhood." *Crusader* 2 (June 1920): 22.

Alexander, Louis. "Durham Streets." *Messenger* 9 (June 1927): 178.

Alexander, Will W. "The Negro in the New South." *AAAPSS* 40 (Nov. 1928): 145–52.

———. "Our Conflicting Racial Policies." *Harper's Magazine* 190 (Jan. 1945): 172–79.

———. "The South's Opportunity: An Indigenous Movement." In *Education and Racial Adjustment: Report of the Peabody Conference on Dual Education in the South*, 72–73. Atlanta: Executive Committee of the Conference, n.d. [1931].

Allen, James S. "America and Neutrality." *National Issues* (Apr. 1939): 13–16.

———. *The Negro Question in the United States.* New York: International, 1936.

———. *Organizing in the Depression South: A Communist's Memoir.* Minneapolis: MEP Publications, 2001.

"American Attempt to Plant Race-Poison in France." In Cunard, *Negro Anthology*, 559. New York: Negro Universities Press, 1934. Originally published in *La Race Nègre* (1930).

"American Kultur in the Island of Haiti." *Crusader* (Oct. 1920): 12–14.

The American Negro in the Communist Party. Washington, DC: Committee on Un-American Activities, Dec. 22, 1954.

Amis, B. D. "For a Strict Leninist Analysis on the Negro Question." *Communist* (Oct. 1932): 944–49.

———. "National Recovery Act in U.S.A. Means Negro Repressive Act." *Negro Worker* 4 (May 1934): 17–18.

"The Anti-Lynching Bill." *Washington Relay*, March 27, 1940, 2.

Aptheker, Herbert., ed. *The Correspondence of W. E. B. Du Bois:* vol. 2, *Selections, 1934–1944.* Amherst: University of Massachusetts Press, 1976.

"Army Can Have Jim Crow Selective Service Act." *Crisis* 48 (Jan. 1941): 22–23.

Avery, Laurence G. "Paul Green at the Top of His Bent." *Carolina Comments* 46 (Sept. 1998): 126.

———, ed. *A Paul Green Reader.* Chapel Hill: University of North Carolina Press, 1998.

———, ed. *Southern Life: Letters of Paul Green, 1916–1981.* Chapel Hill: University of North Carolina Press, 1994.

Baker, Paul Earnest. *Negro-White Adjustment: An Investigation and Analysis of Methods in the Interracial Movement in the United States.* New York: Association Press, 1934.

Balch, Emily Greene, ed. *Occupied Haiti: Being the Report of a Committee of Six Disinterested Americans Representing Organizations Exclusively American, Who, Having Per-*

sonally Studied Conditions in Haiti in 1926, Favor the Restoration of the Independence of the Negro Republic. New York: Writers, 1927.

"The Bantu-European Students' Christian Conference, Fort Hare, June 27th–July 3rd, 1930." *South African Outlook* 60 (Aug. 1, 1930): 146.

Beal, Fred E. *Proletarian Journey: New England, Gastonia, Moscow.* 1937. Reprint, New York: Da Capo Press, 1971.

———. *The Red Fraud: An Exposé of Stalinism.* New York: Tempo, 1949.

Benjamin, Herbert. "The Unemployment Movement in the U.S.A." *Communist* 14 (June 1935): 528–47.

Bernard, Emily, ed. *Remember Me to Harlem: The Letters of Langston Hughes and Carl Van Vechten, 1925–1964.* New York: Knopf, 2001.

Bernard, William S. "Education for Tolerance." *Crisis* 46 (Aug. 1939): 239.

Bernstein, Victor. "Deep South Fights, but Not for 4 Freedoms." *Afro-American*, Sept. 19, 1942. Originally published in *PM* [n.d.]

Berry, Abner W. Introduction to *The Negro and the Democratic Front*, by James Ford. New York: International, 1938.

———. *A Little Closer to Civilization*, ed. Jim Wrenn. Unpublished, in the author's possession.

Bethune, Mary McLeod. "Certain Unalienable Rights." In Logan, ed., *What the Negro Wants*, 248–58.

"Birth of a Filibuster." *Newsweek*, (Jan. 28, 1946): 23.

"The Black Man and Labor." *Crisis* 31 (Dec. 1925): 60.

"Black and Red." *Time* (Nov. 9, 1925): 8.

"Black Shirts versus Night Shirts." *International Press Correspondence* 6 (July 1923): 758.

"Blackout Harlem June 16th." *Black Worker* 7 (June 1942): 1.

Blanshard, Paul. "Communism in Southern Cotton Mills." *Nation* 128 (Apr. 24, 1929): 500–01.

Blossom, F. A. "Rand School." *Messenger* 2 (Jan. 1918): 22.

Boas, Franz. *The Mind of Primitive Man.* New York: Macmillan, 1913. Rev. ed., New York: Free Press, 1963.

———. "The Problem of the American Negro." *Yale Review*, 10 (Jan. 1921): 384–95.

———. "Race." In *Encyclopaedia of the Social Sciences*, ed. Edwin R. A. Seligman and Alvin Johnson, 13:25–36. New York: Macmillan, 1937.

"Bolsheviki." *Messenger* 1 (Jan. 1918): 7.

"Bolshevizing the American Negro." *Independent* (Dec. 5, 1925): 631.

Bond, Horace Mann. "Should the Negro Care Who Wins the War?" *AAAPSS* 223 (Sept. 1942): 81–84.

Brewer, William M. "The Poll Tax and the Poll Taxers." *JNH* 29 (July 1944): 260–99.

Briggs, Cyril. "Bolshevism and Race Prejudice." *Crusader* 2 (Dec. 1919): 541–42.

———. "Fighting Savage Hun and Treacherous Cracker." *Crusader* 1 (Apr. 1919): 3.

———. "Further Notes on Negro Question in Southern Textile Strikes." *Communist* 8 (July 1929): 391–94.

———. "The Klu Klux Klan [*sic*]." *Crusader* 3 (Jan. 1921): 971 (bound vol.).

———. "The Negro Question in Southern Textile Strikes." *Communist* 8 (June 1929): 324–28.

————. "Our Negro Work." *Communist* 8 (Sept. 1929): 494–501.

Browder, Earl. "America and the Second Imperialist War." New York: New York State Committee, Communist Party, 1939.

————. "For National Liberation of the Negroes! War against White Chauvinism!" *Communist* 11 (Apr. 1932): 295–309.

Brown, F. "Toward the Study of Fascization in the United States." *Communist* 14 (June 1935): 558–68.

Brown, George W. "Haiti and the United States." *JNH* 8 (Apr. 1923): 134–52.

Brown, Sterling A. "Count Us In." In Logan, ed., *What the Negro Wants*, 308–44.

————. "Negro Character as Seen by White Authors." *JNE* 2 (Apr. 1933): 170–203.

Bryan, Helen R. "Max Yergan, Uplifter of South Africa." *Crisis* 39 (Dec. 1932): 375–76.

Buell, Raymond Leslie. "Black and White in South Africa." *AAAPSS* 140 (Nov. 1928): 299–305.

Bullock, Ralph W. *In Spite of Handicaps: Brief Biographical Sketches with Discussion Outlines of Outstanding Negroes Now Living Who Are Achieving Distinction in Various Lines of Endeavor.* New York: Association Press, 1927.

Bunche, Ralph J. "A Critique of New Deal Social Planning as It Affects Negroes." *JNE* 5 (Jan. 1936): 59–65.

————. *The Political Status of the Negro in the Age of FDR*, ed. Dewey W. Grantham. Chicago: University of Chicago Press, 1973.

————. "Racial Minorities and the Present International Crisis." *JNE* 10 (July 1941): 567–84.

————. "Triumph? Or Fiasco?" *Race* 1 (Summer 1936): 95.

Buttitta, Anthony. "A Note on *Contempo* and Langston Hughes." In Cunard, *Negro Anthology*, 141–42. New York: Frederick Ungar, 1970.

Cannon, James P. *The Communist League of America, 1932–34: James P. Cannon, Writing and Speeches, 1932–34*, ed. Fred Stanton and Michael Taber. New York: Monad Press, 1985.

————. *The First Ten Years of American Communism: Report of a Participant.* New York: Lyle Stuart, 1962.

————. *James P. Cannon and the Early Years of American Communism: Selected Writings and Speeches, 1920–1928.* New York: Prometheus Research Library, 1992.

Carlson, John Roy [pseud.]. *Under Cover: My Four Years in the Nazi Underworld of America—The Amazing Revelation of How Axis Agents and Our Enemies within Are Now Plotting to Destroy the United States.* New York: Dutton, 1943.

"The Case of Angelo Herndon." New York: Joint Committee to Aid the Herndon Defense, 1935.

Cash, W. J. "The War in the South." *American Mercury* 19 (Feb. 1930): 163–69.

Cayton, Horace R. *Long Old Road.* New York: Trident, 1965.

————. "Negro Morale." *Opportunity* 19 (Dec. 1941): 371–76.

Chandrasekhar, S. "I Meet the Mahatma." *Crisis* 49 (Oct. 1942): 314.

"Charity Begins at Home." *Crisis* 45 (Apr. 1938): 113.

Charney, George. *A Long Journey.* Chicago: Quadrangle Books, 1968.

Christopher, Mary [Dorothy West]. "Room in Red Square." *Challenge* 1 (March 1934): 11.

————. "Russian Correspondence." *Challenge* 1 (Sept. 1934): 14–19.

"C.I. Resolution on Negro Question in U.S." *Communist* 9 (Jan. 1930): 48–55.

Clark, Kenneth B. "Morale of the Negro on the Home Front: World Wars I and II." *JNE* 12 (Summer 1943): 417–28.

Colson, William N. "Confederate-Americanism." *Messenger* 2 (Feb. 1920): 9–10.

Commission of the Central Committee of the C.P.S.U.(B). *History of the Communist Party of the Soviet Union Bolsheviks*. New York: International, 1939.

Commission on Interracial Cooperation. *The Durham Statement, October 20, 1942, The Atlanta Statement, April 8, 1943, The Richmond Statement, June 16, 1943*. Atlanta: Commission on Interracial Cooperation, [1943].

"Communists Champion Negro." *Crusader* 4 (Aug. 1921): 1212.

"The Congress." *Time* (Jan. 28, 1946): 22.

"Congress, the Lusk Committee and the Radical Leaders." *Crusader* 2 (Nov. 1919): 505–06.

"Conscription Bill Gets Amendments on Jim Crow." *Crisis* 47 (Oct. 1940): 324.

Coon, Carleton S. "A Realist Looks at Ethiopia." *Atlantic Monthly* 156 (Sept. 1935): 510–15.

Couch, W. T. "Publisher's Introduction." In Logan, ed., *What the Negro Wants*, ix–xxiii.

"Cropper's Aged Mother." *Workers Defense Bulletin* (Dec. 1940): 1.

Crouch, Paul. *Testimony of Paul Crouch*. Hearings before the Committee on Un-American Activities, House of Representatives, 81st Congr., 1st Sess., May 6, 1949. Washington, DC: Government Printing Office, 1949.

Cummins, E. E. "Workers' Education in the United States." *Social Forces* 14 (May 1936): 507–605.

Cunard, Nancy. "Colour Bar." In Cunard, *Negro Anthology*, 342–45. New York, Frederick Ungar, 1970.

————. *Negro Anthology*. 1934. Reprint of 3d ed., New York: Negro University Press, 1969.

Dabney, Thomas L. "Brookwood Labor College." *Messenger* 8 (Dec. 1926): 377.

Dabney, Virginius. "Nearer and Nearer the Precipice." Condensed from *Atlantic Monthly* and reprinted in *Negro Digest* 1 (Feb. 1943): 47–51.

Damon, Anna. "Fresh Misdeeds of Terrorist Justice in Georgia. *International Press Correspondence* 16 (July 25, 1936): 915–16.

Daniels, Jonathan. "A Native at Large." *Nation* (Dec. 21, 1941): 635.

————. *White House Witness, 1942–1945: An Intimate Diary of the Years with F.D.R.* Garden City, NY: Doubleday, 1975.

Daniels, Josephus. *The Cabinet Diaries of Josephus Daniels, 1913–1921*, ed. David Cronon. Lincoln: University of Nebraska Press, 1963.

Darcy, Sam. "Fight on Lynching Moves Forward." *LD* 1 (Dec. 1930): 251.

Darrow, Clarence. "Scottsboro." *Crisis* 39 (March 1932): 81.

Davenport, Walter. "The Fuehrer of Sugar Creek." *Collier's* 108 (Dec. 6, 1941): 17, 71–73.

Davis, Ben. *Communist Councilman from Harlem: Autobiographical Notes Written in a Federal Penitentiary*. New York: International, 1969.

————. "The Negro People in the Elections." *Communist* 15 (Oct. 1936): 975–87.

————. "Summary for Angelo Herndon Defendant." In Angelo Herndon, *Let Me Live*, 351–54. 1937. Reprint, New York: Arno Press and the *New York Times*, 1969.

———. "Why I Am a Communist." *Phylon* 8 (Second Quarter 1947): 105–16.

Davis, Helen. "The Rise and Fall of George Padmore as a Revolutionary Fighter." *Negro Worker* 4 (Aug. 1934): 15–17, 21.

Davis, John P. "Problems of the Negro under the New Deal." *JNE* 5 (Jan. 1936): 3–12.

"Defending Democracy." *Crisis* 46 (Oct. 1939): 305.

"The Defense Job Front." *Crisis* 48 (Oct. 1941): 327.

Degras, Jane, ed. *The Communist International: 1919–1943, Documents.* 3 vols. London: Cass, 1971.

"Depression Emphasizes Race Discrimination." *Labor Age* 19 (Dec. 1930): 2–3.

Dillard, J. H. "Progress of Education and Race Relations in the South." In *Twenty Year Report of the Phelps-Stokes Fund, 1911–1931*, 52–54.

Dimitrov, George. "The Future Is the Workers." In *Reports of the 7th Congress Communist International*, 3–12. London: Modern Books, [1935].

———. "The Tasks of the Working Class in the War." In *The Communist International, 1919–1943, Documents*, vol. 3, *1929–1943*, ed. Jane Degras, 448–59. Originally published in *World News and Views*, Nov. 11, 1939.

"Discrimination in the Draft." *Crisis* 48 (Jan. 1941): 7.

Dos Passos, John. "Gastonia." *LD* 4 (Aug. 1929): 162.

Douglas, Paul H. "The American Occupation of Haiti I." *Political Science Quarterly* 42 (June 1927): 228–58.

———. "The American Occupation of Haiti II." *Political Science Quarterly* 42 (Sept. 1927): 368–96.

Drew, Allison, ed. *South Africa's Radical Tradition: A Documentary History.* 2 vols. Cape Town: Buchu Books, 1996–97.

Du Bois, W. E. B. *The Autobiography of W. E. B. Du Bois: A Soliloquy on Viewing My Life from the Last Decade of Its First Century.* New York: International, 1968.

———. "Chronicle of Race Relations." *Phylon* 2 (Fourth Quarter 1941): 404.

———. *Darkwater: Voices from within the Veil.* New York: Harcourt, Brace and Howe, 1920.

———. "Gandhi and the American Negroes." In *W. E. B. Du Bois: A Reader*, ed. David Levering Lewis, 90–92. New York: Henry Holt.

———. "Haiti." Reprinted in D. L. Lewis, ed., *W. E. B. Du Bois: A Reader*, 466.

———. "Inter-Racial Implications of the Ethiopian Crisis: A Negro View." *Foreign Affairs* 14 (Oct. 1935): 82–92.

———. "My Evolving Program for Negro Freedom." In Logan, ed., *What the Negro Wants*, 31–70.

———. "Postscript." *Crisis* 40 (May 1933): 117.

———. "Postscript. The Negro and Communism." *Crisis* 38 (Sept. 1931): 313–20.

———. "Propaganda and World War." Reprinted in D. L. Lewis, ed., *W. E. B. Du Bois: A Reader*, 397.

———. "Russia, 1926." *Crisis* 33 (Nov. 1926): 8.

———. "Social Planning for the Negro, Past and Present." *JNE* 5 (Jan. 1936): 110–25.

———. "We Return Fighting." *Crisis* (May 1919): 14.

Dunne, William F. "Gastonia—The Center of the Class Struggle in the New South." *Communist* 8 (July 1929): 375–80.

————. *Gastonia: Citadel of the Class Struggle in the New South.* New York: Workers Library, 1929.

————. "The N.A.A.C.P. Takes a Step Backward." *Workers Monthly* 5 (Aug. 1926): 460–61.

————. "Negroes in American Industry." *Workers Monthly* 4 (March 1925): 206–08, 236.

Durr, Virginia Foster. *Outside the Magic Circle: The Autobiography of Virginia Foster Durr,* ed. Hollinger F. Barnard. University: University of Alabama Press, 1985.

Edgar, Robert R., ed. *An African American in South Africa: The Travel Notes of Ralph J. Bunche, 28 September 1937–1 January 1938.* Athens: Ohio University Press, 1992.

"Editorial." *Christian Century* 62 (Feb. 20, 1946): 227–28.

"Editorial." *Opportunity* 3 (Dec. 1925): 354.

"Editorial." *Southern Textile Bulletin* (Nov. 26, 1931): 11.

"Editorial." *Southern Textile Bulletin* (Dec. 3, 1931): 19.

"Editorial Comment on 'The Negro Question.' " *Communist International* 8 (Feb. 1925): 53–54.

"Editorials." *Messenger* 1 (Jan. 1918): 7.

"Editorials." *Opportunity* 13 (Aug. 1935): 230.

Edmonds, Randolph. "Some Reflections on the Negro in America Drama." *Opportunity* 8 (Oct. 1930): 303–05.

Embree, Edwin R. *Brown Americans: The Story of a Tenth of the Nation,* 2d ed. New York: Viking Press, 1943.

————. *Julius Rosenwald Fund: Review for the Two-Year Period, 1942–1944.* Chicago: Rosenwald Fund, 1943.

Engdahl, J. Louis. "Scottsboro Campaign in England." *Negro Worker* 2 (Aug. 1932): 18–20.

————. "Storm over the U.S." *LD* 5 (June 1930): 115–18.

England, E. *Angelo Herndon.* New York: Repertory Dept., New Theatre League, n.d.

The Evans and Worley Directory of the City of Dallas. Dallas: Evans and Worley, 1896–97.

Eyes on the Prize: America's Civil Rights Years, 1954–1965. Alexandria, VA: Blackside Productions and PBS Video, 1986–1987.

"Fascism." *Opportunity* 14 (June 1936): 165.

"Fascist Terror against Negroes in Germany." *Negro Worker* (Apr.–May 1933): 1–5.

"Federated Farmer-Labor Party." *Messenger* 5 (Aug. 1923): 782 (bound vol.).

Fifth Congress of the Communist International: Abridged Report of Meetings Held at Moscow, June 17–July 8, 1924. London: Communist Party of Great Britain, 1924.

Fish, Hamilton, Jr. "The Menace of Communism." *AAAPSS* 156 (July 1931): 41–61.

Fisher, Isaac. "The Negro—An Untapped Resource in American Life." In *Educational and Racial Adjustment: Report of the Peabody Conference on Dual Education in the South,* 65. Atlanta: Executive Committee of the Conference, [1931].

Fitch, John A. Introduction to *The Great Steel Strike and Its Lessons,* by William Z. Foster. New York: B. W. Huebsch, 1920.

Fonville, W. F. "The South as I Saw It." *A.M.E. Zion Church Quarterly* 4 (July 1894): 419–58.

Ford, James W. "Building the National Negro Congress Movement." *Communist* (June 1936): 552–61.

———. "The Communists' Way out for the Negro." *JNE* 5 (Jan. 1936): 88–99.

———. "The National Negro Congress." *Communist* (Apr. 1936): 316–26.

———. *The Negro and the Democratic Front.* New York: International, 1938.

———. "Political Highlights of the National Negro Congress." *Communist* (May 1936): 437–64.

———. "Racial Question in Soviet Russia." In Foner and Allen, eds. *American Communism and Black Americans: A Documentary History, 1919–1929,* 95–97.

Foreman, Clark. "The Decade of Hope." In *The Negro in Depression and War: Prelude to Revolution, 1930–1945,* ed. Bernard Sternsher, 150–65. Chicago: Quadrangle Books, 1969.

Fort-Whiteman, Lovett. "Garvey's Leadership Imperils Usefulness of U.N.I.A." *Negro Champion,* June 1926.

———. [James Jackson, pseud.]. "The Negro in America." *Communist International* 8 (Feb. 1925): 50–52.

———. "The Nemesis." *Messenger* 1 (Nov. 1917): 29–30.

———. Untitled. *Messenger* 1 (Nov. 1917): 29–30.

———. "Wild Flowers." *Messenger* 5 (Feb. 1923): 603–07.

Foster, William Z. *From Bryan to Stalin.* New York: International, 1937.

———. *The Negro People in American History.* New York: International, 1954.

———. *Pages from a Worker's Life.* 1939. Reprint, New York: International, 1970.

———. "Russia in 1924." *Labor Herald* 3 (July 1924): 138.

———. *Your Questions Answered.* New York: Workers Library, 1939.

Franklin, Francis. "The Cultural Heritage of the Negro People." *Communist* 18 (June 1939): 570–71.

Fry, Charles Luther. "The Negro in the United States—A Statistical Statement," 26–35.

"Funds Needed at Once." *Workers Defense Bulletin* (Nov. 1940): 1.

Garfinkel, Harold. "Color Trouble." *Opportunity* 18 (May 1940): 144–52.

———. "Color Trouble." In *Best Short Stories of 1941,* ed. Edward J. O'Brien, 97–119. New York: Houghton Mifflin, 1941.

General Catalogue of the Officers and Students of Shaw University. Raleigh, NC: Edwards, Broughton, 1882.

"Georgia Students 'Burn' Their Governor in Protest of His Academic Meddling." *Life* (Oct. 27, 1941): 43–45.

Gitlow, Benjamin. *I Confess: The Truth about American Communism.* New York: E. P. Dutton, 1939.

———. *The Whole of Their Lives: Communism in America—A Personal History and Intimate Portrayal of Its Leaders.* New York: Charles Scribner's Sons, 1948.

"Giving Daniels the Lie." *Crusader* 3 (Nov. 1920): 10.

Graves, John Temple. *The Fighting South.* New York: G. P. Putnam's Sons, 1943.

———. "Should Negroes Accept Segregation in the South? Yes." *Negro Digest* 3 (March 1945): 31–42.

———. "The Solid South Is Cracking." *American Mercury* 56 (Apr. 1943): 402.

"Green Pastures," *Time* (March 4, 1935): 35–37.

Green, Paul. *Hymn to the Rising Sun: A Play in One Act.* London: Samuel French, 1936.

———. *In Abraham's Bosom.* London: G. Allen and Unwin, 1929.

Green, William. "Our Negro Worker." *Messenger* 7 (Sept. 1925): 332.

Gruening, Ernest. "Haiti under American Occupation." *Century* 103 (Apr. 1922): 836–45.

Habe, Hans. "Nazi Plan for Negroes." *Nation* 152 (March 1, 1941): 232–35.

"Haiti." *Crisis* 32 (July 1926): 125–27.

"Haiti." *Messenger* 4 (March 1922): 367.

"Haiti Is America's India." *Messenger* 4 (June 1922): 418.

"Haiti: What We Are Really Doing There." *Crisis* 21 (July 1926): 125–27.

"The Haitian Memorial." *Messenger* 3 (July 1921): 209.

Hall, Otto. "Gastonia and the Negro." *LD* 4 (Aug. 1929): 153.

———. "Note." *Communist* 8 (July 1929): 391–94.

Hall, Rob. "New Forces in the South." *Communist* 19 (Aug. 8, 1940): 690–706.

"The Hampton Strike." *Crisis* 34 (Dec. 1927): 345–46.

Hancock, Gordon B. "Race Relations in the United States: A Summary." In Logan, ed., *What the Negro Wants,* 217–47.

"The Hand of Hitler." *Opportunity* 13 (March 1935): 71.

Hankins, Frank H. *The Racial Basis of Civilization: A Critique of the Nordic Doctrine.* New York: Knopf, 1926.

Hard, William. *Raymond Robins' Own Story.* New York: Harper, 1920.

"Harding at Birmingham." *Messenger* 3 (Dec. 1921): 1.

Harris, Abram L. "Lenin Casts His Shadow upon Africa." *Crisis* 31 (Apr. 1926): 272–75.

———. "Negro Labor's Quarrel with White Workingmen." *Current History* 24 (Sept. 1926): 903–08.

———. "The Negro Problem as Viewed by Negro Leaders." *Current History* 18 (June 1923): 410–18.

Harris, Abram L., and Sterling D. Spero. *The Black Worker: The Negro and the Labor Movement.* New York: Atheneum, 1974.

"Has the Negro Gone Bolshevik? *World Outlook* 5 (Oct. 1919): 12–13.

Hathaway, Clarence A. "An Examination of Our Failure to Organize the Unemployed." *Communist* 9 (Sept. 1930): 786–94.

———. "The Struggle for the United Front." *Communist* 14 (June 1935): 510–17.

Haynes, George Edmund. "The Harmon Awards in 1926." *Crisis* 33 (Jan. 1927): 156–57.

———. "Negroes and the Ethiopian Crisis." *Christian Century* 52 (Nov. 20, 1935): 1485–86.

Haywood, Harry. "Against Bourgeois-Liberal Distortions of Leninism on the Negro Question in the United States." *Communist* 9 (Aug. 1930): 694–712.

———. *Black Bolshevik: Autobiography of an Afro-American Communist.* Chicago: Liberator Press, 1978.

———. "Crisis of the Jim-Crow Nationalism of the Negro Bourgeoisie." *Communist* 10 (Apr. 1931): 330–38.

———. *Negro Liberation.* New York: International, 1948.

———. "The Road to Negro Liberation." In Foner and Shapiro, eds., *American Communism and Black Americans: A Documentary History, 1930–1934*, 125–46.

———. "The Theoretical Defenders of White Chauvinism in the Labor Movement." *Communist* 10 (June 1931): 497–508.

Heller, A. A. "U.S.S.R., 1921–1925." Pt. 1. *Workers Monthly* 5 (Nov. 1925): 29–31.

———. "U.S.S.R., 1921–1925." Pt. 2. *Workers Monthly* 5 (Dec. 1925): 107–09.

Herndon, Angelo. "In Memory of Harry Simms." *LD* 10 (Feb. 1934): 17.

———. *Let Me Live.* 1937. Reprint, New York: Arno Press and the *New York Times*, 1969.

———. "You Cannot Kill the Working Class." New York: International Labor Defense and the League of Struggle for Negro Rights, n.d.

"Herndon's Conviction Set Aside." *Christian Century* 54 (May 5, 1937): 572.

Hertzog, J. B. M. "Revolution in South Africa." *Crisis* 31 (March 1926): 246–48.

High, Stanley. "Star-Spangled Fascists." In *The Strenuous Decade: A Social and Intellectual Record of the Nineteen-Thirties*, ed. Daniel Aaron and Robert Bendiner, 339–54. Garden City, NY: Doubleday, 1970. Originally published in *Saturday Evening Post* 211 (May 27, 1939).

Hill, Robert A., ed. *Crusader: A Facsimile of the Periodical.* 3 vols. New York: Garland, 1987.

Hill, T. Arnold. "Communism." *Opportunity* 8 (Sept. 1930): 278.

Hill's Charlotte City Directory, vols. 1–9. Richmond, VA: Hill Directory Company, 1932–40.

"Hitler in Georgia." *America* 65 (Aug. 2, 1941): 462.

House Committee on Un-American Activities. *Report on Southern Conference for Human Welfare.* Washington, DC: Government Printing Office, 1947.

———. *Report on Civil Rights Congress as a Communist Front Organization.* Washington, DC: Government Printing Office, 1947.

"How Can Intelligent Southerners Best Help Their South?" *North Georgia Review* 6 (Winter 1941): 18.

Hughes, Langston. "Ballad of Roosevelt." In *The Collected Poems of Langston Hughes*, ed. Arnold Rampersad, with associate ed., David Roessel, 178–79. New York: Vintage Classics, 1994.

———. *The Big Sea.* New York: Knopf, 1940.

———. "Christ in Alabama." *Contempo* (Dec. 1, 1931): 1.

———. *The Collected Poems of Langston Hughes,* ed. Arnold Rampersad, with associate ed., David Roessel. New York: Vintage Classics, 1994.

———. "Sunset in Dixie." In Hughes, *Good Morning Revolution: Uncollected Social Protest Writings by Langston Hughes,* ed. Faith Berry, 15. New York: Lawrence Hill, 1973. Originally published in *Crisis* 48 (Sept. 1941).

———. "Going South in Russia." *Crisis* 41 (June 1934): 162–63.

———. *I Wonder as I Wander: An Autobiographical Journey.* New York: Rinehart, 1956.

———. *Jim Crow's Last Stand.* New York: Negro Publication Society of America, 1943.

———. "Justice." In *New Masses* 7 (Aug. 1931); 15.

———. "Moscow and Me." In *Good Morning Revolution: Uncollected Social Protest Writings by Langston Hughes,* ed. Faith Berry, 67. Westport, CT: Lawrence Hill, 1973.

————. "My America." In Logan, ed., *What the Negro Wants*, 299–307.

————. "Southern Gentlemen, White Prostitutes, Mill-Owners, and Negroes." *Contempo* (Dec. 1, 1931): 1.

————. *The Ways of White Folks*. New York: Knopf, 1934.

————. "White Shadows in a Black Land." *Crisis* 3 (Apr. 1932): 157.

Hughes, Langston, and Zora Neale Hurston. *Mule Bone: A Comedy of Negro Life*, ed. George Houston Bass and Henry Louis Gates, Jr. New York: Harper Perennial, 1991.

Huiswoud, Otto E. "The October Plenum." In Foner and Allen, eds., *American Communism and Black Americans: A Documentary History, 1919–1929*, 219–21.

————. "Report to the Communist Party Convention." In Foner and Allen, eds., *American Communism and Black Americans: A Documentary History, 1919–1929*, 203–08.

————. "World Aspects of the Negro Question." *Communist* 9 (Feb. 1930): 132–47.

Hutchinson, Glenn. "Jim Crow Challenged in Southern Universities." *Crisis* 46 (Apr. 1939): 103.

"India Speaks." *Crisis* 26 (June 1923): 84.

International Press. *International Press Correspondence*. 18 vols. Berlin: International Press Correspondence, Central Bureau, 1921–38.

"Interview with Dr. Max Yergan: Africa: Next Goal of Communists." *U.S. News & World Report* (May 1, 1953): 52–63.

Irwin, Theodore. "The Klan Kicks Up Again." *American Mercury* 50 (Aug. 1940): 470–76.

Israel, Edward L. "Jew Hatred among Negroes." *Crisis* 43 (Feb. 1936): 39.

"Italy and Abyssinia." *Crisis* 32 (June 1926): 62–66.

"Jacques Romain [*sic*]." *Opportunity* 13 (May 1935): 134–35.

"Japan on American Lynching." *Messenger* 2 (Aug. 1921): 225 (bound vol.).

Jefferson, Alexander, with Lewis H. Carlson. *Red Tail Captured, Red Tail Free: The Memoirs of a Tuskegee Airman and POW*. New York: Fordham University Press, 2005.

Johnpoll, Bernard K., ed. *A Documentary History of the Communist Party of the United States*: vol. 1, *Gestation and Birth, 1918–1928*. Westport, CT: Greenwood Press, 1994.

————. *A Documentary History of the Communist Party of the United States*: vol. 2, *Toil and Trouble, 1928–1933*. Westport, CT: Greenwood Press, 1994.

Johnson, Charles S. *The Negro in American Civilization: A Study of Negro Life and Race Relations in Light of Social Research*. New York: Holt, 1930.

————. "The New Frontier of Negro Labor." *Opportunity* 10 (June 1932): 168–72.

————. "Race Relations and Social Change." In *Race Relations and the Race Problem*, ed. Edgar T. Thompson, 271–304. Durham, NC: Duke University Press, 1939.

————. Review of *A World View of Race*, by Ralph Bunche. *JNE* 7 (Jan. 1938): 61–62.

————. *The Shadow of the Plantation*. Chicago: University of Chicago Press, 1934.

————. "The Southern Welfare Conference: More Southerners Discover the South." *Crisis* 46 (Jan. 1939): 14–15.

Johnson, Charles S., Edwin E. Embree, and W. W. Alexander. *The Collapse of Cotton*

Tenancy: Summary of Field Studies and Statistical Surveys, 1933–1935. Chapel Hill: University of North Carolina Press, 1935.

Johnson, Guy B., and Guion G. Johnson. *Research in Service to Society: The First Fifty Years of the Institute for Research in Social Science at the University of North Carolina.* Chapel Hill: University of North Carolina Press, 1980.

Johnson, James Weldon. *Along This Way: The Autobiography of James Weldon Johnson.* New York: Da Capo, 2000.

———. *The Autobiography of an Ex-Colored Man.* Boston: Sherman, French, 1912.

———. *Black Manhattan.* 1930. Reprint, New York: Arno Press, 1968.

———. *Negro Americans, What Now?* New York: Viking, 1934.

———. "Self-Determining Haiti." *Nation* 111 (Aug. 28, 1920; Sept. 4, 1920; Sept. 11, 1920; Sept. 25, 1920).

Johnson, Tom. *The Reds in Dixie: Who Are the Communists and What Do They Fight For in the South?* New York: Workers Library, 1935.

"Joint Meeting of the L.S.I. and I.F.T.U." *International Press Correspondence* 11 (Jan. 25, 1936): 145–46.

Jones, Thomas Jesse. "Interracial Cooperation." In *Twenty Year Report of the Phelps-Stokes Fund, 1911–1931,* 55–60.

"Judge Hastie Quits the Army." Condensed from *Time. Negro Digest* 1 (March 1943): back cover.

Kabane, M. L. "The All African Convention." *South African Outlook* 66 (Aug. 1, 1936): 187–88.

Kadalie, Clements. "British Color-Bar Bill Provokes Workers' Rebellion among South African Negroes." *Negro Champion* (June 1926).

Kamp, Joseph P. *The Fifth Column in the South.* New Haven, CT: Constitutional Educational League, 1940.

Kempton, Murray. *Part of Our Time: Some Ruins and Monuments of the Thirties.* New York: Simon and Schuster, 1955.

Kennedy, Stetson. *Southern Exposure.* Garden City, NY: Doubleday, 1946.

Kester, Howard. *Revolt among the Sharecroppers.* 1936. Reprint, Knoxville: University of Tennessee Press, 1997.

Khanga, Yelena. *Soul to Soul: A Black Russian Jewish Woman's Search for Her Roots.* New York: Norton, 1992.

Kirchwey, Freda. "Communists and Democracy." *Nation* 149 (Oct. 14, 1939): 399–401.

———. "Red Totalitarianism." *Nation* (May 27, 1939): 605–06.

Klehr, Harvey, John Earl Haynes, and Fridrikh Igorevich Firsov. *The Secret World of American Communism.* Russian documents trans. Timothy D. Sergay. New Haven: Yale University Press, 1995.

Klehr, Harvey, John Earl Haynes, and Kyrill Mikhailovich Anderson. *The Soviet World of American Communism.* New Haven: Yale University Press, 1998.

Kloss, Heinz. *Das Völksgruppenrecht in den Vereinigten Staaten von Amerika* [Essen]: Essener Verlagsanstatt, 1940–[1942]

Knickerbocker, William S. "The Dilemma of the Fugitives." *Contempo* (May 25, 1932): 1.

Konvitz, Milton R. "A Nation within a Nation: The Negro and the Supreme Court." *American Scholar* 2 (Winter 1941–42): 69–78.

Lautier, Louis. "Jim Crow in the Nation's Capital." *Crisis* 47 (Apr. 1940): 107.

Lavine, Harold. *Fifth Column in America*. Garden City, NY: Doubleday, Doran, 1940.

Lecache, Bernard. Letter to the Editor. *Crisis* 41 (Dec. 1934): 375.

Lee, Wallace. "Is Civil Disobedience Practical to Win Full Rights for Negroes?" *Negro Digest* 1 (March 1943): 25.

———. "Will Our War for Democracy Overseas Aid the Negro's Fight for Democracy at Home?" *Negro Digest* 1 (Dec. 1942): 68–69.

Lenin, Vladimir Ilyich. *V. I. Lenin: Collected Works*. 45 vols. Moscow: Progress, 1963–70.

"Lily White Democracy." *Crisis* 46 (Feb. 1939): 49.

Lloyd, Jessie. *Gastonia: A Graphic Chapter in Southern Organization*. New York: National Executive Committee of the Conference for Progressive Labor Action, 1930.

———. "Hoodlum Law in Gastonia." *Labor Age* 18 (Oct. 1929): 12–13.

Locke, Alain, ed. *The New Negro: An Interpretation*. New York: Boni, 1925.

Locke, Alain, and Howard Odum. "Race Relations." In *The Negro in American Civilization*, ed. Charles S. Johnson, 481–83. New York: Holt, 1930.

Logan, Rayford W., ed. *The Attitude of the Southern White Press toward Negro Suffrage, 1932–1940*. Washington, DC: Foundation, 1940.

———. "The Negro Wants First-Class Citizenship." In Logan, ed., *What the Negro Wants*, 1–30.

———, ed. *What the Negro Wants*. Chapel Hill: University of North Carolina Press, [1944].

Loram, C. T. "Native Progress and Improvement in Race Relations in South Africa." In *Twenty Year Report of the Phelps-Stokes Fund, 1911–1931*, 84–92.

Lovestone, Jay. "The Great Negro Migration." *Workers Monthly* 5 (Feb. 1926): 182–84.

———. "Some Issues in the Party Discussion." *Communist* 8 (Jan.–Feb. 1929): 72–74.

"Lovett Fort Whiteman." *Messenger* 2 (Jan. 1918): 22.

Lowie, Robert H. *Are We Civilized? Human Culture in Perspective*. New York: Harcourt, Brace, 1929.

Lyons, Eugene. "Communist False Fronts." *Scribner's Magazine* 99 (Jan. 1936): 18–23.

Mandela, Nelson. "I Am Prepared to Die." www.historyplace.com/index.

Mangum, Charles S., Jr. *The Legal Status of the Negro*. Chapel Hill: University of North Carolina Press, 1940.

Marshall, Thurgood. "The Gestapo in Detroit." *Crisis* 50 (Aug. 1943): 232.

Martin, Louis E. "Fifth Column among Negroes." *Opportunity* 20 (Dec. 1942): 358–60.

———. "The National Negro Congress." *Challenge* 1 (June 1936): 30–34.

———. "The Truth about Sojourner Truth." *Crisis* 49 (Apr. 1942): 112–13.

Mason, Lucy Randolph. *To Win These Rights: A Personal Story of the CIO in the South*. New York: Harper and Brothers, 1952.

Matthews, Ralph. "The Negro Theatre—A Dodo Bird." In Cunard, *Negro Anthology*, 312. New York: Negro Universities Press, 1934.

McKay, Claude. *A Long Way from Home*. 1937. Reprint, London: Pluto, 1985.

———. "Soviet Russia and the Negro." *Crisis* 27 (Dec. 1923): 61–65.

———. "Soviet Russia and the Negro (concluded)." *Crisis* 27 (Jan. 1924): 114.

"McNutt and the FEPC." *Crisis* 49 (Oct. 1942): 325.

Miller, Kelly. "The Negro as a Workingman." *American Mercury* 6 (Nov. 1925): 310–13.

———. *The Negro Sanhedrin: A Call to Conference.* Washington, DC: n.p., 1923.

———. "Race Prejudice in Germany and America." *Opportunity* 14 (Apr. 1936): 102–05.

———. "Radicalism and the Negro." *Competitor* 1 (March 1920): 33–37.

———. "Should Black Turn Red?" Opportunity 11 (Nov. 1933): 328–32, 350.

Miller, Loren. "How 'Left' Is the NAACP?" *New Masses* 16 (July 16, 1935): 12–13.

Miller, R. C. *Testimony of R. C. Miller (Colored), Investigation of Communist Propaganda,* Hearing before a Special Committee to Investigate Communist Activities in the United States, H. Res. 220. Washington, DC: Government Printing Office [1932].

Minor, Robert. "The Black Ten Millions." *Liberator* 7 (March 1924): 15–17.

———. "The First Negro Workers' Congress." *Workers Monthly* 5 (Dec. 1925): 70.

———. "How I Became a Rebel." *Labor Herald* 5 (July 1922): 25–26.

———. "The Negro Finds His Place—and a Sword." *Liberator* 7 (Aug. 1924): 20–23.

———. "The Negro and His Judases." *Communist* 10 (July 1931): 632–39.

Mitchell, H. L. *Mean Things Happening in This Land: The Life and Times of H. L. Mitchell, Co-Founder of the Southern Tenant Farmers Union.* Montclair, NJ: Allanheld, Osmun, 1979.

"Mob Fury and Race Hatred as a National Danger." *Literary Digest* 69 (June 18, 1921): 7–9.

Moon, Henry Lee. "Scottsboro and Its Implications." *Labor Age* 20 (July 1931): 23–24.

———. "Woman under the Soviets." *Crisis* 41 (Apr. 1934): 109.

Moorland, Jesse Edward. "The Young Men's Christian Association and the War." *Crisis* 15 (Dec. 1917): 65–68.

Morrison and Fourmy's General Directory of the City of Dallas, vols. 1888–1889, 1891–1892, 1893–1894, 1894–1895. Galveston, TX: Morrison and Fourmy, 1888–95.

Murray, Pauli. "And the Riots Came." *Call* (Aug. 13, 1943): 1.

———. "A Blueprint for First Class Citizenship." *Crisis* 51 (Nov. 1944): 358–59.

———. *Dark Testament and Other Poems.* [Norwalk, CT]: Silvermine, [1970].

———. "The Historical Development of Race Laws in the United States." *JNE* 22 (Winter 1953): 4–15.

———. "Inquietude." *Challenge* 1 (May 1935): 43.

———. "Mr. Roosevelt Regrets." *Crisis* 50 (Aug. 1943): 252.

———. "Negro Youth's Dilemma." *Threshold* 2 (Apr. 1942): 8–11.

———. "Negroes Are Fed Up." *Common Sense* 12 (Aug. 1943): 274–76.

———. *Proud Shoes: The Story of an American Family.* 1956. Reprint, New York: Harper and Row, 1978.

———. "Song." *Challenge* 1 (March 1934): 15.

———. *Song in a Weary Throat: An American Pilgrimage.* New York: Harper & Row, 1987.

———. "Song of the Highway." In Cunard, *Negro Anthology,* 69–70. New York: Frederick Ungar, 1970.

———. "Three Thousand Miles on a Dime in Ten Days." In Cunard, *Negro Anthology,* 67–70. New York: Frederick Ungar, 1970.

————, and Henry Babcock. "An Alternative Weapon." *South Today* 7 (Autumn/Winter 1942–43): 53–57.

————, and Murray Kempton. " 'All for Mr. Davis': The Story of Sharecropper Odell Waller." In *The Rights of Man Are Worth Defending.* New York: League for Adult Education, 1942.

Muzumdar, Haridas T. *Gandhi versus the Empire.* New York: Universal, 1932.

————. *India's Non-Violent Revolution.* New York: India Today and Tomorrow Series, 1930.

Myers, E. Pauline. *The March on Washington Movement Mobilizes a Gigantic Crusade for Freedom.* [Washington, DC]: March on Washington Movement, n.d.

Myers, James. "Field Notes Textile Strikes in the South." Typescript in the NCC.

Nasanov, N. "Against Liberalism in the American Negro Question." *Communist* 9 (Apr. 1930): 296–308.

"The National Conference on the Economic Crisis and the Negro." *JNE* 5 (Jan. 1936): 1–2.

"National Negro Congress in U.S.A." *Negro Worker* 6 (March 1936): 19.

"National Platform of the Workers (Communist) Party, 1928." In Foner and Allen, eds. *American Communism and Black Americans: A Documentary History, 1919–1929,* 146.

"Nazis, Negroes, Jews and Catholics." *Crisis* 42 (Sept. 1935): 273.

"Negro in National Defense." *Crisis* 48 (July 1941): back cover.

"Negro Women Most Militant Fighters." *Party Organizer* 5 (Feb. 1932): 29.

Nelson, Frederic. "North Carolina Justice." *New Republic* 60 (Nov. 6, 1929): 314–16.

Nerouy, Kantiba. "Tutankh-Amen and Ras Tafari." *Crisis* 29 (Dec. 1924): 64–68.

Newton, Herbert. "The National Negro Congress (U.S.A.)." *Negro Worker* 6 (May–June 1936): 22–27.

Nixon, Herman C. *Forty Acres and Steel Mules.* Chapel Hill: University of North Carolina Press, 1938.

"No Negro Draft Board Members in Many States." *Crisis* 48 (Jan. 1941): 7.

North, Joseph. "Angelo Herndon Back in Atlanta." *New Masses* (Nov. 5, 1935): 15–16.

————. "Chain Gang Governor." *New Masses* (Nov. 12, 1935): 9.

"Now Is the Time Not to Be Silent." *Crisis* 49 (Jan. 1942): 7.

Ntantala, Phyllis. *Life's Mosaic: The Autobiography of Phyllis Ntantala.* Cape Town: David Phillip; Berkeley: University of California Press, 1993.

Odum, Howard W. "Crisis in the Making." *Crisis* 50 (Dec. 1943): 360.

————. "The Epic of Brown America." *Yale Review* 21 (Winter 1932): 419–21.

————. "Lynchings, Fears, and Folkways." *Nation* 133 (Dec. 30, 1931): 719–20.

————. "Negro Children in the Public Schools of Philadelphia." *AAAPSS* 49 (Sept. 1913): 186–208.

————. *Race and Rumors of Race.* Chapel Hill: University of North Carolina Press, 1944.

————. "Social Change in the South." *Journal of Politics* 10 (May 1948): 242–58.

————. *Southern Regions of the United States.* Chapel Hill: University of North Carolina Press, 1936.

————. "What Is the Answer? A Leading Sociologist Has a Plan." *Carolina Magazine* 68 (Feb. 1939): 5–8.

O'Dunne, Eugene. *Report of the Maryland Penitentiary Penal Commission.* Baltimore: Maryland Penitentiary Penal Commission, 1913.

Office of War Information. *Negroes and War.* Washington, DC: Office of War Information, [1944].

O'Flaherty, T. J. "The I.L.D. and Its Mission." *Workers Monthly* 5 (March 1926): 206.

Oldham, J. H. "Developments in the Relations between White and Black in Africa." In *Twenty Year Report of the Phelps-Stokes Fund, 1911–1931*, 76–83.

"Olympians All." *Opportunity* 14 (Aug. 1936): 228.

"Olympic Games, 1936." *Opportunity* 13 (Dec. 1935), 359.

"An Onlooker Writes Us." *Crisis* 34 (Dec. 1927): 345.

Ottley, Roi. *"New World A-Coming": Inside Black America.* New York: Literary Classics, 1943.

Ovington, Mary White. "Max Yergan." In *Portraits in Color*, ed. Mary White Ovington. New York: Viking Press, 1927.

———. "Students Eager for Inter-Racial Forums." *Crisis* 41 (June 1934): 181.

Owen, Chandler. "The South's Triumph!" *Messenger* 4 (Apr. 1922): 386.

Owens, John. "Strike Vignettes." *LD* 4 (Aug. 1929): 101.

Padmore, George. "The Second World War and the Darker Races." *Crisis* 46 (Nov. 1939): 327–28.

Page, Myra. *Gathering Storm: A Story of the Black Belt.* New York: International, 1932.

———. "Inter-Racial Relations among Southern Workers." *Communist* 9 (Feb. 1930): 154–64.

Park, Robert E. "The Bases of Race Prejudice." *AAAPSS* (Nov. 1928): 11–20.

———. "The Nature of Race Relations." In *Race Relations and the Race Problem*, ed. Edgar T. Thompson, 3–45. Durham, NC: Duke University Press, 1939.

Patterson, Haywood, and Earl Conrad. *Scottsboro Boy.* Garden City, NY: Doubleday, 1950.

Patterson, Louise Thompson. "Angelo Herndon Is Free!" *Negro Worker* (June 1937): 3.

———. "With Langston Hughes in the USSR." *Freedomways* 8 (Spring 1968): 152–58.

Patterson, William L. *The Man Who Cried Genocide: An Autobiography.* 1971. Reprint, New York: International. 1991.

———. "A National Negro Congress in America." *International Press Correspondence* (Feb. 1936): 194–95.

Pepper, John. *American Negro Problems.* New York: Workers Library, 1928.

———. "American Negro Problems." *Communist* 8 (Oct. 1929): 628–38.

Pickard, Walter. "The Burlington Dynamite Plot." New York: *LD*, n.d.

Pierce, David H. "Fascism and the Negro." *Crisis* 42 (Apr. 1935): 107.

"The Plot to Make Our Blacks Red." *Literary Digest* 87 (Nov. 21, 1925): 13–14.

Porter, Paul. "Communism Goes South: Gastonia Makes Mill Owners See Red." *New Leader* (June 1, 1929): 8.

Powell, Adam Clayton, Jr. *Marching Blacks.* 1945. Reprint, New York: Dial, 1973.

Powell, Adam Clayton, Sr. *Riots and Ruins.* New York: Richard R. Smith, 1945.

Preece, Harold. "Fascism and the Negro." *Crisis* 41 (Dec. 1934): 355–56.

President's Committee on Civil Rights. *To Secure These Rights: The Report of the President's Committee on Civil Rights.* New York: Simon and Schuster, 1947.

"President's Executive Order." *Crisis* 48 (Sept. 1941): 296.

"Programme of the African Blood Brotherhood." *Communist Review* 2 (Apr. 1922): 449–54.

Puro, H. "The Tasks of Our Party in Agrarian Work." *Communist* 10 (Feb. 1931): 147–52.

Rainey, Glenn W. "America's Relation to the War." *North Georgia Review* 5 (Winter 1940–41): 21.

Raleigh, N.C., Directory, 1909–1910. Richmond, VA: Hill Directory Company, 1910.

Raleigh, N.C., Directory, 1915–1916. Richmond, VA: Hill Directory Company, 1916.

Randolph, A. Philip. "The Case of the Pullman Porter." *Messenger* 7 (July 1925): 254–56.

———. Editorial. *Black Worker* 6 (June 1940): 4.

———. "The Herndon Case." *Black Worker* 1 (June 15, 1935): 4.

———. "Let the Negro Masses Speak." *Black Worker* 7 (March 1941): 4.

———. "March on Washington Movement Presents Program for the Negro." In Logan, ed., *What the Negro Wants*, 133–62.

———. "National Defense." *Black Worker* 6 (June 1940): 4.

———. "Odell Waller Must Not Die." *Black Worker* 7 (June 1942): 1.

———. "President Roosevelt's Statement on Racial Barriers." *Black Worker* 7 (June 1941): 4.

———. "Propaganda against Jews." *Black Worker* 4 (Aug. 1938): 4.

———. "Pullman Porters Need Own Union." *Messenger* 7 (Sept. 1925): 289–90.

———. "The Trade Union Movement and the Negro." *JNE* 5 (Jan. 1936): 54–58.

———. "War." *Black Worker* 5 (Sept. 1939): 4.

———. "Why I Would Not Stand for Re-Election for President of the National Negro Congress." *Black Worker* 6 (May 1940): 1.

"Randolph's Reply to Perry Howard." *Messenger* 7 (Sept. 1925): 350–52.

Raper, Arthur F. *Preface to Peasantry: A Tale of Two Black Belt Counties.* Chapel Hill: University of North Carolina Press, 1936.

Rauschning, Hermann. *The Voice of Destruction.* New York: G. P. Putnam's Sons, 1940.

Reddick, L. D. "What Hitler Says about the Negro." *Opportunity* 17 (Apr. 1939): 108–10.

Redding, Louis L. "Byrnes of South Carolina." *Crisis* 48 (Apr. 1941): 115.

Redpath, James. *Toussaint L'Ouverture: A Biography and Autobiography.* Boston: James Redpath, 1863.

"Refugees and Citizens." *Crisis* 45 (Sept. 1938): 301.

"A Reply to Congressman James F. Byrnes of South Carolina." *Messenger* 2 (Oct. 1919): 11–14.

Report on Southern Conference for Human Welfare. Washington, DC: Government Printing Office, 1947.

"Resolution on the Negro Question in the United States, Final Text, Confirmed by the Political Commission of the E.C.C.I." *Communist* 10 (Feb. 1931): 153–67.

"Resolved: That the terms of the Third International are inacceptable [*sic*] to the Revolutionary Socialists of the world," debate held in Star Casino, New York City, Jan. 16, 1921. New York: Academy Press, [1921].

"A Review of the Case of Fred E. Beal." New York: Non-Partisan Committee for the Defense of Fred Beal, [1938].

"The Revolution in South Africa." *Crisis* 31 (March 1926): 248.

Robeson, Eslanda Goode. *African Journey.* New York: John Day, 1945.

Robeson, Paul. *Here I Stand.* 1958. Reprint, Boston: Beacon, 1971.

Robinson, Robert, with Jonathan Slevin. *Black on Red: My 44 Years inside the Soviet Union.* Washington, DC: Acropolis Books, 1988.

Rogers, J. A. "The Negro's Reception in Europe." *Messenger* 9 (Nov. 1927): 320.

Rubinstein, M. "The Industrialization of the South and the Negro Program." *Communist* 9 (Feb. 1930): 148–53.

Sancton, Thomas. "Big Brass and Jim Crow." *Nation* (Oct. 2, 1948): 365–66.

———. "The Negro Press." *New Republic* 108 (Apr. 26, 1943): 557–60.

———. "Segregation: The Pattern of Failure." *Survey Graphic* 36 (Jan. 1947): 7–11.

———. "Something's Happened to the Negro." *New Republic* 108 (Feb. 8, 1943): 175–79.

———. "The South and the North: A Southern View." *American Scholar* 12 (Winter 1942–43): 105–17.

———. "A Southern View of the Race Question." *Negro Quarterly* 3 (Fall 1942): 197–206.

Saunders, Kenneth. "A Forward Move in Africa." *Southern Workman* 49 (Feb. 1920): 83–85.

Scales, Junius, and Richard Nickson. *Cause at Heart: A Former Communist Remembers.* Athens: University of Georgia Press, 1987.

Schuyler, George S. "Negroes Reject Communism." *American Mercury* 47 (June 1939): 176–81.

Scott, Anne Firor, ed. *Pauli Murray and Caroline Ware: Forty Years of Letters in Black and White.* Chapel Hill: University of North Carolina Press, 2006.

Scott, Emmett J. *Scott's Official History of the American Negro in the World War.* 1919. Reprint, New York: Arno Press, 1969.

"Scottsboro Campaign in Europe." *Negro Worker* 2 (June 1932): 9–11.

"Scottsboro Struggle and the Next Steps." *Communist* (June 1933): 570–82.

Seldes, George. *Facts and Fascism.* New York: In Fact, 1943.

Seligmann, Herbert J. "The Conquest of Haiti." *Nation* 111 (July 10, 1920): 35–36.

———. "The War for Common Humanity." *Crisis* 51 (March 1944): 73–75.

"Seven Negro Editors on Communism." *Crisis* 39 (Apr. 1932): 117–19.

Sgovio, Thomas. *Dear America! The Odyssey of an American Communist Youth Who Miraculously Survived the Harsh Labor Camps of Kolyma.* Kenmore, NY: Partners' Press, 1979.

"Should Congress Pass a Law Prohibiting Employment Discrimination?" *Congressional Record* 24 (June 1945): 163–92.

Simpson, Nancy W., ed. *The Heritage of Wilkes County,* vol. 2. North Wilkesboro, NC: Wilkes Genealogical Society and Hunter Publishing, Winston-Salem, NC, 1990.

Sinatra, Frank. "This Thing Called Prejudice." Condensed from *Magazine Digest.* In *Negro Digest* 3 (Sept. 1945): 11–12.

Smith, Homer. *Black Man in Red Russia: A Memoir.* Chicago: Johnson, 1964.

Smith, Lillian. "Winning the World with Democracy." *South Today* 7 (Spring 1942): 9.

Smith, Robert. "The Poll Tax-Enemy of Democracy." *Crisis* 46 (Apr. 1939): 106, 114.

Smith, Vern. "America's Black Legion." *International Press Correspondence* 16 (July 1936): 914–15.

"Sojourner Truth Homes." *Crisis* 49 (Apr. 1942): 111.

"South Africa." *International Worker's Review* 1 (Jan. 1931): 7–13.

"Southern Bourbons Ignorant." *Messenger* 3 (Aug. 1921): 1.

"Southern Whites Speak." *Crisis* 50 (May 1943): 136.

Special House Committee. *Investigation of Communist Propaganda.* U. S. Congressional Hearings V. 572, 1930–31. Washington, DC: Government Printing Office, 1931.

Stachel, J. "Organization Report to the Sixth Convention of the Communist Party, U.S.A." *Communist* 8 (Apr. 1929): 184.

———. "Organization Report to the Sixth Convention of the Communist Party of the U.S.A." *Communist* 8 (May 1929): 246.

Stalin, Joseph. *Marxism and the National Question: Selected Writings and Speeches.* New York: International, 1942.

"A Statement by the N.A.A.C.P. on the Scottsboro Cases." *Crisis* 39 (March 1932): 82–83.

Steuart, Bradley W., ed. *North Carolina 1870 Census Index*, vol. 3. Bountiful, UT: Precision Indexing, 1989.

Stoddard, Lothrop. "Men of Color Aroused." *Review of Reviews* 92 (Nov. 1935): 35–36.

———. *The Rising Tide of Color against White World-Supremacy.* New York: Scribner, 1920.

Stokes, Anson Phelps. "American Race Relations in War Time." *JNE* 14 (Fall 1945): 545.

———. *Report of Rev. Anson Phelps Stokes on Education, Native Welfare, and Race Relations in East and South Africa.* New York: Carnegie Corporation of New York, 1934.

Stone, I. F. "Swastika over the Senate." *Nation* (Feb. 9, 1946): 158–59.

Stone, Olive. "The Present Position of the Negro Farm Population: The Bottom Rung of the Farm Ladder." *JNE* 5 (Jan. 1936): 20–21.

Stoney, George. "Suffrage in the South, Part I: The Poll Tax." *Survey Graphic* 29 (Jan. 1, 1940): 5–9.

———. "Suffrage in the South, Part II: The One Party System." *Survey Graphic* 29 (March 1, 1940): 163–67.

Street, James H. *Look Away! A Dixie Notebook.* New York: Viking Press, 1936.

Taylor, Millicent. "Through the Editor's Window: *The Races of Mankind.*" *Christian Science Monitor*, Nov. 20, 1943.

Thomas, Norman. "Can America Go Fascist?" *Crisis* 41 (Jan. 1934): 10–11.

———. "The Socialists' Way out for the Negro." *JNE* 5 (Jan. 1936): 100–09.

Thompson, Charles. "The American Negro and the National Defense." *JNE* 9 (Oct. 1940): 547–52.

Thompson, Edgar T., ed. *Race Relations and the Race Problem.* Durham, NC: Duke University Press, 1939.

Thompson, Louise. "Southern Terror." *Crisis* 41 (Nov. 1934): 327–28.

———. "The Soviet Film." *Crisis* 40 (Feb. 1933): 37, 46.

Tippett, Tom. *When Southern Labor Stirs.* New York: Jonathan Cape, 1931.

"To All Who Are Interested in Interracial Peace." Washington, DC: Women's International League for Peace and Freedom, n.d. [1946].

"To Turn Negroes into 'Reds'!" *Literary Digest* 94 (July 30, 1927): 13.

Tobias, Channing H. "The Work of the Young Men's and Young Women's Christian Associations with Negro Youth." *AAAPSS* 140 (Nov. 1928): 283–86.

———. "Max Yergan." *Crisis* 40 (July 1933): 155.

"A Trade Union Programme of Action for Negro Workers." *Communist* 9 (Jan. 1930): 42–47.

"Trade Union Students in Moscow University." *Workers Monthly* 4 (Dec. 1924): 62.

"Trials and Tryouts." *Time* 28 (July 20, 1936): 50–54.

Tribble, Edwin. "Black Shirts in Georgia." *New Republic* 64 (Oct. 8, 1930): 204–06.

Trotter, Joe W., Jr., and Earl Lewis, eds. *African Americans in the Industrial Age: A Documentary History, 1915–1945.* Boston: Northeastern University Press, 1996.

"True Color: Stalin Forces ASU Out into the Open." *Mirror* (Jan. 2, 1940), at www.newdeal.feri.org/students/tc.htm.

Tucker, Robert C., ed. *The Lenin Anthology.* New York: Norton, 1975.

"Tulsa Riot." *Crusader* 4 (July 1921) [bound vol.]: 1173.

Turner, Grace, and Miles S. Philbeck, comp. "Wilkes County North Carolina Will Abstracts, 1777–1910." Typescript in the North Carolina Collection, Wilson Library, University of North Carolina.

Twenty Year Report of the Phelps-Stokes Fund, 1911–1931. New York: Phelps-Stokes Fund, 1932.

"Twenty Years for Free Speech!" New York: American Civil Liberties Union, May 1933.

"University of Missouri Case Won." *Crisis* 46 (Jan. 1939): 10.

Urrutia, Gustavo E. "Racial Prejudice in Cuba." In Cunard, *Negro Anthology,* 473–82. New York: Frederick Ungar, 1970.

U.S. Bureau of the Census. *Fifteenth Census of the United States, 1930.*

———. *Thirteenth Census of the United States, 1910.*

———. *Twelfth Census of the United States, 1900.*

Villard, Oswald Garrison. "Our Attitude toward Russia." *Nation* 131 (Aug. 13, 1930): 172–73.

"The Waller Case." *New Republic* 106 (June 1, 1942): 752.

"Waller Verdict Upheld." *Workers Defense Bulletin* 2 (Nov. 1941): 1.

Ware, C. S. "From Cotton Fields to Steel Mills." *Labor Herald* 2 (Apr. 1923): 13–14.

Washington, Booker T., ed. *Tuskegee and Its People: Their Ideals and Achievements.* 1905. Reprint, New York: Negro Universities Press, 1969.

"We Are Accused of Inciting to Riot and Being Traitors." *Crisis* 49 (June 1942): 183.

"We Must Stand Together." *Crisis* 46 (Jan. 1939): 29. Originally published in *Jewish Frontier* [n.d.].

Weaver, Robert C. "The Defense Program and the Negro." *Opportunity* 18 (Nov. 1940): 324–27.

———. *Negro Labor: A National Problem.* New York: Harcourt, 1946.

"The Week." *New Republic* 80 (Oct. 3, 1934): 197.

Weisbord, Albert. "Passaic—New Bedford—North Carolina." *Communist* 8 (June 1929): 310–23.

Weisbord, Vera Buch. *A Radical Life.* Bloomington: Indiana University Press, 1977.

Wesley, Carter W. "Texans Seek Right to Vote." *Crisis* 47 (Oct. 1940): 312–13.

Wesley, Charles H. *Negro Labor in the United States, 1850–1925.* New York: Russell and Russell, 1927.

West, Don. "Georgia Wanted Me Dead or Alive." In *No Lonesome Road: Selected Prose and Poems*, ed. Jeff Biggers and George Brosi, 30–33. Urbana: University of Illinois Press, 2004. Originally published in *New Masses* (July 1934).

West, Dorothy. "Mary Christopher." *Challenge* 1 (March 1934): 10–15.

———. *The Richer, the Poorer: Stories, Sketches, and Reminiscences.* New York: Doubleday, 1995.

Wexley, John. *They Shall Not Die: A Play.* New York: Knopf, 1934.

"What the South Thinks of Northern Race-Riots." *Literary Digest* 62 (Aug. 16, 1919): 17–18.

White, Walter. "The Color Line in Europe." *Annals of the American Academy of Political and Social Science* 140 (Nov. 1928): 331.

———. "Decline of Southern Liberals." *Negro Digest* 2 (Jan. 1943): 43–46.

———. *A Man Called White: The Autobiography of Walter White.* New York: Viking Press, 1948.

———. "The Negro and the Communists." *Harper's* 164 (Dec. 1931): 62–72.

"White House Blesses Jim Crow." *Crisis* 47 (Nov. 1940): 350–51.

"White Racialism in America." *Crisis* 46 (Oct. 1939): 308. Originally published in *Reconstructionist*, [n.d.].

Whitney, Richard Merrill. *Reds in America.* New York: Beckwith Press, 1924.

"Who Are the Gastonia Prisoners?" *LD* 4 (Sept. 1929): 171–77.

Wilde, Percival. *Contemporary One-Act Plays from Nine Countries.* Boston: Little, Brown, 1936.

Wilkins, Roy, with Tom Mathews. *Standing Fast: The Autobiography of Roy Wilkins.* New York: Viking, 1982.

"Will Alexander and the South." *Crisis* 32 (Aug. 1926): 164–65.

Williams, Charles H. *Sidelights on Negro Soldiers.* Boston: Brimmer, 1923.

Willkie, Wendell. "Quakers, Mormons, Indians, Jews, and Catholics Are Minority Groups Too." *Afro-American*, July 4, 1942. Originally published as "Case for Minorities," *Saturday Evening Post*, [n.d.].

Wilson, Walter. "Georgia Suppresses Insurrection." *Nation* 139 (Aug. 1, 1934): 127–28.

Winner, Percy. "Fascism at the Door." *Scribner's* (Jan. 1936): 33–38.

"Winning the World with Democracy." *South Today* 7 (Spring 1942): 7–24.

Wise, Stephen S. "Parallel between Hitlerism and the Persecution of Negroes in America." *Crisis* 41 (May 1934): 127–79.

World Committee for the Relief of the Victims of German Fascism. *The Reichstag Fire Trial: The Second Brown Book of the Hitler Terror Based on Material Collected by the World Committee for the Relief of the Victims of German Fascism.* London: John Lane, 1934.

World War I Draft Registration Records, 1917–1918. www.ancestry.com.

"Worm Turns." *Crusader* 2 (Nov. 1919): 505–06.

Wright, Richard. "I Tried to Be a Communist." *Atlantic Monthly* 174 (Aug. 1944): 61–70, and (Sept. 1944): 48–56.

———. "Joe Louis Uncovers Dynamite." In *The Strenuous Decade: A Social and Intellectual Record of the 1930s*, ed. Daniel Aaron and Robert Bendiner, 392–97. Garden City, NY: Doubleday, 1970. Originally published in *New Masses* 17 (Oct. 8, 1935).

Yale University. *Historical Register of Yale University, 1701–1937*. New Haven: Yale University, 1939.

Yergan, Max. "The Bantu-European S.C.A. Conference." *South African Outlook* 60 (June 2, 1930): 114.

———. "A Bantu-European Student Christian Conference." *South African Outlook* 60 (March 1, 1930): 52–53.

———. *Christian Students and Modern South Africa: A Report of the Bantu-European Student Christian Conference, Fort Hare*. Alice, South Africa: Student Christian Association, Christian Union, 1930.

———. "The Communist Threat in Africa." In *Africa Today*, ed. C. Grove Haines, 262–80. Baltimore: Johns Hopkins University Press, 1955.

———. *Gold and Poverty in South Africa: A Study of Economic Organization and Standards of Living*. The Hague and New York: International Industrial Relations Institute, 1938.

———. Introduction to *The Shattered Illusion*. New York: American Afro-Asian Educational Exchange, 1966.

———. "The S.C.A. Conference: Students, the Spirit and the Word." *South African Outlook* 60 (May 2, 1930): 94.

———. "A Y.M.C.A. Secretary in Africa." *Southern Workman* 47 (Aug. 1918): 401–02.

———. "Youth's Challenge to Youth." In *Thinking with Africa: Chapters by a Group of Nationals Interpreting the Christian Movement*, ed. Milton Stauffer, 157–84. London: Student Christian Movement, 1928.

Young, Reuben S. "Ethiopia Awakens." *Crisis* 42 (Sept. 1935): 262–63.

Young, Stark. "Negro Material in the Theater." *New Republic* 50 (May 11, 1927): 331–32.

SECONDARY SOURCES

Aaron, Daniel, and Robert Bendiner, eds. *The Strenuous Decade: A Social and Intellectual Record of the 1930s*. Garden City, NY: Doubleday, 1970.

Adams, Frank. *Unearthing Seeds of Fire: The Idea of Highlander*. Winston-Salem, NC: John F. Blair, 1975.

Adams, Thomas K. "Intervention in Haiti: Lessons Relearned." *Military Review* 76 (Sept.–Oct. 1996): 45–56.

Agarwal, N. N. *Soviet Nationalities Policy*. Agra, India: Sri Ram Mehra, 1969.

Aldridge, Daniel W., III. "A War for the Colored Races: Anti-Interventionism and the African American Intelligentsia, 1939–1941." *Diplomatic History* 28 (June 2004): 321–52.

Alexander, Robert J. *The Right Opposition: The Lovestoneites and the International Communist Opposition of the 1930s.* Westport, CT: Greenwood Press, 1981.

Altenbaugh, Richard J. *Education for Struggle: The American Labor Colleges of the 1920s and 1930s.* Philadelphia: Temple University Press, 1990.

Amann, Peter H. "A 'Dog in the Nighttime' Problem: American Fascism in the 1930s." *History Teacher* 19, no. 4 (1986): 559–84.

———. "Vigilante Fascism: The Black Legion as an American Hybrid." *Comparative Studies in Society and History* 25, no. 3 (1983): 490–524.

Anderson, Carol. *Eyes off the Prize: African Americans, the United Nations, and the Struggle for Human Rights, 1944–1955.* New York: Cambridge University Press, 2003.

———. "From Hope to Disillusion: African Americans, the United Nations, and the Struggle for Human Rights, 1944–1947." *Diplomatic History* 20 (Fall 1996): 531–63.

Anderson, Jervis. *A. Philip Randolph: A Biographical Portrait.* New York: Harcourt Brace Jovanovich, 1972.

Anderson, William. *The Wild Man from Sugar Creek: The Political Career of Eugene Talmadge.* Baton Rouge: Louisiana State University Press, 1975.

Andrews, William L., Frances Smith Foster, and Trudier Harris, eds. *The Oxford Companion to African American Literature.* New York: Oxford University Press, 1997.

Anthony, David H. *Max Yergan: Race Man, Internationalist, Cold Warrior.* New York: New York University Press, 2006.

———. "Max Yergan and South Africa: A Transatlantic Interaction." In *Imagining Home: Class, Culture and Nationalism in the African Diaspora,* ed. Sidney J. Lemelle and Robin D. G. Kelley, 185–206. London: Verso, 1994.

———. "Max Yergan in South Africa: From Evangelical Pan-Africanist to Revolutionary Socialist." *African Studies Review* 34 (Sept. 1991): 27–55.

Applebaum, Anne. *Gulag: A History.* New York: Doubleday, 2003.

Armitage, Leia Kaitlyn. "Truth, Falsity, and Schemas of Presentation: A Textual Analysis of Harold Garfinkel's Story of Agnes." *Electronic Journal of Human Sexuality* 4 (Apr. 20, 2001), www.ejhs.org.

Ashby, Warren. *Frank Porter Graham: A Southern Liberal.* Winston-Salem, NC: John F. Blair, 1980.

Athas, Daphne. " 'He Lived to Live': The Story of Ab." *Spectator,* June 13, 1991. In North Carolina Clipping File, North Carolina Collection, Wilson Library, University of North Carolina at Chapel Hill.

Avery, Laurence G. "Paul Green at the Top of His Bent." Speech to the North Carolina Literary and Historical Association and the Federation of North Carolina Historical Societies. *Carolina Comments* 46 (Sept. 1998): 125–35.

Baker, Christina L., and William J. Baker. "Shaking All Corners of the Sky: The Global Response to the Gastonia Strike of 1929." *Canadian Review of American Studies* 21 (Winter 1990): 321–31.

Baker, William J. *Jesse Owens: An American Life.* New York: Free Press, 1986.

Baldwin, Kate A. *Beyond the Color Line and the Iron Curtain: Reading Encounters between Black and Red, 1922–1963.* Durham, NC: Duke University Press, 2002.

Balkin, Jack M., ed. *What "Brown v. Board of Education" Should Have Said: The Nation's*

Top Legal Experts Rewrite America's Landmark Civil Rights Decision. New York: New York University Press, 2001.

"Barnhill, Maurice Victor." *Who Was Who in America*, vol. 8 (1982–85). Chicago: Marquis Who's Who, 1985.

Barrett, James R. *William Z. Foster and the Tragedy of American Radicalism.* Urbana: University of Illinois Press, 1999.

Bates, Beth T. " 'Double V for Victory' Mobilizes Black Detroit, 1941–1946." In *Freedom North: Black Freedom Struggles outside the South, 1940–1980*, ed. Jeanne Theoharis and Komozi Woodard, 17–40. New York: Macmillan, 2003.

Beinart, William. *Twentieth-Century South Africa.* New York: Oxford University Press, 1994.

Belknap, Michael R. *Cold War Political Justice: The Smith Act, the Communist Party, and American Civil Liberties.* Westport, CT: Greenwood Press, 1977.

Bell, Bernard W., Emily Grosholz, and James B. Stewart, eds. *W. E. B. Du Bois on Race and Culture: Philosophy, Politics, and Poetics.* New York: Routledge, 1996.

Bell, Jonathan. *The Liberal State on Trial: The Cold War and American Politics in the Truman Years.* New York: Columbia University Press, 2004.

Bell, Leland V. *In Hitler's Shadow: The Anatomy of American Nazism.* Port Washington, NY: Kennikat Press, 1973.

Bell-Scott, Patricia. "To Write like Never Before: Pauli Murray's Enduring Yearning." *Journal of Women's History* 14 (Summer 2002): 58–61.

Benson, Mary. *The African Patriots: The Story of the African National Congress of South Africa.* London: Faber and Faber, 1963.

Berland, Oscar. "The Emergence of the Communist Perspective on the 'Negro Question' in America: 1919–1931, Part One." *Science and Society* 63 (Winter 1999–2000): 411–32.

———. "The Emergence of the Communist Perspective on the 'Negro Question' in America: 1919–1931, Part Two." *Science and Society* 64 (Summer 2000): 194–217.

———. "Nasanov and the Comintern's American Negro Program." *Science and Society* 64 (Summer 2000): 226–28.

Berman, William. *The Politics of Civil Rights in the Truman Administration.* Columbus: Ohio State University Press, 1970.

Berry, Faith. *Langston Hughes: Before and beyond Harlem.* Westport, CT: Lawrence Hill, 1983.

Beyer, William C. "Creating 'Common Ground' on the Home Front: Race, Class, and Ethnicity in a 1940s Quarterly Magazine." In *The Home-Front War: World War II and American Society*, ed. Kenneth Paul O'Brien and Lynn Hudson Parsons, 41–62. Westport, CT: Greenwood Press, 1995.

Beyond White Supremacy: Towards a New Agenda for the Comparative Histories of South Africa and the United States. Collected Seminar Papers 49. London: Institute of Commonwealth Studies, School of Advanced Study, University of London, 1997.

Biggers, Jeff, and George Brosi, eds. Introduction to *No Lonesome Road: Selected Prose and Poems*, by Don West. Urbana: University of Illinois Press, 2004.

Biles, Roger. *The South and the New Deal.* Lexington: University Press of Kentucky, 1994.

Billingsley, William J. *Communists on Campus: Race, Politics, and the Public University in Sixties North Carolina.* Athens: University of Georgia Press, 1999.

Biondi, Martha. *To Stand and Fight: The Struggle for Civil Rights in Postwar New York City.* Cambridge: Harvard University Press, 2003.

Blagoeva, Stella D. *Dimitrov: A Biography.* Moscow-Leningrad: Co-Operative Publishing Society of Foreign Workers in the U.S.S.R., 1934.

Blakely, Allison. *Russia and the Negro: Blacks in Russian History and Thought.* Washington, DC: Howard University Press, 1986.

Blee, Kathleen M. *Women of the Klan: Racism and Gender in the 1920s.* Berkeley: University of California Press, 1991.

Bloom, Jonathan D. "Brookwood Labor College: The Final Years, 1933–1937." *Labor's Heritage* 2 (Apr. 1990): 37–39.

Bluford, Lucile H. "The Lloyd Gaines Story." *Journal of Educational Sociology* 32 (Feb. 1959): 242–46.

Bogardus, Ralph F., and Fred C. Hobson, eds. *Literature at the Barricades: The American Writer in the 1930s.* University: University of Alabama Press, 1982.

Boger, Gretchen Elisabeth. "Pushing the Envelope: The Civil Rights Activism of Pauli Murray." Senior Essay for the BA, Yale University, 1998.

Borstelmann, Thomas. *The Cold War and the Color Line: American Race Relations in the Global Arena.* Cambridge: Harvard University Press, 2001.

Bracey, John H., and August Meier. "Allies or Adversaries? The NAACP, A. Philip Randolph and the 1941 March on Washington." *Georgia Historical Quarterly* 75 (Spring 1991): 1–17.

Brandenberger, David. *National Bolshevism: Stalinist Mass Culture and the Formation of Modern Russian National Identity, 1931–1956.* Cambridge, Mass.: Harvard University Press, 2002.

Brazeal, Brailsford R. *The Brotherhood of Sleeping Car Porters: Its Origin and Development.* New York: Harper and Brothers, 1946.

Brazil, Wayne D. *Howard W. Odum: The Building Years, 1884–1930.* New York: Garland, 1988.

Brinkmeyer, Robert H., Jr. "Fascism, the Democratic Revival, and the Southern Writer." In *Rewriting the South: History and Fiction,* ed. Lothar Hönnighausen and Valeria Gennaro Lerda, 244–50. Tübingen, Germany: A. Francke Verlag, 1993.

Brock, Adrian. "Was Wundt a 'Nazi'? *Volkerpsychologie*, Racism and Anti-Semitism." *Theory and Psychology* 2 (May 1992): 205–23.

Brooks, Jennifer E. *Defining the Peace: World War II Veterans, Race, and the Remaking of Southern Political Tradition.* Chapel Hill: University of North Carolina Press, 2004.

Brooks, Thomas R. *Walls Come Tumbling Down: A History of the Civil Rights Movement, 1940–1970.* Englewood Cliffs, NJ: Prentice-Hall, 1974.

Brown, Flora Bryant. "NAACP Sponsored Sit-Ins by Howard University Students in Washington, D.C., 1943–1944." *JNH* 85 (Autumn 2000): 274–86.

Bruce, Robert Erik. "Dangerous World, Dangerous Liberties: Rethinking the Smith Act of 1940." Master's thesis, Sonoma State University, 2004.

Buhle, Mari Jo, Paul Buhle, and Dan Georgakas, eds. *Encyclopedia of the American Left.* New York: Oxford University Press, 1998.

Buhle, Paul. *Marxism in the United States: Remapping the History of the American Left.* London: Verso, 1987.

Burns, Augustus Merrimon, III. "Graduate Education for Blacks in North Carolina, 1930–1951." *JSH* 46 (May 1980): 195–218.

———. "North Carolina and the Negro Dilemma, 1930–1950." PhD diss., University of North Carolina at Chapel Hill, 1968.

Burrows, H. R. *A Short Pictorial History of the University College of Fort Hare, 1916–1959.* Lovedale, South Africa: Lovedale Press, 1961.

Campbell, James. *Songs of Zion: The African Methodist Episcopal Church in the United States and South Africa.* Chapel Hill: University of North Carolina Press, 1998.

Canedy, Susan. *America's Nazis: A Democratic Dilemma.* Menlo Park, CA: Markgraf Publications Group, 1990.

Carby, Hazel V. *Race Men.* Cambridge, MA.: Harvard University Press, 1998.

Carter, Dan T. *Scottsboro: A Tragedy of the American South.* Baton Rouge: Louisiana State University Press, 1969.

Carter, Wilmoth A. *Shaw's Universe: A Monument to Educational Innovation.* Raleigh, NC: Shaw University, 1973.

Caute, David. *The Great Fear: The Anti-Communist Purge under Truman and Eisenhower.* New York: Simon & Schuster, 1978.

Cehatopob, A. N. *Sen Katayama.* Mockba: 1988.

Cell, John W. *The Highest Stage of White Supremacy: The Origins of Segregation in South Africa and the American South.* New York: Cambridge University Press, 1982.

Chafe, William H. *Civilities and Civil Rights: Greensboro, North Carolina, and the Black Struggle for Freedom.* New York: Oxford University Press, 1980.

———. *Never Stop Running: Allard Lowenstein and the Struggle to Save American Liberalism.* New York: Basic Books, 1993.

———, et al. *Remembering Jim Crow: African Americans Tell about Life in the Segregated South.* New York: New Press, 2001.

Challen, Paul. *A Sociological Analysis of Southern Regionalism: The Contributions of Howard W. Odum.* Lewiston, NY: Edwin Mellen Press, 1993.

Chalmers, David M. *Hooded Americanism: The First Century of the Ku Klux Klan, 1865–1965.* Garden City, NY: Doubleday, 1965.

Chamberlain, Charles D. *Victory at Home: Manpower and Race in the American South during World War II.* Athens: University of Georgia Press, 2003.

Claudin, Fernando. *The Communist Movement: From Comintern to Cominform.* Harmondsworth, UK: Penguin Books, 1975.

Cobb, James C. *Away down South: A History of Southern Identity.* New York: Oxford University Press, 2005.

Cobley, Alan Gregor. *Class and Consciousness: The Black Petty Bourgeoisie in South Africa, 1924–1950.* Westport, CT: Greenwood Press, 1990.

Cohen, Robert. *When the Old Left Was Young: Student Radicals and America's First Mass Student Movement, 1929–1941.* New York: Oxford University Press, 1993.

Collins, William J. "Race, Roosevelt, and Wartime Production: Fair Employment in World War II Labor Markets." *American Economic Review* 91 (March 2001): 272–86.

Conner, Walker. *The National Question in Marxist-Leninist Theory and Strategy.* Princeton: Princeton University Press, 1984.

Conquest, Robert. *The Harvest of Sorrow: Soviet Collectivization and the Terror-Famine.* New York: Oxford University Press, 1986.

Cooper, John Milton, Jr. *The Warrior and the Priest: Woodrow Wilson and Theodore Roosevelt.* Cambridge, MA: Belknap Press of Harvard University Press, 1983.

Cortner, Richard C. *A Mob Intent on Death: The NAACP and the Arkansas Riot Cases.* Middletown, CT: Wesleyan University Press, 1988.

Crabtree, Beth G. *North Carolina Governors, 1585–1968.* Raleigh, NC: State Department of Archives and History, 1968.

Craig, Gordon A. *Germany: 1866–1945.* New York: Oxford University Press, 1978.

Cripps, Thomas. Introduction to *The Green Pastures,* by Marc Connelly, ed. Thomas Cripps. Madison: University of Wisconsin Press, 1979.

Crouch, John. *Historical Sketches of Wilkes County.* Wilkesboro, NC: Chronicle Job Office, 1902.

Cruse, Harold. *Crisis of the Negro Intellectual.* New York: William Morrow, 1967.

Cullison, Alan. "A Secret Revealed: Stalin's Police Killed Americans." http://204.27.188.70/daily/11-97/11-23-97/a02wn012.htm.

Culver, John C., and John Hyde. *American Dreamer: The Life and Times of Henry A. Wallace.* New York: Norton, 2000.

Cuthbertson, Greg. " 'From White Supremacy to Black Liberation': Intellectual Lineages from South Africa in the 'Making of America.' " *Kleio: A Journal of Historical Studies from Africa* 31 (1999): 99–116.

Dalfiume, Richard M. *Desegregation of the U.S. Armed Forces: Fighting on Two Fronts, 1939–1953.* Columbia: University of Missouri Press, 1969.

———. "The 'Forgotten Years' of the Negro Revolution." *JAH* 55 (June 1968): 90–106.

Dallin, David J., and Boris I. Nicolaevsky. *Forced Labor in Soviet Russia.* New Haven: Yale University Press, 1947.

Dalrymple, Dana. "The Great Famine in Ukraine, 1932–33." *Soviet Studies* 15 (Jan. 1964): 250–85.

Dalton, Dennis. *Mahatma Gandhi: Nonviolent Power in Action.* New York: Columbia University Press, 1993.

Daniel, Pete. *The Shadow of Slavery: Peonage in the South, 1901–1969.* Urbana: University of Illinois Press, 1972.

Davies, R. W., and Stephen G. Wheatcroft. *The Years of Hunger: Soviet Agriculture, 1931–1933.* New York: Palgrave, 2003.

Davis, David Brion. "Jews and Blacks in America." *New York Review of Books* 46 (Dec. 2, 1999): 57–67.

———. *Slavery and Human Progress.* New York: Oxford University Press, 1984.

Davis, Horace B. *Toward a Marxist Theory of Nationalism.* New York: Monthly Review Press, 1978.

Dawidowicz, Lucy S. *The War against the Jews, 1933–1945.* New York: Holt, Rinehart and Winston, 1975.

Degler, Carl N. *In Search of Human Nature: The Decline and Revival of Darwinism in American Social Thought.* New York: Oxford University Press, 1991.

De Jong, Greta. *A Different Day: African American Struggles for Justice in Louisiana.* Chapel Hill: University of North Carolina Press, 2002.

Dekar, Paul R. "The Harlem Ashram, 1940–1946: Gandhian *Satyagraha* in the United States." M. K. Gandhi Institute for Nonviolence, n.d. www.gandhiinstitute.org.

Denning, Michael. *The Cultural Front: The Laboring of American Culture in the Twentieth Century.* London: Verso, 1997.

Diamond, Sander A. *The Nazi Movement in the United States, 1924–1941.* Ithaca, NY: Cornell University Press, 1974.

Dierenfield, Bruce. *Keeper of the Rules: Congressman Howard W. Smith of Virginia.* Charlottesville: University Press of Virginia, 1987.

Diggins, John P. *Mussolini and Fascism: The View from America.* Princeton: Princeton University Press, 1972.

Di Leonardo, Micaela. *Exotics at Home: Anthropologies, Others, American Modernity.* Chicago: University of Chicago Press, 1998.

Diner, Hasia R. *In the Almost Promised Land: American Jews and Blacks, 1915–1935.* Westport, CT: Greenwood Press, 1977.

Dinnerstein, Leo. *The Leo Frank Case.* New York: Columbia University Press, 1968.

Dodd, Donald B., and Wynelle S. Dodd. *Historical Statistics of the South, 1790–1970.* University: University of Alabama Press, 1973.

Doenecke, Justus D. *Storm on the Horizon: The Challenge to American Intervention, 1939–1941.* Lanham, MD: Rowman and Littlefield, 2000.

Dorr, Lisa Lindquist. *White Women, Rape, and the Power of Race in Virginia, 1900–1960.* Chapel Hill: University of North Carolina Press, 2004.

Douglas, Ann. *Terrible Honesty: Mongrel Manhattan in the 1920s.* New York: Farrar, Straus and Giroux, 1995.

Draper, Theodore. *American Communism and Soviet Russia: The Formative Period.* New York: Viking, 1960.

———. "Gastonia Revisited." *Social Research* 38 (Spring 1971): 3–29.

———. *The Rediscovery of Black Nationalism.* New York: Viking, 1970.

———. *The Roots of American Communism.* New York: Viking, 1957.

Drew, Allison. *South Africa's Radical Tradition: A Documentary History,* vol. 2, *1907–1950.* Cape Town: Buchu Books, 1997.

Duberman, Martin Bauml. *Paul Robeson.* New York: Knopf, 1988.

Dubow, Saul. *Racial Segregation and the Origins of Apartheid in South Africa, 1919–1936.* London: Macmillan Press, 1989.

Dudziak, Mary L. *Cold War Civil Rights: Race and the Image of American Democracy.* Princeton: Princeton University Press, 2000.

Dunbar, Anthony P. *Against the Grain: Southern Radicals and Prophets, 1929–1959.* Charlottesville: University Press of Virginia, 1981.

Dykeman, Wilma, and James Stokely. *Seeds of Southern Change: The Life of Will Alexander.* Chicago: University of Chicago Press, 1962.

Eagan, Eileen. *Class, Culture, and the Classroom: The Student Peace Movement of the 1930s.* Philadelphia: Temple University Press, 1981.

Eagles, Charles W. *Jonathan Daniels and Race Relations: The Evolution of a Southern Liberal.* Knoxville: University of Tennessee Press, 1982.

Edwards, John C., and Joseph H. Kitchens, Jr. "Georgia's Anti-Insurrection Law:

Slave Justice for Twentieth-Century Negro Radicals." *Research Studies* 38 (June 1970): 122–33.

Egerton, John. *Speak Now against the Day: The Generation before the Civil Rights Movement in the South.* New York: Knopf, 1995.

Eichelberger, Clark M. *U.N.: The First Ten Years.* New York: Harper and Brothers, 1955.

El-Hai, Jack. "Black and White and Red." *American Heritage* 42 (May–June 1991): 84–85.

Ellis, Mark. *Race, War, and Surveillance: African Americans and the United States Government during World War I.* Bloomington: Indiana University Press, 2001.

Ellis, Stephen, and Tsepo Sechaba. *Comrades against Apartheid: The ANC and the South African Communist Party in Exile.* Bloomington: Indiana University Press, 1992.

Entz, Gary R. "American Negro Labor Congress." In *Organizing Black America: An Encyclopedia of African American Associations,* ed. Nina Mjagkij, 54–56. New York: Garland, 2001.

Fairclough, Adam. *Better Day Coming: Blacks and Equality, 1890–2000.* New York: Viking, 2001.

Fannin, Mark. *Labor's Promised Land: Radical Visions of Gender, Race, and Religion in the South.* Knoxville: University of Tennessee Press, 2003.

Farrar, Hayward. *The Baltimore "Afro-American," 1892–1950.* Westport, CT: Greenwood Press, 1998.

Favor, Martin. *Authentic Blackness: The Folk in the New Negro Renaissance.* Durham, NC: Duke University Press, 1999.

Feimster, Crystal N. " 'Ladies and Lynching': The Gendered Discourse of Mob Violence in the New South, 1880–1930." PhD diss., Princeton University, 2000.

Ferguson, Karen. *Black Politics in New Deal Atlanta.* Chapel Hill: University of North Carolina Press, 2002.

Fink, Gary M. *The Fulton Bag and Cotton Mills Strike of 1914–1915: Espionage, Labor Conflict, and New South Industrial Relations.* Cornell Studies in Industrial and Labor Relations 28. Ithaca, NY: ILR Press, 1993.

———, and Merl E. Reed, eds. *Race, Class, and Community in Southern Labor History.* Tuscaloosa: University of Alabama Press, 1994.

Finkle, Lee. *Forum for Protest: The Black Press during World War II.* Rutherford, NJ: Associated University Presses, Fairleigh Dickinson University Press, 1975.

Flamming, Douglas. *Bound for Freedom: Black Los Angeles in Jim Crow America.* Berkeley: University of California Press, 2005.

Folsom, Franklin. *Impatient Armies of the Poor: The Story of Collective Action by the Unemployed, 1808–1942.* Niwot: University Press of Colorado, 1990.

Folsom, Michael, ed. *Mike Gold: A Literary Anthology.* New York: International, 1972.

Foner, Philip S. *American Socialism and Black Americans: From the Age of Jackson to World War II.* Westport, CT: Greenwood Press, 1977.

Foner, Philip S., and James S. Allen, eds. *American Communism and Black Americans: A Documentary History, 1919–1929.* Philadelphia: Temple University Press, 1987.

Foner, Philip S., and Herbert Shapiro, eds. *American Communism and Black Americans: A Documentary History, 1930–1934.* Philadelphia: Temple University Press, 1991.

Ford, Karen. "Making Poetry Pay: The Commodification of Langston Hughes." In

Marketing Modernisms: Self-Promotion, Canonization, Rereading, ed. Kevin J. H. Dettmar and Stephen Watt, 275–96. Ann Arbor: University of Michigan Press, 1996.

Forman, James R. *Self-Determination and the African-American People*. Seattle: Open Hand, 1981.

Forman, Seth. *Blacks in the Jewish Mind: A Crisis of Liberalism*. New York: New York University Press, 1998.

Fosl, Catherine. "Life and Times of a Rebel Girl: Jane Speed and the Alabama Communist Party." *Southern Historian: A Journal of Southern History* 18 (1997): 45–65.

Fowler, Carolyn. *A Knot in the Thread: The Life and Work of Jacques Roumain*. Washington, DC: Howard University Press, 1980.

Franklin, V. P., Nancy L. Grant, Harold M. Kletnick, and Genna Rae McNeil, eds. *African Americans and Jews in the Twentieth Century: Studies in Convergence and Conflict*. Columbia: University of Missouri Press, 1998.

Fraser, Steven. *Labor Will Rule: Sidney Hillman and the Rise of American Labor*. New York: Free Press, 1991.

Fredrickson, George M. *Black Liberation: A Comparative History of Black Ideologies in the United States and South Africa*. New York: Oxford University Press, 1995.

———. *White Supremacy: A Comparative Study in American and South African History*. New York: Oxford University Press, 1981.

Frederickson, Kari A. *The Dixiecrat Revolt and the End of the Solid South, 1932–1968*. Chapel Hill: University of North Carolina Press, 2001.

Furgurson, Ernest B. *Hard Right: The Rise of Jesse Helms*. New York: Norton, 1986.

Gaines, Kevin Kelly. *American Africans in Ghana: Black Expatriates and the Civil Rights Era*. Chapel Hill: University of North Carolina Press, 2006.

Gallicchio, Marc. *The African American Encounter with Japan and China: Black Internationalism in Asia, 1895–1945*. Chapel Hill: University of North Carolina Press, 2000.

Garb, Paula. *They Came to Stay: North Americans in the U.S.S.R.*. Moscow: Progress, 1987.

Garfinkel, Harold. *Studies in Ethnomethodology*. Englewood Cliffs, NJ: Prentice-Hall, 1967.

Garfinkel, Herbert. *When Negroes March: The March on Washington Movement in the Organizational Politics for FEPC*. 1959. Reprint, with new preface by Lewis M. Killian, New York: Atheneum, 1969.

Garrison, Dee. *Mary Heaton Vorse: The Life of an American Insurgent*. Philadelphia: Temple University Press, 1989.

Gaston, Paul M. "Black Liberation in the United States and South Africa." *South African Historical Journal* 35 (Nov. 1996): 183–91.

Gavins, Raymond. "Within the Shadow of Jim Crow: Black Struggles for Education and Liberation in North Carolina." In *From the Grassroots to the Supreme Court: "Brown v. Board of Education" and American Democracy*, ed. Peter F. Lau, 68–87. Durham, NC: Duke University Press, 2004.

Geisen, Rolf. *Nazi Propaganda Films: A History and Filmography*. Jefferson, NC: McFarland, 2003.

Gershenhorn, Jerry. "*Hocutt v. Wilson* and Race Relations in Durham." *North Carolina Historical Review* 77 (July 2001): 275–308.

———. "Stalling Integration: The Ruse, Rise, and Demise of North Carolina College's Doctoral Program in Education, 1951–1962." *North Carolina Historical Review* 82 (Apr. 2005): 156–92.

Getty, J. Arch, and Oleg V. Naumov. *The Road to Terror: Stalin and the Self-Destruction of the Bolsheviks, 1932–1938.* New Haven: Yale University Press, 1999.

Gibbs, William E. "James Weldon Johnson: A Black Perspective on 'Big Stick' Diplomacy." *Diplomatic History* 8 (Fall 1984): 329–47.

Gilmore, Glenda Elizabeth. "Admitting Pauli Murray." In "Dialogue: Pauli Murray's Notable Connections," ed. Susan Ware. *Journal of Women's History* 14 (Summer 2002): 54–87.

———. *Gender and Jim Crow: Women and the Politics of White Supremacy in North Carolina, 1896–1920.* Chapel Hill: University of North Carolina Press, 1996.

Gish, Steven D. *Alfred B. Xuma: African, American, South African.* New York: New York University Press, 2000.

Glazer, Nathan. *The Social Basis of American Communism.* New York: Harcourt, Brace, 1961.

Glen, John M. *Highlander: No Ordinary School, 1932–1962.* Lexington: University Press of Kentucky, 1988.

Godshalk, David F. *Veiled Visions: The 1906 Atlanta Race Riot and the Reshaping of American Race Relations.* Chapel Hill: University of North Carolina Press, 2005.

Gold, Mike. "William L. Patterson: Militant Leader." *Masses and Mainstream* 4 (Feb. 2, 1951): 34–43.

Goldberg, Chad Alan. "Haunted by the Specter of Communism: Collective Identity and Resource Mobilization in the Demise of the Workers Alliance of America." *Theory and Society* 32 (2003): 725–73.

Goldberg, David J. "Unmasking the Ku Klux Klan: The Northern Movement against the KKK, 1920–1925." *Journal of American Ethnic History* 15 (Summer 1996): 32–48.

Goldfield, Michael. "The Decline of the Communist Party and the Black Question in the U.S.: Harry Haywood's *Black Bolshevik.*" *Review of Radical Political Economics* 12 (Spring 1980): 44–63.

———. "The Failure of Operation Dixie: A Critical Turning Point in American Political Development?" In *Race, Class, and Community in Southern Labor History,* ed. Gary M. Fink and Merl E. Reed, 166–89. Tuscaloosa: University of Alabama Press, 1994.

Goldman, Wendy Z. *Women, the State and Revolution: Soviet Family Policy and Social Life, 1917–1936.* New York: Cambridge University Press, 1993.

Goluboff, Risa L. " 'We Live's in a Free House Such as It Is': Class and the Creation of Modern Civil Rights." *University of Pennsylvania Law Review* (June 2003): 151.

Goodman, James. *Stories of Scottsboro.* New York: Random House, 1995.

Grant, Nathan. "Hughes/Lawrence/Douglass: Power and Resistance in *The Ways of White Folks.*" *Afro-Americans in New York Life and History* 19 (July 31, 1995): 43–52.

Gray, Harold Studley, and Kenneth Irving Brown, eds. *Character "Bad": The Story of a Conscientious Objector.* New York: Harper and Brothers, 1934.

Gray, Richard J. *Literature of Memory: Modern Writers of the American South.* Baltimore: Johns Hopkins University Press, 1976.

Graziosi, Andrea. *The Great Soviet Peasant War: Bolsheviks and Peasants, 1917–1933*. Cambridge, MA: Harvard Papers in Ukrainian Studies, 1996.

———. "Visitors from Other Times: Foreign Workers in the Prewar Five-Year Plans." In Graziosi, *A New Peculiar State: Explorations in Soviet History, 1917–1937*, 223–66. Westport, CT: Praeger, 2000.

Green, Chris, Rachel Rubin, and James Smethurst, eds. *Radicalism in the South since Reconstruction*. New York: Palgrave Macmillan, 2006.

Green, Elna C., ed. *Before the New Deal: Social Welfare in the South, 1830–1930*. Athens: University of Georgia Press, 1999.

———. *The New Deal and Beyond: Social Welfare in the South since 1930*. Athens: University of Georgia Press, 2003.

Green, James R. "Past and Present in Southern History: An Interview with C. Vann Woodward." *Radical History Review* 36 (1986): 80–100.

_____. "Rewriting Southern History: An Interview with C. Vann Woodward." *Southern Exposure* 12 (Nov.–Dec.1984): 87–92.

Greenberg, Cheryl Lynn. "Harold Cruse on Blacks and Jews." In *Harold Cruse's "The Crisis of the Negro Intellectual" Reconsidered*, ed. Jerry Watts, 123–38. New York: Routledge, 2004.

———. *"Or Does It Explode?" Black Harlem in the Great Depression*. New York: Oxford University Press, 1991.

Greenberg, Jack. *Crusaders in the Courts: How a Dedicated Band of Lawyers Fought for the Civil Rights Revolution*. New York: Basic Books, 1994.

———. *Race Relations and American Law*. New York: Columbia University Press, 1959.

Grenville, J. A. S. *A History of the World in the Twentieth Century*. Enlarged ed. Cambridge, MA: Harvard University Press, 2000.

Griffin, Farah Jasmine. "Dorothy West." In *The Oxford Companion to African American Literature*, ed. William L. Andrews, Frances Smith Foster, and Trudier Harris, 176. New York: Oxford University Press, 1997.

Griffith, Barbara S. *The Crisis of American Labor: Operation Dixie and the Defeat of the CIO*. Philadelphia: Temple University Press, 1988.

Griffler, Keith P. "The Black Radical Intellectual and the Black Worker: The Emergence of a Program for Black Labor, 1918–1938." PhD diss., Ohio State University, 1993.

———. *What Price Alliance? Black Radicals Confront White Labor, 1918–1938*. New York: Garland, 1995.

Grill, Johnpeter Horst, and Robert L. Jenkins. "The Nazis and the American South in the 1930s: A Mirror Image?" *JSH* 58 (Nov. 1992): 667–94.

Grossman, James R. *Land of Hope: Chicago, Black Southerners, and the Great Migration*. Chicago: University of Chicago Press, 1989.

Grubbs, Donald. *Cry from the Cotton: The Southern Tenant Farmers' Union and the New Deal*. Chapel Hill: University of North Carolina Press, 1971.

Guttman, Allen. *The Games Must Go On: Avery Brundage and the Olympic Movement*. New York: Columbia University Press, 1984.

Haessley, Jo Lynn. "Mill Mother's Lament: Ella May, Working Women's Militancy, and the 1929 Gaston County Strikes." Master's thesis, University of North Carolina at Chapel Hill, 1987.

Hall, Jacquelyn Dowd. "The Long Civil Rights Movement and the Political Uses of the Past." *JAH* 91 (March 2005): 1233–64.

———. " 'The Mind that Burns in Each Body': Women, Rape, and Racial Violence." In *Powers of Desire: The Politics of Sexuality*, ed. Ann Snitow, Christine Stansell, and Sharon Thompson, 328–49. New York: Monthly Review Press, 1983.

———. "Open Secrets: Memory, Imagination, and the Refashioning of Southern Identity." *American Quarterly* 50.1 (1998): 109–24.

———. "Private Eyes, Public Women: Images of Class and Sex in the Urban South, Atlanta, Georgia, 1913–1915." In *Work Engendered: Toward a New History of American Labor*, ed. Ava Baron, 243–72. Ithaca, NY: Cornell University Press, 1991.

———. *Revolt against Chivalry: Jessie Daniel Ames and the Women's Campaign against Lynching*. 1979. Rev. ed., New York: Columbia University Press, 1993.

———. "Women Writers, the 'Southern Front,' and the Dialectical Imagination." *JSH* 69 (Jan. 2003): 3–38.

———. " 'You Must Remember This': Autobiography as Social Critique." *JAH* 85 (Sept. 1998): 439–65.

James Leloudis, Robert Korstad, Mary Murphy, Lu Ann Jones, and Christopher B. Daly. *Like a Family: The Making of a Southern Cotton Mill World*, 2d ed. Chapel Hill: University of North Carolina Press, 2000.

Halpern, Lena. "Transfer of Inorganic Phosphorus across the Red Blood Cell Membrane." *Journal of Biological Chemistry* 114 (1936): 747–70.

Harris, Joseph E. *African-American Reactions to War in Ethiopia, 1936–1941*. Baton Rouge: Louisiana State University Press, 1994.

Harris, William H. *A. Philip Randolph, Milton P. Webster, and the Brotherhood of Sleeping Car Porters, 1925–1937*. Urbana: University of Illinois Press, 1977.

———. "Federal Intervention in Union Discrimination: FEPC and West Coast Shipyards during World War II." *Labor History* (Summer 1982): 325–47.

Harrison, Alferdteen. ed., *Black Exodus: The Great Migration from the American South*. Jackson: University Press of Mississippi, 1991.

Hatcher, Susan Tucker. "The Senatorial Career of Clyde R. Hoey." PhD diss., Duke University, 1983.

Haynes, John Earl. *Red Scare or Red Menace? American Communism and Anticommunism in the Cold War Era*. Chicago: Ivan Dee, 1996.

———, and Harvey Klehr. *Venona: Decoding Soviet Espionage in America*. New Haven: Yale University Press, 2000.

Heale, M. J. *American Anticommunism: Combating the Enemy Within, 1830–1970*. Baltimore: Johns Hopkins University Press, 1990.

Healey, Dan. "Sexual and Gender Dissent: Homosexuality as Resistance in Stalin's Russia." In *Contending with Stalinism*, ed. Lynne Viola, 139–69. Ithaca, NY: Cornell University Press, 2002.

Hickey, Georgina. *Hope and Danger in the New South City: Working Class Women and Urban Development in Atlanta, 1890–1940*. Athens: University of Georgia Press, 2003.

Higgs, Catherine. *The Ghost of Equality: The Public Lives of D. D. T. Jabavu of South Africa, 1885–1959*. Athens: Ohio University Press, 1997.

Hill, Robert A. "Introduction: Racial and Radical: Cyril V. Briggs, *The Crusader* Magazine, and the African Blood Brotherhood, 1918–1922." In *The Crusader: A Facsimile of the Periodical*, ed. Robert A. Hill, 1:xxvi. New York: Garland, 1987.

———, comp. and ed. *The FBI's RACON: Racial Conditions in America during World War II*. Boston: Northeastern University Press, 1995.

Hirson, Baruch. *Yours for the Union: Class and Community Struggles in South Africa*. London: Zed Books, 1990.

Hodges, James A. *New Deal Labor Policy and the Southern Textile Industry, 1933–1941*. Knoxville: University of Tennessee Press, 1986.

Hoffman, David L. *Stalinist Values: The Cultural Norms of Soviet Modernity, 1917–1941*. Ithaca, NY: Cornell University Press, 2003.

Hoffman, Erwin D. "The Genesis of the Modern Movement for Equal Rights in South Carolina, 1930–1939." In *The Negro in Depression and War: Prelude to Revolution, 1930–1935*, ed. Bernard Sternsher, 203–04. Chicago: Quadrangle Books, 1969.

Holloway, Jonathan S. *Confronting the Veil: Abram Harris, Jr., E. Franklin Frazier, and Ralph Bunche, 1919–1941*. Chapel Hill: University of North Carolina Press, 2002.

Holmes, Michael S. "The Blue Eagle as 'Jim Crow Bird': The NRA and Georgia's Black Workers." *JNH* 57 (July 1972): 276–83.

Honey, Michael. "Black Workers Remember: Industrial Unionism in the Era of Jim Crow." In *Race, Class, and Community in Southern Labor History*, ed. Gary M. Fink and Merl E. Reed, 121–40. Tuscaloosa: University of Alabama Press, 1994.

———. *Southern Labor and Black Civil Rights: Organizing Memphis Workers*. Urbana: University of Illinois Press, 1993.

Hooker, James. *Black Revolutionary: George Padmore's Path from Communism to Pan-Africanism*. New York: Praeger, 1967.

Hoopes, Townsend, and Douglas Brinkley. *FDR and the Creation of the U.N.* New Haven: Yale University Press, 1997.

Horne, Gerald. *Black and Brown: African Americans and the Mexican Revolution, 1910–1920*. New York: New York University Press, 2005.

———. *Black Liberation/Red Scare: Ben Davis and the Communist Party*. Newark: University of Delaware Press, 1994.

———. *Communist Front? The Civil Rights Congress, 1946–1956*. Rutherford, NJ: Fairleigh Dickinson Press; London: Associated University Presses, 1988.

———. "Race from Power: U.S. Foreign Policy and the General Crisis of "White Supremacy.' " *Diplomatic History* 23 (Summer 1999): 450–51.

———. *Race Woman: The Lives of Shirley Graham Du Bois*. New York: New York University Press, 2000.

———. "Who Lost the Cold War? Africans and African Americans." *Diplomatic History* 20 (Fall 1996): 613–26.

Horton, Aimee Isgrig. *The Highlander Folk School: A History of Its Major Programs, 1932–1961*. New York: Carlson, 1989.

Horwitz, Gerry. "Benjamin Davis, Jr., and the American Communist Party: A Study in Race and Politics." *UCLA Historical Journal* 4 (1983): 92–107.

Howe, Irving, and Lewis Coser. *The American Communist Party: A Critical History (1919–1951)*. Boston: Beacon Press, 1957.

Howlett, Charles F. *Brookwood Labor College and the Struggle for Peace and Social Justice in America*. Lewiston, NY: Edwin Mellen Press, 1993.

Huggins, Nathan Irvin. *Harlem Renaissance.* New York: Oxford University Press, 1971.

Hutchinson, Earl Ofari. *Blacks and Reds: Race and Class in Conflict, 1919–1990.* East Lansing: Michigan State University Press, 1995.

Hutchinson, George. *The Harlem Renaissance in Black and White.* Cambridge, MA: Belknap Press of Harvard University Press, 1995.

Ingram, Elwanda D. "Dorothy West." In *Notable Black American Women,* ed. Jessie Carney Smith, 1238–40. Detroit: Gale Research, 1992.

Irons, Janet Christine. *Testing the New Deal: The General Textile Strike of 1934 in the American South.* Urbana: University of Illinois Press, 2000.

Isserman, Maurice. *Which Side Were You On? The American Communist Party during the Second World War.* Middletown, CT: Wesleyan University Press, 1982.

Jackson, Kenneth T. *The Ku Klux Klan and the City, 1915–1930.* New York: Oxford University Press, 1967.

Jackson, Walter A. *Gunnar Myrdal and America's Conscience: Social Engineering and Racial Liberalism, 1938–1987.* Chapel Hill: University of North Carolina Press, 1990.

Jacoby, Karl. "Between North and South: The Alternative Borderlands of William H. Ellis and the African American Colony of 1895." In *Continental Crossroads: Remapping U.S.-Mexico Borderlands History,* ed. Samuel Truett and Elliott Young, 209–40. Durham, NC: Duke University Press, 2004.

Jaffe, Philip J. *The Rise and Fall of American Communism.* New York: Horizon Press, 1975.

Jaffee, Julian F. *Crusade against Radicalism: New York during the Red Scare, 1914–1924.* Port Washington, NY: National University Publications, Kennikat Press, 1972.

James, Sheryl. "A Radical of Long Standing." *St. Petersburg Times,* March 1989. www.aldha.org/donwest.htm.

James, Winston. *Holding Aloft the Banner of Ethiopia: Caribbean Radicalism in Early Twentieth-Century America.* New York: Verso, 1998.

Janken, Kenneth Robert. "African-American Intellectuals Confront the 'Silent South': The *What the Negro Wants* Controversy." *North Carolina Historical Review* 70, no. 2 (1993): 153–79.

———. Introduction to *What the Negro Wants,* by Rayford Logan, rev. ed. Notre Dame, IN: University of Notre Dame Press, 2001.

———. *Rayford W. Logan and the Dilemma of the African-American Intellectual.* Amherst: University of Massachusetts Press, 1993.

———. *White: The Biography of Walter White, Mr. NAACP.* New York: New Press, 2003.

Jefferson, Paul. "Ira De Augustine Reid." In *American National Biography,* vol. 18, ed. John A. Garraty and Mark C. Carnes, 306–08. New York: Oxford University Press, 1999.

Jennings, La Vinia. "Louise Thompson." In *Notable Black American Women,* ed. Jessie Carney Smith, 1133–37. Detroit: Gale Research, 1991.

"Joe Louis." www.cyberboxingzone.com.

Johns, Sheridan. *Raising the Red Flag: The International Socialist League and the Communist Party of South Africa, 1914–1932.* Belville, South Africa: Mayibuye, 1995.

Johnson, Hewlett. *The Soviet Power: The Socialist Sixth of the World.* New York: International, 1940.

Johnson, Phillip J. "The Limits of Interracial Compromise: Louisiana, 1941." *JSH* 69 (May 2003): 319–48.

Johnson, Tom. *The Reds in Dixie: Who Are the Communists and What Do They Fight for in the South?* New York: Workers Library, 1935.

Jones, Anne Goodwyn. *Tomorrow Is Another Day: The Woman Writer in the South, 1859–1936.* Baton Rouge: Louisiana State University Press, 1981.

Jordan, William G. *Black Newspapers and America's War for Democracy, 1914–1920.* Chapel Hill: University of North Carolina Press, 2001.

Joseph, Gilbert M. *Revolution from Without: Yucatan, Mexico, and the United States, 1880–1924.* Durham, NC: Duke University Press, 1988.

Kahn, Albert E. *Treason in Congress: The Record of the House Un-American Activities Committee.* New York: Progressive Citizens of America, n.d. www.trussel.com/hf/treason.htm.

Kanet, Roger E. "The Comintern and the 'Negro Question': Communist Policy in the United States and Africa, 1921–1941." *Survey* 19 (Autumn 1973): 86–122.

Karson, Marc, and Ronald Radosh. "The American Federation of Labor and the Negro Worker, 1984–1949." In *The Negro and the American Labor Movement,* ed. Julius Jacobson, 155–87. Garden City, NY: Doubleday, 1968.

Kass, D. A. "The Issue of Racism at the 1936 Olympics." *Journal of Sports History* 3 (Winter 1976): 223–35.

Katz, Friedrich. *The Secret War in Mexico: Europe, the United States and the Mexican Revolution.* Chicago: University of Chicago Press, 1981.

Katznelson, Ira, Kim Geiger, and Daniel Kryder. "Limiting Liberalism: The Southern Veto in Congress, 1933–1950." *Political Science Quarterly* 108 (Summer 1993): 283–306.

Kearney, Reginald. *African American Views of the Japanese: Solidarity or Sedition?* Albany: State University of New York Press, 1998.

Keith, Jeanette. *Rich Man's War, Poor Man's Fight: Race, Class, and Power in the Rural South during the First World War.* Chapel Hill: University of North Carolina Press, 2004.

Kelley, Robin D. G. " 'Afric's Sons with Banner Red': African American Communists and the Politics of Culture, 1919–1934." In *Imagining Home: Class, Culture and Nationalism in the African Diaspora,* ed. Sidney J. Lemelle and Robin D. G. Kelley, 35–54. New York: Verso, 1994.

———. " 'But a Local Phase of a World Problem': Black History's Global Vision, 1883–1950." *JAH* 86 (Dec. 1999): 1045–77.

———. "Communist Party USA, African Americans and the." In *Africana: The Encyclopedia of the African and African American Experience,* ed. Kwame Anthony Appiah and Henry Louis Gates, Jr., 492–95. New York: Basic Books, 1999.

———. *Hammer and Hoe: Alabama Communists during the Great Depression.* Chapel Hill: University of North Carolina Press, 1990.

———. "A New War in Dixie: Communists and the Unemployed in Birmingham, Alabama, 1930–1933." *Labor History* 30 (Summer 1989): 367–84.

———. "The Religious Odyssey of African Radicals: Notes on the Communist Party of South Africa, 1921–34." *Radical History Review* (Fall 1991): 5–23.

————. "The Third International and the Struggle for National Liberation in South Africa." *Ufahamu: Journal of the African Activist Association* 15, nos. 1–2 (1986): 99–120.

————. " 'We Are Not What We Seem': Rethinking Black Working Class Opposition in the Jim Crow South." *JAH* 80 (June 1993): 75–112.

Kellner, Bruce. "Louise Thompson Patterson." *The Harlem Renaissance: An Historical Dictionary for the Era.* Westport, CT: Greenwood Press, 1984.

Kellogg, Peter J. "Civil Rights Consciousness in the 1940s." *Historian* 42 (Nov. 1979): 18–41.

Kennedy, Elizabeth Lapovsky, and Madeline D. Davis. *Boots of Leather, Slippers of Gold: The History of a Lesbian Community.* New York: Routledge, 1993.

Kennedy, Paul. *The Parliament of Man: The Past, Present, and Future of the United Nations.* New York: Random House, 2006.

Kennedy, Randall. *Race, Crime, and the Law.* New York: Pantheon Books, 1997.

Kennedy, Stetson. *Southern Exposure.* Garden City, NY: Doubleday, 1946.

Kennington, Laura. "African-American Organizing in the Gastonia Textile Strike, 1929." Senior essay for the BA, Yale University, 2001.

Kerr, Alexander. *Fort Hare, 1915–1948: The Evolution of an African College.* London: Shuter and Shooter, Pietermaritzburg, n.d.

Kesselman, Louis Coleridge. *The Social Politics of the FEPC: A Study in Reform Pressure Movements.* Chapel Hill: University of North Carolina Press, 1948.

Kessler, Lou. "Legacy in Black and White." *New Carolinian* (March 1976): 19.

Kieran, John. *The Story of the Olympic Games, 776 B.C.–1936 A.D.* New York: Stokes, 1936.

————, and Arthur Daley. *The Story of the Olympic Games, 776 B.C. to 1968.* Philadelphia: Lippincott, 1969.

King, Kenneth J. "The American Negro as Missionary to East Africa: A Critical Aspect of African Evangelism." *African Historical Studies* 3, no. 1 (1970): 5–22.

————. *Pan-Africanism and Education: A Study of Race Philanthropy and Education in the Southern States of America and East Africa.* Oxford, UK: Clarendon Press, 1971.

King, Richard H. *Race, Culture, and the Intellectuals, 1940–1970.* Washington, DC: Woodrow Wilson Center Press, 2004.

————. *A Southern Renaissance: The Cultural Awakening of the American South, 1930–1955.* New York: Oxford University Press, 1980.

Kirby, Jack Temple. *Media-Made Dixie: The South in the American Imagination,* rev. ed. Athens: University of Georgia Press, 1986.

Kirby, John B. *Black Americans in the Roosevelt Era: Liberalism and Race.* Knoxville: University of Tennessee Press, 1980.

Klarman, Michael J. "*Brown,* Racial Change, and the Civil Rights Movement." *Virginia Law Review* 80 (Feb. 1994): 7–150.

————. "Civil Rights Law: Who Made It and How Much Did It Matter?" *Georgetown Law Journal* 83 (1994): 433–59.

————. *From Jim Crow to Civil Rights: The Supreme Court and the Struggle for Racial Equality.* New York: Oxford University Press, 2004.

————. "Rethinking the Civil Rights and Civil Liberties Revolutions." *Virginia Law Review* 82 (Feb. 1996): 1–67.

Klehr, Harvey. *Communist Cadre: The Social Background of the American Communist Party Elite.* Stanford, CA: Hoover Institution Press, 1978.

———. *The Heyday of American Communism: The Depression Decade.* New York: Basic Books, 1984.

———, and John Earl Haynes. *The American Communist Movement: Storming Heaven Itself.* New York: Twayne, 1992.

———, and William Tompson. "Self-Determination in the Black Belt: Origins of Communist Policy." *Labor History* 30 (Summer 1989): 354–66.

Klibaner, Irwin. "The Travail of Southern Radicals: The Southern Conference Educational Fund, 1946–1976." *JSH* 49 (May 1983): 179–202.

Klinkner, Philip A., and Rogers M. Smith. *The Unsteady March: The Rise and Decline of Racial Equality in America.* Chicago: University of Chicago Press, 1999.

Kluger, Richard. *Simple Justice: The History of "Brown v. Board of Education" and Black America's Struggle for Equality.* New York: Knopf, 1976.

Kneebone, John T. *Southern Liberal Journalists and the Issue of Race, 1920–1944.* Chapel Hill: University of North Carolina Press, 1985.

Kornbluh, Joyce L. *A New Deal for Workers' Education: The Workers' Service Program, 1933–1942.* Urbana: University of Illinois Press, 1987.

Kornweibel, Theodore, Jr. *"Investigate Everything": Federal Efforts to Compel Black Loyalty during World War I.* Bloomington: Indiana University Press, 2002.

———. *No Crystal Stair: Black Life and the Messenger, 1917–1928.* Westport, CT: Greenwood Press, 1975.

———. *Seeing Red: Federal Campaigns against Black Militancy, 1919–1925.* Bloomington: Indiana University Press, 1998.

Korstad, Robert Rodgers. *Civil Rights Unionism: Tobacco Workers and the Struggle for Democracy in the Mid-Twentieth-Century South.* Chapel Hill: University of North Carolina Press, 2003.

———, and Nelson Lichtenstein. "Opportunities Found and Lost: Labor, Radicals, and the Early Civil Rights Movement." *JAH* 75 (Dec. 1988): 786–811.

Kosek, Joseph Kip. "Richard Gregg, Mohandas Gandhi, and the Strategy of Nonviolence." *JAH* 91 (March 2005): 1318–48.

Kouhl, Stefan. *The Nazi Connection: Eugenics, American Racism, and German National Socialism.* New York: Oxford University Press, 1994.

Kousser, J. Morgan. *Shaping of Southern Politics: Suffrage Restriction and the Establishment of the One-Party South, 1880–1910.* New Haven: Yale University Press, 1982.

Kovel, Joel. *Red Hunting in the Promised Land: Anticommunism and the Making of America.* New York: Basic Books, 1994.

Krueger, Thomas A. *And Promises to Keep: The Southern Conference for Human Welfare, 1938–1948.* Nashville, TN: Vanderbilt University Press, 1967.

Kublin, Hyman. *Asian Revolutionary: The Life of Sen Katayama.* Princeton, NJ: Princeton University Press, 1964.

Kuebler, Edward J. "The Desegregation of the University of Maryland." *Maryland Historical Magazine* 71 (Spring 1976): 37–49.

Kuhn, Cliff. *Contesting the New South Order: The 1914–1915 Strike at Atlanta's Fulton Mills.* Chapel Hill: University of North Carolina Press, 2001.

La Botz, Dan. "American 'Slackers' in the Mexican Revolution: International Proletarian Politics in the Midst of a National Revolution." *The Americas* 62, no. 4 (2006): 563–90.

Lal, Shafali. "1930s Multiculturalism: Rachel Davis DuBois and the Bureau for Intercultural Education." *Radical Teacher* 69 (May 2004): 18–22.

Laquer, Walter. *Fascism: Past, Present, and Future.* New York: Oxford University Press, 1996.

Latham, Earl. *The Communist Controversy in Washington: From the New Deal to McCarthy.* Cambridge, MA: Harvard University Press, 1966.

Lawson, Steven F. *Black Ballots: Voting Rights in the South, 1944–1969.* New York: Columbia University Press, 1976.

———. *Civil Rights Crossroads: Nation, Community, and the Black Freedom Struggle.* Lexington; University of Kentucky Press, 2003.

Lay, Shawn. *The Invisible Empire in the West: Toward a New Historical Appraisal of the Ku Klux Klan of the 1920s.* Urbana: University of Illinois Press, 1992.

Layton, Azza Salama. *International Politics and Civil Rights Policies in the United States, 1941–1960.* New York: Cambridge University Press, 2000.

Leab, Daniel J. " 'United We Eat': The Creation and Organization of the Unemployed Councils in 1930." *Labor History* 8 (Fall 1967): 300–15.

Ledeboer, Suzanne G. "The Man Who Would Be Hitler: William Dudley Pelley and the Silver Legion." *California History* 65 (June 1986): 127–55.

Leffler, Melvyn P. *The Specter of Communism: The United States and the Origins of the Cold War, 1917–1953.* New York: Hill and Wang, 1994.

Lentz-Smith, Adriane. "The Great War for Civil Rights." PhD diss., Yale University, 2005.

Levine, Arthur. "Brookwood Remembered." *Change* 13 (Nov.–Dec. 1981): 38–42.

Levine, Daniel. *Bayard Rustin and the Civil Rights Movement.* New Brunswick, NJ: Rutgers University Press, 2000.

Lewis, David Levering. "Parallels and Divergences: Assimilationist Strategies of Afro-American and Jewish Elites from 1910 to the Early 1930s." *JAH* 71 (Dec. 1984): 543–64.

———. *W. E. B. Du Bois: Biography of a Race, 1868–1919.* New York: Holt, 1993.

———. *W. E. B. Du Bois: The Fight for Equality and the American Century, 1919–1963.* New York: Holt, 2000.

———, ed. *W. E. B. Du Bois: A Reader.* New York: Holt, 1995.

———. *When Harlem Was in Vogue.* New York: Penguin, 1997.

Lewis, Earl. *In Their Own Interests; Race, Class, and Power in Twentieth-Century Norfolk, Virginia.* Berkeley, University of California Press, 1991.

Lewis, George. *The White South and the Red Menace: Segregationists, Anticommunism, and Massive Resistance, 1945–1965.* Gainesville: University Press of Florida, 2004.

Lewy, Guenter. *The Cause that Failed: Communism in American Political Life.* New York: Oxford University Press, 1990.

Lichtenstein, Alex. Introduction to *Revolt among the Sharecroppers*, by Howard Kester. Knoxville: University of Tennessee Press, 1997.

Lichtenstein, Nelson. *Labor's War at Home: The CIO in World War II.* Cambridge, UK: Cambridge University Press, 1982.

Lipset, Seymour M., and Earl Raab. *The Politics of Unreason: Right Wing Extremism in America, 1790–1977,* 2d ed. Chicago: University of Chicago Press, 1978.

Lipstadt, Deborah E. *Beyond Belief: The American Press and the Coming of the Holocaust, 1933–1945.* New York: Free Press, 1986.

Logan, Rayford, ed. *The Attitude of the Southern White Press toward Negro Suffrage, 1932–1940.* Washington, DC: Foundation, 1940.

———. *Haiti and the Dominican Republic.* London: issued under the auspices of the Royal Institute of International Affairs [by] Oxford University Press, 1968.

———. "James Weldon Johnson and Haiti." *Phylon* 32 (4th Quarter 1971): 396–402.

Lorence, James J. "Mobilizing the Reserve Army." In *Radicalism in the South since Reconstruction,* eds. Chris Green, Rachel Rubin, and James Smethurst, 67–80.

Lott, Eric. *Love and Theft: Blackface Minstrelsy and the American Working Class.* New York: Oxford University Press, 1993.

Lusane, Clarence. *Hitler's Black Victims: The Historical Experiences of Afro-Germans, European Blacks, Africans, and African Americans in the Nazi Era.* New York: Routledge, 2003.

Lynch, Hollis R. *Black American Radicals and the Liberation of Africa: The Council on African Affairs, 1937–1955.* Ithaca, NY: Cornell University Africana Studies and Research Center, 1978.

Maclean, Frances. " 'They Didn't Speak Our Language; We Didn't Speak Theirs.' " *Smithsonian* 23 (Jan. 1993): 44–55.

MacLean, Nancy. *Behind the Mask of Chivalry: The Making of the Second Ku Klux Klan.* New York: Oxford University Press, 1994.

———. "The Leo Frank Case Reconsidered: Gender and Sexual Politics in the Making of Reactionary Populism." *JAH* 78 (Dec. 1991): 917–48.

"A Man of the People." *Political Affairs* 44 (Sept. 1965): 7–9.

Mandell, Richard D. *The Nazi Olympics.* New York: Macmillan, 1971.

Marable, Manning. *Race, Reform, and Rebellion: The Second Reconstruction in Black America, 1945–1990,* 2d rev. ed. Jackson: University Press of Mississippi, 1991.

Marks, Carole. *Farewell—We're Good and Gone.* Bloomington: Indiana University Press, 1989.

Marks, Shula. *The Ambiguities of Dependence in South Africa.* Baltimore: Johns Hopkins University Press, 1986.

Marks, Shula, and Stanley Trapido. "Politics of Race, Class, and Nationalism." In *The Politics of Race, Class, and Nationalism in Twentieth-Century South Africa,* ed. Marks and Trapido, 1–70. New York: Longman, 1987.

Marks, Shula, and Stanley Trapido. *The Politics of Race, Class and Nationalism in Twentieth-Century South Africa.* New York: Longman, 1987.

Martin, Charles Henry. "The Angelo Herndon Case and Georgia Justice, 1930–1937." PhD diss., Tulane University, 1972.

———. *The Angelo Herndon Case and Southern Justice.* Baton Rouge: Louisiana State University Press, 1976.

———. "Communists and Blacks: The ILD and the Angelo Herndon Case." *JNH* 64 (Spring 1979): 131–41.

———. "White Supremacy and Black Workers: Georgia's 'Black Shirts' Combat the Great Depression." *Labor History* 18, no. 3 (1977): 366–81.

Martin, Robert Francis. *Howard Kester and the Struggle for Social Justice in the South, 1904–1977.* Charlottesville: University Press of Virginia, 1991.

Martin, Tony. *Race First: The Ideological and Organizational Struggles of Marcus Garvey and the Universal Negro Improvement Association.* Westport, CT: Greenwood Press, 1976.

Marx, Anthony W. *Making Race and Nation: A Comparison of South Africa, the United States, and Brazil.* Cambridge, UK: Cambridge University Press, 1998.

Mathieu, Marie Sarah-Jane. "Jim Crow Rides This Train: The Social and Political Impact of African American Sleeping Car Porters in Canada, 1880–1930." PhD diss., Yale University, 2001.

Matthews, Paul. "Park, Robert Ezra." In *American National Biography*, vol. 24, ed. John A. Garraty and Mark C. Carnes, 4–6. New York: Oxford University Press, 1999.

Maxwell, William J. *New Negro, Old Left: African-American Writing and Communism between the Wars.* New York: Columbia University Press, 1999.

Mayeri, Serena. "Reasoning from Race: Legal Feminism in the Civil Rights Era." PhD diss., Yale University, 2006.

McClellan, Woodford. "Africans and Black Americans in the Comintern Schools, 1925–1934." *International Journal of African Historical Studies* 26, no. 2 (1993): 371–90.

McCullough, David G. *Truman.* New York: Simon & Schuster, 1992.

McDowell, Deborah E. "Conversations with Dorothy West." In *The Harlem Renaissance Reexamined*, ed. Victor A. Kramer, 265–81. New York: AMS Press, 1987.

McGovern, James R. *Anatomy of a Lynching: The Killing of Claude Neal.* Baton Rouge: Louisiana State University Press, 1982.

McGuire, Philip. *He, Too, Spoke for Democracy: Judge Hastie, World War II, and the Black Soldier.* Westport, CT: Greenwood Press, 1988.

McMahon, Kevin J. *Reconsidering Roosevelt on Race: How the Presidency Paved the Road to "Brown."* Chicago: University of Chicago Press, 2004.

McNeil, Genna Rae. *Groundwork: Charles Hamilton Houston and the Struggle for Civil Rights.* Philadelphia: University of Pennsylvania Press, 1983.

McWilliams, Tennant S. *The New South Faces the World: Foreign Affairs and the Southern Sense of Self, 1877–1950.* Baton Rouge: Louisiana State University Press, 1988.

Meador, Judith Hay. "A History and Index of *Contempo*." MA thesis, University of Louisville, 1971.

Meier, August, and Elliott Rudwick. *CORE: A Study in the Civil Rights Movement, 1942–1968.* New York: Oxford University Press, 1973.

———. "The Origins of Nonviolent Direct Action in Afro-American Protest: A Note on Historical Discontinuities." In *Along the Color Line: Explorations in the Black Experience*, ed. Meier and Rudwick, 307–404. Urbana: University of Illinois Press, 1976.

Meyerowitz, Joanne. *How Sex Changed: A History of Transsexuality in the United States.* Cambridge, MA: Harvard University Press, 2002.

Miller, James A., Susan D. Pennybacker, and Eve Rosenhaft. "Mother Ada Wright and the International Campaign to Free the Scottsboro Boys, 1931–1934." *AHR* 106 (Apr. 2001): 387–430.

Miller, Loren. *The Petitioners: The Story of the Supreme Court of the United States and the Negro.* Cleveland, OH: Meridian Books, 1966.

Miller, Nina. *Making Love Modern: The Intimate Public Worlds of New York's Literary Women.* New York: Oxford University Press, 1999.

Miller, Sally M. "Socialism and Race." In *Failure of a Dream? Essays in the History of American Socialism,* ed. John H. M. Laslett and Seymour Martin Lipset, 218–31. 1974, rev. ed. Berkeley: University of California Press, 1984.

———. "The Socialist Party and the Negro, 1901–20." *JNH* 56 (July 1971): 220–29.

Modell, John, Marc Goulden, and Sigurdur Magnusson. "World War II in the Lives of Black Americans: Some Findings and an Interpretation." *JAH* 76 (Dec. 1989): 838–48.

Moore, John Hammond. "The Angelo Herndon Case, 1932–1937." *Phylon* 32 (Spring 1971): 60–71.

———. "Communists and Fascists in a Southern City: Atlanta, 1930." *South Atlantic Quarterly* 67 (Summer 1968): 437–54.

Moore, John L., Jon P. Preimesberger, and David R. Tarr, eds. *Congressional Quarterly's Guide to U.S. Elections.* Washington, DC: CQ Press, 2001.

Morgan, Ted. *A Covert Life: Jay Lovestone, Communist, Anti-Communist, and Spymaster.* New York: Random House, 1999.

Morray, Joseph P. *Project Kuzbas: American Workers in Siberia, 1921–1926.* New York: International, 1983.

Morrison, Joseph L. *Governor O. Max Gardner: A Power in North Carolina and New Deal Washington.* Chapel Hill: University of North Carolina Press, 1971.

———. *Josephus Daniels, the Small-d Democrat.* Chapel Hill: University of North Carolina Press, 1966.

Murphy, Robert F. *Robert H. Lowie.* New York: Columbia University Press, 1972.

Murray, Hugh T. "NAACP vs. the Communist Party: The Scottsboro Rape Cases." In *The Negro in Depression and War: Prelude to Revolution, 1935–1940,* ed. Bernard Sternsher, 267–81. Chicago: Quadrangle Books, 1969.

———. Review of *The Angelo Herndon Case and Southern Justice,* by Charles H. Martin. *Journal of Ethnic Studies* 5 (Winter 1978): 90–92.

Naiman, Eric. *Sex in Public: The Incarnation of Early Soviet Ideology.* Princeton, NJ: Princeton University Press, 1997.

Naison, Mark. "Communism and Harlem Intellectuals in the Popular Front: Anti-Fascism and the Politics of Black Culture." *Journal of Ethnic Studies* 9 (Spring 1981): 1–25.

———. *Communists in Harlem during the Depression.* Urbana: University of Illinois Press, 1983.

———. "Remaking America: Communists and Liberals in the Popular Front." In *New Studies in the Politics and Culture of U.S. Communism,* ed. Michael E. Brown, Randy Martin, Frank Rosengarten, and George Snedker, 45–73. New York: Monthly Review Press, 1993.

Nalty, Bernard C. *Strength for the Fight: A History of Black Americans in the Military.* New York: Free Press, 1986.

Nelson, Bruce. *Divided We Stand: American Workers and the Struggle for Black Equality.* Princeton: Princeton University Press, 2001.

Nelson, Claire Nee. "Black and White." In *Encyclopedia of the Harlem Renaissance*, ed. Cary D. Wintz and Paul Finkelman, 1:122–24. New York: Routledge, 2004.

———. "Louise Thompson Patterson." In *Encyclopedia of the Harlem Renaissance*, ed. Cary D. Wintz and Paul Finkelman, 2:960–62. New York: Routledge, 2004.

———. "Louise Thompson Patterson and the Southern Roots of the Popular Front." In *Women Shaping the South: Creating and Confronting Change*, ed. Angela Boswell and Judith N. McArthur, 204–28. Columbia: University of Missouri Press, 2006.

Neu, Charles. "Woodrow Wilson and Colonel House: The Early Years, 1911–1915." In *The Wilson Era: Essays in Honor of Arthur S. Link*, ed. John Milton Cooper Jr. and Charles Neu, 248–55. Princeton: Princeton University Press, 1986.

Newton, Wesley Phillips. *Montgomery in the Good War: Portrait of a Southern City, 1939–1946.* Tuscaloosa: University of Alabama Press, 2000.

Nicholls, David. *From Dessalines to Duvalier: Race, Colour and National Independence in Haiti.* Cambridge, UK: Cambridge University Press, 1979.

Nolan, Paul T. "Marc Connelly's 'Divine Comedy': *Green Pastures* Revisited." *Western Speech* 30 (Fall 1966): 216–24.

Nolte, Ernest. "The Problem of Fascism in Recent Scholarship." In *Reappraisals of Fascism*, ed. Henry Ashby Turner, 24–62. New York: New Viewpoints, 1975.

Norrell, Robert J. *Reaping the Whirlwind: The Civil Rights Movement in Tuskegee.* New York: Knopf, 1985.

North, Joseph. *Robert Minor: Artist and Crusade: An Informal Biography.* New York: International Press, 1956.

Novick, Peter. *The Holocaust in American Life.* Boston: Houghton Mifflin, 1999.

———. *That Noble Dream: The 'Objectivity Question' and the American Historical Profession.* Cambridge, UK: Cambridge University Press, 1988.

Nuechterlein, James A. "The Politics of Civil Rights: The FEPC, 1941–1946." *Prologue* 10 (Fall 1978): 171–91.

O'Brien, Kenneth Paul, and Lynn Hudson Parsons, eds. *The Home-Front War: World War II and American Society.* Westport, CT: Greenwood Press, 1995.

O'Brien, Michael. *The Idea of the American South, 1920–1941.* Baltimore: Johns Hopkins University Press, 1979.

Ogden, Frederic D. *The Poll Tax in the South.* University: University of Alabama Press, 1958.

Oliver, Lawrence J. "Writing from the Right during the 'Red Decade': Thomas Dixon's Attack on W. E. B. Du Bois and James Weldon Johnson in *The Flaming Sword*." *American Literature* 70 (March 1998): 131–52.

Osokina, Elena A. "Economic Disobedience under Stalin." In *Contending with Stalinism: Soviet Power and Popular Resistance in the 1930s*, ed. Lynne Viola, 170–200. Ithaca, NY: Cornell University Press, 2002.

Ottanelli, Fraser M. *The Communist Party of the United States: From the Depression to World War II.* New Brunswick, NJ: Rutgers University Press, 1991.

Painter, Nell Irvin. *The Narrative of Hosea Hudson: His Life as a Negro Communist in the South.* Cambridge, MA: Harvard University Press, 1979.

———. "The Shoah and Southern History." In *Jumpin' Jim Crow: Southern Politics from Civil War to Civil Rights*, ed. Jane Dailey, Bryant Simon, and Glenda Elizabeth Gilmore, 308–10. Princeton, NJ: Princeton University Press, 2000.

Pamphile, Leon D. "America's Policy-Making in Haitian Education, 1915–1934." *JNE* 54 (Winter 1985): 99–108.

———. "NAACP and the American Occupation of Haiti." *Phylon* 47 (First Quarter 1986): 91–100.

Pascoe, Craig S., Karen Trahan Leathem, and Andy Ambrose, eds. *The American South in the Twentieth Century.* Athens: University of Georgia Press, 2005.

Pathe, R. A. "Gene Weltfish." In *Woman Anthropologists: A Biographical Dictionary*, ed. Ute Gacs, 372–81. New York: Greenwood Press, 1988.

Paul, Brad. "Rebels of the New South: The Socialist Party in Dixie, 1897–1920." Master's thesis, Georgia State University, 1994.

Payne, Stanley G. *Fascism: Comparison and Definition.* Madison: University of Wisconsin Press, 1980.

———. *A History of Fascism, 1914–1945.* Madison: University of Wisconsin Press, 1995.

Pederson, Vernon L. *The Communist Party in Maryland, 1919–1957.* Urbana: University of Illinois Press, 2001.

Pfeffer, Paula F. *A. Philip Randolph: Pioneer of the Civil Rights Movement.* Baton Rouge: Louisiana State University Press, 1990.

Phelps, Christopher. *Young Sidney Hook: Marxist and Pragmatist.* Ithaca, NY: Cornell University Press, 1997.

Pilkington, John. "Stark Young." In *Encyclopedia of Southern Culture*, ed. Charles Reagan Wilson and William Ferris, 903–04. Chapel Hill: University of North Carolina Press, 1989.

Pipes, Richard. *Russia under the Bolshevik Regime.* New York: Knopf, 1994.

Pleasants, Julian M. *Buncombe Bob: The Life and Times of Robert Rice Reynolds.* Chapel Hill: University of North Carolina Press, 2000.

———. "A Question of Loyalty: Frank Porter Graham and the Atomic Energy Commission." *North Carolina Historical Review* 69 (Oct. 1992): 414–37.

———, and Augustus M. Burns III. *Frank Porter Graham and the 1950 Senate Race in North Carolina.* Chapel Hill: University of North Carolina Press, 1990.

Plummer, Brenda Gayle. "The Afro-American Response to the Occupation of Haiti, 1915–1934." *Phylon* 43 (2nd Quarter 1982): 135–43.

———. *Haiti and the Great Powers, 1902–1915.* Baton Rouge: Louisiana State University Press, 1988.

———. *Rising Wind: Black Americans and U. S. Foreign Affairs, 1935–1960.* Chapel Hill: University of North Carolina Press, 1996.

Pope, Liston. *Millhands and Preachers.* New Haven: Yale University Press, 1941.

Powell, William Stevens. *The First State University: A Pictorial History of the University of North Carolina.* Chapel Hill: University of North Carolina Press, 1972.

Powers, Richard Gid. *Not without Honor: The History of American Anticommunism.* New York: Free Press, 1995.

Pratt, Virginia Anne. *The Influence of Domestic Controversy on American Participation in the United Nations Commission on Human Rights, 1946–1953.* New York: Garland, 1986.

Presidential Elections since 1789, 4th ed. Washington, DC: Congressional Quarterly, 1987.

Preston, William, Jr. *Aliens and Dissenters: Federal Suppression of Radicals, 1903–1933.* 1963. Reprint, Urbana: University of Illinois Press, 1995.

"Primo Carnera." www.cyberbingzone.com.

Ralston, Richard D. "American Episodes in the Making of an African Leader: A Case Study of Alfred B. Xuma (1893–1962)." *International Journal of African Historical Studies* 6, no. 1 (1973): 72–93.

Rampersad, Arnold. *The Life of Langston Hughes,* vol. 1, *1902–1941: I, Too, Sing America.* New York: Oxford University Press, 1986.

———. *The Life of Langston Hughes,* vol. 2, *1941–1967: I Dream a World.* New York: Oxford University Press, 1988.

———, ed., and David Roessel, associate ed. *The Collected Poems of Langston Hughes.* New York: Vintage Classics, 1994.

Randel, William Pierce. *The Ku Klux Klan: A Century of Infamy.* Philadelphia: Chilton Books, 1965.

Ransby, Barbara. *Ella Baker and the Black Freedom Movement: A Radical Democratic Vision.* Chapel Hill: University of North Carolina Press, 2003.

Read, Anthony, and David Fisher. *The Deadly Embrace: Hitler, Stalin, and the Nazi-Soviet Pact, 1939–1941.* New York: Norton, 1988.

Record, Wilson. "The Development of the Communist Position on the Negro Question in the United States." *Phylon* 19 (Fall 1958): 206–26.

———. *The Negro and the Communist Party.* New York: Atheneum, 1971.

———. *Race and Radicalism: The NAACP and the Communist Party in Conflict.* Ithaca, NY: Cornell University Press, 1964.

Reed, Linda. *Simple Decency and Common Sense: The Southern Conference Movement, 1938–1963.* Bloomington: Indiana University Press, 1991.

Reed, Merl E. "The FEPC, the Black Worker, and the Southern Shipyards." *South Atlantic Quarterly* 74 (Autumn 1975): 446–67.

———. *Seedtime for the Modern Civil Rights Movement: The President's Committee on Fair Employment Practice, 1941–1946.* Baton Rouge: Louisiana State University Press, 1991.

———, Leslie S. Hough, and Gary M. Fink, eds. *Southern Workers and Their Unions, 1880–1975: Selected Papers, the Second Southern Labor History Conference, 1978.* Westport, CT: Greenwood Press, 1981.

Reeve, Carl. "Gastonia: The Strike, the Frameup, the Heritage." *Political Affairs* 62 (Apr. 1984): 23–31.

———. "The Great Gastonia Textile Strike." *Political Affairs* 62 (March 1984): 40.

Renda, Mary A. *Taking Haiti: Military Occupation and the Culture of U.S. Imperialism, 1915–1940.* Chapel Hill: University of North Carolina Press, 2001.

Rice, Arnold S. *The Ku Klux Klan in American Politics.* Washington, DC: Public Affairs Press, 1962.

Richards, Yevette. *Maida Springer: Pan-Africanist and International Labor Leader.* Pittsburgh: University of Pittsburgh Press, 2000.

———. "Race, Gender, and Anticommunism in the International Labor Movement: The Pan-African Connections of Maida Springer." *Journal of Women's History* 11 (Summer 1999): 35–59.

Robbins, Richard. "Charles S. Johnson." In *Black Sociologists: Historical and Contempo-*

rary Perspectives, ed. James E. Blackwell and Morris Jonowitz, 56–82. Chicago: University of Chicago Press, 1974.

———. *Sidelines Activist: Charles S. Johnson and the Struggle for Civil Rights.* Jackson: University Press of Mississippi, 1996.

"Robert Park." In *American National Biography*, vol. 24, ed. John A. Garraty and Mark C. Carnes, 4–6. New York: Oxford University Press, 1999.

Robinson, Cedric J. *Black Marxism: The Making of the Black Radical Tradition.* 1983. Reprint, Chapel Hill: University of North Carolina Press, 2000.

Rodgers, Daniel. "Regionalism and the Burdens of Progress." In *Region Race, and Reconstruction: Essays in Honor of C. Vann Woodward*, ed. J. Morgan Kousser and James M. McPherson. New York: Oxford University Press, 1982, 3–26.

Rogin, Michael. " 'Democracy and Burnt Cork': The End of Blackface, the Beginning of Civil Rights." *Representations* 46 (Spring 1994): 1–34.

Roper, John Herbert. *C. Vann Woodward, Southerner.* Athens: University of Georgia Press, 1987.

———. *Paul Green: Playwright of the Real South.* Athens: University of Georgia Press, 2003.

———. "Paul Green and the Southern Literary Renaissance." *Southern Cultures* 1 (Fall 1994): 75–89.

Rose, Anne C. "Putting the South on the Psychological Map: The Impact of Region and Race on Human Sciences during the 1930s." *JSH* 71 (May 2005): 321–56.

Rosenberg, Gerald N. *The Hollow Hope: Can Courts Bring About Social Change?* Chicago: University of Chicago Press, 1991.

Rosenberg, Jonathan Seth. "For Democracy, Not Hypocrisy: World War and Race Relations in the United States, 1914–1919." *International History Review* 21 (Sept. 1999): 592–625.

———. " 'How Far the Promised Land?' World Affairs and the American Civil Rights Movement from the First World War to Vietnam." PhD diss., Harvard University, 1997.

———. *How Far the Promised Land? World Affairs and the American Civil Rights Movement from the First World War to Vietnam.* Princeton, NJ: Princeton University Press, 2006.

Rosenberg, Rosalind. "Pauli Murray and the Killing of Jane Crow." In *Forgotten Heroes: Inspiring American Portraits from Our Leading Historians*, ed. Susan Ware, 279–87. New York: Free Press, 1998.

Rosenzweig, Roy. "Organizing the Unemployed: The Early Years of the Great Depression, 1929–1933." *Radical America* (July-Aug. 1976): 37–60.

Ross, Felicia G. Jones. "Mobilizing the Masses: The *Cleveland Call and Post* and the Scottsboro Incident." *JNH* 84 (Winter 1999): 48–60.

Roucek, Joseph S. "The Soviet Treatment of Minorities." *Phylon* 22 (Spring 1961): 15–23.

Rubin, Louis D. *The Writer in the South: Studies in a Literary Community.* Athens: University of Georgia Press, 1972.

Rubin, Rachel. "Voice of the Cracker: Don West Reinvents the Appalachian." In *Left of the Color Line: Race, Radicalism, and Twentieth-Century Literature of the United States*, ed. Bill V. Mullen and James Smethurst, 205–22. Chapel Hill: University of North Carolina Press, 2003.

Ruchames, Louis. *Race, Jobs, and Politics: The Story of FEPC.* New York: Columbia University Press, 1953.

Rush, James S., Jr. "The Fair Employment Practice Committee and the Shipyard Hearings of 1943–1944." *Prologue* 29 (Winter 1997): 279–90.

Ryan, James G. *Earl Browder: The Failure of American Communism.* Tuscaloosa: University of Alabama Press, 1997.

"Safarov, Nazir." In *Great Soviet Encyclopedia*, vol. 22, 3d ed. New York: Macmillan, 1979.

Salmond, John A. " 'The Burlington Dynamite Plot': The 1934 Textile Strike and Its Aftermath in Burlington, North Carolina." *North Carolina Historical Review* 75 (Oct. 1998): 398–434.

———. *Gastonia 1929: The Story of the Loray Mill on Strike.* Chapel Hill: University of North Carolina Press, 1995.

———. *The General Textile Strike of 1934: From Maine to Alabama.* Columbia: University of Missouri Press, 2002.

———. *Miss Lucy of the CIO: The Life and Times of Lucy Randolph Mason, 1882–1959.* Athens: University of Georgia Press, 1988.

Salzman, Jack, and Cornel West, eds. *Struggles in the Promised Land: Towards a History of Black-Jewish Relations in the United States.* New York: Oxford University Press, 1997.

Samples, Susan. "African Germans in the Third Reich." In *The African-German Experience: Critical Essays*, ed. Carol Aisha Blackshire-Belay, 53–70. Westport, CT: Praeger, 1996.

Sanders. Lynn Moss. *Howard W. Odum's Folklore Odyssey: Transformation to Tolerance through African American Folk Studies.* Athens: University of Georgia Press, 2003.

Savage, Barbara Dianne. *Broadcasting Freedom: Radio, War, and the Politics of Race, 1938–1948.* Chapel Hill: University of North Carolina Press, 1999.

Schaffer, Samuel L. "Avoiding Friction: Place, Race, and Woodrow Wilson's Worldview." *Proteus* 22 (Spring 2005): 45–52.

Schlesinger, Arthur, Jr. *The Coming of the New Deal.* Boston: Houghton Mifflin, 1959.

Schmidt, Hans. *The United States Occupation of Haiti, 1915–1934.* New Brunswick, NJ: Rutgers University Press, 1971.

"School Honors Legacy of Black Woman." www.cnn.com/2003/education/11/05/poetic.justice.ap/index.html.

Schrecker, Ellen. *Many Are the Crimes: McCarthyism in America.* New York: Little, Brown, 1998.

Schultz, David, and Stephen E. Gottlieb. "Legal Functionalism and Social Change: A Reassessment of Rosenberg's *The Hollow Hope: Can Courts Bring About Social Change?" Journal of Law and Politics* 12 (Winter 1996): 63–91.

Schwarz, Justin. "Cyril Briggs, the African Blood Brotherhood and the Radical New Negro Movement: The Reconciliation of Militant Nationalism and Revolutionary Socialism." Senior essay for the BA, Yale University, 1996.

Scott, Anne Firor. "Introduction." In *Pauli Murray and Caroline Ware: Forty Years of Letters in Black and White.* Chapel Hill: University of North Carolina Press, 2006.

Scott, William R. "Black Nationalism and the Italo-Ethiopian Conflict, 1934–1936." *JNH* 63 (Apr. 1978): 118–34.

Seawright, Sally. "Desegregation at Maryland: The NAACP and the Murray Case in the 1930s." *Maryland Historian* 1 (Spring 1970): 59–73.

Shachtman, Max. *Race and Revolution*, ed. Christopher Phelps. New York: Verso, 2003.

Shedd, Clarence Prouty. *History of the World's Alliance of Young Men's Christian Associations*. London: World's Committee of Young Men's Christian Associations, S.P.C.K., 1955.

Sher, Julian. *White Hoods: Canada's Ku Klux Klan*. Vancouver, BC: New Star Books, 1983.

Sherman, Richard B. *The Case of Odell Waller and Virginia Justice, 1940–1942*. Knoxville: University of Tennessee Press, 1992.

Simon, Bryant. *A Fabric of Defeat: The Politics of South Carolina Millhands, 1910–1948*. Chapel Hill: University of North Carolina Press, 1998.

———. "Introduction." To Howard W. Odum, *Race and Rumors of Race: The American South in the Early Forties*, vii–xxxii. Baltimore: Johns Hopkins University Press, 1997.

———. "Race Reactions: African American Organizing, Liberalism, and White Working-Class Politics in Postwar South Carolina." In *Jumpin' Jim Crow: Southern Politics from Civil War to Civil Rights*, ed. Jane Dailey, Bryant Simon, and Glenda Elizabeth Gilmore, 239–59. Princeton, NJ: Princeton University Press, 2000.

Singal, Daniel Joseph. *The War Within: From Victorian to Modernist Thought in the South, 1919–1945*. Chapel Hill: University of North Carolina Press, 1982.

Sirgiovanni, George. *An Undercurrent of Suspicion: Anti-Communism in America during World War II*. New Brunswick, NJ: Transaction Books, 1990.

Sitkoff, Harvard. *A New Deal for Blacks: The Emergence of Civil Rights as a National Issue*. New York: Oxford University Press, 1978.

———. "Racial Militancy and Interracial Violence in the Second World War." *JAH* 58 (Dec. 1971): 661–81.

Skotnes, Andor. "The Communist Party, Anti-Racism, and the Freedom Movement: Baltimore, 1930–34." *Science and Society* 60 (Summer 1996): 164–94.

Smethurst, James Edward. *The New Red Negro: The Literary Left and African-American Poetry, 1930–1946*. New York: Oxford University Press, 1999.

Smith, Douglas L. *The New Deal in the Urban South*. Baton Rouge: Louisiana State University Press, 1988.

Smith, Edwin W. *Aggrey of Africa: A Study in Black and White*. New York: Friendship Press, 1929.

Smith, Fletcher Charles. "Clyde Johnson, American Communist. His Life in the Labor Movement." PhD diss., University of Arkansas, 1999.

Smith, Geoffrey S. *To Save a Nation: American Countersubversives, the New Deal, and the Coming of World War II*. New York: Basic Books, 1973.

Smith, J. Douglas. *Managing White Supremacy: Race, Politics, and Citizenship in Jim Crow Virginia*. Chapel Hill: University of North Carolina Press, 2002.

Smith, John David. Introduction to *The Flaming Sword*, by Thomas Dixon, rev. ed. Lexington: University of Kentucky Press, 2005.

Sollors, Werner. "W. E. B. Du Bois in Nazi Germany." *Amerikastudien* 44, no. 2 (1999): 207–22.

Solomon, Mark. *The Cry Was Unity: Communists and African Americans, 1917–1936*. Jackson: University Press of Mississippi, 1998.

Sommerville, Dianne Miller. *Rape and Race in the Nineteenth-Century South.* Chapel Hill: University of North Carolina Press, 2004.

Sosna, Morton. *In Search of the Silent South: Southern Liberals and the Race Issue.* New York: Columbia University Press, 1977.

Southern, David W. *Gunnar Myrdal and Black-White Relations: The Use and Abuse of "An American Dilemma," 1944–1969.* Baton Rouge: Louisiana State University Press, 1987.

Spero, Sterling Denhard. *The Black Worker: The Negro and the Labor Movement.* New York: Atheneum, 1968.

Stauffer, Milton, ed. *Thinking with Africa: Chapters by a Group of Nationals Interpreting the Christian Movement.* London: Student Christian Movement, 1928.

Stephens, Michelle. "Black Transnationalism and the Politics of National Identity: West Indian Intellectuals in Harlem in the Age of War and Revolution." *American Quarterly* 50 (Sept. 1998): 592–608.

Sternhell, Zeev, with Mario Sznajder and Maia Asher. *The Birth of Fascist Ideology: From Cultural Rebellion to Political Revolution.* Princeton, NJ: Princeton University Press, 1994.

Stockley, Grif. *Blood in Their Eyes: The Elaine Race Massacres of 1919.* Fayetteville: University of Arkansas Press, 2001.

Stoney, George, Judith Helfand, and Suzanne Rostock, producers. *The Uprising of '34.* VHS. 1934 Strike Consortium, Vera Rony, executive producer. New York: First Run/Icarus Films, 1995.

Storch, Randi. *Red Chicago: American Communism at Its Grassroots, 1928–35.* Urbana: University of Illinois Press, 2007.

Storrs, Landon R. Y. *Civilizing Capitalism: The National Consumers' League, Women's Activism and Labor Standards in the New Deal Era.* Chapel Hill: University of North Carolina Press, 2000.

Strong, Donald S. *Organized Anti-Semitism in America: The Rise of Group Prejudice during the Decade 1930–1940.* Washington, DC: American Council on Public Affairs, 1941.

Stuckey, W. J. *The Pulitzer Prize Novels: A Critical Backward Look.* Norman: University of Oklahoma Press, 1966.

Suggs, Henry Lewis. "The Response of the African American Press to the United States Occupation of Haiti, 1915–1934." *JNH* 73 (Winter-Autumn 1988): 33–45.

Sugrue, Thomas. *Origins of the Urban Crisis: Race and Inequality in Postwar Detroit.* Princeton: Princeton University Press, 1996.

Sullivan, Patricia. *Days of Hope: Race and Democracy in the New Deal Era.* Chapel Hill: University of North Carolina Press, 1996.

Swain, Geoffrey. "Was the Profintern Really Necessary?" *European History Quarterly* 17 (Jan. 1987): 57–77.

Sworakowski, Witold S. *The Communist International and Its Front Organizations.* Stanford, CA: Hoover Institution on War, Revolution, and Peace, 1965.

Taylor, A. J. P. *The Origins of the Second World War.* New York: Fawcett Premier, 1961.

Taylor, Kieran. " 'We Have Just Begun': Black Organizing and White Response in the Arkansas Delta, 1919." *Arkansas Historical Quarterly* 58 (Autumn 1999): 264–84.

Taylor, S. J. *Stalin's Apologist: Walter Duranty, the New York Times's Man in Moscow.* New York: Oxford University Press, 1990.

Taylor, Theman Ray. "Cyril Briggs and the African Blood Brotherhood." PhD diss., University of California, Santa Barbara, 1981.

Teel, Leonard Ray. *Ralph Emerson McGill: Voice of the Southern Conscience.* Knoxville: University of Tennessee Press, 2001.

Thomas, Kendall. *"Rouge et Noir* Reread: A Popular Constitutional History of the Angelo Herndon Case." In *Critical Race Theory: The Key Writings that Formed the Movement,* ed. Kimberle Crenshaw, 465–94. New York: New Press, 1995.

Thompson, Leonard, and Howard Lamar, eds. *The Frontier in History: North America and South Africa Compared.* New Haven: Yale University Press, 1981.

Thurston, Michael. "Black Christ, Red Flag: Langston Hughes on Scottsboro." *College Literature* 22 (Oct. 1995): 30–50.

Tindall, George Brown. *The Emergence of the New South, 1913–1945.* Baton Rouge: Louisiana State University Press, 1967.

———. "The Significance of Howard W. Odum to Southern History: A Preliminary Estimate." *JSH* 24 (Aug. 1958): 285–307.

Torrence, Ridgely. *The Story of John Hope.* New York: Macmillan, 1948.

Trotter, Joe W., Jr. "The Place of Black Workers in Southern Labor History: Introduction." In *Race, Class, and Community in Southern Labor History,* ed. Gary M. Fink and Merl E. Reed, 67–71. Tuscaloosa: University of Alabama Press, 1994.

Tucker, Robert C. *Stalin in Power: The Revolution from Above, 1928–1941.* New York: Norton, 1990.

Turner, Henry Ashby, Jr., ed. *Hitler—Memoirs of a Confidant.* New Haven: Yale University Press, 1985.

———, ed. *Nazism and the Third Reich.* New York: Quadrangle Books, 1972.

———, ed. *Reappraisals of Fascism.* New York: New Viewpoints, 1975.

Turner, Joyce Moore, with the assistance of W. Burghardt Turner. *Caribbean Crusaders and the Harlem Renaissance.* Urbana: University of Illinois Press, 2005.

Turner, W. Burghardt, and Joyce Moore Turner, eds. *Richard B. Moore, Caribbean Militant in Harlem: Collected Writings, 1920–1972.* Bloomington: Indiana University Press, 1988.

Tushnett, Mark. *Making Civil Rights Law: Thurgood Marshall and the Supreme Court, 1936–1961.* New York: Oxford University Press, 1994.

———. *The NAACP's Legal Strategy against Segregated Education, 1925–1950.* Chapel Hill: University of North Carolina Press, 1987.

Tuttle, William M., Jr. *Race Riot: Chicago in the Red Summer of 1919.* New York: Atheneum, 1985.

Tye, Larry. *Rising from the Rails: Pullman Porters and the Making of the Black Middle Class.* New York: Holt, 2004.

Van Zanten, John W. "Communist Theory and the American Negro Question." *Review of Politics* 29 (Oct. 1967): 435–56.

Verich, Thomas M. *The European Powers and the Italo-Ethiopian War 1935–36: A Diplomatic Study.* Salisbury, NC: Documentary Publications, 1980.

Vinson, Robert T. "See Kaffirs: American Negroes and the Gospel of Garveyism in Early Twentieth-Century Cape Town." *Journal of African History* 47 (July 2006): 281–303.

Von Eschen, Penny. "Challenging Cold War Habits: African Americans, Race, and Foreign Policy." *Diplomatic History* 20 (Fall 1996): 627–38.

———. *Race against Empire: Black Americans and Anticolonialism, 1937–1957.* Ithaca, NY: Cornell University Press, 1997.

Wald, Alan M. *Exiles from a Future Time: The Forging of the Mid-Twentieth-Century Literary Left.* Chapel Hill: University of North Carolina Press, 2002.

Walshe, Peter. *The Rise of African Nationalism in South Africa.* Craighall, South Africa: Donker, 1987.

Ware, Gilbert. "*Hocutt*: Genesis of *Brown.*" *JNE* 52 (Summer 1983): 227–33.

———. *William Hastie: Grace under Pressure.* New York: Oxford University Press, 1984.

Ware, Susan, ed. "Dialogue: Pauli Murray's Notable Connections." *Journal of Women's History* 14 (Summer 2002): 54–87.

Warren, Frank A., III. *An Alternative Vision: The Socialist Party in the 1930s.* Bloomington: Indiana University Press, 1974.

———. *Liberals and Communism: The "Red Decade" Revisited.* Bloomington: Indiana University Press, 1966.

Washburn, Patrick S. *A Question of Sedition: The Federal Government's Investigation of the Black Press during World War II.* New York: Oxford University Press, 1986.

Washington, Mary Helen. "I Sign My Mother's Name." In *Mothering the Mind,* ed. Ruth Perry and Martine Watson Brownley, 150–51. New York: Holmes and Meier, 1984.

Weare, Walter B. *Black Business in the New South: A History of the North Carolina Mutual Life Insurance Company.* Urbana: University of Illinois Press, 1973.

Webb, Constance. *Richard Wright: A Biography.* New York: G. P. Putnam's Sons, 1968.

Wedlock, Lunabelle. "Comparisons by Negro Publications of the Plight of the Jew in Germany with that of the Negro in America." In *Strangers and Neighbors: Relations between Blacks and Jews in the United States,* ed. Maurianne Adams and John Bracey, 427–33. Amherst: University of Massachusetts Press, 1999.

Weinberg, Gerhard L. "Hitler's Image of the United States." *AHR* 69 (July 1964): 1006–21.

———. *Hitler's Second Book: The Unpublished Sequel to "Mein Kampf."* New York: Enigma, 2003.

Weinstein, Allen, and Alexander Vassiliev. *The Haunted Wood: Soviet Espionage in America—The Stalin Era.* New York: Random House, 1999.

Weisbord, Robert G., and Arthur Stein. "Negro Perceptions of Jews between World Wars." In *Strangers and Neighbors: Relations between Blacks and Jews in the United States,* ed. Maurianne Adams and John Bracey, 409–26. Amherst: University of Massachusetts Press, 1999. Originally published in *Judaism* 18 (Fall 1969): 428–67.

"Gene Weltfish." www.webster.edu/~woolflm/weltfish.

Wesley, Charles Harris. "Recollections of Carter G. Woodson." *JNH* 83 (Spring 1998): 143–49.

Wiggins, David K. "The 1936 Olympic Games in Berlin: The Response of America's Black Press." *Research Quarterly for Exercise and Sport* 54 (Sept. 1983): 279–82.

Wilkerson, Margaret B. "Excavating Our History: The Importance of Biographies of Women of Color." *Black American Literature Forum* (1990): 73–84.

Wilkerson-Freeman, Sarah. "The Second Battle for Woman Suffrage: Alabama White Women, the Poll Tax, and V. O. Key's Master Narrative of Southern Politics." *JSH* 68 (Spring 2002): 333–74.

———. "Women and the Transformation of American Politics." PhD diss., University of North Carolina at Chapel Hill, 1996.

Williams, Henry. *Black Response to the American Left, 1917–1929*. Princeton Undergraduate Studies in History 1. Princeton: History Department, Princeton University, 1973.

Williams, John. "Struggles of the Thirties in the South." In *The Negro in Depression and War: Prelude to Revolution, 1935–1940*, ed. Bernard Sternsher, 166–78. Chicago: Quadrangle Books, 1969.

Williams, Juan. *Thurgood Marshall: American Revolutionary*. New York: Random House, 1998.

Williamson, Joel. *Crucible of Race: Black/White Relations in the American South since Emancipation*. New York: Oxford University Press, 1984.

Wilson, Charles Reagan, and William Ferris, eds. *Encyclopedia of Southern Culture*. Chapel Hill: University of North Carolina Press, 1989.

Wilson, Emily Herring. *Hope and Dignity: Older Black Women of the South*. Philadelphia: Temple University Press, 1983.

Wilson, Samuel Tyndale. *A Century of Maryville College, 1819–1919*. Maryville, TN: Directors of Maryville College, 1919.

Winchell, Mark Royden. *Where No Flag Flies: Donald Davidson and the Southern Resistance*. Columbia: University of Missouri Press, 2000.

Wittner, Lawrence S. "The National Negro Congress: A Reassessment." *American Quarterly* 22 (Winter 1970): 883–901.

Wolters, Raymond. *The Negro and the Great Depression: The Problem of Economic Recovery*. Westport, CT: Greenwood Press, 1970.

Woodruff, Nan Elizabeth. *American Congo: The African American Freedom Struggle in the Delta*. Cambridge, MA: Harvard University Press, 2003.

Woods, Jeff. *Black Struggle, Red Scare: Segregation and Anti-Communism in the South, 1948–1968*. Baton Rouge: Louisiana State University Press, 2004.

Woodward, C. Vann, *The Strange Career of Jim Crow*. New York: Oxford University Press, 1974.

———. *Thinking Back: The Perils of Writing History*. Baton Rouge: Louisiana State University Press, 1986.

www.ancestry.com.

www/idecisions/isummaries/ilsaesasummary621221.htm.

www.icj-cji.org/icj.

www.mmmc.edu/history2.htm.

www.roots.web.com.

Wyman, David S. *The Abandonment of the Jews: America and the Holocaust, 1941–1945*. New York: Pantheon Books, 1984.

Wynn, Neil A. *The Afro-American and the Second World War*, rev. ed. New York: Holmes and Meier, 1993.

———. "The 'Good War': The Second World War and Postwar American Society." *Journal of Contemporary History* 31 (July 1996): 463–82.

Yarnell, Allen. *Democrats and Progressives: The 1948 Presidential Election as a Test of Postwar Liberalism.* Berkeley: University of California Press, 1974.

Young, Adam. "Stalin's Political Pilgrims." www.mises.org/story/863.

Young, James O. *Black Writers of the Thirties.* Baton Rouge: Louisiana State University Press, 1973.

Zangrando, Robert I. *The NAACP Crusade against Lynching, 1909–1950.* Philadelphia: Temple University Press, 1980.

Zieger, Robert H. *The CIO, 1935–1955.* Chapel Hill: University of North Carolina Press, 1995.

———, ed. *Organized Labor in the Twentieth-Century South.* Knoxville: University of Tennessee Press, 1991.

———. *Southern Labor in Transition, 1940–1995.* Knoxville: University of Tennessee Press, 1997.

PERMISSIONS

INDEX